# MACROECONOMICS
### *Principles and Applications*

**4E**

THOMSON
SOUTH-WESTERN

Macroeconomics: Principles and Applications, Fourth Edition
Robert E. Hall and Marc Lieberman

**VP/Editorial Director:**
Jack W. Calhoun

**VP/Editor-in-Chief:**
Alex von Rosenberg

**Sr. Acquisitions Editor:**
Michael Worls

**Sr. Developmental Editor:**
Susanna C. Smart

**Sr. Marketing Manager:**
John Carey

**Content Project Manager:**
Tamborah Moore

**Manager of Technology, Editorial:**
John Barans

**Marketing Communications Manager:**
Sarah Greber

**Sr. Manufacturing Print Buyer:**
Sandee Milewski

**Production House:**
Lachina Publishing Services

**Printer:**
QuebecorWorld -Taunton
Taunton, MA

**Art Director:**
Michelle Kunkler

**Cover and Internal Designer:**
Albonetti Design/Lisa A. Albonetti

**Cover Images:**
© Dave Cutler/Images.com

**Photography Manager:**
Deanna Ettinger

**Photo Researcher:**
Susan van Etten

Student Edition:
ISBN 13: 978-0-324-42146-0
ISBN 10: 0-324-42146-X

Student Edition with Aplia 1-semester
access:
ISBN 13: 978-0-324-54481-7
ISBN 10: 0-324-54481-2

Instructor's Edition:
ISBN 13: 978-0-324-54484-8
ISBN 10: 0-324-54484-7

Library of Congress Control Number:
2006935808

For more information about our products,
contact us at:

Thomson Learning Academic
Resource Center

1-800-423-0563

**Thomson Higher Education**
5191 Natorp Boulevard
Mason, OH 45040

USA

# MACROECONOMICS
## Principles and Applications

ROBERT E.
# HALL
*Department of Economics*
*Stanford University*


MARC
# LIEBERMAN
*Department of Economics*
*New York University*

**THOMSON**
—∗—
**SOUTH-WESTERN**

Australia · Brazil · Canada · Mexico · Singapore · Spain · United Kingdom · United States

# Brief Contents

# Contents

# PART II: MACROECONOMICS: BASIC CONCEPTS

# PART III: LONG-RUN MACROECONOMICS

# PART IV: SHORT-RUN MACROECONOMICS

# PART V: MONEY, PRICES, AND THE MACROECONOMY

# Preface

*Macroeconomics: Principles and Applications* is about economic principles and how economists use them to understand the world. It was conceived, written, and for the fourth edition, substantially revised to help your students focus on those basic principles and applications.

We originally decided to write this book because we thought that existing books often confused students about economics and what it is all about. In our view, the leading texts tend to fall into one of three categories. In the first category are the encyclopedias—the heavy tomes with a section or a paragraph on every topic or subtopic you might possibly want to present to your students. These books are often useful as reference tools. But because they cover too many topics—many of them superficially—the central themes and ideas can be lost in the shuffle.

The second type of text we call the "scrapbook." In an effort to elevate student interest, these books insert multicolored boxes, news clippings, interviews, cartoons, and whatever else they can find to jolt the reader on each page. While these special features are often entertaining, there is a trade-off: These books sacrifice a logical, focused presentation of the material. Once again, the central themes and ideas are often lost.

Finally, the third type of text, perhaps in response to the first two, tries to do less in every area—a *lot* less. But instead of just omitting extraneous or inessential details, these texts often throw out key ideas, models, and concepts. Students who use these books may think that economics is overly simplified and unrealistic. After the course, they may be less prepared to go on in the field, or to think about the economy on their own.

## A DISTINCTIVE APPROACH

Our approach is very different. We believe that the best way to teach principles is to present economics as a coherent, unified subject. This does not happen automatically. On the contrary, principles students often miss the unity of what we call "the economic way of thinking." For example, they are likely to see the analysis of goods markets, labor markets, and financial markets as entirely different phenomena, rather than as a repeated application of the same methodology with a new twist here and there. So the principles course appears to be just "one thing after another," rather than the coherent presentation we aim for.

## CAREFUL FOCUS

Because we have avoided encyclopedic complexity, we have had to think hard about what topics are most important. As you will see:

### We avoid nonessential material.

When we believed a topic was not essential to a basic understanding of economics, we left it out. However, we have strived to include core material to *support* an instructor who wants to present special topics in class. So, for example, we do not have comprehensive treatments of environmental economics, agricultural economics, urban economics, health care economics, or comparative systems *as separate subject matter*. But instructors should find in the text a good foundation for building any of these areas—and many others-into their course. And we have included examples from each of these areas as *applications* of core theory where appropriate throughout the text.

### We avoid distracting features.

This text does not have interviews, news clippings, or boxed inserts with only distant connections to the core material. The features your students *will* find in our book are there to help them understand and apply economic theory itself, and to help them avoid common mistakes in applying the theory (the Dangerous Curves feature).

### We explain difficult concepts patiently.

By freeing ourselves from the obligation to introduce every possible topic in economics, we can explain the topics we *do* cover more thoroughly and patiently. We lead students, step-by-step, through each aspect of the theory, through each graph, and through each numerical example. In developing this book, we asked other experienced teachers to tell us which aspects of economic theory were hardest for their students to learn, and we have paid special attention to the trouble spots.

### We use concrete examples.

Students learn best when they see how economics can explain the world around them. Whenever possible, we develop the theory using real-world examples. You will find numerous references to real-world corporations and government policies throughout the text. When we employ hypothetical examples because they illustrate the theory more clearly, we try to make them realistic. In addition, almost every chapter ends with a thorough, extended application (the "Using the Theory" section) focusing on an interesting real-world issue.

## FEATURES THAT REINFORCE

To help students see economics as a coherent whole, and to reinforce its usefulness, we have included some important features in this book.

## THE THREE-STEP PROCESS

Most economists, when approaching a problem, begin by thinking about buyers and sellers, and the markets in which they come together to trade. They move on to characterize a market equilibrium, then give their model a workout in a comparative statics exercise. To understand what economics is about, students need to understand this process, and see it in action in different contexts. To help them do so, we have identified and stressed a "three-step process" that economists use in analyzing problems. The three key steps are:

1. **Characterize the Market.** Decide which market or markets best suit the problem being analyzed, and identify the decision makers (buyers and sellers) who interact there.
2. **Find the Equilibrium.** Describe the conditions necessary for equilibrium in the market, and a method for determining that equilibrium.
3. **Determine What Happens When Things Change.** Explore how events or government policies change the market equilibrium.

The steps themselves are introduced toward the end of

Chapter 3. Thereafter, the content of most chapters is organized around this three-step process. We believe this helps students learn how to think like economists, and in a very natural way. And they come to see economics as a unified whole, rather than as a series of disconnected ideas.

## DANGEROUS CURVES

Anyone who teaches economics for a while learns that, semester after semester, students tend to make the same familiar errors. In class, in office hours, and on exams, students seem pulled, as if by gravity, toward certain logical pitfalls in thinking about, and using, economic theory. We've discovered in our own classrooms that merely explaining the theory properly isn't enough; the most common errors need to be *confronted,* and the student needs to be shown *specifically* why a particular logical path is incorrect. This was the genesis of our "Dangerous Curves" feature—boxes that anticipate the most common traps in economics, and warn students just when they are most likely to fall victim to them. We've been delighted to hear from instructors how effective this feature has been in overcoming the most common points of confusion for their students.

## USING THE THEORY

This text is full of applications that are woven throughout the narrative. In addition, almost every chapter ends with an extended application ("Using the Theory") that pulls together several of the tools learned in that chapter. These are not news clippings or world events that relate only tangentially to the material. Rather, they are step-by-step presentations that help students see how the tools of economics can explain things about the world—things that would be difficult to explain without those tools.

## CONTENT INNOVATIONS

In addition to the special features just described, you will find some important differences from other texts in topical approach and arrangement. These, too, are designed to make the theory stand out more clearly, and to make learning easier. These are not pedagogical experiments, nor are they innovation for the sake of innovation. The differences you will find in this text are the product of years of classroom experience.

### Scarcity, Choice, and Economic Systems (Chapter 2):

This early chapter, while covering standard material such as opportunity cost, also introduces some central concepts much earlier than other texts. Most importantly, it introduces the concept of *comparative advantage*, and the basic principle of *specialization and exchange*. We have placed them at the front of our book because we believe they provide important building blocks for much that comes later. International trade (Chapter 17) can be seen as a special application of these principles, extending them to trade between nations.

### Long-Run Macroeconomics (Chapters 7 and 8):

Our text presents long-run growth before short-run fluctuations. Chapter 7 develops the long-run, classical model at a level appropriate for introductory students, mostly using supply and demand. Chapter 8 then *uses* the classical model to explain the causes—and costs—of economic growth in both rich and poor countries.

We believe it is better to treat the long run before the short run, for two reasons. First, the long-run model makes full use of the tools of supply and demand, and thus allows a natural transition from the preliminary chapters (1, 2, and 3) into macroeconomics. Second, we believe that students can best understand economic fluctuations by understanding *how* and *why* the long-run model breaks down over shorter time periods. This, of course, requires an introduction to the long-run model first.

### Economic Fluctuations (Chapter 9):

This unique chapter provides a bridge from the long-run to the short-run macro model, and paves the way for the short-run focus on spending as the driving force behind economic fluctuations.

### Aggregate Demand and Aggregate Supply (Chapter 13):

One of our pet peeves about some introductory texts is the too-early introduction of aggregate demand and aggregate supply curves, *before* teaching where these curves come from. Students then confuse the *AD* and *AS* curves with their microeconomic counterparts, requiring corrective action later. In this text, the *AD* and *AS* curves do not appear until Chapter 13, where they

are fully explained. Our treatment of aggregate supply is based on a very simple mark-up model that our students have found easy to understand.

### Exchange Rates and Macroeconomic Policy (Chapter 16):

Many students find international macroeconomics the most interesting topic in the course, especially the material on exchange rates and what causes them to change. Accordingly, you will find unusually full coverage of exchange rate determination in this chapter. This treatment is kept simple and straightforward, relying exclusively on supply and demand. And it forms the foundation for the discussion of the trade deficit that ends the chapter.

### Comparative Advantage and the Gains from International Trade (Chapter 17):

We've found that international trade is best understood through clear numerical examples, and we've developed them carefully in this chapter. We also try to bridge the gap between the economics and politics of international trade with a systematic discussion of winners and losers.

## ORGANIZATIONAL FLEXIBILITY

We have arranged the contents of each chapter, and the table of contents as a whole, according to our recommended order of presentation. But we have also built in flexibility.

Once the core chapters (4–13) have been taught, the remaining chapters (14–16) can be presented in any order. Some instructors may want to assign selections from Chapter 15 (Spending, Taxes, and the Federal Budget) along with Chapter 10 (The Short-Run Macro Model).

Finally, we have included only those chapters that we thought were both essential and teachable in a year-long course. But not everyone will agree about what is essential. While we—as authors—cringe at the thought of a chapter being omitted in the interest of time, we have allowed for that possibility. Nothing in Chapter 8 (economic growth), Chapter 9 (economic fluctuations), Chapter 14 (inflation and monetary policy), Chapter 15 (fiscal policy and the budget), Chapter 16 (exchange rates and macroeconomic policy), or Chapter 17 (international trade) is required to understand any of the other chapters in the book. Skipping any of these should not cause continuity problems. And in this edition, we've made our first discussion of monetary policy in Chapter 12 (The Money Market and Monetary Policy) more complete, so that an instructor can skip Chapter 14 (Inflation and Monetary Policy) with less sacrifice than previously.

In many cases, a chapter can be assigned selectively. For example, an instructor who is anxious to get to the short-run macro model could freely select among the sections in Chapter 8 (economic growth and rising living standards) and Chapter 9 (economic fluctuations).

## NEW TO THE FOURTH EDITION

For this fourth edition, we've done our most significant revision to date. We've incorporated many excellent suggestions from reviewers and adopters. We've also conducted lengthy interviews with some long-time users to refine their suggestions further. While the overall approach and philosophy of the book remain unchanged, you'll find that almost every chapter has been affected and significantly improved by the revision.

For example, we've worked hard to clarify and simplify figures. We've modified or deleted material that instructors identified as stumbling blocks for their students. We've added several new Dangerous Curves boxes, and removed some that seemed more trouble than they were worth. Several of the "Using the Theory" sections are either entirely new or substantially revised. And, of course, we've updated all tables and figures with new data, adjusted content to reflect economic changes that have taken place over the past few years, and replaced or added dozens of end-of-chapter problems. In doing all this, we've kept our eye on the *essentials* throughout, resulting in a book that is about 100 pages shorter than the previous edition.

In addition, we've made some major changes that all instructors should know about in preparing their course.

- *Chapter 2 (Scarcity, Choice, and Economic Systems)* includes new PPF diagrams to illustrate economic growth.
- *Chapter 3 (Supply and Demand)* now includes a simple circular flow diagram.

- *Chapter 6: (The Price Level and Inflation)* no longer has our discussion of the monetary system and the history of the dollar; these have been moved to Chapter 11.
- *Chapter 7 (The Classical Long-Run Model)*: A few important changes to note. First, the definition of fiscal policy is no longer restricted to its demand-side effects. This and subsequent chapters now stress the distinction between demand-side and supply-side effect of fiscal policy. Second, all material involving a surplus in the loanable funds market has been moved to the end-of-chapter problems. Finally, an (optional) appendix shows how the classical model, and its key conclusions, can be extended to the open economy.
- *Chapter 8 (Economic Growth and Rising Living Standards)* now uses the "employment–population ratio" (EPR) instead of the "labor force participation rate" (LFPR). As you'll see, this greatly simplifies the exposition of factors that contribute to growth.
- *Chapter 9 (Economic Fluctuations)* no longer uses the term "spending shock," because it was creating some confusion (in later chapters) when we begin differentiating between demand shocks and supply shocks.
- *Chapter 10 (The Short-Run Macro Model)* now contains material on countercyclical fiscal policy that used to be in a later chapter.
- *Chapter 12 (The Money Market and Monetary Policy)* has two very important changes. First, the discussion of monetary policy in this and subsequent chapters now revolves around interest rate targets, rather than notions of "passive" or "active" monetary policy. Second, all feedback effects from the Keynesian cross diagram back to the money market have been moved to an optional appendix, enabling a vastly simpler treatment of fiscal and monetary policy for those instructors who prefer it. Discussions in later chapters have been adjusted for those who have not read the appendix.
- *Chapter 17 (International Trade and Comparative Advantage)* has been simplified. Our numerical examples have fewer steps and fewer tables, and they are supplemented with Ricardian PPF graphs. For trade barriers, we've switched from the large-country model (graphs for both exporting and importing countries) to the simpler small-country model (importing-country graphs only).

- The special topic "capstone chapter" on the stock market has been removed in this edition, to create an even greater focus on essentials. Instructors who would like to use this chapter with the fourth edition should contact their South-Western representative.

While we believe these are the issues mostly likely to affect your lectures, they are by no means an exhaustive list of changes in the revision. For those who would like a more extensive list, we have posted one on our Web site at **www.thomsonedu.com/economics/hall.**

## TEACHING AND LEARNING AIDS

To help you present the most interesting principles courses possible, we have created an extensive set of supplementary items. Many of them can be downloaded from the Hall/Lieberman Web site **www.thomsonedu .com/economics/hall.** The list includes:

### FOR THE INSTRUCTOR

- An *Instructor's Manual,* by Dennis Hanseman. The manual provides chapter outlines, teaching ideas, Experiential Exercises for many chapters, suggested answers to the end-of-chapter questions, and solutions to all problems.
- *Instructor's Resource CD-ROM.* This easy-to-use CD allows quick access to instructor ancillaries from your desktop. It also allows you to review, edit, and copy exactly the material you need. Or, you may choose to go to *Instructor Resources* on the *Product Support Web Site.* This site at **www .thomsonedu.com/economics/hall** features the essential resources for instructors, password-protected, in downloadable format: the *Instructor's Manual* in Word, the Test Banks in Word, and PowerPoint® Lecture and Exhibit Slides.
- *Macroeconomics Test Bank,* revised by Robert Guell, Indiana State University. This contains over 2,500 multiple-choice questions. The test questions have been arranged according to chapter headings and subheadings, making it easy to find the material needed to construct examinations.
- *ExamView® Computerized Testing Software.* Exam-View is an easy-to-use test creation package compatible with both Microsoft Windows and Macintosh client software, and contains all of the questions in all of the printed test banks. You can select questions by previewing them on the screen, selecting them by number, or selecting them randomly. Questions, instructions, and answers can be edited, and new questions can easily be added. You can also administer quizzes online-over the Internet, through a local area network (LAN), or through a wide area network (WAN).

- *PowerPoint® Lecture and Exhibit Slides.* Available on the Web site and the IRCD, the PowerPoint presentations consist of speaking points in chapter outline format, accompanied by numerous key graphs and tables from the main text, many with animation, which may be printed for use as transparency masters.

- *Principles of Economics Videotape. Principles of Economics* is a 40-minute videotape that offers students an insightful overview of ten common economic principles: Trade-offs, Opportunity Cost, Marginal Thinking, Incentives, Trade, Markets, Government's Role, Productivity, Inflation, and the Phillips Curve. *Principles of Economics* shows viewers how to apply economic principles to their daily lives. This video is filled with interviews from some of the country's leading economists, includes profiles of real students facing economic choices, and shows the economy's impact on U.S. and foreign companies. The video can be used at the beginning of a term to give students a general overview of economics, or used one section at a time prior to teaching each of these principles.

- *Favorite Ways to Learn Economics: Instructor's Edition.* Authors David Anderson of Centre College and Jim Chasey of Homewood-Flossmoor High School use experiments to bring economic education to life. This is a lab manual for the classroom and for individual study that contains experiments and problem sets that reinforce key economic concepts. The Instructor's Edition provides you the guidance and tips to ensure that these experiments are facilitated successfully.

- *MarketSim.* MarketSim, by Tod Porter at Youngstown State University, is an online simulation designed to help students in microeconomics classes better understand how markets work, by taking on the roles of consumers and producers in a simulated economy. In the simulations, students "make" and "accept" offers to buy and sell labor and goods asynchronously via the Internet. The goal of MarketSim is to provide instructors with a flexible teaching tool that can be used to motivate students to better understand a wide variety of microeconomic concepts.

- **TextChoice.** TextChoice is a custom format of Thomson Learning's online digital content. TextChoice provides the fastest, easiest way for you to create your own learning materials. You may select content from hundreds of best-selling titles, choose material from our numerous databases, and add your own material. Contact your South-Western/Thomson sales representative for more information at **http://thomsoncustom.com.**

- **eCoursepacks.** Create a customizable, easy-to-use, online companion for any course with eCoursepacks, from Thomson companies South-Western and Gale. eCoursepacks give educators access to current content from thousands of popular, professional, and academic periodicals, including NACRA and Darden cases, and business and industry information from Gale. You also have the ability to easily add your own material-even collecting a royalty if you choose. Permissions for all eCoursepack content are already secured, saving you the time and worry of securing rights. eCoursepacks online publishing tools also save you time and energy by allowing you to quickly search the databases and make selections, organize all your content, and publish the final outline product in a clean, uniform, and full-color format. eCoursepacks are the best ways to provide your audience with current information easily, quickly, and inexpensively.

  **http://ecoursepacks.swlearning.com.**

- **WebTutor Toolbox.** WebTutor™ ToolBox provides instructors with links to content from the book companion Web site. It also provides rich communication tools to instructors and students, including a course calendar, chat, and e-mail. For more information about the WebTutor products, please contact your local Thomson sales representative.

## FOR THE STUDENT

- **Hall/Lieberman ThomsonNOW:** Available for purchase with the textbook, access to this robust site provides a powerful set of multimedia learning tools.

  Pre- and Post-Assessment Quizzes offer students diagnostic self-assessment of their comprehension of

each chapter and an individualized plan for directed study based on the areas in which they are found to have a weaker understanding. All testing is automatically graded as the instructor desires.

Master the Learning Objectives give step-by-step instructions associated with each learning objective to guide students systematically through all the activities that will deepen their understanding of that particular concept.

The Graphing Workshop is a one-stop learning resource to help students master the language of graphs — one of the more difficult aspects of an economics course for many learners. It enables students to explore important economic concepts through a unique learning system made up of tutorials, interactive drawing tools, and exercises that teach how to interpret, reproduce, and explain graphs. Key graphs are identified throughout the text.

"Using the Theory" applications ask students to use the three key steps to analyze unique and real-world questions.

Ask the Instructor Video Clips, presented via streaming video, explain and illustrate difficult concepts from each chapter. Featuring Dr. Peter Olson, an economics instructor from Indiana University, these clips provide extremely helpful review and clarification if a student has trouble understanding an in-class lecture or is more of a visual learner.

ABC News Video Segments deliver the "real world" right to students' desktops, giving sudents a context for how economic topics affect world and national events as well as their own daily lives, and helping them learn material by applying it to current events.

ABC News Video Segments within ThomsonNOW give students the context on how economic topics affect world and national events as well as their own daily lives.

- **Tomlinson Economics Videos.** Featuring award-winning teacher and professional communicator, Steven Tomlinson (Ph.D, Stanford), these new Web-based lecture video products—Economic LearningPath and Economic JumpStart®—are sure to engage your students, while reinforcing the economic concepts they need to know. Many of these videos are also part of ThomsonNOW.

- **Complete Online Economics Course.** Whether using these videos to deliver online lectures for a distance learning class or as the required text for your Principles course, *Economics with Steven Tomlinson* presents and develops the fundamentals of economics. While this video text offers comprehensive coverage of economic principles, with more than 40 hours of video lecture, you can offer your students an exceptional value package and a richer learning experience by pairing the video text with one of Thomson South-Western's eight Principles of Economics texts. The videos are also available in Microeconomics and Macroeconomics split versions.

- **Economic LearningPath® and Economic JumpStart Videos.** Great online resources to accompany any Economics text, these segments are like unlimited office hours for your students!. Pre and post tests ensure that students are on track. The JumpStart product contains only the introductory building block principles chapters, while the LearningPath product contains all the topics in either a micro or macro course.

Visit **www.thomsonedu.com/economics/tomlinson/videos** to learn more.

- *Aplia* is an on-line product developed by world-renowned economist Paul Romer and used by thousands of economics students at hundreds of colleges and universities. It includes online interactive problem sets that follow the order of topics within the text. To ensure the highest level of correlation with this textbook, the authors reviewed every Aplia question for suitability, modified hundreds of them for a closer fit, and wrote hundreds of new questions from scratch. And they reviewed each question for this new edition, making further changes whenever necessary. Their involvement has ensured consistency in pedagogical approach and technical language, and will allow students to move seamlessly from the text to Aplia and back again.

- The *Active Learning Guide,* by Geoffrey A. Jehle of Vassar College. This study guide provides numerous exercises and self-tests for problem-solving practice. It is a valuable tool for helping students strengthen their knowledge of economics, and includes a sample multiple-choice final exam, with answers and explanations.

- *WebTutor Advantage:* Available on WebCT and/or Blackboard, this interactive, Web-based student supplement harnesses the power of the Internet to deliver innovative learning aids that actively engage students. Instructors can incorporate WebTutor as an integral part of the course, or students can use it on their own as a study guide. Benefits to students include automatic and immediate feedback from quizzes and exams; interactive, multimedia-rich explanation of concepts; online exercises that reinforce what students have learned; flashcards that include audio support; and greater interaction and involvement through online discussion forums. Visit WebTutor to see a demo and for more information: **http://webtutor.thomsonlearning.com.**

- *The Hall/Lieberman Web site* (**www.thomsonedu.com/economics/hall**). The text Web site contains a wealth of useful teaching and learning resources. Important features available at the Web site include *Interactive Quizzes* with feedback on answers—completed quizzes can be e-mailed directly to the instructor; a sample chapter from the *Active Learning Guide;* and links to other economic resources.

- *Economics: Hits on the Web.* This resource booklet supports your students' research efforts on the World Wide Web. The manual covers materials such as: introduction to the World Wide Web, browsing the Web, finding information on the World Wide Web, e-mail, e-mail discussion groups, newsgroups, and documenting Internet sources for research. It also provides a listing of the hottest economic sites on the Web.

- *9/11: Economic Viewpoints.* The shape, pace, and spirit of the global economy have been greatly impacted by the events that occurred on September 11, 2001. *With 9/11: Economic Viewpoints,* South-Western offers a collection of essays that provides a variety of perspectives on the economic effects of this event. Each essay is written by one of South-Western's economics textbook authors, all of whom are highly regarded for both their academic and professional achievements. This unique collaboration results in one of the most cutting-edge resources available to help facilitate discussions of September 11's impact within the context of economics courses.

- *The Economist's Handbook: A Research and Writing Guide,* 2nd Edition. This reference book, by Thomas Wyrick of Southwest Missouri State University, is designed to help students develop skills in conducting and interpreting economic research. *The Economist's Handbook* provides commonsense explanations, relevant examples, and focused assignments, as well as an extensive glossary of economic terms, information about economics careers, and other useful reference materials.

# ACKNOWLEDGMENTS

Our greatest debt is to the many reviewers who careful-ly read the book and provided numerous suggestions for improvements. While we could not incorporate all their ideas, we did carefully evaluate each one of them. To these reviewers of past editions, we are most grateful:

| | |
|---|---|
| Ljubisa Adamovich | Florida State University |
| Brian A'Hearn | Franklin and Marshall College |
| Rashid Al-Hmoud | Texas Tech University |
| David Aschauer | Bates College |
| Richard Ballman | Augustana College |
| Chris Barnett | Gannon University |
| Parantap Basu | Fordham University |
| Tibor Besedes | Rutgers University |
| Gautam Bhattacharya | University of Kansas |
| Sylvain Boko | Wake Forest University |
| Mark Buenafe | Arizona State University |
| Steven Call | Metropolitan State College |
| Kevin Carey | American University |
| Steven Cobb | Xavier University |
| Dennis Debrecht | Carroll College |
| Selahattin Dibooglu | Southern Illinois University |
| James E. Dietz | California State University, Fullerton |
| Khosrow Doroodian | Ohio University |
| John Duffy | University of Pittsburgh |
| Debra S. Dwyer | SUNY, Stony Brook |
| Stephen Erfle | Dickinson College |
| James Falter | Mount Marty College |
| Sasan Fayazmanesh | California State University, Fresno |
| Lehman B. Fletcher | Iowa State University |
| James R. Gale | Michigan Technological University |
| Sarmila Ghosh | University of Scranton |
| Satyajit Ghosh | University of Scranton |
| Scott Gilbert | Southern Illinois University-Carbondale |
| Michael Gootzeit | University of Memphis |
| John Gregor | Washington and Jefferson University |
| Arunee C. Grow | Mesa Community College |
| Rik Hafer | Southern Illinois University |
| Roger Hewett | Drake University |
| Andrew Hildreth | University of California, Berkeley |
| Shahruz Hohtadi | Suffolk University |
| Thomas Husted | American University |
| Jeffrey Johnson | Sullivan University |
| Jacqueline Khorassani | Marietta College |
| Philip King | San Francisco State University |
| Frederic R. Kolb | University of Wisconsin, Eau Claire |
| Kate Krause | University of New Mexico |
| Brent Kreider | Iowa State University |
| Viju Kulkarni | San Diego State University |
| Nazma Latif-Zaman | Providence College |
| Teresa Laughlin | Palomar College |
| Bruce Madariaga | Montgomery College |
| Judith Mann | University of California, San Diego |
| Mark McCleod | Virginia Tech University |
| Steve McQueen | Barstow Community College |
| William R. Melick | Kenyon College |
| Shahruz Mohtadi | Suffolk University |
| Paul G. Munyon | Grinnell College |
| Rebecca Neumann | University of Wisconsin, Milwaukee |
| Chris Niggle | University of Redlands |
| Emmanuel Nnadozie | Truman State University |
| Farrokh Nourzad | Marquette University |
| Jim Palmieri | Simpson College |
| Zaohong Pan | Western Connecticut State University |
| Yvon Pho | American University |
| Gregg Pratt | Mesa Community College |
| Teresa Riley | Youngstown State University |
| William Rosen | Cornell University |
| Alannah Orrison Rosenberg | Saddleback Community College |
| Thomas Sadler | Pace University |
| Jonathan Sandy | University of San Diego |
| Ramazan Sari | Texas Tech University |
| Ghosh Sarmila | University of Scranton |
| Edward Scahill | University of Scranton |
| Robert F. Schlack | Carthage College |
| Pamela M. Schmitt | U.S. Naval Academy |
| Mary Schranz | University of Wisconsin, Madison |
| Alden Shiers | California Polytechnic State University |
| Kevin Siqueira | Clarkson University |
| Kevin Sontheimer | University of Pittsburgh |
| Richard Steinberg | Indiana University-Purdue University Indianapolis |

| | |
|---|---|
| Martha Stuffler | Irvine Valley College |
| Mohammad Syed | Miles College |
| John Vahaly | University of Louisville |
| Mikayel Vardanyan | Oregon State University |
| Thomas Watkins | Eastern Kentucky University |
| Glen Whitman | California State University, Northridge |
| Robert Whaples | Wake Forest University |
| Michael F. Williams | University of St. Thomas |
| Dirk Yandell | University of San Diego |
| Petr Zemcik | Southern Illinois University, Carbondale |

We are especially grateful to the reviewers of this fourth edition:

| | |
|---|---|
| Gerald Scott | Florida Atlantic University |
| Thomas McCaleb | Florida State University |
| Jeff Rubin | Rutgers University |
| Mark Frascatore | Clarkson College |
| Arthur M. Diamond, Jr. | University of Nebraska at Omaha |
| Arsen Melkumian | West Virginia University |
| Richard Fowles | University of Utah |
| Frank Mixon | University of Southern Mississippi |
| Barry Bomboy | J Sargeant Reynolds Community College |
| Michael Heslop | Northern Virginia C.C. |
| Daniel Horton | Cleveland State |
| Barry Falk | Iowa State University |
| Kiril Tochkov | Binghamton University |
| Manjuri Talukdar | Northern Illinois University |
| William Doyle Smith | University of Texas - El Paso |
| Rose Rubin | U* of Memphis |
| Scott Redenius | Bryn Mawr College |
| Thomas Pogue | University of Iowa |
| Nick Noble | Miami University-Ohio |
| Jeff Gropp | DePauw |
| Dennis Debrecht | Carroll College |
| Ali Akarca | University of Illinois-Chicago |

We also wish to acknowledge the talented and dedicated group of instructors who helped put together a supplementary package that is second to none. Geoffrey A. Jehle of Vassar College cowrote the *Active Learning Guide* and created numerous improvements to this edition making it even more user-friendly and *active*. Dennis Hanseman revised the *Instructor's Manual*, and the Test Banks were carefully revised by Robert Guell of Indiana State University. Finally, special thanks go to Dennis Hanseman, who was our development editor for the first edition; his insights and ideas are still present in this fourth edition, and his continued assistance has proved invaluable.

The beautiful book you are holding would not exist except for the hard work of a talented team of professionals. Book production was overseen by Tamborah Moore, Content Project Manager at South-Western, and undertaken by Katherine Wilson at Lachina Publishing Services. Tamborah and Katherine showed remarkable patience, as well as an unflagging concern for quality throughout the process. We couldn't have asked for better production partners. Two NYU students—Andrea Schiferl and Sara-Ashley Orr—helped to locate and fix the few remaining errors.

The overall look of the book and cover was planned by Michelle Kunkler and executed by Lisa Albonetti. Deanna Ettinger managed the photo program, and Sandee Milewski made all the pieces come together in her role as Manufacturing Coordinator.

We are especially grateful for the hard work of the dedicated and professional South-Western editorial, marketing, and sales teams. Mike Worls, Senior Acquisitions Editor, has once again shepherded this text through publication with remarkable skill and devotion. John Carey, Senior Marketing Manager, has done a first-rate job getting the message out to instructors and sales reps. Susan Smart, who has been Senior Development Editor on several editions, once again delved into every chapter and contributed to their improvement. With each new edition, she has shown greater patience, flexibility, and skill in managing both content and authors. Dana Cowden, Technology Project Editor, has put together a wonderful package of media tools and the Thomson South-Western sales representatives have been extremely persuasive advocates for the book. We sincerely appreciate all their efforts!

Finally, we want to acknowledge the amazing team at Aplia, who helped us as we modified existing Aplia problems, and wrote new ones, to create the closest possible fit with our textbook. In particular, Paul Romer (CEO and Founder), Kristen Ford (Managing Editor) and Perkin Chung (Senior Content Developer) showed remarkable skill, knowledge, and patience in working with us on content, and in coming up with clever ways to make our job easier. It was a pleasure to work with them.

## A REQUEST

Although we have worked hard on the first three editions of this book, we know there is always room for further improvement. For that, our fellow users are indispensable. We invite your comments and suggestions wholeheartedly. We especially welcome your suggestions for additional "Using the Theory" sections and Dangerous Curves. You may send your comments to either of us care of South-Western.

Bob Hall
Marc Lieberman

# About the Authors

## Robert E. Hall

is a prominent applied economist. He is the Robert and Carole McNeil Professor of Economics at Stanford University and Senior Fellow at Stanford's Hoover Institution where he conducts research on inflation, unemployment, taxation, monetary policy, and the economics of high technology. He received his  Ph.D. from MIT and has taught there as well as at the University of California, Berkeley. Hall is Director of the research program on Economic Fluctuations of the National Bureau of Economic Research, and Chairman of the Bureau's Committee on Business Cycle Dating, which maintains the semiofficial chronology of the U.S. business cycle. He has published numerous monographs and articles in scholarly journals, and coauthored a popular intermediate text. Hall has advised the Treasury Department and the Federal Reserve Board on national economic policy, and has testified on numerous occasions before congressional committees.

## Marc Lieberman

is Clinical Associate Professor of Economics at New York University. He received his Ph.D. from Princeton University. Lieberman has presented his extremely popular Principles of Economics course at Harvard, Vassar, the University of California, Santa Cruz, and the University of Hawaii, as well as at NYU, where he  won the university's Golden Dozen teaching award and also the Economics Society Award for Excellence in Teaching. He is coeditor and contributor to *The Road to Capitalism: Economic Transformation in Eastern Europe and the Former Soviet Union*. Lieberman has consulted for the Bank of America and the Educational Testing Service. In his spare time, he is a professional screenwriter, and teaches screenwriting at NYU's School of Continuing and Professional Studies.

# What Is Economics?

*Economics.* The word conjures up all sorts of images: manic stock traders on Wall Street, an economic summit meeting in a European capital, a somber television news anchor announcing good or bad news about the economy. . . . You probably hear about economics several times each day. What exactly *is* economics?

First, economics is a *social science*, so it seeks to explain something about *society*. In this sense, it has something in common with psychology, sociology, and political science. But economics is different from these other social sciences because of *what* economists study and *how* they study it. Economists ask different questions, and they answer them using tools that other social scientists find rather exotic.

## ECONOMICS, SCARCITY, AND CHOICE

A good definition of economics, which stresses the difference between economics and other social sciences, is the following:

> *Economics is the study of choice under conditions of scarcity.*

**Economics** The study of choice under conditions of scarcity.

This definition may appear strange to you. Where are the familiar words we ordinarily associate with economics: "money," "stocks and bonds," "prices," "budgets," . . .? As you will soon see, economics deals with all of these things and more. But first, let's take a closer look at two important ideas in this definition: scarcity and choice.

## SCARCITY AND INDIVIDUAL CHOICE

Think for a moment about your own life. Is there anything you don't have that you'd *like* to have? Anything you'd like *more* of? If your answer is "no," congratulations! You are well advanced on the path of Zen self-denial. The rest of us, however, feel the pinch of limits to our material standard of living. This simple truth is at the very core of economics. It can be restated this way: We all face the problem of **scarcity**.

At first glance, it may seem that you suffer from an infinite variety of scarcities. There are so many things you might like to have right now—a larger room or apartment, a new car, more clothes . . . the list is endless. But a little reflection suggests

**Scarcity** A situation in which the amount of something available is insufficient to satisfy the desire for it.

that your limited ability to satisfy these desires is based on two other, more basic limitations: scarce *time* and scarce *spending power*.

> As individuals, we face a scarcity of time and spending power. Given more of either, we could each have more of the goods and services that we desire.

The scarcity of spending power is no doubt familiar to you. We've all wished for higher incomes so that we could afford to buy more of the things we want. But the scarcity of time is equally important. So many of the activities we enjoy—seeing a movie, taking a vacation, making a phone call—require time as well as money. Just as we have limited spending power, we also have a limited number of hours in each day to satisfy our desires.

Because of the scarcities of time and spending power, each of us is forced to make *choices*. We must allocate our scarce *time* to different activities: work, play, education, sleep, shopping, and more. We must allocate our scarce *spending power* among different goods and services: housing, food, furniture, travel, and many others. And each time we choose to buy something or do something, we also choose *not* to buy or do something else.

Economists study the choices we make as individuals and also the *consequences* of those choices. For example, over the next decade, the fraction of high school graduates choosing to attend college is expected to rise to record levels. What does this mean for state and federal budgets? What will happen to the wages and salaries of those with college degrees, and those without them? What are the implications for our ability to reform health care, to reduce poverty, and to deal with other problems? Economics is uniquely equipped to analyze these questions.

Economists also study the more subtle and indirect effects of individual choice on our society. Will most Americans continue to live in houses or—like Europeans—will most of us end up in apartments? As the population ages, what will happen to the quality and accessibility of health care for the elderly? Will traffic congestion in our cities continue to worsen or is there relief in sight? These questions hinge, in large part, on the separate decisions of millions of people. To answer them requires an understanding of how individuals make choices under conditions of scarcity.

## SCARCITY AND SOCIAL CHOICE

**Resources** The labor, capital, land and natural resources, and entrepreneurship that are used to produce goods and services.

Now let's think about scarcity and choice from *society*'s point of view. What are the goals of our society? We want a high standard of living for our citizens, clean air, safe streets, good schools, and more. What is holding us back from accomplishing all of these goals in a way that would satisfy everyone? You already know the answer: scarcity. In society's case, the problem is a scarcity of **resources**—the things we use to make goods and services that help us achieve our goals.

### The Four Resources

**Labor** The time human beings spend producing goods and services.

Economists classify resources into four categories:

1. **Labor** is the time human beings spend producing goods and services.

**Capital** A long-lasting tool that is used to produce other goods.

2. **Capital** is a long-lasting tool that we produce to help us make other goods and services.

    It's useful to distinguish two different types of capital. **Physical capital** consists of things like machinery and equipment, factory buildings, computers, and

**Physical capital** The part of the capital stock consisting of physical goods, such as machinery, equipment, and factories.

even hand tools like hammers and screwdrivers. These are all long-lasting *physical* goods that are used to make other things.

**Human capital** consists of the skills and knowledge possessed by workers. These satisfy our definition of capital: They are *produced* (through education and training), they help us produce *other* things, and they last for many years, typically through an individual's working life.[1]

Note the word *long-lasting* in the definition. If something is used up quickly in the production process—like the flour a baker uses to make bread—it is generally *not* considered capital. A good rule of thumb is that capital should last at least a year, although most types of capital last considerably longer.

The **capital stock** is the total amount of capital at a nation's disposal at any point in time. It consists of all the physical and human capital made in previous periods that is still productively useful.

3. **Land** refers to the physical space on which production takes place, as well as useful materials—*natural resources*—found under it or on it, such as crude oil, iron, coal, or fertile soil.

4. **Entrepreneurship** is the ability (and the willingness to *use* it) to combine the *other* resources into a productive enterprise. An entrepreneur may be an *innovator* who comes up with an original idea for a business or a *risk taker* who provides her own funds or time to nurture a project with uncertain rewards.

Anything *produced* in the economy comes, ultimately, from some combination of these four resources. Think about the last lecture you attended at your college. You were consuming a service—a college lecture. What went into producing that service? Your instructor was supplying labor. Many types of physical capital were used as well, including desks, chairs, a chalkboard or transparency projector, the classroom building itself, and the computer your instructor may have used to compose lecture notes. There was human capital—your instructor's specialized knowledge and lecturing skills. There was land—the property on which your classroom building sits, and natural resources like oil or natural gas to heat or cool the building. And some individual or group had to play the role of innovator and risk taker in order to combine the labor, capital, and natural resources needed to create and guide your institution in its formative years. (If you attend a public college or university, this entrepreneurial role was largely filled by the state government, with the state's taxpayers assuming the risk.)

> *As a society, our resources—land, labor, capital, and entrepreneurship—are insufficient to produce all the goods and services we might desire. In other words, society faces a scarcity of resources.*

This stark fact about the world helps us understand the choices a society must make. Do we want a more educated citizenry? Of course. But that will require more labor—construction workers to build more classrooms and teachers to teach in them. It will require more land for classrooms and lumber to build them. And it will require more capital—bulldozers, cement mixers, trucks, and more. These very same resources, however, could instead be used to produce *other* things that we find desirable, things

**Human capital** The skills and training of the labor force.

**Capital stock** The total amount of capital in a nation that is productively useful at a particular point in time.

**Land** The physical space on which production takes place, as well as the natural resources that come with it.

**Entrepreneurship** The ability and willingness to combine the *other* resources—labor, capital, and natural resources—into a productive enterprise.

---

[1] An individual's human capital is ordinarily supplied along with her labor time. (When your instructor lectures or holds office hours, she is providing both labor time and her skills as an economist and teacher.) Still, it's often useful to distinguish the *time* a worker provides (her labor) from any skills or *knowledge* possessed (human capital).

such as new homes, hospitals, automobiles, or feature films. As a result, every society must have some method of *allocating* its scarce resources—choosing which of our many competing desires will be fulfilled and which will not be.

Many of the big questions of our time center on the different ways in which resources can be allocated. The cataclysmic changes that rocked Eastern Europe and the former Soviet Union during the early 1990s arose from a very simple fact: The method these countries used for decades to allocate resources was not working. Closer to home, the never-ending debates between Democrats and Republicans in the United States about tax rates, government services, and even foreign policy reflect subtle but important differences of opinion about how to allocate resources. Often, these are disputes about whether the private sector can handle a particular issue of resource allocation on its own or whether the government should be involved.

**Input** Anything (including a resource) used to produce a good or service.

**DANGEROUS CURVES**

**Resources versus Inputs** The term *resources* is often confused with another, more general term—**inputs**. An input is *anything* used to make a good or service. Inputs include not only resources but also many other things made from them (cement, rolled steel, electricity), which are, in turn, used to make goods and services. *Resources*, by contrast, are the *special* inputs that fall into one of four categories: labor, land, capital, and entrepreneurship. They are the ultimate source of everything that is produced.

## SCARCITY AND ECONOMICS

The scarcity of resources—and the choices it forces us to make—is the source of all of the problems you will study in economics. Households have limited incomes for satisfying their desires, so they must choose carefully how they allocate their spending among different goods and services. Business firms want to make the highest possible profit, but they must pay for their resources; so they carefully choose *what* to produce, *how much* to produce, and *how* to produce it. Federal, state, and local government agencies work with limited budgets, so they must carefully choose which goals to pursue. Economists study these decisions made by households, firms, and governments to explain how our economic system operates, to forecast the future of our economy, and to suggest ways to make that future even better.

## THE WORLD OF ECONOMICS

The field of economics is surprisingly broad. It extends from the mundane—why does a pound of steak cost more than a pound of chicken?—to the personal and profound—how do couples decide how many children to have? With a field this broad, it is useful to have some way of classifying the different types of problems economists study and the different methods they use to analyze them.

### MICROECONOMICS AND MACROECONOMICS

**Microeconomics** The study of the behavior of individual households, firms, and governments; the choices they make; and their interaction in specific markets.

The field of economics is divided into two major parts: microeconomics and macroeconomics. **Microeconomics** comes from the Greek word *mikros*, meaning "small." It takes a close-up view of the economy, as if looking through a microscope. Microeconomics is concerned with the behavior of *individual* actors on the economic scene—households, business firms, and governments. It looks at the choices they make and how they interact with each other when they come together to trade *specific* goods and services. What will happen to the cost of movie tickets over the next five years? How many management-trainee jobs will open up for college graduates? How would U.S. phone companies be affected by a tax on imported cell phones? These are all microeconomic questions because they analyze individual *parts* of an economy rather than the *whole*.

Macroeconomics—from the Greek word *makros*, meaning "large"—takes an *overall* view of the economy. Instead of focusing on the production of carrots or computers, macroeconomics lumps all goods and services together and looks at the economy's *total output*. Instead of focusing on employment of management trainees or manufacturing workers, it considers *total employment* in the economy. Instead of asking why credit card loans carry higher interest rates than home mortgage loans, it asks what makes interest rates *in general* rise or fall. In all of these cases, macroeconomics focuses on the big picture and ignores the fine details.

**Macroeconomics** The study of the behavior of the overall economy.

## POSITIVE AND NORMATIVE ECONOMICS

The micro versus macro distinction is based on the level of detail we want to consider. Another useful distinction has to do with our *purpose* in analyzing a problem. **Positive economics** deals with *how* the economy works, plain and simple. If someone says, "Recent increases in spending for domestic security have slowed the growth rate of the U.S. economy," she is making a positive economic statement. A statement need not be accurate or even sensible to be classified as positive. For example, "Government policy has no effect on our standard of living" is a statement that virtually every economist would regard as false. But it is still a positive economic statement. Whether true or not, it's about how the economy works and its accuracy can be tested by looking at the facts—and just the facts.

**Positive economics** The study of how the economy works.

**Normative economics** concerns itself with what *should be*. It is used to make judgments about the economy and prescribe solutions to economic problems. Rather than limiting its concerns to just "the facts," it goes on to say what we should *do* about them and therefore depends on our values.

**Normative economics** The study of what *should be*; it is used to make judgments about the economy, and prescribe solutions.

If an economist says, "We should cut total government spending," she is engaging in normative economic analysis. Cutting government spending would benefit some citizens and harm others, so the statement rests on a value judgment. A normative statement—like the one about government spending above—cannot be proved or disproved by the facts alone.

Positive and normative economics are intimately related in practice. For one thing, we cannot properly argue about what we should or should not do unless we know certain facts about the world. Every normative analysis is therefore based on an underlying positive analysis. But while a positive analysis can, at least in principle, be conducted without value judgments, a normative analysis is always based, at least in part, on the values of the person conducting it.

**Seemingly Positive Statements** Be alert to statements that may *seem* positive but are actually normative. Here's an example: "If we want to reduce pollution, our society will have to use less gasoline." This may *sound* positive, because it seems to refer only to facts about the world. But it's actually normative. Why? Cutting back on gasoline is just *one* policy among many that could reduce pollution. To say that we *must* choose this method makes a value judgment about its superiority to other methods. A purely positive statement on this topic would be, "Using less gasoline—with no other change in living habits—would reduce pollution."

Similarly, be alert to statements that use vague terms with hidden value judgments. An example: "All else equal, the less gasoline we use, the better our quality of life." Whether you agree or disagree, this is *not* a positive statement. Two people who agree about the facts—in this case, the consequences of using less gasoline—might disagree over the meaning of the phrase "quality of life," how to measure it, and what would make it better. This disagreement could not be resolved just by looking at the facts.

DANGEROUS CURVES

### Why Economists Disagree

The distinction between positive and normative economics can help us understand why economists sometimes disagree. Suppose you are watching a television interview in which two economists are asked whether the United States should eliminate all government-imposed barriers to trading with the rest of the world. The first economist says, "Yes, absolutely," but the other says, "No, definitely not." Why the sharp disagreement?

The difference of opinion may be *positive* in nature: The two economists may have different views about what would actually happen if trade barriers were eliminated. Differences like this sometimes arise because our knowledge of the economy is imperfect or because certain facts are in dispute.

In some cases, however, the disagreement will be *normative*. Economists, like everyone else, have different values. In this case, both economists might agree that opening up international trade would benefit *most* Americans, but harm *some* of them. Yet they may still disagree about the policy move because they have different values. The first economist might put more emphasis on benefits to the overall economy, while the second might put more emphasis on preventing harm to a particular group. Here, the two economists have come to the same *positive* conclusion, but their *different values* lead them to different *normative* conclusions.

In the media, economists are rarely given enough time to express the basis for their opinions, so the public hears only the disagreement. People may then conclude that economists cannot agree about how the economy works, even when the *real* disagreement is over goals and values.

## WHY STUDY ECONOMICS?

If you've gotten this far into the chapter, chances are you've already decided to allocate some of your scarce time to studying economics. We think you've made a wise choice. But it's worth taking a moment to consider what you might gain from this choice.

Why study economics?

### TO UNDERSTAND THE WORLD BETTER

Applying the tools of economics can help you understand global and catastrophic events such as wars, famines, epidemics, and depressions. But it can also help you understand much of what happens to you locally and personally—the worsening traffic conditions in your city, the raise you can expect at your job this year, or the long line of people waiting to buy tickets for a popular concert. Economics has the power to help us understand these phenomena because they result, in large part, from the choices we make under conditions of scarcity.

Economics has its limitations, of course. But it is hard to find any aspect of life about which economics does not have *something* important to say. Economics cannot explain why so many Americans like to watch television, but it *can* explain how TV networks decide which programs to offer. Economics cannot protect you from a robbery, but it *can* explain why some people choose to become thieves and why no society has chosen to eradicate crime completely. Economics will not improve your love life, resolve unconscious conflicts from your childhood, or help you overcome a fear of flying, but it *can* tell us how many skilled therapists, ministers, and counselors are available to help us solve these problems.

## To Achieve Social Change

If you are interested in making the world a better place, economics is indispensable. There is no shortage of serious social problems worthy of our attention—unemployment, hunger, poverty, disease, child abuse, drug addiction, violent crime. Economics can help us understand the origins of these problems, explain why previous efforts to solve them haven't succeeded, and help us to design new, more effective solutions.

## To Help Prepare for Other Careers

Economics has long been a popular college major for individuals intending to work in business. But it has also been popular among those planning careers in politics, international relations, law, medicine, engineering, psychology, and other professions. This is for good reason: Practitioners in each of these fields often find themselves confronting economic issues. For example, lawyers increasingly face judicial rulings based on the principles of economic efficiency. Doctors will need to understand how new technologies or changes in the structure of health insurance will affect their practices. Industrial psychologists need to understand the economic implications of workplace changes they may advocate, such as flexible scheduling or on-site child care.

## To Become an Economist

Only a tiny minority of this book's readers will decide to become economists. This is welcome news to the authors, and after you have studied labor markets in your *microeconomics* course you will understand why. But if you do decide to become an economist—obtaining a master's degree or even a Ph.D.—you will find many possibilities for employment. The economists with whom you have most likely had personal contact are those who teach and conduct research at colleges and universities. But about equal numbers of economists work outside and inside of academia. Economists are hired by banks to assess the risk of investing abroad; by manufacturing companies to help them determine new methods of producing, marketing, and pricing their products; by government agencies to help design policies to fight crime, disease, poverty, and pollution; by international organizations to help create and reform aid programs for less developed countries; by the media to help the public interpret global, national, and local events; and by nonprofit organizations to provide advice on controlling costs and raising funds more effectively.

## THE METHODS OF ECONOMICS

One of the first things you will notice as you begin to study economics is the heavy reliance on *models*.

You've no doubt encountered many models in your life. As a child, you played with model trains, model planes, or model people—dolls. You may have also seen architects' cardboard models of buildings. These are physical models, three-dimensional replicas that you can pick up and hold. Economic models, on the other hand, are built not with cardboard, plastic, or metal but with words, diagrams, and mathematical statements.

What, exactly, is a model?

**Model** An abstract representation of reality.

> A **model** is an abstract representation of reality.

The two key words in this definition are *abstract* and *representation*. A model is not supposed to be exactly like reality. Rather, it *represents* the real world by *abstracting* or *taking from* the real world that which will help us understand it. By definition, a model leaves out features of the real world.

## THE ART OF BUILDING ECONOMIC MODELS

When you build a model, how do you know which real-world details to include and which to leave out? There is no simple answer to this question. The right amount of detail depends on your purpose in building the model in the first place. There is, however, one guiding principle:

> A model should be as simple as possible to accomplish its purpose.

This means that a model should contain only the *necessary* details.

To understand this a little better, think about a map. A map is a model that represents a part of the earth's surface. But it leaves out many details of the real world. First, a map leaves out the third dimension—height—of the real world. Second, maps always ignore small details, such as trees and houses and potholes. But when you buy a map, how much detail do you want it to have?

Let's say you are in Boston, and you need a map to find the best way to drive from Logan Airport to the downtown convention center. In this case, you would want a very detailed city map, with every street, park, and plaza in Boston clearly illustrated and labeled as in the map on the left in Figure 1. A highway map, which ignores these details, wouldn't do at all.

But now suppose your purpose is different: to select the best driving route from Boston to Cincinnati. Now you want a highway map such as the one on the right in Figure 1. A map that shows every street between Boston and Cincinnati would have *too much* detail. All of that extraneous information would only obscure what you really need to see.

The same principle applies in building economic models. The level of detail that would be just right for one purpose will usually be too much or too little for another. When you feel yourself objecting to a model in this text because something has been left out, keep in mind the purpose for which the model is built. In introductory economics, the purpose is entirely educational. The models are designed to help you understand some simple, but powerful, principles about how the economy

---

**FIGURE** **1**

**Maps as Models**

*These maps are models. But each would be used for a different purpose.*

operates. Keeping the models simple makes it easier to see these principles at work and remember them later.

Of course, economic models have other purposes besides education. They can help businesses make decisions about pricing and production, help households decide how and where to invest their savings, and help governments and international agencies formulate policies. Models built for these purposes will be much more detailed than the ones in this text, and you will learn about them if you take more advanced courses in economics. But even complex models are built around very simple frameworks—the same frameworks you will be learning here.

## ASSUMPTIONS AND CONCLUSIONS

Every economic model begins with *assumptions* about the world. There are two types of assumptions in a model: simplifying assumptions and critical assumptions.

A **simplifying assumption** is just what it sounds like—a way of making a model simpler without affecting any of its important conclusions. The purpose of a simplifying assumption is to rid a model of extraneous detail so its essential features can stand out more clearly. A road map, for example, makes the simplifying assumption, "There are no trees" because trees on a map would only get in the way. Similarly, in an economic model, we might assume that there are only two goods that households can choose from or that there are only two nations in the world. We make such assumptions *not* because they are true, but because they make a model easier to follow and do not change any of the important insights we can get from it.

A **critical assumption,** by contrast, is an assumption that affects the conclusions of a model in important ways. When you use a road map, you make the critical assumption, "All of these roads are open." If that assumption is wrong, your conclusion—the best route to take—might be wrong as well.

In an economic model, there are always one or more critical assumptions. You don't have to look very hard to find them because economists like to make these assumptions explicit right from the outset. For example, when we study the behavior of business firms, our model will assume that firms try to earn the highest possible profit for their owners. By stating this critical assumption up front, we can see immediately where the model's conclusions spring from.

## THE THREE-STEP PROCESS

As you read this textbook, you will learn how economists use economic models to address a wide range of problems. In Chapter 2, for example, you will see how a simple economic model can give us important insights about society's production choices. And subsequent chapters will present still different models that help us understand the U.S. economy and the global economic environment in which it operates. As you read, it may seem to you that there are a lot of models to learn and remember . . . and, indeed, there are.

But there is an important insight about economics that—once mastered—will make your job easier than you might think. The insight is this: There is a remarkable similarity in the types of models that economists build, the assumptions that underlie those models, and what economists actually *do* with them. In fact, you will see that economists follow the same *three-step process* to analyze almost any economic problem. The first two steps explain how economists *build* an economic model, and the last explains how they *use* the model.

**Simplifying assumption** Any assumption that makes a model simpler without affecting any of its important conclusions.

**Critical assumption** Any assumption that affects the conclusions of a model in an important way.

What are these three steps that underlie the economic approach to almost any problem? Sorry for the suspense, but you'll have to wait a bit (until the end of Chapter 3) for the answer. By that time, you'll have learned a little more about economics, and the three-step process will make more sense to you.

## MATH, JARGON, AND OTHER CONCERNS...

Economists often express their ideas using mathematical concepts and a special vocabulary. Why? Because these tools enable economists to express themselves more precisely than with ordinary language. For example, someone who has never studied economics might say, "When gas is expensive, people don't buy big, gas-guzzling cars." That statement might not bother you right now. But once you've finished your first economics course, you'll be saying it something like this: "When the price of gas rises, the demand curve for big, gas-guzzling cars shifts leftward."

Does the second statement sound strange to you? It should. First, it uses a special term—a *demand curve*—that you haven't yet learned. Second, it uses a mathematical concept—a *shifting curve*—with which you might not be familiar. But while the first statement might mean a number of different things, the second statement—as you will see in Chapter 3—can mean only *one* thing. By being precise, we can steer clear of unnecessary confusion.

If you are worried about the special vocabulary of economics, you can relax. All of the new terms will be defined and carefully explained as you encounter them. Indeed, this textbook does not assume you have any special knowledge of economics. It is truly meant for a "first course" in the field.

But what about the math? Here, too, you can relax. While professional economists often use sophisticated mathematics to solve problems, only a little math is needed to understand basic economic *principles*. And virtually all of this math comes from high school algebra and geometry.

Still, if you have forgotten some of your high school math, a little brushing up might be in order. This is why we have included an appendix at the end of this chapter. It covers some of the most basic concepts—such as interpreting graphs, the equation for a straight line, and the concept of a slope—that you will need in this course. You may want to glance at this appendix now, just so you'll know what's there. Then, from time to time, you'll be reminded about it when you're most likely to need it.

## HOW TO STUDY ECONOMICS

As you read this book or listen to your instructor, you may find yourself following along and thinking that everything makes perfect sense. Economics may even seem easy. Indeed, it *is* rather easy to *follow* economics, since it's based so heavily on simple logic. But *following* and *learning* are two different things. You will eventually discover (preferably *before* your first exam) that economics must be studied actively, not passively.

If you are reading these words lying back on a comfortable couch, a phone in one hand and a remote control in the other, you are going about it in the wrong way. Active studying means reading with a pencil in your hand and a blank sheet of paper in front of you. It means closing the book periodically and *reproducing* what you have learned. It means listing the steps in each logical argument, retracing the flow of cause and effect in each model, and drawing the graphs that represent the model. It does require some work, but the payoff is a good understanding of economics and a better understanding of your own life and the world around you.

## Summary

*Economics* is the study of choice under conditions of scarcity. As individuals, and as a society, we have unlimited desires for goods and services. Unfortunately, the *resources*—land, labor, capital, and entrepreneurship—needed to produce those goods and services are scarce. Therefore, we must choose which desires to satisfy and how to satisfy them. Economics provides the tools that explain those choices.

The field of economics is divided into two major areas. *Microeconomics* studies the behavior of individual households, firms, and governments as they interact in specific markets. *Macroeconomics*, by contrast, concerns itself with the behavior of the entire economy. It considers variables such as total output, total employment, and the overall price level.

Economics makes heavy use of *models*—abstract representations of reality. These models are built with words, diagrams, and mathematical statements that help us understand how the economy operates. All models are simplifications, but a good model will have *just enough detail for the purpose at hand*.

When analyzing almost any problem, economists follow a three-step process in building and using economic models. This three-step process will be introduced at the end of Chapter 3.

## Problem Set  *Answers to even-numbered Questions and Problems can be found on the text Web site at www.thomsonedu.com/economics/hall.*

1. Discuss whether each statement is an example of positive economics or normative economics or if it contains elements of both:
   a. An increase in the personal income tax will slow the growth rate of the economy.
   b. The goal of any country's economic policy should be to increase the well-being of its poorest, most vulnerable citizens.
   c. Excess regulation of small business is stifling the economy. Small business has been responsible for most of the growth in employment over the last 10 years, but regulations are putting a severe damper on the ability of small businesses to survive and prosper.
   d. The 1990s were a disastrous decade for the U.S. economy. Income inequality increased to its highest level since before World War II.
2. For each of the following, state whether economists would consider it a *resource*, and if they would, identify which of the four types of resources the item is.
   a. A computer used by an FBI agent to track the whereabouts of suspected criminals.
   b. The office building in which the FBI agent works.
   c. The time that an FBI agent spends on a case.
   d. A farmer's tractor.

   e. The farmer's knowledge of how to operate the tractor.
   f. Crude oil.
   g. A package of frozen vegetables.
   h. A food scientist's knowledge of how to commercially freeze vegetables.
   i. The ability to bring together resources to start a frozen food company.
   j. Plastic bags used by a frozen food company to hold its product.
3. Suppose you are using the second map in Figure 1, which shows main highways only. You've reached a conclusion about the fastest way to drive from the Boston city center to an area south of the city. State whether each of the following assumptions of the map would be a *simplifying* or *critical* assumption for your conclusion, and explain briefly. (Don't worry about whether the assumption is true or not.)
   a. The thicker, numbered lines are major highways without traffic lights.
   b. The earth is two-dimensional.
   c. When two highways cross, you can get from one to the other without going through city traffic.
   d. Distances on the map are proportional to distances in the real world.

# APPENDIX

## Graphs and Other Useful Tools

### TABLES AND GRAPHS

A brief glance at this text will tell you that graphs are important in economics. Graphs provide a convenient way to display information and enable us to immediately *see* relationships between variables.

Suppose that you've just been hired at the advertising department of Len & Harry's—an up-and-coming manufacturer of high-end ice cream products, located in Texas. You've been asked to compile a report on how advertising affects the company's sales. It turns out that the company's spending on advertising has changed repeatedly in the past, so you have lots of data on monthly advertising expenditure and monthly sales revenue, both measured in thousands of dollars.

Table A.1 shows a useful way of arranging this data. The company's advertising expenditure in different months are listed in the left-hand column, while the right-hand column lists total sales revenue ("sales" for short) during the same months. Notice that the data here is organized so that spending on advertising increases as we move down the first column. Often, just looking at a table like this can reveal useful patterns. Here, it's clear that higher spending on advertising is associated with higher monthly sales. These two variables—advertising and sales—have a *positive relationship*. A rise in one is associated with a rise in the other. If higher advertising had been associated with *lower* sales, the two variables would have a *negative* or *inverse relationship:* A rise in one would be associated with a fall in the other.

We can be even more specific about the positive relationship between advertising and sales: Logic tells us that the association is very likely *causal*. We'd expect that sales revenue *depends on* advertising outlays, so we call sales our *dependent variable* and advertising our *independent variable*. Changes in an independent variable cause changes in a dependent variable, but not the other way around.

To explore the relationship further, let's graph it. As a rule, the *independent* variable is measured on the *horizontal* axis and the *dependent* variable on the *vertical* axis. In economics, unfortunately, we do not always stick to this rule, but for now we will. In Figure A.1, monthly advertising outlays—our independent variable—are measured on the horizontal axis. If we start at the *origin*—the corner where the two axes intersect—and move rightward along the horizontal axis, monthly advertising outlays increase from $0 to $1,000 to $2,000 and so on. The vertical axis measures monthly sales—the dependent variable. Along this axis, as we move upward from the origin, sales rise.

The graph in Figure A.1 shows six labeled points, each representing a different pair of numbers from our table. For example, point *A*—which represents the numbers in the first row of the table—shows us that when the firm spends $2,000 on advertising, sales are $24,000 per month. Point *B* represents the *second* row of the table, and so on. Notice that all of these points lie along a *straight line*.

| TABLE A.1 | Advertising Expenditures ($1,000 per Month) | Sales ($1,000 per Month) |
|---|---|---|
| Advertising and Sales at Len & Harry's | 2 | 24 |
| | 3 | 27 |
| | 6 | 36 |
| | 7 | 39 |
| | 11 | 51 |
| | 12 | 54 |

## STRAIGHT-LINE GRAPHS

You'll encounter straight-line graphs often in economics, so it's important to understand one special property they possess: The "rate of change" of one variable compared with the other is always the same. For example, look at what happens as we move from point *A* to point *B*: Advertising rises by $1,000 (from $2,000 to $3,000), while sales rise by $3,000 (from $24,000 to $27,000). If you study the graph closely, you'll see that anywhere along this line, whenever advertising increases by $1,000, sales increase by $3,000. Or, if we define a "unit" as "one thousand dollars," we can say that every time advertising increases by one unit, sales rise by three units. So the "rate of change" is three units of sales for every one unit of advertising.

The rate of change of the *vertically* measured variable for a one-unit change in the *horizontally* measured variable is also called the *slope* of the line. The slope of the line in Figure A.1 is three, and it remains three no matter where along the line we measure it. For example, make sure you can see that from point *C* to point *D*, advertising rises by one unit and sales rise by three units.

What if we had wanted to determine the slope of this line by comparing points *D* and *E*, which has advertising rising by four units instead of just one? In that case, we'd have to calculate the rise in one variable *per unit* rise in the other. To do this, we divide the change in the vertically measured variable by the change in the horizontally measured variable.

$$\text{Slope of a straight line} = \frac{\text{Change in vertical variable}}{\text{Change in horizontal variable}}.$$

We can make this formula even simpler by using two shortcuts. First, we can call the variable on the vertical axis "Y" and the variable on the horizontal axis "X." In our case, Y is sales, while X is advertising outlays. Second, we use the Greek letter Δ ("delta") to denote the words "change in." Then, our formula becomes:

$$\text{Slope of straight line} = \frac{\Delta Y}{\Delta X}.$$

Let's apply this formula to get the slope as we move from point *D* to point *E*, so that advertising (X) rises from 7 units to 11 units. This is an increase of 4, so ΔX = 4. For this move, sales rise from 39 to 51, an increase of 12, so ΔY = 12. Applying our formula,

$$\text{Slope} = \frac{\Delta Y}{\Delta X} = \frac{12}{4} = 3.$$

This is the same value for the slope that we found earlier. Not surprising, since it's a straight line and a straight line has the same slope everywhere. The particular pair of points we choose for our calculation doesn't matter.

## CURVED LINES

Although many of the relationships you'll encounter in economics have straight-line graphs, many others do

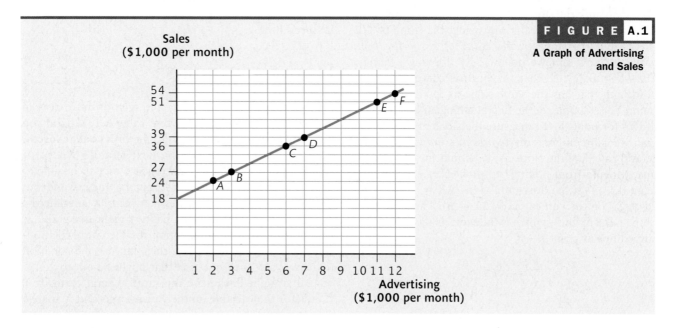

**FIGURE A.1**

**A Graph of Advertising and Sales**

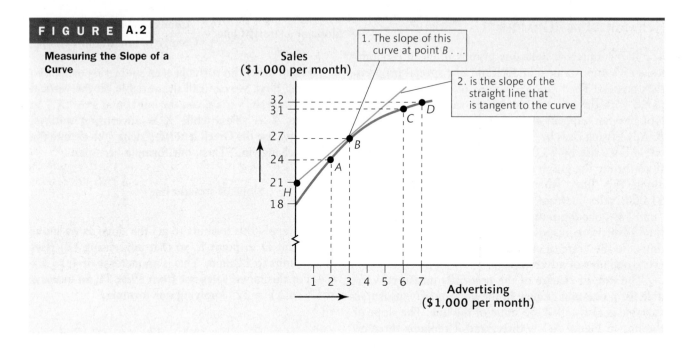

**FIGURE A.2**

**Measuring the Slope of a Curve**

1. The slope of this curve at point *B* . . .

2. is the slope of the straight line that is tangent to the curve

Sales ($1,000 per month)

Advertising ($1,000 per month)

---

not. Figure A.2 shows *another* possible relationship between advertising and sales that we might have found from a different set of data. As you can see, the line is curved. But as advertising rises, the curve gets flatter and flatter. Here, as before, each time we spend another $1,000 on advertising, sales rise. But now, the rise in sales seems to get smaller and smaller. This means that the *slope* of the curve is *itself changing* as we move along this curve. In fact, the slope is getting smaller.

How can we measure the slope of a curve? First, note that since the slope is different at every point along the curve, we aren't really measuring the slope of "the curve" but the slope of the curve *at a specific point along it*. How can we do this? By drawing a *tangent line*—a straight line that touches the curve at just one point and that has the same slope as the curve at that point. For example, in the figure, a tangent line has been drawn for point *B*. To measure the slope of this tangent line, we can compare any two points on it, say *H* and *B*, and calculate the slope as we would for any straight line. Moving from point *H* to point *B*, we are moving from 0 to 3 on the horizontal axis ($\Delta X = 3$) and from 21 to 27 on the vertical axis ($\Delta Y = 6$). Thus, the slope of the tangent line—which is the same as the slope of the curved line at point *B*—is

$$\frac{\Delta Y}{\Delta X} = \frac{6}{3} = 2.$$

This says that, at point *B*, the rate of change is two units of sales for every one unit of advertising. Or, going back to dollars, the rate of change is $2,000 in sales for every $1,000 spent on advertising.

The curve in Figure A.2 slopes everywhere upward, reflecting a positive relationship between the variables. But a curved line can also slope downward to illustrate a negative relationship between variables, or slope first one direction and then the other. You'll see plenty of examples of each type of curve in later chapters, and you'll learn how to interpret each one as it's presented.

## LINEAR EQUATIONS

Let's go back to the straight-line relationship between advertising and sales, as shown in Table A.1. What if you need to know how much in sales the firm could expect if it spent $5,000 on advertising next month? What if it spent $8,000, or $9,000? It would be nice to be able to answer questions like this without having to pull out tables and graphs to do it. As it turns out, anytime the relationship you are studying has a straight-line graph, it is easy to figure out an equation for the entire relationship—a *linear equation*. You then can use the equation to answer any such question that might be put to you.

All straight lines have the same general form. If *Y* stands for the variable on the vertical axis and *X* for the variable on the horizontal axis, every straight line has an equation of the form

$$Y = a + bX,$$

where *a* stands for some number and *b* for another number. The number *a* is called the vertical *intercept*, because it marks the point where the graph of this equation hits (intercepts) the vertical axis; this occurs when *X* takes the value zero. (If you plug *X* = 0 into the equation, you will see that, indeed, *Y* = *a*.) The number *b* is the slope of the line, telling us how much *Y* will change every time *X* changes by one unit. To confirm this, note that as *X* increases from 0 to 1, *Y* goes from *a* to *a* + *b*. The number *b* is therefore the change in *Y* corresponding to a one-unit change in *X*—exactly what the slope of the graph should tell us.

If *b* is a positive number, a one-unit increase in *X* causes *Y* to *increase* by *b* units, so the graph of our line would slope upward, as illustrated by the line in the upper left panel of Figure A.3. If *b* is a negative number, then a one-unit increase in *X* will cause *Y* to *decrease* by

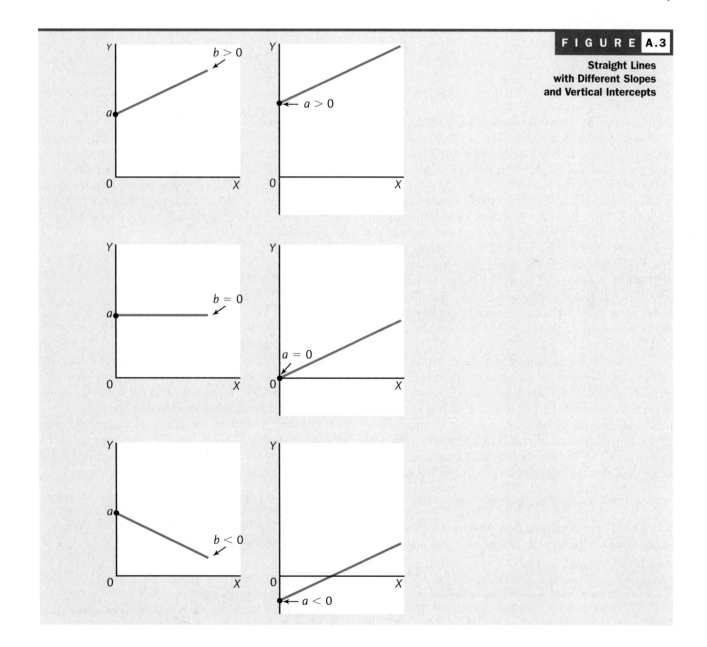

**FIGURE A.3**

**Straight Lines with Different Slopes and Vertical Intercepts**

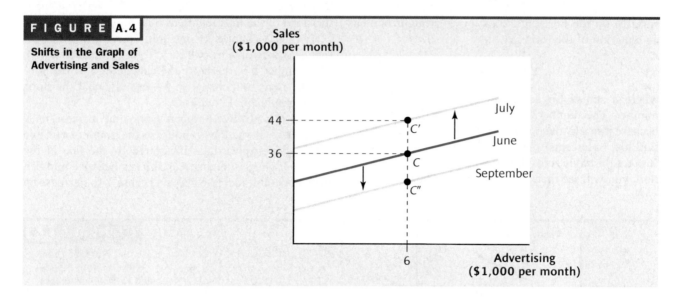

**FIGURE A.4**

**Shifts in the Graph of Advertising and Sales**

*b* units, so the graph would slope downward, as the line does in the lower left panel. Of course, *b* could equal zero. If it does, a one-unit increase in *X* causes no change in *Y*, so the graph of the line is flat, like the line in the middle left panel.

The value of *a* has no effect on the slope of the graph. Instead, different values of *a* determine the graph's position. When *a* is a positive number, the graph will intercept the vertical *Y*-axis above the origin, as the line does in the upper right panel of Figure A.3. When *a* is negative, however, the graph will intercept the *Y*-axis *below* the origin, like the line in the lower right panel. When *a* is zero, the graph intercepts the *Y*-axis right at the origin, as the line does in the middle right panel.

Let's see if we can figure out the equation for the relationship depicted in Figure A.1. There, *X* denotes advertising and *Y* denotes sales. Earlier, we calculated that the slope of this line, *b*, is 3. But what is *a*, the vertical intercept? In Figure A.1, you can see that when advertising outlays are zero, sales are $18,000. That tells us that *a* = 18.[2] Putting these two observations together, we find that the equation for the line in Figure A.1 is

$$Y = 18 + 3X.$$

*Now* if you need to know how much in sales to expect from a particular expenditure on advertising

(both in thousands of dollars), you'd be able to come up with an answer: You'd simply multiply the amount spent on advertising by 3, add 18, and that would be your sales in thousands of dollars. To confirm this, plug in for *X* in this equation any amount of advertising in dollars from the left-hand column of Table A.1. You'll see that you get the corresponding amount of sales in the right-hand column.

## HOW STRAIGHT LINES AND CURVES SHIFT

So far, we've focused on relationships where some variable *Y* depends on a single other variable, *X*. But in many of our theories, we recognize that some variable of interest to us is actually affected by more than just one other variable. When *Y* is affected by both *X* and some third variable, changes in that third variable will usually cause a *shift* in the graph of the relationship between *X* and *Y*. This is because whenever we draw the graph between *X* and *Y*, we are holding fixed every other variable that might possibly affect *Y*.

*A graph between two variables X and Y is only a picture of their relationship when all other variables affecting Y are held constant.*

But suppose one of these other variables *does* change? What happens then?

Think back to the relationship between advertising and sales. Earlier, we supposed sales depend only on advertising. But suppose we make an important discovery: Ice cream sales are *also* affected by how hot the

[2] We could also use direct logic to find the vertical intercept. In Figure A.1, locate any point—we'll use point A as our example, where *X* = 2 and *Y* = 24. From this point, to get to the vertical intercept, we'd have to decrease *X* by two units. But with a slope of 3, a two-unit decrease in *X* will cause a six-unit decrease in *Y*. Therefore, *Y* will decrease from 24 to 18. Summing up, we've found that when *X* = 0, *Y* = 18, so our vertical intercept is 18.

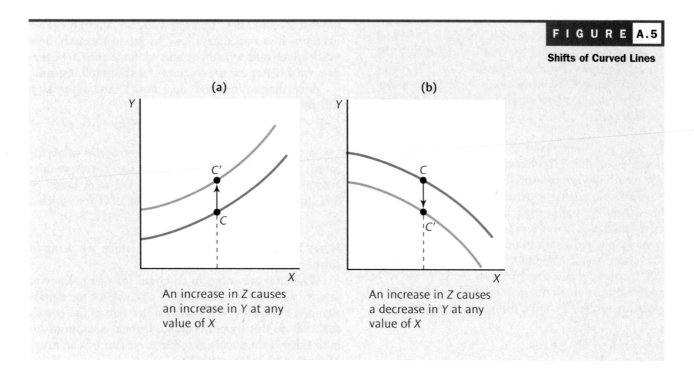

**F I G U R E  A.5**

**Shifts of Curved Lines**

**(a)**

An increase in Z causes
an increase in Y at any
value of X

**(b)**

An increase in Z causes
a decrease in Y at any
value of X

weather is. What's more, all of the data in Table A.1 on which we previously based our analysis turns out to have been from the month of June in different years, when the average temperature in Texas is 80 degrees. What's going to happen in July, when the average temperature rises to 100 degrees?

In Figure A.4 we've redrawn the graph from Figure A.1, this time labeling the line "June." Often, a good way to determine how a graph will shift is to perform a simple experiment like this: Put your pencil tip anywhere on the graph labeled June—let's say at point C. Now ask the following question: If I hold advertising constant at $6,000, do I expect to sell more or less ice cream as temperature rises in July? If you expect to sell more, then the amount of sales corresponding to $6,000 of advertising will be *above* point C, at a point such as C' (pronouned "C prime"), representing sales of $44,000. From this, we can tell that the graph will *shift upward* as temperature rises. In September, however, when temperatures fall, the amount of sales corresponding to $6,000 in advertising would be less than it is at point C. It would be shown by a point such as C" (pronounced "C double-prime"). In that case, the graph would shift downward.

The same procedure works well whether the original graph slopes upward or downward and whether it is a straight line or a curved one. Figure A.5 sketches two examples. In panel (a), an increase in some third variable, Z, increases the value of Y for each value of X,

so the graph of the relationship between X and Y shifts upward as Z increases. We often phrase it this way: "An increase in Z causes an increase in Y, *at any value of X.*" In panel (b), an increase in Z *decreases* the value of Y, at any value of X, so the graph of the relationship between X and Y shifts *downward* as Z increases.

You'll notice that in Figures A.4 and A.5, the original line is darker, while the new line after the shift is drawn in a lighter shade. We'll use this convention—a lighter shade for the new line after a shift—throughout this book.

## SHIFTS VERSUS MOVEMENTS ALONG A LINE

If you look back at Figure A.1, you'll see that when advertising increases (say, from $2,000 to $3,000), we *move along* our line, from point A to point B. But you've just learned that when average temperature changes, the entire line *shifts*. This may seem strange to you. After all, in both cases, an independent variable changes (either advertising or temperature). Why should we move *along* the line in one case and *shift* it in the other?

The reason for the difference is that in one case (advertising), the independent variable is *in our graph*, measured along one of the axes. When an independent variable in the graph changes, we simply move along the line. In the other case (temperature), the independent variable does *not* appear in our graph. Instead, it's been in the background, being held constant.

Here's a very simple—but crucial—rule:

*Suppose* Y *is the dependent variable, which is measured on one of the axes in a graph. If the independent variable **measured on the other axis changes, we move along** the line. But if **any other** independent variable changes, the **entire line shifts.***

Be sure you understand the phrase "any other independent variable." It refers to any variable that actually *affects* Y but is *not* measured on either axis in the graph.

This rule applies to straight lines as well as curved lines. And it applies even in more complicated situations, such as when *two different* lines are drawn in the same graph, and a shift of one causes a movement along the other. (You'll encounter this situation in Chapter 3.) But for now, make sure you can see how we've been applying this rule in our example, where the three variables are total sales, advertising, and temperature.

## SOLVING EQUATIONS

When we first derived the equation for the relationship between advertising and sales, we wanted to know what level of sales to expect from different amounts of advertising. But what if we're asked a slightly different question? Suppose, this time, you are told that the sales committee has set an ambitious goal of $42,000 for next month's sales. The treasurer needs to know how much to budget for advertising, and you have to come up with the answer.

Since we know how advertising and sales are related, we ought to be able to answer this question. One way is just to look at the graph in Figure A.1. There, we could first locate sales of $42,000 on the vertical axis. Then, if we read over to the line and then down, we find the amount of advertising that would be necessary to gener-

ate that level of sales. Yet even with that carefully drawn diagram, it is not always easy to see just exactly how much advertising would be required. If we need to be precise, we'd better use the equation for the graph instead.

According to the equation, sales ($Y$) and advertising ($X$) are related as follows:

$$Y = 18 + 3X.$$

In the problem before us, we know the value for sales, and we need to solve for the corresponding amount of advertising. Substituting the sales target of $42, for $Y$, we need to find that value of $X$ for which

$$42 = 18 + 3X.$$

Here, $X$ is the unknown value for which we want to solve.

Whenever we solve an equation for one unknown, say, $X$, we need to *isolate* $X$ on one side of the equals sign and everything else on the other side of the equals sign. We do this by performing identical operations on both sides of the equals sign. Here, we can first subtract 18 from both sides, getting

$$24 = 3X.$$

We can then divide both sides by 3 and get

$$8 = X.$$

This is our answer. If we want to achieve sales of $42,000, we'll need to spend $8,000 on advertising.

Of course, not all relationships are linear, so this technique will not work in every situation. But no matter what the underlying relationship, the idea remains the same:

*To solve for* X *in any equation, rearrange the equation, following the rules of algebra, so that* X *appears on one side of the equals sign and everything else in the equation appears on the other side.*

# Scarcity, Choice, and Economic Systems

What does it cost you to go to the movies? If you answered nine or ten dollars, because that is the price of a movie ticket, then you are leaving out a lot. Most of us are used to thinking of "cost" as the money we must pay for something. A Big Mac costs $3.15, a new Toyota Corolla costs $16,000, and the baby-sitter costs $8.00 an hour. Certainly, the money we pay for a good or service is a *part* of its cost. But economics takes a broader view of costs, recognizing monetary as well as non-monetary components.

## THE CONCEPT OF OPPORTUNITY COST

The total cost of any choice we make—buying a car, producing a computer, or even reading a book—is everything we must *give up* when we take that action. This cost is called the *opportunity cost* of the action, because we give up the opportunity to have other desirable things.

> The **opportunity cost** of any choice is what we must forego when we make that choice.

**Opportunity cost** What is given up when taking an action or making a choice.

Opportunity cost is the most accurate and complete concept of cost—the one we should use when making our own decisions or analyzing the decisions of others.

### Opportunity Cost for Individuals

Virtually every action we take as individuals uses up scarce money, scarce time, or both. This money or time *could* have been used for other things that you value. Thus, the true cost of any choice you make—the *opportunity cost*—is everything you actually sacrifice in making the choice.

Suppose, for example, it's 8 P.M. on a weeknight and you're spending a couple of hours reading this chapter. As authors, that thought makes us very happy, especially because we know there are many other things you could be doing: going to a movie, having dinner with friends, playing ping pong, earning some extra money, watching TV. . . . But, assuming you're still reading—and you haven't just run out the door to do something else—let's relate this to opportunity cost.

What *is* the opportunity cost of reading this chapter? Is it *all* of those other possibilities we've listed? Not really, because if you weren't reading for these two hours, you'd probably have time to do only *one* of them. And you'd no doubt choose whichever one among these alternatives you regarded as best. So, by reading, you sacrifice only the best choice among the alternatives that you could be doing instead.

> *When the alternatives to a choice are mutually exclusive, only the* next best *choice—the one that would actually be chosen—is used to determine the opportunity cost of the choice.*

For many choices, a large part of the opportunity cost is the money sacrificed. If you spend $15 on a new DVD, you have to part with $15, which is money you could have spent on something else (whatever the best choice among the alternatives turned out to be). But for other choices, money may be only a small part, or no part, of what is sacrificed. If you walk your dog a few blocks, it will cost you time but not money. Still, economists often like to attach a monetary value even to the parts of opportunity cost that *don't* involve money. By translating a sacrifice into a dollar value, we can express the opportunity cost of a choice as a single number, albeit a roughly estimated one. That, in turn, enables us to compare the cost of a choice with its benefits, which we also often express in dollars.

### An Example: The Opportunity Cost of College

Let's consider an important choice you've made for this year: to attend college. What is the opportunity cost of this choice? A good starting point is to look at the actual monetary costs—the annual out-of-pocket expenses borne by you or your family for a year of college. Table 1 shows the College Board's estimates of these expenses for the average student (ignoring scholarships). For example, the third column of the table shows that the average in-state resident at a four-year state college pays $5,491 in tuition and fees, $894 for books and supplies, $6,636 for room and board, and $2,545 for transportation and other expenses, for a total of $15,566 per year.

So, is that dollar figure the opportunity cost of a year of college for the average student at a public institution? Not really. Even if the entries are what you or your family actually pays out for college, there are two problems with using these figures to calculate the opportunity cost.

| **TABLE  1**  Average Cost of a Year of College, 2005–2006 | Type of Institution | Two-year Public | Four-year Public | Four-year Private |
|---|---|---|---|---|
| | Tuition and fees | $ 2,191 | $ 5,491 | $21,236 |
| | Books and supplies | $    801 | $    894 | $    904 |
| | Room and board | $ 5,909 | $ 6,636 | $ 7,791 |
| | Transportation and other expenses | $ 2,791 | $ 2,545 | $ 1,986 |
| | Total out-of-pocket costs | $11,692 | $15,566 | $31,917 |

*Source: Trends in College Pricing, 2005, The College Board, New York, NY.*
Notes: Averages are enrollment-weighted by institution, to reflect the average experience among students across the United States. Average tuition and fees at public institutions are for in-state residents only. Room and board charges are for students living on campus at four-year institutions, and off-campus (but not with parents) at two-year institutions.

First, the table includes some expenses that are *not* part of the opportunity cost of college. For example, room and board is something you'd need no matter *what* your choice. That's obvious if, as part of your best choice among the alternatives, you'd have lived in an apartment and paid rent. But even the alternative of living in your old room at home doesn't eliminate this cost: Your family *could* have rented out the room to someone else, or used it for some other valuable purpose. Either way, something is sacrificed. Let's suppose, for simplicity, that if you weren't in college, you or your family would be paying the same amount for room and board as your college charges. Then, the $6,636 for room and board expense should be excluded from the opportunity cost of going to college. And the same applies to transportation and other expenses, at least the part that you would have spent anyway even if you weren't in college.

Now we're left with payments for tuition and fees, and for books and supplies. For an in-state resident going to a state college, this averages $5,491 + $894 = $6,385 per year. Since these dollars are paid only when you attend college, they represent something sacrificed for that choice and are part of its opportunity cost. Costs like these—for which dollars are actually paid out—are called **explicit costs**, and they are *part* of the opportunity cost.

But college also has **implicit costs**—sacrifices for which no money changes hands. The biggest sacrifice in this category is *time*. But what is that time worth? That depends on what you *would* be doing if you weren't in school. For many students, the alternative would be working full-time at a job, something most students can't manage while attending college. If you are one of these students, attending college requires the sacrifice of the income you *could* have earned at a job—a sacrifice we call *foregone income*.

How much income is foregone when you go to college for a year? In 2005, the average total of an 18- to 24-year-old high school graduate who worked full-time was about $22,000. If we assume that only nine months of work must be sacrificed to attend college, and that you could still work full-time in the summer, then foregone income is about 9/12 of $22,000, or $16,500.

Summing the explicit and implicit costs gives us a rough estimate of the opportunity cost of a year in college. For a public institution, we have $6,385 in explicit costs and $16,500 in implicit costs, giving us a total of $22,885 per year. Notice that this is significantly greater than the total charges estimated by the college board we calculated earlier. When you consider paying this opportunity cost for four years, its magnitude might surprise you. Without financial aid in the form of tuition grants or other fee reductions, the average in-state resident will sacrifice about $90,000 to get a bachelor's degree at a state college and about $153,000 at a private one.

Our analysis of the opportunity cost of college is an example of a general, and important, principle:

> *The opportunity cost of a choice includes both* **explicit costs** *and* **implicit costs**.

### A Brief Digression: Is College the Right Choice?

Before you start questioning your choice to be in college, there are a few things to remember. First, for many students, scholarships reduce the costs of college below those in our example. Second, in addition to its high cost, college has substantial *benefits*, including financial ones. In fact, over a 40-year work life, the average

**Explicit cost** The dollars sacrificed—and actually paid out—for a choice.

**Implicit cost** The value of something sacrificed when no direct payment is made.

college graduate will make about $2.5 million, which is about a million dollars *more* than the average high school graduate.[1]

True, much of that income is earned in the future, and a dollar gained years from now is worth less than a dollar spent today. Also, *some* of the higher earnings of college graduates result from the personal characteristics of people who are likely to attend college, rather than from the education or the degree itself. But even when we make reasonable adjustments for these facts, attending college appears to be one of the best *financial* investments you can make.[2]

Finally, remember that we've left out of our discussion many important aspects of this choice that would be harder to estimate in dollar terms, but could be very important to you. Do you *enjoy* being at college? If so, your enjoyment is an added benefit, even though it may be difficult to value that enjoyment in dollars. (Of course, if you *hate* college and are only doing it for the financial rewards or to satisfy your parents, that's an implicit cost—which is part of your opportunity cost—that we haven't included.)

### Time Is Money

Our analysis of the opportunity cost of college points out a general principle, one understood by economists and noneconomists alike. It can be summed up in the expression, "Time is money." Those three words contain a profound truth: The sacrifice of time often means the sacrifice of money—in particular, the money that *could* have been earned during that time.

As a rule, economists have a simple technique to estimate the dollar value of time. First, we assume that working additional hours for pay is the best among the alternatives to the choice being considered. Then, each hour sacrificed for the choice is multiplied by the individual's hourly wage. (Even someone paid a monthly salary has an implied hourly wage: their total monthly income divided by the total monthly hours of work.)

For example, suppose Jessica is a freelance writer who decides to see a movie. The ticket price is $10, and the entire activity—including getting there and back—will take three hours out of her evening. What is the opportunity cost of seeing this movie? Let's suppose that Jessica earns $20 per hour as a freelance writer. We'll also assume that she can choose to take on additional work at that same wage rate. Therefore, each hour that Jessica chooses *not* to work causes her to give up $20 in earnings. Then for Jessica, the opportunity cost is the sum of the explicit costs ($10 for the ticket) and the implicit costs ($20 × 3 hrs = $60 in foregone income), giving her a total opportunity cost of $70.

The idea that a movie "costs" $70 might seem absurd to you. But if you think about it, $70 is a much better estimate than $10 of what the movie costs for Jessica. After all, she gives up three hours that *could* have been spent working on an article that, on average, would provide her with another $60. Thus, in a very real sense, Jessica sacrifices $70 for the movie.[2]

Our examples about the cost of college and the cost of a movie point out an important lesson about opportunity cost:

---

[1] Jennifer C. Day and Eric C. Newburger, "The Big Payoff: Educational Attainment and Synthetic Estimates of Work-Life Earnings," in *Current Population Reports* (U.S. Census Bureau), July 2002.

[2] If you are using the microeconomics or combined micro/macro version of this book, we'll revisit the value of college as an investment in the Using the Theory section of Chapter 13. In that chapter, you'll also learn the general technique economists use to compare future earnings with current costs.

> *The explicit (direct money) cost of a choice may only be a part—and sometimes a small part—of the opportunity cost of a choice.*

Indeed, the higher an individual's income, the less important is the direct money cost, and the more important the time cost of an activity. For example, suppose that Samantha is an attorney who bills out her time at $100 per hour. For her, the opportunity cost of the same movie—which entails three hours and the ticket—would be $310 dollars!

You might wonder if Samantha would ever see a movie at such a high cost. The answer for Samantha is the same as for Jessica or anyone else: yes, as long as the benefits of the movie are greater than the explicit and implicit costs. It's easy to see why Samantha might decide to see a movie. Imagine that she begins taking on more and more clients, working longer and longer hours, and earning more and more income. At some point, she will realize that leisure activities like movies are very important, while earning more income will seem less important. And taking time off to see a movie might be well worth sacrificing the $310 that she could have had.

The concept of opportunity cost also explains why you'll never see a rebate coupon like the doctored one in Figure 1. For most of us, the opportunity cost—including the cost of the stamp and the value of the time sacrificed to follow the instructions—is greater than the $1 that is being offered.

## OPPORTUNITY COST AND SOCIETY

For an individual, opportunity cost arises from the scarcity of time or money. But for society as a whole, opportunity cost arises from a different source: the scarcity of society's *resources*. Our desire for goods is limitless, but we have limited resources to produce them. Therefore,

---

**FIGURE 1**

**Something You'll Never See**

*The opportunity cost of this rebate (the value of the time lost plus the cost of a postage stamp) would exceed its benefit (one dollar).*

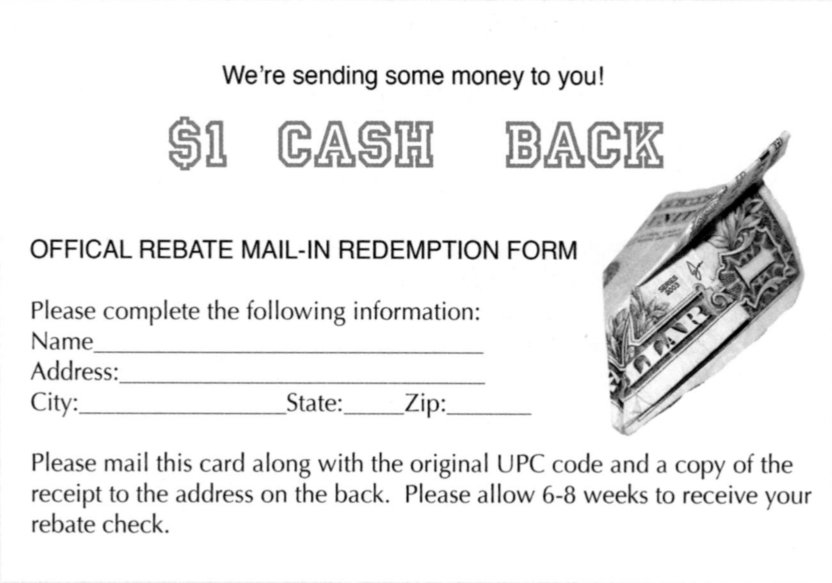

We're sending some money to you!

$1 CASH BACK

OFFICAL REBATE MAIL-IN REDEMPTION FORM

Please complete the following information:
Name_____
Address:_____
City:_____State:_____Zip:_____

Please mail this card along with the original UPC code and a copy of the receipt to the address on the back. Please allow 6-8 weeks to receive your rebate check.

*virtually all production carries an opportunity cost: To produce more of one thing, society must shift resources away from producing something else.*

For example, we'd all agree that we'd like better health for our citizens. What would be needed to achieve this goal? Perhaps more frequent medical checkups for more people and greater access to top-flight medicine when necessary. These, in turn, would require more and better-trained doctors, more hospital buildings and laboratories, and more high-tech medical equipment. In order for us to produce these goods and services, we would have to pull resources—land, labor, capital, and entrepreneurship—out of producing other things that we also enjoy. The opportunity cost of improved health care, then, consists of those other goods and services we would have to do without.

### An Example: Military versus Consumer Goods

Let's build a simple model to help us understand the opportunity cost we must pay to have more of something. To be specific, we'll look at a society's choice between producing military goods (represented here by tanks) and producing consumer goods (represented by wheat).

Table 2 lists some possible combinations of yearly tank production and yearly wheat production this society could manage, given its available resources and the currently available production technology. For example, the first row of the table tells us what would happen if all available resources were devoted to wheat production and no resources at all to producing tanks. The resulting quantity of wheat—1 million bushels per year—is the most this society could possibly produce. In the second row, society moves enough resources into tank production to make 1,000 tanks per year. This leaves fewer resources for wheat production, which now declines to 950,000 bushels per year. As we go down the left column, tank production increases by increments of 1,000. The right column shows us the maximum quantity of wheat that can be produced for each given quantity of tanks. Finally, look at the last row. It shows us that when society throws all of its resources into tank production (with none for wheat), tank production is 5,000 while wheat production is zero.

The table gives us a quantitative measure of opportunity cost for this society. For example, suppose this society currently produces 1,000 tanks per year, along with

| TABLE  2                                   | Tank Production (number per year) | Wheat Production (bushels per year) |
|--------------------------------------------|-----------------------------------|-------------------------------------|
| **Production of Tanks and Wheat**          |                                   |                                     |
|                                            | 0                                 | 1,000,000                           |
|                                            | 1,000                             | 950,000                             |
|                                            | 2,000                             | 850,000                             |
|                                            | 3,000                             | 700,000                             |
|                                            | 4,000                             | 400,000                             |
|                                            | 5,000                             | 0                                   |

950,000 bushels of wheat (the second row). What would be the opportunity cost of producing another 1,000 tanks? Moving down to the third row, we see that producing another 1,000 tanks (for a total of 2,000) would require wheat production to drop from 950,000 to 850,000 bushels, a decrease of 100,000 bushels. Thus, the opportunity cost of 1,000 more tanks is 100,000 bushels of wheat. In this simple model with just two goods, the opportunity cost of having more of one good is measured in the units of the other good that must be sacrificed.

### Production Possibilities Frontiers

We can see opportunity cost even more clearly in Figure 2, where the data in Table 2 has been plotted on a graph. In the figure, tank production is measured along the horizontal axis, and wheat production along the vertical axis. Each of the six points labeled *A* through *F* corresponds to a combination of the two goods as given by one of the rows of the table. For example, point *B* represents the combination in the second row: 1,000 tanks and 950,000 bushels of wheat. When we connect these points with a smooth line, we get a curve called society's **production possibilities frontier (PPF)**. Specifically, this PPF tells us the maximum quantity of wheat that can be produced for each quantity of tanks produced. Alternatively, it tells us the maximum number of tanks that can be produced for each different quantity of wheat. Positions outside the frontier are unattainable with the technology and resources at the economy's disposal. Society's choices are limited to points on or inside the PPF.

**Production possibilities frontier (PPF)** A curve showing all combinations of two goods that can be produced with the resources and technology currently available.

Now recall our earlier example of a change in production in Table 2: When tank production increased from 1,000 to 2,000, wheat production decreased from 950,000 to 850,000. In the graph, this change would be represented by a movement along the PPF from point *B* to point *C*. We're moving rightward (1,000 more tanks) and also downward (100,000 fewer bushels of wheat). Thus, the opportunity cost of 1,000 more tanks can be viewed as the vertical drop along the PPF as we move from point *B* to point *C*.

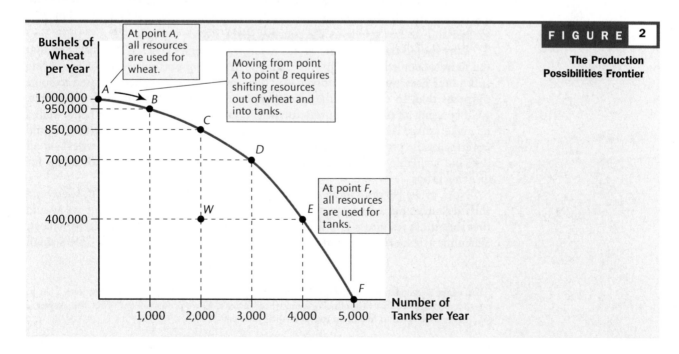

**FIGURE 2**

**The Production Possibilities Frontier**

### Increasing Opportunity Cost

Suppose we have arrived at point *C* and society then decides to produce still more tanks. Once again, resources must be shifted into tank production to make an additional 1,000 of them, moving from point *C* to point *D*. This time, however, there is an even *greater opportunity cost*: Production of wheat falls from 850,000 to 700,000 bushels, a sacrifice of 150,000 bushels. The opportunity cost of 1,000 more tanks has risen. Graphically, the vertical drop along the curve is greater for the same move rightward.

You can see that as we continue to increase tank production by increments of 1,000—moving from point *C* to point *D* to point *E* to point *F*—the opportunity cost of producing an additional 1,000 tanks keeps rising, until the last 1,000 tanks costs us 400,000 bushels of wheat. (You can also see this in the table, by running down the numbers in the right column. Each time tank production rises by 1,000, wheat production falls by more and more.)

The behavior of opportunity cost described here—the more tanks we produce, the greater the opportunity cost of producing still more—applies to a wide range of choices facing society. It can be generalized as the *law of increasing opportunity cost*.

> *According to the law of increasing opportunity cost, the more of something we produce, the greater the opportunity cost of producing even more of it.*

The law of increasing opportunity cost causes the PPF to have a concave (upside-down bowl) shape, becoming steeper as we move rightward and downward. That's because the slope of the PPF—the change in the quantity of wheat divided by the change in the quantity of tanks—can be interpreted as the change in wheat *per additional tank*. If we remove the minus sign from this slope and consider just its absolute value, it tells us the opportunity cost of *one more tank*.

Now—as we've seen—this opportunity cost increases as we move rightward. Therefore, the absolute value of the PPF's slope must rise as well. The PPF gets steeper and steeper, giving us the concave shape we see in Figure 2.[3]

Why should there be a law of increasing opportunity cost? Why must it be that the more of something we produce, the greater the opportunity cost of producing still more? Because most resources—by their very nature—are better suited to some purposes than to others. If the economy were operating at point *A*, for example, we'd be using *all* of our resources for wheat, even those that are much better suited to make tanks. People who would be better at factory work than farming would nevertheless be pressed into working on farms. And we'd be growing wheat on all the land available, even land that would be fine for a tank factory but awful for growing crops.

Now, as we begin to move rightward along the PPF, say from *A* to *B*, we would shift resources out of wheat production and into tank production. But we would first shift those resources *best suited* to tank production—and least suited for wheat. When these resources are shifted, an additional thousand tanks causes only a small

---

[3] You might be wondering if the law of increasing opportunity cost applies in both directions. That is, does the opportunity cost of producing more wheat increase as we produce more of it? The answer is yes, as you'll be asked to find in an end-of-chapter problem.

drop in wheat production. This is why, at first, the PPF is very flat: a small vertical drop for the rightward movement.

As we continue moving rightward, however, we are forced to shift away from wheat production resources that are less and less suited to tanks and more and more suited to wheat. As a result, the PPF becomes steeper. Finally, we arrive at point $F$, where all resources—no matter how well suited for wheat—are used to make tanks.

The principle of increasing opportunity cost applies to most of society's production choices, not just that between wheat and tanks. If we look at society's choice between food and oil, we would find that some land is better suited to growing food and other land is better suited to drilling for oil. As we continue to produce more oil, we would find ourselves drilling on land that is less and less suited to producing oil, but better and better for producing food. The opportunity cost of producing additional oil will therefore increase. The same principle applies if we want to produce more health care, more education, more automobiles, or more computers: The more of something we produce, the greater the opportunity cost of producing still more.

## THE SEARCH FOR A FREE LUNCH

This chapter has argued that every decision to produce *more* of something requires us to pay an opportunity cost by producing less of something else. Nobel Prize–winning economist Milton Friedman summarized this idea in his famous remark, "There is no such thing as a free lunch." Friedman was saying that, even if a meal is provided free of charge to someone, society still uses up resources to provide it. Therefore, a "free lunch" is not *really* free: Society pays an opportunity cost by not producing other things with those resources. Therefore, some members of society will have to make do with less.

The same logic applies to other supposedly "free" goods and services. From society's point of view, there is no such thing as free Internet service, free broadcast television, or free medical care, even if those who enjoy these things don't pay for them as individuals. Providing any of these things requires us to sacrifice *other* things, as illustrated by a movement along society's PPF.

But there are some situations that seem, at first glance, to violate Freidman's dictum. Let's explore them.

### Productive Inefficiency

What if an economy is not living up to its productive potential, but is instead operating *inside* its PPF? For example, in Figure 2, suppose we are currently operating at point $W$, where we are producing 2,000 tanks and 400,000 bushels of wheat. Then we could move from point $W$ to point $E$ and produce 2,000 more tanks, with no sacrifice of wheat. Or, starting at point $W$, we could move to point $C$ (more wheat with no sacrifice of tanks), or to a point like $D$ (more of *both* wheat and tanks).

But why would an economy ever operate inside its PPF?

One possibility is that, although all of its resources are being used, they are not being used in the most productive way. Suppose, for example, that many people who could be outstanding wheat farmers are instead making tanks, and many who would be great at tank production are instead stuck on farms. Then switching people from one job to the other could enable us to have more of *both* tanks *and* wheat.

That is, because of the mismatch of workers and jobs, we would be *inside* the PPF at a point like *W*. Creating better job matches would then move us to a point *on* the PPF (such as point *E*).

Economists use the phrase *productive inefficiency* to describe this type of situation that puts us inside our PPF.

**Productively inefficient** A situation in which more of at least one good can be produced without sacrificing the production of any other good.

> *A firm, an industry, or an entire economy is* **productively inefficient** *if it could produce more of at least one good without pulling resources from the production of any other good.*

The phrase *productive efficiency* means the absence of any productive *ineffi-ciency*. For example, if the computer industry is producing the maximum possible number of computers with the resources it is currently using, we would describe the computer industry as productively efficient. In that case, there would be no way to produce any more computers except to use more resources and shift them from the production of some other good. For an entire *economy* to be productively efficient, there must be no way to produce more of *any* good except by pulling resources from the production of some other good.

Although no firm, industry, or economy is ever 100 percent productively effi-cient, cases of gross inefficiency are not as common as you might think. When you study microeconomics, you'll learn that business firms have strong incentives to iden-tify and eliminate productive inefficiency, since any waste of resources increases their costs and decreases their profit. When one firm discovers a way to eliminate waste, others quickly follow.

For example, empty seats on an airline flight represent productive inefficiency. Since the plane is making the trip anyway, filling the empty seat would enable the airline to serve more people with the flight (produce more transportation services) without using any additional resources (other than the trivial resources of in-flight snacks). Therefore, more people could fly without sacrificing any other good or service. When American Airlines developed a computer model in the late 1980s to fill its empty seats by altering schedules and fares, the other airlines followed its example very rapidly. And when—in the late 1990s—Priceline.com enabled airlines to auction off empty seats on the Internet, several airlines jumped at the chance and others quickly followed. As a result of this—and similar efforts to eliminate waste in personnel, aircraft, and office space—many cases of productive inefficiency in the airline industry were eliminated.

Starbucks provides a recent example of reducing productive inefficiency.[4] In 2000, it created a special department of "store operations engineering," tasked with analyzing beverage preparation in order to identify and eliminate waste. Among the recommendations that were instituted: rearranging labor within each store, elimi-nating signatures on small credit-card purchases, and using larger scoops so that iced drinks can be made with one dip into the ice machine instead of two. These and other efforts—all using existing technologies—enabled more coffee drinks to be pre-pared each day with the same amount of labor and store space, thus eliminating a source of productive inefficiency. (For those in a hurry, the changes also reduced the average wait time from $3\frac{1}{2}$ minutes in 2000 to three minutes in 2006.)

---

[4] Steven Gray, "Coffee on the Double," *Wall Street Journal*, April 12, 2005.

Economists, logistics experts, and engineers are continually working to identify and design policies to eliminate cases of productive inefficiency. But many instances remain. Does that mean we are freed from having to pay an opportunity cost when we want to produce more of something?

Not necessarily. Many sources of productive inefficiency create benefits for individuals or groups who will resist changes in the status quo. For example, the government currently requires every taxpayer to file a federal tax return. About 40 percent of these returns are so simple that they merely provide the Internal Revenue Service (IRS) with information it already has, and contain calculations that the IRS duplicates anyway, to check for mistakes. Yet each taxpayer in this 40 percent group must spend hours doing his or her own return, or else pay someone to do it. Why not have the IRS send these people filled-out returns, requiring only a signature if they approve?

One economist[5] has estimated that this simple change would save a total of 250 million hours per year (for those who currently fill out their own returns), and $2 billion per year (for those who pay accountants). With resources freed up by this change, we could produce and enjoy more of all the things that we value. But if you reread this paragraph, you can probably guess who might lobby the government to oppose this change, if and when it is seriously considered.

Since political obstacles often make it difficult to reduce inefficiency, producing more of one thing we value typically results in taking resources away from something else we value, rather than getting "free" resources from greater efficiency. Productive inefficiency does create a theoretical possibility for a free lunch. But in practice, it does not offer as many hearty meals as you might think.

## Recessions

Another reason an economy might operate inside its PPF is a *recession*—a slowdown in overall economic activity. During recessions, many resources are idle. For one thing, there is widespread *unemployment*—people *want* to work but are unable to find jobs. In addition, factories shut down, so we are not using all of our available capital. An end to the recession would move the economy from a point *inside* its PPF to a point *on* its PPF—using idle resources to produce more goods and services without sacrificing anything.

This simple observation can help us understand an otherwise confusing episode in U.S. economic history. During the early 1940s, after the United States entered World War II and began using massive amounts of resources to produce military goods and services, the standard of living in the United States did *not* decline as we might have expected but actually improved slightly. Why?

When the United States entered the war in 1941, it was still suffering from the Great Depression—the most serious and long-lasting economic downturn in modern history, which began in 1929 and hit most of the developed world. For reasons you will learn when you study macroeconomics, joining the allied war effort helped end the Depression in the United States. As shown in Figure 3, this moved our economy from a point like *A*, *inside* the PPF, to a point like *B*, *on* the frontier. Military production like tanks increased, but so did the production of civilian goods such as wheat. Although there were shortages of some consumer goods, the overall result

---

[5] Austan Goolsbee, "Why Tell the I.R.S. What It Already Knows?" *New York Times*, April 7, 2006.

**FIGURE 3**

**Production and Unemployment**

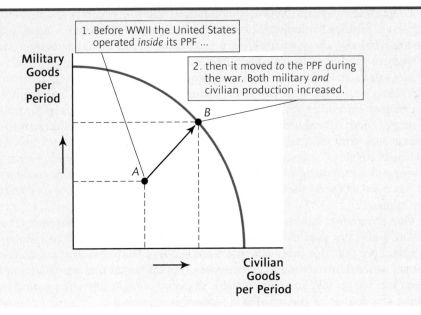

1. Before WWII the United States operated *inside* its PPF …

2. then it moved *to* the PPF during the war. Both military *and* civilian production increased.

Military Goods per Period

Civilian Goods per Period

**False Benefits from Employment** Often, you'll hear an evaluation of some economic activity that includes "employment" as one of the benefits. For example, a recent article in the online magazine *Slate*, after discussing the costs of email spam, pointed out that spam also has "a corresponding economic payoff. Anti-spam efforts keep well-paid software engineers employed."[6]

This is usually an error. True, when the economy is in a recession, an increase in employment can be regarded as a gain for those who get jobs. But in most years we are *not* in a recession. And once a recession ends, the software engineers—if not for the spam—would be employed elsewhere. At that point, employment in the spam-fighting industry—far from being a benefit—is actually part of the *opportunity cost* of spam: we sacrifice the goods and services these spam-fighting engineers would otherwise produce.

was a rise in total production and an increase in the material well-being of the average U.S. citizen.

An economic downturn, such as the Great Depression of the 1930s, does seem to offer the possibility of a free lunch. And a war is only one factor that can reverse a downturn. (In fact, no rational nation would ever *choose* war as an economic policy designed to cure a recession, since there are always economically superior alternatives to accomplish this goal.) Still, eliminating a recession is not *entirely* cost-free. When you study macroeconomics, you will learn that policies to cure or avoid recessions can have risks and costs of their own. Of course, we may feel it is worth the possible costs, but they are costs nonetheless. Once again, a truly free lunch is hard to find.

### Economic Growth

If the economy is already operating *on* its PPF, we cannot exploit the opportunity to have more of everything by moving *to* it. But what if the PPF itself were to change? Couldn't we then produce more of everything? This is exactly what happens when an economy's productive capacity grows.

---

[6] Jeff Merron, "Workus Interruptus," *Slate*, posted March 16, 2006, 12:06pm ET.

Many factors contribute to economic growth, but they can be divided into two categories. First, the quantities of available *resources* can increase. An increase in physical capital—more factories, office buildings, tractors, or high-tech medical equipment—enables the economy to produce more of *everything* that uses these tools. The same is true for an increase in human capital—the skills of doctors, engineers, construction workers, software writers, and so on. In thinking about growth from greater resources, economists focus mostly on capital because, over time, increases in the capital stock have contributed more to higher living standards than increases in other resources (such as land or labor).

The second main factor behind economic growth is *technological change*, which enables us to produce more from a *given* quantity of resources. For example, the development of the Internet has enabled people to retrieve information in a few seconds that used to require hours of searching in a library. As a result, teachers, writers, government officials, attorneys, and physicians can produce more of their services without working longer hours.

These two main causes of economic growth—increases in resources and technological change—often go hand in hand. In order for the Internet (a technological change) to be widely used, the economy had to produce and install servers, Internet-capable computers, and fiber-optic cable (increases in capital). In any case, both technological change and increases in the capital stock have the same type of effect on the PPF.

Figure 4 shows three examples of economic growth, and how they might affect the PPF. Panel (a) illustrates the case of a technological change in wheat farming—say, the discovery of a new type of seed that yields more wheat for any given amount of land, labor, and capital. First, look at point *A*, which shows maximum wheat production when *all* of our resources are used to grow wheat, but without the new seeds. The introduction of the new seeds would enable us to grow even *more* wheat with all of our resources than before. For that reason, the vertical intercept of the PPF rises from point *A* to a point like *A'*, where the economy could produce 1,200,000 bushels per year.

Now consider point *F*, where we assume that *none* of our resources would be used to grow wheat, and all would be used to make tanks. The new seeds have no impact on this maximum possible tank production, so introducing them would not change the horizontal intercept of the PPF.

As you can see, the impact of the new seeds is to stretch the PPF upward along the vertical axis. Society could then choose any point along the new PPF. For example, it could move from point *D* on the original PPF to point *H* on the new one. For this move, all of the benefits of the new seeds would be devoted to giving us more wheat, with unchanged production of tanks. Or society could choose to move from point *D* to point *J* where, as you can verify, more of *both* goods are produced. Indeed, a society could choose to take advantage of the new seeds in a surprising way: more tanks and the same quantity of wheat as before. (See if you can identify this point on the new PPF.)

You may be wondering: How does a new type of seed enable greater production of *tanks*? The answer is: After the new, more productive seeds are introduced, society can choose to shift resources out of farming without decreasing wheat production at all. (Although there are smaller quantities of resources in the wheat industry, the new seeds make up for that.) The shifted resources can be used to increase tank production.

One more thing about panel (a): It can also be used to illustrate the change in the PPF from an increase in resources that can be used *only* in wheat farming. For example, an increase in the quantity of farm tractors would shift the vertical intercept of the PPF as in panel (a) but leave the horizontal intercept unchanged because tractors have no direct impact on tank production.

Panel (b) illustrates the opposite type of change in the PPF—from a technological change in producing tanks, or an increase in resources usable only in the tank industry. This time, the *horizontal* intercept of the PPF increases, while the vertical intercept remains unchanged. (Can you explain why?) As before, we could choose to produce more tanks, more wheat, or more of both. (See if you can identify points on the new PPF in panel (b) to illustrate all three cases.)

Finally, panel (c) illustrates the case where technological change occurs in both the wheat and the tank industries, or there is an increase in resources (such as workers or computers) that could be used in either. Now both the horizontal and the vertical intercepts of the PPF increase. But as before, society can choose to locate anywhere along the new PPF, producing more tanks, more wheat, or more of both.

Panels (a) and (b) can be generalized to an important principle about economic growth:

## FIGURE 4

**Economic Growth and the PPF**

*All three panels show economic growth from an increase in resources or a technological change. In panel (a), the additional resources or technological advance directly affect only wheat production. However, society can choose to have more wheat and more tanks if it desires, such as at point J. In panel (b), the additional resources or technological advance directly affect only tank production. But once again, society can choose to have more of both goods. In panel (c), the additional resources or technological advance directly affect production of both goods.*

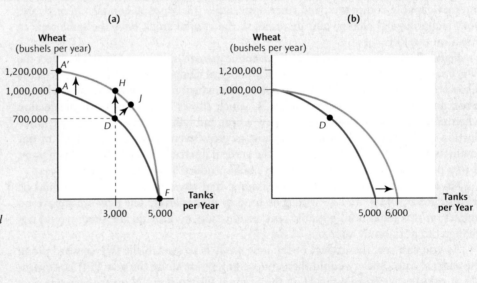

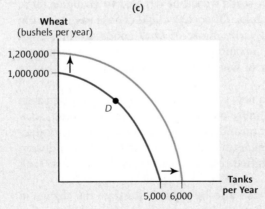

> *A technological change or an increase in the capital stock, even when the direct impact is to increase production of just one type of good, allows us to choose greater production of all types of goods.*

This conclusion certainly *seems* like a free lunch. After all, if we can produce more of the things that we value, without having to produce less of anything else, haven't we escaped from paying an opportunity cost?

Yes . . . and no. Figure 4 tells only *part* of the story because it leaves out the steps needed to *create* this shift in the PPF in the first place.

## CONSUMPTION VERSUS GROWTH

In the previous section, you saw that increases in capital or technological advances can shift the economy's PPF outward along one or both axes, enabling us to produce more of everything we desire. Clearly, economic growth gives us benefits. But in this section, we'll see that it also entails an opportunity cost.

Consider the case of having more capital. First, note that capital plays a dual role in the economy. On the one hand, capital is a *resource*—a long-lasting tool that we use to produce goods and services. On the other hand, capital is itself a good and needs to be produced using . . . resources. A tractor, for example, is produced using land, labor, entrepreneurship, and *other* capital (a tractor factory and all of the manufacturing equipment inside the factory).

Each year, society must choose how much of its available resources to devote to producing capital. The more long-lasting capital we produce this year, the more we will have available in future years to help us produce the goods and services that we enjoy. But there is a tradeoff: Any resources used to produce capital this year are *not* being used to produce *consumer goods*—food, automobiles, movies, health care, books, and other things that we enjoy right now and that contribute to our current living standard. For example, food (a consumer good) that we produce this year contributes directly to this year's standard of living. But the tractors (a capital good) that we produce this year contribute to our standard of living only indirectly, over time, as the tractors are used to produce more food.

The tradeoff in having more capital is illustrated in Figure 5. In each panel, the quantity of capital goods is measured on the horizontal axis, and consumption goods are measured on the vertical axis. (Notice that we've lumped all capital goods together into one broad category and all consumer goods into another. Our purpose is to illustrate the general tradeoff between one type of good and the other, rather than make statements or measurements involving specific goods.) In each panel, the solid curve shows the economy's PPF this year—the maximum production of one type of good for any given production of the other type.

Now look at panel (a). Point A on the PPF shows one choice that society could make this year: relatively high production of consumer goods and little production of capital goods. This choice gives us a relatively high standard of living this year (lots of consumer goods) but adds little to our total stock of capital. As a result, next year's PPF—shown by the dotted line—does shifts outward (because we have more capital), but not by much.

Panel (b) illustrates a different choice. By locating at point A' on this year's PPF, we sacrifice considerably more consumption goods now, and shift even more resources toward capital than in panel (a). Living standards are lower this year. But next year, with considerably more capital, the PPF shifts outward even more. As a

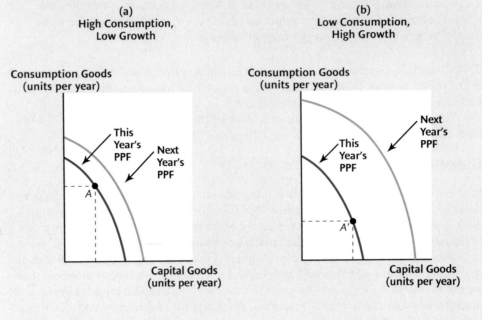

**FIGURE 5**

**How Current Production Affects Economic Growth**

*In panel (a), production is tilted toward current consumption goods, with relatively few resources devoted to production of capital goods. As a result, in the future, there will not be much of an increase in productive resources, so the PPF will not shift out much in the future. In panel (b), production is tilted more toward capital goods, with a greater sacrifice of current consumption. As a result, there will be a greater increase in productive resources, so the PPF will shift out more in the future.*

result, we can choose a point on next year's PPF, with much greater production of consumer goods than we could have chosen in panel (a). Panel (b), while requiring greater sacrifice this year, leads to a greater rise in living standards next year.

A similar tradeoff exists when we look at technological change as a cause of economic growth. Technological change doesn't just "happen." Rather, resources must be used to create it—mostly by the research and development (R&D) departments of large corporations. In 2003, corporations used about $200 billion worth of resources for R&D, and the federal government kicked in about another $100 billion.[7] These resources *could* have been used to produce other things that we'd enjoy right now. For example, doctors who are working in the R&D departments of pharmaceutical companies trying to develop drugs for the future could instead be providing health care to patients right now.

We could illustrate the sacrifice needed for technological change using a pair of PPFs similar to those in Figure 5. The vertical axis would still measure consumer goods production. But on the horizontal axis, instead of capital goods, we'd have a measure of "Research and Development Production"—such as the expenditures made by corporations and government agencies to run scientific laboratories or design new products. And we would come to the same conclusion we came to earlier about economic growth from more capital.

---

[7] For data on R&D in U.S. industries, see "Increases in U.S. Industrial R&D Expenditures Reported for 2003 Makes Up for Earlier Decline," *National Science Foundation Brief*, December 2005 (at http://www.nsf.gov). For the government's contribution, see "Federal Funds for R&D: FYs 2002, 2003 and 2004" *National Science Foundation* (at http://www.nsf.gov).

*In order to produce more goods and services in the future, we must shift resources toward R&D and capital production, and away from the production of things we'd enjoy right now.*

We must conclude that although economic growth—at first glance—*appears* to be a free lunch, someone ends up paying the check. In this case, the bill is paid by those members of society who will have to make do with less in the present.

## ECONOMIC SYSTEMS

As you read these words—perhaps sitting at home or in the library—you are experiencing a very private moment. It is just you and this book; the rest of the world might as well not exist. Or so it seems. . . .

Actually, even in this supposedly private moment, you are connected to the rest of the world in ways you may not have thought about. In order for you to be reading this book, the authors had to write it. Someone had to edit it, to help make sure that all necessary material was covered and explained as clearly as possible. Someone else had to prepare the graphics. Others had to run the printing presses and the binding machines, and still others had to pack the book, ship it, unpack it, put it on a store shelf, and then sell it to you.

And there's more. People had to manufacture all kinds of goods: paper and ink, the boxes used for shipping, the computers used to keep track of inventory, and so on. It is no exaggeration to say that thousands of people were involved in putting this book in your hands.

And there is still more. The chair or couch on which you are sitting, the light shining on the page, the heat or the air conditioning in the room, the clothes you are wearing—all these things that you are using right now were *produced by somebody else*. So even now, as you sit alone reading this book, you are economically linked to others in hundreds—even thousands—of different ways.

Take a walk in your town or city, and you will see even more evidence of our economic interdependence: People are collecting garbage, helping schoolchildren cross the street, transporting furniture across town, constructing buildings, repairing roads, painting houses. Everyone is producing goods and services for *other people.*

Why is it that so much of what we consume is produced by other people? Why are we all so heavily dependent on each other for our material well-being? Why don't we all—like Robinson Crusoe on his island—produce our own food, clothing, housing, and anything else we desire? And how did it come about that *you*—who did not produce any of these things yourself—are able to consume them?

These are all questions about our *economic system*—the way our economy is organized. Ordinarily, we take our economic system for granted, like the water that runs out of our faucets. But now it's time to begin looking at the plumbing—to learn how our economy serves so many millions of people, enabling them to survive and prosper.

### SPECIALIZATION AND EXCHANGE

If we were forced to, many of us could become economically *self-sufficient*. We could stake out a plot of land, grow our own food, make our own clothing, and

**Specialization** A method of production in which each person concentrates on a limited number of activities.

**Exchange** The act of trading with others to obtain what we desire.

build our own homes. But in no society is there such extreme self-sufficiency. On the contrary, every economic system has been characterized by two features: (1) **specialization**, in which each of us concentrates on a limited number of productive activities, and (2) **exchange**, in which most of what we desire is obtained by trading with others rather than producing for ourselves.

> *Specialization and exchange enable us to enjoy greater production and higher living standards than would otherwise be possible. As a result, all economies exhibit high degrees of specialization and exchange.*

There are three reasons why specialization and exchange enable us to enjoy greater production. The first has to do with human capabilities: Each of us can learn only so much in a lifetime. By limiting ourselves to a narrow set of tasks—fixing plumbing, managing workers, writing music, or designing Web pages—we are each able to hone our skills and become experts at one or two things instead of remaining amateurs at a lot of things. It is easy to see that an economy of experts will produce more than an economy of amateurs.

A second gain from specialization results from the time needed to switch from one activity to another. When people specialize, and thus spend more time doing one task, there is less unproductive "downtime" from switching activities.

Adam Smith first explained these gains from specialization in his book *An Inquiry into the Nature and Causes of the Wealth of Nations*, published in 1776. Smith explained how specialization within a pin factory dramatically increased the number of pins that could be produced there. In order to make a pin . . .

> *One man draws out the wire, another straightens it, a third cuts it, a fourth points it, a fifth grinds it at the top for receiving the head; to make the head requires three distinct operations; to put it on is a [separate] business, to whiten the pins is another; it is even a trade by itself to put them into the paper; and the important business of making a pin is, in this manner, divided into about eighteen distinct operations, which, in some manufactories, are all performed by distinct hands.*

Smith went on to observe that 10 people, each working separately, might make 200 pins in a day, but through specialization they were able to make 48,000! What is true for a pin factory can be generalized to the entire economy: Total production will increase when workers specialize.

Notice that the gains from specialization we've been discussing—and that Adam Smith described so well—do *not* depend on any differences in individuals' capabilities. Even in a society where initially everyone is *identical* to everyone else, specialization would still yield gains for the two reasons we've discussed: People would develop expertise over time, and there would be less downtime from switching tasks.

Of course, in the real world, workers are *not* identically suited to different kinds of work. Nor are all plots of land, all natural resources, or all types of capital equipment identically suited for different tasks. This observation brings us to the *third* source of gains from specialization—one based on individual differences.

## FURTHER GAINS TO SPECIALIZATION: COMPARATIVE ADVANTAGE

Imagine a shipwreck in which there are only two survivors—let's call them Maryanne and Gilligan—who wash up on opposite shores of a deserted island.

| | **Labor Required for:** | | TABLE 3 |
|---|---|---|---|
| | **1 Fish** | **1 Cup of Berries** | **Labor Requirements for Fish and Berries** |
| Maryanne | 1 hour | 1 hour | |
| Gilligan | 3 hours | $1\frac{1}{2}$ hours | |

Initially they are unaware of each other, so each is forced to become completely self-sufficient. And there are only two kinds of food on the island: fish and berries.

Table 3 shows how much time it takes for each castaway to pick a cup of berries or catch one fish. For simplicity, we'll assume that the time requirement remains constant no matter how much time is devoted to these activities.

On one side of the island, Maryanne finds that it takes her 1 hour to catch a fish and 1 hour to pick one cup of berries, as shown in the first row of the table. On the other side of the island, Gilligan—who is less adept at both tasks—requires 3 hours to catch a fish and $1\frac{1}{2}$ hours to pick a cup of berries, as listed in the second row of the table. Since both castaways would want some variety in their diets, we can assume that each would spend part of the week catching fish and part picking berries.

Suppose that, one day, Maryanne and Gilligan discover each other. After rejoicing at the prospect of human companionship, they decide to develop a system of production that will work to their mutual benefit. Let's rule out any of the gains from specialization that we discussed earlier (minimizing downtime or developing expertise). Will it still pay for these two to specialize? The answer is yes, as you will see after a small detour.

## Absolute Advantage: A Detour

When Gilligan and Maryanne sit down to figure out who should do what, they might fall victim to a common mistake: basing their decision on *absolute advantage*.

> *An individual has an **absolute advantage** in the production of some good when he or she can produce it using* fewer resources *than another individual can.*

**Absolute advantage** The ability to produce a good or service, using fewer resources than other producers use.

On the island, the only resource being used is labor time, so the reasoning might go as follows: Maryanne can catch a fish more quickly than Gilligan (see Table 3), so she has an *absolute advantage* in fishing. It seems logical, then, that Maryanne should be the one to catch fish.

But wait! Maryanne can also pick berries more quickly than Gilligan, so she has an absolute advantage in that as well. If absolute advantage is the criterion for assigning work, then Maryanne should do *both* tasks. This, however, would leave Gilligan doing nothing, which is certainly *not* in the pair's best interests. What can we conclude from this example? That absolute advantage is an unreliable guide for allocating tasks to different workers.

## Comparative Advantage

The correct principle to guide the division of labor on the island is comparative advantage:

**Comparative advantage** The ability to produce a good or service at a lower opportunity cost than other producers.

> *A person has a **comparative advantage** in producing some good if he or she can produce it with a smaller opportunity cost than some other person can.*

Notice the important difference between absolute advantage and comparative advantage: You have an *absolute* advantage in producing a good if you can produce it using fewer *resources* than someone else can. But you have a *comparative* advantage if you can produce it with a smaller *opportunity cost*. As you'll see, these are not necessarily the same thing.

Let's see who has a *comparative* advantage in fishing, by calculating—for each of the castaways—the opportunity cost of catching one fish. For Maryanne, catching a fish takes an hour. This is time that could instead be used to pick one cup of berries. Thus, for Maryanne, the *opportunity cost of one more fish is one cup of berries.* It takes Gilligan three hours to catch a fish, time which he could use to pick two cups of berries instead. Thus, for Gilligan, the *opportunity cost of one more fish is two cups of berries.* These opportunity costs are listed in the first column of Table 4. As you can see by comparing the entries, the opportunity cost for one more fish is lower for Maryanne than for Gilligan. Therefore, *Maryanne has a comparative advantage in fishing.*

Now let's determine who has a comparative advantage in berries. From Table 3, Maryanne needs an hour to pick a cup of berries, time that could be used to catch one fish. Thus, for Maryanne, the *opportunity cost of one more cup of berries is one fish.* For Gilligan, it takes $1\frac{1}{2}$ hours to pick a cup of berries, time that could be used instead to catch one-half of a fish. Thus, for Gilligan the *opportunity cost of one cup of berries is one-half fish.* (Of course, no one would ever catch half a fish unless they were using a machete. The number just tells us the rate of tradeoff of one good for the other.)

These opportunity costs are listed in the second column of Table 4. As you can see, when it comes to berries, it is *Gilligan* who has the lower opportunity cost. Therefore, Gilligan—who has an *absolute* advantage in nothing—has a *comparative advantage in berries.*

What happens when the two decide to produce more of the good in which they have a comparative advantage? The results are shown in Table 5. In the first row, we have Maryanne catching one more fish each day. This requires an additional hour, which she shifts out of picking berries. So Maryanne produces one more fish ($+1$) and one fewer cup of berries ($-1$). In the second row, we have Gilligan producing one fewer fish ($-1$). This frees up three hours. Since it takes Gilligan $1\frac{1}{2}$ hours to produce a cup of berries, he can use those three hours to produce two cups of berries ($+2$).

Now look at the last row. It shows what has happened to production of both goods on the island as a result of this little shift between the two. While fish

*Even castaways do better when they specialize and exchange with each other, instead of trying to be self-sufficient.*

© COURTESY NEAL PETERS COLLECTION

| TABLE 4 | | Opportunity Cost of: | |
|---|---|---|---|
| **Opportunity Costs for Fish and Berries** | | **One More Fish** | **One More Cup of Berries** |
| | Maryanne | 1 cup berries | 1 fish |
| | Gilligan | 2 cups berries | $\frac{1}{2}$ fish |

| | Change in Fish Production | Change in Berry Production | TABLE 5 |
|---|---|---|---|
| | | | A Beneficial Change in Production |
| Maryanne | +1 | −1 | |
| Gilligan | −1 | +2 | |
| Total Island | +0 | +1 | |

production remains unchanged, berry production has risen by one cup. And because total production has increased, so does total consumption. If the castaways can find some way of trading with each other, they can both come out ahead: consuming the same quantity of fish as before, but more berries.

As you can see in Table 5, when each castaway moves toward producing more of the good in which he or she has a *comparative advantage*, total production rises. Now, let's think about this. Because the castaways gain when they make this small shift toward their comparative advantage goods, why not make the change again? And again after that? In fact, why not keep repeating it until the opportunities for increasing total island production are exhausted, which occurs when one or both of them is devoting all of their time to producing just their comparative advantage good, and none of the other? In the end, the castaways enjoy a higher standard of living when they try to specialize and exchange goods with each other, compared to the level they'd enjoy under self-sufficiency.[8]

What is true for our shipwrecked island dwellers is also true for the entire economy:

> *Total production of every good or service will be greatest when individuals specialize according to their comparative advantage. This is another reason why specialization and exchange lead to higher living standards than does self-sufficiency.*

When we turn from our fictional island to the real world, is production, in fact, consistent with the principle of comparative advantage? Indeed, it is. A journalist may be able to paint her house more quickly than a house painter, giving her an *absolute* advantage in painting her home. Will she paint her own home? Except in unusual circumstances, no, because the journalist has a *comparative* advantage in writing news articles. Indeed, most journalists—like most college professors, attorneys, architects, and other professionals—hire house painters, leaving themselves more time to practice the professions in which they enjoy a comparative advantage.

Even comic book superheroes seem to behave consistently with comparative advantage. Superman can no doubt cook a meal, fix a car, chop wood, and do virtually *anything* faster than anyone else on the earth. Using our new vocabulary, we'd say that Superman has an absolute advantage in everything. But he has a clear *comparative* advantage in catching criminals and saving the universe from destruction, which is exactly what he spends his time doing.

---

[8] In this example, production of berries rises while fish production remains unchanged. But the castaways could instead choose to produce more fish and the same quantity of berries, or even more of both goods. Some end-of-chapter problems will guide you to these other outcomes.

### Specialization in Perspective

The gains from specialization, whether they arise from developing expertise, minimizing downtime, or exploiting comparative advantage, can explain many features of our economy. For example, college students need to select a major and then, upon graduating, to decide on a specific career. Those who follow this path are often rewarded with higher incomes than those who dally. This is an encouragement to specialize. Society is better off if you specialize, since you will help the economy produce more, and society rewards you for this contribution with a higher income.

The gains from specialization can also explain why most of us end up working for business firms that employ dozens, or even hundreds or thousands, of other employees. Why do these business firms exist? Why isn't each of us a *self-employed* expert, exchanging our production with other self-employed experts? Part of the answer is that organizing production into business firms pushes the gains from specialization still further. Within a firm, some people can specialize in working with their hands, others in managing people, others in marketing, and still others in keeping the books. Each firm is a kind of minisociety within which specialization occurs. The result is greater production and a higher standard of living than we would achieve if we were all self-employed.

## RESOURCE ALLOCATION

Ten thousand years ago, the Neolithic revolution began, and human society switched from hunting and gathering to farming and simple manufacturing. At the same time, human wants grew beyond mere food and shelter to the infinite variety of things that can be *made*. Ever since, all societies have been confronted with three important questions:

1. *Which* goods and services should be produced with society's resources?
2. *How* should they be produced?
3. *Who* should get them?

Together, these three questions constitute the problem of **resource allocation.**

Let's first consider the *which* question. Should we produce more health care or more movies, more goods for consumers or more capital goods for businesses? Where on its production possibilities frontier should the economy operate? As you will see, there are different methods societies can use to answer these questions.

The *how* question is more complicated. Most goods and services can be produced in a variety of different ways, each method using more of some resources and less of others. For example, there are many ways to dig a ditch. We could use *no capital at all* and have dozens of workers digging with their bare hands. We could use *a small amount of capital* by giving each worker a shovel and thereby use less labor, since each worker would now be more productive. Or we could use *even more capital*—a power trencher—and dig the ditch with just one or two workers. In every economic system, there must always be some mechanism that determines how goods and services will be produced from the infinite variety of ways available.

Finally, the *who* question. Here is where economics interacts most strongly with politics. There are so many ways to divide ourselves into groups: men and women, rich and poor, skilled and unskilled, workers and owners, families and single people, young and old . . . the list is endless. How should the products of our economy be distributed among these different groups and among individuals within each group?

**Resource allocation** A method of determining which goods and services will be produced, how they will be produced, and who will get them.

Determining *who* gets the economy's output is always the most controversial aspect of resource allocation. Over the last half-century, our society has become more sensitized to the way goods and services are distributed, and we increasingly ask whether that distribution is fair. For example, men get a disproportionately larger share of our national output than women do, whites get more than African-Americans and Hispanics, and middle-aged workers get more than the very old and the very young. As a society, we want to know *why* we observe these patterns (a positive economic question) and *what* we should do about them (a normative economic question).

## The Three Methods of Resource Allocation

Throughout history, every society has relied primarily on one of three mechanisms for allocating resources. In a **traditional economy**, resources are allocated according to the long-lived practices of the past. Tradition was the dominant method of resource allocation for most of human history and remains strong in many tribal societies and small villages in parts of Africa, South America, Asia, and the Pacific. Typically, traditional methods of production are handed down by the village elders, and traditional principles of fairness govern the distribution of goods and services.

**Traditional economy** An economy in which resources are allocated according to long-lived practices from the past.

Economies in which resources are allocated mostly by tradition tend to be stable and predictable. But these economies have one serious drawback: They don't grow. With everyone locked into the traditional patterns of production, there is little room for innovation and technological change. Traditional economies are therefore likely to be stagnant economies.

In a **command economy**, resources are allocated mostly by explicit instructions from some higher authority. *Which* goods and services should we produce? The ones we're *ordered* to produce. *How* should we produce them? The way we're *told* to produce them. *Who* will get the goods and services? Whoever the authority *tells* us should get them.

**Command or centrally planned economy** An economic system in which resources are allocated according to explicit instructions from a central authority.

In a command economy, a government body *plans* how resources will be allocated. That is why command economies are also called **centrally planned economies**. But command economies are disappearing fast. Until about 20 years ago, examples would have included the former Soviet Union, Poland, Rumania, Bulgaria, Albania, China, and many others. Beginning in the late 1980s, all of these nations began abandoning central planning. The only examples left today are Cuba and North Korea, and even these economies—though still dominated by central planning—occasionally take steps away from it.

The third method of allocating resources—and the one with which you are no doubt most familiar—is "the market." In a **market economy**, neither long-held traditions nor commands from above guide most economic behavior. Instead, people are largely free to do what they want with the resources at their disposal. In the end, resources are allocated as a result of individual decision making. *Which* goods and services are produced? The ones that producers *choose* to produce. *How* are they produced? However producers *choose* to produce them. *Who* gets these goods and services? Anyone who *chooses* to buy them.

**Market economy** An economic system in which resources are allocated through individual decision making.

Of course, in a market system, freedom of choice is constrained by the resources one controls. And in this respect, we do not all start in the same place in the economic race. Some of us have inherited great intelligence, talent, or beauty; and some, such as the children of successful professionals, are born into a world of helpful personal contacts. Others, unfortunately, will inherit none of these advantages. In a market system, those who control more resources will have more choices available to them than those who control fewer resources. Nevertheless, given these different starting points, individual choice plays the major role in allocating resources in a market economy.

But wait . . . isn't there a problem here? People acting according to their own desires, without command or tradition to control them? This sounds like a recipe for chaos! How, in such a free-for-all, could resources possibly be *allocated*?

The answer is contained in two words: *markets* and *prices*.

### The Nature of Markets

The market economy gets its name from something that nearly always happens when people are free to do what they want with the resources they possess. Inevitably, people decide to specialize in the production of one or a few things—often organizing themselves into business firms—and then sellers and buyers *come together to trade*. A **market** is a collection of buyers and sellers who have the potential to trade with one another.

**Market** A group of buyers and sellers with the potential to trade with each other.

In some cases, the market is *global*; that is, the market consists of buyers and sellers who are spread across the globe. The market for oil is an example of a global market, since buyers in any country can buy from sellers in any country. In other cases, the market is local. Markets for restaurant meals, haircuts, and taxi service are examples of local markets.

Markets play a major role in allocating resources by forcing individual decision makers to consider very carefully their decisions about buying and selling. They do so because of an important feature of every market: the *price* at which a good is bought and sold.

### The Importance of Prices

**Price** The amount of money that must be paid to a seller to obtain a good or service.

A **price** is *the amount of money a buyer must pay to a seller for a good or service.* Price is not always the same as *cost*. In economics, as you've learned in this chapter, cost means *opportunity cost*—the *total* sacrifice needed to buy the good. While the price of a good is a *part* of its opportunity cost, it is not the only cost. For example, the price does not include the value of the time sacrificed to buy something. Buying a new jacket will require you to spend time traveling to and from the store, trying on different styles and sizes, and waiting in line at the cash register.

Still, in most cases, the price of a good is a significant part of its opportunity cost. For large purchases such as a home or automobile, the price will be *most* of the opportunity cost. And this is why prices are so important to the overall working of the economy: They confront individual decision makers with the costs of their choices.

Consider the example of purchasing a car. Because you must pay the price, you know that buying a new car will require you to cut back on purchases of other things. In this way, the opportunity cost to *society* of making another car is converted to an opportunity cost *for you*. If you value a new car more highly than the other things you must sacrifice for it, you will buy it. If not, you won't buy it.

Why is it so important that people face the opportunity costs of their actions? The following thought experiment can answer this question.

### A Thought Experiment: Free Cars

Imagine that the government passes a new law: When anyone buys a new car, the government will reimburse that person for it immediately. The consequences would be easy to predict. First, on the day the law was passed, everyone would rush out to buy new cars. Why not, if cars are free? The entire stock of existing automobiles would be gone within days—maybe even hours. Many people who didn't value cars much at all, and who hardly ever used them, would find themselves owning several—one for each day of the week or to match the different colors in their wardrobe. Others who weren't able to act in time—including some who desperately needed a new car for their work or to run their households—would be unable to find one at all.

Over time, automobile companies would drastically increase production to meet the surge in demand for cars. So much of our available labor, capital, land, and entrepreneurial talent would be diverted to the automobile industry that we'd have to sacrifice huge quantities of all other goods and services. Thus, we'd end up *paying* for those additional cars in the end, by making do with less education, less medical care, perhaps even less food—all to support the widespread, frivolous use of cars. Almost everyone would conclude that society had been made worse off with the new "free-car" policy. By eliminating a price for automobiles, and severing the connection between the opportunity cost of producing a car and the individual's decision to get one, we would have created quite a mess for ourselves.

> *When resources are allocated by the market, and people must* pay *for their purchases, they are forced to consider the opportunity cost to society of their individual actions. In this way, markets are able to create a sensible allocation of resources.*

### Resource Allocation in the United States

The United States has always been considered the leading example of a market economy. Each day, millions of distinct items are produced and sold in markets. Our grocery stores are always stocked with broccoli and tomato soup, and the drugstore always has Kleenex and aspirin—all due to the choices of individual producers and consumers. The goods that are traded, the way they are traded, and the price at which they trade are determined by the traders themselves. No direction from above is needed to keep markets working.

But even in the United States, there are numerous cases of resource allocation *outside* the market. For example, families are important institutions in the United States, and many economic decisions are made within them. Families tend to operate like traditional villages, not like market economies. For example, few parents make their children pay for goods and services provided inside the home.

Our economy also allocates some resources by command. Various levels of government collect, in total, about one-third of our incomes as taxes. We are *told* how much tax we must pay, and those who don't comply suffer serious penalties, including imprisonment. Government—rather than individual decision makers—spends the tax revenue. In this way, the government plays a major role in allocating resources—especially in determining which goods are produced and who gets them.

There are also other ways, aside from strict commands, that the government limits our market freedoms. Regulations designed to protect the environment, maintain safe workplaces, and ensure the safety of our food supply are just a few examples of government-imposed constraints on our individual choice.

What are we to make, then, of resource allocation in the United States? Markets are, indeed, constrained. But for each example we can find where resources are allocated by tradition or command, or where government restrictions seriously limit some market freedom, we can find hundreds of examples where individuals make choices according to their own desires. The things we buy, the jobs at which we work, the homes in which we live—in almost all cases, these result from market choices. The market, though not pure, is certainly the dominant method of resource allocation in the United States.

## RESOURCE OWNERSHIP

So far, we've been concerned with how resources are allocated. Another important feature of an economic system is how resources are *owned*. The owner of a resource—a parcel of land, a factory, or one's own labor time—determines how it can be used and receives income when others use it. And there have been three primary modes of resource ownership in human history.

Under *communal* ownership, resources are owned by everyone—or by no one, depending on your point of view. They are simply there for the taking; no person or organization imposes any restrictions on their use or charges any fees.

**Communism** A type of economic system in which most resources are owned in common.

It is hard to find economies with significant communal ownership of resources. Karl Marx believed that, in time, all economies would evolve toward communal ownership, and he named this predicted system **communism**. In fact, none of the economies that called themselves communist (such as the former Soviet Union) ever achieved Marx's vision. This is not surprising: Communal ownership on a broad scale can work only when individuals have no conflicts over how resources are used. Therefore, communism requires the end of *scarcity*—an unlikely prospect in the foreseeable future.

Nevertheless, there are examples of communal ownership on a smaller scale. Traditional villages maintain communal ownership of land and sometimes cattle. Closer to home, most families operate on the principle of communal ownership. The house, television, telephone, and food in the refrigerator are treated as if owned jointly. More broadly, who "owns" our sidewalks, streets, and public beaches? No one does, really. In practice, all citizens are free to use them as much and as often as they would like. This is essentially communal ownership.

**Socialism** A type of economic system in which most resources are owned by the state.

Under **socialism**, the *state* owns most of the resources. The prime example is the former Soviet Union, where the state owned all of the land and capital equipment in the country. In many ways, it also owned the labor of individual households, since it was virtually the only employer in the nation and unemployment was considered a crime.

State ownership also occurs in nonsocialist economies. In the United States, national parks, state highway systems, military bases, public colleges and universities, and government buildings are all state-owned resources. Over a third of the land in the country is owned by the federal government. The military, even under our current volunteer system, is an example in which the state owns the labor of soldiers—albeit for a limited period of time.

**Capitalism** A type of economic system in which most resources are owned privately.

Finally, the third system. When most resources are owned *privately*—as in the United States—we have **capitalism**. Take the book you are reading right now. If you turn to the title page, you will see the imprint of the company that published this book. This is a corporation owned by thousands of individual stockholders. These individuals own the buildings, the land under them, the office furniture and computer equipment, and even the reputation of the company. When these facilities are used to produce and sell a book, the company's profits belong to these stockholders.

Similarly, the employees of the company are private individuals. They are selling a resource they own—their labor time—to the company, and they receive income—wages and salaries—in return.

The United States is one of the most capitalistic countries in the world. True, there are examples of state and communal ownership, as we've seen. But the dominant mode of resource ownership in the United States is *private* ownership. Resource owners keep most of the income they earn from supplying their resources, and they have broad freedom in deciding how their resources are used.

## TYPES OF ECONOMIC SYSTEMS

We've used the phrase *economic system* a few times already in this book. But now it's time for a formal definition.

> An **economic system** *is composed of two features: a mechanism for allocating resources and a mode of resource ownership.*

**Economic system** A system of resource allocation and resource ownership.

Let's leave aside the rare economies in which communal ownership is dominant and those in which resources are allocated primarily by tradition. That leaves us with four basic types of economic systems, indicated by the four quadrants in Figure 6. In the upper left quadrant, we have *market capitalism*. In this system, resources are *allocated* primarily by the market and *owned* primarily by private individuals. Today, most nations have market capitalist economies, including all of the countries of North America and Western Europe, and most of those in Asia, Latin America, and Africa.

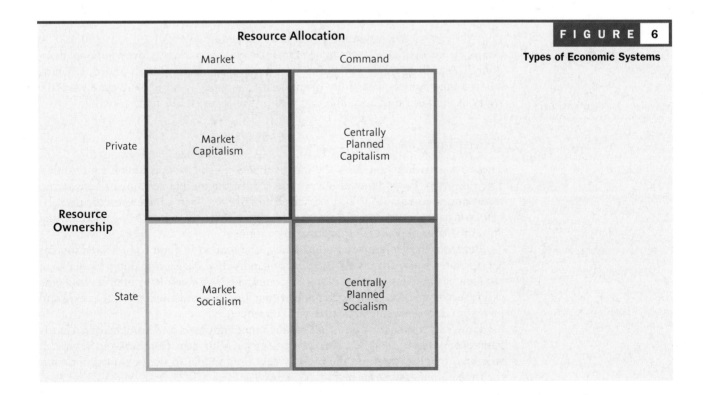

**FIGURE 6**

**Types of Economic Systems**

In the lower right quadrant is *centrally planned socialism*, under which resources are mostly allocated by command and mostly owned by the state. This *was* the system in the former Soviet Union and the nations of Eastern Europe until the late 1980s. But since then, these countries' economies have gone through cataclysmic change by moving from the lower right quadrant to the upper left. That is, these nations have simultaneously changed both their method of resource allocation and their systems of resource ownership.

Although market capitalism and centrally planned socialism have been the two paramount economic systems in modern history, there have been others. The upper right quadrant represents a system of *centrally planned capitalism*, in which resources are owned by private individuals yet allocated by command. In the recent past, countries such as Sweden and Japan—where the government has been more heavily involved in allocating resources than in the United States—have flirted with this type of system. Nations at war—like the United States during World War II—also move in this direction, as governments find it necessary to direct resources by command in order to ensure sufficient military production.

Finally, in the lower left quadrant is *market socialism*, in which resources are owned by the state yet allocated by the market mechanism. The possibility of market socialism has fascinated many social scientists, who believed it promised the best of both worlds: the freedom and efficiency of the market mechanism and the fairness and equity of socialism. There are, however, serious problems—many would say "unresolvable contradictions"—in trying to mix the two. The chief examples of market socialism in modern history were short-lived experiments—in Hungary and the former Yugoslavia in the 1950s and 1960s—in which the results were mixed at best.

### Economic Systems and This Book

Over the past two decades, the world has changed dramatically: About 300 million people in Europe have come under the sway of the market as their nations abandoned centrally planned socialism; more than a billion have been added as China has changed course. The study of modern economies is now, more than ever, the study of market capitalism, and that will be the focus of our text.

### Understanding the Market

The market is simultaneously the most simple and the most complex way to allocate resources. For individual buyers and sellers, the market is simple. There are no traditions or commands to be memorized and obeyed. Instead, we enter the markets we *wish* to trade in, and we respond to prices there as we *wish* to, unconcerned about the overall process of resource allocation.

But from the economist's point of view, the market is quite complex. Resources are allocated indirectly, as a *by-product* of individual decision making, rather than through easily identified traditions or commands. As a result, it often takes some skillful economic detective work to determine just how individuals are behaving and how resources are being allocated as a consequence.

How can we make sense of all of this apparent chaos and complexity? That is what economics is all about. And you will begin your detective work in Chapter 3, where you will learn about the most widely used model in the field of economics: the model of supply and demand.

# USING THE THEORY

## Are We Saving Lives Efficiently?

Earlier in this chapter, you learned that instances of gross productive inefficiency are not as easy to find in our economy as one might imagine. But many economists argue that our allocation of resources to lifesaving efforts is a glaring exception. In this section, we'll use some of the tools and concepts you've learned in this chapter to ask whether we are saving lives efficiently.

We can view "saving lives" as the output—a service—produced by the "lifesaving industry." This industry consists of private firms (such as medical practices and hospitals), as well as government agencies (such as the Department of Health and Human Services or the Environmental Protection Agency). In a productively efficient economy, we must pay an opportunity cost whenever we choose to save additional lives. That's because any lifesaving action we might take—building another emergency surgery center, running an advertising campaign to encourage healthier living, or requiring the substitution of costly but safe materials for less costly but toxic ones—would require us to use additional land, labor, capital, and entrepreneurship. And these resources could be used to produce other goods and services that we value.

Figure 7 illustrates this opportunity cost with a production possibilities frontier. The number of lives saved per year is measured along the horizontal axis, and the quantity of all other goods (lumped together into a single category) is measured on the vertical axis. A productively efficient economy would be *on* the frontier, producing the maximum quantity of all other goods for any given number of lives saved. Equivalently, productive efficiency would mean saving the maximum possible number of lives for any given quantity of other goods

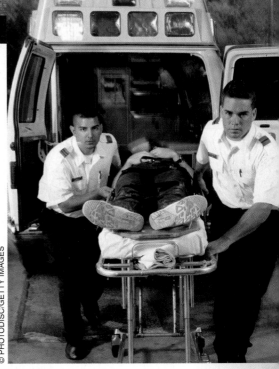

© PHOTODISC/GETTY IMAGES

### FIGURE 7

**Efficiency and Inefficiency in Saving Lives**

*This PPF shows society's choice between saving lives (measured along the horizontal axis) and all other production (on the vertical axis). Operating on the curve (at a point like A) would be productively efficient. But if the life-saving industry is not efficient, then society is operating inside the PPF (at a point like B). Eliminating the inefficiency would enable us to save more lives, or have more of other goods, or both.*

Quantity of All Other Goods per Year

$Q_2$

B       A

$Q_1$    Number of Lives Saved per Year

produced. Point *A* on the PPF is one such productively efficient point, where we would save $Q_1$ lives per year, and produce the quantity $Q_2$ of all other goods. Once we are on the frontier, we can only save more lives by pulling resources away from producing other goods, and paying an opportunity cost in other goods foregone.

But what if there is productive *in*efficiency in the economy? And what if the source of the inefficiency is in the lifesaving industry itself? More specifically, what if more lives could be saved with the current quantity of resources used by the industry simply by reallocating those resources among different types of lifesaving activities? In that case, the economy would be operating at a point like *B*, *inside* the PPF. By eliminating the inefficiency, we could move *to* the frontier. For example, we could save more lives with no sacrifice of other goods (a move from point *B* to point *A*) or have more of other goods while saving the same number of lives (a move vertically upward from point *B* to a new, unmarked point on the PPF) or have more of both (upward and rightward from point *B*).

Economists argue that the United States and most other countries do, in fact, operate at a point like *B* because of productive inefficiency in saving lives. How have they come to such a conclusion?

The first step in the analysis is to remember that, in a market economy, resources sell at a price. This allows us to use the dollar cost of a lifesaving method to measure the value of the resources used up by that method.

Moreover, we can compare the "cost per year of life saved" of different methods. For example, in the United States we currently spend about $253 million on heart transplants each year and thereby add about 1,600 years to the lives of heart patients. Thus, the cost per year of life saved from heart transplants is $253,000,000/1,600 = $158,000 (rounded to the nearest thousand).

Table 6 lists several of the methods we currently use to save lives in the United States. Some of these methods reflect legal or regulatory decisions (such as the ban on asbestos) and others reflect standard medical practices (such as annual mammograms for women over 50). Other methods effectively save lives only sporadically (such as seat belts in school buses). You can see that the cost per life saved ranges widely—from $150 per year of life saved for a physician warning a patient to quit smoking, to over $66,000,000 per year of life saved from the ban on asbestos in automatic transmissions.

The table indicates that some lifesaving methods are highly cost effective. For example, our society probably exhausts the potential to save lives from brief physician antismoking intervention. Most doctors *do* warn their smoking patients to quit.

But the table also indicates some serious productive *in*efficiency in lifesaving. For example, screening and treating African-American newborns for sickle cell anemia is one of the least costly ways of saving a year of life in the United States—only $236 per year of life saved. Nevertheless, 20 percent of African-American newborns do *not* get this screening at all. Similarly, intensive intervention to discourage smoking is far from universal in the U.S. health care system, even though it has the relatively low cost of $2,587 per year of life saved.

Why is the less than universal use of these lower cost methods *productively inefficient*? To answer, let's do some thought experiments. First, let's imagine that we shift resources from heart transplants to *intensive* antismoking efforts. Then for each year of life we decided *not* to save with heart transplants, we would free up $157,821 in medical resources. If we applied those resources toward intensive antismoking efforts, at a cost of $2,587 per year of life saved, we could then save an additional $157,821/$2,587 = 61 life-years. In other words, we could increase the

| Method | Cost per Life-Year Saved | |
|---|---|---|
| | | TABLE 6 |
| | | **The Cost of Saving Lives** |
| Brief physician antismoking intervention: | | |
| Single personal warning from physician to stop smoking | $150 | |
| Sickle cell screening and treatment for African-American newborns | $236 | |
| Replacing ambulances with helicopters for medical emergencies | $2,454 | |
| Intensive physician antismoking intervention: | | |
| Physician identification of smokers among their patients; three physician counseling sessions; two further sessions with smoking-cessation specialists; and materials—nicotine patch or nicotine gum | $2,587 | |
| Mammograms: Once every three years, for ages 50–64 | $2,700 | |
| Chlorination of water supply | $4,000 | |
| Next step after suspicious lung X-ray: | | |
| PET Scan | $3,742 | |
| Exploratory Surgery | $4,895 | |
| Needle Biopsy | $7,116 | |
| Vaccination of all infants against strep infections | $80,000 | |
| Mammograms: Annually, for ages 50–64 | $108,401 | |
| Exercise electrocardiograms as screening test: | | |
| For 40-year-old males | $124,374 | |
| Heart transplants | $157,821 | |
| Mammograms: Annually, for age 40–49 | $186,635 | |
| Exercise electrocardiograms as screening test: | | |
| For 40-year-old females | $335,217 | |
| Seat belts on school buses | $2,760,197 | |
| Asbestos ban in automatic transmissions | $66,402,402 | |

*Sources:* Compiled from various publications. Individual sources available from authors upon request.

number of life-years saved without any increase in resources flowing to the health care sector, and therefore, without any sacrifice in other goods and services. If you look back at the definition of productive inefficiency given earlier in this chapter, you'll see why this is an example of it.

But why pick on heart transplants? Our ban on asbestos in automobile transmissions—which requires the purchase of more costly materials with greater quantities of scarce resources—costs us about $66 million for each life-year saved. Suppose these funds were spent instead to buy the resources needed to provide women aged 40 to 49 with annual mammograms (currently *not* part of most physicians' recommendations). Then for each life-year lost to asbestos, we'd save $66 million/186,635 = 354 life-years from earlier detection of breast cancer.

Of course, allocating lifesaving resources is much more complicated than our discussion so far has implied. For one thing, the benefits of lifesaving efforts are not fully captured by "life-years saved" (or even by an alternative measure, which accounts for improvement in *quality* of life). The cost per life-year saved from mandating seat belts on school buses is extremely high—almost $3 million. This is mostly because very few children die in school bus accidents—about 11 per year in the entire United States—and, according to the National Traffic Safety Board, few of these deaths would have been prevented with seat belts. But mandatory seat belts—rightly or wrongly—might decrease the anxiety of millions of parents as they send their children off to school. How should we value such a reduction in anxiety? Hard to say. But it's not unreasonable to include it as a benefit—at least in some way—when deciding about resources.

Another difficulty in allocating our lifesaving resources efficiently—which has become profoundly more serious in the last few years—is uncertainty. Consider, for example, our efforts to prevent a terrorist attack via hijacked airliners. What is the cost per life-year saved? We cannot know. An earlier study of antiterrorist efforts in the mid-1990s had estimated the cost at $8,000,000 per life-year saved, which seems productively inefficient.[9] But this study made two critical assumptions to arrive at that number. First, it assumed that without the new procedures 37 people would perish each year from airline-related terrorist incidents—equal to the rate we had had in the late 1980s and early 1990s. Second, the study assumed that the safety procedures being evaluated would be 100 percent effective in eliminating attacks. Clearly, trying to gauge and improve our productive efficiency in saving lives—which was never an exact science—has become even *less* exact in the post-9/11 era.

## Summary

One of the most fundamental concepts in economics is *opportunity cost*. The opportunity cost of any choice is what we give up when we make that choice. At the individual level, opportunity cost arises from the scarcity of time or money; for society as a whole, it arises from the scarcity of resources—land, labor, capital, and entrepreneurship. To produce and enjoy more of one thing, we must shift resources away from producing something else. The correct measure of cost is not just the money price we pay, but the opportunity cost: what we must give up when we make a choice. The *law of increasing opportunity cost* tells us that the more of something we produce, the greater the opportunity cost of producing still more.

In a world of scarce resources, each society must have an economic system—its way of organizing economic activity. All *economic systems* feature *specialization*, where each person and firm concentrates on a limited number of productive activities, and *exchange*, through which we obtain most of what we desire by trading with others. Specialization and exchange enable us to enjoy higher living standards than would be possible under self-sufficiency. One way that specialization increases living standards is by allowing each of us to concentrate on tasks in which we have a comparative advantage.

Every economic system determines how resources are owned and how they are allocated. In a market capitalist economy, resources are owned primarily by private individuals and allocated primarily through markets. Prices play an important role in markets by forcing decision makers to take account of society's opportunity cost when they make choices.

## Problem Set    *Answers to even-numbered Questions and Problems can be found on the text Web site at www.thomsonedu.com/economics/hall.*

1. Redraw Figure 2, but this time identify a different set of points along the frontier. Starting at point F (5,000 tanks, zero production of wheat), have each point you select show equal increments in the quantity of wheat produced. For example, a new point H should correspond to 200,000 bushels of wheat, point J to 400,000 bushels, point K to 600,000 bushels, and so on. Now observe what happens to the opportunity cost of "200,000 more bushels of wheat"

[9] "The Cost of Anti-terrorist Rhetoric," The Cato Review of Business and Government, Dec. 17, 1996, and authors' calculations to convert "per life saved" to "per year of life saved."

as you move leftward and upward along this PPF. Does the law of increasing opportunity cost apply to the production of wheat? Explain briefly.

2. Suppose that you are considering what to do with an upcoming weekend. Here are your options, from least to most preferred: (1) Study for upcoming midterms; (2) fly to Colorado for a quick ski trip; (3) go into seclusion in your dorm room and try to improve your score on a computer game. What is the opportunity cost of a decision to play the computer game all weekend?

3. How would a technological innovation in lifesaving—say, the discovery of a cure for cancer—affect the PPF in Figure 7?

4. How would a technological innovation in the production of *other* goods—say, the invention of a new kind of robot that speeds up assembly-line manufacturing—affect the PPF in Figure 7?

5. Suppose that one day, Gilligan (the castaway) eats a magical island plant that turns him into an expert at everything. In particular, it now takes him just half an hour to pick a quart of berries, and 15 minutes to catch a fish.
   a. Redo Table 3 in the chapter.
   b. Who—Gilligan or Maryanne—has a comparative advantage in picking berries? In fishing? When the castaways discover each other, which of the two should specialize in which task?
   c. Can *both* castaways benefit from Gilligan's new abilities? How?

6. Suppose that two different castaways, Mr. and Mrs. Howell, end up on a different island. Mr. Howell can pick 1 pineapple per hour, or 1 coconut. Mrs. Howell can pick 2 pineapples per hour, but it takes her two hours to pick a coconut.
   a. Construct a table like Table 3 showing Mr. and Mrs. Howell's labor requirements.
   b. Who—Mr. or Mrs. Howell—has a comparative advantage in picking pineapples? In picking coconuts? Which of the two should specialize in which tasks?
   c. Assume that Mr. and Mrs. Howell had originally washed ashore on different parts of the island, and that they originally each spent 12 hours per day working, spending 6 hours picking pineapples and 6 hours picking coconuts. How will their total production change if they find each other and begin to specialize?

7. You and a friend have decided to work jointly on a course project. Frankly, your friend is a less than ideal partner. His skills as a researcher are such that he can review and outline only two articles a day. Moreover, his hunt-and-peck style limits him to only 10 pages of typing a day. On the other hand, in a day you can produce six outlines or type 20 pages.
   a. Who has an absolute advantage in outlining, you or your friend? What about typing?
   b. Who has a comparative advantage in outlining? In typing?
   c. According to the principle of comparative advantage, who should specialize in which task?

8. One might think that performing a mammogram once each year—as opposed to once every three years—would triple the cost per life saved. But according to Table 6, peforming the exam annually raises the cost per life-year saved by about 40 times. Does this make sense? Explain.

9. Use the information in Table 1 as well as the assumption about foregone income made in the chapter to calculate the average opportunity cost of a year in college for a student at a four-year private institution under each the following assumptions:
   a. The student receives free room and board at home at no opportunity cost to the parents.
   b. The student receives an academic scholarship covering all tuition and fees (in the form of a grant, not a loan or a work study aid).
   c. The student works half time while at school at no additional emotional cost.

10. Use the information in Table 1 as well as the assumption about foregone income made in the chapter to compare the opportunity cost of attending a year of college for a student at a two-year public college under each of the following assumptions:
    a. The student receives free room and board at home at no opportunity cost to the parents.
    b. The student receives an academic scholarship covering all tuition and fees (in the form of a grant, not a loan or a work study aid).
    c. The student works half time while at school at no additional emotional cost.

11. Consider Kylie, who has been awarded academic scholarships covering all tuition and fees at three different colleges. College #1 is a two-year public college. College #2 is a four-year public college, and College #3 is a four-year private college. Explain why, if the decision is based solely on opportunity cost, Kylie will turn down her largest scholarship offers. (Use Table 1 in the chapter.)

12. Suppose the Internet enables more production of other goods *and* helps to save lives (for simplicity, assume proportional increases).
    a. Show how the PPF in Figure 7 would be affected.
    b. Does this affect any of the general conclusions about economic growth?

13. Suppose that an economy's PPF is a straight line, rather than a bowed out, concave curve. What would this say about the nature of opportunity cost as production is shifted from one good to the other?

# Supply and Demand

Father Guido Sarducci, a character on the early *Saturday Night Live* shows, once observed that the average person remembers only about five minutes worth of material from college. He therefore proposed the "Five Minute University," where you'd learn only the five minutes of material you'd actually remember and dispense with the rest. The economics course would last only 10 seconds, just enough time for students to learn to recite three words: "supply and demand."

Of course, there is much more to economics than these three words. But many people *do* regard the phrase "supply and demand" as synonymous with economics and the concept is often misused. But surprisingly few people actually understand what the phrase means. In a debate about health care, poverty, recent events in the stock market, or the high price of housing, you might hear someone say, "Well, it's just a matter of supply and demand," as a way of dismissing the issue entirely. Others use the phrase with an exaggerated reverence, as if supply and demand were an inviolable physical law, like gravity, about which nothing can be done. So what does this oft-repeated phrase really mean?

First, supply and demand is just an economic model—nothing more and nothing less. It's a model designed to explain *how prices are determined in certain types of markets*.

Why has this model taken on such an exalted role in the field of economics? Because prices themselves play such an exalted role in the economy. In a market system, once the price of something has been determined, only those willing to pay that price will get it. Thus, prices determine which households will get which goods and services and which firms will get which resources. If you want to know why the cell phone industry is expanding while the video rental industry is shrinking, or why homelessness is a more pervasive problem in the United States than hunger, you need to understand how prices are determined. In this chapter, you will learn how the model of supply and demand works and how to use it. You will also learn about the strengths and limitations of the model. It will take more time than Guido Sarducci's 10-second economics course, but in the end you will know much more than just those three words.

## MARKETS

Put any compound in front of a chemist, ask him what it is and what it can be used for, and he will immediately think of the basic elements—carbon, hydrogen, oxygen, and so on. Ask an economist almost any question about the economy, and he will immediately think about *markets*.

In ordinary language, a market is a specific location where buying and selling take place: a supermarket, a flea market, and so on. In economics, a market is not a place, but rather a collection of *traders*. More specifically,

> *a market is a group of buyers and sellers with the potential to trade with each other.*

Economists think of the economy as a collection of markets. In each of these markets, the collection of buyers and sellers will be different, depending on what is being traded. There is a market for oranges, another for automobiles, another for real estate, and still others for corporate stocks, labor services, land, euros, and anything else that is bought and sold.

However, unlike chemistry—in which the set of basic elements is always the same—in economics, we can define a market in *different* ways, depending on our purpose. In fact, in almost any economic analysis, the first step is to define and characterize the market or collection of markets to analyze.

## HOW BROADLY SHOULD WE DEFINE THE MARKET?

Suppose we want to study the personal computer industry in the United States. Should we define the market very broadly ("the market for computers"), or very narrowly ("the market for ultra-light laptops"), or something in between ("the market for laptops")? The right choice depends on the problem we're trying to analyze.

For example, if we're interested in why computers *in general* have come down in price over the past decade, there would be no reason to divide computers into desktops and laptops. Such a distinction would only get in the way. Thus, we'd treat all types of computers as if they were the same good. Economists call this process **aggregation**—combining a group of distinct things into a single whole.

**Aggregation** The process of combining distinct things into a single whole.

But suppose we're asking a different question: Why do laptops always cost more than desktops with similar computing power? Then we'd aggregate all laptops together as one good, and all desktops as another, and look at each of these more narrowly defined markets.

The same general principle applies to the *geographic* breadth of the market. If we want to predict how instability in the Persian Gulf will affect gasoline prices around the world, we'd use the "global market for oil," in which the major oil producers in about 20 countries sell to buyers around the globe. But if we want to explain why gasoline is cheaper in the United States than in most of the rest of the world, we'd want to look at the "U.S. market for oil." In this market, global sellers choose how much oil to sell to U.S. buyers.

> *In economics, **markets** can be defined broadly or narrowly, depending on our purpose.*

How broadly or narrowly markets are defined is one of the most important differences between *macro*economics and *micro*economics. In macroeconomics, goods and services are aggregated to the highest levels. Macro models even lump all consumer goods—breakfast cereals, cell phones, blue jeans, and so forth—into the single category "consumption goods" and view them as if they are traded in a single, broadly defined market, "the market for consumption goods." Similarly, instead of recognizing different markets for shovels, bulldozers, computers, and factory buildings, macro models analyze the market for "capital goods." Defining markets this broadly allows macroeconomists to take an overall view of the economy without getting bogged down in the details.

In microeconomics, by contrast, markets are defined more narrowly. Instead of asking how much we'll spend on *consumer goods*, a microeconomist might ask how much we'll spend on *health care* or *video games*. Although microeconomics always involves some aggregation, the process stops before it reaches the highest level of generality.

## PRODUCT AND RESOURCE MARKETS

**Circular flow** A simple model that shows how goods, resources, and dollar payments flow between households and firms.

Figure 1 displays the **circular flow** model of the economy, which helps us organize our thinking about markets. It shows how we can divide markets into two major categories, and how each category fits into the big picture.

**Product markets** Markets in which firms sell goods and services to households

The upper half of the diagram shows **product markets**, where goods and services such as soft drinks, word-processing software, gasoline, DVDs, college educational services, medical services, and more are bought and sold. The outer arrows represent the flow of *goods and services* from business firms (the sellers) to households (the buyers). The inner arrows show the associated flow of funds, where household payments for goods and services ($ Expenditures) become the receipts of businesses ($ Revenue).

**Resource markets** Markets in which households that own resources sell them to firms.

The lower half of the diagram depicts another type of market: **resource markets**, where labor, land, capital, and entrepreneurship are bought and sold. In these markets, as shown by the outer arrows, households (the ultimate owners of resources) act as sellers. Business firms, which use resources to make goods and services, are the buyers. The inner arrows in the lower half of the diagram show us that when businesses pay for the resources they use ($ Resource Payments), the funds flow to households ($ Income).

There is, of course, much more to the economy than this simple model captures. For example, we've left out the government, which buys many goods and services, and also produces some for the general public. And we've left out some markets entirely, such as markets where borrowing and lending takes place, or markets where foreign currencies are traded.

But for many problems, the simple circular flow model can help us understand and identify the participants and the type of market we are discussing. In this chapter, for example, our focus is on *product markets*, so we'll view households as buyers and business firms as sellers. Later in this book (in both microeconomics and macroeconomics), you'll encounter resource markets where these roles are reversed.

## COMPETITION IN MARKETS

A final issue in defining a market is how individual buyers and sellers view the price of the product. In many cases, individual buyers or sellers have an important influence over the price. For example, in the national market for cornflakes, Kellogg's—an individual *seller*—simply sets its price every few months. It can raise the price and sell fewer boxes of cereal or lower the price and sell more. In a small-town, a major buyer of antiques may be able to negotiate special discount prices with the local antique shops. These are examples of *imperfectly competitive* markets.

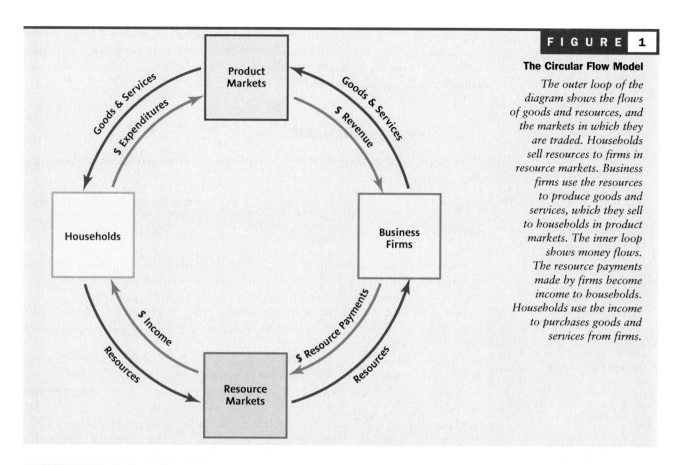

**FIGURE 1**

**The Circular Flow Model**

*The outer loop of the diagram shows the flows of goods and resources, and the markets in which they are traded. Households sell resources to firms in resource markets. Business firms use the resources to produce goods and services, which they sell to households in product markets. The inner loop shows money flows. The resource payments made by firms become income to households. Households use the income to purchases goods and services from firms.*

> *In **imperfectly competitive markets**, individual buyers or sellers can influence the price of the product.*

**Imperfectly competitive market** A market in which a single buyer or seller has the power to influence the price of the product.

But now think about the national market for wheat. Can an individual seller have any impact on the market price? Not really. On any given day there is a going price for wheat—say, $5.80 per bushel. If a farmer tries to charge more than that—say, $5.85 per bushel—he won't sell any wheat at all! His customers will instead go to one of his many competitors and buy the identical product from them for less. Each wheat farmer must take the price of wheat as a "given."

The same is true of a single wheat *buyer:* If he tries to negotiate a lower price from a seller, he'd be laughed off the farm. "Why should I sell my wheat to you for $5.75 per bushel, when there are others who will pay me $5.80?" Accordingly, each buyer must take the market price as a given.

The market for wheat is an example of a *perfectly competitive market.*

> *In **perfectly competitive markets** (or just **competitive markets**), each buyer and seller takes the market price as a given.*

**Perfectly competitive market** A market in which no buyer or seller has the power to influence the price.

What makes some markets imperfectly competitive and others perfectly competitive? You'll learn the complete answer, along with more formal definitions, when you are further into your study of *microeconomics*. But here's a hint: In perfectly competitive markets, there are many small buyers and sellers, each is a small part of the market, and the product is standardized, like wheat. Imperfectly competitive markets, by contrast, have just a few large buyers or sellers, or else the product of each seller is unique in some way.

## USING SUPPLY AND DEMAND

Why is it important to know about perfectly competitive markets when using the supply and demand model? For one simple reason:

> *The supply and demand model is designed to explain how prices are determined in perfectly competitive markets.*

But wait. In the real world, perfectly competitive markets—in which an individual buyer or seller has *no* influence on market price—are rare. Does that mean the supply and demand model can't be used when analyzing most markets?

Not at all. Many markets, while not *strictly* perfectly competitive, come rather close. Choosing to view these markets as if they were perfectly competitive is often a useful approximation.

Think of the market for fast-food hot dogs in a big city. On the one hand, every hot dog stand is somewhat different from every other one in terms of location, quality of service, and so on. This means an individual vendor has *some* influence over the price of his hot dogs. For example, if his competitors are all charging $1.50 for a hot dog, but he sells in a more convenient location, he might be able to charge $1.60 or $1.70 without losing too many customers. In this sense, the market for sidewalk hot dogs does not seem perfectly competitive.

On the other hand, there are rather narrow limits to an individual seller's freedom to change his price. With so many vendors in a big city, who are not *that* different from one another, one who charged $2.00 or $2.25 might soon find that he's lost all of his customers to the other vendors who are charging the market price of $1.50. Since no single seller can deviate *too* much from the market price, we could—if we wanted to—view the market as more or less perfectly competitive.

How, then, do we decide whether to consider a market, such as the market for big-city hot dogs, as perfectly or imperfectly competitive? You won't be surprised to hear that it depends on the question we want to answer. If we want to explain why there are occasional price wars among hot dog vendors, or why some of them routinely charge higher prices than others, viewing the market as perfectly competitive would not work well—it would hide, rather than reveal, the answer. For these questions, we'd choose a *different* model—one designed for a type of *im*perfectly competitive market. (If your current course is *micro*economics, you will soon learn about these models and how to use them.)

But if we want to know why hot dogs are cheaper than most other types of fast foods, the simplest approach is to view the market for hot dogs as perfectly competitive. True, each hot dog vendor does have *some* influence over the price. But that influence is so small, and the prices of different sellers are so similar, that our assumption of perfect competition works pretty well.

Perfect competition then, is a matter of degree, rather than an all-or-nothing characteristic. While there are very few markets in which sellers and buyers take the price as completely given, there are many markets in which a *narrow range* of prices is treated as a given (as in the market for hot dogs). In these markets, supply and demand often provides a good approximation to what is going on. This is why it has proven to be the most versatile and widely used model in the economist's tool kit. Neither laptop computers nor orange juice is traded in a perfectly competitive market. But ask an economist to tell you why the price of laptops decreases every year, or why the price of orange juice rises after a freeze in Florida, and he or she will invariably reach for supply and demand to find the answer.

Supply and demand are like two blades of a scissors: To analyze a market, we need both of them. In this and the next section, we will be sharpening those blades, learning separately about supply and demand. Then, we'll put them together and put them to use. Let's start with demand.

## DEMAND

It's tempting to think of the "demand" for a product as just a psychological phenomenon, a pure "want" or "desire." But that notion can lead us astray. For example, you *want* all kinds of things: a bigger apartment, a better car, nicer clothes, more and better vacations. The list is endless. But you don't always *buy* them. Why not?

Because in addition to your wants—which you'd very much like to satisfy—you also face *constraints*. First, you have to *pay*. Second, you have limited funds with which to buy things, so every decision to buy one thing is also a decision *not* to buy something else (or a decision to save less, and have less buying power in the future). As a result, every purchase confronts you with an opportunity cost. Your "wants," together with the real-world constraints that you face, determine what you will choose to buy in any market. Hence, the following definition:

> The **quantity demanded** of a good or service is the number of units that all buyers in a market would choose to buy over a given time period, given the constraints that they face.

**Quantity Demanded** The amount of a good that all buyers in a market would choose to buy during a period of time, given their constraints.

Since this definition plays a key role in any supply and demand analysis, it's worth taking a closer look at it.

*Quantity Demanded Implies a* **Choice.** Quantity demanded doesn't tell us the amount of a good that households feel they "need" or "desire" in order to be happy. Instead, it tells us how much households would choose to buy *when they take into account the opportunity cost* of their decisions. The opportunity cost arises from the constraints households face, such as having to pay a given price for the good, limits on spendable funds, and so on.

*Quantity Demanded Is* **Hypothetical.** Will households actually be *able* to purchase the amount they want to purchase? As you'll soon see, usually yes. But there are special situations—analyzed in microeconomics—in which households are frustrated in buying all that they would like to buy. Quantity demanded makes no assumptions about the availability of the good. Instead, it's the answer to a hypothetical question: How much would households buy, given the constraints that they face, if the units they wanted to buy were available.

*Quantity Demanded Depends on* **Price.** The price of the good is just one variable among many that influences quantity demanded. But because one of our main purposes in building a supply and demand model is to explain how prices are determined, we try to keep that variable front-and-center in our thinking. This is why for the next few pages we'll assume that all other influences on demand are held constant, so we can explore the relationship between price and quantity demanded.

## THE LAW OF DEMAND

How does a change in price affect quantity demanded? You probably know the answer to this already: When something is more expensive, people tend to buy less of it. This common observation applies to air travel, magazines, guitars, and virtually everything else that people buy. For all of these goods and services, price and quantity are *negatively related*: that is, when price rises, quantity demanded falls; when price falls, quantity demanded rises. This negative relationship is observed so regularly in markets that economists call it the *law of demand*.

**Law of demand** As the price of a good increases, the quantity demanded decreases.

> The **law of demand** states that when the price of a good rises and everything else remains the same, the quantity of the good demanded will fall.

Read that definition again, and notice the very important words, "everything else remains the same." The law of demand tells us what would happen *if* all the other influences on buyers' choices remained unchanged, and only one influence—the price of the good—changed.

This is an example of a common practice in economics. In the real world, many variables change *simultaneously*. But to understand changes in the economy, we must first understand the effect of each variable *separately*. So we conduct a series of mental experiments in which we ask: "What would happen if this one influence—and only this one—were to change?" The law of demand is the result of one such mental experiment, in which we imagine that the price of the good changes, but all other influences on quantity demanded remain constant.

**Ceteris paribus** Latin for "all else remaining the same."

Mental experiments like this are used so often in economics that we sometimes use a shorthand Latin expression to remind us that we are holding all but one influence constant: *ceteris paribus* (formally pronounced KAY-ter-is PAR-ih-bus, although it's acceptable to pronounce the first word as SEH-ter-is). This is Latin for "all else the same," or "all else remaining unchanged." Even when it is not explicitly stated, the *ceteris paribus* assumption is virtually always implied. The exceptions are cases where we consider two or more influences on a variable that change simultaneously, as we will do toward the end of this chapter.

## THE DEMAND SCHEDULE AND THE DEMAND CURVE

To make our discussion more concrete, let's look at a specific market: the market for real maple syrup in the United States. In this market, we'll view the buyers as U.S. households, whereas the sellers (to be considered later) are maple syrup producers in the United States or Canada.

**Demand schedule** A list showing the quantities of a good that consumers would choose to purchase at different prices, with all other variables held constant.

Table 1 shows a hypothetical **demand schedule** for maple syrup in this market. This is *a list of different quantities demanded at different prices, with all other variables that affect the demand decision assumed constant.* For example, the demand schedule tells us that when the price of maple syrup is $2.00 per bottle, the quantity demanded will be 60,000 bottles per month. Notice that the demand schedule obeys

| Price (per bottle) | Quantity Demanded (bottles per month) | TABLE 1 |
|---|---|---|
| | | **Demand Schedule for Maple Syrup in the United States** |
| $1.00 | 75,000 | |
| $2.00 | 60,000 | |
| $3.00 | 50,000 | |
| $4.00 | 40,000 | |
| $5.00 | 35,000 | |

the law of demand: As the price of maple syrup increases, *ceteris paribus*, the quantity demanded falls.

Now look at Figure 2. It shows a diagram that will appear again and again in your study of economics. In the figure, each price-and-quantity combination in Table 1 is represented by a point. For example, point *A* represents the price $4.00 and quantity 40,000, while point *B* represents the pair $2.00 and 60,000. When we connect all of these points with a line, we obtain the famous *demand curve*, labeled with a *D* in the figure.

> *The **demand curve** shows the relationship between the price of a good and the quantity demanded in the market, holding constant all other variables that influence demand. Each point on the curve shows the total quantity that buyers would choose to buy at a specific price.*

**Demand curve** The graphical depiction of a demand schedule; a curve showing the quantity of a good or service demanded at various prices, with all other variables held constant.

Notice that the demand curve in Figure 2—like virtually all demand curves—*slopes downward*. This is just a graphical representation of the law of demand.

## SHIFTS VERSUS MOVEMENTS ALONG THE DEMAND CURVE

Markets are affected by a variety of events. Some events will cause us to *move along* the demand curve; others will cause the entire demand curve to *shift*. It is crucial to distinguish between these two very different types of effects.

Let's go back to Figure 2. There, you can see that when the price of maple syrup rises from $2.00 to $4.00 per bottle, the number of bottles demanded falls from 60,000 to 40,000. This is a movement *along* the demand curve, from point *B* to point *A*. In general,

> *a change in the price of a good causes a movement* along *the demand curve.*

In Figure 2, a *fall* in price would cause us to move *rightward* along the demand curve (from point *A* to point *B*), and a *rise* in price would cause us to move *leftward* along the demand curve (from *B* to *A*).

Remember, though, that when we draw a demand curve, we assume all other variables that might influence demand are *held constant* at some particular value. For example, the demand curve in Figure 2 might have been drawn to give us quantity demanded at each price when average household income in the United States remains constant at, say, $40,000 per year.

But suppose average income increases to $50,000? With more income, we'd expect households to buy more of *most* things, including maple syrup. This is illus-

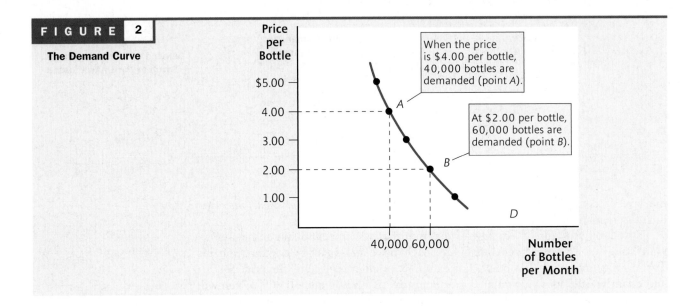

**FIGURE 2**

**The Demand Curve**

trated in Table 2. At the original income level, households would choose to buy 60,000 bottles of maple syrup at $2.00 per bottle. But after income rises, they would choose to buy more at that price—80,000 bottles, according to Table 2. A similar change would occur at any other price for maple syrup: After income rises, households would choose to buy more than before. In other words, the rise in income *changes the entire relationship between price and quantity demanded*. We now have a *new* demand curve.

Figure 3 plots the new demand curve from the quantities in the third column of Table 2. The new demand curve lies to the *right* of the old curve. For example, at a price of $2.00, quantity demanded increases from 60,000 bottles on the old curve (point *B*) to 80,000 bottles on the *new* demand curve (point *C*). As you can see, the rise in household income has *shifted* the demand curve to the right.

More generally,

> *a change in any variable that affects demand—except for the good's price—causes the demand curve to shift.*

When buyers would choose to buy a greater quantity at any price, the demand curve shifts *rightward*. If they would decide to buy a smaller quantity at any price, the demand curve shifts *leftward*.

## "Change in Quantity Demanded" versus "Change in Demand"

Language is important when discussing demand. The term *quantity demanded* means a *particular amount* that buyers would choose to buy at a specific price, represented by a single point on a demand curve. *Demand*, by contrast, means the *entire relationship* between price and quantity demanded, represented by the entire demand curve.

For this reason, when a change in the price of a good moves us *along* a demand curve, we call it a **change in quantity demanded**. For example, in Figure 2, the movement from point *A* to point *B* is an *increase* in quantity demanded. This is a change from one number (40,000 bottles) to another (60,000 bottles).

**Change in quantity demanded** A movement along a demand curve in response to a change in price.

| Price (per bottle) | Original Quantity Demanded (bottles per month) | New Quantity Demanded After Increase in Income (bottles per month) | TABLE 2 |
|---|---|---|---|
| $1.00 | 75,000 | 95,000 | Increase in Demand for Maple Syrup in the United States |
| $2.00 | 60,000 | 80,000 | |
| $3.00 | 50,000 | 70,000 | |
| $4.00 | 40,000 | 60,000 | |
| $5.00 | 35,000 | 55,000 | |

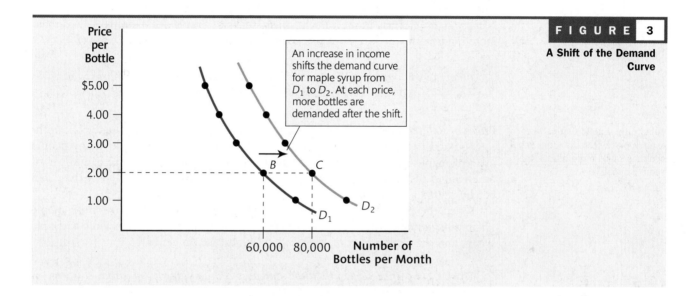

**FIGURE 3**

**A Shift of the Demand Curve**

An increase in income shifts the demand curve for maple syrup from $D_1$ to $D_2$. At each price, more bottles are demanded after the shift.

When something *other* than the price changes, causing the entire demand curve to shift, we call it a **change in demand**. In Figure 3, for example, the shift in the curve would be called an *increase in demand*.

**Change in demand** A shift of a demand curve in response to a change in some variable other than price.

## FACTORS THAT SHIFT THE DEMAND CURVE

Let's take a closer look at what might cause a change in demand (a shift of the demand curve). Keep in mind that for now, we're exploring *one factor at a time*, always keeping *all other determinants of demand constant*.

*Income.* In Figure 3, an increase in **income** shifted the demand for maple syrup to the right. In fact, a rise in income has the same effect on the demand for *most* goods. We call these **normal goods**. Housing, automobiles, health club memberships, and real maple syrup are all examples of normal goods.

But not all goods are normal. For some goods—called **inferior goods**—a rise in income would *decrease* demand—shifting the demand curve *leftward*. Regular-grade ground chuck is a good example. It's a cheap source of protein, but not as high in quality as sirloin. With higher income, households could more easily afford better types of meat—ground sirloin or steak, for example. As a result, higher

**Income** The amount that a person or firm earns over a particular period.

**Normal good** A good that people demand more of as their income rises.

**Inferior good** A good that people demand less of as their income rises.

incomes for buyers might cause the demand for ground chuck to *decrease*. For similar reasons, we might expect that Greyhound bus tickets (in contrast to airline tickets) and single-ply paper towels (in contrast to two-ply) are inferior goods.

> *A rise in income will* increase *the demand for a* normal *good, and* decrease *the demand for an* inferior *good.*

**Wealth**  The total value of everything a person or firm owns, at a point in time, minus the total value of everything owed.

*Wealth.*  Your **wealth** at any point in time is the total value of everything you *own* (cash, bank accounts, stocks, bonds, real estate or any other valuable property) minus the total dollar amount you *owe* (home mortgage, credit card debt, auto loan, student loan, and so on). Although income and wealth are different, (see the nearby Dangerous Curves box), they have similar effects on demand. Increases in wealth among buyers—because of an increase in the value of their stocks or bonds, for example—gives them more funds with which to purchase goods and services. As you might expect,

> *an increase in wealth will* increase *demand (shift the curve rightward) for a normal good, and* decrease *demand (shift the curve leftward) for an inferior good.*

**Substitute**  A good that can be used in place of some other good and that fulfills more or less the same purpose.

*Prices of Related Goods.*  A **substitute** is a good that can be used in place of another good and that fulfills more or less the same purpose. For example, many people use real maple syrup to sweeten their pancakes, but they could use a number of other things instead: honey, sugar, jam, or *artificial* maple syrup. Each of these can be considered a substitute for real maple syrup.

When the price of a substitute rises, people will choose to buy *more* maple syrup. For example, when the price of jam rises, some jam users will switch to maple syrup, and the demand for maple syrup will increase. In general,

> *a rise in the price of a substitute increases the demand for a good, shifting the demand curve to the right.*

**DANGEROUS CURVES**

**Income versus Wealth**  It's easy to confuse *income* with *wealth*, because both are measured in dollars and both are sources of funds that can be spent on goods and services. But they are not the same thing. Your income is how much you earn *per period of time* (such as, $20 *per hour*, $3,500 *per month*, or $40,000 *per year*). Your wealth, by contrast, is the value of what you *own* minus the value of what you *owe* at a particular *moment in time*. (Such as, on December 31, 2005, the value of what you own is $12,000, but the value of what you owe is $9,000, so you have $3,000 in wealth.)

To help you see the difference: suppose you get a good job after you graduate, but you have very little in the bank, and you still have large, unpaid student loans. Then you'd have a moderate-to-high *income* (what you earn at your job each period), but your wealth would be negative (since what you would *owe* is greater than what you *own*).

Of course, if the price of a substitute falls, we have the opposite result: Demand for the original good decreases, shifting its demand curve to the left.

There are countless examples in which a change in a substitute's price affects demand for a good. A drop in the rental price of DVDs, *ceteris paribus*, would decrease the demand for movies at theaters. A rise in the price of beef, *ceteris paribus*, would increase the demand for chicken.

**Complement**  A good that is used *together with* some other good.

A **complement** is the opposite of a substitute: It's used *together with* the good we are interested in. Pancake mix is a complement to maple syrup, since these two goods are used frequently in combination. If the price of pancake mix rises, some consumers will switch to other breakfasts—bacon and eggs, for example—that *don't* include maple syrup. The demand for maple syrup will decrease.

> *A rise in the price of a complement decreases the demand for a good, shifting the demand curve to the left.*

For this reason, we'd expect a higher price for automobiles to decrease the demand for gasoline. (To test yourself: How would a lower price for milk affect the demand for breakfast cereal?)

*Population.* As the population increases in an area, the number of buyers will ordinarily increase as well, and the demand for a good will increase. The growth of the U.S. population over the last 50 years has been an important reason (but not the only reason) for rightward shifts in the demand curves for food, housing, automobiles, and many other goods and services.

*Expected Price.* If buyers expect the price of maple syrup to rise next month, they may choose to purchase more *now* to stock up before the price hike. If people expect the price to drop, they may postpone buying, hoping to take advantage of the lower price later.

> *In many markets, an expectation that price will rise in the future shifts the* current *demand curve rightward, while an expectation that price will fall shifts the current demand curve leftward.*

Expected price changes are especially important in the markets for financial assets such as stocks and bonds and in the market for real estate. People want to buy more stocks, bonds, and real estate when they think their prices will rise in the near future. This shifts the demand curves for these items to the right.

*Tastes.* Suppose we know the number of buyers in the United States, their expectations about the future price of maple syrup, the prices of all related goods, and the average levels of income and wealth. Do we have all the information we need to draw the demand curve for maple syrup? Not really. Because we have not yet considered the psychological component—the habits and tastes that determine the basic desire people have for maple syrup. How many Americans eat breakfast every day? Of these, how many eat pancakes or waffles? How often? How many of them *like* maple syrup, and how much do they like it? And what about all of the other goods and services competing for consumers' dollars: How do buyers feel about *them*?

The questions could go on and on, pinpointing various characteristics about buyers that influence their attitudes toward maple syrup. The approach of economics is to lump all of these characteristics of buyers together and call them, simply, *tastes* or *preferences.* Economists are sometimes interested in where these tastes come from or what makes them change. But for the most part, economics deals with the *consequences* of a change in tastes, whatever the reason for its occurrence.

When tastes change *toward* a good (people favor it more), demand increases, and the demand curve shifts to the right. When tastes change *away* from a good, demand decreases, and the demand curve shifts to the left. An example of this is the change in tastes away from cigarettes over the past several decades. The cause may have been an aging population, a greater concern about health among people of *all* ages, or successful antismoking advertising. But regardless of the cause, the effect has been to decrease the demand for cigarettes, shifting the demand curve to the left.

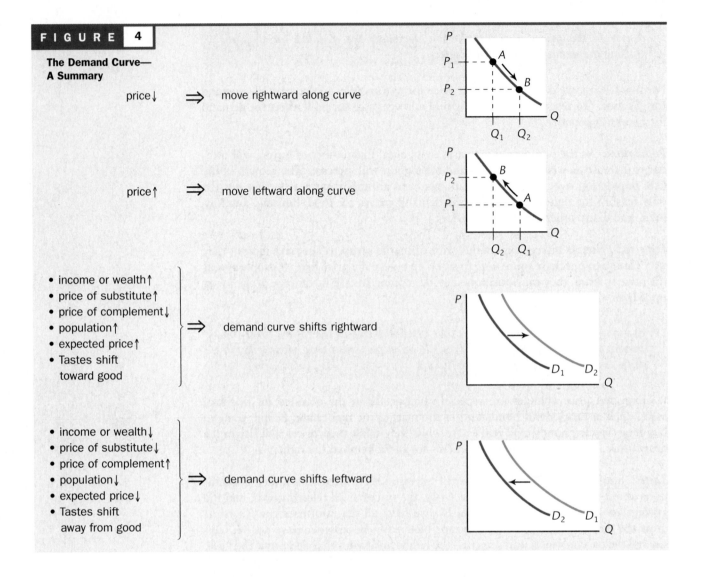

**FIGURE 4**

The Demand Curve—
A Summary

price↓ ⟹ move rightward along curve

price↑ ⟹ move leftward along curve

- income or wealth↑
- price of substitute↑
- price of complement↓
- population↑
- expected price↑
- Tastes shift toward good

⟹ demand curve shifts rightward

- income or wealth↓
- price of substitute↓
- price of complement↑
- population↓
- expected price↓
- Tastes shift away from good

⟹ demand curve shifts leftward

## DEMAND: A SUMMARY

Figure 4 summarizes the variables we've discussed that affect the demand side of the market and how their effects are represented with a demand curve. Notice the important distinction between movements *along* the demand curve and *shifts* of the entire curve.

Keep in mind that other variables, besides those listed in Figure 4, can influence demand. For example, government subsidies such as Federal Pell Grants for college shift the demand curve for higher education rightward. Expectations other than future price

**DANGEROUS CURVES**

**Does Supply Affect Demand?** A troubling thought may have occurred to you. Among the variables that shift the demand curve in Figure 3, shouldn't we include the amount of syrup available? Or to put the question another way, doesn't supply influence demand?

No—at least not directly. The demand curve by asking people a series of hypothetical questions about how much they *would like* to buy at each different price. A change in the amount available would not affect the answers to these questions, and so doesn't affect the curve itself, As you'll see later, a change in supply *will* change the *price* of the good, but this causes a movement along—not a shift of—the demand curve.

matter too. If buyers expect a recession and fear their incomes may fall in the future, their demand for many goods may decrease *now*, even though current income remains unchanged. Some of these other *shift-variables* for demand curves will be discussed in future chapters, as they become relevant in each case. But we'll always use the same logic we used here: If an event makes buyers want to purchase more or less of a good *at any price*, it causes the demand curve to shift.

## SUPPLY

When most people hear the word *supply*, their first thought is that it's the amount of something "available," as if this amount were fixed in stone. For example, someone might say, "We can only drill so much oil from the ground," or "There are only so many apartments for rent in this town." And yet, the world's known oil reserves—as well as yearly production of oil—have increased dramatically over the last half century, as oil companies have found it worth their while to look harder for oil. Similarly, in most towns and cities, short buildings have been replaced with tall ones, and the number of apartments has increased. Supply, like demand, can change, and the amount of a good supplied in a market depends on the *choices* made by those who produce it.

What governs these choices? We assume that business firms' managers have a goal: to earn the highest profit possible. But they also face constraints. First, in a competitive market, the price they can charge for their product is a *given*—the market price. Second, firms have to pay the *costs* of producing and selling their product. These costs will depend on the production process they use, the prices they must pay for their inputs, and more. Business firms' desire for profit, together with the real-world constraints that they face, determines how much they will choose to sell in any market. Hence, the following definition:

> *Quantity supplied is the number of units of a good that* all *sellers in the market would choose to sell over some time period, given the constraints that they face.*

**Quantity supplied** The specific amount of a good that *all* sellers in the market would choose to sell over some time period, given (1) a particular price for the good; (2) all other constraints on firms.

Let's briefly go over the notion of quantity supplied to clarify what it means and doesn't mean.

*Quantity Supplied Implies a* Choice. We assume that the managers of business firms have a simple goal—to earn the highest possible profit. But they also face constraints: the specific price they can charge for the good, the cost of any inputs used, and so on. Quantity supplied doesn't tell us the amount of, say, maple syrup that sellers would like to sell *if* they could charge a thousand dollars for each bottle, and *if* they could produce it at zero cost. Instead, it's the quantity that firms *choose* to sell—the quantity that gives them the highest profit given the constraints they face.

*Quantity Supplied Is* Hypothetical. Will firms actually be *able* to sell the amount they want to sell at the going price? You'll soon see that they usually can. But the definition of quantity supplied makes no assumptions about firms' *ability* to sell the good. Quantity supplied answers the hypothetical question: How much *would* firms' managers sell, given the constraints they face, if they were able to sell all that they wanted.

*Quantity Supplied Depends on* **Price.** The price of the good is just one variable among many that influences quantity supplied. But—as with demand—we want to keep that variable foremost in our thinking. This is why for the next couple of pages we'll assume that all other influences on supply are held constant, so we can explore the relationship between price and quantity supplied.

## THE LAW OF SUPPLY

How does a change in price affect quantity supplied? When a seller can get a higher price for a good, producing and selling it become more profitable. Producers will devote more resources toward its production—perhaps even pulling resources from other goods they produce—so they can sell more of the good in question. For example, a rise in the price of laptop computers will encourage computer makers to shift resources out of the production of other things (such as desktop computers) and toward the production of laptops.

In general, price and quantity supplied are *positively related:* When the price of a good rises, the quantity supplied will rise as well. This relationship between price and quantity supplied is called the law of supply, the counterpart to the law of demand we discussed earlier.

**Law of supply** As the price of a good increases, the quantity supplied increases.

> The **law of supply** *states that when the price of a good rises, and everything else remains the same, the quantity of the good supplied will rise.*

Once again, notice the very important words "everything else remains the same—*ceteris paribus.*" Although many other variables influence the quantity of a good supplied, the law of supply tells us what would happen if all of them remained unchanged and only one—the price of the good—changed.

## THE SUPPLY SCHEDULE AND THE SUPPLY CURVE

Let's continue with our example of the market for maple syrup in the United States. Who are the suppliers in this market? Maple syrup producers are located mostly in the forests of Vermont, upstate New York, and Canada. The market quantity supplied is the amount of syrup all of these producers together would offer for sale at each price for maple syrup in the United States.

**Supply schedule** A list showing the quantities of a good or service that firms would choose to produce and sell at different prices, with all other variables held constant.

Table 3 shows the **supply schedule** for maple syrup—a *list of different quantities supplied at different prices, with all other variables held constant.* As you can see, the supply schedule obeys the law of supply: As the price of maple syrup rises, the quantity supplied rises along with it. But how can this be? After all, maple trees must be about 40 years old before they can be tapped for syrup, so any rise in quantity supplied now or in the near future cannot come from an increase in planting. What, then, causes quantity supplied to rise as price rises?

Many things. First, with higher prices, firms will find it profitable to tap existing trees more intensively. Second, evaporating and bottling can be done more carefully, so that less maple syrup is spilled and more is available for shipping. Finally, the product can be diverted from other areas and shipped to the United States instead. For example, if the price of maple syrup rises in the United States but not in Canada, producers would shift deliveries away from Canada so they could sell more in the United States.

| Price (per bottle) | Quantity Supplied (bottles per month) | TABLE 3 |
|---|---|---|
| | | Supply Schedule for Maple Syrup in the United States |
| $1.00 | 25,000 | |
| $2.00 | 40,000 | |
| $3.00 | 50,000 | |
| $4.00 | 60,000 | |
| $5.00 | 65,000 | |

Now look at Figure 5, which shows a very important curve—the counterpart to the demand curve we drew earlier. In Figure 5, each point represents a price-quantity pair taken from Table 3. For example, point *F* in the figure corresponds to a price of $2.00 per bottle and a quantity of 40,000 bottles per month, while point *G* represents the price-quantity pair $4.00 and 60,000 bottles. Connecting all of these points with a solid line gives us the *supply curve* for maple syrup, labeled with an *S* in the figure.

> The **supply curve** *shows the relationship between the price of a good and the quantity supplied in the market, holding constant the values of all other variables that affect supply. Each point on the curve shows the quantity that sellers would choose to sell at a specific price.*

**Supply curve** A graphical depiction of a supply schedule; a curve showing the quantity of a good or service supplied at various prices, with all other variables held constant.

Notice that the supply curve in Figure 5—like all supply curves for goods and services—is *upward sloping*. This is the graphical representation of the law of supply.

## SHIFTS VERSUS MOVEMENTS ALONG THE SUPPLY CURVE

As with the demand curve, it's important to distinguish those events that will cause us to *move along* a given supply curve for the good, and those that will cause the entire supply curve to *shift*.

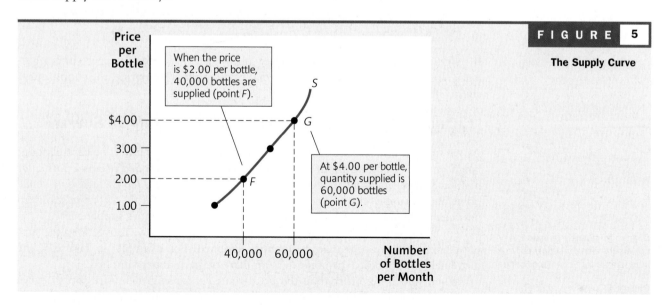

FIGURE 5

The Supply Curve

If you look once again at Figure 5, you'll see that if the price of maple syrup rises from $2.00 to $4.00 per bottle, the number of bottles supplied rises from 40,000 to 60,000. This is a movement *along* the supply curve, from point *F* to point *G*. In general,

> *a change in the price of a good causes a movement* along *the supply curve.*

In the figure, a *rise* in price would cause us to move *rightward* along the supply curve (from point *F* to point *G*) and a *fall* in price would move us *leftward* along the curve (from point *G* to point *F*).

But remember that when we draw a supply curve, we assume that all other variables that might influence supply are *held constant* at some particular values. For example, the supply curve in Figure 5 might tell us the quantity supplied at each price when the cost of an important input—transportation from the farm to the point of sale—remains constant.

But suppose the cost of transportation drops. Then, at any given price for maple syrup, firms would find it more profitable to produce and sell it. This is illustrated in Table 4. With the original transportation cost, and a selling price of $4.00 per bottle, firms would choose to sell 60,000 bottles. But after transportation cost falls, they would choose to produce and sell more—80,000 bottles in our example—assuming they could still charge $4.00 per bottle. A similar change would occur for any other price of maple syrup we might imagine: After transportation costs fall, firms would choose to sell more than before. In other words, *the entire relationship between price and quantity supplied has changed*, so we have a *new* supply curve.

Figure 6 plots the new supply curve from the quantities in the third column of Table 4. The new supply curve lies to the *right* of the old one. For example, at a price of $4.00, quantity supplied increases from 60,000 bottles on the old curve (point *G*) to 80,000 bottles on the *new* supply curve (point *J*). The drop in the transportation costs has *shifted* the supply curve to the right.

In general,

> *a change in any variable that affects supply—except for the good's price—causes the supply curve to shift.*

If sellers want to sell a greater quantity at any price, the supply curve shifts *rightward*. If sellers would prefer to sell a smaller quantity at any price, the supply curve shifts *leftward*.

## "CHANGE IN QUANTITY SUPPLIED" VERSUS "CHANGE IN SUPPLY"

As we stressed in our discussion of the demand side of the market, be careful about language when thinking about supply. The term *quantity supplied* means a *particular amount* that sellers would choose to sell at a *particular* price, represented by a single point on the supply curve. The term *supply*, however, means the *entire relationship* between price and quantity supplied, as represented by the entire supply curve.

For this reason, when the price of the good changes, and we move *along* the supply curve, we have a **change in quantity supplied**. For example, in Figure 5, the movement from point *F* to point *G* is an *increase* in quantity supplied.

When something *other* than the price changes, causing the entire supply curve to shift, we call it a **change in supply**. The shift in Figure 6, for example, would be called an *increase in supply*.

**Change in quantity supplied** A movement along a supply curve in response to a change in price.

**Change in supply** A shift of a supply curve in response to some variable other than price.

| Price (per bottle) | Original Quantity Supplied (bottles/month) | Quantity Supplied After Decrease in Transportation Cost | TABLE 4 |
|---|---|---|---|
| | | | Increase in Supply of Maple Syrup in the United States |
| $1.00 | 25,000 | 45,000 | |
| $2.00 | 40,000 | 60,000 | |
| $3.00 | 50,000 | 70,000 | |
| $4.00 | 60,000 | 80,000 | |
| $5.00 | 65,000 | 90,000 | |

## FACTORS THAT SHIFT THE SUPPLY CURVE

Let's take a closer look at some of the *causes* of a change in supply (a shift of the supply curve). As always, we're considering *one* variable at a time, keeping all other determinants of supply constant.

*Input Prices.* In Figure 6, we saw that a drop in transportation costs shifted the supply curve for maple syrup to the right. But producers of maple syrup use a variety of other inputs besides transportation: land, maple trees, evaporators, sap pans, labor, glass bottles, bottling machinery, and more. A lower price for any of these means a lower cost of producing and selling maple syrup, making it more profitable. As a result, we would expect producers to shift resources into maple syrup production, causing an increase in supply.
    In general,

*a fall in the price of an input causes an increase in supply, shifting the supply curve to the right.*

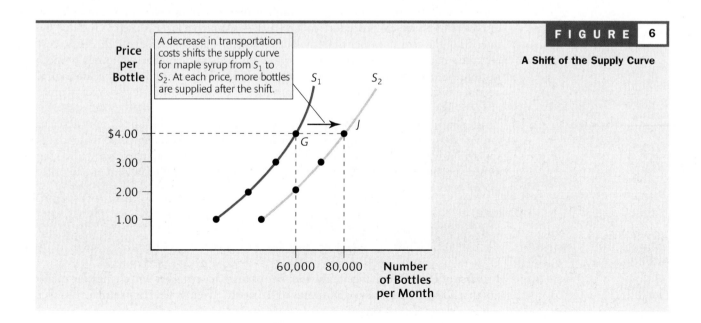

**FIGURE 6**

**A Shift of the Supply Curve**

Similarly, a rise in the price of an input causes a decrease in supply, shifting the supply curve to the left. If, for example, the wages of maple syrup workers rose, the supply curve in Figure 6 would shift to the left.

*Price of Alternatives.* Many firms can switch their production rather easily among several different goods or services, all of which require more or less the same inputs. For example, a dermatology practice can rather easily switch its specialty from acne treatments for the young to wrinkle treatments for the elderly. An automobile producer can—without too much adjustment—switch to producing light trucks. And a maple syrup producer could dry its maple syrup and produce maple *sugar* instead. Or it could even cut down its maple trees and sell maple wood as lumber. These other goods that firms *could* produce are called **alternate goods** and their prices influence the supply curve.

**Alternate goods** Other goods that a firm could produce, using some of the same types of inputs as the good in question.

For example, if the price of maple *sugar* rose, then at any given price for maple *syrup*, producers would choose to shift some production from syrup to sugar. This would be a decrease in the supply of maple syrup. If firms already are producing maple sugar, and its price *falls*, the supply of syrup would increase.

Another alternative for the firm is to sell the *same* good in a *different* market, which we'll call an **alternate market**. For example, since we are considering the market for maple syrup in the United States, the maple syrup market in Canada is an alternate market for producers. For any given price in the United States, a rise in the price of maple syrup in Canada will cause producers to shift some sales from the United States to Canada. In the U.S. market, this will cause the supply curve to shift leftward.

**Alternate market** A market other than the one being analyzed in which the same good could be sold.

> *When the price for an alternative rises—either an alternate good or the same good in an alternate market—the supply curve shifts leftward.*

Similarly, a decrease in the price of an alternate good (or a lower price in an alternate market) will shift the supply curve rightward.

*Technology.* A *technological advance* in production occurs whenever a firm can produce a given level of output in a new and cheaper way than before. For example, the discovery of a surgical procedure called Lasik—in which a laser is used to reshape the interior of the cornea rather than the outer surface—has enabled eye surgeons to correct their patients' vision with fewer follow-up visits and smaller quantities of medication than were used with previous procedures. This example is a technological advance because it enables firms to produce the same output (eye surgery) more cheaply than before.

In maple syrup production, a technological advance might be a new, more efficient tap that draws more maple syrup from each tree, or a new bottling method that reduces spillage. Advances like these would reduce the cost of producing maple syrup, making it more profitable, and producers would want to make and sell more of it at any price.

In general,

> *cost-saving technological advances increase the supply of a good, shifting the supply curve to the right.*

*Number of Firms.* A change in the number of firms in a market will change the quantity that all sellers together would want to sell at any given price. For example, if—over time—more people decided to open up maple syrup farms because it was a profitable business, the supply of maple syrup would increase. And if maple syrup farms began closing down, their number would be reduced and supply would decrease.

> *An increase in the number of sellers—with no other change—shifts the supply curve rightward.*

***Expected Price.*** Imagine you're the president of Sticky's Maple Syrup, Inc., and you expect that the market price of maple syrup—over which you, as an individual seller, have no influence—to rise next month. What would you do? You'd certainly want to postpone selling your maple syrup until the price is higher and your profit greater. Therefore, at any given price *now*, you might slow down production, or just slow down sales by warehousing more of what you produce. If other firms have similar expectations of a price hike, they'll do the same. Thus, an expectation of a *future* price hike will decrease supply *in the present*.

Suppose instead you expect the market price to *drop* next month. Then—at any given price—you'd want to sell more *now*, by stepping up production and even selling out of your inventories. So an expected future drop in the price would cause an increase in supply in the present.

**Does Demand Affect Supply?** In the list of variables that shift the supply curve in Figure 7 we've left out the amount that buyers would like to buy. Is this a mistake? Doesn't demand affect supply?

The answer is no—at least, not directly. The supply curve tells us how much sellers would like to sell at each different price. Buyers' behavior doesn't affect this hypothetical quantity, so buyers cannot cause the supply curve to shift. As you'll soon see, buyers *can* affect the price of the good, which in turn affects quantity supplied. But this causes a movement *along* the supply curve—not a shift.

**DANGEROUS CURVES**

> *In many markets, an expectation of a* future price rise *shifts the current supply curve leftward. Similarly, an expectation of a* future price drop *shifts the current supply curve* rightward.

***Changes in Weather and Other Natural Events.*** Weather conditions are an especially important determinant of the supply of agricultural goods.

> Favorable weather *increases crop yields, and causes a* rightward *shift of the supply curve for that crop.* Unfavorable weather *destroys crops and shrinks yields, and shifts the supply curve* leftward.

In addition to bad weather, natural disasters such as fires, hurricanes, and earthquakes can destroy or disrupt the productive capacity of *all* firms in a region. If many sellers of a particular good are located in the affected area, the supply curve for that good will shift leftward. For example, after Hurricanes Katrina and Rita struck the U.S. Gulf Coast in August and September of 2005, 20 percent of the nation's oil refining capacity was taken out for several weeks, causing a sizable leftward shift of the supply curve for gasoline.

## SUPPLY—A SUMMARY

Figure 7 summarizes the various factors we've discussed that affect the supply side of the market, and how we illustrate them using a supply curve. But the short list

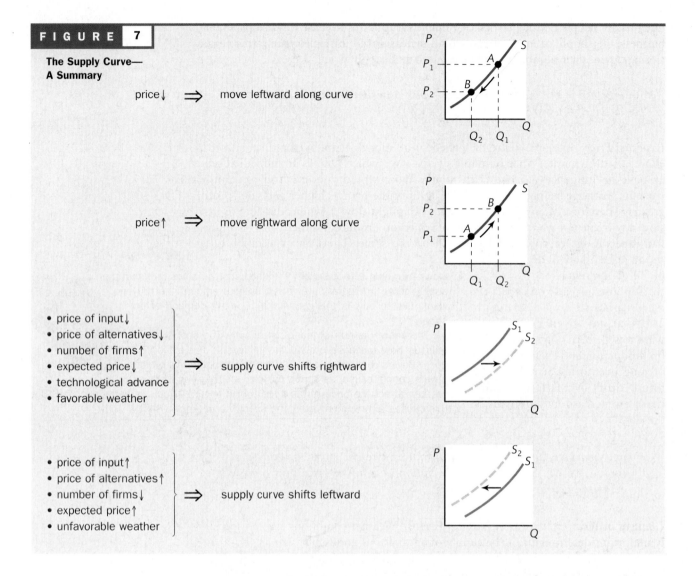

**FIGURE 7**

**The Supply Curve—
A Summary**

price↓  ⟹  move leftward along curve

price↑  ⟹  move rightward along curve

- price of input↓
- price of alternatives↓
- number of firms↑
- expected price↓
- technological advance
- favorable weather

⟹  supply curve shifts rightward

- price of input↑
- price of alternatives↑
- number of firms↓
- expected price↑
- unfavorable weather

⟹  supply curve shifts leftward

of *shift-variables* for supply is far from exhaustive. For example, a government tax on a good—or a government subsidy paid to producers—will shift the supply curve. So can other government policies, such as environmental and safety regulations.

Some of the other shift-variables for supply curves will be discussed as they become relevant in future chapters. The basic principle, however, is always the same: Anything that makes sellers want to sell more or less of a good *at any given price* will shift the supply curve.

## PUTTING SUPPLY AND DEMAND TOGETHER

What happens when buyers and sellers, each having the desire and the ability to trade, come together in a market? The two sides of the market certainly have different agendas. Buyers would like to pay the lowest possible price, while sellers would like to charge the highest possible price. Is there chaos when they meet, with buyers and sellers endlessly chasing after each other or endlessly bargaining for advantage, so that trade never takes place? A casual look at the real world suggests not. In most markets, most of the time, there is order and stability in the encounters between buyers and sellers. In most cases, prices do not fluctuate wildly from moment to moment but seem to hover around a stable value. Even when this stability is short-lived—lasting only a day, an hour, or even a minute in some markets—for this short-time the market seems to be at rest. Whenever we study a market, therefore, we look for this state of rest—a price and quantity at which the market will settle, at least for a while.

Economists use the word *equilibrium* when referring to a state of rest. When a market is in equilibrium, both the price of the good and the quantity bought and sold have settled into a state of rest. More formally,

> the **equilibrium price** and **equilibrium quantity** are values for price and quantity in the market that, once achieved, will remain constant—unless and until the supply curve or the demand curve shifts.

What is the *equilibrium* price of maple syrup in our example, and what is the *equilibrium* quantity that will be bought and sold? These are precisely the questions that the supply and demand model is designed to answer.

Look at Table 5, which combines the supply and demand schedules for maple syrup from Tables 1 and 3. We'll use Table 5 to find the equilibrium price in this market through the process of elimination.

Let's first ask what would happen if the price were $1.00 per bottle. At this price, Table 5 tells us that buyers would want to buy 75,000 bottles each month, while sellers would offer to sell only 25,000. There would be an **excess demand** of 50,000 bottles. What would happen? Buyers would compete with each other to get more maple syrup than was available, and would offer to pay a higher price rather than do without. The price would then rise. The same would occur if the price were $2.00, or any other price below $3.00.

We conclude that any price less than $3.00 cannot be an equilibrium price. If the price starts below $3.00, it would start rising—*not* because the supply curve or the demand curve had shifted, but from natural forces within the market itself. This directly contradicts our definition of equilibrium price.

Figure 8 illustrates the same process by putting the supply and demand curves together on the same graph. As you can see, at a price of $1.00, quantity supplied

**Equilibrium price** The market price that, once achieved, remains constant until either the demand curve or supply curve shifts.

**Equilibrium quantity** The market quantity bought and sold per period that, once achieved, remains constant until either the demand curve or supply curve shifts.

**Excess demand** At a given price, the amount by which quantity demanded exceeds quantity supplied.

| Price (per bottle) | Quantity Demanded (bottles per month) | Quantity Supplied (bottles per month) | Excess Demand or Supply? | Consequence |
|---|---|---|---|---|
| $1.00 | 75,000 | 25,000 | Excess Demand | Price will Rise |
| $2.00 | 60,000 | 40,000 | Excess Demand | Price will Rise |
| **$3.00** | **50,000** | **50,000** | **Neither** | **No Change in price** |
| $4.00 | 40,000 | 60,000 | Excess Supply | Price will Fall |
| $5.00 | 35,000 | 65,000 | Excess Supply | Price will Fall |

**TABLE 5**

**Finding the Market Equilibrium**

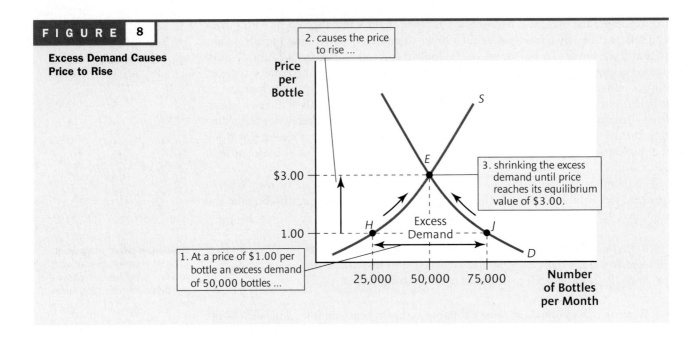

FIGURE 8

**Excess Demand Causes
Price to Rise**

2. causes the price
to rise ...

*Price
per
Bottle*

*S*

*E*

$3.00

3. shrinking the excess
demand until price
reaches its equilibrium
value of $3.00.

*H*        Excess      *J*
1.00         Demand

1. At a price of $1.00 per
bottle an excess demand
of 50,000 bottles ...

*D*

25,000   50,000   75,000      **Number
of Bottles
per Month**

---

of 25,000 bottles is found at point *H* on the supply curve, while quantity demanded is at point *J* on the demand curve. The horizontal difference between the two
curves at $1.00 is a graphical representation of the excess demand at that price.

At this point, we should ask another question: If the price were initially $1.00,
would it ever *stop* rising? Yes. Since excess demand is the reason for the price to rise,
the process will stop when the excess demand is gone. And as you can see in Figure
8, the rise in price *shrinks* the excess demand in two ways. First, as price rises, buyers demand a smaller quantity—a leftward movement along the demand curve.
Second, sellers increase supply to a larger quantity—a rightward movement along
the supply curve. Finally, when the price reaches $3.00 per bottle, the excess
demand is gone and the price stops rising.

This logic tells us that $3.00 is an *equilibrium* price in this market—a value that
won't change as long as the supply and demand curves stay put. But is it the *only*
equilibrium price? We've shown that any price *below* $3.00 is not an equilibrium,
but what about a price *greater* than $3.00? Let's see.

Suppose the price of maple syrup was, say, $5.00 per bottle. Look again at Table 5
and you'll find that, at this price, quantity supplied would be 65,000 bottles per
month, while quantity demanded would be only 35,000 bottles. There is an **excess
supply** of 30,000 bottles. Sellers would compete with each other to sell more maple
syrup than buyers wanted to buy, and the price would fall. Thus, $5.00 cannot
be the equilibrium price.

Figure 9 provides a graphical view of the market in this situation. With a price of
$5.00, the excess supply is the horizontal distance between points *K* (on the demand
curve) and *L* (on the supply curve). In the figure, the resulting drop in price would
move us along both the supply curve (leftward) and the demand curve (rightward).
As these movements continued, the excess supply of maple syrup would shrink until
it disappeared, once again, at a price of $3.00 per bottle. Our conclusion: If the price
happens to be above $3.00, it will fall to $3.00 and then stop changing.

You can see that $3.00 is the equilibrium price—and the *only* equilibrium price—
in this market. Moreover, at this price, sellers would want to sell 50,000 bottles—the

**Excess supply** At a given price,
the amount by which quantity
supplied exceeds quantity
demanded.

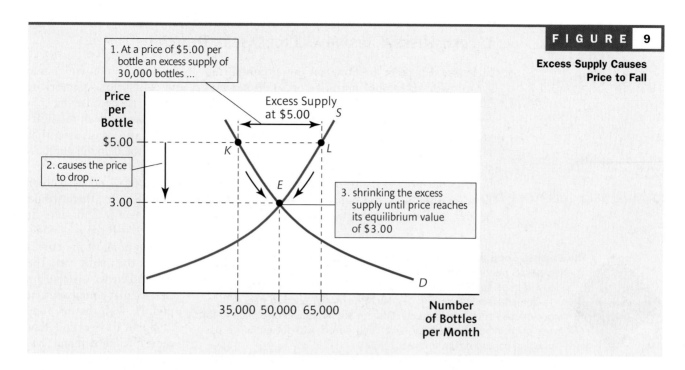

**FIGURE 9**

**Excess Supply Causes Price to Fall**

1. At a price of $5.00 per bottle an excess supply of 30,000 bottles ...

2. causes the price to drop ...

3. shrinking the excess supply until price reaches its equilibrium value of $3.00

Excess Supply at $5.00

Price per Bottle

$5.00

3.00

35,000  50,000  65,000

Number of Bottles per Month

same quantity that households would want to buy. So, when price comes to rest at $3.00, quantity comes to rest at 50,000 per month—the *equilibrium quantity*.

No doubt, you have noticed that $3.00 happens to be the price at which the supply and demand curves cross. This leads us to an easy, graphical technique for locating our equilibrium:

> *To find the equilibrium price and quantity in a competitive market, draw the supply and demand curves. The equilibrium price and equilibrium quantity can then be found on the vertical and horizontal axes, respectively, where the two curves cross.*

Notice that in equilibrium, the market is operating on *both* the supply curve *and* the demand curve so that—at a price of $3.00—quantity demanded and quantity supplied are equal. There are no dissatisfied buyers unable to find goods they want to purchase, nor are there any frustrated sellers unable to sell goods they want to sell. Indeed, this is why $3.00 is the equilibrium price. It's the only price that creates consistency between what buyers choose to buy and sellers choose to sell.

But we don't expect a market to stay at any particular equilibrium forever, as you're about to see.

## WHAT HAPPENS WHEN THINGS CHANGE?

Remember that in order to draw the supply and demand curves in the first place, we had to assume particular values for all the other variables—besides price—that affect demand and supply. If one of these variables changes, then either the supply curve or the demand curve will shift, and our equilibrium will change as well. Let's look at some examples.

## INCOME RISES, CAUSING AN INCREASE IN DEMAND

In Figure 10, point *E* shows an initial equilibrium in the U.S. market for maple syrup, with an equilibrium price of $3.00 per bottle, and equilibrium quantity of 50,000 bottles per month. Suppose that the incomes of buyers rise because the U.S. economy recovers rapidly from a recession. We know that income is one of the shift-variables in the demand curve (but not the supply curve). We also can reason that maple syrup is a *normal good,* so the rise in income will cause the demand curve to shift rightward. What happens then?

The old price—$3.00—is no longer the equilibrium price. How do we know? Because if the price *did* remain at $3.00 after the demand curve shifts, there would be an excess demand that would drive the price upward. The new equilibrium—at point *E'*—is the new intersection point of the curves *after* the shift in the demand curve. Comparing the original equilibrium at point *E* with the new one at point *E'*, we find that the shift in demand has caused the equilibrium price to rise (from $3.00 to $4.00) and the equilibrium quantity to rise as well (from 50,000 to 60,000 bottles per month).

Notice, too, that in moving from point *E* to point *E'*, we move *along* the supply curve. That is, a shift of the demand curve has caused a movement along the supply curve. Why is this? The demand shift causes the *price* to rise, and a rise in price always causes a movement *along* the supply curve. But the supply curve itself does not shift because none of the variables that affect sellers—other than the price of the good—has changed.

**The Endless Loop of Erroneous Logic**  In trying to work out what happens after, say, a rise in income, you might find yourself caught in an endless loop. It goes something like this: "A rise in income causes an increase in demand. An increase in demand causes the price to rise. A higher price causes supply to increase. Greater supply causes the price to fall. A lower price increases demand . . ." and so on, without end. The price keeps bobbing up and down, forever.

What's the mistake here? The first two statements ("a rise in income causes an increase in demand" and "an increase in demand causes price to rise") are entirely correct. But the next statement ("a higher price causes an increase in supply") is flat wrong, and so is everything that follows. A higher price does *not* cause an "increase in supply" (a shift of the supply curve). It causes an increase in *quantity supplied* (a movement *along* the supply curve).

Here's the correct sequence of events: "A rise in income causes an increase in demand. An increase in demand causes price to rise. A higher price causes an increase in *quantity supplied,* moving us along the supply curve until we reach the new equilibrium, with a higher price and greater quantity." End of story.

**DANGEROUS CURVES**

In this example, the equilibrium price and quantity changed because income rose. But *any* event that shifted the demand curve rightward would have the same effect. For example, if tastes changed in favor of maple syrup, or a substitute good like jam rose in price, or a complementary good like pancake mix became cheaper, the demand curve for maple syrup would shift rightward, just as it did in Figure 10. So, we can summarize our findings as follows:

*A rightward shift in the demand curve causes a rightward movement* along *the supply curve. Equilibrium price and equilibrium quantity both rise.*

## BAD WEATHER CAUSES A DECREASE IN SUPPLY

Bad weather can affect supply for most agricultural goods, including maple syrup. An example occurred in January 1998, when New England and Quebec were struck

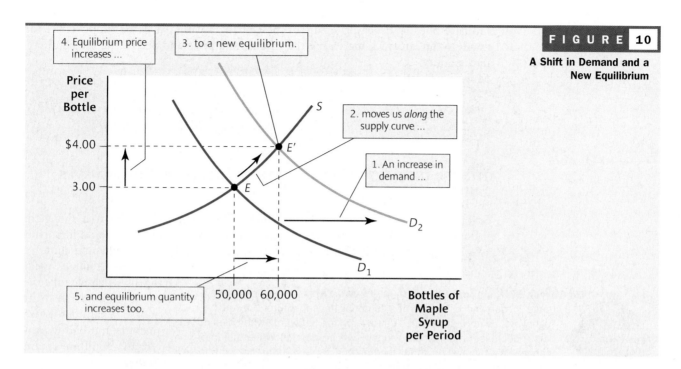

**F I G U R E   10**

**A Shift in Demand and a New Equilibrium**

4. Equilibrium price increases ...

3. to a new equilibrium.

2. moves us *along* the supply curve ...

1. An increase in demand ...

5. and equilibrium quantity increases too.

by a severe ice storm. Hundreds of thousands of maple trees were downed, and many more were damaged. In Vermont alone, 10 percent of the maple trees were destroyed. How did this affect the market for maple syrup?

As you've learned, weather can be shift-variable for the supply curve. Look at Figure 11. Initially, the supply curve for maple syrup is $S_1$, with the market in equilibrium at Point $E$. When had weather hits, the supply curve shifts leftward—say, to $S_2$. The result: a rise in the equilibrium price of maple syrup (from $3.00 to $5.00 in the figure) and a fall in the equilibrium quantity (from 50,000 to 35,000 bottles).

In this case, it is bad weather that shifts the supply curve leftward. But suppose, instead, that the wages of maple syrup workers increase, or that evaporators become more expensive, or that some maple syrup producers go out of business and sell their

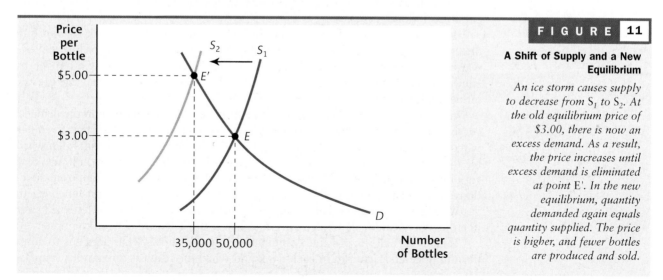

**F I G U R E   11**

**A Shift of Supply and a New Equilibrium**

*An ice storm causes supply to decrease from $S_1$ to $S_2$. At the old equilibrium price of $3.00, there is now an excess demand. As a result, the price increases until excess demand is eliminated at point E'. In the new equilibrium, quantity demanded again equals quantity supplied. The price is higher, and fewer bottles are produced and sold.*

farms to housing developers. Any of these changes would shift the supply curve for maple syrup leftward, increasing the equilibrium price and decreasing the equilibrium quantity.

More generally,

> *A leftward shift of the supply curve causes a leftward movement* along *the demand curve. Equilibrium price rises, but equilibrium quantity falls.*

## HIGHER INCOME AND BAD WEATHER TOGETHER: BOTH CURVES SHIFT

So far, we've considered examples in which just one curve shifts due to a change in a single variable that influences *either* demand or supply. But what would happen if two changes affected the market simultaneously? Then both curves would shift.

**Do Curves Shift Up and Down? Or Right and Left?** When describing an increase in demand or supply, it's tempting to substitute "upward" for "rightward," and to substitute "downward" for "leftward" when describing a decrease in demand or supply. But be careful! While this interchangeable language works for the demand curve, it does *not* work for the supply curve. To prove this to yourself, look at Figure 6. There you can see that a rightward shift of the supply curve (an increase in supply) is also a *downward* shift of the curve. In later chapters, it will sometimes make sense to describe shifts as upward or downward. For now, it's best to avoid these terms and stick with *rightward* and *leftward*.

Figure 12 shows what happens when we take the two factors we've just explored separately (a rise in income and bad weather) and combine them together. The rise in income causes the demand curve to shift rightward, from $D_1$ to $D_2$. The bad weather causes the supply curve to shift leftward, from $S_1$ to $S_2$. The result of all this is a change in equilibrium from point $E$ to point $E'$, where the new demand curve $D_2$ intersects the new supply curve $S_2$.

Notice that the equilibrium price rises from $3.00 to $6.00 in our example. This should come as no surprise. A rightward shift in the demand curve, with no other change, causes price to rise. And a leftward shift in the supply curve, with no other change, causes price to rise. So when we combine the two shifts together, the price must rise. In fact, the increase in the price will be greater than would be caused by either shift alone.

But what about equilibrium quantity? Here, the two shifts work in *opposite* directions. The rightward shift in demand works to increase quantity, while the leftward shift in supply works to decrease quantity. We can't say what will happen to equilibrium quantity until we know which shift is greater and thus has the greater influence. Quantity could rise, fall, or remain unchanged.

In Figure 12, it just so happens that the supply curve shifts more than the demand curve, so equilibrium quantity falls. But you can easily prove to yourself that the other outcomes are possible. First, draw a graph where the demand curves shifts rightward by more than the supply curve shifts leftward. In your graph, you'll see that equilibrium quantity rises. Then, draw one where both curves shift (in opposite directions) by equal amounts, and you'll see that equilibrium quantity remains unchanged.

We can also imagine other combinations of shifts. A rightward or leftward shift in either curve can be combined with a rightward or leftward shift in the other.

Table 6 lists all the possible combinations. It also shows what happens to equilibrium price and quantity in each case, and when the result is ambiguous (a ques-

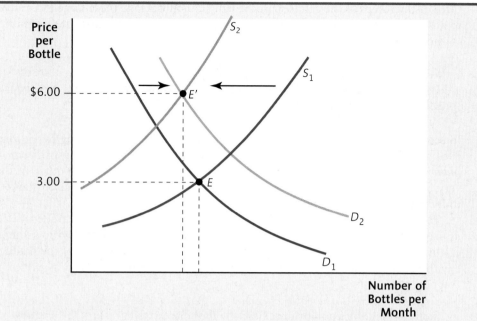

FIGURE 12

**A Shift in Both Curves and a New Equilibrium**

*An increase in income shifts the demand curve rightward from $D_1$ to $D_2$. At the same time, bad weather shifts the supply curve leftward from $S_1$ to $S_2$. The equilibrium moves from point E to point E'. While the price must rise after these shifts, quantity could rise or fall or remain the same, depending on the relative sizes of the shifts. In the figure, quantity happens to fall.*

tion mark). For example, the top left entry tells us that when both the supply and demand curves shift rightward, the equilibrium *quantity* will always rise, but the equilibrium price could rise, fall, or remain unchanged, depending on the relative *size* of the shifts.

Do *not* try to memorize the entries in Table 6. Instead, remember the advice in Chapter 1: to study economics actively, rather than passively. This would be a good time to put down the book, pick up a pencil and paper, and see whether you can draw a graph to illustrate each of the nine possible results in the table. When you see a question mark (?) for an ambiguous result, determine which shift would have to be greater for the variable to rise or to fall.

## THE THREE-STEP PROCESS

In this chapter, we built a model—a supply and demand model—and then used it to analyze price changes in several markets. You may not have noticed it, but we took

| | Increase in Demand (Rightward Shift) | No Change in Demand | Decrease in Demand (Leftward Shift) | TABLE 6 |
|---|---|---|---|---|
| • **Increase in Supply** (Rightward Shift) | $P? \; Q\uparrow$ | $P\downarrow \; Q\uparrow$ | $P\downarrow \; Q?$ | **Effect of Supply and Demand Shifts on Equilibrium Price ($P$) and Quantity ($Q$)** |
| • **No Change in Supply** | $P\uparrow \; Q\uparrow$ | No change in $P$ or $Q$ | $P\downarrow \; Q\downarrow$ | |
| • **Decrease in Supply** (Leftward Shift) | $P\uparrow \; Q?$ | $P\uparrow \; Q\downarrow$ | $P? \; Q\downarrow$ | |

three distinct steps as the chapter proceeded. Economists take these same three steps to answer many questions about the economy, as you'll see throughout this book.

Let's review these steps:

> **Step 1—Characterize the Market:** *Decide which market or markets best suit the problem being analyzed, and identify the decision makers (buyers and sellers) who interact there.*

In economics, we make sense of the very complex, real-world economy by viewing it as a collection of *markets*. Each of these markets involves a group of *decision makers*—buyers and sellers—who have the potential to trade with each other. At the very beginning of any economic analysis, we must decide which market or markets to look at and how these markets should be *defined*.

To define a market, we decide how to view (a) the thing being traded (such as maple syrup); (b) the decision makers in the market (such as maple syrup producers in New England and Canada selling to U.S. households); and (c) the trading environment (in this chapter, we viewed the market for maple syrup as perfectly competitive).

> **Step 2—Find the Equilibrium:** *Describe the conditions necessary for equilibrium in the market, and a method for determining that equilibrium.*

Once we've defined a market, and put buyers and sellers together, we look for the point at which the market will come to rest—the equilibrium. In this chapter, we used supply and demand to find the equilibrium price and quantity in a perfectly competitive market, but this is just one example of how economists apply Step 2.

> **Step 3—What Happens When Things Change:** *Explore how events or government policies change the market equilibrium.*

Once you've found the equilibrium, the next step is to ask how different events will *change* it. In this chapter, for example, we explored how rising income or bad weather (or both together) would affect the equilibrium price and quantity for maple syrup.

Economists follow this same three-step procedure to analyze important *microeconomic* questions. Why does government intervention to lower the price of a good (such as apartment rents) often backfire and sometimes harm the very people it was designed to help? Why do some people earn salaries that are hundreds of times higher than others? What would happen to the price of oil in world markets if supplies from the Persian Gulf were suddenly cut off? If you're studying *micro*economics, you'll soon see how the three-step process helps us answer all of those questions.

Economists also use the procedure to address important *macroeconomic* questions. What caused the recession that began in early 2001, and what can we do to help avoid recessions in the future? Why has the United States experienced such low inflation in recent years, and how long can we expect our recent good fortune to continue? Why has the U.S. economy been growing so much more rapidly than the economies of continental Europe? In *macro*economics, the three steps help us answer once again.

In this book, we'll be taking these three steps again and again, and we'll often call them to your attention.

# USING THE THEORY

© ASSOCIATED PRESS

## Explaining Changes in Price and Quantity: Avian Flu in Early 2006

In 2005 and early 2006, the avian influenza virus was spreading rapidly among chicken flocks in Asia and Europe. More than a hundred million chickens in the affected countries had either died from the virus or been destroyed in an unsuccessful effort to slow its spread. But in early 2006, the virus had *not* yet struck flocks in the United States.

The spread of the avian flu virus raised many important questions for economists, health care professionals, medical researchers, and government agencies. But here we focus on a narrower topic: something that was happening in markets for chicken meat.

Here are two relevant facts about these markets toward the end of 2005 and into early 2006.[1]

- In Europe, people were buying substantially *less* chicken. (For example, over a period of a few months in early 2006, chicken consumption dropped by 20 percent in France, and a whopping 70 percent in Italy.)
- In the United States, people were buying *more* chicken.

At first glance (and especially to someone who has not studied supply and demand), the explanation might seem obvious. It would go something like this: "Since chickens were dying or being killed off in Europe, the Europeans had to make do with less chicken. But in the United States, where chicken flocks were unaffected, there was no such problem. And since in most years, the U.S. population rises and income goes up, American chicken consumption probably rose just like it usually does."

That sounds sensible. But an economist, hearing this explanation, would hesitate. There is an easy way to test this explanation: find out what happened to the *price* of chicken in Europe and the United States.

If the first-glance explanation is correct, then chicken prices should have risen in both Europe and the United States. The explanation for Europe (fewer chickens available) implies that the *supply* curve for chicken shifted *leftward*, raising equilibrium price. (Look back, for example, at Figure 11.) The explanation for the United States (the usual increases in income and population) implies that the *demand* curve for chicken shifted *rightward*, once again, raising the price of chicken. (Look back, for example, at Figure 10).

So what happened to chicken prices in Europe and the United States?

They fell in both markets. In fact, they plummeted. From June 2005 to March 2006, the price of chicken in both Europe and the United States dropped by about 70 percent.

So, what really happened? As you're about to see, the three-step process just discussed will help us find the answer.

---

[1] Scott Kilman and Jane Zhang, "Avian-Flu Concerns Overseas Damp U.S. Chicken Exports," *The Wall Street Journal*, March 11–12, 2006, p. A5. Other data on chicken markets comes from the Food and Agriculture Organization, "Poultry Trade Prospects for 2006 Jeopardized by Escalating AI Outbreaks," at www.fao.org, accessed on 3/16/06.

FIGURE 13

**The European Market for Chicken**

*The Avian flu led to the destruction of a relatively small fraction of the world's chicken supply. In the market for dark-meat chicken in Europe, this caused a relatively small leftward shift in the supply curve, from S₂₀₀₅ to S₂₀₀₆. At the same time, fear of Avian flu among Europeans caused a larger leftward shift in the demand curve, from D₂₀₀₅ to D₂₀₀₆. The market equilibrium moved from point A to point B, with a decrease in equilibrium quantity from Q₁ to Q₂. Because the demand shift was greater than the supply shift, the market price fell, from $0.42 to $0.14 per pound.*

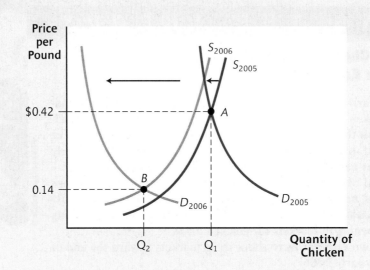

First, let's *characterize the market.* We are interested in explaining why things were *different* in Europe and the United States, so it makes sense to look at two geographic markets for chicken: one in Europe, and the other in the United States.

In Figure 13, we first illustrate the market in Europe. Because chicken (especially when frozen) is easily shipped from country to country, the supply side of this market consists of chicken producers around the world. These producers sell some portion of their chicken to buyers in Europe—the demand side of this market.

Now the second step: *Find the equilibrium.* Our starting point will be the summer of 2005, with demand curve $D_{2005}$ and supply curve $S_{2005}$. The equilibrium occurs at the intersection of the two curves (point *A*), with quantity $Q_1$ and price equal to the dollar equivalent of about $0.42 per pound. (In this analysis, we're using the approximate wholesale price of dark-meat chicken. But other chicken-related prices behaved similarly during this period.)

Finally, the third step: *What happens when things change?* From 2005 to 2006, millions of chickens around the world died or were destroyed, so at any given price, suppliers would choose to sell fewer chickens in *any* market, including the European market. In Figure 13, the supply curve shifts leftward, to $S_{2006}$. But notice that this shift is depicted as rather small. That's because the millions of birds eliminated were only a tiny percentage of total world supply. (According to the Food and Agriculture Organization, the total number of chickens in the world is about 16 *trillion*, a significant fraction of which are brought to market each year.) Still, if this had been the only change in the market (as in the "first glance" explanation), chicken prices in Europe would have risen.

Since chicken prices actually *fell*, we know something else must have changed in this market. And indeed it did. As the avian influenza virus spread from Asia to Europe, consumers in Europe were gripped by a chicken panic. Even though there

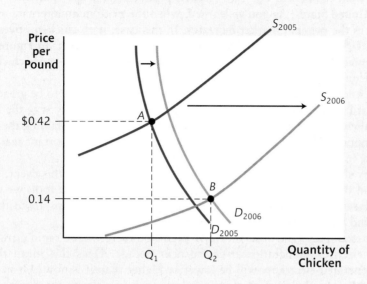

**FIGURE 14**

**The U.S. Market for Chicken**

*As chicken prices declined in Europe (an alternate market for U.S. producers), the supply curve in the U.S. market shifted rightward, from $S_{2005}$ to $S_{2006}$. At the same time, normal increases in income and population caused a (smaller) rightward shift in demand, from $D_{2005}$ to $D_{2006}$. The market equilibrium moved from point A to point B with an increase in equilibrium quantity from $Q_1$ to $Q_2$. Because the supply shift was greater, the market price fell, from $0.42 to $0.14 per pound.*

was no danger from eating infected chickens (cooking kills the virus), millions of consumers in Europe decided to take no chances. They simply stopped eating chicken. This is represented by the sizable *leftward shift in the demand curve*, to $D_{2006}$ in Figure 13. The equilibrium price of dark meat chicken fell from about $0.42 per pound to about $0.14 per pound.

We know the leftward shift in the demand curve was greater than the leftward shift in the supply curve, because that is the only way to explain the drop in price that actually occurred. So, although a decrease in supply played *some* role in explaining the drop in European consumption (as in the first-glance explanation), a more important reason for the drop in consumption was a decrease in demand.

Now let's consider the *U.S. market*. The demand side of the market is chicken buyers in the United States. And once again, the supply side of the market consists of chicken producers around the world who have the potential to sell their chicken to Americans. However, in practice, the supply side of the market is limited to American chicken farmers. This is because the United States is a chicken *exporter*: it produces all the chickens demanded in the home market, and then some. This fact will turn out to be important.

Figure 14 depicts the U.S. chicken market. The initial equilibrium in June 2005 was at point *A*, with the price at about $0.42, the same price as in Europe.

Now let's look at what changed. In early 2006, there was no "chicken panic" in the United States since the virus had not yet affected U.S. chicken flocks. (Remember: The chicken in U.S. supermarkets was American-produced chicken.) And it is true that the United States was experiencing a healthy rate of income and population growth, so the demand for chicken—a normal good—rose. In Figure 14, we've shifted the demand curve rightward a bit, to $D_{2006}$. If this had been the only change, U.S. chicken prices would have risen somewhat.

But remember that chicken prices actually *fell*, so something else was going on. Here's what happened: For U.S. chicken producers, Europe is an *alternate market* to the United States. As you've learned, when the price in an alternate market falls, supply in the original market increases. In this case, with chicken prices in Europe falling, U.S. producers shifted sales back to the home market. In Figure 14, this is represented by a *rightward shift* in the supply curve to $S_{2006}$—more chicken offered in the United States at any given price.

We know that the rightward shift in the supply curve had to be greater than the rightward shift in the demand curve, because that is the only way the price could have fallen.[2] So, while rising demand played *some* role in explaining the rise in U.S. consumption (as in the first-glance explanation), a more important reason was the increase in supply.

Why should we worry about the proper explanation for this event, which happened in the past? Because, as you'll see in later chapters, the tools we've just used to analyze this past event can help us make proper predictions about the future as well. And they can be applied to *any* competitive market.

For example, some observers have predicted there will be rapid growth in solar-power electricity-generation over the next decade. Does this mean the price of solar-generated electricity will be lower or higher than it is now? Or in the market for health care, the price of many services, such as visits to the doctor or hospital stays, is likely to rise over the next decade. Will this be accompanied by an *increase* in the quantity of these services supplied? Or a decrease?

As you probably suspect, the answer to these questions, and hundreds more like them, depends on which force—demand or supply—is the dominant change in the market. You'll be asked to look at a few cases similar to these in the end-of-chapter problems.

## Summary

In a market economy, prices are determined through the interaction of buyers and sellers in *markets*. *Perfectly competitive* markets have many buyers and sellers, and none of them individually can affect the market price. If an individual, buyer, or seller has the power to influence the price of a product, the market is *imperfectly competitive*.

The model of *supply and demand* explains how prices are determined in perfectly competitive markets. The *quantity demanded* of any good is the total amount buyers would choose to purchase given the constraints that they face. The *law of demand* states that quantity demanded is negatively related to price; it tells us that the *demand curve* slopes downward. The demand curve is drawn for given levels of income, wealth, tastes, prices of substitute and complementary goods, population, and expected future price. If any of those factors changes, the demand curve will shift.

The *quantity supplied* of a good is the total amount sellers would choose to produce and sell given the constraints that they face. According to the *law of supply*, supply curves slope upward. The supply curve will shift if there is a change in the price of an input, the price of an alternate good, the price in an alternate market, the number of firms, expectations of future prices, or (for some goods) a change in weather.

Equilibrium price and quantity in a market are found where the supply and demand curves intersect. If either of these curves shifts, price and quantity will change as the market moves to a new equilibrium.

Economists frequently use a three-step process to answer questions about the economy. The three steps—taken several times in this chapter—are to (1) characterize the market or markets involved in the question; (2) find the equilibrium in the market; and (3) ask what happens when something changes. This three-step process will be used throughout the textbook.

---

[2] In the figure, you'll notice that the supply curve shifts just enough to bring the price down to $0.14 per pound—the same as the new price in Europe. The U.S. price has to drop to about the same level as the price in Europe, because if not, U.S. producers would continue shifting sales away from Europe and into the United States, causing further price declines in the United States.

# Problem Set   *Answers to even-numbered Questions and Problems can be found on the text Web site at www.thomsonedu.com/economics/ball.*

1. Consider the following statement: "In 2005 and 2006, as at many other times, new home building in most American cities slowed, and the price of housing came down. Therefore, one way for a city to bring down home prices is to use zoning regulations that slow down new home building." True or false? Explain.

2. In the late 1990s and through 2000, the British public became increasingly concerned about "Mad Cow Disease," which could be deadly to humans if they ate beef from these cattle. Fearing the disease, many consumers switched to other meats, like chicken, pork, or lamb. At the same time, the British government ordered the destruction of thousands of head of cattle. Illustrate the effects of these events on the equilibrium price and quantity in the market for British beef. Can we determine with certainty the direction of change for the quantity? For the price? Explain briefly.

3. Discuss, and illustrate with a graph, how each of the following events will affect the market for coffee:
   a. A blight on coffee plants kills off much of the Brazilian crop.
   b. The price of tea declines.
   c. Coffee workers organize themselves into a union and gain higher wages.
   d. Coffee is shown to cause cancer in laboratory rats.
   e. Coffee prices are expected to rise rapidly in the near future.

4. The following table gives hypothetical data for the quantity of two-bedroom rental apartments demanded and supplied in Peoria, Illinois:

| Monthly Rent | Quantity Demanded (thousands) | Quantity Supplied (thousands) |
|---|---|---|
| $  800 | 30 | 10 |
| $1,000 | 25 | 14 |
| $1,200 | 22 | 17 |
| $1,400 | 19 | 19 |
| $1,600 | 17 | 21 |
| $1,800 | 15 | 22 |

   a. Graph the demand and supply curves.
   b. Find the equilibrium price and quantity.
   c. Explain briefly why a rent of $1,000 cannot be the equilibrium in this market.
   d. Suppose a tornado destroys a significant number of apartment buildings in Peoria, but doesn't affect people's desire to live there. Illustrate on your graph the effects on equilibrium price and quantity.

5. The following table gives hypothetical data for the quantity of alarm clocks demanded and supplied per month.

| Price per Alarm Clock | Quantity Demanded | Quantity Supplied |
|---|---|---|
| $  5 | 3,500 | 700 |
| $10 | 3,000 | 900 |
| $15 | 2,500 | 1,100 |
| $20 | 2,000 | 1,300 |
| $25 | 1,500 | 1,500 |
| $30 | 1,000 | 1,700 |
| $35 | 500 | 1,900 |

   a. Graph the demand and supply curves.
   b. Find the equilibrium price and quantity.
   c. Illustrate on your graph how a decrease in the price of telephone wake-up services would affect the market for alarm clocks.
   d. What would happen if there was a decrease in the price of wake-up services at the same time that the price of the plastic used to manufacture alarm clocks rose?

6. The following table gives hypothetical data for the quantity of electric scooters demanded and supplied per month.

| Price per Electric Scooter | Quantity Demanded | Quantity Supplied |
|---|---|---|
| $150 | 500 | 250 |
| $175 | 475 | 350 |
| $200 | 450 | 450 |
| $225 | 425 | 550 |
| $250 | 400 | 650 |
| $275 | 375 | 750 |

   a. Graph the demand and supply curves.
   b. Find the equilibrium price and quantity.
   c. Illustrate on your graph how an increase in the wage rate paid to scooter assemblers would affect the market for electric scooters.
   d. What would happen if there was an increase in the wage rate paid to scooter assemblers at the same time that tastes for electric scooters increased?

7. The following table gives hypothetical data for the quantity of gasoline demanded and supplied in Los Angeles per month.

| Price per Gallon | Quantity Demanded (millions of gallons) | Quantity Supplied (millions of gallons) |
|---|---|---|
| $1.20 | 170 | 80 |
| $1.30 | 156 | 105 |
| $1.40 | 140 | 140 |
| $1.50 | 123 | 175 |
| $1.60 | 100 | 210 |
| $1.70 | 95 | 238 |

a. Graph the demand and supply curves.

b. Find the equilibrium price and quantity.

c. Illustrate on your graph how a rise in the price of automobiles would affect the gasoline market.

8. How would each of the following affect the market for blue jeans in the United States? Illustrate each answer with a supply and demand diagram.

a. The price of denim cloth increases.

b. An economic slowdown in the United States causes household incomes to decrease.

9. Indicate which curve shifted—and in which direction—for each of the following. Assume that only one curve shifts.

a. The price of furniture rises as the quantity bought and sold falls.

b. Apartment vacancy rates increase while average monthly rent on apartments declines.

c. The price of personal computers continues to decline as sales skyrocket.

10. Consider the following forecast: "In 2008, we predict that the demand curve for solar panels will continue its shift rightward, which will tend to raise price and quantity. However, with a higher price, supply will increase as well, shifting the supply curve rightward. A rightward shift of the supply curve will tend to lower price and raise quantity. We conclude that as 2008 proceeds, quantity will increase but the price of solar panels may either rise or fall." There is a serious mistake of logic in this forecast. Can you find it? Explain.

11. A couple of months after Hurricane Katrina, an article in *The New York Times* contained the following passage: "Gasoline prices—the national average is now $2.15, according to the Energy Information Administration—have fallen because higher prices held down demand and Gulf Coast supplies have been slowly restored."[3] The statement about supply is entirely correct and explains why gas prices came down. But the statement about demand confuses two concepts you learned about in this chapter.

a. What two concepts does the statement about demand seem to confuse? Explain briefly.

b. On a supply and demand diagram, show what most likely caused gasoline prices to rise when Hurricane Katrina shut down gasoline refineries on the Gulf Coast.

c. On another supply and demand diagram, show what most likely happened in the market for gasoline as Gulf Coast refineries were repaired—and began operating again—after the Hurricane.

d. What role did the *demand* side of the market play in explaining the rise and fall of gas prices?

12. Draw supply and demand diagrams for market A for each of the following. Then use your diagrams to illustrate the impact of the following events. In each case, determine what happens to price and quantity in each market.

a. A and B are substitutes, and the price of good B rises.

b. A and B satisfy the same kinds of desires, and there is a shift in tastes away from A and toward B.

c. A is a normal good, and incomes in the community increase.

d. There is a technological advance in the production of good A.

e. B is an input used to produce good A, and the price of B rises.

## More Challenging

13. Suppose that demand is given by the equation $Q^D = 500 - 50P$, where $Q^D$ is quantity demanded, and $P$ is the price of the good. Supply is described by the equation $Q^S = 50 + 25P$, where $Q^S$ is quantity supplied. What is the equilibrium price and quantity? (See Appendix.)

14. While crime rates have fallen across the country over the past few years, they have fallen especially rapidly in Manhattan. At the same time, there are some neighborhoods in the New York metropolitan area in which the crime rate has remained constant. Using supply and demand diagrams for rental housing, explain how a falling crime rate in Manhattan could make the residents in *other* neighborhoods *worse off*. (Hint: As people from around the country move to Manhattan, what happens to rents there? If people cannot afford to pay higher rent in Manhattan, what might they do?)

15. A Wall Street analyst observes the following equilibrium price-quantity combinations in the market for restaurant meals in a city over a four-year period:

| Year | P | Q (thousands of meals per month) |
|------|------|------|
| 1 | $12 | 20 |
| 2 | $15 | 30 |
| 3 | $17 | 40 |
| 4 | $20 | 50 |

She concludes that the market defies the law of demand. Is she correct? Why or why not?

[3] "Economic Memo: Upbeat Signs Hold Cautions for the Future," *New York Times*, November 30, 2005.

## Solving for Equilibrium Algebraically

In the body of this chapter, notice that the supply and demand curves for maple syrup were *not* graphed as straight lines. This is because the data they were based on (as shown in the tables) were not consistent with a straight-line graph. You can verify this if you look back at Table 1: When the price rises from $1.00 to $2.00, quantity demanded drops by 15,000 (from 75,000 to 60,000). But when the price rises from $2.00 to $3.00, quantity demanded drops by 10,000 (from 60,000 to 50,000). Since the change in the independent variable (price) is $1.00 in both cases, but the change in the dependent variable (quantity demanded) is different, we know that when the relationship between quantity demanded and price is graphed, it will not be a straight line.

We have no reason to expect demand or supply curves in the real world to be straight lines (to be *linear*). However, it's often useful to approximate a curve with a straight line that is reasonably close to the original curve. One advantage of doing this is that we can then express both supply and demand as simple equations, and solve for the equilibrium using basic algebra.

For example, suppose the demand for take-out pizzas in a modest-size city is represented by the following equation:

$$Q^D = 64,000 - 3,000\,P$$

where $Q^D$ stands for the quantity of pizzas demanded per week. This equation tells us that every time the price of pizza rises by $1.00, the number of pizzas demanded each week *falls* by 3,000. As we'd expect, there is a negative relationship between price and quantity demanded. Moreover, since quantity demanded always falls at the same rate (3,000 fewer pizzas for every $1.00 rise in price), the equation is linear.[1]

Now we'll add an equation for the supply curve:

$$Q^S = -20,000 + 4,000\,P$$

where $Q^S$ stands for the quantity of pizzas supplied per week. This equation tells us that when the price of pizza rises by $1.00, the number of pizzas supplied per week *rises* by 4,000—the positive relationship we expect of a supply curve.[2] And like the demand curve, it's linear: Quantity supplied continues to rise at the same rate (4,000 more pizzas for every $1.00 increase in price).

We know that if this market is in equilibrium, quantity demanded ($Q^D$) will equal quantity supplied ($Q^S$). So let's *impose* that condition on these curves. That is, let's require $Q^D = Q^S$. This allows us to use the definitions for $Q^D$ and $Q^S$ that have price as a variable, and set those equal to each other in equilibrium:

$$64,000 - 3,000\,P = -20,000 + 4,000\,P$$

This is one equation with a single unknown—$P$—so we can use the rules of algebra to isolate $P$ on one side of the equation. We do this by adding 3,000 $P$ to both sides, which isolates $P$ on the right, and adding 20,000 to both sides, which moves everything that *doesn't* involve $P$ to the left, giving us:

$$84,000 = 7,000\,P$$

Finally, dividing both sides by 7,000 gives us

$$84,000/7,000 = P$$

or

$$P = 12$$

---

[1] If you try to graph the demand curve, don't forget that supply and demand graphs reverse the usual custom of where the independent and dependent variables are plotted. Quantity demanded is the dependent variable (it *depends* on price), and yet it's graphed on the *horizontal* axis.

[2] Don't be troubled by the negative sign ($-20,000$) in this equation. It helps determine a minimum price that suppliers must get in order to supply any pizza at all. Using the entire equation, we find that if price were $5.00, quantity supplied would be zero, and that price has to rise *above* $5.00 for any pizzas to be supplied in this market. But since a "negative supply" doesn't make sense, this equation is valid only for prices of $5.00 or greater.

We've found our equilibrium price: $12.

What about equilibrium quantity? In equilibrium, we know quantity demanded and quantity supplied are equal, so we can *either* solve for $Q^D$ using the demand equation, or solve for $Q^S$ using the supply equation, and we should get the same answer. For example, using the demand equation, and using the equilibrium price of $12:

$$Q^D = 64,000 - 3,000\,(12)$$

or

$$Q^D = 28,000$$

To confirm that we didn't make any errors, we can also use the supply equation.

$$Q^S = -20,000 + 4,000\,(12)$$

or

$$Q^S = 28,000$$

We've now confirmed that the equilibrium quantity is 28,000.

# What Macroeconomics Tries to Explain

You have no doubt seen photographs of the earth taken from satellites thousands of miles away. Viewed from that great distance, the world's vast oceans look like puddles, and its mountain ranges like wrinkles on a bedspread. In contrast to our customary view from the earth's surface—of a car, a tree, a building—this is a view of the big picture.

These two different ways of viewing the earth—from up close or from thousands of miles away—are analogous to two different ways of viewing the economy. When we look through the *microeconomic lens—from up close—we see the behavior of individual decision makers and individual markets.* When we look through the macroeconomic lens—from a distance—these smaller features fade away, and we see only the broad outlines of the economy.

Which view is better? That depends on what we're trying to do. If we want to know why computers are getting better and cheaper each year, or why the earnings of business professors are rising so rapidly, we need the close-up view of microeconomics. But to answer questions about the *overall* economy—about the overall level of economic activity, our standard of living, or the percentage of our potential workforce that is unemployed—we need the more comprehensive view of *macroeconomics.*

## MACROECONOMIC GOALS

While there is some disagreement among economists about *how* to make the macroeconomy perform well, there is widespread agreement about the goals we are trying to achieve:

> *Economists—and society at large—agree on three important macroeconomic goals: economic growth, full employment, and stable prices.*

Why is there such universal agreement on these three goals? Because achieving them gives us the opportunity to make *all* of our citizens better off. Let's take a closer look at each of these goals and see why they are so important.

### ECONOMIC GROWTH

Imagine that you were a typical American worker living at the beginning of the 20th century. You would work about 60 hours every week, and your yearly salary—about $450—would buy a bit less than $9,000 would buy today. You could expect to die at the age of 47. If you fell seriously ill before then, your doctor wouldn't be able to help much: There were no X-ray machines or blood tests, and little effective medicine for the few diseases that could be diagnosed. You would probably never hear the sounds produced by the best musicians of the day, or see the performances of the best actors, dancers, or singers. And the most exotic travel you'd enjoy would likely be a trip to a nearby state.

Today, the typical worker has it considerably better. He or she works about 35 hours per week and is paid about $40,000 per year, not to mention fringe benefits such as health insurance, retirement benefits, and paid vacation. Thanks to advances in medicine, nutrition, and hygiene, the average worker can expect to live into his or her late 70s. And more of a worker's free time today is really free: There are machines to do laundry and dishes, cars to get to and from work, telephones for quick communication, and personal computers to keep track of finances, appointments, and correspondence. Finally, during their lifetimes, most Americans will have traveled—for enjoyment—to many locations in the United States or abroad.

**Economic growth** The increase in our production of goods and services that occurs over long periods of time.

What is responsible for these dramatic changes in economic well-being? The answer is: **economic growth**—the increase in our production of goods and services that occurs over long periods of time. In the United States, as in most developed economies, the annual output of goods and services has risen over time, and risen faster than the population. As a result, the average person can consume much more today—more food, clothing, housing, medical care, entertainment, and travel—than in the year 1900.

Economists monitor economic growth by keeping track of *real gross domestic product* (*real GDP*): the total quantity of goods and services produced in a country over a year. When real GDP rises faster than the population, output per person rises, and so does the average standard of living.

Figure 1 shows real GDP in the United States from 1929 to the first half of 2006, measured in dollars of output at 2000 prices. As you can see, real GDP has increased dramatically. Part of the reason for the rise is an increase in population: More workers can produce more goods and services. But real GDP has actually increased *faster* than the population: During this period, while the U.S. population did not quite triple, annual production of goods and services has increased more than tenfold. Hence, the remarkable rise in the average American's living standard.

But when we look more closely at the data, we discover something important: Although output has grown, the *rate* of growth has varied over the decades. From 1959 to 1973, real GDP grew, on average, by 4.2 percent per year. But from 1973 to 1991, average annual growth slowed to 2.7 percent. Then, from 1991 to 2006, growth picked up again, averaging 3.3 percent per year. These may seem like slight differences. But over long periods of time, such small differences in growth rates can cause huge differences in living standards. For example, suppose that in each of the 20 years between 1986 and 2006, real GDP had grown by just one percentage point more than its actual rate. Then, over that entire period, the United States would have produced about $20 trillion *more* in goods and services than we *actually* produced (valuing these goods and services at 2000 prices). That amounts to more than $65,000 for each person in the population.

Growth increases the size of the economic pie, so it becomes possible—at least in principle—for every citizen to have a larger slice. But in practice, growth does *not* benefit everyone. Living standards will always rise more rapidly for some groups than for others, and some may even find their slice of the pie shrinking.

For example, since the late 1970s, economic growth has improved the living standards of the highly skilled, while less-skilled workers have benefited very little.

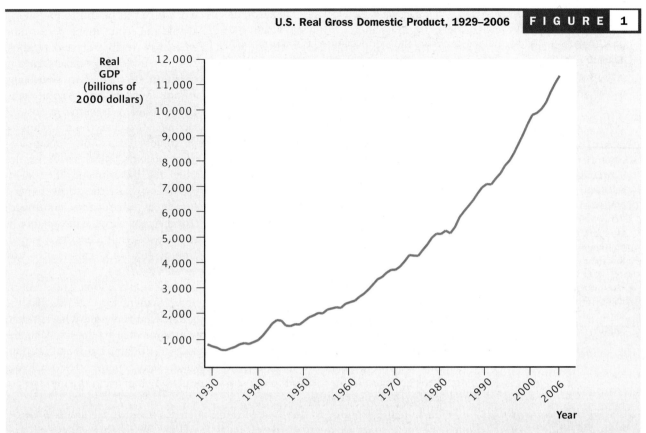

**U.S. Real Gross Domestic Product, 1929–2006** | **FIGURE 1**

*Real GDP has increased dramatically over the past 75 years. In the figure, real GDP is measured in dollars of output valued at 2000 prices. (The measurement of real GDP will be discussed in more detail in the next two chapters.)*

Partly, this is due to improvements in technology that have lowered the earnings of workers whose roles can be taken by computers and machines. But very few economists would advocate a halt to growth as a solution to the problems of unskilled workers. Some believe that, in the long run, everyone will indeed benefit from growth. Others see a role for the government in taxing successful people and providing benefits to those left behind by growth. But in either case, economic growth, by increasing the size of the overall pie, is seen as an important part of the solution.

Macroeconomics helps us understand a number of issues surrounding economic growth. What makes real GDP grow in the first place? Why does it grow more rapidly in some decades than in others? Why do some countries experience very rapid growth—some much faster than the United States—while others seem unable to grow at all? Can government policy do anything to alter the growth rate? And are there any downsides to such policies?

## HIGH EMPLOYMENT (OR LOW UNEMPLOYMENT)

Economic growth is one of our most important goals, but not the only one. Suppose our real GDP were growing at, say, a 3 percent annual rate, but 10 percent of the

**Growth Rates from Graphs** In Figure 1, it looks like real GDP has not only been growing, but growing at a faster and faster rate, since the line becomes steeper over time. But the real GDP line would get steeper even if the growth rate were *constant* over the entire period. That's because as real GDP rises from an increasingly higher and higher level, the same *percentage* growth rate is a greater and greater *absolute* increase in GDP.

For example, when real GDP is $5 trillion, 3 percent growth would be a rise of $5 trillion × 0.03 = $0.15 trillion that year. But when real GDP is $10 trillion, the same 3 percent growth would be $10 trillion × 0.03 = $0.30 trillion. Since the slope of the line depends on the *absolute* rise rather than the *percentage* rise, the line gets steeper when the growth rate remains constant.

In fact, the line can become steeper even if the percentage growth rate *decreases* over time. As you've read, real GDP actually grew faster from 1959 to 1973 (where the line is flatter) than during any subsequent period (where the line is steeper). In subsequent chapters, you'll see other graphs that make it easier to see changes in the growth rate of real GDP.

workforce was unable to find work. Would the economy be performing well? Not really, for two reasons. First, unemployment affects the distribution of economic well-being among our citizens. People who cannot find jobs suffer a loss of income. And even though many of the jobless receive some unemployment benefits and other assistance from the government, the unemployed typically have lower living standards than the employed. Concern for those without jobs is one reason that consistently high employment—or consistently low *unemployment*—is an important macroeconomic goal.

But in addition to the impact on the unemployed themselves, joblessness affects *all* of us—even those who *have* jobs. A high unemployment rate means that the economy is not achieving its full economic potential: Many people who *want* to work and produce additional goods and services are not able to do so. With the same number of people—but fewer goods and services to distribute among that population—the average standard of living will be lower. This general effect on living standards gives us another reason to strive for consistently high rates of employment and low rates of unemployment.

One measure economists use to keep track of employment is the *unemployment rate*—the percentage of the workforce that is searching for a job but hasn't found one. Figure 2 shows the average unemployment rate during each of the past 86 years. Notice that the unemployment rate is never zero; there are always *some* people looking for work, even when the economy is doing well. But in some years, unemployment is unusually high. The worst example occurred during the Great Depression of the 1930s, when millions of workers lost their jobs and the unemployment rate reached 25 percent. One in four potential workers could not find a job. More recently, in 1982 and 1983, the unemployment rate averaged almost 10 percent.

The nation's commitment to high employment has twice been written into law. With the memory of the Great Depression still fresh, Congress passed the *Employment Act of 1946*, which required the federal government to "promote maximum employment, production, and purchasing power." It did not, however, dictate a target rate of unemployment the government should aim for. A numerical target was added in 1978, when Congress passed the *Full Employment and Balanced Growth Act,* which called for an unemployment rate of 4 percent.

A glance at Figure 2 shows how seldom we have hit this target over the last few decades. In fact, we did not hit it at all through the 1970s and 1980s. But in the 1990s, we came closer and closer and finally, in December 1999, we reached the 4 percent target for the first time since the 1960s. But it did not stay there long. In the early 2000s, the average unemployment rate has fluctuated, ranging from a high of 6.0 percent in 2003 to a low of 4.6 percent for most of 2006.

Why has the unemployment rate been above its target so often? Why were we able to reach 4 percent unemployment at the end of the 1990s, but not maintain it through the early 2000s? And what causes the average unemployment rate to

© TONY FREEMAN/PHOTOEDIT

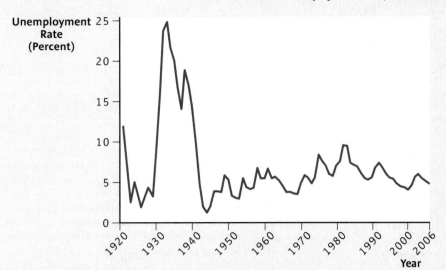

U.S. Unemployment Rate, 1920–2006   **F I G U R E   2**

*The unemployment rate fluctuates over time. During the Great Depression of the 1930s, unemployment was extremely high, reaching 25 percent in 1933. In the early 1980s, the rate averaged 10 percent. And during the 1990s, it fell rapidly, reaching 4 percent before turning up in the early 2000s.*

fluctuate from year to year, as shown in Figure 2? These are all questions that your study of macroeconomics will help you answer.

### Employment and the Business Cycle

When firms produce more output, they hire more workers; when they produce less output, they tend to lay off workers. We would thus expect real GDP and employment to be closely related, and indeed they are. In recent years, each 1 percent drop in output has been associated with the loss of more than half a million jobs. Consistently high employment, then, requires a high, stable level of output.

Unfortunately, output has *not* been very stable. If you look back at Figure 1, you will see that while real GDP has climbed upward over time, it has been a bumpy ride. The periodic fluctuations in GDP—the bumps in the figure—are called **business cycles.**

Figure 3 shows a close-up view of a hypothetical business cycle. First, notice the thin upward-sloping line. This shows the long-run upward trend of real GDP, which we refer to as *economic growth.* The thicker line shows the business cycle that occurs *around* the long-run trend. When output rises, we are in the **expansion** phase of the cycle; when output falls, we are in the *contraction* or **recession** phase. (Officially, a recession is a contraction considered significant in terms of depth, breadth, and duration.)

Of course, real-world business cycles never look quite like the smooth, symmetrical cycle in Figure 3, but rather like the jagged, irregular cycles of Figure 1. Recessions can be severe or mild, and they can last several years or less than a single year. When a recession is particularly severe and long lasting, it is called a **depression.** In the 20th century, the United States experienced just one decline in output serious enough to be considered a depression—the worldwide *Great Depression* of the

**Business cycles** Fluctuations in real GDP around its long-term growth trend.

**Expansion** A period of increasing real GDP.
**Recession** A period of significant decline in real GDP.

**Depression** An unusually severe recession.

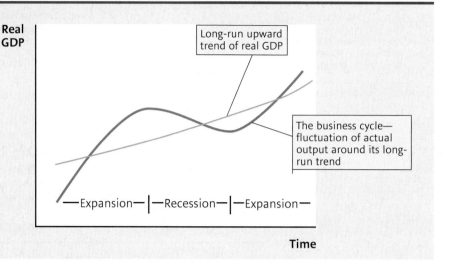

**FIGURE 3**

**The Business Cycle**

*Over time, real GDP fluctuates around an overall upward trend. Such fluctuations are called* business cycles. *When output rises, we are in the* expansion *phase of the cycle; when output falls, we are in a* recession.

**Expansion versus Economic Growth** Although the terms *expansion* and *economic growth* both refer to increases in real GDP, they are not the same. *Economic growth* refers to the long-run upward trend in output over a long period of time, usually more than a decade. It is measured as the *average* annual change in output over the entire period. An *expansion* refers to a usually shorter period of time during which output increases quarter by quarter or year by year.

Here's an example of the difference: From 1973 to 1991, output increased at an *average rate* of 2.7 percent per year over the entire period. This was the rate of economic growth during the period. But during a *part* of this long period—the early 1980s—output *fell* for several quarters. This was a contraction. During another part of this long period—the mid- and late 1980s—output rose every quarter. This was an expansion.

1930s. From 1929 to 1933, the first four years of the Great Depression, U.S. output dropped by more than 25 percent.

But even during more normal times, the economy has gone through many recessions. Since 1959, we have suffered through two severe recessions (in 1974–75 and 1981–82) and several more mild ones, such as the recession from March to November of 2001.

Why are there business cycles? Is there anything we can do to prevent recessions from occurring, or at least make them milder and shorter? And why—even after a period of severe depression as in the 1930s—does the economy eventually move back toward its long-run growth trend? These are all questions that macroeconomics helps us answer.

## STABLE PRICES

Figure 4 shows the annual inflation rate—the percentage increase in the average level of prices—from 1922 to the first half of 2006.[1] With very few exceptions, the inflation rate has been positive: On average, prices have risen in each of those years. But notice the wide variations in inflation. In 1979 and 1980, we had double-digit inflation: Prices rose by more than 12 percent in both years. During that time, polls showed that people were more concerned about inflation than any other national problem—more than unemployment, crime, poverty, pollution, or anything else. During the 1990s, the inflation rate averaged less than 3 percent per year, and it has

---

[1] Figure 4 is based on the Consumer Price Index, the most popular measure of the price level, as well as historical estimates of what this index *would* have been in the early part of the 20th century, before the index existed. We'll discuss the Consumer Price Index and other measures of inflation in more detail in later chapters.

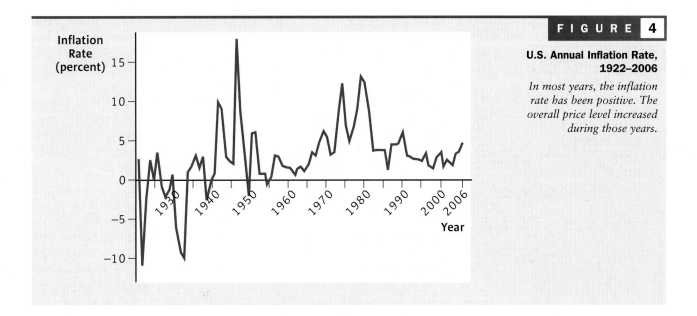

F I G U R E   4

**U.S. Annual Inflation Rate,
1922–2006**

*In most years, the inflation
rate has been positive. The
overall price level increased
during those years.*

averaged about 2.8 percent during the 2000s (through mid-2006). As a result, we hardly seem to notice it at all. Pollsters no longer include "rising prices" as a category when asking about the most important problems facing the country.

Other countries have not been so lucky. In the 1980s, several Latin American nations experienced inflation rates of thousands of percent per year. In the early 1990s, some of the newly emerging nations of Central Europe and the former Soviet Union suffered annual inflation rates in the triple digits.

An extreme case was the new nation of Serbia, where prices rose by 1,880 percent in the single month of August 1993. If prices had continued to rise at that rate all year, the annual inflation rate would have been 363,000,000,000,000,000 percent. A more recent example is Zimbabwe. The annual inflation rate has been consistently above 200 percent since 2003, and it reached 1,000 percent in mid-2006.

Why are stable prices—a low inflation rate—an important macroeconomic goal? Because inflation is *costly* to society. With annual inflation rates in the thousands of percent, the costs are easy to see: The purchasing power of the currency declines so rapidly that people are no longer willing to hold it. This breakdown of the monetary system forces people to waste valuable time and resources bartering with each other—for example, trading plumbing services for dentistry services. With so much time spent trying to find trading partners, there is little time left for producing goods and services. As a result, the average standard of living falls.

With inflation rates of 12 or 13 percent—such as the United States experienced in the late 1970s—the costs to society are less obvious and less severe. But they are still significant. And when it comes time to bring down the inflation rate, painful corrective actions by government are sometimes required. These actions can cause output to decline and unemployment to rise. For example, in order to bring the inflation rate down from the high levels of the late 1970s (see Figure 4), government policy purposely caused a severe recession in 1981–82, reducing output and increasing unemployment.

Economists regard *some* inflation as good for the economy. In fact, in 2001 and 2002, policy makers worried that the inflation rate might fall *too low,* and that the economy might experience a harmful *deflation*—a period of *decreasing* prices. Price stabilization requires not only preventing the inflation rate from rising too high, but also preventing it from falling too *low*, where it would be dangerously close to turning negative.

The previous paragraphs may have raised a number of questions in your mind. What causes inflation or deflation? How would a *moderately* high inflation rate of 7 or 8 percent harm society? How does a recession bring down the inflation rate, and how does the government actually *create* a recession? And why might a period of decreasing prices—which sounds so wonderful—be a threat to the economy? Your study of macroeconomics will help you answer all of these questions.

## THE MACROECONOMIC APPROACH

If you have already studied microeconomics, you will notice much that is familiar in macroeconomics. The *three-step process* introduced in Chapter 3 plays an important role in both branches of the field. But the macroeconomic approach differs from the microeconomic approach in significant ways. Most importantly, in *microeconomics*, we typically apply our three steps to *one market at a time*—the market for soybeans, for neurosurgeons, or for car washes. In *macroeconomics*, by contrast, we want to understand how the entire economy behaves. Thus, we apply the steps to *all markets simultaneously*. This includes not only markets for goods and services, but also markets for labor and for financial assets like stocks and bonds.

How can we possibly hope to deal with all of these markets at the same time? One way would be to build a gigantic model that included every individual market in the economy. The model would have tens of thousands of supply and demand curves, which could be used to determine tens of thousands of prices and quantities. With today's fast, powerful computers, we could, in principle, build this kind of model.

But it would not be easy. We would need to gather data on every good and service in the economy, every type of labor, every type of financial asset, and so on. As you might guess, this would be a formidable task, requiring thousands of workers just to gather the data alone. And in the end, the model would not prove very useful. We would not learn much about the economy from it: With so many individual trees, we could not see the forest.

Moreover, the model's predictions would be highly suspect: With so much information and so many moving parts, high standards of accuracy would be difficult to maintain. Even the government of the former Soviet Union, which directed production throughout the economy until the 1990s, was unable to keep track of all the markets under its control. In a market economy, where production decisions are made by individual firms, the task would be even harder.

What, then, is a macroeconomist to do? The answer is a word that you will become very familiar with in the chapters to come: *aggregation*.

### AGGREGATION IN MACROECONOMICS

**Aggregation** The process of combining different things into a single category.

**Aggregation** is the process of combining different things into a single category, and treating them as a whole. It is a basic tool of reasoning, one that you often use without being aware of it. If you say, "I applied for five jobs last month," you are aggregating five very different workplaces into the single category, *jobs*. Whenever you say, "I'm going out with my friends," you are combining several different people into a single category: people you consider *friends*.

Aggregation plays a key role in both micro- and macroeconomics. Microeconomists will speak of the market for automobiles, lumping Toyotas, Fords, BMWs, and other types of cars into a single category. But in macroeconomics, we take aggregation to the extreme. Because we want to consider the entire economy at once, and yet keep our model as simple as possible, we must aggregate all markets into the broadest possible categories. For example, we lump together all the goods and services that households buy—newspapers, pizza, couches, and haircuts—into the single category *consumption goods*. We combine all the different types of capital purchased by business firms—forklifts, factory buildings, office computers, and trucks—into the single category *investment goods*. Often we go even further, lumping consumption, investment, and all other types of goods into the single category *output* or *real GDP*. And in macroeconomics, we typically combine the thousands of different types of workers in the economy—doctors, construction workers, plumbers, college professors—into the category, *labor*. By aggregating in this way, we can create workable and reasonably accurate models that teach us a great deal about how the overall economy operates.

**"Micro" versus "Macro"** In many English words, the prefix *macro* means "large" and *micro* means "small." As a result, you might think that in microeconomics, we study economic units in which small sums of money are involved, while in macroeconomics we study units involving greater sums. But this is not correct: The annual output of General Motors is considerably greater than the total annual output of many small countries, such as Estonia or Guatemala. Yet when we study the behavior of General Motors, we are practicing *microeconomics,* and when we study changes in output in Estonia, we are practicing *macroeconomics.* Why? Microeconomics is concerned with the behavior and interaction of *individual* firms and markets, even if they are very large; macroeconomics is concerned with the behavior of *entire economies,* even if they are very small.

**DANGEROUS CURVES**

## MACROECONOMIC CONTROVERSIES

Macroeconomics is full of disputes and disagreements. Indeed, modern macroeconomics, which began with the publication of *The General Theory of Employment, Interest, and Money* by British economist John Maynard Keynes in 1936, originated in controversy. Keynes was taking on the conventional wisdom of his time, *classical economics*, which held that the macroeconomy worked very well on its own, and the best policy for the government to follow was *laissez-faire*—"leave it alone." As he was working on *The General Theory,* Keynes wrote to his friend, the playwright George Bernard Shaw, "I believe myself to be writing a book on economic theory which will largely revolutionize—not, I suppose, at once but in the course of the next ten years—the way the world thinks about economic problems."

Keynes's prediction was on the money. After the publication of his book, economists argued about its merits, but 10 years later, the majority of the profession had been won over: They had become Keynesians. This new school of thought held that the economy does *not* do well on its own (one needed only to look at the Great Depression for evidence) and requires continual guidance from an activist and well-intentioned government.

From the late 1940s until the early 1960s, events seemed to prove the Keynesians correct. Then, beginning in the 1960s, several distinguished economists began to challenge Keynesian ideas. Their counterrevolutionary views, which in many ways mirrored those of the classical economists, were strengthened by events in the 1970s, when the economy's behavior began to contradict some Keynesian ideas. Today, much of this disagreement has been resolved and a modern consensus—incorporating both Keynesian and classical ideas—has emerged. But there are still controversies.

Consider, for example, the controversy over the Bush administration's $350 billion 10-year tax cut. In May 2003, the tax cut was approved by 231 to 200 in the House of Representatives, and passed the Senate only when Vice President Cheney cast his vote to break a 50–50 tie. Within hours of passage, the following appeared on CNN's Web site:

> "This is a great victory for the American people," said Senate Majority Leader Bill Frist, R-Tennessee. "The wonderful thing is it really boils down to greater job security for people."

> "This is a policy of debt, deficits, and decline," said Sen. Kent Conrad, D-North Dakota, adding, "This is a scandal in the making. We're going to read there are perverse results as a result of this tax policy."[2]

Similar opposing views were expressed by economists associated with the Bush administration on the one hand, and those associated with the Democratic Party on the other. What are we to make of macroeconomic policy controversies like these, which occur so often on the political scene?

Remember the distinction between *positive (what is)* and *normative (what should be)*? Some of these disagreements are *positive* in nature. While economists and policy makers often agree on the broad outlines of how the macroeconomy works, they may disagree on some of the details. For example, they may disagree about the economy's current direction or momentum, or the relative effectiveness of different policies in altering the economy's course. Indeed, the two opposing senators quoted above were expressing at least in part a positive disagreement: a disagreement about the *impact* that tax cuts would have on the economy.

But disagreements that *sound* positive often have *normative* origins. For example in 2003, Democrats in Congress criticized the Bush tax cut as unfair, because it gave the biggest tax reduction to those with the highest incomes. Republicans in Congress countered that the tax cut was fair, because taxpayers with the highest incomes paid higher taxes to begin with. In the competitive and confrontational arena of politics—with each side trying to muster all the arguments it can—positive economics is often enlisted. In 2003, Republicans who began with the view that the Bush tax cut was fair invariably *also* argued that it was the most effective policy to spur the economy into a healthy expansion phase (see Figure 3). And they found a number of economists—who may have had similar normative views—to support that argument. Democrats who began with the view that the tax cut was *un*fair invariably *also* argued that it would cause great harm to the economy. And they found a number of economists—who may have had similar normative views—to support *that* argument.

Because of such political battles, people who follow the news often think that there is little agreement among economists about how the macroeconomy works. In fact, the profession has come to a consensus on many basic principles, and we will stress these as we go. And even when there are disagreements, there is surprising consensus on the approach that should be taken to resolve them.

You won't find this consensus expressed in a hot political debate. But you *will* find it in academic journals and conferences, and in reports issued by certain non-partisan research organizations or government agencies. And—we hope—you will find it in the chapters to come.

[2] "Congress Approves Tax-Cut Package," CNN.com/Inside Politics, May 23, 2002.

## AS YOU STUDY MACROECONOMICS ...

Macroeconomics is a fascinating and wide-ranging subject. You will find that each piece of the macroeconomic puzzle connects to all of the other pieces in many different ways. Each time one of your questions is answered, ten more will spring up in your mind, each demanding immediate attention. This presents a problem for textbook writers, and for your instructor as well: What is the best order in which to present the principles of macroeconomics? One way is to follow the order of questions as they would occur to a curious reader. For example, learning about unemployment raises questions about international trade, so we could then skip to that topic. But it also raises questions about government spending, economic growth, wages, banking, and much, much more. And each of these topics raises questions about still others. Organizing the material in this way would make you feel like a ball in a pinball machine, bouncing from bumper to bumper. This pinball approach—bouncing from topic to topic—is the one taken by the media when reporting on the economy. If you have ever tried to learn economics from a newspaper, you know how frustrating this approach can be.

In our study of macroeconomics, we will follow a different approach: presenting material as it is *needed* for what follows. In this way, what you learn in one chapter will form the foundation for the material in the next, and your understanding of macroeconomics will deepen as you go.

But be forewarned: This approach requires considerable patience on your part. Many of the questions that will pop into your head will have to be postponed until the proper foundations for answering them have been established. It might help, though, to give you a *brief* indication of what is to come.

In the next two chapters, we will discuss three of the most important aggregates in macroeconomics: output, employment, and the price level. You will see why each of these is important to our economic well-being, how we keep track of them with government statistics, and how to interpret these statistics with a critical eye.

Then, in the remainder of the book, we study how the macroeconomy operates. We'll start with the long run: What makes an economy grow over long periods of time, and which government policies are likely to help or hinder that growth.

Then, we turn our attention to the short run. You will learn why the economy behaves differently in the short run than in the long run, why we have business cycles, and how these cycles may be affected by government policies. We'll also expand our analysis to include the banking system and the money supply, and the special challenges they pose for government policy makers.

Finally, we'll turn our attention to the special problems of a global economy. You'll learn how trade with other nations constrains and expands our macro policy options at home and how economic events abroad influence our own economy. You will also learn why the United States has run persistent trade deficits with the rest of the world and what that means for our citizens.

This sounds like quite a lot of ground to cover, and, indeed, it is. But it's not as daunting as it might sound. Remember that the study of macroeconomics—like the macroeconomy itself—is not a series of separate units, but an integrated whole. As you go from chapter to chapter, each principle you learn is a stepping-stone to the next one. Little by little, your knowledge and understanding will accumulate and deepen. Most students are genuinely surprised at how well they understand the macroeconomy after a single introductory course, and find the reward well worth the effort.

# Summary

Macroeconomics is the study of the economy as a whole. It deals with issues such as economic growth, unemployment, inflation, and government policies that might influence the overall level of economic activity.

Economists generally agree about the importance of three main macroeconomic goals. The first of these is economic growth. If output, real gross domestic product, grows faster than population, the average person can enjoy an improved standard of living.

High employment is another important goal. When employment is low (unemployment is high), it harms not only the unemployed themselves, but also society in general: Society loses output that could have been produced.

The third macroeconomic goal is stable prices. This goal is important because inflation—especially very high inflation—imposes costs on society and can lower living standards.

Because an economy like that of the United States is so large and complex, the models we use to analyze the economy must be highly aggregated. For example, we lump together millions of different goods to create an aggregate called "output." We combine all their prices into a single "price index."

Macroeconomics is often controversial. It may seem that macroeconomists agree on very little, but there is actually broad consensus on many positive economic issues. The roots of most macroeconomic controversies are normative.

# Problem Set   *Answers to even-numbered Questions and Problems can be found on the text Web site at www.thomsonedu.com/economics/hall.*

1. In 1973, real GDP (at 2000 prices) was $4,342 billion. In 2000, it was $9,817 billion. During the same period, the U.S. population rose from 212 million to 281 million.
   a. What was the total percentage increase in real GDP from 1973 to 2000?
   b. What was the total percentage increase in the U.S. population during this period?
   c. Calculate real GDP per person in 1973 and in 2000. By what percentage did output per person grow over this period?

2. Suppose that real GDP had grown by 8 percent per year from 1973 to 2000. Using the data from problem 1:
   a. What would real GDP have been in 2000?
   b. How much would output *per person* in 2000 have increased (compared to its actual value in 2000) if annual growth in real GDP over this period had been 8 percent?

3. a. The average growth rate for real GDP in the United States was 3.7 percent from 1991 to 2000. Use the information in the following table (which gives the actual GDP numbers measured in 2000 dollars) to calculate how much more we would have produced in 2000 if real GDP had grown by 4.7 percent per year over that period.

   b. Calculate, for a 2000 population of 281 million people, how much higher the average output per person would have been in 2000 if the growth rate had been 4.7 percent per year over this period.

4. Assume that the country of Ziponia produced real GDP equal to $5,000 (in billions) in the year 2000.
   a. Calculate Ziponia's output from 2000 to 2006, assuming that it experienced a constant growth rate of 6 percent per year over this period. Use your answers to construct a graph similar to the one in Figure 1. Is the slope of this graph constant? Explain.
   b. Calculate Ziponia's output from 2000 to 2006, assuming that its growth rate was 6 percent from 2000 to 2001, and then the growth rate fell by 1 percentage point each year. Plot these points onto your graph from part (a). Is the slope of this graph constant? Explain.

| Year | Real GDP (Billions of 2000 dollars) |
|------|-------------------------------------|
| 1991 | $7,100.5 |
| 1992 | $7,336.6 |
| 1993 | $7,532.7 |
| 1994 | $7,835.5 |
| 1995 | $8,031.7 |
| 1996 | $8,328.9 |
| 1997 | $8,703.5 |
| 1998 | $9,066.9 |
| 1999 | $9,470.3 |
| 2000 | $9,817.0 |

# Production, Income, and Employment

On the first Friday of every month, at 8:00 A.M., dozens of journalists mill about in a room in the Department of Labor. They are waiting for the arrival of the press officer from the government's Bureau of Labor Statistics. When he enters the room, carrying a stack of papers, the buzz of conversation stops. The papers contain the monthly report on the experience of the American workforce. They summarize everything the government knows about hiring and firing at businesses across the country; about the number of people working, the hours they worked, and the incomes they earned; and about the number of people *not* working and what they did instead. But one number looms large in the journalists' minds as they scan the report and compose their stories: the percentage of the labor force that could not find jobs, or the nation's *unemployment rate*.

Every three months, a similar scene takes place at the Department of Commerce. In this case, the reporters are there for the quarterly report on the nation's output of goods and services and the incomes we have earned from producing it. Once again, there is tremendous detail. Output is broken down by the industry that produced it and by the sector that purchased it. Income is broken down into different types of earners. And once again, the reporters' eyes will focus on a single number, a number that will dominate their stories and create headlines in newspapers across the country: the nation's *gross domestic product.*

The government knows that its reports on employment and production will have a major impact on the American political scene, and on financial markets in the United States and around the world. So it takes great pains to ensure fair and equal access to the information. For example, the Bureau of Labor Statistics allows journalists to look at the employment report at 8:00 A.M. on the day of the release (the first Friday of every month). But they must stay inside a room—appropriately called the lockup room—and cannot contact the outside world until the official release time of 8:30 A.M. At 8:29 A.M., the reporters are permitted to hook up their laptop modems, and then a countdown begins. At precisely 8:30 A.M., the reporters are permitted to transmit their stories. At the same instant, the Bureau posts its report on an Internet Web site (*http://www.bls.gov*).

And the world reacts. Within seconds, wire-service headlines appear on computer screens: "Unemployment Rate Up Two-Tenths of a Percent" or "Nation's Production Steady." Within minutes, financial traders, for whom these news flashes provide clues about the economy's future, make snap decisions to buy or sell, moving stock and bond prices. And throughout the day, politicians and pundits will respond with sound bites, attacking or defending the administration's economic policies.

In this chapter, we will take our first look at production and employment in the economy, focusing on two key variables: *gross domestic product* and the *unemployment rate*. The purpose here is not to explain what causes these variables to rise or fall. That will come a few chapters later, when we begin to study macroeconomic models. Here, we focus on the reality behind the numbers: what the statistics tell us about the economy, how the government obtains them, and how they are sometimes misused.

## PRODUCTION AND GROSS DOMESTIC PRODUCT

You have probably heard the phrase *gross domestic product*—or its more familiar abbreviation, GDP—many times. It is one of those economic terms that is frequently used by the media and by politicians. In the first half of this chapter, we take a close look at GDP.

### GDP: A DEFINITION

The U.S. government has been measuring the nation's total production since the 1930s. You might think that this is an easy number to calculate, at least in theory: Simply add up the output of every firm in the country during the year. Unfortunately, measuring total production is not so straightforward, and there are many conceptual traps and pitfalls. This is why economists have come up with a very precise definition of GDP.

**Gross domestic product (GDP)**
The total value of all final goods and services produced for the marketplace during a given year, within the nation's borders.

> The nation's **gross domestic product** (GDP) *is the total value of all final goods and services produced for the marketplace during a given period, within the nation's borders.*

Quite a mouthful. But every part of this definition is absolutely necessary. To see why, let's break the definition down into pieces and look more closely at each one.

*The total value . . .*
An old expression tells us that "you can't add apples and oranges." But that is just what government statisticians must do when they measure our total output. In a typical day, American firms produce millions of *loaves* of bread, thousands of *pounds* of peanut butter, hundreds of *hours* of television programming, and so on. These are different products, and each is measured in its own type of units. Yet, somehow, we must combine all of them into a single number. But how?

The approach of GDP is to add up the *dollar value* of every good or service—the number of dollars each product is sold for. As a result, GDP is measured in dollar units. For example, in 2005, the GDP of the United States was about $12,456,000,000,000—give or take a few billion dollars. (That's about $12.5 trillion.)

Using dollar values to calculate GDP has two important advantages. First, it gives us a common unit of measurement for very different things, thus allowing us to add up "apples and oranges." Second, it ensures that a good that uses more resources to produce (a computer chip) will count more in GDP than a good that uses fewer resources (a tortilla chip).

However, using the dollar prices at which goods and services actually sell also creates a problem: If prices rise, then GDP will rise, even if we are not actually *producing* more. For this reason, when tracking changes in production over time, GDP must be adjusted to take away the effects of inflation. We'll come back to this issue again a bit later in the chapter.

### . . . of all final . . .

When measuring production, we do not count *every* good or service produced in the economy, but only those that are sold to their *final users*. An example will illustrate why.

Figure 1 shows a simplified version of the stages of production for a ream (500 sheets) of notebook paper: A lumber company cuts down trees and produces $1.00 worth of wood chips. These are sold to a paper mill for $1.00. The mill cooks, bleaches, and refines the wood chips, turning them into paper rolls. These are sold to an office supplies manufacturer for $1.50. This manufacturer cuts the paper, prints lines and margins on it, and sells it to a wholesaler for $2.25. The wholesaler sells it to a retail store for $3.50, and then, finally, it is sold to a consumer—perhaps you—for $5.00.

Should we add the value of *all* this production, and include $1.00 + $1.50 + $2.25 + $3.50 + $5.00 = $13.25 in GDP each time a ream of notebook paper is produced? No, this would clearly be a mistake because all of this production ends up creating a good worth only $5 in the end. In fact, the $5 you pay for this good already *includes* the value of all the other production in the process.

In our example, the goods sold by the lumber company, paper mill, office supplies manufacturer, and wholesaler are all **intermediate goods**—goods used up in the process of producing something else. But the retailer (say, your local stationery store) sells a **final good**—a product sold to its *final user* (you). If we separately added in the production of intermediate goods when calculating GDP, we would be counting them more than once, since they are already included in the value of the final good.

**Intermediate goods** Goods used up in producing final goods.

**Final good** A good sold to its final user.

> *To avoid overcounting intermediate products when measuring GDP, we add up the value of final goods and services only. The value of all intermediate products is automatically included in the value of the final products they are used to create.*

### . . . goods and services . . .

We all know a good when we see one: We can look at it, feel it, weigh it, and, in some cases, eat it, strum it, or swing a bat at it. Not so with a service: When you

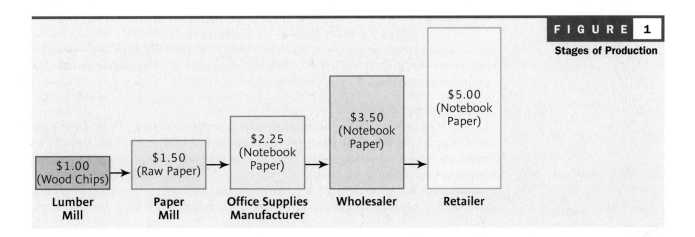

**FIGURE 1**

**Stages of Production**

get a medical checkup, a haircut, or a car wash, the *effects* of the service may linger, but the service itself is used up the moment it is produced. Nonetheless, final services count in GDP in the same way as final goods.

Services have become an increasingly important part of our total output in recent decades. The service sector has grown from about a third of U.S. output in 1950 to well over half of our output in 2006. These include the services produced by Internet providers, the health care industry, the banking industry, the educational system, and the entertainment industry.

### . . . produced . . .

GDP counts only things that are *produced*. This may sound obvious, but it is easy to forget. Every day, Americans buy billions of dollars worth of things that are *not* produced, or at least not produced during the period being considered. These are not counted in that period's GDP. For example, people may buy land, or they may buy financial assets such as stocks or bonds. While these things cost money, they are not counted in GDP because they are not "goods and services *produced*." Land, for example, is not produced at all. Stocks and bonds represent a claim to ownership or to receive future payments, but they are not themselves produced goods or services.

**The Services of Dealers, Brokers, and Other Sellers** You've learned that GDP excludes the value of many things that are bought and sold—such as land, financial assets, and used goods—because they are not *currently produced goods and services*. But all of this buying and selling *can* contribute to GDP indirectly. How? If a dealer or broker is involved in the transaction, then that dealer or broker is producing a current service: bringing buyer and seller together. The value of this service is part of current GDP.

For example, suppose you bought a secondhand book at your college bookstore for $50. Suppose, too, that the store had bought the book from another student for $30. Then the purchase of the used book will contribute $20 to this year's GDP. Why? Because $20 is the value of the bookstore's services; it's the premium you pay to buy the book in the store, rather than going through the trouble to find the original seller yourself. The remainder of your purchase—$30—represents the value of the used book itself, and is *not* counted in GDP. The book was already counted when it was newly produced, in this or a previous year.

### . . . for the marketplace . . .

GDP does not include *all* final goods and services produced in the economy. Rather, it includes only the ones produced for the marketplace, that is, with the intention of being *sold*. Because of this restriction, we exclude many important goods and services from our measure. For example, when you clean your own home, you have produced a final service—housecleaning—but it is *not* counted in GDP because you are doing it for yourself, not for the marketplace. If you hire a housecleaner to clean your home, however, this final service *is* included in GDP; it has become a market transaction.

The same is true for many services produced in the economy. Taking care of your children, washing your car, mowing your lawn, walking your dog—none of these services is included in GDP if you do it for yourself, but all *are* included if you pay someone else to do them for you.

### . . . during a given period . . .

GDP measures production during some specific period of time. Only goods produced during that period are counted. But people and businesses spend billions of dollars each year on *used* goods, such as secondhand cars, previously occupied homes, used furniture, or an old signed photo of Elvis. These goods were all *produced*, but not necessarily in the current period. And even if they *were* produced in the current period, they would only count when sold the *first* time, as new goods.

If we counted them again each time they were resold, we would overestimate total production for the period.

What duration of time should we use for GDP? In theory, we could use any duration. In 2005, for example, the United States produced an average of $34 billion worth of output each day, $1 trillion each month, and $12.5 trillion for the year as a whole. Thus, we could measure daily GDP, monthly GDP, and so on. In practice, however, GDP is measured for *each quarter* and then reported as an *annual rate* for that quarter.

To understand this, look at Table 1, which shows how GDP was actually reported by the government during the course of 2005. A few months after the end of each quarter, the government releases its estimates for GDP for that quarter, and then revises the estimates periodically as new information is obtained. Look at the row for 2005—I, the first quarter (January through March of 2005). During that quarter the U.S. economy *actually* produced about $3,043 billion in final goods and services. But you won't see that number in the table. What you *will* see is how much we *would* have produced during an entire year if we produced at that quarter's rate for *four* full quarters (4 × $3,043.3 billion = $12,173.2 billion).[1] Once the fourth-quarter figures are in, the government also reports the official GDP figure for the entire year—what we *actually* produced during the entire year. For 2005, that was $12,445.8 billion.

### . . . within the nation's borders.

U.S. GDP measures output produced *within U.S. borders,* regardless of whether it was produced by Americans. This means we *include* output produced by foreign-owned resources and foreign citizens located in the United States, and we *exclude* output produced by Americans located in other countries. For example, when the rock band U2, whose members reside in Ireland, gives a concert tour in the United States, the value of their services is counted in U.S. GDP but not in Ireland's GDP. Similarly, the services of an American nurse working in an Ethiopian hospital are part of Ethiopian GDP and not U.S. GDP.

## THE EXPENDITURE APPROACH TO GDP

The Commerce Department's Bureau of Economic Analysis (BEA), the agency responsible for measuring the nation's production, calculates GDP in several different ways. The most important of these is the *expenditure approach.* Because this method of measuring GDP tells us so much about the structure of our economy, we'll spend the next several pages on it.

In the expenditure approach, we divide output into four categories according to which group in the economy purchases it as the final user. The four categories are:

| TABLE | 1 |
|---|---|

**Quarterly and Annual GDP in 2005**

| Quarters | GDP ($ billions) |
|---|---|
| 2005—I | $12,173.2 |
| 2005—II | $12,346.1 |
| 2005—III | $12,573.5 |
| 2005—IV | $12,730.5 |
| **Year** | |
| 2005 | $12,455.8 |

*Source:* Bureau of Economic Analysis (*www.bea.gov*), August 30, 2006 revision.

---

[1] There is one other twist to the government's reporting: Before multiplying by 4, each quarter's production is *seasonally adjusted*—raised or lowered to eliminate any changes that usually occur during that time of year.

1. *Consumption goods and services (C)*, purchased by households;
2. *Private investment goods and services (I)*, purchased by businesses;
3. *Government goods and services (G)*, purchased by government agencies;
4. *Net exports (NX)*, purchased by foreigners.

This is an exhaustive list: Everyone who purchases a good or service included in U.S. GDP must be either a U.S. household, U.S. business, or U.S. government agency (including state and local government); otherwise, they are part of the foreign sector. Thus, when we add up the purchases of all four groups, we must get GDP:

**Expenditure approach** Measuring GDP by adding the value of goods and services purchased by each type of final user.

> *In the **expenditure approach** to measuring GDP, we add up the value of the goods and services purchased by each type of final user:*
>
> $$GDP = C + I + G + NX$$

Table 2 shows the part of GDP purchased by each sector during the entire year 2005. Ignore the finer details for now and just concentrate on the last number in each column. Applying the expenditure approach to GDP in 2005 gives us GDP = $C + I + G + NX$ = \$8,742 + \$2,057 + \$2,373 + (−\$716) = \$12,456 billion.

Now let's take a closer look at each of the four components of GDP.

### Consumption Spending

Consumption (C) is the largest component of GDP—making up about 70 percent of total production in recent years—and the easiest to understand:

**Consumption (*C*)** The part of GDP purchased by households as final users.

> *Consumption is the part of GDP purchased by households as final users.*

### TABLE 2  GDP in 2005: The Expenditure Approach

| Consumption Purchases ($ billion) | | Private Investment Purchases ($ billion) | | Government Purchases ($ billion) | | Net Exports ($ billion) | |
|---|---|---|---|---|---|---|---|
| Services | $5,170 | Plant, Equipment, and Software | $1,266 | Government Consumption | $1,976 | Exports | $1,303 |
| Nondurable Goods | $2,539 | New-Home Construction | $ 770 | Government Investment | $ 397 | Imports | $2,019 |
| Durable Goods | $1,033 | Changes in Business Inventories | $ 21 | | | | |
| **Consumption =** | **$8,742** | **Private Investment =** | **$2,057** | **Government Purchases =** | **$2,373** | **Net Exports =** | **−$ 716** |

GDP = $C + I + G + NX$

= \$8,742 + \$2,057 + \$2,373 + (−\$716)

= \$12,456 billion

*Source*: Bureau of Economic Analysis, "National Income and Product Account Tables" (*www.bea.gov*).

Almost everything that households buy during the year—restaurant meals, gasoline, new clothes, doctors' visits, movies, electricity, and more—is included as part of consumption spending when we calculate GDP.

But notice the word *almost*.

Some of the things that households buy are *not* part of consumption in GDP. First, used goods that households buy are excluded. As discussed earlier, these were already counted when they were originally sold as new goods.

Second, households buy assets—like stocks, bonds, and land—that are *not* goods and services. These are excluded from consumption, as well as from GDP.

Third, *newly constructed homes*—even though part of GDP and usually purchased directly by households—are included as investment, rather than consumption. We'll discuss the reasons for this in the next section.

Finally, there are two things included in consumption even though households don't actually buy them: (1) the total value of food products produced on farms that are consumed by the farmers and their families themselves; and (2) the total value of housing services provided by owner-occupied homes. The government estimates how much the food consumed on farms *could* have been sold for, and how much owner-occupied homes *could* have been rented for. These estimates are included as part of consumption spending, and therefore included in GDP as well.

### Private Investment

In Chapter 2, you learned that one of the four resources is capital, a long-lasting tool used in production, and which is *itself* produced. Examples are oil drilling rigs, cash registers, office telephone equipment, and wireless phone towers. When we sum the value of all capital goods like these in the country, we get our *capital stock*.

Understanding the concept of capital stock helps us understand and define the concept of investment. A rough definition of **private investment** is *capital formation*— the *increase* in the nation's capital stock during the year.

More specifically,

> *private investment has three components: (1) business purchases of plant, equipment, and software; (2) new-home construction; and (3) changes in business firms' inventory stocks (changes in stocks of unsold goods).*

**Private investment (*I*)** The sum of business plant, equipment, and software purchases, new-home construction, and inventory changes; often referred to as just *investment*.

Each of these components requires some explanation.

*Business Purchases of Plant, Equipment, and Software.* This category might seem confusing at first glance. Why aren't plant, equipment, and software considered intermediate goods? After all, business firms buy these things in order to produce other things. Doesn't the value of their final goods include the value of their plant, equipment, and software as well?

Actually, no, and if you go back to the definition of intermediate goods, you will see why. Intermediate goods are *used up* in producing the current year's GDP. But a firm's plant, equipment, and software are intended to last for many years; only a small part of them is used up to make the current year's output. Thus, we regard new plant, equipment, and software as final goods, and we regard the firms that buy them as the final users of those goods.

For example, suppose our paper mill—the firm that turns wood chips into raw paper—builds a new factory building that is expected to last for 50 years. Then only a small fraction of that factory building—one-fiftieth—is used up in any one year's production of raw paper, and only this small part of the factory building's value will be reflected in the value of the firm's paper production. But since the entire factory is produced during the year, we must include its full value *somewhere* in our measure of production. We therefore count the whole factory building as investment in GDP.

Plant, equipment, and software purchases are always the largest component of private investment. And 2005 was no exception, as you can see in the second column of Table 2. That year, businesses purchased and installed $1,266 billion worth of plant, equipment, and software, which was almost two-thirds of total private investment.

*New-Home Construction.* As you can see in Table 2, new-home construction made up a significant part of total private investment in 2005. But it may strike you as odd that this category is part of investment spending at all, since most new homes are purchased by households and could reasonably be considered consumption spending instead. Why is new-home construction counted as investment spending in GDP?

Largely because residential housing is an important part of the nation's *capital stock.* Just as an oil-drilling rig will continue to provide oil-drilling services for many years, so, too, a home will continue to provide housing services into the future. Because we want our measure of private investment to roughly correspond to the increase in the nation's capital stock, we include this important category of capital formation as part of private investment.

Unsold goods, like those pictured in this warehouse, are considered inventories. The change *in these inventories is included as investment when calculating GDP.*

*Changes in Inventories.* Inventories are goods that have been produced but not yet sold. They include goods on store shelves, goods making their way through the production process in factories, and raw materials waiting to be used. We count the *change* in firms' inventories as part of investment in measuring GDP. Why? When goods are produced but not sold during the year, they end up in some firm's inventory stocks. If we did *not* count changes in inventories, we would be missing this important part of current production. Remember that GDP is designed to measure total *production*, not just the part of production that is sold during the year.

To understand this more clearly, suppose that in some year, the automobile industry produced $100 billion worth of automobiles, and that $80 billion worth was sold to consumers. Then the other $20 billion remained unsold and was added to the auto companies' inventories. If we counted consumption spending alone ($80 billion), we would underestimate automobile production in GDP. To ensure a proper measure, we must include not only the $80 billion in cars sold (consumption), but also the $20 billion *change* in inventories (private investment). In the end, the contribution to GDP is $80 billion (consumption) + $20 billion (private investment) = $100 billion, which is, indeed, the total value of automobile production during the year.

What if inventory stocks *decline* during the year, so that the change in inventories is negative? Our rule still holds: We include the change in inventories in our measure of GDP. But in this case, we add a *negative* number. For example, if the automobile industry produced $100 billion worth of cars this year, but consumers bought $120 billion, then $20 billion worth must have come from inventory stocks. This $20 billion worth of cars was produced (and counted) in previous years, so it should not be counted in this year's GDP. In this case, the consumption spending of $120 billion *overestimates* automobile production during the year, so subtracting $20 billion corrects for this overcount. In the end, GDP would rise by $120 billion (consumption) + [−$20 billion (private investment)] = $100 billion.

But why are inventory changes included in investment, rather than some other component of GDP? Because unsold goods are part of the nation's capital stock. They will provide services in the future, when they are finally sold and used. An increase in inventories represents capital formation. A decrease in inventories—negative investment—is a decrease in the nation's capital.

Inventory changes are generally the smallest component of private investment, but the most highly volatile in percentage terms. In 2005, for example, inventories rose by $21 billion; one year earlier, they rose by $55 billion—almost three times as much. Part of the reason for this volatility is that, while some inventory investment is intended, much of it is *unintended*. As the economy begins to slow, for example, businesses may be unable to sell all of the goods they have produced and had planned to sell. The unsold output is added to inventory stocks—an unintended increase in inventories. During rapid expansions, the opposite may happen: Businesses find themselves selling more than they produced—an unintended (though welcome) decrease in inventories.

*Private Investment and the Capital Stock: Some Provisos.* A few pages ago, it was pointed out that private investment corresponds only *roughly* to the increase in the nation's capital stock. Why this cautious language? Because changes in the nation's capital stock are somewhat more complicated than we are able to capture with private investment alone.

First, private investment *excludes* some production that adds to the nation's capital stock. Specifically, private investment does not include:

- *Government investment.* An important part of the nation's capital stock is owned and operated not by businesses, but by government—federal, state, and local. Courthouses, police cars, fire stations, schools, weather satellites, military aircraft, highways, and bridges are all examples of government capital. If you look at the third column of Table 2, for example, you'll see that the BEA estimated government investment to be $397 billion in 2005; that was the part of government spending that was devoted to capital formation in 2005.
- *Consumer durables.* Goods such as furniture, automobiles, washing machines, and personal computers for home use can be considered capital goods because they will continue to provide services for many years. In 2005, households purchased $1,033 billion worth of consumer durables (see Table 2, first column).
- *Human capital.* Think about a surgeon's skills in performing a heart bypass operation, or a police detective's ability to find clues and solve a murder, or a Web page designer's mastery of HTML and Java. These types of knowledge will continue to provide valuable services well into the future, just like plant and equipment or new housing. To measure the increase in the capital stock most broadly, then, we *should* include the additional skills and training acquired by the workforce during the year.

In addition to excluding some types of capital formation, private investment also errs in the other direction: It ignores *depreciation*—the capital that is used up during the year. Fortunately, the BEA estimates depreciation of the private and public capital stock, allowing us to calculate **net investment** (total investment minus depreciation) for these sectors. For example, for 2005, the BEA estimates that $1,353 billion of the private capital stock depreciated during the year (not shown in Table 2). So net private investment that year was only $2,057 billion − $1,353 billion = $704 billion.

**Net investment** Investment minus depreciation.

Similarly, the BEA estimates that $252 billion in government capital depreciated in 2005, so net government investment that year was $397 billion − $252 billion = $145 billion.

### Government Purchases

**Government purchases (G)**
Spending by federal, state, and local governments on goods and services.

In 2005, the government bought $2,373 billion worth of goods and services that were part of GDP—almost a fifth of the total. This component of GDP is called **government purchases,** although in recent years the Department of Commerce has begun to use the phrase *government consumption and investment purchases.* Government *investment,* as discussed earlier, refers to capital goods purchased by government agencies. The rest of government purchases is considered government *consumption:* spending on goods and services that are used up during the period. This includes the salaries of government workers and military personnel, and raw materials such as computer paper for government offices, gasoline for government vehicles, and the electricity used in government buildings.

There are a few things to keep in mind about government purchases in GDP. First, we include purchases by state and local governments as well as the federal government. In macroeconomics, it makes little difference whether the purchases are made by a local government agency like the parks department of Kalamazoo, Michigan, or a huge federal agency such as the U.S. Department of Defense.

**DANGEROUS CURVES**

**Investment: Economics versus Ordinary English** Be *extremely* careful when using the term *investment* in your economics course. In economics, investment refers to capital formation, such as the building of a new factory, home, or hospital, or the production and installation of new capital equipment, or the accumulation of inventories by business firms. In everyday language, however, *investment* has a very different meaning: a place to put your wealth. Thus, in ordinary English, you invest whenever you buy stocks or bonds or certificates of deposit or when you lend money to a friend who is starting up a business. But in the language of economics, you have not invested but merely changed the form in which you are holding your wealth (say, from checking account balances to stocks or bonds). To avoid confusion, remember that investment takes place when there is new production of capital goods— that is, when there is *capital formation.*

Second, government purchases include *goods*—like fighter jets, police cars, school buildings, and spy satellites—and *services*—such as those performed by police, legislators, and military personnel.

The government is considered to be the final purchaser of these things even if it uses them to make other goods or services. For example, if you are taking economics at a public college or university that produces educational services, then your professor is selling teaching services to a state or city government. His or her salary enters into GDP as part of government purchases.

**Transfer payment** Any payment that is not compensation for supplying goods, services, or resources.

Finally, it's important to distinguish between government *purchases*—which are counted in GDP—and government *outlays* as measured by local, state, and federal budgets and reported in the media. What's the difference? In addition to their purchases of goods and services, government agencies also disburse money for **transfer payments.** These funds are *given* to people or organizations—*not* to buy goods or services from them, but rather to fulfill some social obligation or goal. For example, Social Security payments by the federal government, unemployment insurance and welfare payments by state governments, and money disbursed to homeless shelters and soup kitchens by city governments are all examples of transfer payments. They are not included in government purchases, because the government itself has not actually purchased any goods and services with these funds.

The important thing to remember about transfer payments is this:

*Transfer payments represent money redistributed from one group of citizens (taxpayers) to another (the poor, the unemployed, the elderly). While transfers are included in government budgets as outlays, they are not included in the government purchases component of GDP.*

### Net Exports

There is one more category of buyers of output produced in the United States: *the foreign sector.* Looking back at Table 2, the fourth column tells us that in 2005, purchasers *outside* the nation bought approximately $1,303 billion of U.S. goods and services—about 10 percent of our GDP. These exports are part of U.S. production of goods and services and so are included in GDP.

However, in recognizing dealings with the rest of the world, we must correct an inaccuracy in our measure of GDP the way we've reported it so far. Americans buy many goods and services every year that were produced *outside* the United States (Chinese shoes, Japanese cars, Mexican beer, Costa Rican coffee). When we add up the final purchases of households, businesses, and government agencies, we *overcount* U.S. production because we include goods and services produced abroad. But these are *not* part of U.S. output. To correct for this overcount, we deduct all U.S. *imports* during the year, leaving us with just the output produced in the United States. In 2005, these imports amounted to $2,019 billion, an amount equal to about 16 percent of our GDP.

Let's recap: To obtain an accurate measure of GDP, we must include U.S. production that is purchased by foreigners: total exports. But to correct for including goods produced abroad, we must subtract Americans' purchases of goods produced outside of the United States: total imports. In practice, we take both of these steps together by adding **net exports (NX)**, which are total exports minus total imports.

**Net exports (NX)** Total exports minus total imports.

*To properly account for output sold to, and bought from, foreigners, we must include net exports—the difference between exports and imports—as part of expenditure in GDP.*

In 2005, when total exports were $1,303 billion and total imports were $2,019 billion, net exports (as you can see in Table 2) were $1,303 − $2,019 = −$716 billion. The negative number indicates that the imports we're subtracting from GDP are greater than the exports we're adding.

## OTHER APPROACHES TO GDP

In addition to the expenditure approach, in which we calculate GDP as $C + I + G + NX$, there are other ways of measuring GDP. You may be wondering: Why bother? Why not just use one method—whichever is best—and stick to it?

Actually, there are two good reasons for measuring GDP in different ways. The first is practical. Each method of measuring GDP is subject to measurement errors. By calculating total output in several different ways and then trying to resolve the differences, the BEA gets a more accurate measure than would be possible with one method alone.

The second reason is that the different ways of measuring total output give us different insights into the structure of our economy. Let's take a look at two more ways of measuring—and thinking about—GDP.

### The Value-Added Approach

In the expenditure approach, we record goods and services only when they are sold to their final users—at the end of the production process. But we can also measure GDP by adding up each *firm's* contribution to the product *as it is produced*.

A firm's contribution to a product is called its *value added*. More formally,

**Value added** The revenue a firm receives minus the cost of the intermediate goods it buys.

> *a firm's **value added** is the revenue it receives for its output, minus the cost of all the intermediate goods that it buys.*

Look back at Figure 1, which traces the production of a ream of notebook paper. The paper mill, for example, buys $1.00 worth of wood chips (an intermediate good) from the lumber company. It turns wood chips into raw paper, which it sells for $1.50. The value added by the paper mill is $1.50 − $1.00 = $0.50. Similarly, the office supplies maker buys $1.50 worth of paper (an intermediate good) from the paper mill and sells it for $2.25. Its value added is $2.25 − $1.50 = $0.75. If we total the value added by each firm, we should get the final value of the notebook paper, as shown in Table 3. (Notice that we assume the first producer in this process—the lumber company—uses no intermediate goods.)

The total value added is $1.00 + $0.50 + $0.75 + $1.25 + $1.50 = $5.00, which is equal to the final sales price of the ream of paper. For any good or service, it will always be the case that the sum of the values added by all firms equals the final sales price. This leads to our second method of measuring GDP:

**Value-added approach** Measuring GDP by summing the values added by all firms in the economy.

> *In the **value-added approach**, GDP is the sum of the values added by all firms in the economy.*

### The Factor Payments Approach

If a bakery sells $200,000 worth of bread during the year and buys $25,000 in intermediate goods (flour, eggs, yeast), then its value added is $200,000 − $25,000 = $175,000. This is also the sum that will be *left over* from its revenue after the bakery pays for its intermediate goods.

| TABLE 3 | | | |
|---|---|---|---|
| **Value Added at Different Stages of Production** | | | |
| **Firm** | **Cost of Intermediate Goods** | **Revenue** | **Value Added** |
| Lumber Company | $  0 | $1.00 | $1.00 |
| Paper Mill | $1.00 | $1.50 | $0.50 |
| Office Supplies Manufacturer | $1.50 | $2.25 | $0.75 |
| Wholesaler | $2.25 | $3.50 | $1.25 |
| Retailer | $3.50 | $5.00 | $1.50 |
| | | | Total: $5.00 |

Where does this $175,000 go? Since we've already deducted the payment for intermediate goods, the rest must go to pay for the *resources* used by the bakery during the year: the land, labor, capital, and entrepreneurship that it used to add value to its intermediate goods.

Payments to owners of resources are called **factor payments,** because resources are also called the factors of production. Owners of capital (such as those who lend funds to the firm so that *it* can buy its buildings and machinery) receive *interest payments.* Owners of land and natural resources receive *rent.* And those who provide labor to the firm receive *wages and salaries.*

**Factor payments** Payments to the owners of resources that are used in production.

Finally, there is one additional resource used by the firm: *entrepreneurship.* In every capitalist economy, the entrepreneurs are those who visualize society's needs, mobilize and coordinate the other resources so that production can take place, and gamble that the enterprise will succeed. The people who provide this entrepreneurship (often the owners of the firms) receive a fourth type of factor payment: *profit.*

Now let's go back to our bakery, which received $200,000 in revenue during the year. We've seen that $25,000 of this went to pay for intermediate goods, leaving $175,000 in value added earned by the factors of production. Let's suppose that $110,000 went to pay the wages of the bakery's employees, $10,000 was paid out as interest on loans, and $15,000 was paid in rent for the land under the bakery. That leaves $175,000 − $110,000 − $10,000 − $15,000 = $40,000. This last sum—since it doesn't go to anyone else—goes to the owners of the bakery. It, too, is a factor payment—profit—for the entrepreneurship they provide. Thus, when all of the factor payments, including profit, are added together, the total will be $110,000 + $10,000 + $15,000 + $40,000 = $175,000—precisely equal to the value added at the bakery. More generally,

> *in any year, the value added by a firm is equal to the total factor payments made by that firm.*

Earlier, we learned that GDP equals the sum of all firms' value added; now we've learned that each firm's value added is equal to its factor payments. Thus, GDP must equal the total factor payments made by all firms in the economy. Since all of these factor payments are received by households in the form of wages and salaries, rent, interest, or profit, we have our *third* method of measuring GDP:

> *In the **factor payments approach,** GDP is measured by adding up all of the income—wages and salaries, rent, interest, and profit—earned by all households in the economy.*[2]

**Factor payments approach** Measuring GDP by summing the factor payments earned by all households in the economy.

At first glance, the factor payments approach seems the same as the value-added approach. Each firm's value added is also its factor payments. But the difference is in the way the numbers are added up. In the value-added approach, we go firm by firm and add each one's value added. In the factor payments approach, we go household by household and add up the various types of factor payments earned by each one. Then we get subtotals for each type of factor payment—total wages and

---

[2] Actually, this is just an approximation. Before a firm pays its factors of production, it first deducts a small amount for depreciation of its plant and equipment, and another small amount for the sales taxes it must pay to the government. Thus, GDP and total factor payments are slightly different. We ignore this difference in the text.

salaries earned by all households, total interest, total rent, and total profit. Finally, we add these subtotals together to get total factor payments.

As stated earlier, having alternative methods to get GDP helps deal with measurement errors. But the factor payments approach, in particular, also gives us a key insight about the macroeconomy. On the one hand, total factor payments are just another way of measuring GDP. On the other hand, total factor payments are equal to total household income. Therefore,

> *the total output of the economy (GDP) is equal to the total income earned in the economy.*

This simple idea—output equals income—follows directly from the factor payments approach to GDP. It explains why macroeconomists use the terms *output* and *income* interchangeably: They are one and the same. If output rises, income rises by the same amount; if output falls, income falls by an equal amount. We'll be using this very important insight in several chapters to come.

## MEASURING GDP: A SUMMARY

You've now learned three different ways to calculate GDP:

*Expenditure Approach*: GDP = C + I + G + NX

*Value-Added Approach*: GDP = Sum of value added by all firms

*Factor Payments Approach*: GDP = Sum of factor payments earned by all households

= Wages and salaries + interest

+ rent + profit

= Total household income

We will use these three approaches to GDP again and again as we study what makes the economy tick. But for now, make sure you understand why each one of them should, in theory, give us the same number for GDP.

## REAL VERSUS NOMINAL GDP

Since GDP is measured in dollars, we have a serious problem when we want to track the change in output over time. The problem is that the value of the dollar—its purchasing power—is itself changing. As prices have risen over the years, the value of the dollar has steadily fallen. Trying to keep track of GDP using dollars in different years is like trying to keep track of a child's height using a ruler whose length changes each year. If we find that the child is three rulers tall in one year and four rulers tall in the next, we cannot know how much the child has grown, if at all, until we adjust for the effects of a changing ruler. The same is true for GDP and for any other economic variable measured in dollars: We usually need to adjust our measurements to reflect changes in the value of the dollar.

*When a variable is measured in dollars, with no adjustment for the dollar's changing value, it is called a **nominal variable**. When a variable is adjusted for the dollar's changing value, it is called a **real variable**.*

**Nominal variable** A variable measured without adjustment for the dollar's changing value.

**Real variable** A variable adjusted for changes in the dollar's value.

Most government statistics are reported in both nominal and real terms, but economists focus almost exclusively on real variables. This is because changes in nominal variables don't really tell us much. For example, from the second to the third quarter of 2001 (not shown in earlier tables), nominal GDP increased from $10,050 billion to $10,098 billion, an increase of one-half of 1 percent. But production as measured by *real GDP* actually *decreased* over that period. The increase in nominal GDP was due entirely to a rise in prices. Real GDP corrects for this rise in prices by recognizing that the dollar's value (its purchasing power) declined, and by measuring production in adjusted dollars.

The distinction between nominal and real values is crucial in macroeconomics. The public, the media, and sometimes even government officials have been confused by a failure to make this distinction. Whenever we want to track significant changes in key macroeconomic variables—such as the average wage rate, wealth, income, and GDP or any of its components—we always use *real* variables.

*When comparing variables measured in dollars over time, it is important to translate nominal values (which are measured in current dollars) to real values (which adjust for the dollar's changing value).*

In the next chapter, you'll learn how economists translate some important nominal variables into real variables.

## How GDP Is Used

We've come a long way since 1931. In that year—as the United States plummeted into the worst depression in its history—Congress summoned economists from government agencies, from academia, and from the private sector to testify about the state of the economy. They were asked the most basic questions: How much output was the nation producing, and how much had production fallen since 1929? How much income were Americans earning, and how much were they spending? How much profit were businesses earning, and what were they doing with their profits? To the surprise of the members of Congress, no one could answer any of these questions, because *no one was keeping track of our national income and output!* The most recent measurement, which was rather incomplete, had been made in 1929.

Thus began the U.S. system of national income accounts, a system whose value was instantly recognized around the world and rapidly copied by other countries. Today, the government's reports on GDP are used to steer the economy over both the short run and the long run.

In the short run, sudden changes in real GDP can alert us to the onset of a recession or a too-rapid expansion that can overheat the economy. Many (but not all) economists believe that, if alerted in time, policies can be designed to help keep the economy on a more balanced course.

GDP is also used to measure the long-run growth rate of the economy's output. Indeed, we typically define the average *standard of living* as *output per capita*: real GDP divided by the population. In order for output per capita to rise, real GDP must grow faster than the population. Since the U.S. population tends to grow by

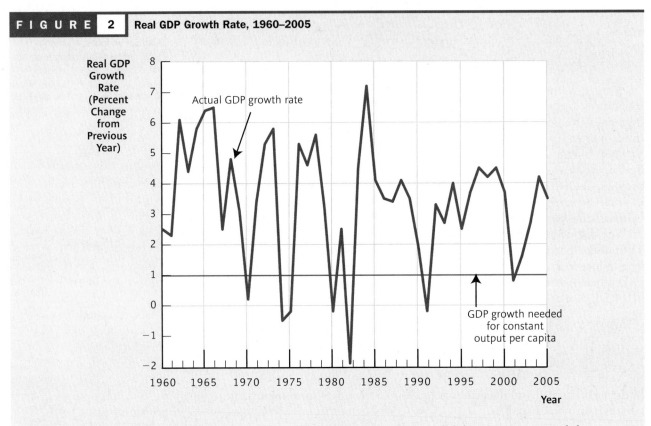

**FIGURE** **2** **Real GDP Growth Rate, 1960–2005**

Although the growth rate of real GDP has fluctuated over time, it has on average exceeded the 1 percent rate needed to maintain output per capita.

Source: Bureau of Economic Analysis, *National Economic Accounts*, Table 1.1.1.

about 1 percent per year, a real GDP growth rate of 1 percent per year is needed just to *maintain* our output per capita; higher growth rates are needed to increase it.

Look at Figure 2, which shows the annual percentage change in real GDP from 1960 through 2005. The lower horizontal line indicates the 1 percent growth needed to just maintain output per capita. You can see that, on average, real GDP has grown by more than this. This tells us that output per capita has steadily increased over time.

But growth in real GDP is also important for another reason: to ensure that the economy generates sufficient new *jobs* for a workforce that is not only growing in number, but also becoming more productive. Each year, the average worker is capable of producing more output, due to advances in technology, increases in the capital stock, and the greater skills of workers themselves. But if each worker can produce more output, then output must increase even *faster* than the population to create enough jobs for everyone who wants to work. If not, the unemployment rate will rise. For example, suppose that output per worker doubled over some period of time. If *total* output doubled as well, the number of *jobs* would remain constant. But unemployment would rise because the workforce would be growing, while the number of jobs would not.

Over the period shown in Figure 2, real GDP needed to grow by an average of about 3.3 percent per year to prevent the unemployment rate from rising. And although growth fluctuated widely, the average annual growth rate of the period was, in fact, about 3.3 percent. Most economists are confident that, over the long run, real GDP will rise fast enough to generate the jobs needed by a growing and more productive workforce, just as it has in the past. Later, you'll learn the reasons for this confidence.

To sum up: We use GDP to guide the economy in two ways. In the short run, it alerts us to recessions and give us a chance to stabilize the economy. And over long periods it tells us whether our economy is growing fast enough to raise output per capita and our standard of living, and fast enough to generate sufficient jobs for a growing population.

## PROBLEMS WITH GDP

You have seen that GDP is an extremely useful concept. But the measurement of GDP is plagued by some serious problems.

### Quality Changes

Suppose a new ballpoint pen comes out that lasts four times as long as previous versions. What *should* happen to GDP? Ideally, each new pen should count the same as four old pens, since one new pen offers the same *writing services* as four old ones. But the analysts at the Bureau of Economic Analysis would most likely treat this new pen the same as an old pen and record an increase in GDP only if the total number of pens increased. Why? Because the BEA has a limited budget. While it does include the impact of quality changes for many goods and services (such as automobiles and computers), the BEA simply does not have the resources to estimate quality changes for millions of different goods and services. These include many consumer goods (such as razor blades that shave closer and last longer), medical services (increased surgery success rates and shorter recovery periods), and retail services (faster checkout times due to optical scanners). Ignoring these quality improvements causes GDP to understate the true growth in output from year to year.

### The Underground Economy

Some production is hidden from government authorities, either because it is illegal (drugs, prostitution, most gambling) or because those engaged in it are avoiding taxes. Production in these hidden markets, which comprise the *underground economy*, cannot be measured accurately, so the BEA must estimate it. Many economists believe that the BEA's estimates are too low. As a result, GDP may understate total output. However, because the *relative* importance of the underground economy does not change rapidly, the BEA's estimates of *changes* in GDP from year to year should not be seriously affected.

### Nonmarket Production

With a few exceptions, GDP does not include **nonmarket production:** goods and services that are produced but not sold in the marketplace. All of the housecleaning, typing, sewing, lawn mowing, and child rearing that people do themselves, rather than hiring someone else, are excluded from GDP. Whenever a nonmarket transaction (say, cleaning your apartment) becomes a market transaction (hiring a housecleaner to do it for you), GDP will rise, even though total production (cleaning one apartment) has remained the same.

**Nonmarket production** Goods and services that are produced but not sold in a market.

Over the last half-century, much production has shifted away from the home and to the market. Parenting, which was not counted in past years' GDP, has become day care, which *does* count—currently contributing several billion dollars annually to GDP. Similarly, home-cooked food has been replaced by takeout, talking to a friend has been replaced by therapy, and the neighbor who watches your house while you're away has been replaced by a store-bought alarm system or an increase in police protection. In all of these cases, real GDP increases, even though production has not. This can exaggerate the growth in GDP over long periods of time.

### Other Aspects of Economic Well-Being

Earlier we mentioned that output per capita (real GDP divided by the population) is often referred to as a country's standard of living. And for good reason: Our economic well-being depends to a large extent on the quantity of goods and services available per person. Food, clothing, transportation, and health care are all examples of things that contribute to our economic satisfaction, and all are included in our measure of GDP.

But output per capita is an imperfect measure of living standards. First, many things that contribute to our economic welfare are not captured by GDP at all: leisure time, an equitable distribution of income, a sense of community, and more. GDP also ignores economic "bads"—crime, pollution, traffic congestion, and more—which make us worse off.

Finally, GDP does not distinguish between production that makes us better off and production that only prevents us from becoming worse off. For example, every year hundreds of thousands of automobile accidents result in billions of dollars spent on car repair, medical expenses, insurance, and legal services—production that counts in GDP as much as any other production. But we'd be better off if the same total output of goods and services was devoted to doing things that we enjoy, rather than to coping with things that harm us.

## USING GDP PROPERLY

The previous discussion suggests that, for certain purposes, GDP must be used with caution. One example is interpreting changes in GDP growth over the long run. Suppose, for example, that over the next 10 or 15 years, growth in real GDP per capita slows down a bit. It might mean that something is going wrong, and we should change course. But it *could* be partly a measurement problem: the underground economy or unrecorded quality changes may be becoming more important. Or it could be a willing tradeoff: less output growth in exchange for more leisure time. Similarly, if GDP growth gradually accelerates, it could mean faster growth in our economic welfare. But some of the improvement might come from economic activity shifting out of the home and into the market even more rapidly than in the past.

Caution is also required for some comparisons of economic well-being across countries. Everyone agrees that economic welfare is substantially greater in the United States than in Pakistan or Cambodia. Output per capita—which is almost 20 times greater in the United States—captures most of this difference.

But what about the United States versus, say, Germany? Output per capita is about 40 percent greater in the United States. But a greater fraction of Americans work, and the average American worker spends about 30 percent more hours on the job each year than the average German. So Americans have more goods, but Germans have more leisure. Who is economically better off? And by how much?

There is no objective answer, but using output per capita as the sole criterion would be misleading.

GDP works very well, however, as a guide to the short-run performance of the economy. Look back at the list of problems with GDP. The distortion in GDP measurement caused by each problem is likely to remain fairly constant from quarter to quarter. If GDP suddenly drops, it is extremely unlikely that the underground economy has suddenly become more important, or that there has been a sudden shift from market to nonmarket activities, or that we are suddenly missing more quality changes than usual. Rather, we can be reasonably certain that output and economic activity are slowing down.

> *Short-term changes in real GDP are fairly accurate reflections of the state of the economy. A significant quarter-to-quarter change in real GDP indicates a change in actual production, rather than a measurement problem.*

This is why policy makers, businesspeople, and the media pay such close attention to GDP as a guide to the economy from quarter to quarter.

# EMPLOYMENT AND UNEMPLOYMENT

When you think of unemployment, you may have an image in your mind that goes something like this: As the economy slides into recession, an anxious employee is called into an office and handed a pink slip by a grim-faced manager. "Sorry," the manager says, "I wish there were some other way. . . ." The worker spends the next few months checking the classified ads, pounding the pavement, and sending out résumés in a desperate search for work. And perhaps, after months of trying, the laid-off worker gives up, spending days at the neighborhood bar, drinking away the shame and frustration, and sinking lower and lower into despair and inertia.

For some people, joblessness begins and ends very much like this—a human tragedy, and a needless one. On one side, we have people who want to work and support themselves by producing something; on the other side is the rest of society, which could certainly use more goods and services. Yet somehow, the system isn't working, and the jobless cannot find work. The result is often hardship for the unemployed and their families, and a loss to society in general.

But this is just one face of unemployment, and there are others. Some instances of unemployment, for example, have little to do with macroeconomic conditions. And frequently, unemployment causes a lot less suffering than in our grim story.

## TYPES OF UNEMPLOYMENT

In the United States, people are considered unemployed if they are: (1) not working and (2) actively seeking a job. But unemployment can arise for a variety of reasons, each with its own policy implications. This is why economists have found it useful to classify unemployment into four different categories, each arising from a different cause and each having different consequences.

### Frictional Unemployment

Short-term joblessness experienced by people who are between jobs or who are entering the labor market for the first time or after an absence is called **frictional**

**Frictional unemployment**
Joblessness experienced by people who are between jobs or who are just entering or reentering the labor market.

**unemployment**. In the real world, it takes time to find a job—time to prepare your résumé, to decide where to send it, to wait for responses, and then to investigate job offers so you can make a wise choice. It also takes time for different employers to consider your skills and qualifications and to decide whether you are right for their firms. If you are not working during that time, you will be unemployed: searching for work but not working.

Because frictional unemployment is, by definition, short term, it causes little hardship to those affected by it. In most cases, people have enough savings to support themselves through a short spell of joblessness, or else they can borrow on their credit cards or from friends or family to tide them over. Moreover, this kind of unemployment has important benefits: By spending time searching rather than jumping at the first opening that comes their way, people find jobs for which they are better suited and in which they will ultimately be more productive. As a result, workers earn higher incomes, firms have more productive employees, and society has more goods and services.

### Seasonal Unemployment

**Seasonal unemployment**
Joblessness related to changes in weather, tourist patterns, or other seasonal factors.

Joblessness related to changes in weather, tourist patterns, or other seasonal factors is called **seasonal unemployment**. For example, most ski instructors lose their jobs every April or May, and many construction workers are laid off each winter.

Seasonal unemployment, like frictional unemployment, is rather benign: It is short term and, because it is entirely predictable, workers are often compensated in advance for the unemployment they experience in the off-season. Construction workers, for example, are paid higher-than-average hourly wages, in part to compensate them for their high probability of joblessness in the winter.

However, seasonal unemployment complicates the interpretation of unemployment data. Seasonal factors push the unemployment rate up in certain months of the year and pull it down in others, even when overall conditions in the economy remain unchanged. For example, each June, unemployment rises as millions of high school and college students—who do not want to work during the school year—begin looking for summer jobs. If the government reported the actual rise in unemployment in June, it would *seem* as if labor market conditions were deteriorating. In fact, the rise is just a predictable and temporary seasonal change. To prevent any misunderstandings, the government usually reports the *seasonally adjusted* rate of unemployment, a rate that reflects only those changes beyond normal for the month. For example, if the unemployment rate in June is typically one percentage point higher than during the rest of the year, then the seasonally adjusted rate for June will be the actual rate minus one percentage point.

### Structural Unemployment

Sometimes, there are jobs available and workers who would be delighted to have them, but job seekers and employers are mismatched in some way. For example, in 2005, there were plenty of job openings for business professors; for nurses and nurse practitioners; for translators of strategic languages like Arabic, Persian, and Urdu; and in many other professions. Many of the unemployed, however, had been laid off from the airline, automobile, and textile industries and did not have the skills and training to work where the jobs were going begging. This is a *skill* mismatch.

The mismatch can also be *geographic,* as when construction jobs go begging in Northern California, Oregon, and Washington, but unemployed construction workers live in other states.

Unemployment that results from these kinds of mismatches is called **structural unemployment,** because it arises from *structural change* in the economy: when old, dying industries are replaced with new ones that require different skills and are located in different areas of the country. Structural unemployment is generally a stubborn, *long-term* problem, often lasting several years or more. Why? Because it can take considerable time for the structurally unemployed to find jobs—time to relocate to another part of the country or time to acquire new skills. To make matters worse, the structurally unemployed—who could benefit from financial assistance for job training or relocation—usually cannot get loans because they don't have jobs.

In recent decades, structural unemployment has been a much bigger problem in other countries, especially in Europe, than it is in the United States. Table 4 shows average unemployment rates in the United States and several European countries from 1995 to 2005 as well as in early 2006. Unemployment rates were consistently higher in continental Europe than in the United States during this decade and, in most of these countries, were still high in early 2006. And the unemployed remain jobless longer in Europe (where more than a third of all the unemployed have been so for more than a year) than in the United States (where only one in ten has been jobless for more than a year).

Within the United States, some areas have higher structural unemployment than others. For example, in early 2006 when the U.S. unemployment rate was 4.7 percent, the rate in Ohio was 5.5 percent; in South Carolina, 6.6 percent; and in Michigan, 7.2 percent.

The types of unemployment we've considered so far—frictional, structural, and seasonal—arise largely from *microeconomic* causes; that is, they are attributable to changes in specific industries and specific labor markets, rather than to the overall level of production in the country. This kind of unemployment cannot be entirely eliminated, as people will always spend some time searching for new jobs, there will always be seasonal industries in the economy, and structural changes will, from time to time, require workers to move to new locations or gain new job skills. Some amount of microeconomic unemployment is a sign of a dynamic economy. It allows

**Structural unemployment**
Joblessness arising from mismatches between workers' skills and employers' requirements or between workers' locations and employers' locations.

| T A B L E | 4 |

**Average Unemployment Rates in Several Countries, 1995–2005 and early 2006**

| Country | Average Unemployment Rate, 1995–2005 | Unemployment Rate, early 2006 |
|---------|--------------------------------------|-------------------------------|
| France | 10.2 % | 9.3 % |
| Italy | 9.9 % | 7.8 % |
| Canada | 7.2 % | 5.6 % |
| United Kingdom | 6.2 % | 5.2 % |
| Germany | 8.9 % | 8.8 % |
| Sweden | 7.2 % | 6.3 % |
| United States | 5.2 % | 4.7 % |

*Source*: "Comparative Unemployment Rates in Nine Countries, 1995–2006," available online at Bureau of Labor Statistics, Foreign Labor Statistics page (*www.bls.gov/fls/home.htm*). European rates have been adjusted by the BLS for comparability to U.S. rates. Ten-year averages were calculated by authors from the BLS data. Early 2006 unemployment rates are for March 2006 except for Italy (4th quarter, 2005), the United Kingdom (February 2006), and Sweden (1st quarter, 2005).

workers to sort themselves into the best possible jobs, enables us to enjoy seasonal goods and services like winter skiing and summers at the beach, and permits the economy to go through structural changes when needed.

But frictional, structural, and seasonal unemployment rates are not fixed in stone, and government policy may be able to influence them. In the United States, many economists believe that we can continue to enjoy the benefits of a fast-changing and flexible economy with a lower unemployment rate. To achieve this goal, they advocate programs to help match the unemployed with employers and to help the jobless relocate and learn new skills.

In Europe, by contrast, most economists believe that government labor and regulatory policies have been a *cause* of the structural unemployment problem. For example, government regulations make it costly or impossible for many European firms to lay off workers once they are hired. That encourages firms to retain any *currently* employed workers. But it also discourages new hiring, because firms regard any newly hired worker as a permanent obligation, even if future production turns down and the new worker is no longer needed.

France, in particular, has been plagued by this problem. The unemployment rate among the young (under age 26) is 23 percent, and rises to around 40 percent in the mostly minority suburbs around Paris. In early 2006, the French government announced a new policy: For the first two years at a new job, young workers could be fired by their employers without the usual costly and time-consuming bureaucratic procedures. But when the proposal led to street riots in Paris, the government backed down.

European unemployment benefits may also play a role in high structural unemployment. Benefits in Europe are more generous than in the United States, and the benefits are given for longer durations with a greater fraction of the potential labor force eligible to receive them. While this certainly helps the unemployed deal with the hardship of job loss, it also means that European workers have less incentive to seek new work once they lose a job.

Note, however, that in both Europe and the United States, the proposed solutions for high seasonal, frictional, or structural unemployment are changes in labor or regulatory policies, rather than changes in macroeconomic policy.

Our fourth and last type of unemployment, however, has an entirely *macroeconomic* cause and requires macroeconomic solutions.

### Cyclical Unemployment

When the economy goes into a recession and total output falls, the unemployment rate rises. Many previously employed workers lose their jobs and have difficulty finding new ones. At the same time, there are fewer openings, so new entrants to the labor force must spend more than the usual time searching before they are hired. This type of unemployment—because it is caused by the business cycle—is called **cyclical unemployment.**

**Cyclical unemployment**
Joblessness arising from changes in production over the business cycle.

Look at Figure 3, which shows the unemployment rate in the United States for each quarter from 1960 to mid-2006, and notice the rises that occurred during periods of recession (shaded). For example, in the recessions of the early 1980s, the unemployment rate rose from about 6 percent to more than 10 percent. And during the more recent recession from March to November of 2001, the unemployment rate rose from 4.2 percent to 5.6 percent. These were rises in cyclical unemployment.

Since it arises from conditions in the overall economy, cyclical unemployment is a problem for *macroeconomic* policy. This is why macroeconomists focus almost

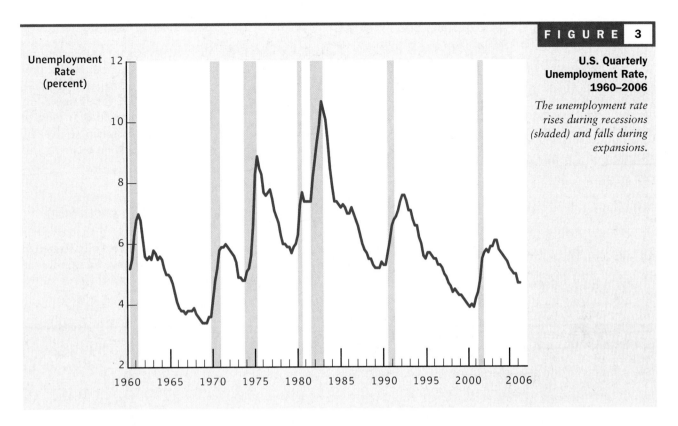

**FIGURE 3**

**U.S. Quarterly Unemployment Rate, 1960–2006**

*The unemployment rate rises during recessions (shaded) and falls during expansions.*

exclusively on cyclical unemployment, rather than the other types of joblessness. Reflecting this emphasis, macroeconomists say we have reached **full employment** when *cyclical unemployment is reduced to zero,* even though substantial amounts of frictional, seasonal, and structural unemployment may remain:

> *In macroeconomics, full employment means zero* cyclical *unemployment. But the overall unemployment rate at full employment is greater than zero because there are still positive levels of frictional, seasonal, and structural unemployment.*

How do we tell how much of our unemployment is cyclical? Many economists believe that today, normal amounts of frictional, seasonal, and structural unemployment account for an unemployment rate of between 4.5 and 5.0 percent in the United States. Therefore, any unemployment beyond this is considered cyclical unemployment. For example, when the actual unemployment rate was 5.6 percent in November 2001, we would say that 0.6 to 1.1 percent of the labor force was cyclically unemployed.

**Full employment** A situation in which there is no cyclical unemployment.

## THE COSTS OF UNEMPLOYMENT

Why are we so concerned about achieving a low rate of unemployment? What are the *costs* of unemployment to our society? We can identify two different types of costs: economic costs (those that can be readily measured in dollar terms) and broader costs (which are difficult to measure in dollars, but still affect us in important ways).

### Economic Costs

The chief economic cost of unemployment is the *opportunity cost* of lost output: the goods and services the jobless *would* produce if they were working but do not produce because they cannot find work. This cost is borne by our society in general, although the burden may fall more on one group than another. If, for example, the unemployed were simply left to fend for themselves, then *they* would bear most of the cost. In fact, the unemployed are often given government assistance, so that the costs are spread somewhat among citizens in general. But there is no escaping this central fact:

> *When there is cyclical unemployment, the nation produces less output, and therefore some group or groups within society must consume less output.*

**Potential output** The level of output the economy could produce if operating at full employment.

One way of viewing the economic cost of cyclical unemployment is illustrated in Figure 4. The green line shows real GDP over time, while the orange line shows the path of our **potential output**—the output we *could* have produced if the economy were operating at full employment.

---

**F I G U R E   4   Actual and Potential Real GDP, 1960–2005**

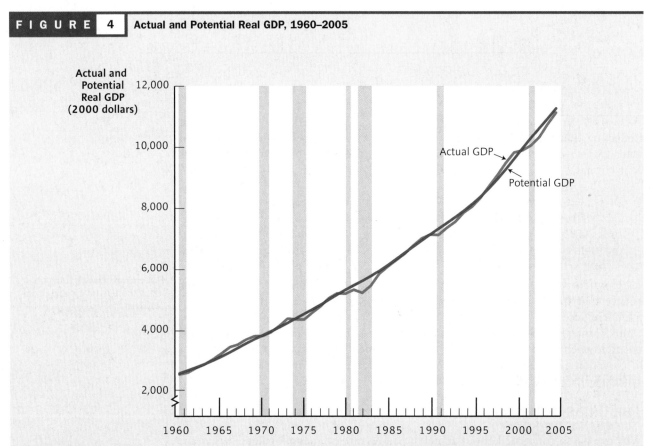

*Measured in 2000 dollars.*

*Sources*: Real GDP from Bureau of Economic Analysis, "National Economic Accounts," Table 1.1.6 (*www.bea.gov*); Potential Real GDP from Congressional Budget Office, "Data Underlying Table 2-2: Key Assumptions in CBO's Projection of Potential Output" (By calendar year), The Budget and Economic Outlook: Fiscal Years 2006–2016, January 2006 (*www.cbo.gov*).

Notice that actual output is sometimes *above* potential output. At these times, unemployment is *below* the full-employment rate. For example, during the expansion in the late 1960s, cyclical unemployment was eliminated, and the sum of frictional, seasonal, and structural unemployment dropped below 4.5 percent, its normal level for those years. At other times, real GDP is *below* potential output, most often during and following a recession. At these times, unemployment rises above the full-employment rate. During the 2001 recession, the unemployment rate rose from 4.2 percent to 5.6 percent, then hovered near or above 6 percent for the next two years.

In the figure, you can see that we have spent more of the last 40 years operating *below* our potential than above it. That is, the cyclical ups and downs of the economy have, on balance, led to lower living standards than we would have had if the economy had always operated just at potential output.

### Broader Costs

There are also costs of unemployment that go beyond lost output. Unemployment—especially when it lasts for many months or years—can have serious psychological and physical effects. Some studies have found that increases in unemployment cause noticeable rises in the number of heart attack deaths, suicides, and admissions to state prisons and psychiatric hospitals. The jobless are more likely to suffer a variety of health problems, including high blood pressure, heart disorders, troubled sleep, and back pain. There may be other problems—such as domestic violence, depression, and alcoholism—that are more difficult to document. And, tragically, most of those who lose their job and remain unemployed for long periods also lose their health insurance, increasing the likelihood that these problems will have serious consequences.

Unemployment also causes setbacks in achieving important social goals. For example, most of us want a fair and just society where all people have an equal chance to better themselves. But our citizens do not bear the burden of unemployment equally. In a recession, we do not all suffer a reduction in our work hours; instead, some people are laid off entirely, while others continue to work roughly the same hours.

Moreover, the burden of unemployment is not shared equally among different groups in the population, but tends to fall most heavily on minorities, especially minority youth. As a rough rule of thumb, the unemployment rate for blacks is twice that for whites; and the rate for *teenage* blacks is triple the rate for blacks overall. Table 5 shows that the unemployment rates for May 2006 are roughly consistent with this general experience. Notice the extremely high unemployment rate for black teenagers: 25 percent. This contributes to a vicious cycle of poverty and discrimination: When minority youths are deprived of that all-important first job, they remain at a disadvantage in the labor market for years to come.

## HOW UNEMPLOYMENT IS MEASURED

In May 2006, about 155 million Americans were not employed, according to official government statistics. Were all of these people

| | TABLE 5 |
|---|---|

**Unemployment Rates for Various Groups, May 2006**

| Group | Unemployment Rate |
|---|---|
| Whites | 4.1% |
| Hispanics | 5.0% |
| Blacks | 8.9% |
| White Teenagers | 12.7% |
| Black Teenagers | 25.0% |

*Source: The Employment Situation: May 2006,* Bureau of Labor Statistics (seasonally adjusted data).

unemployed? Absolutely not. In theory, the unemployed are those who are *willing and able* to work but do not have jobs. Most of the 155 million nonworking Americans were either *unable* or *unwilling* to work. For example, the very old, the very young, and the very ill were unable to work, as were those serving prison terms. Others were able to work, but preferred not to, including millions of college students, homemakers, and retired people. Still others were in the military and are counted in the population, but not counted when calculating civilian employment statistics.

But how, in practice, can we determine who is willing and able? This is a thorny problem, and there is no perfect solution to it. In the United States, we determine whether a person is willing and able to work by his or her *behavior*. More specifically, to be counted as unemployed, you must have recently *searched* for work. But how can we tell who has, and who has not, recently searched for work?

### The Census Bureau's Household Survey

Every month, thousands of interviewers from the United States Census Bureau— acting on behalf of the U.S. Bureau of Labor Statistics—conduct a survey of 60,000 households across America. This sample of households is carefully selected to give information about the entire population. Household members who are under 16, in the military, or currently residing in an institution like a prison or hospital are excluded from the survey. The interviewer will then ask questions about the remaining household members' activities during the *previous week*.

Figure 5 shows roughly how this works. First, the interviewer asks whether the household member has worked one or more hours for pay or profit. If the answer is yes, the person is considered employed; if no, another question is asked: Has she been *temporarily* laid off from a job from which she is waiting to be recalled? A yes means the person is unemployed whether or not the person searched for a new job; a no leads to one more question: Did the person actively *search* for work during the previous four weeks. If yes, the person is unemployed; if no, she is not in the labor force.

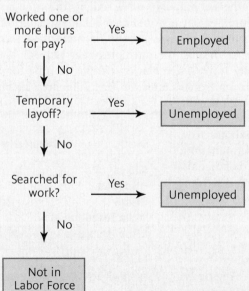

**FIGURE 5**

**How the BLS Measures Employment Status**

*BLS interviewers ask a series of questions to determine whether an individual is employed, unemployed, or not in the labor force.*

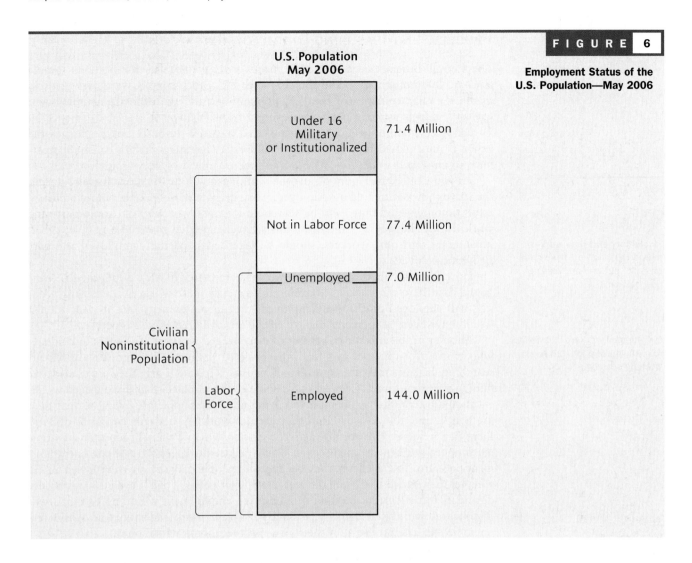

FIGURE 6

Employment Status of the
U.S. Population—May 2006

**U.S. Population
May 2006**

| | |
|---|---|
| Under 16 Military or Institutionalized | 71.4 Million |
| Not in Labor Force | 77.4 Million |
| Unemployed | 7.0 Million |
| Employed | 144.0 Million |

Civilian Noninstitutional Population

Labor Force

Figure 6 illustrates how the BLS, extrapolating from its 60,000-household sample, classified the U.S. population in May 2006. First, note that about 71 million people were ruled out from consideration because they were under 16 years of age, living in institutions, or in the military. The remaining 228 million people made up the civilian, noninstitutional population, and of these, 144.0 million were employed and 7.0 million were unemployed. Adding the employed and unemployed together gives us the **labor force**, equal to 144.0 million + 7.0 million = 151.0 million.

Finally, we come to the official **unemployment rate**, which is defined as the percentage of the labor force that is unemployed:

$$\text{Unemployment rate} = \frac{\text{Unemployed}}{\text{Labor force}} = \frac{\text{Unemployed}}{(\text{Unemployed} + \text{Employed})}$$

Using the numbers in Figure 6, the U.S. unemployment rate in May 2006 was calculated as 7.0/(7.0 + 144.0) = .046 or 4.6 percent. This was the number released to journalists at 8:00 A.M. on the first Friday of June 2006, and the number that made headlines in your local newspaper the next day.

**Labor force** Those people who have a job or who are looking for one.

**Unemployment rate** The fraction of the labor force that is without a job.

## Problems in Measuring Unemployment

The Census Bureau earns very high marks from economists for both its sample size—60,000 households—and the characteristics of its sample, which very closely match the characteristics of the U.S. population. Still, the official unemployment rate suffers from some important measurement problems.

Many economists believe that our official measure seriously underestimates the extent of unemployment in our society. There are two reasons for this belief: the treatment of *involuntary part-time workers* and the treatment of *discouraged workers.*

As you can see in Figure 5, anyone working one hour or more for pay during the survey week is treated as employed. This includes many people who would like a full-time job—and may even be searching for one—but who did some part-time work during the week. Some economists have suggested that these people, called **involuntary part-time workers,** should be regarded as partially employed and partially unemployed.

How many involuntary part-time workers are there? In May 2006, the BLS estimated that there were about 4.0 million. If each of these workers were considered, say, half-employed and half-unemployed, the unemployment rate in that month would have been 6.0 percent, instead of the officially reported 4.6 percent.

Another problem is the treatment of **discouraged workers.** These are individuals who would like to work but feel little hope of finding a job and have given up searching. Because they are not taking active steps to find work, they are considered "not in the labor force" (see Figure 5). Some economists feel that discouraged workers should be counted as unemployed. After all, these people are telling us that they are willing and able to work, but they are not working. It seems wrong to exclude them just because they are not actively seeking work. Others argue that counting discouraged workers as unemployed would reduce the objectivity of our unemployment measure. Talk is cheap, they believe, and people may *say* anything when asked whether they would like a job; the real test is what people *do.* Yet even the staunchest defenders of the current method of measuring employment would agree that *some* discouraged workers are, in fact, willing and able to work and should be considered unemployed. The problem, in their view, is determining which ones.

How many discouraged workers are there? No one knows for sure. The BLS tries to count them, but defining who is genuinely discouraged is yet another thorny problem. Using the BLS's rather strict criteria, there were 323,000 discouraged workers in May 2006. But with a looser, unofficial definition of "discouraged worker"— people who are not working but say they want a job—the count rises to 5.2 million. Including some or all of these people among the unemployed could raise the unemployment rate significantly.

Still, the unemployment rate, as currently measured, tells us something important: the number of people who are *searching* for jobs, but have not yet found them. It is not exactly the same as the percentage of those willing and able to work that is jobless. But if we could obtain a perfect measure of the latter, the unemployment rate, as currently measured, would be highly correlated with it.

Moreover, the unemployment rate tells us something unique about conditions in the macroeconomy. When the unemployment rate is relatively low—so that few people are actively seeking work—a firm that wants to hire more workers may be forced to lure them from other firms, by offering a higher wage rate. This puts upward pressure on wages and can lead to future inflation. A high unemployment rate, by contrast, tells us that firms can more easily expand by hiring those who are

**Involuntary part-time workers** Individuals who would like a full-time job, but who are working only part time.

**Discouraged workers** Individuals who would like a job, but have given up searching for one.

actively seeking work, without having to lure new workers from another firm and without having to offer higher wages. This suggests little inflationary danger. Later in the book, we will discuss the connection between unemployment and inflation more fully.

# USING THE THEORY

© 2005 GETTY IMAGES

## SUDDEN DISASTERS AND GDP

People are sometimes surprised that some horrific national disasters—man-made and natural—have had relatively little impact on U.S. GDP. Such events may cause thousands of deaths, devastate a city or region, disrupt economic activity on a wide scale, and hold the national attention for months. Yet when we look back at the behavior of the nation's real GDP, the effects are almost imperceptible.

For example, look at Figure 7, which shows quarterly GDP from 1998 through early 2006. Two major disasters occurred within this period. The first was the terrorist attack of September 2001, which killed more than 3,000 people, destroyed one of the largest office complexes in the United States, and led to major disruptions of production in lower Manhattan for weeks. If you search for the impact in Figure 7, you may think you've found it in the widening gap between actual and potential real GDP around that time. But look closely: GDP began to flatten in mid-2000, more than a year *before* the attack, due to a slowdown from other causes. Even though the attack no doubt worsened and prolonged that slowdown, a separate impact on production is hardly discernible.

Now consider Hurricanes Katrina and Rita, which hit the Gulf Coast in August and September of 2005. The hurricanes devastated huge areas of Louisiana and Mississippi, destroyed hundreds of thousands of homes, and left most of the city of New Orleans uninhabitable for months. About 250,000 people in the area lost their jobs—many of them for a few months or longer. But once again, the impact on GDP appears to be slight: a barely noticeable slowdown in growth from the third to the fourth quarter of 2005, and then the effect seems to disappear. And if you look for an effect on *yearly* GDP in Figure 4, it is not apparent at all.

Why is GDP so stubbornly unmoved by such cataclysmic events? Disasters such as the terrorist attack of 2001 or the hurricanes of 2005 generally have two types of effects on real GDP. One is the *direct* impact of the event itself. The other is the *indirect* effects that follow as economic decision makers respond to the event. Let's consider each of these types of effects in turn for the hurricanes of 2005.

### DIRECT EFFECTS: DESTRUCTION AND DISRUPTION

Table 6 shows a range of estimates for the physical destruction caused by Hurricanes Katrina and Rita in 2005. The total loss—between $69 billion and $130 billion—included about 287,000 homes destroyed or damaged (about half of them in New Orleans), as well as severe damage to oil and natural gas platforms and pipelines. Even though much of this property destruction was insured, the insurance merely redistributes the financial burden; it does not affect the total value of the loss.

**Quarterly GDP During Two Recent Disasters**

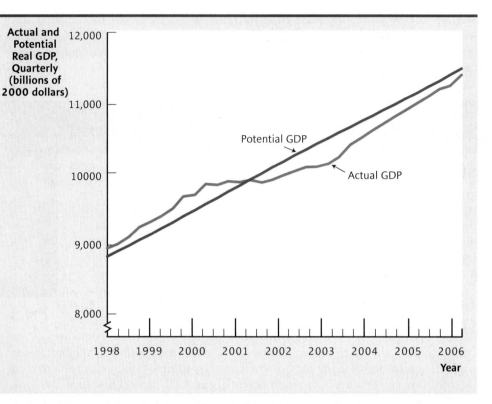

**FIGURE** 7

**TABLE** 6

**Property Destruction from Hurricanes Katrina and Rita, 2005**

| Type of Property | Estimated Loss |
|---|---|
| Residential housing | $17 billion to $33 billion |
| Consumer durables (autos, furniture, appliances) | $5 billion to $9 billion |
| Energy infrastructure | $18 billion to $31 billion |
| Nonenergy business property | $16 billion to $32 billion |
| Public infrastructure | $13 billion to $25 billion |
| **Total** | **$69 billion to $130 billion** |

*Source:* Based on Douglas Holtz-Eakin, "The Macroeconomic and Budgetary Effects of Hurricanes Katrina and Rita," *CBO Testimony before the Committee on the Budget, U.S. House of Representatives*, October 6, 2005.

How does all this destruction affect GDP? Not nearly as much as you might think. A disaster destroys part of the nation's *capital stock*. But remember that GDP does *not* measure the resources at our disposal, but rather the production we get *from* those resources.[3] The impact on GDP is therefore limited to the loss of output that the destroyed resources would otherwise have enabled us to produce. Destroyed

---

[3] Destruction of capital does, however, directly affect *net national product*, which is defined as GDP minus depreciation of the capital stock during the period. Destruction of capital from a disaster is considered depreciation, and is therefore deducted when calculating net national product.

factory buildings, oil rigs, and office buildings mean less production of manufactured goods, energy, and services. And every destroyed home is one that is no longer producing housing services (which are also part of GDP). This is how physical destruction has a direct impact on GDP.

How much *production* did we lose from the loss of these resources? Table 7 shows how the U.S. Congressional Budget Office (CBO) answered this question. The first three rows of numbers refer to the direct impact of the destruction and disruption of economic activity from the hurricanes. Notice that the CBO uses the value-added approach to estimate this impact. That is, the effects on GDP are categorized by the sector that produces it—energy, agricultural, or housing services—rather than by the final user that buys the production. This is for practical reasons. When productive capital is destroyed, it is easier to identify the decrease in production at its source. For example, after the destruction of energy infrastructure, it is relatively easy to estimate the total decrease in energy production (value added by the oil and gas industries). It would be much more difficult to determine which final users would have bought goods and services produced with this energy (consumers, businesses, government, or foreigners).

If you subtotal the decrease in value added by these three sectors for the second half of 2005, you'll find that the direct impact of the hurricanes was a decrease in production of between $20 billion and $32 billion.[4] While this is a large number, it is very small compared to the size of the economy. In the second half of 2005, GDP was running at an annual rate of $12.6 trillion. Thus, the direct impact on production was at most 0.25 percent (a quarter of 1 percent) of GDP during that period.[5]

| | Second Half, 2005 | First Half, 2006 | Second Half, 2006 | TABLE 7 |
|---|---|---|---|---|
| | | | | Estimated and Projected Effects of Hurricanes Katrina and Rita on GDP (billions of 2005 dollars at annual rates) |
| **Direct effects** | | | | |
| Energy production | −18 to −28 | −8 to −10 | −5 to −7 | |
| Housing services | −1 to −2 | −2 to −4 | −1 to −3 | |
| Agricultural production | −1 to −2 | 0 | 0 | |
| **Indirect effects** | | | | |
| Reduced consumption spending (beyond direct effects) | −14 to −22 | −7 to −11 | −3 to −8 | |
| Replacement investment | +6 to +12 | +16 to +34 | +16 to +35 | |
| Increased government spending on goods and services | +6 to +10 | +12 to +18 | +14 to +20 | |
| **Total impact on real GDP** | **−22 to −32** | **+11 to +27** | **+21 to +37** | |

*Source*: Based on Douglas Holtz-Eakin, "The Macroeconomic and Budgetary Effects of Hurricanes Katrina and Rita," *CBO Testimony before the Committee on the Budget, U.S. House of Representatives*, October 6, 2005.

[4] Remember that GDP figures for periods shorter than a year are always reported at an annual rate—how much the production *would* be if it continued at that rate for a year. So the actual direct loss in production for the second half of 2005 was between $10 billion and $16 billion.

[5] Another way to understand why the effect is relatively small is to compare the total destruction of capital in Table 6—$69 billion to $130 billion—to the nation's total physical capital stock in 2005, which was $38 trillion. Thus, the hurricanes destroyed at most 0.34 percent of the nation's capital.

## INDIRECT EFFECTS: GOVERNMENT AND PRIVATE RESPONSES

We've seen that the direct effect of the hurricanes on GDP was relatively small. (And the direct effects of September 11 were even smaller.) But what about the indirect effects—those that result from decisions made afterward? These have the *potential* to be more harmful and long-lasting. But in fact, any indirect decreases in production are usually smaller than the direct decrease—and very short-lived. One reason is changes in macroeconomic policy that are designed to counteract the decrease in production. (You will learn about these efforts and how they work in subsequent chapters.) But another reason is that the indirect effects themselves work in both directions: Some tend to decrease production, while others work to increase it. Within a short time, the forces that increase production come to dominate.

The indirect effects of the hurricanes are reported in the second three rows of numbers in Table 7. Notice that these effects are estimated using the expenditure approach to GDP. This too is for practical reasons. The indirect effects come from decisions about *spending* by different sectors of the economy—households, businesses, and government agencies. Thus, the effects are most easily estimated by looking at each type of final user whose spending is likely to change.

Of the three indirect effects, only one is negative: the decrease in consumption spending. For the hurricanes, this decrease came about for two reasons. First (as happens in *any* regional disaster), those who lived in the affected region and lost jobs and property saw significant reductions in their income and wealth. As a result, they reduced their spending on goods and services produced by firms across the country. These firms responded by producing less.

But there was also a special impact on consumption, because the hurricanes knocked out large chunks of the nation's energy infrastructure, including pipelines and refineries. This caused a spike in energy prices—for gasoline, natural gas, and electricity. Nationwide, as consumers spent more on energy-related products, they cut back on their purchases of other goods and services.

Working against these negative effects was spending to rebuild and repair damage, and government purchases of food, housing, and medical care to distribute to those in need. If you subtotal the effects of these spending changes, you'll see that even in the second half of 2005, the net impact was only slightly negative. By the first half of 2006, the impact turns positive.

## THE TOTAL IMPACT ON GDP

The last row of Table 7 traces the total impact of the hurricanes on GDP over time. In the second half of 2005, the direct impact of the destruction and the further decrease in consumption spending dominate. But notice that even in this early period, they are substantially mitigated by the positive effects of reconstruction and government assistance. The total impact in the second half of 2005 is a reduction in the annual rate of GDP by $22 billion to $32 billion—a reduction of 0.25 percent.

But by the first half of 2006, the impact of the hurricanes on GDP turns *positive* and remains positive for the second half as well. That is, production is greater throughout 2006 than it would have been if there had been no hurricane. As you can see, this happens because the negative effects on production gradually weaken, while the positive effects of replacement investment and government assistance gradually grow and ultimately dominate.

## DRAWING CONCLUSIONS

One conclusion we can draw from this analysis is that *local* disasters generally have relatively small effects on the nation's GDP. This is especially true when the locality affected produces only a small fraction of the country's total output. In the case of the hurricanes, Louisiana and Mississippi—the two states most affected—together produce only about 2 percent of the nation's GDP. And Manhattan—the area most profoundly affected by the attacks of September 11—produces about 1.5 percent of our GDP.[6] And although the response of consumers can cause further decreases in production, the need to replace destroyed capital and government assistance help to counter these effects.

However, there are two mistakes to avoid in analyzing the economic impacts of disasters. One mistake is to think that, because a disaster actually increases production (as it did in 2006), we end up economically better off for it. Actually, we do not. Aside from the human tragedy of lives lost and communities destroyed, we must remember that much of the additional production after a disaster is used to bring our capital stock back to where it was beforehand. Although the disaster causes us to produce more, it does not enable us to *enjoy* more goods and services than we would if the disaster had not occurred. This is one of those cases we discussed in the chapter, in which GDP—which measures only production, rather than its purpose— provides an imperfect measure of economic well-being.

The second mistake is to extrapolate too broadly from past disasters to future ones. The direct effects of recent disasters—such as the attack of 2001 or the hurricanes of 2005—affected specific cities or a region of the country, leaving the rest unaffected. But disasters can occur on a larger scale. A flu pandemic, for example, would impact the entire country within a short period of time, creating a human tragedy of larger magnitude than any of our recent disasters. The purely economic effect would be much greater as well. The Congressional Budget Office has estimated that even a mild pandemic would reduce real GDP by about 1.5 percent. And a more serious pandemic caused by a more virulent strain of flu virus could reduce real GDP by as much as 5 percent—an impact 20 times greater than that of the hurricanes of 2005.[7]

---

[6] This assumes that Manhattan's share of GDP is equal to its share of personal income, as estimated by the Bureau of Economic Analysis.

[7] *A Potential Influenza Pandemic: An Update on Possible Macroeconomic Effects and Policy Issues,* Congressional Budget Office, May 22, 2006.

# Summary

This chapter discusses how two key macroeconomic aggregates are measured and reported. One is *gross domestic product*—the total value of all final goods and services produced for the marketplace during a given period, within a nation's borders. GDP is a measure of an economy's total production.

In the *expenditure approach*, GDP is calculated as the sum of spending by households, businesses, government agencies, and foreigners on domestically produced goods and services. The *value-added approach* computes GDP by adding up each firm's contributions to the total product as it is being produced. Value added at each stage of production is the revenue a firm receives minus the cost of the intermediate inputs it uses. The *factor payments approach* sums the wages and salaries, rent, interest, and profit earned by all households. The three approaches reflect three different ways of viewing and measuring GDP.

Since nominal GDP is measured in current dollars, it changes when either production or prices change. *Real GDP* is nominal GDP adjusted for price changes; it rises only when production rises.

Real GDP is most useful in the short run, for giving warnings about impending recessions. For other uses, it is plagued by important inaccuracies. It does not fully reflect quality changes or production in the underground economy, and it does not include many types of nonmarket production. GDP is only a very rough measure of economic welfare because it excludes many aspects of the economy that add to or detract from economic well-being.

When real GDP grows, employment tends to rise and—if real GDP grows fast enough—the unemployment rate falls. In the United States, a person is considered unemployed if he or she does not have a job but is actively seeking one. Economists have found it useful to classify unemployment into four different categories. *Frictional unemployment* is short-term unemployment experienced by people between jobs or by those who are just entering the job market. *Seasonal unemployment* is related to changes in the weather, tourist patterns, or other predictable seasonal changes. *Structural unemployment* results from mismatches, in skills or location, between jobs and workers. Finally, *cyclical unemployment* occurs because of the business cycle. Seasonal and frictional unemployment can be beneficial to the economy. Structural and cyclical unemployment, however, create harm to the individuals involved, and the economy as a whole suffers the loss of output that the unemployed could have produced. From a macroeconomic perspective, we say the economy is at *full employment* when there is no cyclical unemployment, even though normal amounts of frictional, seasonal, and structural unemployment remain.

# Problem Set    *Answers to even-numbered Questions and Problems can be found on the text Web site at www.thomsonedu.com/economics/hall.*

1. Using the expenditure approach, which of the following would be directly counted as part of U.S. GDP? For those that count, state whether the action causes an increase in $C$, $I$, $G$, or $NX$. (If you need to make any special assumptions, state them.)

   a. A new personal computer produced by IBM, which remained unsold at the year's end
   b. A physician's services to a household
   c. Produce bought by a restaurant to serve to customers
   d. The purchase of 1,000 shares of Disney stock
   e. The sale of 50 acres of commercial property
   f. A real estate agent's commission from the sale of property
   g. A transaction in which you clean your roommate's apartment in exchange for his working on your car
   h. An Apple iMac computer produced in the United States and purchased by a French citizen
   i. The government's Social Security payments to retired people

2. Calculate the total change in a year's GDP for each of the following scenarios:

   a. A family sells a home, without using a broker, for $150,000. They could have rented it on the open market for $700 per month. They buy a 10-year-old condominium for $200,000; the broker's fee on the transaction is 6 percent of the selling price. The condo's owner was formerly renting the unit at $500 per month.
   b. General Electric uses $10 million worth of steel, glass, and plastic to produce its dishwashers. Wages and salaries in the dishwasher division are $40 million; the division's only other expense is $15 million in interest that it pays on its bonds. The division's revenue for the year is $75 million.
   c. On March 31, you decide to stop throwing away $50 a month on convenience store nachos. You buy $200 worth of equipment, cornmeal, and cheese and make your own nachos for the rest of the year.
   d. You win $25,000 in your state's lottery. Ever the entrepreneur, you decide to open a Ping-Pong ball washing service, buying $15,000 worth of equipment from SpiffyBall Ltd. of Hong Kong and $10,000 from Ball-B-Kleen of Toledo, Ohio.
   e. Tone-Deaf Artists, Inc., produces 100,000 new CDs that it prices at $15 apiece. Ten thousand CDs are sold abroad, but, alas, the rest remain unsold on warehouse shelves.

3. The country of Freedonia uses the same method to calculate the unemployment rate as the U.S. Bureau of Labor Statistics uses. From the following data, compute Freedonia's unemployment rate.

| Population | 10,000,000 |
|---|---|
| Under 16 | 3,000,000 |
| Over 16 | |
| In military service | 500,000 |
| In hospitals | 200,000 |
| In prison | 100,000 |
| Worked one hour or more in previous week | 4,000,000 |
| Searched for work during previous four weeks | 1,000,000 |

4. Toward the end of this chapter, it was stated that if half of the 4.0 million involuntary part-time workers in May 2006 were counted as unemployed, then the unemployment rate that month would have been 6.0 percent instead of 4.6 percent. Do the necessary calculations to confirm this statement, using the information in Figure 6. (Hint: The labor force will not be affected.)

5. In December 2005, the BLS estimated there were 7.4 million unemployed, 142.8 million employed, 451,000 discouraged workers, and 4.8 million people (including discouraged workers) who were not working but said they wanted a job. What would the unemployment rate have been in December 2005 if it had included among the unemployed:
   a. All officially discouraged workers?
   b. All those who were not working but said they wanted a job? (Hint: Don't forget about how these inclusions would affect the labor force.)

6. Ginny asks, "If I buy a sweater that was produced in Malaysia, why is its purchase price subtracted from GDP?" How should you answer her question? (You may assume, for simplicity, that there was no value added to the sweater in the United States.)

7. Suppose that in one year household consumption falls by $20 billion (compared to the year before), but business firms continue to produce consumer goods at an unchanged rate. If there is no other change affecting real GDP that year, what will happen to total real GDP? What will happen to each of its components?

8. a. The country of Ziponia uses the same method to calculate the unemployment rate as the U.S. Bureau of Labor Statistics uses. From the data below, compute Ziponia's unemployment rate.

| Population | 60,000 |
|---|---|
| Under 16 | 9,000 |
| Over 16 | |
| In military service | 600 |
| In hospitals | 60 |
| In prison | 200 |
| Worked one hour or more in previous week | 46,000 |
| Searched for work during previous four weeks | 2,140 |
| Did not work in previous week but would have taken a job if one were offered | 200 |

b. How large is Ziponia's labor force?
c. How many discouraged workers (loosely defined) live in Ziponia?
d. Not all of Ziponia's citizens are accounted for in part (a). How are the missing citizens classified? Give some examples of what they may be doing.
e. How many of Ziponia's citizens are not in the labor force?

9. Refer to question 8. The 2,140 Ziponians who searched for work during the previous four weeks included: 54 ski resort employees who lost their winter jobs but expect to get them back in late fall; 200 recent high school graduates; 258 former textile workers who lost their jobs when their employers moved their operations overseas; 143 mothers and 19 fathers who had stayed at home to raise their children but who recently decided to reenter the work force; 394 high school and college students who want summer jobs; 127 people who live in West Ziponia and lost their jobs when their employers moved operations to East Ziponia, but who are not qualified for the remaining jobs in the west; 110 recent college graduates; and 32 retirees who decided to return to the workforce. The remaining job seekers lost their jobs due to a recession. Use this information to:
   a. Classify the job seekers by their type of unemployment, and calculate how many fell into each category.
   b. Find the frictional, seasonal, structural, and cyclical unemployment rates.

10. The following table shows an estimate of the destruction caused by the terrorist attacks of September 11:

| Type of Property | Estimated Loss |
|---|---|
| World Trade Center Complex buildings | $ 6.7 billion |
| Contents of Buildings in World Trade Center Complex | $ 5.2 billion |
| Buildings nearby | $ 4.5 billion |
| Public infrastructure (subway, commuter rail, and utilities) | $ 3.7 billion |
| **Total** | **$20.1 billion** |

*Source*: Modified from Jason Bram, James Orr, and Carol Rapaport, "Measuring the Effects of the September 11 Attack on New York City," *Federal Reserve Bank of New York Policy Review*, November 2002.

Use the following two facts (from the Bureau of Economic Analysis) as needed to answer the questions below:
   Fact #1: GDP in 2001 was $10 trillion.
   Fact #2: Manhattan produces 1.5 percent of the nation's GDP.

a. Assume that each dollar of destroyed property reduces annual production by 10 cents (a rough estimate of the general impact of capital destruction on GDP), and that none of the destroyed property was replaced over the next 12 months. Estimate the percentage impact on

GDP during the 12 months after the attacks due to the physical destruction alone.

b. Suppose that, in addition to the property destruction, the attack created disruption of economic activity, and that Manhattan's production was cut in half for 2 weeks. Estimate the percentage impact on GDP for the *quarter* due to this disruption alone.

c. Again, suppose Manhattan's production was cut in half for 2 weeks. Estimate the percentage impact on GDP for the *year* due to this disruption alone.

## More Challenging

11. Suppose, in a given year, someone buys a General Motors automobile for $30,000. That same year, GM produced the car in Michigan, using $10,000 in parts imported from Japan. However, the parts imported from Japan themselves contained $3,000 in components produced in the United States.

 a. By how much does U.S. GDP rise?

 b. Using the expenditure approach, what is the change in each component (*C, I, G,* and *NX*) of U.S. GDP?

 c. What is the change in Japan's GDP and each of its components?

12. After the attacks of September 11, 2001, U.S. businesses began to spend more on security, and continue to do so today. For example, airlines and package delivery services run more background checks on their employees, and office buildings hire more security guards than they did before the attack. What impact have these decisions had on real GDP? (Hint: Is the new spending considered to be purchases of final goods?)

# The Price Level and Inflation

About a hundred years ago, you could buy a pound of coffee for 15 cents, see a Broadway play for 40 cents, buy a new suit for $6, and attend a private college for $200 in yearly tuition.[1] Needless to say, the price of each of these items has gone up considerably since then. Microeconomic causes—changes in individual markets—can explain only a tiny fraction of these price changes. For the most part, these price rises came about because of a continually rising **price level**—the average level of prices in the economy.

When the price level rises, the value of the dollar—its purchasing power—falls. And this presents a problem. We measure many economic variables—such as income, production, or the wage rate—in dollars. But over time, how can we keep track of them when our unit of measurement—the dollar—has a changing value? It would be like trying to monitor a child's height over the years with a yardstick whose length changes every year. To make sensible comparisons of variables measured in dollars, we must know how the dollar's purchasing power changes from period to period. And this requires us to know how the price level is changing.

In this chapter, we'll discuss how the price level and its rate of change are measured, and some of the difficulties and controversies involved. We'll postpone until later chapters the question of *why* prices change from year to year.

**Price level** The average level of prices in the economy.

## MEASURING THE PRICE LEVEL AND INFLATION

Economists use several different measures of the price level, depending on their purpose. But all of them have one thing in common: They are all calculated and reported as *index numbers*. Because index numbers have some special features, it's worth discussing them more generally before we look specifically at price indexes.

### INDEX NUMBERS IN GENERAL

Most measures of the price level are reported in the form of an **index**—a series of numbers, each one representing a different period. Index numbers are meaningful only in a *relative* sense: We compare one period's index number with that of another period and can quickly see which one is larger and by what percentage. But the actual value of an index number for a particular period has no meaning in and of itself.

**Index** A series of numbers used to track a variable's rise or fall over time.

[1] Scott Derks, ed., *The Value of the Dollar: Prices and Incomes in the United States: 1860–1989* (Detroit, MI: Gale Research Inc., 1994), various pages.

In general, an index number for any measure is calculated as

$$\frac{\text{Value of measure in current period}}{\text{Value of measure in base period}} \times 100.$$

Let's see how index numbers work with a simple example. Suppose we want to measure how violence on TV has changed over time, and we have data on the number of violent acts shown in each of several years. We could then construct a TV-violence index. Our first step would be to choose a *base period*—a period to be used as a benchmark. Let's choose 2000 as our base period, and suppose that there were 10,433 violent acts on television in that year. Then our violence index in any current year would be calculated as

$$\frac{\text{Number of violent acts in current year}}{10,433} \times 100.$$

In 2000, the base year, the index will have the value $(10,433/10,433) \times 100 = 100$. Look again at the general formula for index numbers, and you will see that this is always true: *An index will always equal 100 in the base period.*

Now let's calculate the value of our index in another year. If there were 14,534 violent acts in 2005, then the index that year would have the value

$$\frac{14,534}{10,433} \times 100 = 139.3.$$

Index numbers compress and simplify information so that we can see how things are changing at a glance. Our media violence index, for example, tells us at a glance that the number of violent acts in 2005 was 139.3 percent of the number in 2000. Or, more simply, TV violence grew by 39.3 percent between 2000 and 2005.

## THE CONSUMER PRICE INDEX

**Consumer Price Index** An index of the cost, through time, of a fixed market basket of goods purchased by a typical household in some base period.

The most widely used measure of the price level in the United States is the **Consumer Price Index (CPI)**. This index, which is designed to track the prices paid by the typical consumer, is compiled and reported by the Bureau of Labor Statistics.

Measuring the prices paid by the typical consumer is not easy. The BLS must solve a number of conceptual problems before it begins (such as deciding which items to include and what weight to give to each item). Then there are a host of practical problems. Let's discuss how all these problems are dealt with in the CPI.

### Which Items to Include?

The goal of the CPI is to track the prices paid by *consumers*, and no one else. So, as a start, the CPI includes the part of GDP that consumers purchase as final users (new clothes, new furniture, new cars, haircuts, or restaurant meals). But it also includes two types of goods and services that consumers buy, even though they are *not* part of GDP: (1) household purchases of used goods such as used cars or used computers and (2) household purchases of imports from other countries—French cheese, Japanese cars, and Mexican tomatoes.

The CPI does *not* include goods and services purchased by anyone other than consumers. It leaves out purchases by businesses (for capital equipment, raw materials, or wholesale goods). It leaves out goods and services purchased by government agencies (military equipment and the services of police officers and public school teachers). And it leaves out goods and services that are purchased by foreigners (U.S. exports).

Finally, remember that the CPI tracks the prices of goods and services only. Consumers also buy assets, such as stocks, bonds, and homes. The prices paid for these assets are *not* included in the CPI. For housing, the CPI (like GDP) includes the price of housing *services* rather than the value of the home or apartment itself. So for rental units, the CPI tracks the average rent people pay; for owner-occupied units, the CPI uses the rent that owners *would* pay if they had to rent their homes instead of owning them.

## How Much Weight for Each Item?

In any given month, different prices will change by different amounts. The average price of doctors' visits might rise by 1 percent, the price of blue jeans might rise by a tenth of a percent, the price of milk might fall by half a percent, and so on. When prices change at different rates, and when some are rising while others are falling, how can we track the change in the *average* price level? It would be a mistake to use a simple average of all prices, adding them up and dividing by the number of goods. A proper measure must recognize that we spend very little of our incomes on some goods—such as Tabasco sauce—and much more on others—like gasoline or rent.

The CPI's approach is to track the cost of the *CPI market basket*—the collection of goods and services that the typical consumer buys. If the market basket's cost rises by 10 percent over some period, then the price level, as reported by the CPI, will rise by 10 percent. This way, goods and services that are relatively unimportant in the typical consumer's budget will have little weight in the CPI. Tabasco sauce could triple in price and have no noticeable impact on the cost of the complete market basket. Goods that are more important—such as gas or rent—will have more weight.

To determine the CPI market basket, the BLS surveys thousands of families every couple of years, and records their spending in detail. It uses these spending patterns to construct a market basket containing thousands of different goods and services, with each one weighted according to its relative importance in the average family's budget.[2]

Figure 1 shows the broadest categories of the CPI market basket, and the proportion of total spending on each one in December 2005. For example, all the items in the category "food and beverages" together made up 15.0 percent of the typical consumer's spending, while all of the items included in "housing" amounted to 42.4 percent. The communication category—amounting to 3.1 percent—includes phone and Internet service, as well as computer hardware and software.

## Tracking and Reporting the Price Level

Each month, hundreds of BLS employees visit thousands of stores, gas stations, medical offices, and apartments across the country. Their job is to record the prices of specific goods and services in the market basket—about 80,000 price quotes in all. All this information is fed into a central database, and used to determine the new cost of the CPI market basket for that month.

---

[2] More specifically, the Bureau of Labor Statistics compiles two different types of market baskets to reflect the spending habits of two different types of people: (1) "All Urban Workers," resulting in the CPI-U; and (2) "Urban Wage Earners and Clerical Workers," resulting in the CPI-W. The CPI-U is the index most commonly reported and followed in the media, and it is used throughout this chapter.

FIGURE 1

**FIGURE** **1**

**Broad Categories and
Relative Importance in
the CPI, December 2005**

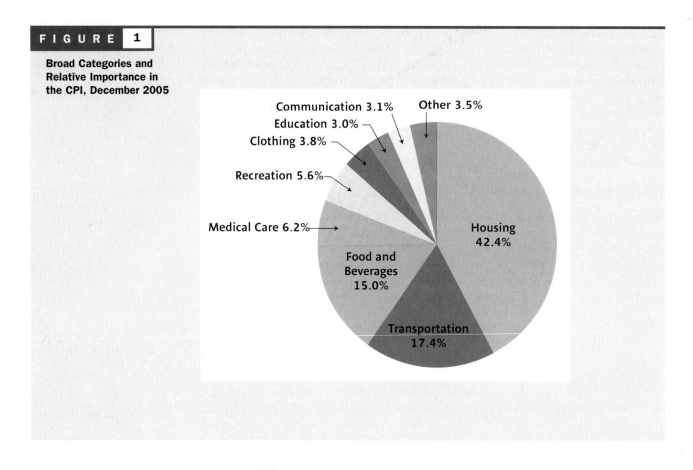

In recent years, the base period for the CPI has been July 1983. Following our general formula for price indexes, the CPI is calculated as follows:

$$\text{CPI} = \frac{\text{Cost of market basket in current period}}{\text{Cost of market basket in July 1983}} \times 100.$$

This simple formula shows us what the CPI tracks: the changing cost of a basket of goods.[3] In July 1983, the value of the CPI is 100. In any month in which the basket cost more than July 1983, the CPI's value is greater than 100. For periods (before July 1983) in which the basket's cost was lower, the CPI is less than 100. The appendix to this chapter provides a more detailed example of how the CPI is calculated.

Table 1 shows the actual value of the CPI for December of selected years. Because it is reported in index number form, we can easily see how much the price level has changed over different time intervals. In December 2005, for example, the CPI had a value of 196.8, telling us that the typical market basket in that year cost 96.8 percent more than it would have cost in the July 1983 base period. In December 1970, the CPI was 39.8, so the cost of the market basket in that year was only 39.8 percent of its cost in July 1983.

---

[3] The formula, however, ignores another feature of the CPI: the periodic updating of items and their relative importance in the CPI market basket. Each time the market basket is updated, the BLS splices a new CPI series onto the old one. But it retains July 1983 as the base period for index number calculation.

## FROM PRICE INDEX TO INFLATION RATE

The Consumer Price Index is a measure of the price *level* in the economy. The **inflation rate** measures how fast the price level is changing. More specifically, it tells us the percentage change in the price level from one period to the next. For example, let's calculate the inflation rate for the year 2005. Table 1 tells us that, from December 2004 to December 2005, the CPI rose from 190.3 to 196.8. Therefore, the annual inflation rate over the year 2005 was (196.8−190.3) / 190.3 = 0.034, or 3.4 percent.

The CPI is reported monthly, but the reported rate is virtually always seasonally adjusted and reported as an annual rate. For example, from April 2006 to May 2006, the seasonally adjusted CPI rose from 201.0 to 201.9. Therefore, the percentage increase in the CPI for May was (201.9 − 201.0 )/201.0 = 0.0045 or 0.45 percent. But the media reported inflation for May as 5.5 percent. That's because inflation of 0.45 percent per month for 12 months would, over a year, result in annual inflation of 5.5 percent.

Figure 2 shows the annual rate of inflation, as measured by the CPI, since 1950. For each year, the inflation rate is calculated as the percentage change in the CPI from December of the previous year to December of that year. For example, the CPI in December 2004 was 190.3, and in December 2005 it was 196.8. The inflation rate for 2005 was therefore (196.8 − 190.3)/190.3 = 0.034 or 3.4 percent.

Whenever the price level rises, as it usually does, the inflation rate will be positive. When the price level falls, as it did during the Great Depression (not shown) and in 1954 (shown in Figure 2), we have negative inflation, which is called **deflation**. As you can see in the figure, the U.S. inflation rate was low in the 1950s, began to creep up in the 1960s, then spiked upward in the 1970s and early 1980s, and has been low ever since. In later chapters, you will learn what causes the inflation rate to rise and fall, and some of the reasons it has behaved as it has over the past several decades.

| | TABLE 1 |
|---|---|
| **Consumer Price Index, December, Selected Years, 1970–2005** | |

| Year | Consumer Price Index (December) |
|---|---|
| 1970 | 39.8 |
| 1980 | 86.3 |
| 1990 | 133.8 |
| 2000 | 174.0 |
| 2001 | 176.7 |
| 2002 | 180.9 |
| 2003 | 184.3 |
| 2004 | 190.3 |
| 2005 | 196.8 |

*Source*: Bureau of Labor Statistics, Consumer Price Index—All Urban Consumers (*www.bls.gov*).

**Inflation rate** The percentage change in the price level from one period to the next.

**Deflation** A *decrease* in the price level from one period to the next.

## HOW THE CPI IS USED

The CPI is the most important and widely used measure of prices in the United States. It is used in three ways:

*As a Policy Target.* In the introductory macroeconomics chapter, we saw that price stability—or a low inflation rate—is one of the nation's important macroeconomic goals. One of the measures used to gauge our success in achieving low inflation is the CPI.

*To Index Payments.* An **indexed payment** is one that is periodically adjusted so that it rises and falls by the same percentage as a price index. Indexing a payment makes up for any loss of purchasing power caused by inflation. Ideally, indexing would adjust a nominal payment by just enough to keep its purchasing power unchanged. In the United States, more than 50 million Social Security recipients

**Indexed payment** A payment that is periodically adjusted in proportion with a price index.

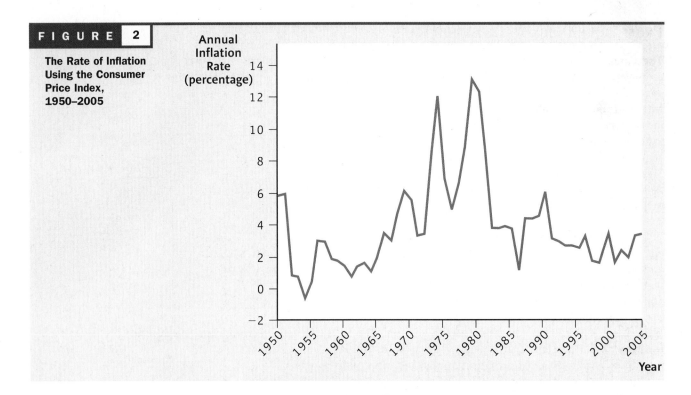

**FIGURE 2**

**The Rate of Inflation Using the Consumer Price Index, 1950–2005**

and government retirees have their benefit payments indexed to the CPI. More than 2 million workers have labor contracts that index their wages to the CPI. The U.S. income tax is indexed as well: The threshold income levels—at which people move into higher tax brackets—rise along with the CPI. And the government sells bonds that are indexed to the CPI. The owner of an indexed bond receives a payment each year to make up for the loss of purchasing power when the CPI rises.

*To Translate from Nominal to Real Values.* In order to compare economic values from different periods, we must translate *nominal variables*, measured in the number of dollars, into *real variables,* which are adjusted for the change in the dollar's purchasing power. The CPI is often used for this translation. Since calculating real variables is one of the most important uses of the CPI, let's discuss this in more detail.

## REAL VARIABLES AND ADJUSTMENT FOR INFLATION

Suppose that from December 2007 to December 2012, your nominal wage—what you are paid in dollars—rises from $15 to $30 per hour. Will you be better off? That depends. You will be earning twice as many dollars. But you should care not about how many green pieces of paper you earn, but how many goods and services you can buy with that paper. How, then, can we tell what happens to your purchasing power?

**DANGEROUS CURVES**

**Rising Prices versus Rising Inflation** People often confuse the statement "prices are rising" with the statement "inflation is rising," but they do not mean the same thing. Remember that the inflation rate is the *rate of change* of the price level. To have rising inflation, the price level must be rising by a greater and greater percentage each period. But we can also have rising prices and *falling* inflation. For example, from 1996 to 1998, the CPI rose each year: "Prices were rising." But they rose by a smaller percentage each year than the year before, so "inflation was falling"—from 3.4 percent in 1996 to 1.7 percent in 1997 and to 1.6 percent in 1998.

By focusing not on the *nominal wage* (the number of *dollars* you earn) but on the *real wage* (the *purchasing power* of your wage). To track your real wage, we need to look at the number of dollars you earn *relative to the price level*.

Since the "typical worker" and the "typical consumer" are pretty much the same, the CPI is usually the price index used to calculate the real wage. The real-wage formula is as follows:

$$\text{Real wage in any year} = \frac{\text{Nominal wage in that year}}{\text{CPI in that year}} \times 100.$$

To see that this formula makes sense, let's go back to our fictional example: From 2007 to 2012, your nominal wage doubles from $15 to $30 per hour. Now, suppose the price of everything that you buy doubles at the same time. It is easy to see that in this case, your purchasing power would remain unchanged. And that is just what our formula tells us: If prices double, the CPI doubles as well. With 2007 as our base year, the CPI would increase from 100 in 2007, to 200 in the year 2012. The *real* wage would be ($15/100) × 100 = $15 in 2007, and ($30/200) × 100 = $15 in 2012. The real wage would remain unchanged.

Now suppose that prices doubled over this period but your nominal wage remains unchanged at $15. In this case, your purchasing power would be cut in half. You'd have the same number of dollars, but each one would buy half as much as it did before. Our formula gives us a real wage of ($15/100) × 100 = $15 in 2007 and ($15/200) × 100 = $7.50 in 2012. The real wage falls by half.

Now look at Table 2, which shows the average hourly earnings of wage earners (people who are paid by the hour) over the past three decades. In the first two columns, you can see that the average American wage earner was paid $4.87 per hour in December 1975, and more than triple that—$16.37—in December 2005. Does this mean the average hourly worker was paid more in 2005 than in 1975? In *dollars*, the answer is clearly yes. But what about in *purchasing power*? Or, using the new terminology you've learned: What happened to the *real wage* over this period?

Let's see. We know that the *nominal wage* rose from $4.87 in 1975 to $16.37 in 2005. But, according to the table, the CPI rose from 55.5 to 196.8 over the same period. Using our formula, we find that:

| TABLE | 2 |
| --- | --- |

**Nominal and Real Wages (in December of Each Year)**

| Year | Nominal Wage (dollars per hour) | CPI | Real Wage (1983 dollars per hour) |
| --- | --- | --- | --- |
| 1975 | 4.87 | 55.5 | 8.77 |
| 1980 | 7.12 | 86.3 | 8.25 |
| 1985 | 8.86 | 109.3 | 8.11 |
| 1990 | 10.35 | 133.8 | 7.74 |
| 1995 | 11.79 | 153.5 | 7.68 |
| 2000 | 14.29 | 174.0 | 8.21 |
| 2005 | 16.37 | 196.8 | 8.32 |

*Source*: Bureau of Labor Statistics, Statistical Tables, *http://www.bls.gov*. Wage and CPI data for December of each year. Nominal wage: average hourly earnings of production or nonsupervisory workers in nonfarm private sector; CPI: CPI-All Urban Consumers.

$$\text{Real wage in 1975} = \frac{\$4.87}{55.5} \times 100 = \$8.77$$

$$\text{Real wage in 2005} = \frac{\$16.37}{196.8} \times 100 = \$8.32.$$

Thus, although the average worker earned more *dollars* in 2005 than in 1975, when we use the CPI as our measure of prices, her purchasing power seems to have fallen over those years.

### Important Provisos About Wage Data

It is tempting to come to a sweeping conclusion from information such as that in Table 2 and our previous discussion: that nonsupervisory workers were economically worse off in 2005 than in 1975. This would be a mistake, for several reasons. Here, we'll highlight just two of them.

First, over the past three decades, an increasing share of worker compensation has been nonwage benefits, such as employer contributions to retirement accounts and health insurance. By 2005, these benefits reached more than a quarter of total compensation for hourly workers, but they are not included in the hourly wage in Table 2. If benefits were included, real hourly pay would be greater in 2005 than in 1975.

Second, as we'll discuss later in this chapter, changes in the CPI overestimate inflation somewhat. Over a long time period such as three decades, this can make a big difference. A more accurate measure of the price level would show a rise in the hourly wage (even excluding benefits) over this period.

Still, while the adjustment for inflation in Table 2 is imperfect, no one would argue that we would get a clearer picture of worker pay by leaving the adjustment out. Using the nominal wage, we would conclude that worker pay (excluding benefits) more than tripled during this period. This is *not* a meaningful description of what happened. The important point to remember here is that

> *when comparing dollar values over time, we care not about the number of dollars, but about their purchasing power. Thus, we translate nominal values into real values using the formula*
>
> $$\text{Real value} = \frac{\text{Nominal value}}{\text{Price index}} \times 100.$$

This formula, usually using the CPI as the price index, is how most real values in the economy are calculated. But there is one important exception: To calculate real GDP, the government uses a different procedure, to which we now turn.

## THE GDP PRICE INDEX AND REAL GDP

In the previous chapter, we discussed the difference between nominal GDP and real GDP. After reading this chapter, you might think that real GDP is calculated just like the real wage: dividing nominal GDP by the Consumer Price Index. But the Consumer Price Index is *not* used to calculate real GDP. Instead, a special price index—which we can call the **GDP price index**—is used.

**GDP price index** An index of the price level for all final goods and services included in GDP.

The most important differences between the CPI and the GDP price index are in the types of goods and services covered by each index. First, the GDP price index *includes* some prices that the CPI ignores. In particular, while the CPI tracks only the prices of goods bought by American *consumers*, the GDP price index must also include the prices of goods purchased by the government, investment goods purchased by businesses, and exports, which are purchased by foreigners.

Second, the GDP price index *excludes* some prices that are part of the CPI. In particular, the GDP price index leaves out used goods and imports, both of which are included in the CPI. This makes sense, because while used goods and imports are part of the typical consumer's market basket, they do not contribute to current U.S. GDP.

We can summarize the chief difference between the CPI and the GDP price index this way:

> *The GDP price index measures the prices of all goods and services that are included in U.S. GDP, while the CPI measures the prices of all goods and services bought by U.S. households.*[4]

 ## THE COSTS OF INFLATION

A high rate of inflation—whether it is measured by the CPI or the GDP price index—is never welcome news. What's so bad about inflation? As we've seen, it certainly makes your task as an economics student more difficult: Rather than taking nominal variables at face value, you must do those troublesome calculations to convert them into real variables.

But inflation causes much more trouble than this. It can impose costs on society and on each of us individually. Yet when most people are asked *what* the cost of inflation is, they come up with an incorrect answer.

### THE INFLATION MYTH

Most people think that inflation, merely by making goods and services more expensive, erodes the average purchasing power of income in the economy. The reason for this belief is easy to see: The higher the price level, the fewer goods and services a given number of dollars will buy. It stands to reason, then, that inflation—which raises prices—must be destroying the purchasing power of our incomes. Right?

Actually, this statement is mostly wrong.

To see why, remember that every market transaction involves *two* parties—a buyer and a seller. When a price rises, buyers of that good must pay more, but sellers get more revenue when they sell it. The loss in buyers' real income is matched by the rise in sellers' real income. Inflation may *redistribute* purchasing power, but it does not change the *average* purchasing power, when we include both buyers and sellers in the average.

In fact, most people in the economy participate on both sides of the market. On the one hand, they are consumers—as when they shop for food or clothing or furniture. On the other hand, they work in business firms that *sell* products and may benefit (in the form of higher wages or higher profits) when their firms' revenues rise. Thus, when prices rise, a particular person may find that her purchasing power has either risen or fallen, depending on whether she is affected more as a seller or as a

---

[4] The technical name for the GDP price index is the *chain-type annual weights GDP price index*. It differs from the CPI not only in goods covered, but also in its mathematical formula.

buyer. But regardless of the outcome for individuals, our conclusion remains the same:

> *Inflation can redistribute purchasing power from one group to another, but it does not directly decrease the average real income in the economy.*

Why, then, do people continue to believe that inflation robs the average citizen of real income? Largely because real incomes sometimes do decline—for *other* reasons. Inflation—while not the *cause* of the decline—will often be the *mechanism* that brings it about. Just as we often blame the messenger for bringing bad news, so too we often blame inflation for lowering our purchasing power when the real cause lies elsewhere.

Let's consider an example. In Table 2, notice the decline in real wages during the late 1970s. The real wage (excluding benefits) fell from $8.77 in 1975 to $8.25 in 1980, a decline of about 6 percent. Other data show that during this period, not only wage earners but also salaried workers, small-business owners, and corporate shareholders all suffered stagnant or declining real incomes. What was the cause?

There were several reasons, but one of the most important was the dramatic rise in the price of imported oil—from $3 per barrel in 1973 to $34 in 1981, an increase of more than 1,000 percent. The higher price for oil meant that oil-exporting countries, like Saudi Arabia, Kuwait, and Iraq, got more goods and services for each barrel of oil they supplied to the rest of the world, including the United States. But with these countries claiming more of America's output, less remained for the typical American. That is, the typical American family had to suffer a decline in real income. As always, a rise in price shifted income from buyers to sellers. But in this case, the sellers were *foreigners*, while the buyers were Americans. Thus, the rise in the price of foreign oil caused average purchasing power in the United States to decline.

But what was the mechanism that brought about the decline? Since real income is equal to (Nominal income/Price index) $\times$ 100, it can decrease in one of two ways: a fall in the numerator (nominal income) or a rise in the denominator (the price index). The decline in real income in the 1970s came entirely from an increase in the denominator.

Look back at Figure 2. You can see that this period of declining real income in the United States was also a period of unusually high inflation; at its peak in 1979, the inflation rate exceeded 13 percent. As a result, most people blamed *inflation* for their loss of purchasing power. But inflation was not the cause; it was just the *mechanism*. The cause was a change in the terms of trade between the United States and the oil-exporting countries—a change that resulted in higher oil prices.

To summarize, the common idea that inflation imposes a cost on society by directly decreasing average real income in the economy is incorrect. But inflation *does* impose costs on society, as the next section shows.

## THE REDISTRIBUTIVE COST OF INFLATION

One cost of inflation is that it often redistributes purchasing power *within* society. But because the winners and losers are chosen haphazardly—rather than by conscious social policy—the redistribution of purchasing power is not generally desirable. In some cases, the shift in purchasing power is downright perverse—harming the needy and helping those who are already well off.

How does inflation sometimes redistribute real income? An increase in the price level reduces the purchasing power of any payment that is specified in *nominal* terms. For example, some workers have contracts that set their nominal wage for two or three years, regardless of any future inflation. The nationally set minimum wage, too, is set for several years and specified in nominal dollars. Under these circumstances, inflation can harm ordinary workers, since it erodes the purchasing power of their prespecified nominal wage. Real income is redistributed from these workers to their employers, who benefit by paying a lower real wage.

But the effect can also work the other way: benefiting ordinary households and harming businesses. For example, many homeowners sign fixed-dollar mortgage agreements with a bank. These are promises to pay the bank the same nominal sum each month. Inflation can reduce the *real* value of these payments, thus redistributing purchasing power away from the bank and toward the average homeowner.

In general,

*inflation can shift purchasing power away from those who are awaiting future payments specified in dollars, and toward those who are obligated to make such payments.*

But does inflation *always* redistribute income from one party in a contract to another? Actually, no; if the inflation is *expected* by both parties, it should not redistribute income. The next section explains why.

## Accurately Expected Inflation Does *Not* Shift Purchasing Power

Suppose a labor union is negotiating a 3-year contract with an employer, and both sides agree that each year, workers should get a 3 percent increase in their *real wage*. Labor contracts, like most other contracts, are usually specified in nominal terms: The firm will agree to give workers so many additional *dollars per hour* each year. If neither side anticipates any inflation, they should simply negotiate a 3 percent *nominal* wage hike. With an unchanged price level, the *real* wage would then also rise by the desired 3 percent.

But suppose instead that both sides anticipate 10 percent inflation each year for the next three years. Then, they must agree to *more* than a 3 percent nominal wage increase in order to raise the real wage by 3 percent. How much more?

We can answer this question with a simple mathematical rule:

*Over any period, the percentage change in a real value (%∆Real) is approximately equal to the percentage change in the associated nominal value (%∆Nominal) minus the percentage change in the price level (%∆P):*

$$\%\Delta Real = \%\Delta Nominal - \%\Delta P$$

Over each year, if the inflation rate is 10 percent and the real wage is to rise by 3 percent, then the change in the nominal wage must (approximately) satisfy the equation

$$3 \text{ percent} = \%\Delta \text{Nominal} - 10 \text{ percent}$$

$$\%\Delta \text{Nominal} = 13 \text{ percent}.$$

The required nominal wage hike is 13 percent.

You can see that as long as both sides correctly anticipate the inflation, and no one stops them from negotiating a 13 percent nominal wage hike, inflation will *not* affect either party in real terms:

> *If inflation is correctly anticipated, and if both parties take it into account, then inflation will not redistribute purchasing power.*

We come to a similar conclusion about contracts between lenders and borrowers. When you lend someone money, you receive a reward—an interest payment—for letting that person use your money instead of spending it yourself. The annual *interest rate* is the interest payment divided by the amount of money you have lent. For example, if you lend someone $1,000 and receive back $1,040 one year later, then your interest is $40, and the interest *rate* on the loan is $40/$1,000 = 0.04, or 4 percent.

But there are actually *two* interest rates associated with every loan. One is the **nominal interest rate**—the percentage increase in the lender's *dollars* each year from making the loan. The other is the **real interest rate**—the percentage increase in the lender's *purchasing power* each year from making the loan. It is the *real* rate—the change in purchasing power—that lenders and borrowers should care about.

In the absence of inflation, real and nominal interest rates would always be equal. A 4 percent increase in the lender's *dollars* would always imply a 4 percent increase in her purchasing power. But if there is inflation, it will reduce the purchasing power of the money paid back. Does this mean that inflation redistributes purchasing power? Not if the inflation is correctly anticipated, and if there are no restrictions on making loan contracts.

For example, suppose both parties anticipate annual inflation of 5 percent and want to arrange a contract whereby the lender will be paid a 4 percent *real* interest rate each year. What *nominal* interest rate should they choose? Since the annual interest rate is the *percentage change* in the lender's funds over the year, we can use our approximation rule,

$$\%\Delta \text{ Real} = \%\Delta \text{ Nominal} - \%\Delta P.$$

For each year of the loan, this becomes

$$\%\Delta \text{ in lender's purchasing power} = \%\Delta \text{ in lender's dollars} - \text{Rate of inflation}$$

or

$$\text{Real interest rate} = \text{Nominal interest rate} - \text{Rate of inflation}.$$

In our example, where we want the real interest rate to equal 4 percent per year when the inflation rate is 5 percent per year, we must have

$$4 \text{ percent} = \text{Nominal interest rate} - 5 \text{ percent}$$

or

$$\text{Nominal interest rate} = 9 \text{ percent}.$$

Once again, we see that as long as both parties correctly anticipate the inflation rate, and face no restrictions on contracts (that is, they are free to set the nominal interest rate at 9 percent), then no one gains or loses.

When inflation is *not* correctly anticipated, however, our conclusion is very different.

**Nominal interest rate** The annual percent increase in a lender's dollars from making a loan.

**Real interest rate** The annual percent increase in a lender's purchasing power from making a loan.

### Unexpected Inflation *Does* Shift Purchasing Power

Suppose that, expecting no inflation, you agree to lend money at a 4 percent nominal interest rate for one year. You and the borrower think that this will translate into a 4 percent real rate. But it turns out you are both wrong: The price level actually rises by 3 percent, so the *real* interest rate ends up being 4 percent − 3 percent = 1 percent. As a lender, you have given up the use of your money for the year, expecting to be rewarded with a 4 percent increase in purchasing power. But you get only a 1 percent increase. Your borrower was willing to pay 4 percent in purchasing power, but ends up paying only 1 percent. *Unexpected* inflation has led to a better deal for your borrower and a worse deal for you, the lender.

That will not make you happy. But it could be even worse. Suppose the inflation rate is higher—say, 6 percent. Then your real interest rate ends up at 4 percent − 6 percent = −2 percent, a negative real interest rate. You get back *less* in purchasing power than you lend out. You are *paying* (in purchasing power) for the privilege of lending out your money. The borrower is *rewarded* (in purchasing power) for borrowing!

Negative real interest rates like this are not just a theoretical possibility. In the late 1970s, when inflation was higher than expected for several years in a row, many borrowers ending up "paying" negative real interest rates to lenders.

Now, let's consider one more possibility: Expected inflation is 6 percent, so you negotiate a 10 percent nominal rate, thinking this will translate to a 4 percent real rate. But the actual inflation rate turns out to be zero, so the real interest rate is 10 percent − 0 percent = 10 percent. In this case, inflation turns out to be *less* than expected, so the *real* interest rate is higher than either of you anticipated. The borrower is harmed and you (the lender) benefit.

These examples apply, more generally, to any agreement on future payments: to a worker waiting for a wage payment and the employer who has promised to pay it; to a doctor who has sent out a bill and the patient who has not yet paid it; or to a supplier who has delivered goods and his customer who hasn't yet paid for them.

> *When inflationary expectations are inaccurate, purchasing power is shifted between those obliged to make future payments and those waiting to be paid. An inflation rate higher than expected harms those awaiting payment and benefits the payers; an inflation rate lower than expected harms the payers and benefits those awaiting payment.*

## THE RESOURCE COST OF INFLATION

In addition to its possible redistribution of income, inflation imposes another cost upon society. To cope with inflation, we are forced to use up time and other resources as we go about our daily economic activities (shopping, selling, saving) that we could otherwise have devoted to productive activities. Thus, inflation imposes an *opportunity cost* on society as a whole and on each of its members:

> *When people must spend time and other resources coping with inflation, they pay an opportunity cost—they sacrifice the goods and services those resources could have produced instead.*

Let's first consider the resources used up by *consumers* to cope with inflation. Suppose you shop for clothes twice a year. You've discovered that both The Gap and Banana Republic sell clothing of similar quality and have similar service, and you naturally want to shop at the one with the lower prices. If there is no inflation, your task is easy: You shop first at The Gap and then at Banana Republic; thereafter, you rely on your memory to determine which is less expensive.

With inflation, however, things are more difficult. Suppose you find that prices at Banana Republic are higher than you remember them to be at The Gap. It may be that Banana Republic is the more expensive store, or it may be that prices have risen at *both* stores. How can you tell? Only a trip back to The Gap will answer the question—a trip that will cost you extra time and trouble. If prices are rising very rapidly, you may have to visit both stores on the same day to be sure which one is cheaper. Now, multiply this time and trouble by all the different types of shopping you must do on a regular or occasional basis—for groceries, an apartment, a car, concert tickets, compact discs, restaurant meals, and more. Inflation can make you use up valuable time—time you could have spent earning income or enjoying leisure activities. True, if you shop for some of these items on the Internet, you can compare prices in less time, but not zero time. And most shopping is *not* done over the Internet.

Inflation also forces *sellers* to use up resources. First, remember that sellers of goods and services are also buyers of resources and intermediate goods. They, too, must do comparison shopping when there is inflation, which uses up hired labor time. Second, each time sellers raise prices, labor is needed to put new price tags on merchandise, to enter new prices into a computer scanning system, to update the HTML code on a Web page, or to change the prices on advertising brochures or menus.

Finally, inflation makes us all use up resources managing our financial affairs. When the inflation rate is high, we'll try to keep our funds in accounts that pay high nominal interest rates, in order to preserve our purchasing power. And we'll try to keep as little as possible in cash or in low-interest checking accounts. Of course, this means more frequent trips to the bank or the automatic teller machine, to transfer money into our checking accounts or get cash each time we need it.

All of these additional activities—inspecting prices at several stores or Web sites, changing price tags or price entries, going back and forth to the automatic teller machine—use up time and other resources. From society's point of view, these resources could have been used to produce *other* goods and services that we'd enjoy.

You may not have thought much about the resource cost of inflation because in recent years, U.S. inflation has been so low—averaging about 3 percent during the 1990s, and about 2.75 percent from 2000 to mid-2006. Such a low rate of inflation is often called *creeping inflation;* from week to week or month to month, the price level creeps up so slowly that we hardly notice the change. The cost of coping with creeping inflation is negligible. And (as you'll see in a later chapter) low, creeping inflation may actually be good for the economy.

But it has not always been this way. Three times during the last 50 years, we have had double-digit inflation: about 14 percent during 1947–48, 12 percent in 1974, and 13 percent during 1979 and 1980. Going back farther, the annual inflation rate reached almost 20 percent during World War I and rose above 25 percent during the Civil War.

And as serious as these episodes of American inflation have been, they pale in comparison to the experiences of other countries. In the 1980s, several South American countries experienced inflation greater than 1,000 percent per year, and in mid-2006, Zimbabwe's inflation rate approached that level as well. In Germany during the 1920s, the inflation rate reached thousands of percent per *month*. And even worse was the Yugoslavian inflation of 1993–94. In one month alone—January 1994—the price level rose by 313 million percent.

When inflation reaches extremely high rates like these, normal economic life breaks down. No one wants to hold the national currency—or even accept it as payment—because it loses its value so rapidly. For some transactions, people will use a foreign currency, such as the U.S. dollar. But because there are insufficient quantities of foreign currency available in the country, most people are forced to barter—trading goods for goods rather than goods for money. Buying and selling becomes so inefficient and time consuming that production and living standards plummet.

## IS THE CPI ACCURATE?

The Bureau of Labor Statistics spends millions of dollars gathering data to ensure that its measure of inflation is accurate. To determine the market basket of the typical consumer, the BLS analyzes the spending habits of thousands of households. Every month, the bureau's shoppers visit 23,000 retail stores and about 50,000 housing units (rental apartments and owner-occupied homes) to record 80,000 different prices.

The BLS is a highly professional agency. Billions of dollars are at stake for each 1 percent change in the CPI, and the BLS deserves high praise for keeping its measurement honest and free of political manipulation. Nevertheless, conceptual problems and resource limitations make the CPI fall short of the ideal measure of inflation. Economists—even those who work in the BLS—widely agree that the CPI overstates the U.S. inflation rate. By how much?

According to a report by an advisory committee of economists in 1996, the overall bias was at least 1.1 percent during the 1980s and early 1990s.[5] That is, in a typical year, the reported rise in the CPI was about 1 percentage point greater than the true rise in the price level. The BLS has been working hard to reduce this upward bias and—especially in the late 1990s—it made some progress. But significant bias remains.

### SOURCES OF BIAS IN THE CPI

There are several reasons for the upward bias in the CPI.

#### Substitution Bias

Until recently, the CPI almost completely ignored a general principle of consumer behavior: People tend to *substitute* goods that have become relatively cheaper in place of goods that have become relatively more expensive. For example, in the seven years from 1973 to 1980, the retail price of oil-related products—like gasoline and home heating oil—increased by more than 300 percent, while the prices of most other goods and services rose by less than 100 percent. As a result, people found ways to conserve on oil products. They joined carpools, used public transportation, insulated their homes, and in many cases moved closer to their workplaces to shorten their commute. Yet throughout this period, the CPI basket—based on a survey of buying patterns in 1972–73—assumed that consumers were buying unchanged quantities of oil products.

[5] See *Toward a More Accurate Measure of the Cost of Living*, Report to the Senate Finance Committee from the Advisory Commission to Study the Consumer Price Index, December 1996.

The treatment of oil products is an example of a more general problem that has plagued the CPI for decades. Until recently, the CPI used fixed *quantities* to determine the relative importance of each item. That is, it assumed that households continued to buy each good or service in the same quantities in which they bought it during the most recent household survey—until the next household survey. Compounding the problem, the survey to determine spending patterns—and to update the market basket—was taken only about once every 10 years or so. So by the end of each 10-year period, the CPI's assumptions about spending habits could be far off the mark, as they were in the case of oil in the 1970s.

The BLS has *partially* fixed this problem, in two ways.[6] First, beginning in 2002, it began updating the market basket with a household survey every 2 years instead of every 10 years. This is widely considered an important improvement in CPI measurement.

Second, since January 1999, the CPI has no longer assumed that the typical consumer continues to buy the same *quantity* of each good that he bought in the last household "market basket" survey. Instead, the CPI now assumes that when a good's relative price rises by 10 percent, consumers buy 10 percent less of it, and switch their purchases to other goods whose prices are rising more slowly.

However, this is only a partial fix. The CPI still only recognizes the possibility of such substitution *within* categories of goods and *not among* them. For example, if the price of steak rises relative to the price of hamburger meat, the CPI now assumes that consumers will substitute away from steak and toward hamburger meat, since both are in the same category: *beef*. However, if the price of all beef products rises relative to chicken and pork, the CPI assumes that there is *no* substitution at all from beef toward chicken and pork. As a result, beef products still would be overweighted in the CPI until the next survey.

> *Although the BLS has partially fixed the problem, the CPI still suffers from substitution bias. That is, categories of goods whose prices are rising most rapidly are overweighted in the CPI market basket and categories of goods whose prices are rising most slowly are underweighted.*

### New Technologies

New technologies are another source of upward bias in the CPI. One problem is that goods using new technologies are introduced into the BLS market basket only after a lag. These goods often drop rapidly in price after they are introduced, helping to balance out price rises in other goods. By excluding a category of goods whose prices are dropping, the CPI overstates the rate of inflation. For example, even though many consumers were buying and using cellular phones throughout the 1990s, they were not included in the BLS basket of goods until 1998. As a result, the CPI missed the rapid decline in the price of cell phones. Now that the market basket of the typical consumer is updated every 2 years instead of every 10, this source of bias has been reduced but not completely eliminated.

But there is another issue with new technologies: They often offer consumers a lower cost alternative for obtaining the same service. For example, the introduction

---

[6] For a discussion of these and other recent changes in the CPI, see Robert J. Gordon, "The Boskin Commission Report: A Retrospective One Decade Later," *International Productivity Monitor*, Spring 2006.

of cable television lowered the cost of entertainment significantly by offering a new, cheaper alternative to going out to see movies. This should have registered as a drop in the price of "seeing movies." But the CPI does not have any good way to measure this reduction in the cost of living. Instead, it treats cable television as an entirely separate service.

> The CPI excludes new products that tend to drop in price when they first come on the market. When those products are included, the CPI regards them as entirely separate from existing goods and services, instead of recognizing that they lower the cost of achieving a given level of service.

## Changes in Quality

Many products are improving over time. Cars are much more reliable than they used to be and require much less routine maintenance. They have features like air bags and antilock brakes that were unknown in the early 1980s. The BLS struggles to deal with these changes. As far back as 1967, it has recognized that when the price of a car rises, some of that price hike is not really inflation, but instead the result of charging more because the consumer is *getting* more. In recent years, the BLS has adopted some routine statistical procedures to automatically adjust price changes for quality improvements for certain goods, such as personal computers and televisions. And in 1997, it introduced a major change in its treatment of health care costs. Before then, the CPI would track the price of individual health care components, such as "a night in the hospital" or "a post-surgery checkup." But after 1997, it began tracking the overall cost of treating specific diseases or conditions. Thus, the introduction of a new type of heart surgery that requires fewer days of hospitalization (and no change in other inputs) would be recorded as a *decrease* in the price of heart surgery.

But most goods and services do not get this special treatment. There is no explicit recognition that home appliances are more reliable, that audio equipment has better sound, that many medical treatments are more *effective* at prolonging life and health (aside from reducing hospital stays or doctor visits), that home power tools are safer, and so on.[7]

Take the Internet. Every year, it offers more information and entertainment content, a greater number of retailers from which to buy things, and faster and more intelligent search engines to help you find it all. Yet, the Internet—which was introduced into the CPI in 1998—has been treated as a service whose quality has not changed. If the price of Internet service rises, the CPI considers it inflation rather than paying more to *get* more. And if the price stays the same, the CPI ignores the *decrease* in the cost per unit of available content and treats the price as unchanged.

> The CPI fails to fully account for quality improvements in the goods and services in its market basket and, therefore, overestimates how fast the price of the basket is rising.

---

[7] There is, however, some implicit adjusting for quality. When a new model of a good is introduced at a higher price, the BLS assumes that the entire price increase is due to quality improvement rather than inflation. But the BLS does *not* recognize the possibility of more "bang for the buck"—that the value of the new model's higher quality might exceed any rise in its price.

© ASSOCIATED PRESS, AP

## Growth in Discounting

When a Wal-Mart opens up, many people begin to shop there. And for good reason: Prices at Wal-Mart are substantially lower than at other stores. For example, identical food items cost between 15 and 25 percent less at a Wal-Mart than at the typical supermarket (unless the supermarket has to compete with a nearby Wal-Mart).[8]

The BLS recognizes that people shop at Wal-Mart, and tracks changes in the prices of items sold there. But it fails to register a drop in prices when a new Wal-Mart first opens and people can suddenly buy the same goods for less. Wal-Mart and other discount chains have expanded rapidly in recent years, and continue to do so; the CPI systematically misses the price drop from the shift to these discounters.

> *The CPI does not recognize that a new discount outlet lowers the prices on many items for the people who begin shopping there. As a result, as discount outlets expand into new areas, the CPI overstates the inflation rate for food, electronic appliances, clothing, and other items sold there.*

## THE OVERALL BIAS AND ITS CONSEQUENCES

While the BLS has fixed some of the problems with the CPI, economists are in general agreement that it continues to overestimate inflation. By how much? That depends on what we mean by "inflation." If we mean the rate of price increase for the typical consumer's market basket, then the overestimate—after the improvements made in the late 1990s—is probably a bit less than one percentage point per year. But if we define inflation the way it is often interpreted—as the percentage change in the *cost of living*—then the CPI's overestimate of annual inflation is unknown, but much greater. This is largely because of how the CPI responds to technological change.

When a new good comes to market, it is dropped into the CPI market basket at some point, and the CPI tracks changes in its price from that time forward. But the increase in economic well-being made possible by *introducing* the good in the first place—and from its continued availability—is never accounted for. Even if the BLS was able to incorporate the good as soon as it came to market, and even if it accurately adjusted for subsequent quality improvements, it would still be missing the most important factor: the rise in living standards made possible by the new good's availability.

For example, we've already discussed the CPI's failure to account for quality improvements in the Internet after it was dropped into the basket in 1998. But beyond this problem, the CPI has *never* recognized how the Internet has lowered the cost of achieving any given level of economic satisfaction (think of email, news, online entertainment, online purchases, online dating, blogs, and more). The same is true for new medical procedures or prescription drugs that can treat or cure formerly untreatable diseases: The CPI ignores the longer and healthier lives that the new treatments often make possible. In this way, the CPI misses a highly relevant

---

[8] Hausman, J. and E. Leibtag, "CPI Bias from Supercenters: Does the BLS Know that Wal-Mart Exists?" NBER Working Paper No. 10712, National Bureau of Economic Research, Inc., Cambridge, MA, August 2004.

fact: New goods raise the living standard we can achieve at any given dollar cost. Or, equivalently, they lower the dollar cost of achieving any given living standard.

How serious is this problem? No one knows for sure. But many economists believe that the error from ignoring the effect of new goods on living standards could be substantial—much larger than the combined effects of the other biases in the CPI discussed in this chapter.[9]

> *The upward bias in the CPI depends on what we are trying to measure. If the target is the cost of the typical consumer's market basket, then the current upward bias is probably less than one percentage point per year. If the target is the cost of achieving a given standard of living, the upward bias is substantially greater.*

What are the implications of this bias in the CPI? That depends on our purpose in using it. If we are trying to measure inflationary tendencies in the economy, to help guide macroeconomic policy, then the CPI's failure to track the cost of achieving a given living standard is irrelevant. The policy goal is to avoid the costs to society when the price level—however it is interpreted—changes rapidly. The CPI is one of several useful tools to help achieve this goal.

But there are other purposes for which the measurement errors in the CPI matter a great deal. One such purpose is to determine the behavior of real wages over long periods of time. Look back at Table 2, which shows the behavior of the real hourly wage (not including benefits) over the past 40 years. It tells us that the real hourly wage was lower in 2005 than in 1975. Can we have faith in that result? Not really. Aside from the problem discussed earlier (the exclusion of increasingly important non-wage benefits), we have the problem of CPI bias. With the errors in each year's CPI accumulating over time, the overstatement of the price level after 40 years is huge. (An end-of-chapter problem will help you see this.) Moreover, the CPI is never revised retroactively, so any improvements in measurement made in later years—which reduce the bias—leave the historical record unchanged.[10]

Another purpose for which measurement errors matter is indexing. Millions of people have their retirement benefits, wages, interest payments, or federal tax brackets adjusted for inflation as determined by the CPI. Thus, any errors have important implications for the government budget, as well as the economy. In the Using the Theory section, we look at one example of this issue: the controversy over indexing Social Security benefits to the CPI.

Still, as imperfect as the CPI is for some purposes, no one would argue that we get a clearer picture of economic values by not adjusting for inflation at all. As long as the measurement errors are relatively small, even an imperfect adjustment for inflation will come closer to the truth than no adjustment at all.

---

[9] See, for example, the suggestions of Jerry Hausman, "Sources of Bias and Solutions to Bias in the CPI," *Journal of Economic Perspectives*, Vol. 17, No. 1, Winter 2003.

[10] The Bureau of Labor Statistics has published experimental price indexes, which correct some of its earlier errors and are revised retroactively. And, since 1999, it has been publishing an improved index that largely solves the substitution bias, called the Chained Consumer Price Index for All Urban Consumers. But these other price indexes are not widely reported in the media and are not used for indexing.

# USING THE THEORY

## THE CONTROVERSY OVER INDEXING SOCIAL SECURITY BENEFITS

In recent years, the Social Security system—which provides benefits to almost 50 million retired workers in the United States—has become embroiled in controversy. On the one hand, it has been of immense benefit to millions of people. For most of them, it provides an important supplement to other sources of retirement income. For about 10 million retirees, Social Security is the *only* source of income. This has made the program immensely popular.

On the other hand, Social Security is one of the largest and most expensive of all federal government programs, paying out more than $500 billion in 2005. And as the baby-boom generation begins to retire over the next several years, the costs of the system will balloon, adding to the government's projected budget deficits. This has led to calls to reduce the budgetary costs by changing the way that benefits are determined.

Let's consider how Social Security benefits are determined. First, the benefits of each year's *new* retirees are tied to the average wage rate in the economy at the time of retirement. As living standards and wages rise over time, each new group of retirees is granted a higher real benefit payment when they first retire. This part is not controversial.

But once a retiree's initial benefit is assigned, his payments in future years are indexed to the CPI. That is, his nominal (dollar) benefit automatically increases at the same percentage rate as the CPI. This is the controversial part.

The justification for indexing is to preserve the purchasing power of the benefit payment for all retirees for as long as they live. But because changes in the CPI *overstate* inflation, benefits are *over*indexed. That is, the nominal payment rises by more than the actual rise in the price level. As a result, the real benefit payment rises over time.

Table 3 illustrates how this works, with a hypothetical example. We assume that someone retires in 2006 with an initial promise of $25,000 per year in benefits (about the maximum initial benefit payable that year). The benefit payment is then indexed to the CPI for the next 20 years. We also assume that an accurate price index would rise at 2 percent per year (that is, we assume the inflation rate is actually 2 percent per year). Column (1) shows the value of this accurate price index in each year, using 2006 as our base year.

In columns (2) and (3), we assume that the CPI—to which benefits are indexed—is accurate. Accordingly, column (2) shows nominal benefits starting at $25,000 and then growing by 2 percent per year with the CPI. For example, in the second year, benefits rise to $25,000 × 1.02 = $25,500. In the third year, they rise by another 2 percent, to $25,500 × 1.02 = $26,010. Continuing in this way, the nominal payment in the twentieth year would reach $25,000 × (1.02)$^{20}$ = $37,149.

Column (3) shows the real benefit payment in each year. It is obtained using our formula:

$$\text{Real value} = \frac{\text{Nominal value}}{\text{Price index}} \times 100.$$

| | | Benefits Indexed to Accurate CPI (rising at 2%) | | Benefits Indexed to Overstated CPI (rising at 3%) | | TABLE 3 |
|---|---|---|---|---|---|---|
| **Year** | **(1) Accurate Price Index (2006 = 100)** | **(2) Nominal Annual Benefit (indexed at 2% per year)** | **(3) Real Annual Benefit, [(2) ÷ (1)] × 100** | **(4) Nominal Annual Benefit (indexed at 3% per year)** | **(5) Real Annual Benefit, [(4) ÷ (1)] × 100** | **Indexing and "Overindexing" Social Security Benefits** |
| 2006 | 100.00 | $25,000 | $25,000 | $25,000 | $25,000 | |
| 2007 | 102.00 | $25,500 | $25,000 | $25,750 | $25,245 | |
| 2008 | 104.04 | $26,010 | $25,000 | $26,523 | $25,493 | |
| 2009 | 106.12 | $26,532 | $25,000 | $27,318 | $25,742 | |
| . . . | . . . | . . . | . . . | . . . | . . . | |
| 2026 | 148.59 | $37,149 | $25,000 | $45,153 | $30,388 | |

In our example, each value in column (2) is divided by the accurate price index in column (1) to obtain the real payment in column (3). For example, in the second year, with the price index equal to 102, the real payment is

$$\text{Real payment} = \frac{\$25,500}{102} \times 100 = \$25,000.$$

As you can see, when the benefit payment is indexed to an accurate CPI, the real payment remains unchanged at $25,000 (in 2006 dollars). This is not surprising. The purpose of indexing is to keep a real payment constant. With no inaccuracy in the CPI, this is exactly what indexing does.

Now, let's see what happens when benefits are indexed to a CPI that *overestimates* inflation by one percentage point each year. That is, we'll continue to assume that inflation is actually 2 percent per year, but nominal benefit payments will now rise with the (erroneous) CPI at 3 percent per year. In column (4), nominal benefits start at $25,000. In the second year, benefits are $25,000 × 1.03 = $25,750; in the third year, they rise to $25,750 × 1.03 = $26,523, and so on.

Finally, we calculate the real benefit payment each year. But remember: The real benefit is its *actual* purchasing power. In this scenario, although the CPI reports inflation of 3 percent, prices are *actually* rising at only 2 percent per year. So, to determine the real benefit in any year, we must divide the overindexed nominal payment in column (4) by the actual price level in column (1). In the second year, the real payment is

$$\text{Real payment} = \frac{\$25,750}{102} \times 100 = \$25,245.$$

In the third year, the real payment is

$$\text{Real payment} = \frac{\$26,523}{104.04} \times 100 = \$25,493.$$

As you can see, rather than just maintaining the real benefit over time, indexing to an upward-biased CPI results in a *continually increasing real benefit payment*. By the last year of retirement, the real benefit payment rises to $30,388—an increase of more than 21 percent.

This will suit Social Security recipients just fine. And it may suit the rest of us too—when the economy is growing at a rapid pace. After all, why shouldn't retirees get a larger slice of the economic pie when the pie itself is growing rapidly and everyone else's slice is growing as well? But note that the increase in real benefits happens *automatically*, due to overindexing, *regardless* of the rate of economic growth. If real GDP growth slows down or disappears, the average Social Security recipient will *still* get a growing slice of the pie each year, even if everyone else's slice is shrinking. (Because Social Security is financed by tax payments from the rest of society, any increase in real benefits shrinks the after-tax real income of nonretirees.)

More generally,

> *when a payment is indexed and the price index overstates inflation, the real payment increases over time. Purchasing power is automatically shifted toward those who are indexed and away from the rest of society.*

This general principle applies whether the economy is growing rapidly or slowly, and it applies to anyone who is indexed: Social Security recipients, government pensioners, union workers with indexed wage contracts, or anyone else.

Because it is widely recognized that the CPI overstates inflation, there have been calls to adjust the indexing formula for Social Security. One proposal is to index to the CPI minus one-half of a percentage point, to correct for at least some of measurement error. Other proposals are to more aggressively fix the problems of the CPI itself, which might decrease the reported annual inflation rate by a half percentage point or more.

But some economists have argued that the system should be left alone. For one thing, the elderly consume a different market basket than the "typical consumer." They spend a greater fraction of their income on health care (for which prices are rising rapidly) and much less on new technology goods like laptop computers or cell phones (for which prices are falling). According to this argument, any overstatement of inflation by the CPI helps to compensate for the higher inflation faced by the elderly.

The Bureau of Labor Statistics has been compiling an experimental index, the CPI-E ("E" for elderly), based on a market basket more representative for those receiving benefits. From 1982 to 2005, the CPI-E has risen faster than the version of the CPI used for indexing Social Security,[11] by about 0.4 percentage points each year. But this tells us that reasonable estimates of the upward bias of the CPI have *more* than compensated for the higher inflation faced by the elderly, suggesting that some change to indexing may still be needed.

Another argument used by advocates of the current system is that it helps to reduce a source of inequity among retirees.[12] Remember that each group's initial benefit is determined by the average wage at their time of retirement. Thus, those who retired in earlier years were awarded a lower initial real benefit than those who retired in later years. Overindexing for inflation thus helps to reduce the difference in real benefits among retirees, because the longer someone has been retired, the more they have gained from the upward bias in the CPI.

---

[11] Social Security benefits are indexed to the CPI-W, which is based on the typical market basket of urban wage earners and clerical workers. Over the past few decades, it has risen slightly more slowly than the CPI-U, which covers all urban workers.

[12] This point has been made by Martin Neil Baily, "Policy Implications of the Boskin Commission Report," *International Productivity Monitor*, Spring 2006.

# Summary

The value of a dollar is its purchasing power, and this changes as the prices of the things we buy change. The overall trend of prices is measured using a price index. Like any index number, a price index is calculated as: (Value in current period/Value in base period) × 100. The most widely used price index in the United States is the *Consumer Price Index (CPI)*, which tracks the prices paid for a typical consumer's "market basket." The percentage change in the CPI is the inflation rate.

The most common uses of the CPI are for indexing payments, as a policy target, and to translate from nominal to real variables. Many nominal variables, such as the nominal wage, can be corrected for price changes by dividing by the CPI and then multiplying by 100. The result is a real variable, such as the real wage, that rises and falls only when its purchasing power rises and falls. Another price index in common use is the GDP price index. It tracks prices of all final goods and services included in GDP.

Inflation, a rise over time in a price index, is costly to our society. One of inflation's costs is an arbitrary redistribution of purchasing power. Unanticipated inflation shifts purchasing power away from those awaiting future dollar payments and toward those obligated to make such payments. Another cost of inflation is the resource cost: People use valuable time and other resources trying to cope with inflation.

It is widely agreed that the CPI has overstated inflation in recent decades. As a result, the official statistics on real variables may contain errors, and people whose incomes are indexed to the CPI may be overindexed, enjoying an increase in real income that is paid for by the rest of society. The Bureau of Labor Statistics has been trying to eliminate the upward bias in the CPI. Much progress has been made, but some upward bias remains. The CPI is especially inaccurate as an index of the cost of achieving a given standard of living.

# Problem Set

*Answers to even-numbered Questions and Problems can be found on the text Web site at www.thomsonedu.com/economics/hall.*

1. Calculate each of the following from the data in Table 1 in this chapter.
   a. The inflation rate for the year 2005
   b. *Total* inflation (the total percentage change in the price level) from December 1970 to December 2005

2. Using the data in Table 2, calculate the following for the period 2000–2005:
   a. The total percentage change in the nominal wage
   b. The total percentage change in the price level

3. Use your answers from problems 2(a) and 2(b) to obtain the total percentage change in the real wage (excluding benefits) from 2000 to 2005. (Hint: Use the rule given earlier in the chapter for obtaining the percentage change in a real variable from the percentage change in the nominal variable and the percentage change in the price level.)

4. Calculate the total percentage change in the real wage (excluding benefits) from 2000 to 2005 using the last column of Table 2. Compare your answer to the answer in problem 3. Which is the more accurate answer?

5. In Table 2, you can see that the CPI rose from 55.5 in December 1975 to 196.8 in December 2005. The *average* annual inflation rate from 1975 to 2005 was 4.31 percent. That is, $55.5 \times (1.0431)^{30} = 196.8$. Suppose that this average annual rate of inflation overstates the actual annual inflation rate by one percentage point.
   a. What would be the value of an accurate CPI in December 2005?
   b. What would be an accurate value for the real wage (excluding benefits) in December 2005? (Use information in Table 2.)
   c. Determine the total percentage change in the real wage (excluding benefits) from December 1975 to December 2005 using your answer in (b).

6. Given the following *year-end* data, calculate both the inflation rate and the real wage for years 2, 3, and 4.

| Year | CPI | Inflation Rate | Nominal Wage | Real Wage |
|------|-----|----------------|--------------|-----------|
| 1 | 100 | | $10.00 | — |
| 2 | 110 | — | $12.00 | — |
| 3 | 120 | — | $13.00 | — |
| 4 | 115 | — | $12.75 | — |

7. If there is 5 percent inflation each year for 8 years, what is the *total* amount of inflation (i.e., the total percentage rise in the price level) over the entire 8-year period? (Hint: The answer is *not* 40 percent.)

8. Given the following data, calculate the approximate real interest rate for years 2, 3, and 4. (Assume that each CPI number tells us the price level at the *end* of each year.)

| End of Year | CPI | Nominal Interest Rate | Real Interest Rate |
|-------------|-----|-----------------------|--------------------|
| 1 | 100 | | |
| 2 | 110 | 15% | — |
| 3 | 120 | 13% | — |
| 4 | 115 | 8% | — |

If you lent $200 to a friend at the beginning of year 2 at the prevailing nominal interest rate of 15 percent, and your friend returned the money, with the interest, at the end of year 2, did you benefit from the deal?

9. (Requires appendix) An economy has only two goods, whose prices and typical consumption quantities are as follows:

|  | Dec. 2005 | | Dec. 2006 | |
|---|---|---|---|---|
|  | Price | Quantity | Price | Quantity |
| Fruit (lbs) | $1.00 | 100 | $1.00 | 150 |
| Nuts (lbs) | $3.00 | 50 | $4.00 | 25 |

a.  Using December 2005 as the base period for calculations and also as the year for measuring the typical consumer's market basket, calculate the CPI in December 2005 and December 2006.

b.  What is the annual inflation rate for 2006?

c.  Do you think your answer in (b) would understate the actual inflation rate in 2006? Briefly, why or why not?

10. Complete the following table. (CPI numbers are for the end of each year.)

| Year | CPI | Inflation Rate | Nominal Wage | Real Wage |
|---|---|---|---|---|
| 1 | 37 | — | $ 5.60 | |
| 2 | 48 | | $ 7 | |
| 3 | | 10% | $11.26 | |
| 4 | | 19% | | $25 |
| 5 | 60 | | $15 | |

11. a.  Jodie earned $25,000 at the end of year 1, when the CPI was 460. If the CPI at the end of year 2 is 504, what would Jodie have to earn at the end of year 2 to maintain a constant real wage?

b.  What would she have to earn in year 2 to obtain a 5 percent increase in her real wage? What percentage increase in the nominal wage is this?

12. During the late 19th and early 20th centuries, many U.S. farmers favored inflationary government policies. Why might this have been the case? (Hint: Do farmers typically pay for their land in full at the time of purchase?)

13. As in Table 3, consider someone who retires in 2006 with $25,000 in initial Social Security benefits per year, and that the actual inflation rate is 2 percent per year over the next 20 years. But now, suppose that the CPI overstates inflation as 4 percent per year (i.e., an overstatement of 2 full percentage points).

a.  What would the *real* benefit payment be in 2026?

b.  What would be the *total percentage increase* in the real benefit payment from 2006 to 2026?

## More Challenging

14. Suppose we want to change the base period of the CPI from July 1983 to December 2000. Recalculate December's CPI for each of the years in Table 1, so that the table gives the same information about inflation, but the CPI in December 2000 now has the value 100 instead of 174.0.

15. Inflation is sometimes said to be a tax on nominal money holdings. If you hold $100 and the price level increases by 10 percent, the purchasing power of that $100 falls by about 10 percent. Who benefits from this inflation tax?

# APPENDIX

## *Calculating the Consumer Price Index*

The Consumer Price Index (CPI) is the government's most popular measure of inflation. It tracks the cost of the collection of goods, called the *CPI market basket,* bought by a typical consumer in some *base period.* This appendix demonstrates how the Bureau of Labor Statistics calculates the CPI. To help you follow the steps clearly, we'll do the calculations for a very simple economy with just two goods: hamburger meat and oranges (not a pleasant world, but a manageable one). Table A.1 shows prices for each good, and the quantities produced and consumed, in two different periods: December 2004 (the base period) and December 2005. The market basket (measured in the base period) is given in the third column of the table: In December 2004, the typical consumer buys 30 pounds of hamburger and 50 pounds of oranges. Our formula for the CPI in any period *t* is

CPI in period *t*

$$= \frac{\text{Cost of market basket at prices in period } t}{\text{Cost of market basket at 2004 prices}} \times 100$$

where each year's prices are measured in December of that year.

Table A.2 shows the calculations we must do to determine the CPI in December 2004 and December 2005. In the table, you can see that the cost of the 2004 market basket at 2004 prices is $200. The cost of the *same* market basket at 2005's higher prices is $235.

To determine the CPI in December 2004—the base period—we use the formula with period *t* equal to 2004, giving us

CPI in 2004

$$= \frac{\text{Cost of 2004 basket at 2004 prices}}{\text{Cost of 2004 basket at 2004 prices}} \times 100$$

$$= \frac{\$200}{\$200} \times 100 = 100.$$

That is, the CPI in December 2004—the base period—is equal to 100. (The formula, as you can see, is set up so that the CPI will always equal 100 in the base period, regardless of which base period we choose.)

### TABLE A.1

**Prices and Weekly Quantities in a Two-Good Economy**

| | December 2004 | | December 2005 | |
|---|---|---|---|---|
| | Price (per lb) | Quantity (lbs) | Price (per lb) | Quantity (lbs) |
| Hamburger Meat | $5.00 | 30 | $6.00 | 10 |
| Oranges | $1.00 | 50 | $1.10 | 100 |

### TABLE A.2

**Calculations for the CPI**

| | At December 2004 Prices | At December 2005 Prices |
|---|---|---|
| Cost of 30 lbs of Hamburger | $5.00 × 30 = $150 | $6.00 × 30 = $180 |
| Cost of 50 lbs of Oranges | $1.00 × 50 = $50 | $1.10 × 50 = $55 |
| Cost of Entire Market Basket | $150 + $50 = $200 | $180 + $55 = $235 |

Now let's apply the formula again, to get the value of the CPI in December 2005:

CPI in 2005

$$= \frac{\text{Cost of 2004 basket a...}}{\text{Cost of 2004 basket a...}}$$

$$= \frac{\$235}{\$200} \times 10...$$

From December 2004 to Dece... from 100 to 117.5. The rate ... 2005 is therefore 17.5 percent ...

Notice that the CPI give... changes of goods that are mo... sumer's budget. In our exampl... the CPI (17.5 percent) is closer t... the price of hamburger (20 percen... centage price rise of oranges (1... because a greater percentage of the budget is *spent* on hamburger than on oranges, so hamburger carries more weight in the CPI.

But one of the CPI's problems, discussed in the body of the chapter, is *substitution bias*. The CPI recognizes that consumers substitute *within* categories of goods. For example, if we had a third good, steak, the CPI would recognize that consumers will buy more steak if

the price of hamburger rises faster than the price of ... assumes there is no substitution ... tween beef products and fruit, for ... ow much the relative price of beef ... ger rises, the CPI assumes that peo- ... uy the same quantity of it, rather ... in other categories like oranges. ... ice of hamburger rises, the CPI ... d a greater and greater percentage ... hamburger gets *increasing weight* ... ample, spending on hamburger is ... $150/$200 = 0.75, or 75 percent ... udget, to $180/$235 = 0.766, or ... however, the rapid rise in price ... substitute *away* from hamburger ... hose prices are rising more slowly. ... rs in our two-good example, as ... column of Table A.1. In 2005, the quantity of hamburger purchased drops to 10, and the quantity of oranges rises to 100. In an ideal measure, the decrease in the quantity of hamburger would reduce its weight in determining the overall rate of inflation. But the CPI ignores the information in the last column of Table A.1, which shows the new quantities purchased in 2005. This failure to correct for substitution bias across categories of goods is one of the reasons the CPI overstates inflation.

# The Classical Long-Run Model

Economists often disagree with each other. In news interviews, class lectures, and editorials, they give differing opinions about even the simplest matters. To the casual observer, it might seem that economics is little more than guesswork, where anyone's opinion is as good as anyone else's. But there is actually much more agreement among economists than there appears to be.

Take the following typical example: At a time when the economy is performing well, two distinguished economists appear on *CNN NewsNight*. In a somber tone, the anchor asks each of them what should be done to maintain the health of the economy. "We need to reduce the government's budget deficit by cutting government spending or raising taxes," replies the first economist. "This will enable private businesses to borrow more, so they can purchase new capital and the economy can grow faster." (Don't worry if this chain of logic isn't clear to you yet; it will be by the end of the next chapter.)

"No, no, no," the second economist might interrupt. "Cutting the deficit is the *worst* thing we could do right now. The economy appears to be slowing, and if we raise taxes or cut government spending, we'd reduce the take-home pay of households, causing them to cut their own spending. We'd push the economy toward a recession—one that the U.S. Federal Reserve might not be able to prevent." (You'll begin learning what's behind this argument a few chapters later.)

Which of these economists would be right? Surprisingly, it's entirely possible for *both* of them to be correct. But how can this be? Aren't the two responses contradictory? Not necessarily, because each economist might be hearing—and answering—a different question. The first economist is addressing the likely *long-run* impact of a cut in the government's budget deficit: the impact we might expect after several years have elapsed. The second economist, by contrast, is focusing on a possible *short-run* impact: the effects we might see over the next year.

Once the distinction between the long run and the short run becomes clear, many apparent disagreements among macroeconomists dissolve. If the news anchor had asked our two economists about the *long-run* impact of cutting the deficit, both may well have agreed that it would lead to more investment by business firms and faster economic growth. If asked about the *short-run* impact, both may have agreed about the potential danger of recession. If no time horizon is specified, however, an economist is likely to focus on the horizon he or she feels is most important—something about which economists sometimes *do* disagree. The real dispute, though, is less over how the economy *works* and more about what our priorities should be in guiding it.

Ideally, we would like our economy to do well in both the long run and the short run. Unfortunately, there is often a tradeoff between these two goals: Doing better in the short run can require some sacrifice of long-run goals, and vice versa. The problem for policy makers is much like that of the captain of a ship sailing through the North Atlantic. On the one hand, he wants to reach his destination (his long-run goal); on the other hand, he must avoid icebergs along the way (his short-run goal). As you might imagine, avoiding icebergs may require the captain to deviate from an ideal long-run course. At the same time, reaching port might require risking the occasional iceberg.

The same is true of the macroeconomy. If you flip back two chapters and look at Figure 4, you will see that there are two types of movements in total output. The long-run trajectory shows the growth of potential output. The short-run movements around that trajectory we call economic fluctuations or business cycles. Macroeconomists are concerned with both types of movements. But, as you will see, policies that can help us smooth out economic fluctuations may prove harmful to growth in the long run, while policies that promise a high rate of growth might require us to put up with more severe fluctuations in the short run.

## MACROECONOMIC MODELS: CLASSICAL VERSUS KEYNESIAN

**Classical model** A macro-economic model that explains the long-run behavior of the economy.

The **classical model,** developed by economists in the 19th and early 20th centuries, was an attempt to explain a key observation about the economy: Over periods of several years or longer, the economy performs rather well. That is, if we step back from current conditions and view the economy over a long stretch of time, we see that it operates reasonably close to its potential output. And even when it deviates, it does not do so for very long. Business cycles may come and go, but the economy eventually returns to full employment. Indeed, if we think in terms of decades rather than years or quarters, the business cycle fades in significance much like the waves in a choppy sea disappear when viewed from a jet plane.

In the classical view, this behavior is no accident: Powerful forces are at work that drive the economy toward full employment. Many of the classical economists went even further, arguing that these forces operated within a reasonably short period of time. And even today, an important group of macroeconomists continues to believe that the classical model is useful even in the shorter run.

Until the Great Depression of the 1930s, there was little reason to question these classical ideas. True, output fluctuated around its trend, and from time to time there were serious recessions, but output always returned to its potential, full-employment level within a few years or less, just as the classical economists predicted. But during the Great Depression, output was stuck far below its potential for many years. For some reason, the economy wasn't working the way the classical model said it should.

In 1936, in the midst of the Great Depression, the British economist John Maynard Keynes offered an explanation for the economy's poor performance. His new model of the economy—soon dubbed the *Keynesian model*—changed many economists' thinking.[1] Keynes and his followers argued that, while the classical model might

---

[1] Keynes's attack on the classical model was presented in his book *The General Theory of Employment, Interest and Money* (1936). Unfortunately, it's a very difficult book to read, though you may want to try. Keynes's assumptions were not always clear, and some of his text is open to multiple interpretations. As a result, economists have been arguing for decades about what Keynes really meant.

explain the economy's operation in the long run, the long run could be a very long time in arriving. In the meantime, production could be stuck below its potential, as it seemed to be during the Great Depression.

Keynesian ideas became increasingly popular in universities and government agencies during the 1940s and 1950s. By the mid-1960s, the entire profession had been won over: Macroeconomics *was* Keynesian economics, and the classical model was removed from virtually all introductory economics textbooks. You might be wondering, then, why we are bothering with the classical model here. After all, it's an older model of the economy, one that was largely discredited and replaced, just as the Ptolemaic view that the sun circled the earth was supplanted by the more modern, Copernican view. Right?

Not really. The classical model is still important, for two reasons. First, in recent decades, there has been an active counterrevolution against Keynes's approach to understanding the macroeconomy. Many of the counterrevolutionary new theories are based largely on classical ideas. In some cases, the new theories are just classical economics in modern clothing, but in other cases significant new ideas have been added. By studying classical macroeconomics, you will be better prepared to understand the controversies centering on these newer schools of thought.

The second—and more important—reason for us to study the classical model is its usefulness in understanding the economy over the long run. Even the many economists who find the classical model inadequate for understanding the economy in the short run find it extremely useful in analyzing the economy in the long run.

*Keynes's ideas and their further development help us understand economic fluctuations—movements in output around its long-run trend. But the classical model has proven more useful in explaining the long-run trend itself.*

This is why we will use the terms "classical view" and "long-run view" interchangeably in the rest of the book; in either case, we mean "the ideas of the classical model used to explain the economy's long-run behavior."

## ASSUMPTIONS OF THE CLASSICAL MODEL

Remember from Chapter 1 that all models begin with *assumptions* about the world. The classical model is no exception. Many of its assumptions are *simplifying;* they make the model more manageable, enabling us to see the broad outlines of economic behavior without getting lost in the details. Typically, these assumptions involve aggregation. We combine the many different interest rates in the economy and refer to a single interest rate. We combine the many different types of labor in the economy into a single aggregate labor market. These simplifications are usually harmless: Adding more detail would make our work more difficult, but it would not add much insight; nor would it change any of the central conclusions of the classical view.

There is, however, one assumption in the classical model that goes beyond mere simplification. This is an assumption about how the world works, and it is critical to the conclusions we will reach in this and the next chapter. We can state it in two words: *Markets clear.*

*A critical assumption in the classical model is that **markets clear***: *The price in every market will adjust until quantity supplied and quantity demanded are equal.*

**Market clearing** Adjustment of prices until quantities supplied and demanded are equal.

Does the market-clearing assumption sound familiar? It should: It was the basic idea behind our study of supply and demand. When we look at the economy through the classical lens, we assume that the forces of supply and demand work fairly well throughout the economy and that markets do reach equilibrium. An excess supply of anything traded will lead to a fall in its price; an excess demand will drive the price up.

The market-clearing assumption, which permeates classical thinking about the economy, provides an early hint about why the classical model does a better job over longer time periods (several years or more) than shorter ones. In some markets, prices might not fully adjust to their equilibrium values for many months or even years after some change in the economy. An excess supply or excess demand might persist for some time. Still, if we wait long enough, an excess supply in a market will eventually force the price down, and an excess demand will eventually drive the price up. That is, *eventually*, the market will clear. Therefore, when we are trying to explain the economy's behavior over the long run, market clearing seems to be a reasonable assumption.

In the remainder of the chapter, we'll use the classical model to answer a variety of important questions about the economy in the long run, such as:

- How is total employment determined?
- How much output will we produce?
- What role does total spending play in the economy?
- What happens when things change?

Keep in mind that, in our discussion of the classical model, we will focus on *real* variables: real GDP, the real wage, real saving, and so on. These variables are typically measured in the dollars of some base year, and their numerical values change only when their *purchasing power* changes. Even though our *actual* measures of the price level are imperfect, you can think of a real variable as one that reflects *true* purchasing power—the value we'd obtain if we used a perfectly accurate price index.

## HOW MUCH OUTPUT WILL WE PRODUCE?

Over the last decade, on average, the U.S. economy produced about $10 trillion worth of goods and services per year (valued in 2000 dollars). How was this average level of output determined? Why didn't we produce $14 trillion per year? Or just $2 trillion? There are so many things to consider when answering this question, variables you constantly hear about in the news: wages, interest rates, investment spending, government spending, taxes, and more. Each of these concepts plays an important role in determining total output, and our task in this chapter is to show how they all fit together.

But what a task! How can we disentangle the web of economic interactions we see around us? Our starting point will be the first step of our *three-step process*, introduced toward the end of Chapter 3. To review, that first step was to *characterize the market*—to decide which market or markets best suit the problem being analyzed, which means identifying the buyers and sellers and the type of environment in which they trade.

But which market should we start with?

The classical approach is to start at the beginning, with the *reason* for all this production in the first place: our desire for goods and services, and our need for income in order to buy them. In a market economy, people get their income from supplying labor and other resources to firms. Firms, in turn, use these resources to make the goods and services that people demand. Thus, a logical place to start our analysis is the markets for resources: labor, land, capital, and entrepreneurship.

For now we'll concentrate our attention on just one type of resource: labor. We'll assume that firms are already using the available quantities of the other resources. Moreover, because we are building a *macroeconomic* model, we'll aggregate all the different types of labor—office workers, construction workers, factory workers, teachers, waiters, writers, and more—into a single variable, simply called *labor*.

Our question is: How many workers will be employed in the economy?

## THE LABOR MARKET

The classical labor market is illustrated in Figure 1. The number of workers is measured on the horizontal axis, and the real hourly wage rate is measured on the vertical axis. Remember that the *real wage*—which is measured in the dollars of some base year—tells us the amount of goods that workers can buy with an hour's earnings.

Now look at the two curves in the figure. These are supply and demand curves, similar to the supply and demand curves for maple syrup, but there is one key difference: For a *good* such as maple syrup, households are the demanders and firms the suppliers. But for labor, the roles are reversed: Households supply labor and firms demand it.

The curve labeled $L^S$ is the **labor supply curve** in this market; it tells us how many people will want to work at each wage. The upward slope tells us that the greater the real wage, the greater the number of people who will want to work. Why does the labor supply curve slope upward?

**Labor supply curve** Indicates how many people will want to work at various real wage rates.

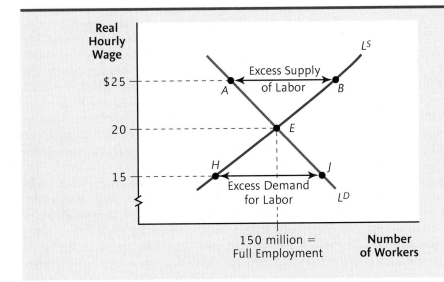

**FIGURE 1**

**The Labor Market**

*The equilibrium wage rate of $20 per hour is determined at point E, where the upward-sloping labor supply curve crosses the downward-sloping labor demand curve. At any other wage, an excess demand or excess supply of labor will cause an adjustment back to equilibrium.*

To earn income, you must go to work and give up other activities such as school, parenting, or leisure. Thus, each of us will want to work only if the income we will earn *at least* compensates us for the other activities that we will give up.

Of course, people value their time differently. But for each of us, there is some critical wage rate above which we would decide that we're better off working. Below that wage, we would be better off not working. In Figure 1,

> *the labor supply curve slopes upward because, as the wage rate increases, more and more individuals are better off working than not working. Thus, a rise in the wage rate increases the number of people in the economy who want to work—to supply their labor.*

**Labor demand curve** Indicates how many workers firms will want to hire at various real wage rates.

The curve labeled $L^D$ is the **labor demand curve**, which shows the number of workers firms will want to hire at any real wage. Why does this curve slope downward?

In deciding how much labor to hire, a firm's goal is to earn the greatest possible profit: the difference between sales revenue and costs. A firm will want to keep hiring additional workers as long as the output produced by those workers adds more to the firm's revenue than it adds to costs.

Now think about what happens as the wage rate rises. Some workers that added more to revenue than to cost at the lower wage will now cost more than they add in revenue. Accordingly, the firm will not want to employ these workers at the higher wage.

> *As the wage rate increases, each firm in the economy will find that, to maximize profit, it should employ fewer workers than before. When all firms behave this way together, a rise in the wage rate will decrease the quantity of labor demanded in the economy.*

Remember that in the classical view, *all markets clear*, and that includes the market for labor. Specifically, the real wage adjusts until the quantities of labor supplied and demanded are equal. In the labor market in Figure 1, the market-clearing wage is $20 per hour because that is where the labor supply and labor demand curves intersect. While every worker would prefer to earn $25 rather than $20, at $25 there would be an excess supply of labor equal to the distance *AB*. With not enough jobs to go around, competition among workers would drive the wage downward. Similarly, firms might prefer to pay their workers $15 rather than $20, but at $15, the excess demand for labor (equal to the distance *HJ*) would drive the wage upward. When the wage is $20, however, there is neither an excess demand nor an excess supply of labor, so the wage will neither increase nor decrease. Thus, $20 is the equilibrium wage in the economy. Reading along the horizontal axis, we see that at this wage, 150 million people will be working.

Notice that, in the figure, labor is fully employed; that is, the number of workers that firms want to hire is equal to the number of people who want jobs. Therefore, everyone who wants a job at the market wage of $20 should be able to find one. Small amounts of frictional unemployment might exist, since it takes some time for new workers or job switchers to find jobs. And there might be structural unemployment, due to some mismatch between those who want jobs in the market and the types of jobs available. But there is no *cyclical* unemployment of the type we discussed two chapters ago.

Full employment of the labor force is an important feature of the classical model. As long as we can count on markets (including the labor market) to clear, government action is not needed to ensure full employment; it happens automatically:

*In the classical view, the economy achieves full employment on its own.*

Automatic full employment may strike you as odd, since it contradicts the cyclical unemployment we sometimes see around us. For example, in the recession of 2001, millions of workers around the country, in all kinds of professions and labor markets, were unable to find jobs for many months. Remember, though, that the classical model takes the long-run view, and over long periods of time, full employment is a fairly accurate description of the U.S. labor market. Cyclical unemployment, by definition, lasts only as long as the current business cycle itself; it is not a permanent, long-run problem.

## Determining the Economy's Output

So far, we've focused on the labor market to determine the economy's level of employment. In our example, 150 million people will have jobs. Now we ask: How much output (real GDP) will these 150 million workers produce? The answer depends on two things: (1) the amount of other resources available for labor to use; and (2) the state of *technology*, which determines how much output we can produce with those resources.

In this chapter, remember that we're focusing on only one resource—labor—and we're treating the quantities of all other resources firms use as fixed during the period we're analyzing. Now we'll go even further: We'll assume that technology does not change.

Why do we make these assumptions? After all, in the real world technology *does* change, the capital stock *does* grow, new natural resources *can* be discovered, and the number and quality of entrepreneurs *can* change. Isn't it unrealistic to hold all of these things constant?

Yes, but our assumption is only temporary. The most effective way to master a macroeconomic model is "divide and conquer": Start with a part of the model, understand it well, and then add in other parts. Accordingly, our classical analysis of the economy is divided into two separate questions: (1) What would be the long-run equilibrium of the economy *if* there were a constant state of technology and *if* quantities of all resources besides labor were fixed? And (2) What happens to this long-run equilibrium when technology and the quantities of other resources change? In this chapter, we focus on the first question. In the next chapter on economic growth, we'll address the second question.

### The Production Function

With a constant technology, and given quantities of all resources other than labor, only one variable can affect total output: the quantity of labor. So it's time to explore the relationship between total employment and total production in the economy. This relationship is given by the economy's *aggregate production function*.

*The **aggregate production function** (or just **production function**) shows the total output the economy can produce with different quantities of labor, given constant amounts of other resources and the current state of technology.*

**Aggregate production function**
The relationship showing how much total output can be produced with different quantities of labor, with quantities of all other resources held constant.

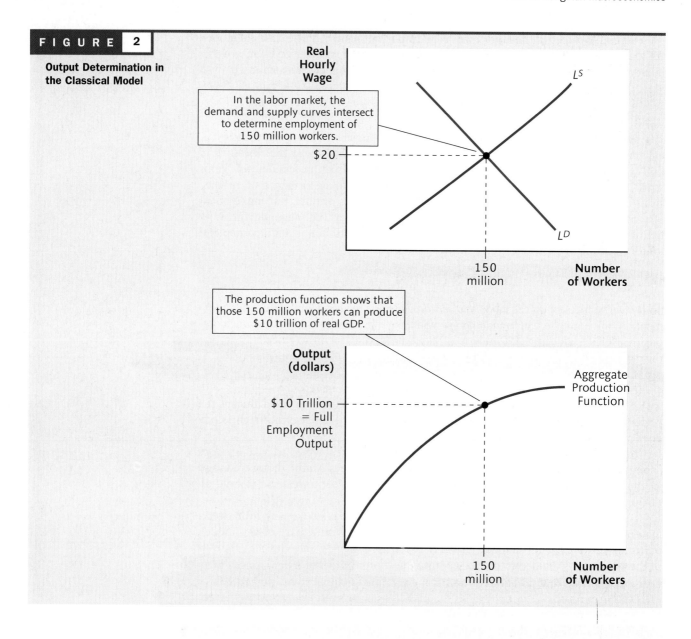

**FIGURE 2**

**Output Determination in the Classical Model**

In the labor market, the demand and supply curves intersect to determine employment of 150 million workers.

The production function shows that those 150 million workers can produce $10 trillion of real GDP.

The bottom panel of Figure 2 shows what a nation's aggregate production function might look like. The upward slope tells us that an increase in the number of people working will increase the quantity of output produced. But notice the shape of the production function: It flattens out as we move rightward along it.

The declining slope of the aggregate production function is the result of *diminishing returns to labor:* Output rises when another worker is added, but the rise is smaller and smaller with each successive worker.

Why does this happen? For one thing, as we keep adding workers, gains from specialization are harder and harder to come by. Moreover, as we continue to add workers, each one will have less and less of the other resources to work with. For example, each time more agricultural workers are added to a fixed amount of farmland, output might rise. But as we continue to add workers and there are more and more workers per acre, output will rise by less and less with each new worker. The same is true when more factory workers are added to a fixed amount of factory floor space and machinery, or more professors are added to a fixed number of classrooms: Output continues to rise, but by less and less with each added worker.

Figure 2 also illustrates how the aggregate production function, together with the labor market, determines the economy's total output or real GDP. In our example, the labor market (upper panel) automatically generates full employment of 150 million workers, and the production function (lower panel) tells us that 150 million workers—together with the available amounts of other resources and the current state of technology—can produce $10 trillion worth of output. Since $10 trillion is the output produced by a fully employed labor force, it is also the economy's potential output level.

> *In the classical, long-run view, the economy reaches its potential output automatically.*

This last statement is an important conclusion of the classical model and an important characteristic of the economy in the long run: Output tends toward its potential, full-employment level *on its own*, with no need for government to steer the economy toward it. And we have arrived at this conclusion merely by assuming that the labor market clears and observing the relationship between employment and output.


## THE ROLE OF SPENDING

Something may be bothering you about the classical view of output determination, a potential problem we have so far carefully avoided: What if business firms are unable to sell all the output produced by a fully employed labor force? Then business firms will not continue to employ workers who produce output that is not being sold, and the economy will not remain at full employment for very long. Thus, if we are asserting that potential output is the economy's equilibrium, we had better be sure that *total spending* on output is equal to *total production* during any given year. But can we be sure of this?

In the classical view, the answer is, absolutely yes! We'll demonstrate this in two stages: first, in a very simple (but very unrealistic) economy, and then, under more realistic conditions.

### Total Spending in a Very Simple Economy

Imagine a world much simpler than our own, a world with just two types of economic units: households and business firms. In this world, households spend all of their income on goods and services. They do not save any of their income, nor do they pay taxes, nor do they buy any products from abroad. Such an economy is illustrated in Figure 3.

Let's assume that $10 trillion worth of goods and services are produced in this economy during the year. As you learned two chapters ago, the value of the total

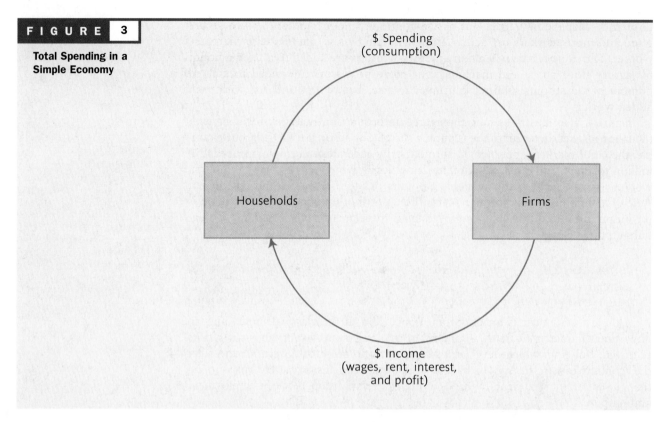

**FIGURE 3**

**Total Spending in a Simple Economy**

output of firms is equal to the total income (factor payments) of households. So with firms producing $10 trillion in output, they also pay out $10 trillion to households in the form of wages, rent, interest, and profit. What happens to this $10 trillion in household income? In this simple economy, with no saving, no taxes, and no goods purchased from abroad, the $10 trillion has nowhere to go except to be spent on domestically produced output. Thus, household consumption spending will equal $10 trillion—the same as the value of output that firms are producing.

In general,

> *in a simple economy with just households and firms, in which households spend all of their income on domestic output, total spending must be equal to total output.*

**Say's law** The idea that total spending will be sufficient to purchase the total output produced.

This simple proposition is called **Say's law,** after the early 19th-century economist Jean Baptiste Say, who popularized the idea. Say noted that each time a good or service is produced, an equal amount of income is created. This income is spent, so it comes back to the business sector to purchase its goods and services. In Say's own words:

> A product *is no sooner created than it, from that instant, affords a market for other products to the full extent of its own value. . . . Thus, the mere circumstance of the creation of one product immediately opens a vent for other products.*[2]

[2]  J. B. Say, *A Treatise on Political Economy,* 4th ed. (London: Longman, 1821), Vol. I, p. 167.

For example, each time a shirt manufacturer produces a $25 shirt, it creates $25 in factor payments to households. (Forgot why? Go back two chapters and refresh your memory about the factor payments approach to GDP.) But in the simple economy we're analyzing, that $25 in factor payments will lead to $25 in total spending—just enough to buy the very shirt produced. Of course, the households who receive the $25 in factor payments won't necessarily buy a shirt with it; the shirt manufacturer must still worry about selling its own specific output. But in the *aggregate,* we needn't worry about there being sufficient demand for the total output produced. Business firms—by producing output—also create a demand for goods and services equal to the value of that output.

> *Say's law states that by producing goods and services, firms create a total demand for goods and services equal to what they have produced. Or, more simply, supply creates its own demand.*

Say's law is crucial to the classical view of the economy. Why? Remember that because the labor market is assumed to clear, firms will hire all the workers who want jobs and produce our *potential* or *full-employment* output level. But firms will only *continue* to produce this level of output if they can *sell* it all. In the simple economy of Figure 3, Say's law assures us that, in the aggregate, spending will be just high enough for firms to sell all the output that a fully employed labor force can produce. As a result, full employment can be maintained.

But the economy in Figure 3 leaves out some important details of economies in the real world. Does Say's law also apply in a more realistic economy? Let's see.

## Total Spending in a More Realistic Economy

The real-world economy is more complicated than the imaginary one we've just considered. One complication is trade with the rest of the world. We'll deal with international trade in the appendix to this chapter. For now, we'll continue to assume that we're in a *closed economy*—one that does not have any economic dealings with the rest of the world. But here we'll add some features that we ignored before.

In the real world:

- Households don't spend *all* their income. Rather, some of their income is saved or goes to pay taxes.
- Households are not the only spenders in the economy. Rather, businesses and the government also buy final goods and services.

With these added details, will Say's law still apply?

Let's consider the economy of Classica, a fictional economy that behaves according to the classical model, but more realistically than the economy of Figure 3. Data on Classica's economy in 2006 are given in Table 1. Notice that total output and total income are both equal to $10 trillion in 2006, which is assumed to be Classica's full-employment or potential output level.

Next come three entries that refer to spending by the final users who purchase Classica's GDP. Note that, unlike the households in Figure 3, Classica's households spend only *part* of their income, $7 trillion, on consumption goods (*C*). Skipping down to government purchases (*G*), we find that Classica's government sector—combining its national, regional, and local government agencies—purchases $2 trillion in goods and services.

| TABLE 1 | | |
| --- | --- | --- |
| **Flows in the Economy of Classica, 2006** | Total Output (GDP) | $10 trillion |
| | Total Income | $10 trillion |
| | Consumption Spending ($C$) | $7 trillion |
| | Planned Investment Spending ($I^p$) | $1 trillion |
| | Government Purchases ($G$) | $2 trillion |
| | Net Taxes ($T$) | $1.25 trillion |
| | Household Saving ($S$) | $1.75 trillion |

### Some New Macroeconomic Variables

In addition to consumption and government purchases—with which you are already familiar—Table 1 includes some new variables. Since these will be used throughout the rest of this book, it's worth defining and discussing them here.

*Planned Investment Spending ($I^p$).* Two chapters ago, you learned that total investment spending—the component labeled $I$ in the expenditure approach to GDP—includes not only business spending on new capital but also *changes in firms' inventories* over a period of time. Inventory changes occur when firms produce more than they sell (an increase in inventories) or sell more than they produce (a decrease in inventories).

Our ultimate goal is to find out if Say's law works in Classica—if total spending exactly matches Classica's total output. Therefore, it would be a mistake to include inventory changes—which represent the mismatch between sales and production—as part of investment spending. When we exclude inventory changes from investment spending, we're left with *planned investment spending*.

**Planned investment spending**
Business purchases of plant and equipment.

> *Planned investment spending* ($I^p$) *over a period of time is total investment spending* ($I$) *minus the change in inventories over the period:*
>
> $$I^p = I - \Delta\ inventories.$$

Here, we're using the Greek letter $\Delta$ ("delta") to indicate a change in a variable.

Why do we call this new variable *planned* investment? In the real world, some inventory changes are, in fact, planned by firms. But they can also come as a surprise. For example, suppose Calvin Klein produces $40 million in clothing during a quarter, planning to sell all of it. But during the quarter, it actually ships and sells only $35 million. Then $5 million in unsold output would be an *unplanned increase in inventories*—a surprise, rather than a planned result. On the other hand, if Calvin Klein sold $43 million, then $3 million in sales would come out of inventories. This would be an *unplanned decrease in inventories*—a surprise in the other direction.

Changes in inventories are generally the only component of spending in GDP that is not planned. A firm does not "discover" at the end of a quarter that it has purchased a new factory. This type of investment is intended and planned in advance. And—other than Homer in *The Simpsons*—a consumer doesn't "discover" that he has purchased a new car or a lifetime supply of slurpies; consumption spending is intentional.

In this and future chapters, to keep our discussions simple we'll regard *all* inventory changes as unplanned surprises. This is why, after deducting inventory changes from total investment, we call what is left *planned investment*. In Table 1, you can see that Classica's planned investment spending—which excludes any changes in inventories—is $1 trillion.

*Net Tax Revenue (T).* Recall (from two chapters ago) that *transfer payments* are government outlays that are *not* spent on goods and services. These transfers— which include unemployment insurance, welfare payments, and Social Security benefits—are just *given* to people, either out of social concern (welfare payments), to keep a promise (Social Security payments), or elements of both (unemployment insurance).

In the macroeconomy, government transfer payments are like negative taxes: They represent the part of tax revenue that the government takes from one set of households (taxpayers) but gives right back to another set of households (such as Social Security recipients), and are not available for government purchases. Because transfer payments stay *within* the household sector, we can treat them as if they were never paid to the government at all. We do this by focusing on *net taxes*:

> *Net taxes* (**T**) *are total government tax revenue minus government transfer payments:*
>
> T = *Total tax revenue − Transfers.*

**Net taxes** Government tax revenues minus transfer payments.

For example, in 2006 net taxes in Classica are $1.25 trillion. This number might result from total tax revenue of $2 trillion and $0.75 trillion in government transfer payments. It could also result from $3 trillion in tax revenue and $1.75 trillion in transfers. From the macroeconomic perspective, net taxes—what the government has available for purchases—are $1.25 trillion in either case.

*Household Saving (S).* We'll define household saving in two steps. First, we determine how much income the household sector has left after payment of net taxes. This is the household sector's **disposable income**:

**Disposable income** Household income minus net taxes, which is either spent or saved.

$$\text{Disposable income} = \text{Total income} - \text{Net taxes.}$$

The household sector can *dispose* of this disposable (after-tax) income in only two ways: either by spending it (C) or by *not* spending it. The part that is *not* spent is defined as (**household**) **saving** (S):

**(Household) saving** The portion of after-tax income that households do not spend on consumption.

$$S = \text{Disposable income} - C.$$

The last entry in Table 1 tells us that in Classica, household saving is $1.75 trillion. Let's check this using disposable income. From the table, total income is $7 trillion and net taxes are $1.25 trillion, so disposable income (not shown in the table) is $10 trillion − $1.25 trillion = $8.75 trillion. Consumption spending is $7 trillion, so:

$$S = \text{Disposable income} - C = \$8.75 \text{ trillion} - \$7 \text{ trillion} = \$1.75 \text{ trillion}$$

**Total Spending in Classica**

In Classica, total spending is the sum of the purchases made by the household sector (C), the business sector ($I^p$), and the government sector (G):

$$\text{Total spending} = C + I^P + G.$$

Or, using the numbers in Table 1:

$$\text{Total spending} = \$7 \text{ trillion} + \$1 \text{ trillion} + \$2 \text{ trillion} = \$10 \text{ trillion}.$$

This may strike you as suspiciously convenient: Total spending is exactly equal to total output, just as we'd like it to be if we want Classica to continue producing its potential output of $10 trillion. And just what we needed to illustrate Say's law in this more realistic economy.

But we haven't yet proven anything; we've just cooked up an example that made the numbers come out this way. The question is, do we have any reason to *expect* the economy to give us numbers like these automatically, with total spending precisely equal to total output?

The rectangles in Figure 4 provide some perspective on this question and suggest the way to an answer. Total output (represented by the first rectangle) is, by definition, always equal in value to total income (the second rectangle). As we've seen in Figure 3, if households *spent* all of this income, then consumption spending would equal total output.

But in Classica, households do *not* spend all of their income. Some income goes to pay net taxes ($1.25 trillion), and some is saved ($1.75 trillion). We can think of

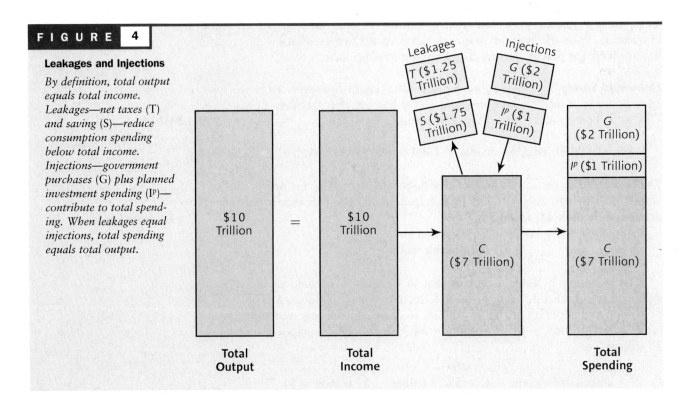

**FIGURE 4**

**Leakages and Injections**

*By definition, total output equals total income. Leakages—net taxes (T) and saving (S)—reduce consumption spending below total income. Injections—government purchases (G) plus planned investment spending ($I^p$)—contribute to total spending. When leakages equal injections, total spending equals total output.*

Leakages

T ($1.25 Trillion)

S ($1.75 Trillion)

Injections

G ($2 Trillion)

$I^p$ ($1 Trillion)

$10 Trillion = $10 Trillion

C ($7 Trillion)

G ($2 Trillion)

$I^p$ ($1 Trillion)

C ($7 Trillion)

Total Output          Total Income                                    Total Spending saving and net taxes as **leakages** out of spending: income that households receive, but do not spend. Leakages reduce consumption spending below total income, as you can see in the third, lower rectangle. In Classica, total leakages = $1.75 trillion + $1.25 trillion = $3 trillion, and this must be subtracted from income of $10 trillion to get consumption spending of $7 trillion. Thus, if consumption spending were the only spending in the economy, business firms would be unable to sell their entire potential output of $10 trillion.

Fortunately, in addition to leakages, there are **injections**—spending from sources *other* than households. Injections boost total spending and enable firms to produce and sell a level of output greater than just consumption spending.

There are two types of injections in the economy. First is the government's purchases of goods and services. When government agencies—federal, state, or local—buy aircraft, cleaning supplies, cellular phones, or computers, they are buying a part of the economy's output.

The other injection is planned investment spending ($I^p$). When business firms purchase new computers, trucks, or machinery, or they build new factories or office buildings, they are buying a part of the GDP along with consumers and the government.

Take another look at the rectangles in Figure 4. Notice that in going from total output to total spending, leakages are subtracted and injections are added. Clearly, total output and total spending will be equal only if leakages and injections are equal as well.

> *Total spending will equal total output if and only if total leakages in the economy are equal to total injections—that is, only if the sum of saving and net taxes is equal to the sum of planned investment spending and government purchases.*

And here is a surprising result: In the classical model, this condition will automatically be satisfied. To see why, we must first take a detour through another important market. Then we'll come back to the equality of leakages and injections.

## THE LOANABLE FUNDS MARKET

The **loanable funds market** is where households make their saving available to those who need additional funds. When you save—that is, when you have income left over after paying taxes and buying consumption goods—you can put your surplus funds in a bank, buy a bond or a share of stock, or use the funds to buy a variety of other assets. In each of these cases, you would be a supplier in the loanable funds market.

Households supply funds because they receive a reward for doing so. But the reward comes in different forms. When the suppliers *lend* out funds, the reward is *interest payments*. When the funds are provided through the stock market, the suppliers become part owners of the firm and their payment is called *dividends*. To keep our discussion simple, we'll assume that all funds made available by households are *loaned* and that the payment is simply *interest*.

> *The total supply of loanable funds is equal to household saving. The funds supplied are loaned out, and households receive interest payments on these funds.*

**Leakages** Income earned, but not spent, by households during a given year.

**Injections** Spending from sources other than households.

**Loanable funds market** The market in which households make their saving available to borrowers.

On the other side of the market are those who want to obtain funds—demanders in this market. Business firms are one set of demanders of funds. When Avis wants to add cars to its automobile rental fleet, when McDonald's wants to build a new beef-processing plant, or when the local dry cleaner wants to buy new dry cleaning machines, it will likely raise the funds in the loanable funds market. It may take out a bank loan, sell bonds, or sell new shares of stock. In each of these cases, a firm's planned investment spending would be equal to the funds it obtains from the loanable funds market. To keep the discussion simple, we'll assume that business firms *borrow* the funds they obtain in the loanable funds market.

> *Businesses' demand for loanable funds is equal to their planned investment spending. The funds obtained are borrowed, and firms* pay interest *on their loans.*

Aside from households and business firms, the other major player in the loanable funds market is the government sector. Government participates in the market whenever it runs a budget deficit or a budget surplus.

When government purchases of goods and services ($G$) are greater than net taxes ($T$), the government runs a **budget deficit** equal to $G - T$. When government purchases of goods and services ($G$) are less than net taxes ($T$), the government runs a **budget surplus** equal to $T - G$.

In our example in Table 1, Classica's government is running a budget deficit: Government purchases are $2 trillion, while net taxes are $1.25 trillion, giving us a deficit of $2 trillion − $1.25 trillion = $0.75 trillion. This deficit is financed by borrowing in the loanable funds market. In any year, the government's demand for funds is equal to its deficit.

> *When the government runs a budget deficit, its demand for loanable funds is equal to its deficit. The funds are borrowed, and the government* pays interest *on its loans.*

(What if Classica's government were running a surplus? You'll be asked to consider that in the end-of-chapter problems.)

We can summarize our view of the loanable funds market so far with these two points:

- The supply of funds is household saving.
- The demand for funds is the sum of the business sector's planned investment spending and the government sector's budget deficit, if any.

Now let's take a closer look at the behavior of each of the key players—households, business firms, and the government—in the market for loanable funds.

## THE SUPPLY OF FUNDS CURVE

Since interest is the reward for saving and supplying funds to the financial market, a rise in the interest rate *increases* the quantity of funds supplied (household saving), while a drop in the interest rate decreases it. This relationship is illustrated by Classica's upward-sloping **supply of funds curve** in Figure 5. If the interest rate is 3 percent, households save $1.5 trillion, and if the interest rate rises to 5 percent, people save more and the quantity of funds supplied rises to $1.75 trillion.

**Budget deficit** The excess of government purchases over net taxes.

**Budget surplus** The excess of net taxes over government purchases.

**Supply of funds curve** Indicates the level of household saving at various interest rates.

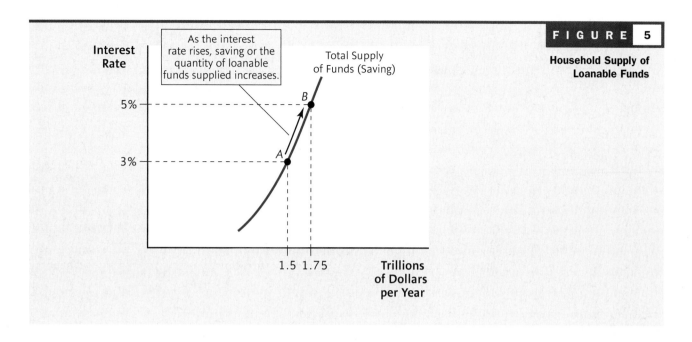

**FIGURE 5**

**Household Supply of Loanable Funds**

*The quantity of funds supplied to the financial market depends positively on the interest rate. This is why the saving or supply of funds curve slopes upward.*

Of course, other things can affect saving besides the interest rate: tax rates, expectations about the future, and the general willingness of households to post-pone consumption, to name a few. In drawing the supply of funds curve, we assume each of these variables is constant. In the next chapter, we'll explore what happens when some of these variables change.

## THE DEMAND FOR FUNDS CURVE

Businesses buy plant and equipment when the expected benefits exceed the costs. Since businesses obtain the funds for their investment spending from the loanable funds market, a key cost of any investment project is the interest rate that must be paid on borrowed funds. As the interest rate rises and investment costs increase, fewer projects will look attractive, and planned investment spending will decline. This is the logic of the downward-sloping **business demand for funds curve** in Figure 6. At a 5 percent interest rate, firms would borrow $1 trillion and spend it on capital equipment; at an interest rate of 3 percent, business borrowing and investment spending would rise to $1.5 trillion.

**Business demand for funds curve** Indicates the level of investment spending firms plan at various interest rates.

*When the interest rate falls, investment spending and the business borrow-ing needed to finance it rise.*

What about the government's demand for funds? Will it, too, be influenced by the interest rate? Probably not very much. Government seems to be cushioned from the cost–benefit considerations that haunt business decisions. Any company president who ignored interest rates in deciding how much to borrow would be quickly out of a job. U.S. presidents and legislators have often done so with little political cost.

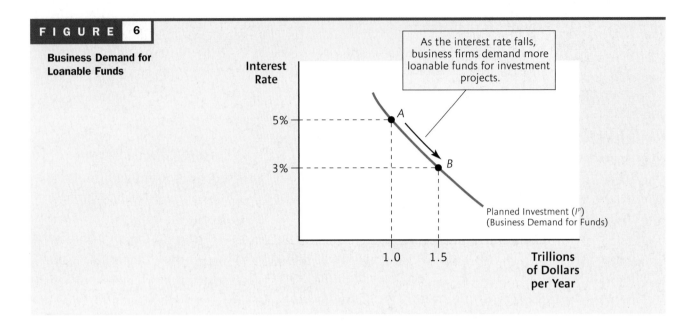

**FIGURE 6**

**Business Demand for Loanable Funds**

For this reason, when government is running a budget deficit, our classical model treats government borrowing as independent of the interest rate: No matter what the interest rate, the government sector's deficit—and its borrowing—is the same. This is why we have graphed the **government's demand for funds curve** as a vertical line in panel (b) of Figure 7.

> *The government sector's deficit and, therefore, its demand for funds are independent of the interest rate.*

**Government demand for funds curve** Indicates the amount of government borrowing at various interest rates.

In the figure, the government deficit—and hence the government's demand for funds—is equal to $0.75 trillion at any interest rate.

Figure 7 also shows that the **total demand for funds curve** is found by horizontally summing the business demand curve [panel (a)] and the government demand curve [panel (b)]. For example, if the interest rate is 5 percent, firms demand $1 trillion in funds and the government demands $0.75 trillion, so that the total quantity of loanable funds demanded is $1.75 trillion. A drop in the interest rate—to 3 percent—increases business borrowing to $1.5 trillion while the government's borrowing remains at $0.75 trillion, so the total quantity of funds demanded rises to $2.25 trillion.

**Total demand for funds curve** Indicates the total amount of borrowing at various interest rates.

> *As the interest rate decreases, the quantity of funds demanded by business firms increases, while the quantity demanded by the government remains unchanged. Therefore, the total quantity of funds demanded rises.*

## EQUILIBRIUM IN THE LOANABLE FUNDS MARKET

In the classical view, the loanable funds market—like all other markets—is assumed to clear: The interest rate will rise or fall until the quantities of funds supplied and demanded are equal. Figure 8 illustrates the loanable funds market of Classica, our

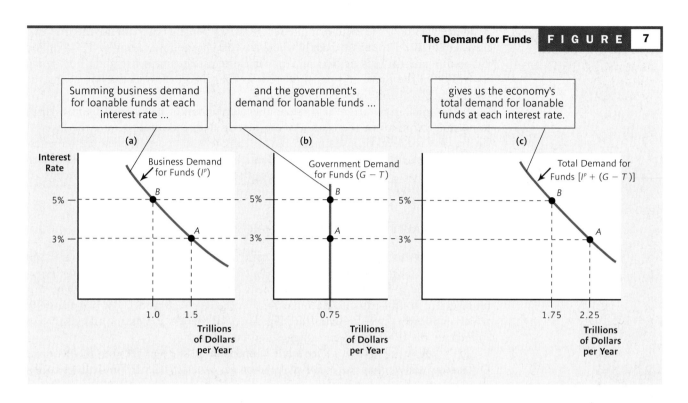

**The Demand for Funds**   **FIGURE**   **7**

Summing business demand for loanable funds at each interest rate ...

and the government's demand for loanable funds ...

gives us the economy's total demand for loanable funds at each interest rate.

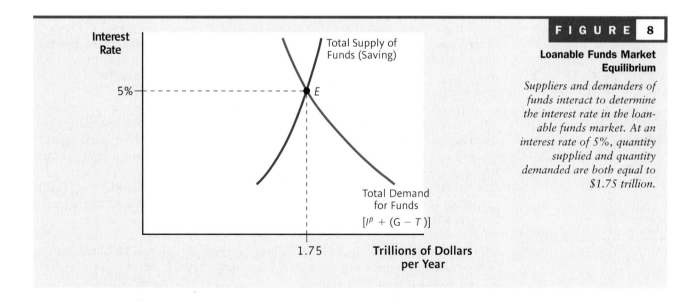

**FIGURE**   **8**

**Loanable Funds Market Equilibrium**

*Suppliers and demanders of funds interact to determine the interest rate in the loanable funds market. At an interest rate of 5%, quantity supplied and quantity demanded are both equal to $1.75 trillion.*

fictional economy. Equilibrium occurs at point *E*, with an interest rate of 5 percent and total saving equal to $1.75 trillion. (To convince yourself that 5 percent is the equilibrium interest rate, mark an interest rate of 4 percent on the graph. Would there be an excess demand or an excess supply of loanable funds at this rate? How would the interest rate change? Then do the same for an interest rate of 6 percent.)

Once we know the equilibrium interest rate (5 percent), we can use the first two panels of Figure 7 to tell us exactly where the total household saving of $1.75 billion ends up. Panel (a) tells us that at 5 percent interest, business firms are borrowing $1 trillion of the total, and panel (b) tells us that the government is borrowing the remaining $0.75 trillion to cover its deficit.

So far, our exploration of the loanable funds market has shown us how three important variables in the economy are determined: the interest rate, the level of saving, and the level of investment. But it really tells us more. Remember the question that sent us on this detour into the loanable funds market in the first place: Can we be sure that all of the output produced at full employment will be purchased? We now have the tools to answer this question.

## THE LOANABLE FUNDS MARKET AND SAY'S LAW

In Figure 4 of this chapter, you saw that total spending will equal total output if and only if *total leakages* in the economy (saving plus net taxes) are equal to *total injections* (planned investment plus government purchases). Now we can see why this requirement will be satisfied automatically in the classical model. Look at Figure 9, which duplicates the rectangles from Figure 4. But there is something added: arrows to indicate the flows between leakages and injections.

Let's follow the arrows to see what happens to all the leakages out of spending. One arrow shows that the entire leakage of net taxes ($1.25 trillion) flows to the government, which spends it.

Now look at the other two arrows that show us what happens to the $1.75 trillion leakage of household saving. $0.75 trillion of this saving is borrowed by the government, while the rest—$1 trillion—is borrowed by business firms.

But let's step back from the numbers, and focus on the logic of Figure 9. Remember our question: Will total spending be sufficient to purchase the economy's total output? And remember what created some doubt about the answer: The household sector spends only *part* of its income, because of the leakages of net taxes and saving.

Figure 9 shows us that net taxes and savings don't just disappear from the economy. Net taxes go to the government, which *spends them*. And any funds saved go either to the government—which spends them—or to business firms—which spend them.

But wait . . . how do we know that *all* funds that are saved will end up going to either the government or businesses? Because the loanable funds market clears: The interest rate adjusts until the quantity of loanable funds supplied (saving) is equal to the quantity of loanable funds demanded (government and business borrowing).

We can put all this together as follows: Every dollar of output creates a dollar of household income, by definition. And—as long as the loanable funds market clears—every dollar of income will either be spent by households themselves or passed along to some *other* sector of the economy that will spend it in their place.

Or, to put it even more simply,

> *as long as the loanable funds market clears, Say's law holds: Total spending equals total output. This is true even in a more realistic economy with saving, taxes, investment, and a government deficit.*

Here's another way to see the same result, in terms of a simple equation. Because the loanable funds market clears, we know that the interest rate—the price in this

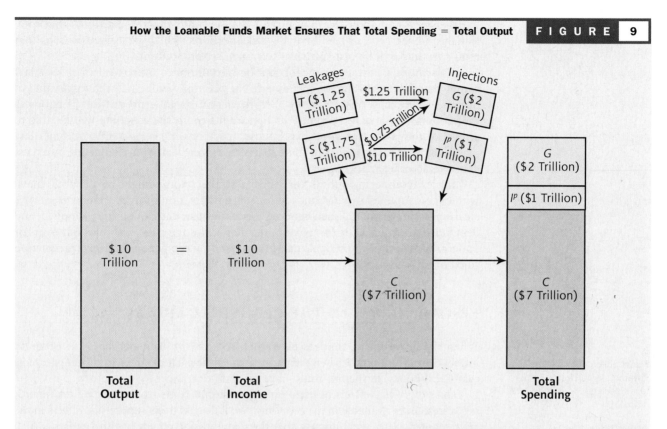

**How the Loanable Funds Market Ensures That Total Spending = Total Output** FIGURE 9

Because the loanable funds market clears, we know that total leakages will automatically equal total injections. The leakage of net taxes goes to the government and is spent on government purchases. If the government is running a budget deficit, it will also borrow part of the leakage of household saving and spend that too. Any household saving left over will be borrowed by business firms and spent on capital. Thus, every dollar of leakages turns into spending by either government or private business firms.

market—will rise or fall until the quantity of funds supplied (savings, $S$) is equal to the quantity of funds demanded (planned investment plus the deficit, or $I^p + (G - T)$):

Loanable funds market clears ⇒ $S$ = $I^p + (G - T)$.

Quantity of          Quantity of
funds supplied    funds demanded

Rearranging this equation by moving $T$ to the left side, we have:

Loanable funds market clears ⇒ $S + T$ = $I^p + G$

Leakages       Injections

Finally, remember that

Leakages = Injections ⇒ Total spending = Total output

In other words, market clearing in the loanable funds market *assures us* that total leakages in the economy will equal total injections, which in turn *assures us* that total spending will be just sufficient to purchase total output.

Say's law is a powerful concept. But be careful not to overinterpret it. Say's law shows that the *total* value of spending in the economy will equal the *total* value of output, which rules out a *general* overproduction or underproduction of goods in the economy. It does not promise us that each firm in the economy will be able to sell all of the particular good it produces. It is perfectly consistent with Say's law that there be excess supplies in some markets, as long as they are balanced by excess demands in other markets.

But lest you begin to think that the classical economy might be a chaotic mess, with excess supplies and demands in lots of markets, don't forget about the *market-clearing* assumption. In each market, prices adjust until quantities supplied and demanded are equal. For this reason, the classical, long-run view rules out over- or underproduction in individual markets, as well as the generalized overproduction ruled out by Say's law.

## FISCAL POLICY IN THE CLASSICAL MODEL

**Fiscal policy** A change in government purchases or net taxes designed to change total output.

**Demand-side effects** Macroeconomic policy effects on total output that work through changes in total spending.

When the government changes either net taxes or its own purchases in order to influence total output, it is engaging in **fiscal policy**. There are two different effects that fiscal policy, in theory, could have on total output.

The *supply-side* effects of fiscal policy on output come from changing the quantities of resources available in the economy. We'll discuss these supply-side effects in the next chapter. Here, we'll discuss only the **demand-side effects** of fiscal policy, which are entirely different. These effects arise from fiscal policy's impact on total spending.

At first glance, using fiscal policy to change total spending and thereby change the economy's real GDP seems workable. For example, if the government cuts taxes or increases transfer payments, households would have more income, so their consumption spending would increase. Or the government itself could purchase more goods and services. In either case, if total spending rises, and business firms *sell* more output, they should want to hire more workers and *produce* more output as well. The economy's real GDP would rise.

It sounds reasonable. Does it work?

Not if the economy behaves according to the classical model. As you are about to see, in the classical model *fiscal policy has no demand-side effects at all*.

### AN INCREASE IN GOVERNMENT PURCHASES

Let's first see what would happen if the government of Classica attempted to increase employment and output by increasing government purchases. More specifically, suppose the government raised its spending by $0.5 trillion, hiring people to fix roads and bridges, or hiring more teachers, or increasing its spending on goods and services for homeland security. What would happen?

To answer this, we must first answer another question: Where will Classica's government get the additional $0.5 trillion it spends? If net taxes are unchanged (as we are assuming), then the government deficit will rise, so the government must dip into the loanable funds market to *borrow* the additional funds.

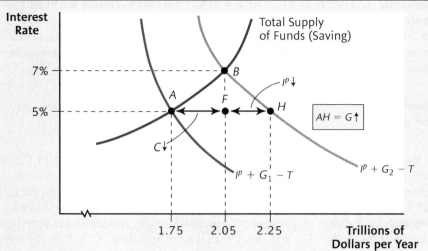

FIGURE 10

**Crowding Out from an Increase in Government Purchases**

*Beginning from equilibrium at point A, an increase in the budget deficit caused by additional government purchases shifts the demand for funds curve from $I^p + G_1 - T$ to $I^p + G_2 - T$. At point H, the quantity of funds demanded exceeds the quantity supplied, so the interest rate begins to rise. As it rises, households are led to save more, and business firms invest less. In the new equilibrium at point B, both consumption and investment spending have been completely crowded out by the increased government spending.*

Figure 10 illustrates the effects. Initially, with government purchases equal to $2 trillion, the demand for funds curve is $I^p + G_1 - T$, where $G_1$ represents the initial level of government purchases. The equilibrium occurs at point $A$ with the interest rate equal to 5 percent. If government purchases increase by $0.5 trillion, with no change in taxes, the budget deficit increases by $0.5 trillion and so does the government's demand for funds. The demand for funds curve shifts rightward by $0.5 trillion to $I^p + G_2 - T$, where $G_2$ represents an amount $0.5 trillion greater than $G_1$. After the shift, there would be an excess demand for funds at the original interest rate of 5 percent. The total quantity of funds demanded would be $2.25 trillion (point $H$), while the quantity supplied would continue to be $1.75 trillion (point $A$). Thus, the excess demand for funds would be equal to the distance $AH$ in the figure, or $0.5 trillion. This excess demand drives up the interest rate to 7 percent. As the interest rate rises, two things happen.

First, a higher interest rate chokes off some investment spending, as business firms decide that certain investment projects no longer make sense. For example, the local dry cleaner might wish to borrow funds for a new machine at an interest rate of 5 percent, but not at 7 percent. In the figure, we move along the new demand for funds curve from point $H$ to point $B$. Planned investment drops by $0.2 trillion (because the total demand for funds falls from $2.25 trillion to $2.05 trillion). (Question: How do we know that only business borrowing, and not also government borrowing, adjusts as we move from point $H$ to point $B$?) Thus, one consequence of the rise in government purchases is a *decrease in planned investment spending*.

But that's not all: The rise in the interest rate also causes saving to increase. Of course, when people save more of their incomes, they spend less, so another consequence of the rise in government purchases is a *decrease in consumption spending*. In the figure, we move from point $A$ to point $B$ along the saving

**G and T Are Separate Variables** It is common to think that a rise in government purchases ($G$) implies an equal rise in net taxes ($T$) to pay for it. But as you've seen in our discussion, economists treat $G$ and $T$ as two separate variables. Unless stated otherwise, we use the *ceteris paribus* assumption: When we change $G$, we assume $T$ remains constant, and when we change $T$, we assume $G$ remains constant. It is the budget deficit (or surplus) that changes when $T$ or $G$ changes.

DANGEROUS CURVES

curve. As saving increases from $1.75 trillion to $2.05 trillion—a rise of $0.3 trillion—consumption falls by $0.3 trillion.

Let's recap: As a result of the increase in government purchases, both planned investment spending and consumption spending decline. We say that the government's purchases have *crowded out* the spending of households ($C$) and businesses ($I^p$).

**Crowding out** A decline in one sector's spending caused by an increase in some other sector's spending.

> **Crowding out** *is a decline in one sector's spending caused by an increase in some other sector's spending.*

But we are not quite finished. If we sum the drop in $C$ and the drop in $I^p$, we find that total private sector spending has fallen by $0.3 trillion + $0.2 trillion = $0.5 trillion. That is, the drop in private sector spending is *precisely equal* to the rise in government purchases, $G$. Not only is there crowding out, there is **complete crowding out**: Each dollar of government purchases causes private sector spending to decline by a full dollar. The net effect is that total spending ($C + I^p + G$) does not change at all!

**Complete crowding out** A dollar-for-dollar decline in one sector's spending caused by an increase in some other sector's spending.

> *In the classical model, a rise in government purchases completely crowds out private sector spending, so total spending remains unchanged.*

A closer look at Figure 10 shows that this conclusion always holds, regardless of the particular numbers used or the shapes of the curves. When $G$ increases, the demand for funds curve shifts rightward by the same amount that $G$ rises, or the distance from point $A$ to point $H$. Then the interest rate rises, moving us along the supply of funds curve from point $A$ to point $B$. As a result, saving rises (and consumption falls) by the distance $AF$. But the rise in the interest rate *also* causes a movement along the demand for funds curve, from point $H$ to point $B$. As a result, investment spending falls by the amount $FH$.

The final impact can be summarized as follows:

- $G\uparrow = AH$

- $C\downarrow = AF$

- $I^p\downarrow = FH$

And since $AF + FH = AH$, we know that the combined decrease in $C$ and $I^p$ is precisely equal to the increase in $G$.

Because there is complete crowding out in the classical model, a rise in government purchases cannot change total spending. And the logic behind this result is straightforward. Each additional dollar the government spends is obtained from the loanable funds market, where *it would have been spent by someone else* if the government hadn't borrowed it. How do we know this? Because the loanable funds market funnels every dollar of household saving—no more and no less—to either the government or business firms. If the government borrows more, it just removes funds that would have been spent by businesses (the drop in $I^p$) or by consumers (the drop in $C$).

Remember that the goal of this increase in government purchases was to increase output and employment *by increasing total spending*. But now we see that the policy fails to increase spending at all. Therefore, *in the classical model, an increase in government purchases has no demand-side effects on total output or total employment.*

Of course, the opposite sequence of events would happen if government purchases *decreased*: The drop in G would *shrink* the deficit. The interest rate would decline, and private sector spending (C and $I^p$) would rise by the same amount that government purchases had fallen. (See if you can draw the graphs to prove this to yourself.) Once again, total spending and total output would remain unchanged.

## A DECREASE IN NET TAXES

Suppose that the government, instead of increasing its own purchases by $0.5 trillion, tried to increase total spending through a $0.5 trillion cut in net taxes. For example, the government could decrease income tax collections by $0.5 trillion, or increase transfer payments such as unemployment benefits by that amount. What would happen?

In general, households respond to a cut in net taxes by spending some of it and saving the rest. But let's give this policy every chance of working by making an extreme assumption in its favor: We'll assume that households *spend the entire $0.5 trillion tax cut* on consumption goods; they save none of it.

Figure 11 shows what will happen in the market for loanable funds. Initially, the demand for funds curve is $I^p + G - T_1$, where $T_1$ is the initial level of net taxes. The equilibrium is at point A, with an interest rate of 5 percent. If we cut net taxes (T) by $0.5 trillion, while holding government purchases constant, the budget deficit increases by $0.5 trillion, and so does the government's demand for funds. The demand for funds curve shifts rightward to $I^p + G - T_2$, where $T_2$ is an amount $0.5 trillion less than $T_1$.

The increase in the demand for funds drives the interest rate up to 7 percent, until we reach a new equilibrium at point B. As the interest rate rises, two things happen.

First, a higher interest rate will encourage more saving, which means a decrease in consumption spending. This is a movement along the supply of funds curve, from point A to point B, with saving rising (and consumption falling) by $0.3 trillion.

Second, a higher interest rate will decrease investment spending. This is shown by the movement from H to B along the new demand for funds curve. Planned investment decreases by $0.2 trillion.

What has happened to *total* spending? Only two components of spending have changed in this case: C and $I^p$. Let's first consider what's happened to consumption (C). First, we had a $0.5 trillion *rise* in consumption from the tax cut (remember: we assumed the entire tax cut was spent). This is equal to the horizontal distance AH. Then, because the interest rate rose, we had a $0.3 billion *decrease* in consumption. This decrease is equal to the horizontal distance AF. Taking both effects together, the net effect is a rise of $0.5 trillion − $0.3 trillion = $0.2 trillion. This net rise in consumption is shown by the distance FH.

Now remember what has happened to planned investment spending: It fell by $0.2 billion (the distance FH)—the same amount that consumption spending rose. In other words, the tax cut increases consumption but decreases planned investment by the same amount. We can say that higher consumption spending *completely crowds out* planned investment spending, leaving total spending unchanged.

**Crowding Out from a Tax Cut**

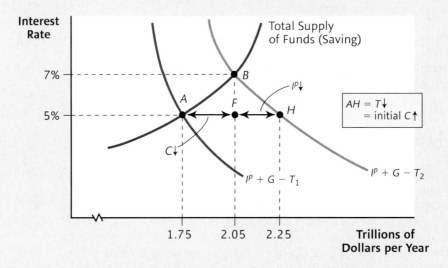

*Beginning from equilibrium at point A, an increase in the budget deficit caused by a tax cut shifts the demand for funds curve from $I^p + G - T_1$ to $I^p + G - T_2$. If the tax cut is entirely spent, consumption initially rises by the distance AH.*

*At the original interest rate of 5 percent, the quantity of funds demanded now exceeds the quantity supplied. This causes the interest rate to rise.*

*As the interest rate rises, we move from A to B along the supply of funds curve. Saving rises (and consumption falls) by the distance AF. The final rise in consumption is FH. We also move along the demand for funds curve from H to B, so investment falls by the distance FH. In the new equilibrium at point B, consumption (which has risen by FH) has completely crowded out investment (which has dropped by FH).*

> *In the classical model, a cut in net taxes raises consumption, which completely crowds out planned investment. Total spending remains unchanged, so the tax cut has no demand-side effects on total output or employment.*

## THE CLASSICAL MODEL: A SUMMARY

You've just completed a first tour of the classical model, our framework for understanding the economy in the long run. In the (optional) appendix, we extend this model to the global economy. And in the next chapter, we'll be using the classical model to understand economic growth. But before we do, let's review what we've done, and what we've concluded.

We began with a critical assumption: All markets clear. We then applied the three-step process to organize our thinking of the economy. First, we focused on an important market—the labor market. We identified the buyers and sellers in that market (Step 1), and then found equilibrium employment (Step 2) by assuming that the labor market cleared. We went through a similar process with the loanable funds market, identifying the suppliers and demanders (Step 1) and finding the equilibrium in that market as well (Step 2). We then showed that total spending will be just sufficient to purchase our potential output, reinforcing our confidence in the full-employment equilibrium we found. Finally, we explored what happens when things change (Step 3). In particular, we saw that fiscal policy changes have no demand-side effects on total output and total employment.

Our explorations have considered just some of the possible scenarios under which the economy might operate. For example, we've assumed that the government runs a budget deficit. But we could also explore what happens when the government starts out with a budget *surplus*, collecting more in net taxes than it spends on its purchases. We also assumed that any tax cut was entirely spent by households on consumption goods. But we could also ask what happens when some or all of a tax cut is saved.

You'll be asked to explore some of these other scenarios in the end-of-chapter problems. When you do, you'll see that the graphs may look different, but the important conclusions still hold. These general conclusions are:

- In the classical model, the government needn't worry about employment. The economy will achieve full employment on its own.
- In the classical model, the government needn't worry about total spending. The economy will generate just enough spending on its own to buy the output that a fully employed labor force produces.
- In the classical model, fiscal policy has no *demand-side effects* on output or employment.

### Using the Theory

This chapter does not end with the usual Using the Theory section. Instead, we will spend the next entire chapter using the classical model to explore a topic for which the model is very well-suited: Economic Growth.

## Summary

The classical model is an attempt to explain the behavior of the economy over long time periods. Its most critical assumption is that markets clear—that prices adjust in every market to equate quantities demanded and supplied. The labor market is the starting point of the classical model. When the labor market clears, we have full employment and the economy produces the potential level of output.

The economy's production function shows the total output that can be produced with different quantities of labor and for given amounts of other resources and a given state of technology. When the labor market is at full employment, the production function can be used to determine the economy's potential level of output.

According to Say's law, total spending in the economy will always be just sufficient to purchase the amount of total output produced. By producing and selling goods and services, firms create a total demand equal to what they have produced. Taxes are channeled to the government, which spends them. If households do not spend their entire after-tax incomes, the excess is channeled, as saving, into the loanable funds market, where it is borrowed and spent by businesses and government.

In the loanable funds market, the quantity of funds supplied equals household saving, which depends positively on the interest rate. The quantity of funds demanded equals planned investment, which depends negatively on the interest rate, and any government budget deficit, if there is one. The interest rate adjusts so that the quantity of funds supplied always equals the quantity demanded. Equivalently, it adjusts so that saving ($S$) equals the sum of planned investment spending ($I^p$) and the government budget deficit ($G - T$).

Fiscal policy has no demand-side effects on output in the classical model. An increase in government purchases results in complete crowding out of planned investment and consumption spending. A tax cut causes greater consumption spending to completely crowd out investment spending. In both cases, fiscal policy leaves total spending unchanged.

# Problem Set   *Answers to even-numbered Questions and Problems can be found on the text Web site at www.thomsonedu.com/economics/hall.*

1. Use a diagram similar to Figure 2 to illustrate the effect, on aggregate output and the real hourly wage, of (a) an increase in labor demand and (b) an increase in labor supply.

2. Draw a diagram (similar to Figure 10 in this chapter) illustrating the impact of a *decrease* in government purchases. Assume the government is running a budget deficit both before and after the change in government purchases. On your diagram, identify distances that represent:
   a. The decrease in government purchases
   b. The increase in consumption spending
   c. The increase in planned investment spending

3. Consider the following statement: "In the classical model, just as an *increase* in government purchases causes complete crowding *out*, so a *decrease* in government purchases causes complete crowding *in*."
   a. In this statement, explain what is meant by "crowding in" and "complete crowding in."
   b. Is the statement true? (Hint: Look at the diagram you drew in problem 2.)

4. The following data ($ millions) are for the island nation of Pacifica.

   | | |
   |---|---|
   | Total output | $10 |
   | Total income | $10 |
   | Consumption | $ 6 |
   | Government spending | $ 3 |
   | Total tax revenue | $ 2.5 |
   | Transfer payments | $ 0.5 |

   a. Use this information to find Pacifica's net taxes, disposable income, and savings.
   b. Determine whether the government is running a budget surplus, budget deficit, or balanced budget.
   c. Find planned investment by calculating how much is available in the loanable funds market after the government has borrowed what it might need.
   d. Does total output equal total spending?
   e. Show your answers on a diagram similar to the one in Figure 9 in the chapter.

5. Return to problem 4. What will happen if consumption spending starts to rise? Assume no change in net taxes. Show the effect on the loanable funds market, and explain what will happen to C, $I^p$, and G. (Note: You won't be able to find specific numbers.)

6. As the baby boomers retire, spending on Social Security benefits is expected to rise dramatically. Show the impact on a diagram of the loanable funds market, assuming that the government is initially running a budget deficit, and that all the additional Social Security benefits are *spent*. If there is no other change in policy, what would you expect to be the total impact on consumption spending? On planned investment spending?

7. The following data give a complete picture of the household, business, and government sectors for 2006 in the small nation of Sylvania. (All dollar figures are in billions.)

   | | |
   |---|---|
   | Consumption spending | $ 50 |
   | Capital stock (end of 2005) | $100 |
   | Capital stock (end of 2006) | $103 |
   | Change in inventories | $ 0 |
   | Government welfare payments | $ 5 |
   | Government unemployment insurance payments | $ 2 |
   | Government payroll | $ 3 |
   | Government outlays for materials | $ 2 |
   | Depreciation | $ 7 |
   | Interest rate | 6% |

   Assuming the government budget for 2006 was in balance, $(G = T)$, calculate each of the following (in order):
   a. Government purchases
   b. Net taxes
   c. Total planned investment
   d. Real GDP
   e. Total saving
   f. Total leakages
   g. Total injections

8. For the economy in problem 7, suppose that the government had purchased $2 billion more in goods and services than you found in that problem, with no change in taxes.
   a. Explain how each of the variables you calculated in problem 7 would be affected (i.e., state whether it would increase or decrease).
   b. Draw a graph illustrating the impact of the $2 billion increase in government purchases on the loanable funds market. Clearly label the equilibrium interest rate, saving, and total quantity of funds demanded at both the original and the new level of government purchases. (Note: You won't be able to find specific numbers.)

9. When the government runs a budget surplus $(T > G)$, it deposits any unspent tax revenue into the banking system, thus adding to the supply of loanable funds. In this case, the supply of loanable funds is household saving plus the budget surplus $[S + (T − G)]$, while the demand for funds is just planned investment ($I^p$).
   a. Draw a diagram of the loanable funds market with a budget surplus, showing the equilibrium interest rate and quantity of funds demanded and supplied.
   b. Prove that when the loanable funds market is in equilibrium, total leakages $(S + T)$ are equal to total injections $(I^p + G)$. (Hint: Use the same method as used in the chapter for the case of a budget deficit.)
   c. Show (on your graph) what happens when government purchases increase, identifying any decrease in consumption and planned investment on the graph (similar to what was done in Figure 10).
   d. When the government is running a budget surplus, does

an increase in government purchases cause complete crowding out? Explain briefly.

## More Challenging

10. Figure 11 shows the impact of a tax cut on the loanable funds market when the entire tax cut is spent. What if, instead, the entire tax cut had been *saved*?

   a. Draw a diagram of the loanable funds market showing the impact of a tax cut that is entirely saved. (Assume the government is already running a budget deficit.)

   b. What happens to the interest rate after the tax cut? Explain briefly.

   c. In Figure 11, the tax cut caused consumption spending to crowd out planned investment spending. How does a tax cut that is entirely saved affect the components of total spending?

11. [Requires appendix] Suppose that the government budget is balanced ($G = T$), and household saving is $1 trillion.

   a. If this is a closed economy, what is the value of planned investment ($I^P$)?

   b. If this is an open economy with balanced trade ($IM = X$), will investment have the same value as you found in (a)? Briefly, why or why not?

   c. If this is an open economy with a trade deficit ($IM > X$), will planned investment have the same value as you found in (a)? Briefly, why or why not?

12. [Requires appendix] Suppose that Classica has international trade, but it is running a trade surplus ($X > IM$) rather than a trade deficit as in the appendix. Suppose, too, that Classica's government is running a budget deficit.

   a. Draw a diagram for Classica's loanable funds market, being careful to include the trade surplus in the label for one of the curves. (Hint: When Classica runs a trade surplus equal to $X - IM$, foreigners spend more dollars on Classica's goods than they get by selling their goods to Classica. From where do you think foreigners get these dollars?)

   b. Label the initial equilibrium point $A$.

   c. Give an equation showing that, in equilibrium, the quantity of loanable funds demanded (on one side) is equal to the quantity of loanable funds supplied (on the other side).

   d. Rearrange your equation to show that, even when Classica runs a trade surplus, its leakages and injections are equal.

# APPENDIX

## The Classical Model in an Open Economy

So far in this chapter, we've been working with a *closed economy*—one that has no trade with other nations. What is different in an *open economy* with imports and exports of goods and services? The most general answer is: not much. All of the conclusions of the classical model still hold. But there are a few added complications in showing that Say's law holds—that total spending equals total output.

Let's suppose that in Classica (the economy used in the chapter), households, business firms, and government agencies spend $1.5 trillion on *imports* from other countries. This $1.5 trillion is income received by households, but *not* spent on Classica's output. It is an additional *leakage* in the economy. Total leakages are now imports (*IM*) along with the other leakages of saving (*S*) and taxes (*T*).

But once we recognize international trade, we must add foreign spending on Classica's *exports* as an *injection* into Classica's spending. Total injections are now exports (*X*) along with planned investment (*I^p*) and government purchases (*G*).

Finally, total spending on Classica's output must be modified. When we add together the spending of Classica's households, business firms, and government, we've included some imports in each category. We've thus *over*estimated total spending on Classica's output. To correct for this error, we must subtract imports (*IM*) from $C + I^p + G$ to get total spending by Classicans on their own country's output. Then we must add exports (*X*) to get the total spending from *all* sources on Classica's output. These modifications give us

$$\text{Total spending} = C + I^p + G + (X - IM)$$

Will this new expression for total spending be equal to total output? We'll explore this under two different scenarios.

## BALANCED TRADE: EXPORTS = IMPORTS

With *balanced* trade, exports (*X*) and imports (*IM*) are equal, so the last term added in total spending ($X - IM$) is zero. In this case, total spending in Classica will be $C + I^p + G$, just as it was in a closed economy.

Will total spending of $C + I^p + G$ be equal to total output, even though there are exports and imports? The answer is yes, as we can see by thinking about leakages and injections. In the case of balanced trade, the $1.5 trillion that leaks out of Classica's spending to buy imports (*IM*) is equal to the $1.5 billion that comes back to Classica to buy its exports (*X*). Because total leakages and total injections were equal in the closed economy (before we included imports and exports), they must be equal now as well.

But what happens if trade is *not* balanced?

In the next section, we'll consider what happens to spending when a country imports more than it exports. You'll be invited to analyze the opposite case (exports exceed imports) in an end-of-chapter problem.

## UNBALANCED TRADE: IMPORTS > EXPORTS

Suppose, as before, that Classica's households import $1.5 trillion in goods produced in other countries. But now, residents of these other countries want to purchase only $1 trillion in goods from Classica. Classica will then be running a *trade deficit* equal to the excess of its imports (*IM*) over its exports (*X*):

$$\text{Trade deficit} = IM - X = \$1.5 \text{ trillion} - \$1 \text{ trillion} = \$0.5 \text{ trillion}.$$

Now, it seems we have a problem. With imports greater than exports, won't Classica's leakages ($S + T +$

$IM$) be greater than injections ($I^p + G + X$)? And won't total spending therefore be less than total output?

The answer is no.

To see why, let's assume (as we've done all along in the chapter) that Classica's currency is the dollar. The 1.5 trillion in dollars that Classica's households spend on imports during the year does not just disappear. Rather, the dollars are passed along to the foreign countries producing the goods that Classica imports. In our current example, the residents of these foreign countries return $1 trillion of the $1.5 trillion back to Classica as spending on Classica's exports. But what about the other $0.5 trillion? If foreigners are rational, they will not want to just keep this money, because dollars by themselves pay no interest or other return. Foreigners will, instead, want to purchase Classica's stocks or bonds, or even just deposit funds in a bank in Classica. If they do any of these things, they *supply funds to Classica's loanable funds market* and make them available to Classica's borrowers.[3]

> When a country runs a trade deficit (imports exceed exports), foreigners will supply loanable funds to that country equal to its trade deficit.

With a trade deficit, the supply of funds in Classica becomes household saving ($S$) *plus* the flow of funds coming from foreigners ($IM - X$):

$$\text{Total supply of funds} = S + (IM - X)$$

The total demand for funds is still business borrowing ($I^p$) plus the government's budget deficit ($G - T$):

$$\text{Total demand for funds} = I^p + (G - T)$$

Figure A.1 shows the loanable funds market in Classica, where we've added Classica's trade deficit to its supply of loanable funds. Equilibrium occurs at point $E$, with an interest rate of 5 percent and $2.25 trillion in loanable funds supplied and demanded. Of this $2.25 trillion, we know that foreigners are supplying $0.5 trillion of the total, so households must be supplying (saving) the other $1.75 trillion.

In equilibrium, the quantity of funds supplied and demanded are equal:

Loanable funds market clears $\Rightarrow$

$$\underbrace{S + (IM - X)}_{\substack{\text{Quantity of} \\ \text{funds supplied}}} = \underbrace{I^p + (G - T)}_{\substack{\text{Quantity of} \\ \text{funds demanded}}}$$

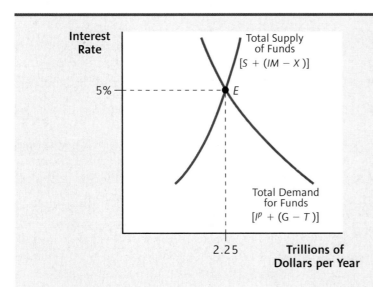

**FIGURE A.1**

**The Loanable Funds Market with a Trade Deficit**

*When Classica runs a trade deficit (its imports exceed its exports), foreigners earn more dollars (Classica's currency) selling goods to Classica than they spend on goods from Classica. The excess dollars are returned to Classica's loanable funds market, where they become part of the supply of loanable funds. When the loanable funds market clears, we have $S + IM - X = I^p + G - T$. This, in turn, means that total leakages ($S + T + IM$) equal total injections ($I^p + G + X$).*

Interest Rate

Total Supply of Funds [$S + (IM - X)$]

5% — — — — — — $E$

Total Demand for Funds [$I^p + (G - T)$]

2.25    **Trillions of Dollars per Year**

[3] There is another part of the story we are leaving out here: the foreign exchange market. When Classica's households import goods, they may pay in dollars, but the foreign firms are paid in their own local currencies. Someone must exchange Classica's dollars for foreign currency— a bank or a foreign government. It is these banks or foreign governments that, in turn, supply the excess dollars to Classica's loanable funds market. We'll deal more explicitly with foreign exchange markets in the last chapter of this book.

Let's now rearrange this equation by moving $T$ over to the left and $X$ over to the right:

Loanable funds market clears $\Rightarrow$

$$\underbrace{S + T + IM}_{\text{Leakages}} = \underbrace{I^p + G + X}_{\text{Injections}}$$

This last equation shows us that total leakages and total injections are equal in Classica, even when it runs a trade deficit. But if leakages and injections are equal, then total spending must equal total output. Even with a trade deficit, Say's law still holds.

Let's take a step back and understand the reasoning behind this result about spending. Even though Classica is running a trade deficit, every dollar of the $10 trillion that households earn will still be spent on Classica's production—either by households themselves or by some other sector that spends it in their place. The dollars spent on imports are either spent on Classica's exports or put into its loanable funds market, where they are borrowed and spent by business firms or the government. And, as before, taxes and saving are also spent by either the government or business firms.

# Economic Growth and Rising Living Standards

Economist Thomas Malthus, writing in 1798, came to a striking conclusion: "Population, when unchecked, goes on doubling itself every twenty-five years, or increases in a geometrical ratio. . . . The means of subsistence . . . could not possibly be made to increase faster than in an arithmetic ratio."[1] From this simple logic, Malthus forecast a horrible fate for the human race. There would be repeated famines and wars to keep the rapidly growing population in balance with the more slowly growing supply of food and other necessities.

But history has proven Malthus wrong . . . at least in part. In the industrialized nations, living standards have increased beyond the wildest dreams of anyone alive in Malthus's time. Economists today are optimistic about these nations' long-run material prospects. At the same time, living standards in many of the less developed countries have remained stubbornly close to survival level and, in some cases, have fallen below it.

What are we to make of this? Why have living standards steadily increased in some nations but not in others? And what, if anything, can governments do to speed the rise in living standards? These are questions about economic growth—the long-run increase in an economy's output of goods and services.

In this chapter, you will learn what makes economies grow. Our approach will make use of the classical model, focusing on Step 3 of the three-step process: What Happens When Things Change? As you'll see, growth arises from *shifts* of the curves of the classical model. And by the end of this chapter, you will know why increasing the rate of economic growth is not easy. Even though nations can take measures to speed growth, each measure carries an opportunity cost. More specifically,

> *achieving a higher rate of growth in the long run generally requires some sacrifice in the short run.*

## THE IMPORTANCE OF GROWTH

Why should we be concerned about economic growth? For one simple reason:

> *When output grows faster than the population, GDP per capita, our measure of the **average standard of living**, will rise. When output grows more slowly than the population, the average standard of living will fall.*

**Average standard of living** Total output (real GDP) per person.

[1] Thomas Robert Malthus, *An Essay on the Principle of Population*, 1798.

Measuring the standard of living by GDP per capita may seem limiting. After all, as we saw three chapters ago, many important aspects of our quality of life are not captured in GDP. Leisure time, workplace safety, good health, a clean environment—we care about all of these. Yet they are not considered in GDP.

Still, many aspects of our quality of life *are* counted in GDP: food, housing, medical care, education, transportation services, and movies, to name a few. It is not surprising, then, that economic growth—measured by increases in GDP—remains a vital concern in every nation.

Economic growth is especially important in countries with income levels far below those of Europe, Japan, and the United States. The average standard of living in some third-world nations is so low that many families can barely acquire the basic necessities of life, and many others perish from disease or starvation.

Table 1 lists GDP per capita, infant mortality rates, life expectancies, and adult literacy rates for some of the richest and poorest countries. The statistics for the poor countries are grim enough, but even they capture only part of the story. Unsafe and unclean workplaces, inadequate housing, and other sources of misery are part of daily life for most people in these countries. Other than emigration, economic growth is their only hope.

Growth is a high priority in prosperous nations, too. As we know, resources are scarce, and we cannot produce enough of everything to satisfy all of our desires simultaneously. We want more and better medical care, education, vacations, entertainment . . . the list is endless. When output per capita is growing, it's at least *possible* for everyone to enjoy an increase in material well-being without anyone having to cut back. We can also accomplish important social goals—helping the

| TABLE 1 | | | | |
|---|---|---|---|---|
| **Some Indicators of Economic Well-Being in Rich and Poor Countries, 2003** | **Country** | **Real GDP per Capita** | **Infant Mortality Rate (per 1,000 Live Births)** | **Life Expectancy at Birth** | **Adult Literacy Rate** |
| | **Rich Countries** | | | | |
| | United States | $37,562 | 7 | 77.4 | Greater than 99% |
| | Japan | $27,967 | 3 | 82.0 | Greater than 99% |
| | Germany | $27,756 | 4 | 78.7 | Greater than 99% |
| | France | $27,677 | 4 | 79.5 | Greater than 99% |
| | United Kingdom | $27,147 | 5 | 78.4 | Greater than 99% |
| | Italy | $27,119 | 4 | 80.1 | 98.5% |
| | **Poor Countries** | | | | |
| | Azerbaijan | $3,617 | 75 | 66.9 | 98.8% |
| | Ghana | $2,238 | 59 | 56.8 | 54.1% |
| | Pakistan | $2,097 | 81 | 63.0 | 48.7% |
| | Cambodia | $2,078 | 97 | 56.2 | 73.6% |
| | Zambia | $  877 | 102 | 37.5 | 67.9% |
| | Sierra Leone | $  548 | 166 | 40.8 | 29.6% |

*Sources:* United Nations Development Programme, *Human Development Report,* 2005, pp. 219–222 and 250–253.

poor, improving education, cleaning up the environment—by asking those who are doing well to sacrifice part of the rise in their material well-being, rather than suffer a drop.

But when output per capita stagnates, material gains become a fight over a fixed pie: The more purchasing power my neighbor has, the less is left for me. With everyone struggling for a larger piece of this fixed pie, conflict replaces cooperation. Efforts to help the less fortunate, wipe out illiteracy, reduce air pollution—all are seen as threats, rather than opportunities.

In the 1950s and 1960s, economic growth in the wealthier nations seemed to be taking care of itself. Economists and policy makers focused their attention on short-run movements around full-employment output, rather than on the growth of full-employment output itself. The real payoff for government seemed to be in preventing recessions and depressions—in keeping the economy operating as close to its potential as possible.

All of that changed starting in the 1970s, and economic growth became a national and international preoccupation. Like most changes in perception and thought, this one was driven by experience. Table 2 tells the story. It gives the average yearly growth rates of real GDP per capita for the United States and some of our key trading partners.

Over most of the postwar period, output in the more prosperous industrialized countries (such as the United States, the United Kingdom, and Canada) grew by 2 or 3 percent per year, while output in the less wealthy ones—those with some catching up to do—grew even faster. But beginning in the mid-1970s, all of these nations saw their growth rates slip.

In the late 1990s and early 2000s, only the United States and the United Kingdom returned to their previous high rates of growth, while the other industrialized countries continued to grow more slowly than their historical averages.

Looking at the table, you might think that this slowing in growth was rather insignificant. Do the tiny differences between the pre-1972 and the post-1972 growth rates really matter? Indeed, they do. Recall our example a few chapters ago in which an increase in the U.S. growth rate of around one percentage point over the past 20 years would mean $20 trillion in additional output over the entire period. Seemingly small differences in growth rates matter a great deal.

**TABLE 2**

**Average Annual Growth Rate of Real GDP per Capita**

| Country | 1948–1972 | 1972–1988 | 1988–1995 | 1995–2004 |
|---------|-----------|-----------|-----------|-----------|
| United States | 2.2% | 1.7% | 1.0% | 2.3% |
| United Kingdom | 2.4 | 2.1 | 0.9 | 2.5 |
| Canada | 2.9 | 2.6 | 0.6 | 2.4 |
| France | 4.3 | 2.1 | 1.2 | 1.8 |
| Italy | 4.9 | 2.8 | 1.6 | 1.3 |
| West Germany | 5.7 | 2.2 | 1.3 | 1.2 |
| Japan | 8.2 | 3.3 | 2.1 | 1.3 |

*Sources:* Angus Maddison, *Phases of Capitalist Development* (Oxford: Oxford University Press, 1982); U.S. Census Bureau IDB Summary Demographic Data (*http://www.census.gov/ipc/www/idbsum.html*); *Economic Report of the President*, 2002, 2005, Table B-112; and various OECD publications. *Note:* Data for Germany includes West Germany only through 1995, and all of Germany after 1995.

# WHAT MAKES ECONOMIES GROW?

A useful way to start thinking about long-run growth is to look at what determines our potential GDP in any given period. Starting this process is very simple: We can say that real GDP depends on

- The amount of output the average worker can produce in an hour
- The number of hours the average worker spends at the job
- The fraction of the population that is working
- The size of the population

If you spend a moment considering each of these variables, you'll see that—all else equal—if any one of them increases, real GDP rises.

Before we start working with these determinants of growth, let's briefly discuss how the first three are measured. The amount of output the average worker produces in an hour is called **labor productivity**, or just **productivity**. It is measured by taking the total output (real GDP) of the economy over a period of time and dividing by the total number of hours that *everyone* worked during that period.

**Labor productivity** The output produced by the average worker in an hour.

$$\text{Productivity} = \text{Output per hour} = \frac{\text{Total output}}{\text{Total hours worked}}$$

For example, if during a given year all workers in the United States spent a total of 300 billion hours at their jobs and produced \$12 trillion worth of output, then on average, labor productivity would be \$12 trillion/300 billion hours = \$40 per hour. Or in words, the average worker would produce \$40 worth of output in an hour. As you'll see later in this chapter, increases in productivity are one of the most important contributors to economic growth.

Next, the hours of the average worker can be found by dividing the total hours worked over a period by total employment (the *number* of people who worked during the period).

$$\text{Average hours} = \frac{\text{Total hours}}{\text{Total employment}}$$

For example, if total employment is 150 million people and they work a total of 300 billion hours per year, then average annual hours would be 300 billion hours/150 million workers = 2,000 hours.

Now let's turn to the fraction of the population that is working. This is called the **employment–population ratio (EPR)** and is found by dividing total employment by the population:[2]

**Employment–population ratio (EPR)** The percentage of the population that is working.

$$\text{EPR} = \frac{\text{Total employment}}{\text{Population}}$$

Now that we understand how these variables are measured, let's multiply them together and cancel out the like terms:

$$\frac{\text{Total output}}{\text{Total hours}} \times \frac{\text{Total hours}}{\text{Total employment}} \times \frac{\text{Total employment}}{\text{Population}} \times \text{Population}$$

$$= \text{Total output}.$$

[2] In actual practice in the United States and many other countries, the population base for the EPR is more limited. In the United States, for example, the EPR is technically the fraction of the *civilian, non-institutional population over the age of 16* that is employed. We'll ignore this technical definition in our analysis and consider the EPR to be the fraction of the entire population that is working.

where the last inequality follows after canceling terms that appear in both a numerator and a denominator. Thus, we can write our equation for total output as:

Total output = Productivity × Average hours × EPR × Population.

Now we'll borrow a rule from mathematics that states that if two variables $A$ and $B$ are multiplied together, then the percentage change in their product is approximately equal to the sum of their percentage changes. In symbols:

$$\%\Delta\,(A \times B) \approx \%\Delta A + \%\Delta B.$$

Applying this rule to all four variables in the right side of our equation, as well as to total output on the left, we find that the growth rate of total output over any period of time is

$$\%\Delta\,\text{Total output} \approx \%\Delta\,\text{Productivity} + \%\Delta\,\text{Average hours} +$$

$$\%\Delta\,\text{EPR} + \%\Delta\,\text{Population}.$$

This last equation, which we'll call the economy's **growth equation**, shows how four different variables contribute to the growth rate of real GDP.

Now look at Table 3, which shows how each of these variables has contributed to output growth during different periods of recent U.S. history, as well as a six-year future projection. For example, the first column tells us that from 1953 to 1973, real GDP grew, on average, by 3.6 percent per year. Of that growth, 1.6 percentage points were due to a growing population, and 0.1 percentage points were due to a rise in the employment–population ratio. Average hours—which decreased during the period—contributed negatively to growth, reducing it by a third of a percentage point. Finally, growth in labor productivity contributed 2.2 percent during this period.

Going across the rows and moving from period to period, you can see that almost all of the growth in real GDP over the last 50 years (and projected for the near future) has come from two factors: population growth and productivity growth. Increases in the employment–population ratio have contributed somewhat in the past, and average hours have decreased slightly, slowing growth in real GDP.

**Growth equation** An equation showing the percentage growth rate of output as the sum of the growth rates of productivity, average hours, the employment–population ratio, and population.

| Annual Percentage Growth in Real GDP Due to: | 1953 to 1973 | 1973 to 1995 | 1995 to 2005 | 2005 to 2010 (projected) |
|---|---|---|---|---|
| Population | 1.6 | 1.4 | 1.2 | 1.1 |
| EPR | 0.1 | 0.4 | 0.0 | −0.1 |
| Average Hours | −0.3 | −0.3 | −0.2 | −0.1 |
| Productivity | 2.2 | 1.3 | 2.3 | 2.3 |
| Total | 3.6 | 2.8 | 3.3 | 3.2 |

**TABLE 3**

**Factors Contributing to Growth in U.S. Real GDP**

*Source: Economic Report of the President*, 2006, Table 1–2, p. 44, and author calculations. (The *Economic Report* lists nonfarm business productivity only. In this table, annual productivity growth has been reduced by 0.2 to 0.5 percentage points in each period to account for slightly slower output growth in the government and farm sectors.)

## ECONOMIC GROWTH AND LIVING STANDARDS

Ultimately, growth in real GDP—by itself—does not guarantee a rising standard of living. Imagine, for example, that real GDP grew by 10 percent over some period while the population doubled. With 10 percent more output divided among twice as many people, the average standard of living would clearly decrease even though real output was growing. What matters for the standard of living is *real GDP per capita*—our total output of goods and services *per person*. Over the long run, since real GDP tends to hover near *potential* output, living standards will depend on *potential* output per person.

To see more clearly what causes potential output per person to rise, let's go back to our basic growth equation:

$$\text{Total output} = \text{Productivity} \times \text{Average hours} \times \text{EPR} \times \text{Population}.$$

If we divide both sides of this equation by the population, we get:

$$\frac{\text{Total output}}{\text{Population}} = \text{Productivity} \times \text{Average hours} \times \text{EPR}.$$

And, in terms of percentage growth rates:

$$\%\Delta \text{ Total output per person} \approx \%\Delta \text{ Productivity} +$$

$$\%\Delta \text{ Average hours} + \%\Delta \text{ EPR}.$$

Notice that population drops out of the equation. This tells us that the only way to raise the average standard of living is to increase productivity, increase average hours, or increase the percentage of the population that is working.

But as we saw in Table 3, average hours in the United States have decreased over the past several decades and are projected to remain constant for several years. In continental Europe, the decrease in average hours has been even greater. This is why we'll focus our discussion on the remaining two factors in our equation: the EPR and productivity.

> *To explain growth in output per person and living standards in the United States and other developed nations, economists look at two factors: increases in the employment–population ratio and growth in productivity.*

Now it's time to look more closely at *how* these two factors raise the average standard of living. And the classical model that you learned in the last chapter is very well suited to helping us understand this. We'll start by considering increases in the labor force participation rate.

## GROWTH IN THE EMPLOYMENT–POPULATION RATIO (EPR)

Over the long run, the employment–population ratio rises only when total employment increases at a faster rate than the population. For example, if total employment is

50 million out of a population of 100 million, then the EPR is 50 million/100 million = 0.5. If both total employment and population grow by 10 percent, then the EPR will be 55 million/110 million = 0.5, the same as before. With population growth of 10 percent, total employment would have to grow by *more* than 10 percent in order for the EPR to rise and thereby contribute to growth in living standards. And if total employment were to grow by *less* than 10 percent, the EPR would fall, contributing to a drop in living standards.

If we treat the rate of population growth as a given, then the growth rate of total employment will determine what happens to the EPR. More specifically,

> *for a given growth rate of the population, the greater the growth of total employment, the greater will be the rise (or the smaller will be the drop) in the EPR.*

But what causes employment to grow? The classical model can help us answer this question.

One possibility is an increase in labor *supply:* a rise in the number of people who would like to work at any given wage. This is illustrated in Figure 1 by a rightward shift in the labor supply curve. We'll discuss *why* the labor supply curve might shift later; here, we'll concentrate on the consequences of the shift.

Before the shift, the labor supply curve is $L_1^S$, the market clears at a wage of $20 per hour, and the fully employed labor force is 150 million workers. The aggregate production function tells us that, with the given amounts of other resources in the economy, and the given state of technology, 150 million workers can produce $10 trillion in goods and services—the initial value of full-employment output. When the labor supply curve shifts to $L_2^S$, the market-clearing wage drops to $16. Business firms, finding labor cheaper to hire, increase the number of workers employed along the labor demand curve, from point *A* to point *B*. The labor force increases to 180 million workers, and full-employment output rises to $11.5 trillion.

But growth in employment can also arise from an increase in labor demand: a rise in the number of workers that firms would like to hire at any given wage. Once again, we'll consider the *causes* of labor demand changes momentarily; here, we focus on the *consequences*.

Graphically, an increase in labor demand is represented by a rightward shift in the labor demand curve, as in Figure 2. As the wage rate rises from $20 to its new equilibrium of $22, we move along the labor supply curve from point *A* to point *B*. More people decide they want to work as the wage rises. Equilibrium employment once again rises from 150 million to 180 million workers, so full-employment output will rise. Thus,

> *growth in employment can arise from an increase in labor supply (a rightward shift in the labor supply curve) or an increase in labor demand (a rightward shift of the labor demand curve).*

You may have noticed one very important difference between the labor market outcomes in Figures 1 and 2: When labor *supply* increases, the wage rate falls (from $20 to $16 in Figure 1); when labor *demand* increases, the wage rate rises (from $20 to $22 in Figure 2). Which of the figures describes the actual experience of the U.S. labor market?

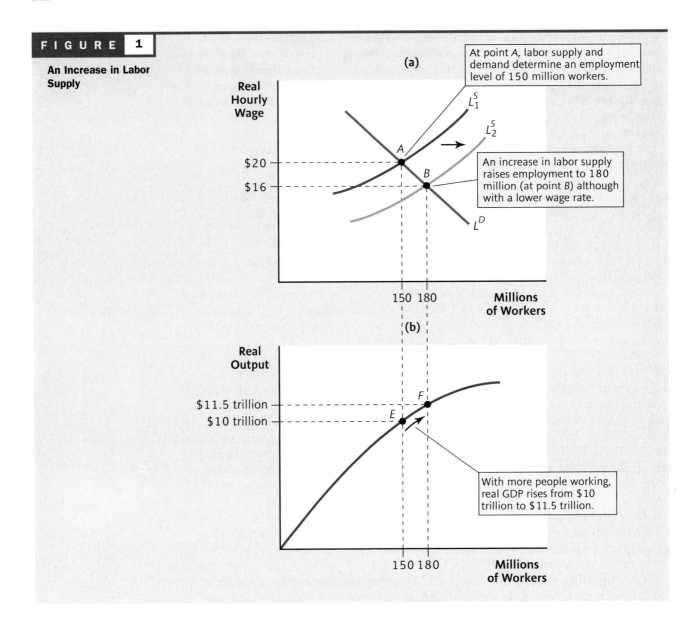

**FIGURE 1**

**An Increase in Labor Supply**

(a)

Real Hourly Wage

At point A, labor supply and demand determine an employment level of 150 million workers.

$L_1^S$

$L_2^S$

$20

$16

A

B

An increase in labor supply raises employment to 180 million (at point B) although with a lower wage rate.

$L^D$

150 180    **Millions of Workers**

(b)

Real Output

$11.5 trillion

$10 trillion

E

F

With more people working, real GDP rises from $10 trillion to $11.5 trillion.

150 180    **Millions of Workers**

Actually, a combination of both. Over most of the past century, the U.S. labor supply curve shifted steadily rightward, sometimes slowly, sometimes more rapidly. Why the shift in labor supply? In part, the reason was steady population growth: The more people there are, the more will want to work at any wage. But another reason was an important change in tastes: an increase in the desire of women (especially married women) to work.

But as the labor supply curve shifted rightward, the labor demand curve shifted rightward as well. Firms acquired more and better capital equipment for their employees to use. Managers and accountants began keeping track of inventories and other important accounts with lightning-fast computer software instead of account ledgers. Supermarket clerks began using electronic scanners instead of hand-entry cash registers. And college professors or their research assistants began gathering

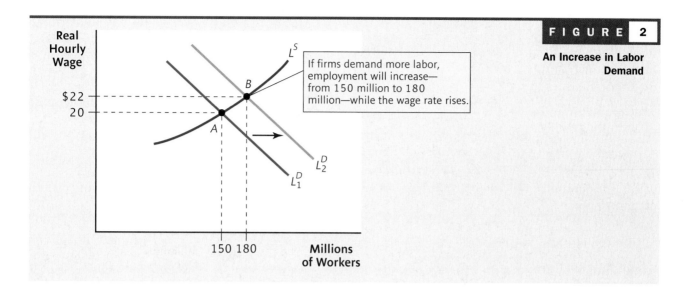

**FIGURE 2**

**An Increase in Labor Demand**

Real Hourly Wage

$22
20

If firms demand more labor, employment will increase—from 150 million to 180 million—while the wage rate rises.

150 180

**Millions of Workers**

data by searching for a few minutes on the Web instead of a few hours in the library. At the same time, workers became better educated and better trained. These changes increased the amount of output a worker could produce in any given period, so firms wanted to hire more of them at any wage.[3]

In fact, over the past century, increases in labor demand outpaced increases in labor supply, so that, on balance, the average wage rate rose and employment increased. This is illustrated in Figure 3, which shows a shift in the labor supply curve from $L_1^S$ to $L_2^S$, and an even greater shift in the labor demand curve from $L_1^D$ to $L_2^D$.

The impact of these changes on total employment has been dramatic. Between 1948 and 2006, employment rose from 56 million to about 145 million. But what about the employment–population ratio? It, too, rose: from 57 percent of the (adult) population to about 63 percent. This tells us that employment grew *faster* than the population during this period. And as you've learned, such an increase in the EPR causes not just real GDP, but real GDP *per capita*, to grow. However, most of the rise in the EPR was due to a special factor that is unlikely to be repeated: the greater labor force participation rate of women—especially married women—during the 1960s, 1970s, and 1980s. In the 1990s—as the female EPR stabilized—this source of growth disappeared.

Currently, the U.S. Bureau of Labor Statistics predicts employment growth of 1 percent per year until the year 2010—about the same as the growth rate of the population. Thus, the employment–population ratio is not expected to grow at all. Employment growth—while it will raise real GDP—will not increase real GDP per capita, and so will not contribute to a rise in living standards.

Could we do anything about this? Could we speed up the rightward shifts in the labor demand and labor supply curves over the next few years, so that employment grows faster than the 1 percent annual growth rate of the population? Yes, we could.

---

[3] These changes in physical and human capital have also shifted the economy's production function, but we'll consider that in the next section.

**The U.S. Labor Market Over a Century**

*Over the past century, increases in labor demand have outpaced increases in supply. As a result, both the level of employment and the average wage have risen.*

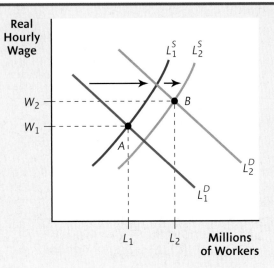

But as you read on, keep in mind that these measures to increase employment are not necessarily socially desirable. They would, most likely, accomplish the goal, but they would also have costs—costs that Americans may or may not be willing to pay. Later, we'll discuss these costs.

## HOW TO INCREASE EMPLOYMENT AND THE EPR

One set of policies to speed the rise in employment focuses on changing labor supply. And an often-proposed example of this type of policy is a decrease in income tax rates. Imagine that you have a professional degree in accounting, physical therapy, or some other field, and you are considering whether to take a job. Suppose the going rate for your professional services is $30 per hour. If your average tax rate is 33 percent, then one-third of your income will be taxed away, so your take-home pay would be only $20 per hour. But if your tax rate were cut to 20 percent, you would take home $24 per hour. Since you care about your take-home pay, you will respond to a tax cut in the same way you would respond to a wage increase—even if the wage your potential employer pays does not change at all. If you would be willing to take a job that offers a take-home pay of $24, but not one that offers $20, then the tax cut would be just what was needed to get you to seek work.

When we extend your reaction to the population as a whole, we can see that a cut in the income tax rate can convince more people to seek jobs at any given wage, shifting the labor supply curve rightward. This is why economists and politicians who focus on the economy's long-run growth often recommend lower taxes on labor income to encourage more rapid growth in employment. They point out that many American workers must pay combined federal, state, and local taxes of more than 40 cents out of each additional dollar they earn, and that this may be discouraging labor market participation in the United States.

Indeed, this was an important part of the logic behind the two tax cuts engineered by President Bush early in his administration. For example, the first tax cut, which Congress passed after much debate in June 2001, called for gradually reduced tax rates over 10 years. It reduced the cumulative tax burden on households by about $1.35 trillion over that period.

In addition to tax rate changes, some economists have advocated changes in government transfer programs to speed the growth in employment. They argue that the current structure of many government programs creates disincentives to work. For example, families receiving welfare payments, food stamps, unemployment benefits, and Social Security retirement payments all face steep losses in their benefits if they go to work or increase their work effort. Redesigning these programs might therefore stimulate growth in labor supply.

This reasoning was an important motive behind the sweeping reforms in the U.S. welfare system passed by Congress, and signed by President Clinton, in August 1996. Among other things, the reforms reduced the number of people who were eligible for benefits, cut the benefit amount for many of those still eligible, and set a maximum coverage period of five years for most welfare recipients. Later in this chapter, we'll discuss some of the *costs* of potentially growth-enhancing measures like these. Here, we only point out that changes in benefit programs have the potential to change labor supply.

> *A cut in tax rates increases the reward for working, while a cut in benefits to the needy increases the hardship of not working. Either policy can speed the rightward shifts in the labor supply curve and speed the growth in employment, raising the EPR and output per person.*

Government policies can also affect the labor *demand* curve. In recent decades, subsidies for education and training, such as government-guaranteed loans for college students or special training programs for the unemployed, have helped to increase the skills of the labor force and made workers more valuable to potential employers. Government also subsidizes employment more directly—by contributing part of the wage when certain categories of workers are hired—the disabled, college work-study participants, and, in some experimental programs, inner-city youth. By enlarging these programs, government could increase the number of workers hired at any given wage and thus shift the labor demand curve to the right:

> *Government policies that help increase the skills of the workforce or that subsidize employment more directly speed the rightward shift in the labor demand curve, increasing the EPR and output per person.*

Efforts to create growth in the employment–population ratio are sometimes controversial. In recent decades, those who prefer an activist government have favored policies to increase labor *demand* through government-sponsored training programs, more aid to college students, employment subsidies to firms, and similar programs. Those who prefer a more *laissez-faire* approach have generally favored policies to increase the labor *supply* by *decreasing* government involvement—lower taxes or a less generous social safety net.

In any case, the employment–population ratio is unlikely to contribute to growth in the near future. For one thing, the retirement of the baby boomers is expected to *decrease* the EPR over the next few decades. And the sorts of employment policies we've discussed here would, at best, lead to a one-time rise in the EPR, rather than a continually rising EPR that would contribute to sustained economic growth.

## GROWTH IN PRODUCTIVITY

If you look back at Table 3, you'll see that growth in productivity has been responsible for most of the growth in real GDP over the last 50 years. (The period from 1973 to 1995, when population growth led slightly, is the exception.) And as you've learned, population growth—while it can raise real GDP—cannot raise real GDP *per capita*. If we restrict ourselves to the three factors in Table 3 that *can* raise real GDP per capita, we see that

> *over the past several decades, and into the near future, virtually all growth in the average standard of living can be attributed to growth in productivity.*

Not surprisingly, when economists analyze rising living standards, they think first and foremost about growth in productivity.

Table 3 shows that productivity is expected to grow at about 2.3 percent over the next several years. Can we make it grow even faster?

### GROWTH IN THE CAPITAL STOCK

One key to productivity growth is the nation's capital stock or, more precisely, the amount of capital available for the average worker in the economy. You can dig more ditches with a shovel than with your hands, and even more with a backhoe. And the economy can produce more automobiles, medical services, and education when the average employee in these industries has more machinery, technical equipment, and computers to work with.

**Capital per worker** The total capital stock divided by total employment.

A rise in **capital per worker**—the total capital stock divided by the labor force—results in greater productivity. Figure 4 shows this from the perspective of the

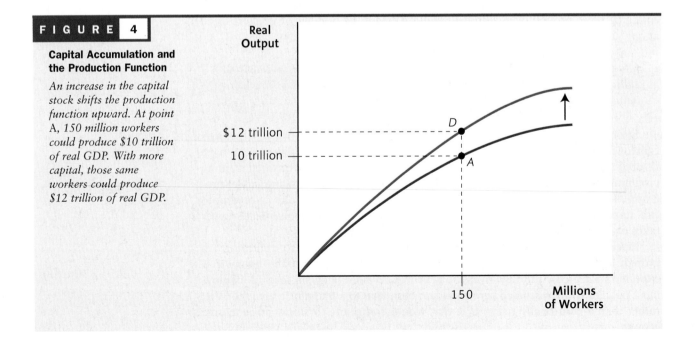

**FIGURE 4**

**Capital Accumulation and the Production Function**

*An increase in the capital stock shifts the production function upward. At point A, 150 million workers could produce $10 trillion of real GDP. With more capital, those same workers could produce $12 trillion of real GDP.*

classical model. Initially, the economy operates at point *A* on the lower aggregate production function, where 150 million workers produce $10 trillion in output. An increase in the capital stock shifts the production function upward, since any given number of workers can produce more output if there is more capital to work with. Assuming that the labor force remains at 150 million, there will be more capital per worker, greater productivity, and the economy will move to point *D*. At this point, 150 million workers produce $12 trillion in output.

However, in the real world, as the capital stock grows, so does the labor force. While any increase in capital will shift up the production function as in the figure, productivity will rise only if capital *per worker* increases—that is, only if the nation's total capital stock grows *faster* than the labor force.

*As business firms acquire more machinery and other capital equipment, the economy's production function shifts upward.*

> *All else equal, if the capital stock grows faster than the labor force, then capital per worker will rise, and labor productivity will increase along with it. But if the capital stock grows more slowly than the labor force, then capital per worker will fall, and labor productivity will fall as well.*

In the United States and most other developed countries, the capital stock has grown more rapidly than the labor force. This is one reason that labor productivity has risen over time. But in some developing countries, the capital stock has grown at about the same rate as, or even more slowly than, the labor force, and labor productivity has remained stagnant or fallen. We will return to this problem in the Using the Theory section of this chapter.

## INVESTMENT AND THE CAPITAL STOCK

What determines how fast the capital stock rises, and whether it will rise faster than the labor force? The answer is: the rate of *planned investment spending* in the economy. Investment spending and the capital stock are related to each other, but they are different *kinds* of variables. Specifically, capital is a *stock* variable while investment spending is a *flow* variable.

> *A **stock variable** measures a quantity at a moment in time. A **flow variable** measures a process over a period of time.*

**Stock variable** A variable measuring a quantity at a moment in time.

**Flow variable** A variable measuring a *process* over some period of time.

To use an analogy, think of a bathtub being filled with water. The water *in* the tub is a stock variable—so many gallons at any given moment. The water *flowing into* the tub is a flow variable—so many gallons *per minute* or *per hour*. You can always identify a flow variable by the addition of "per period" in its definition. Even when not explicitly stated, some period of time is always implied in a flow variable.

The capital stock—the total amount of plant and equipment that exists in the economy—is like the quantity of water *in* the tub. It can be measured at any given moment. Investment spending—the amount of *new* capital being installed over some time interval—is like the water flowing *into* the tub. Investment spending is defined *per period*—such as *per quarter* or *per year*. In the simplest terms, investment spending *adds* to the capital stock over time.

But there is one more flow involved in the capital–investment relationship: *depreciation*. Each period, some of the capital stock is used up. If a computer is expected to last only three years, for example, then each year the computer depreciates by about a third of its initial value. Depreciation tends to *reduce* the capital stock over time. (In our tub analogy, depreciation is like the flow of water draining *out* each period.) *As long as investment is greater than depreciation* (more water flows into the tub than drains out), *the capital stock will rise.* Moreover, for any rate of depreciation, the greater the flow of investment spending, the faster the rise in the capital stock.

Pulling all of this together leads us to an important conclusion about investment spending and the capital stock:

> *For a given rate of depreciation and a given growth rate of employment, a higher rate of investment spending causes faster growth in capital per worker and productivity, and faster growth in the average standard of living.*

This is why when economists think about raising productivity via the capital stock, they focus on raising the rate of investment spending.

## HOW TO INCREASE INVESTMENT

A government seeking to spur investment has more than one weapon in its arsenal. It can direct its efforts toward businesses themselves, toward the household sector, or toward its own budget.

### Targeting Businesses: Increasing the Incentive to Invest

One kind of policy to increase investment targets the business sector itself, with the goal of increasing planned investment spending. Figure 5 shows how this works. The figure shows a simplified view of the loanable funds market where—to focus on investment—we assume that there is no budget deficit, so there is no government demand for funds. The initial equilibrium in the market is at point *A*, where household saving (the supply of funds) and investment (the demand for funds) are both equal to $1.5 trillion and the interest rate is 3 percent. Now suppose that the government takes steps to make investment more profitable so that—at any interest rate—firms will want to purchase $0.75 trillion more in capital equipment than

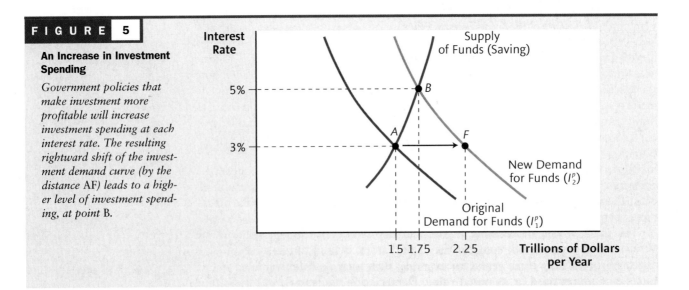

**F I G U R E   5**

**An Increase in Investment Spending**

*Government policies that make investment more profitable will increase investment spending at each interest rate. The resulting rightward shift of the investment demand curve (by the distance AF) leads to a higher level of investment spending, at point B.*

before. Then the investment curve would shift rightward by \$0.75 trillion and the interest rate would rise from 3 percent to 5 percent. Note that, as the interest rate rises, some—but not all—of the original increase in planned investment is choked off. In the end, investment rises from \$1.5 trillion to \$1.75 trillion, and so each year \$0.25 trillion more is added to the capital stock than would otherwise be added.

These are the mechanics of a rightward shift in the investment curve. But what government measures would *cause* such a shift in the first place? That is, how could the government help to make investment spending more profitable for firms?

One such measure would be a reduction in the **corporate profits tax,** which would allow firms and their owners to keep more of the profits they earn from investment projects. Another, even more direct, policy is an **investment tax credit,** which subsidizes corporate investment in new capital equipment.

> *Reducing business taxes or providing specific investment incentives can shift the investment curve rightward, thereby creating faster growth in physical capital. This leads to faster growth in productivity and output per capita.*

Of course, the same reasoning applies in reverse: An *increase* in the corporate profits tax or the *elimination* of an investment tax credit would shift the investment curve to the left, slowing the rate of investment, the growth of the capital stock, and the rise in living standards.

### Targeting Households: Increasing the Incentive to Save

An increase in investment spending can also originate in the household sector, through an increase in the desire to save. This is illustrated in Figure 6. If households decide to save more of their incomes at any given interest rate, the supply of funds curve will shift rightward. The increase in saving drives down the interest rate, from 5 percent to 3 percent, which, in turn, causes investment to increase. With a lower interest rate, NBC might decide to borrow funds to build another production studio, or the corner grocery store may finally decide to borrow the funds it needs for a new electronic scanner at the checkout stand. In this way, an increase in the desire to save is translated, via the loanable funds market, into an increase in investment and faster growth in the capital stock.

What might cause households to increase their saving? The answer is found in the reasons people save in the first place. And to understand these reasons, you needn't look farther than yourself or your own family. You might currently be saving for a large purchase (a car, a house, a vacation, college tuition) or to build a financial cushion in case of hard times ahead. You might even be saving to support yourself during retirement, though this is a distant thought for most college students.

Given these motives, what would make you save *more?* Several things: greater uncertainty about your economic future, an increase in your life expectancy, anticipation of an earlier retirement, a change in tastes toward big-ticket items, or even just a change in your attitude about saving. Any of these changes—if they occurred in many households simultaneously—would shift the saving curve (the supply of funds curve) to the right, as in Figure 6.

But government policy can increase household saving as well. One way is to decrease the **capital gains tax.** A capital gain is the profit you earn when you sell an

**Corporate profits tax** A tax on the profits earned by corporations.

**Investment tax credit** A reduction in taxes for firms that invest in new capital.

**Capital gains tax** A tax on profits earned when a financial asset is sold at more than its acquisition price.

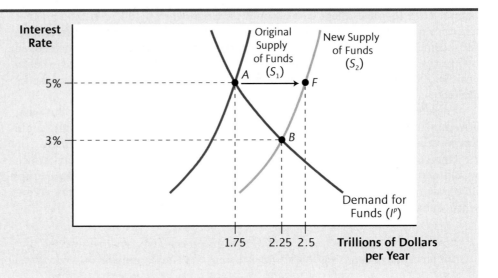

FIGURE 6

**An Increase in Saving**

*If households decide to save more of their incomes, the supply of funds curve will shift rightward (by the distance AF). With more funds available, the interest rate will fall. Businesses will respond by increasing their borrowing, and investment will increase from $1.75 trillion to $2.25 trillion.*

asset, such as a share of stock or a bond, at a higher price than you paid for it. By lowering the special tax rate for capital gains, households would be able to keep more of the capital gains they earn. As a result, stocks and bonds would become more rewarding to own, and you might decide to reduce your current spending in order to buy them. If other households react in the same way, total saving would rise, and the supply of funds to the loanable funds market would increase.

This was the logic behind a key component of the Bush administration's second tax cut, signed into law in May 2003. The tax cut included a reduction in the capital gains tax, from 20 percent to 15 percent for higher income households, and from 10 percent to 5 percent (and down to 0 percent in 2008) for lower income households. The lower tax rates applied only to *long-term* capital gains—gains on assets held for a year or longer—to encourage people to put their funds into stocks and other assets and keep them there, rather than engage in short-term speculation.

The 2003 tax cut on capital gains was controversial for two reasons. First, there was an equity issue: Because most of the capital gains in the economy are earned by higher income households, high-income households benefited more than low-income households. Second, the government was already running a substantial budget deficit in 2003, and the tax cuts threatened to raise it further. As you'll see in the next section, higher budget deficits can work *against* economic growth.

Another frequently proposed measure is to switch from the current U.S. income tax—which taxes all income whether it is spent or saved—to a **consumption tax**, which would tax only the income that households spend. A consumption tax could work just like the current income tax, except that you would deduct your saving from your income and pay taxes on the remainder. This would increase the reward for saving. By saving, you would earn additional interest on the part of your income that would have been taxed away under an income tax. Currently, individual retirement accounts (IRAs) and employer-sponsored 401(k) plans allow households to deduct limited amounts of saving from their incomes before paying taxes. A general consumption tax would go much further and allow *all* saving to be deducted.

**Consumption tax** A tax on the part of their income that households spend.

Another change that would increase household saving—if we were to choose this route—would be to modify the government programs that form our social safety net. Social Security payments to the elderly, unemployment insurance payments for those who lose their jobs, and Medicaid for those too poor to afford health care—all help to guarantee a basic floor for living standards. But by reducing the fear and anxiety of possible adverse economic outcomes, these government transfer programs also reduce households' incentive to save as a precaution.

> *Government can alter the tax and transfer system to increase incentives for saving. This would make more funds available for investment, speed growth in the capital stock, and speed the rise in living standards.*

(Do any of these methods of increasing saving disturb you? Remember, we are not advocating any measures here; rather, we are merely noting that such measures would increase saving and promote economic growth. We'll discuss the *costs* of growth-promoting measures later.)

## Shrinking the Budget Deficit

A final pro-investment measure is directed at the government sector itself. The previous chapter showed that an increase in government purchases, financed by borrowing in the financial market, completely crowds out consumption and investment. A *decrease* in government purchases has the opposite effect: raising consumption and investment.

Figure 7 reintroduces the government to the loanable funds market to show how this works. Initially, the budget deficit is $0.75 trillion, equal to the distance *EA*. The total demand for funds is the sum of investment and the government's budget deficit, given by the curve labeled $I^p + (G - T)$. The demand for funds curve intersects the supply of funds curve at point *A*, creating an equilibrium interest rate of 5 percent and equilibrium saving of $1.75 trillion. At this interest rate, investment spending is only $1 trillion. The part of saving not going to finance investment

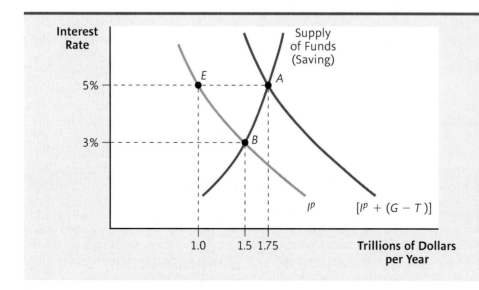

**FIGURE 7**

**Deficit Reduction and Investment Spending**

*Eliminating the government's budget deficit will reduce government borrowing in the loanable funds market. As a result, the total demand for funds will fall, as will the interest rate. At a lower interest rate, businesses will increase their investment spending from $1.0 trillion (point E) to $1.5 trillion (point B).*

spending ($1.75 trillion − $1 trillion = $0.75 trillion) is being used to finance the budget deficit.

Now consider what happens if the government eliminates the deficit—say, by reducing its purchases by $0.75 trillion. The demand for funds would consist of investment spending only. Since there would be no other borrowing, the new equilibrium would be point B, with an interest rate of 3 percent and investment equal to $1.5 trillion—greater than before. By balancing its budget, the government no longer needs to borrow in the loanable funds market, which frees up funds to flow to the business sector instead.

The link between the government budget, the interest rate, and investment spending is the major reason the U.S. government, and governments around the world, try to reduce and, if possible, eliminate budget deficits. They have learned that

> *a shrinking deficit or a rising surplus tends to reduce interest rates and increase investment, thus speeding the growth in the capital stock.*

In the 1990s, Congress set strict limits on the growth of government spending, and the budget deficit began shrinking. The restraints on spending, and rapid economic growth during the 1990s, finally turned the federal budget from deficit to surplus in 1998, and continued surpluses were projected for more than a decade. These surpluses were viewed as positive for economic growth: They would help keep the interest rate low, which in turn would lead to greater business investment spending.

When President George W. Bush took office in 2001, the direction of growth policy shifted away from preserving budget surpluses and toward lower tax rates. The first Bush tax cut in 2001( a total of $1.35 trillion over 10 years) purposely cut into potential future surpluses in order to reduce the tax burden on American households. Shortly afterward, a series of events pushed the budget into deficit. These included a continuing recession that had begun in March 2001 and the attacks of September 11, which resulted in large increases in military and homeland security spending. And a second tax cut in 2003—amounting to $350 billion over 10 years—increased current and projected deficits further.

The tax cuts included some elements (discussed earlier) to increase investment spending, such as a lower tax rate for capital gains and tax incentives for investment by small businesses. Also, you've learned that cutting income tax rates can have some effect on the labor force participation rate by shifting the labor supply curve rightward. But the tax cuts—by raising current and future budget deficits—would ultimately drive the interest rate higher than it would otherwise be, which works in opposition to the growth benefits of the tax cut. We'll discuss budget deficits and their effects on the economy more thoroughly toward the end of this book, in the chapter on fiscal policy.

### An Important Proviso about the Budget Deficit

A reduction in the deficit or an increase in the surplus—even if they stimulate private investment—are not *necessarily* pro-growth measures. It depends on *how* the budget changes. By an increase in taxes? A cut in government spending? And if the latter, which government programs will be cut? Welfare? National defense? Highway repair? The answers can make a big difference to the impact on growth.

For example, in our discussions of the capital stock so far, we've ignored government capital—roads, communication lines, bridges, and dams. To understand the importance of government capital, just imagine what life would be like without it. How would factories obtain their raw materials or distribute their goods if no one repaired the roads? How would contracts between buyers and sellers be enforced if there were no public buildings to house courts and police departments? It is clear that

> *government investment in new capital and the maintenance of existing capital make important contributions to economic growth.*

This important observation complicates our view of deficit reduction. It is still true that a decrease in government spending will lower the interest rate and increase private investment. But if the budget cutting falls largely on government investment, the negative effect of smaller *public* investment will offset some of the positive impact of greater *private* investment. Shrinking the deficit will then alter the *mix* of capital—more private and less public—and the effect on growth could go either way. A society rife with lawlessness, deteriorating roads and bridges, or an unreliable communications network might benefit from a shift toward public capital. For example, a study of public budgets in African nations—which have poor road conditions—found that each one-dollar-per-year cut in the road-maintenance budget increased vehicle operating costs by between $2 and $3 per year, and, in one case, by as much as $22 per year.[4] This is an example of a cut in government spending that, even if it reduces the deficit, probably hinders growth. By contrast, in Sweden—a country with a fully developed and well-maintained public infrastructure—recent governments have decided to shift the mix away from public and toward private capital, in part because they believed this would speed growth.

> *The impact of deficit reduction on economic growth depends on which government programs are cut. Shrinking the deficit by cutting government investment will not stimulate growth as much as would cutting other types of government spending.*

## HUMAN CAPITAL AND ECONOMIC GROWTH

So far, the only type of capital we've discussed is physical capital—the plant and equipment workers use to produce output. But when we think of the capital stock most broadly, we include *human capital* as well. Human capital—the skills and knowledge possessed by workers—is as central to economic growth as is physical capital. After all, most types of physical capital—computers, CAT scanners, and even shovels—will contribute little to output unless workers know how to use them. And when more workers gain skills or improve their existing skills, output rises just as it does when workers have more physical capital:

> *An increase in human capital works like an increase in physical capital to increase output: It causes the production function to shift upward, raises productivity, and increases the average standard of living.*

[4] This World Bank study was cited in *The Economist*, June 10, 1995, p. 72.

There is another similarity between human and physical capital: Both are *stocks* that are increased by *flows* of investment. The stock of human capital increases whenever investment in new skills during some period, through education and training, exceeds the depreciation of existing skills over the same period, through retirement, death, or disuse. Therefore, greater investment in human capital will speed the growth of the human capital stock, increasing the growth rate of productivity and living standards.

Human capital investments are made by business firms (when they help to train their employees), by government (through public education and subsidized training), and by households (when they pay for general education or professional training). Human capital investments have played an important role in recent U.S. economic growth. Can we do anything to increase our rate of investment in human capital?

In part, we've already answered this question: Some of the same policies that increase investment in *physical* capital also work to raise investment in human capital. For example, a decrease in the budget deficit would lower the interest rate and make it cheaper for households to borrow for college loans and training programs. A change in the tax system that increases the incentive to save would have the same impact, since this, too, would lower interest rates. And an easing of the tax burden on business firms could increase the profitability of *their* human capital investments, leading to more and better worker training programs.

But there is more: Human capital, unlike physical capital, cannot be separated from the person who provides it. If you own a building, you can rent it out to one firm and sell your labor to another. But if you have training as a doctor, your labor and your human capital must be sold together, as a package. Moreover, your wage or salary will be payment for both your labor and your human capital. This means that income tax reductions—which we discussed earlier as a means of increasing labor supply—can also increase the profitability of human capital to households, and increase their rate of investment in their own skills and training.

For example, suppose an accountant is considering whether to attend a course in corporate financial reporting, which would increase her professional skills. The course costs $4,000 and will increase the accountant's income by $1,000 per year for the rest of her career. With a tax rate of 40 percent, her take-home pay would increase by $600 per year, so her annual rate of return on her investment would be $600/$4,000 = 15 percent. But with a lower tax rate—say, 20 percent—her take-home pay would rise by $800 per year, so her rate of return would be $800/$4,000 = 20 percent. The lower the tax rate, the greater is the rate of return on the accountant's human capital investment, and the more likely she will be to acquire new skills. Thus,

> *many of the pro-growth policies discussed earlier—policies that increase employment or increase investment in physical capital—are also effective in promoting investment in human capital.*

## TECHNOLOGICAL CHANGE

**Technological change** The invention or discovery of new inputs, new outputs, or new production methods.

So far, we've discussed how productivity growth is increased by greater investment in physical or human capital. But another important source of growth is **technological change**—the invention or discovery of new inputs, new outputs, or new methods of production. Indeed, it is largely because of technological change that Malthus's horrible prediction (cited at the beginning of this chapter) has not come true. In the last 60 years, for example, the inventions of synthetic fertilizers, hybrid corn, and chemical pesticides have enabled world food production to increase faster than population.

New technology affects the economy in much the same way as do increases in the capital stock. Flip back to Figure 4 of this chapter. There, you saw that an increase in the capital stock would shift the production function upward and increase output. New technology, too, shifts the production function upward because it enables any given number of workers to produce more output.

It follows that

> *the faster the rate of technological change, the greater the growth rate of productivity, and the faster the rise in living standards.*

It might seem that technological change is one of those things that just happens. Thomas Edison invents electricity, or Steve Jobs and Steve Wozniak develop the first practical personal computer in their garage. But the pace of technological change is not as haphazard as it seems. The transistor was invented as part of a massive research and development effort by AT&T to improve the performance of communications electronics. Similarly, the next developments in computer technology, transportation, and more will depend in part on how much money is spent on research and development (R&D) by the leading technology firms:

> *The rate of technological change in the economy depends largely on firms' total spending on R&D. Policies that increase R&D spending will increase the pace of technological change.*

What can the government do to increase spending on R&D? First, it can increase its own direct support for R&D by carrying out more research in its own laboratories or increasing funding for universities and tax incentives to private research labs.

Second, the government can enhance **patent protection**, which increases rewards for those who create new technology by giving them exclusive rights to use it or sell it. Hundreds of thousands of new patents are issued every year in the United States: to pharmaceutical companies for new prescription drugs, to telecommunications companies for new cellular technologies, and to the producers of a variety of household goods ranging from can openers to microwave ovens.

**Patent protection** A government grant of exclusive rights to use or sell a new technology.

Because patent protection increases the rewards that developers can expect from new inventions, it encourages them to spend more on R&D. By broadening patent protection—issuing patents on a wider variety of discoveries—or by lengthening patent protection—increasing the number of years during which the developer has exclusive rights to market the invention—the government could increase the expected profits from new technologies. That would increase total spending on R&D and increase the pace of technological change.

Finally, R&D spending is in many ways just like other types of investment spending: The funds are drawn from the loanable funds market, and R&D programs require firms to buy something now (laboratories, the services of research scientists, materials for prototypes) for the uncertain prospect of profits in the future. Therefore, almost any policy that stimulates investment spending in general will also increase spending on R&D. Cutting the tax rate on capital gains or on corporate profits, or lowering interest rates by encouraging greater saving or by reducing the budget deficit, can each help to increase spending on R&D and increase the rate of technological change.

## GROWTH POLICIES: A SUMMARY

In this chapter, you've learned about the forces that affect economic growth, as well as a host of government policies that can make the economy grow faster. If you are having trouble keeping it all straight, Table 4—which summarizes all of this information—might help.

As you look at the table, you'll notice that many of the policies that affect economic growth are *fiscal policies*—changes in government purchases or net taxes designed to affect total output. In the previous chapter, you learned that fiscal policy has no *demand-side* effects on output. But in this chapter, you've seen that fiscal policy *can* affect output in a different way—by changing the resources available in the economy. For example, tax rates influence the number of people who want to work and change the quantity of labor employed. Fiscal changes can also change the rate of investment spending and therefore influence the capital stock firms will have in the future. These effects of fiscal policy—changing total output by changing the resources available in the economy—are called **supply-side effects**.

**Supply-side effects**
Macroeconomic policy effects on total output that work by changing the quantities of resources available.

> In the long run, while fiscal policy cannot influence total output by changing total spending (demand-side effects), it can influence output by changing the quantity of resources available for production (supply-side effects).

Table 4 also shows that some pro-growth policies can work through multiple channels. For example, a less-generous social safety net would have three separate impacts on growth: (1) an increase in labor supply (by making alternatives to working more draconian); (2) an increase in the incentive to save (because people would worry more about their future); and (3) a reduction in the budget deficit (through lower transfer payments). The first effect raises the EPR, and the other two raise investment and productivity.

Finally, the table shows that some policies that *increase* economic growth through one channel can simultaneously work *against* growth through another channel. For example, in the first row of the table, you can see that a *decrease* in income tax rates contributes to growth by increasing employment. But farther down, you'll see that an *increase* in taxes can aid growth by shrinking a budget deficit (implying that a *decrease* in taxes would have the opposite effect and harm growth). Thus, a decrease in tax rates simultaneously helps growth through one channel and harms growth through another.

The fact that a single policy can have two competing effects on the economy helps us understand one reason for controversy in macroeconomic policy. When we cut income taxes, for example, the ultimate effect on economic growth will depend on which of the two effects is stronger, something over which economists can and do disagree. The Bush tax cut in 2001 was seen by some economists as a growth-enhancing measure (those who stressed the impact on employment) and by others as harmful to

| Factors That Influence Growth in Output per Capita | | | TABLE 4 |
|---|---|---|---|
| **Examples of Pro-Growth Policies** | **Method of Impact** | **Immediate Goal** | **Effect on Growth Equation** |
| • Decrease income or payroll tax rates<br>• Less-generous social safety net | Increase in labor supply | Employment ↑ | EPR growth rate ↑ |
| • Specific employment subsidies<br>• Any policy that raises labor productivity (e.g., all policies below) | Increase in labor demand | | |
| • Investment tax credit<br>• Decrease corporate profits tax rate<br>• Greater subsidies for student loans | Direct impact on investment | Greater investment in:<br>• Human capital<br>• Physical capital<br>• R&D | Productivity growth rate ↑ |
| • Tax incentives for saving [IRAs, 401(k)s]<br>• Decrease capital gains tax rate<br>• Less-generous social safety net | Increase in saving $\Rightarrow$ $r\downarrow \Rightarrow I^p\uparrow$ | | |
| • Decrease in government purchases<br>• Increase in taxes<br>• Decrease in transfer payments | Decrease in budget deficit $\Rightarrow r\downarrow \Rightarrow I^p\uparrow$ | | |

economic growth (those who stressed the effect on the government's budget, and the consequences for interest rates and investment).

The biggest controversies regarding growth policies, however, are not about their effectiveness but about their *costs*.

## THE COSTS OF ECONOMIC GROWTH

So far in this chapter, we've discussed a variety of policies that could increase the rate of economic growth and speed the rise in living standards. Why don't all nations pursue these policies and push their rates of economic growth to the maximum? For example, why did the U.S. standard of living (output per capita) grow by 2.1 percent per year between 1995 and 2005? Why not 4 percent per year? Or 6 percent? Or even more?

In this section, you will see that

> *promoting economic growth involves unavoidable tradeoffs: It requires some groups, or the nation as a whole, to give up something else that is valued.*

Economics is famous for making the public aware of policy tradeoffs. One of the most important things you will learn in your introductory economics course is that there are no costless solutions to society's problems. Just as individuals face an opportunity cost when they take an action (they must give up something else that they value), so, too, policy makers face an opportunity cost whenever they pursue a policy: They must compromise on achieving some other social goal.

What are the costs of growth?

## BUDGETARY COSTS

If you look again at Table 4, you'll see that many of the pro-growth policies we've analyzed involve some kind of tax cut. Cutting the income tax rate may increase the labor force participation rate. Cutting taxes on capital gains or corporate profits will increase investment directly. And cutting taxes on saving will increase household saving, lower interest rates, and thus increase investment spending indirectly. Unfortunately, implementing any of these tax cuts would force the government to choose among three unpleasant alternatives: increase some other tax to regain the lost revenue, cut government spending, or permit the budget deficit to rise.

Who will bear the burden of this budgetary cost? That depends on which alternative is chosen. Under the first option—increasing some other tax—the burden falls on those who pay the other tax. For example, if income taxes are cut, real estate taxes might be increased. A family might pay lower income taxes, but higher property taxes. Whether it comes out ahead or behind will depend on how much income the family earns relative to how much property it owns.

The second option, cutting government spending, imposes the burden on those who currently benefit from government programs. This includes those who directly benefit from specific programs—like welfare recipients or farmers. It also includes those who benefit from government spending more indirectly. Even though you may earn your income in the private sector, if government spending is cut, you may suffer from a deterioration of public roads, decreased police protection, or poorer schools for your children.

The third option—a larger budget deficit or a smaller budget surplus—is more complicated. Suppose a tax cut causes the government to end up with a larger deficit. Then greater government borrowing will increase the total amount of government debt outstanding—called the *national debt*. This means greater interest payments by future generations and higher taxes.

But that is not all. From the previous chapter, we know that a rise in the budget deficit (by increasing the demand for funds) drives up the interest rate. The higher interest rate will reduce investment in physical capital and R&D by businesses, as well as investment in human capital by households, and both effects will work to decrease economic growth. It is even possible that so much private investment will be crowded out that the tax cut, originally designed to boost economic growth, ends up slowing growth instead. At best, the growth-enhancing effects of the tax cut will be weakened. This is why advocates of high growth rates usually propose one of the other options—a rise in some other tax or a cut in government spending—as part of a pro-growth tax cut.

In sum,

> *even though properly targeted tax cuts can increase the rate of economic growth, they will generally force us to either redistribute the tax burden or cut government programs.*

## CONSUMPTION COSTS

Any pro-growth policy that works by increasing investment—in physical capital, human capital, or R&D—requires a sacrifice of current consumption spending. We use *resources* to construct new oil rigs or factory buildings, or to build and staff new training facilities and research laboratories. These resources could have been used instead to produce clothing, automobiles, video games, and other consumer goods. In other words, we face a tradeoff: The more capital goods we produce in any given year, the fewer consumption goods we can enjoy in that year.

The role of this tradeoff in economic growth can be clearly seen with a familiar tool from Chapter 2: the production possibilities frontier (PPF). Figure 8 shows the PPF for a nation with some given amount of land, labor, capital, and entrepreneurship that must be allocated to the production of two types of output: capital goods and consumption goods. At point *K*, the nation is using all of its resources to produce capital goods and none to produce consumption goods. Point *C* represents the opposite extreme: all resources used to produce consumption goods and none for capital goods. Ordinarily, a nation will operate at an intermediate point such as *A*, where it is producing both capital and consumption goods.

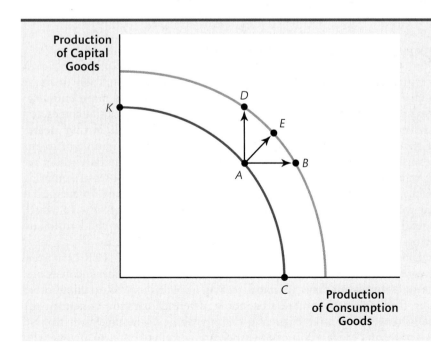

**FIGURE** 8

**Consumption, Investment, and Economic Growth**

*In the current period, a nation can choose to produce only consumer goods (point C), or it can produce some capital goods by sacrificing some current consumption, as at point A. If investment at point A exceeds capital depreciation, the capital stock will grow, and the production possibilities frontier will shift outward. After it does, the nation can produce more consumption goods (point B), more capital goods (point D), or more of both (point E).*

Now, as long as capital production at point *A* is greater than the depreciation of existing capital, the capital stock will grow. In future periods, the economy—with more capital—can produce more output, as shown by the outward shift of the PPF in the figure. If a nation can produce more output, then it can produce more consumption goods and the same quantity of capital goods (moving from point *A* to point *B*), or more capital goods and the same quantity of consumption goods (from point *A* to point *D*) or more of both (from point *A* to point *E*).

Let's take a closer look at how this sacrifice of current consumption goods might come about. Suppose that some change in government policy—an investment tax credit or a lengthening of the patent period for new inventions—successfully increases investment. (Go back to Figure 5.) What will happen? Businesses— demanding more loanable funds—will drive up the interest rate, and households all over the country will find that saving has become more attractive. As families increase their saving, we move rightward along the economy's supply of funds curve. In this way, firms get the funds they need to purchase new capital. But a decision to *save more* is also a decision to *spend less*. As current saving rises, current consumption spending necessarily falls. By driving up the interest rate, *the increase in investment spending causes a voluntary decrease in consumption spending by households.* Resources are freed from producing consumption goods and diverted to producing capital goods instead.

Although this decrease in consumption spending is voluntary, it is still a cost that we pay. And in some cases, a painful cost: Some of the increase in the household sector's net saving results from a decrease in borrowing by households that—at higher interest rates—can no longer afford to finance purchases of homes, cars, or furniture. In sum,

> *greater investment in physical capital, human capital, or R&D will lead to faster economic growth and higher living standards in the future, but we will have fewer consumer goods to enjoy in the present.*

## OPPORTUNITY COSTS OF WORKERS' TIME

An increase in the employment–population ratio or average hours will increase living standards, as measured by output per capita. There will be more output to divide among a given population. But this increase in output per capita comes at a cost: a decrease in time spent in nonmarket activities. For example, with a greater fraction of the population working, a smaller fraction is spending time at home. This might mean that more students have summer jobs, more elderly workers are postponing their retirement, or more previously nonworking spouses are entering the labor force. Similarly, an increase in average working hours would mean that the average worker will have less time for other activities—less time to watch television, read novels, garden, fix up the house, teach his or her children, or do volunteer work.

Thus, when economic growth comes about from increases in the EPR or in average hours, we face a tradeoff: On the one hand, we can enjoy higher incomes and more goods and services; on the other hand, we will have less time to do things other than work in the market. In a market economy, where choices are voluntary, the value of the income gained must be greater than the value of the time given up. No one forces us to reenter the labor force or to increase working hours. So anyone who takes either of these actions must be better off for doing so. Still, we must recognize that *something* of value is always given up when employment or hours increase:

> *An increase in the employment–population ratio or a rise in average hours will increase living standards as measured by output per capita, but also require us to sacrifice time previously spent in nonmarket activities.*

## SACRIFICE OF OTHER SOCIAL GOALS

Rapid economic growth is an important social goal, but it's not the only one. Some of the policies that quicken the pace of growth require us to sacrifice other goals that we care about. For example, you've seen that restructuring and even reducing government transfer payments could increase saving, leading to more investment and faster growth. But such a move would cut the incomes of those who benefit from the current system and force some citizens into levels of poverty that society may find unacceptable. You've learned that extending patent protection would increase incentives for research and development. But it would also extend the monopoly power exercised by patent holders and force consumers to pay higher prices for drugs, electronic equipment, and even packaged foods in the present.

Of course, the argument cuts both ways: Just as government policies to stimulate investment require us to sacrifice other goals, so, too, can the pursuit of other goals impede investment spending and economic growth. Most of us would like to see a cleaner environment and safer workplaces. But safety and environmental regulations can reduce the rate of profit on new capital and shrink investment spending.

Does this mean that business taxes and government regulations should be reduced to the absolute minimum? Not at all. As in most matters of economic policy, we face a tradeoff:

> *Achieving greater worker safety, a cleaner environment, and other social goals requires the sacrifice of some economic growth along the way. Alternatively, achieving greater economic growth may require some compromise on other things we care about.*

When values differ, people will disagree on just how much we should sacrifice for economic growth or how much growth we should sacrifice for other goals.

# USING THE THEORY

## Economic Growth in the Less-Developed Countries

In most countries, Malthus's dire predictions (cited at the beginning of this chapter) have not come true. One reason is that increases in the capital stock have raised productivity and increased the average standard of living. Increases in the capital stock are even more important in the less-developed countries (LDCs), which have relatively little capital to begin with. In these countries, even small increases in capital formation can have dramatic effects on living standards.

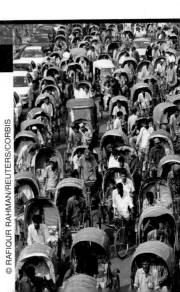

© RAFIQUR RAHMAN/REUTERS/CORBIS

But how does a nation go about increasing its capital stock? As you've learned, there are a variety of measures, all designed to accomplish the same goal: shifting resources away from consumer-goods production toward the production of physical and human capital. A very simple formula.

Some countries that were once LDCs—like Hong Kong, Singapore, South Korea, and India—have applied the formula very effectively. Output per capita in these countries has grown by an average of 4 or 5 percent per year for the past two decades. China's output per capita has grown even faster over this period, with an average annual increase of 8 percent. All these countries were able to shift resources from consumption goods into capital goods in part by pursuing many of the growth-enhancing measures discussed in this chapter: large subsidies for human and physical capital investments, pro-growth tax cuts to encourage saving and investment, and the willingness to sacrifice other social goals—especially a clean environment—for growth.[5] These economies gave up large amounts of potential consumption during a period of intensive capital formation.

But other LDCs have had great difficulty raising living standards. Table 5 shows growth rates for several of them, over the periods 1975–1990 and 1990–2003. In some cases, such as Bangladesh, Ghana, and Benin, there is at least some cause for optimism: Stagnating or declining living standards in the earlier period have given way to slow but consistent growth. In other cases—such as Kenya—living standards have barely budged over the past few decades. In still other cases—for example, Haiti and Sierra Leone—output per capita has been falling ever more rapidly. Why do some LDCs have such difficulty achieving economic growth?

Much of the explanation for the low growth rates of many LDCs lies with three characteristics that they share:

1. *Very low current output per capita.* Living standards are so low in some LDCs that they cannot take advantage of the tradeoff between producing consumption goods and producing capital goods. In these countries, pulling resources out of consumption would threaten the survival of many families.

| TABLE 5 | | |
|---|---|---|

**Economic Growth in Selected Poor Countries**

| | Average Annual Growth Rate of Output per Capita | |
|---|---|---|
| Country | 1975–1990 | 1990–2003 |
| Bangladesh | 0.9 | 3.1 |
| Ghana | −0.8 | 1.8 |
| Benin | −0.6 | 2.2 |
| Kenya | 0.9 | −0.6 |
| Haiti | −1.9 | −2.8 |
| Sierra Leone | −1.5 | −5.3 |

*Source:* United Nations Development Programme, *Human Development Report 2005*, pp. 266–269, and author calculations.

[5] Some of these countries also had some special advantages—such as a high level of human capital to start with.

At the household level, the problem is an inability to save: Incomes are so low that households must spend all they earn on consumption.

2. *High population growth rates.* Low living standards and high population growth rates are linked together in a cruel circle of logic. On the one hand, rapid population growth by itself tends to reduce living standards. On the other hand, a low standard of living tends to increase population growth. Why? First, the poor are often uneducated in matters of family planning. Second, high mortality rates among infants and children encourage families to have many offspring, to ensure the survival of at least a few to care for parents in their old age. As a result, while the average woman in the United States will have fewer than two children in her lifetime, the average woman in Haiti will have four children; in Kenya, five children; and in Sierra Leone, more than six.

3. *Poor infrastructure.* Political instability, poor law enforcement, corruption, and adverse government regulations make many LDCs unprofitable places to invest. Low rates of investment mean a smaller capital stock and lower productivity. Infrastructure problems also harm worker productivity in another way: Citizens must spend time guarding against thievery and trying to induce the government to let them operate businesses—time they could otherwise spend producing output.

These three characteristics—low current production, high population growth, and poor infrastructure—interact to create a vicious circle of continuing poverty, which we can understand with the help of the familiar PPF between capital goods and consumption goods. Look back at Figure 8, and now imagine that it applies to a poor, developing country. In this case, an outward shift of the PPF does not, in itself, guarantee an increase in the standard of living. In the LDCs, the population growth rate is often very high, and employment grows at the same rate as the population. If employment grows more rapidly than the capital stock, then even though the PPF is shifting outward, capital per worker will decline. Unless some other factor—such as technological change—is raising productivity, then living standards will fall.

*In order to have rising capital per worker—an important source of growth in productivity and living standards—a nation's stock of capital must not only grow but grow faster than its population.*

Point N in Figure 9 shows the minimum amount of investment needed to maintain capital per worker, and therefore labor productivity and living standards, for a given rate of population growth. For example, if the population is growing at 4 percent per year, then point N indicates the annual investment needed to increase the total capital stock by 4 percent per year. If investment is just equal to N, then capital per worker—and living standards—remains constant. If investment exceeds N, then capital per worker—and living standards—will rise. Of course, the greater the growth in population, the higher point N will be on the vertical axis, since greater investment will be needed just to keep up with population growth. (We assume throughout this discussion that the labor force and employment are both rising at the same rate as the population.)

The PPF in Figure 9 has an added feature: Point S shows the minimum acceptable level of consumption, the amount of consumer goods the economy *must* produce

**LDC Growth and Living Standards**

*In order to increase capital per worker when population is growing, yearly investment spending must exceed some minimum level N. In any year, there is a minimum level of consumption, S, needed to support the population. If output is currently at point H, capital per worker and living standards are stagnant. But movement to a point like J would require an unacceptably low level of consumption.*

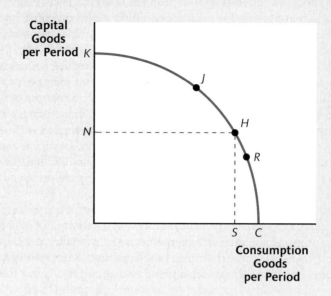

in a year. For example, *S* might represent the consumption goods needed to prevent starvation among the least well off, or to prevent unacceptable social consequences, such as violent revolution.

Now we can see the problem faced by some less-developed economies. Output is currently at a point like *H* in Figure 9, with annual investment just equal to *N*. The capital stock is not growing fast enough to increase capital per worker, and so labor productivity and living standards are stagnant. In this situation, the PPF shifts outward each year, but not quickly enough to improve people's lives. In the most desperate countries, the situation is worse: They operate at a point like *R*, with investment *below N*. Even though the capital stock is growing, it does not grow fast enough, so capital per worker and living standards decline.

The solution to this problem appears to be an increase in capital production beyond point *N*—a movement *along* the PPF from point *H* to a point such as *J*. As investment rises above *N*, capital per worker rises, and the PPF shifts outward rapidly enough over time to raise living standards. In a wealthy country, like the United States, such a move could be engineered by changes in taxes or other government policies. But in the LDCs depicted here, such a move would be intolerable: At point *H*, consumption is already equal to *S*, the lowest acceptable level. Moving to point *J* would require reducing consumption *below S*.

> *The poorest LDCs are too poor to take advantage of the tradeoff between consumption and capital production in order to increase their living standards. Since they cannot reduce consumption below current levels, they cannot produce enough capital to keep up with their rising populations.*

In recent history, a variety of methods have been attempted to break out of this vicious circle of poverty.

- *Brute force.* The most tragic way to break out of the cycle is to simply force the economy from a point like *H* to a point like *J*, even though consumption falls below the minimally acceptable level *S*.

     An example occurred during the 1930s, when the dictator Joseph Stalin moved the Soviet economy in this way by ordering farmers into the city to produce capital equipment rather than food. With fewer people working on farms, agricultural production declined and there was not enough food to go around. Stalin's solution was to confiscate food from the remaining farmers and give it to the urban workforce. Of course, this meant starvation for millions of farmers. Millions more who complained too loudly, or who otherwise represented a political threat, were rounded up and executed.

- *Target the wealthy.* In this method, the economy moves from point *H* to point *J* while limiting the sacrifice of consumption to the wealthy. Figure 10(a) shows this graphically. The minimally acceptable level of consumption moves leftward, from *S* to *S′*, because total consumption can be reduced to a lower level than before without threatening the survival of the poor. The drop in consumption to point *J* (which is now acceptable) frees up resources for investment. However, this method is not often practical because the wealthy have the most influence with government in LDCs. Being more mobile, they can easily relocate to other countries, taking their savings with them. This is why efforts to shift the sacrifice to the wealthy are often combined with restrictions on personal liberties, such as the freedom to travel or to invest abroad. These moves often backfire in the long run, since restrictions on personal and economic freedom are remembered long after they are removed and make the public—especially foreigners—hesitant to invest in that country.

- *Decrease population growth.* Consider a nation producing at point *H* in Figure 10(b). Capital production is just sufficient to keep up with a rising population. The PPF shifts outward each year, but because capital per worker remains constant, living standards remain constant. If this nation can reduce its population growth rate, however, the level of capital production needed to just maintain capital per worker moves downward, from *N* to *N′*. The economy can then continue to operate at point *H*, but now—with the population growing more slowly than the capital stock—capital per worker and living standards rise.

     Reducing population growth was an important part of China's growth strategy, bringing the number of births per woman down from six in 1970 to less than two in 1980 (and to 1.7 in 2000). But it has involved severe restrictions on the rights of individual families to have children, including heavy fines and, in many cases, forced abortions and sterilizations. Although restrictions and enforcement have been loosened considerably, China's government continues to regulate childbearing as part of its effort to raise living standards, and announced in 2006 that it would continue to do so through at least 2010.

- *Foreign assistance.* Since the 1940s, assistance from wealthier countries—either individually or through international organizations such as the World Bank or the International Monetary Fund—has been viewed as the most humane way for LDCs to break out of poverty. Providing capital goods to an LDC allows its capital stock to grow faster with no decrease in consumption goods. This is illustrated in Figure 10(c), where the additional capital allows the country to operate *beyond* its PPF, moving from point *H* to point *F*. The LDC still *produces* at point *H*. But point *F* shows the new combination of consumption goods and capital goods the country obtains over the year.

## FIGURE 10 Some Growth Options for LDCs

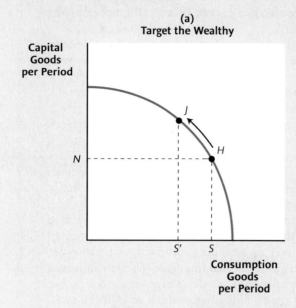

**(a)**
**Target the Wealthy**

Capital
Goods
per Period

J

N

H

S'    S

Consumption
Goods
per Period

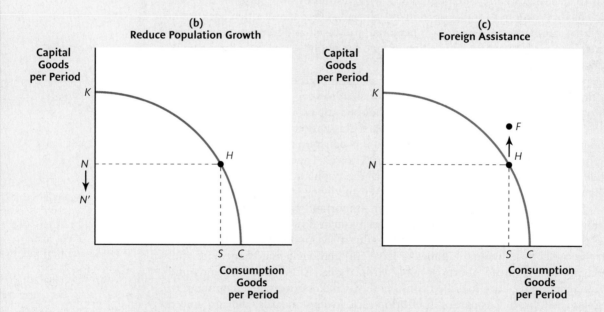

**(b)**
**Reduce Population Growth**

Capital
Goods
per Period

K

N
↓
N'

H

S    C

Consumption
Goods
per Period

**(c)**
**Foreign Assistance**

Capital
Goods
per Period

K

● F

N

H

S    C

Consumption
Goods
per Period

*In all three panels, an LDC is initially producing at point H, where consumption is just equal to the amount needed for survival (S), and capital production is just equal to the amount needed to keep up with a rising population (N).*

*In panel (a), resources are shifted from producing capital goods to producing consumer goods. But because any decrease in consumption is limited to the wealthy, the minimum-survival level of consumption decreases from S to S'. At point J, the LDC can produce more capital and raise living standards over time while still meeting survival needs for consumption.*

*In panel (b), the LDC reduces the population growth rate, so that capital production needed to keep up with a rising population decreases from N to N'. Although production remains at point H, capital per worker now rises, raising living standards over time.*

*In panel (c), capital goods are obtained externally, through foreign investment or foreign assistance. The economy continues to produce at point H, but with the total amount of capital added each period greater than N (at point F), capital per worker and living standards rise over time.*

Alternatively, foreign assistance could provide consumption goods, allowing the country to free up its own resources for capital production while maintaining minimal levels of consumption. In Figure 10(c), the country would move leftward along the PPF (not shown), but the combination of consumption and capital goods would once again be at point *F*. Either form of assistance could enable the capital stock to grow faster than the population for some time, setting the stage for sustained growth in living standards.

At least, that's the theory. But the failure of so many poor countries to gain traction, despite trillions of dollars in foreign assistance over the past half century, has made many economists skeptical. They put much of the blame on one of the features of LDCs discussed earlier: poor institutional infrastructure. When corrupt or undeveloped legal systems fail to protect property rights or enforce contracts, savers will not lend to domestic borrowers, and entrepreneurs will not start productive businesses. When corrupt governments siphon off most of the foreign aid dollars toward military spending or lavish lifestyles for the politically connected, little is left for improving the health and education of the population or increasing the stock of productive capital.

Although most economists believe that foreign assistance is still important, they are paying increasing attention to the institutional infrastructure of the recipient countries. This was the thinking behind the *Millennium Challenge Account* established by the Bush administration in 2004. It provides significantly increased amounts of foreign aid . . . with a catch: Countries must meet guidelines for reducing corruption, improving the environment for entrepreneurship, and working to improve the health and human capital of their citizens. The program has been given high marks for its design, but it is still too early to judge its ultimate effectiveness.

## Summary

The growth rate of real GDP is a key determinant of economic well-being. If output grows faster than the population, then output per person—and the average standard of living—will rise. But in order for output per person to rise, either average working hours, the *employment–population ratio (EPR)*, or productivity must increase. In developed countries, average hours have been decreasing and are unlikely to rise in the future. Growth in the EPR has been responsible for considerable past growth in the United States and several other countries. It can be increased by policy changes that increase labor supply (such as tax cuts) or labor demand (such as subsidized job training or employment subsidies). But in the future, continual rises in the EPR are unlikely. This leaves increases in *productivity*—a major contributor to growth in the past—as the main source of growth in the future.

Productivity increases when capital per worker rises or there are advances in technology. When the flow of investment spending is greater than the flow of depreciation over some period of time, the capital stock will rise. An increase in the capital stock shifts the production function upward, enabling any given number of workers to produce more output. If the capital stock rises at a faster rate than the labor force, then *capital per worker* rises, and so does productivity.

Investment can be encouraged by government policies. It can be stimulated directly through reductions in the corporate profits tax rate or through subsidies. Or investment can be increased indirectly through government policies that bring about lower interest rates, such as changes in tax policy to encourage more saving or reductions in the government's budget deficit.

*Technological change*—the application of new inputs or new methods of production—also raises productivity. The rate of technological change depends partly on spending on research and development, either by government or private firms. Almost any government policy that increases investment spending in general will also increase spending on research and development, and therefore increase the pace of technological change. In addition, patent protection can specifically influence research and development of new, patentable products and technologies.

Economic growth is not costless. Tax cuts that stimulate employment, capital formation, or technological progress require increases in other taxes, cuts in spending programs, or an increase in the national debt. Any increase in employment from a given population requires a sacrifice of leisure time and other nonmarket activities. More broadly, any increase in investment requires the sacrifice of consumption today.

# Problem Set   *Answers to even-numbered Questions and Problems can be found on the text Web site at www.thomsonedu.com/economics/hall.*

1. For each of the following, (1) determine the impact on full-employment output and (2) illustrate the immediate and long-run impact using the classical model (labor market, production function, or loanable funds market).
   a. Increased immigration
   b. An aging of the population with an increasing proportion of retirees
   c. A decline in the tax rate on corporate profits
   d. A reduction of unemployment benefits
   e. The development of the Internet

2. Below are GDP and growth data for the United States and four other countries:

| | 1950 Real GDP per Capita (in 1990 dollars) | 1990 Real GDP per Capita (in 1990 dollars) | Average Yearly Growth Rate |
|---|---|---|---|
| United States | $9,573 | $21,558 | 2.0% |
| France | $5,221 | $17,959 | 3.0% |
| Japan | $1,873 | $19,425 | 5.7% |
| Kenya | $ 609 | $ 1,055 | 1.3% |
| India | $ 597 | $ 1,348 | 2.0% |

*Source:* Angus Maddison, *Monitoring the World Economy, 1820–1992* (Paris: OECD, 1995).

   a. For both years, calculate each country's per capita GDP as a percentage of U.S. per capita GDP. Which countries appeared to be catching up to the United States, and which were lagging behind?
   b. If all these countries had continued to grow (from 1990 onward) at the average growth rates given, in what year would France have caught up to the United States? In what years (respectively) would India and Kenya have caught up to the United States?

3. Below are hypothetical data for the country of Barrovia:

| | Population (millions) | Employment (millions) | Average Yearly Hours | Labor Productivity (output per hour) | Total Yearly Output |
|---|---|---|---|---|---|
| 2002 | 100 | 50 | 2,000 | $4.75 | — |
| 2003 | 104 | 51 | 2,000 | $4.75 | — |
| 2004 | 107 | 53 | 1,950 | $5.00 | — |
| 2005 | 108 | 57 | 1,950 | $5.00 | — |
| 2006 | 110 | 57 | 2,000 | $5.00 | — |

   a. Fill in the entries for total output in each of the five years.
   b. Calculate the following for each year (except 2002):
      (1) Population growth rate (from previous year)
      (2) Growth rate of output (from previous year)
      (3) Growth rate of per capita output (from previous year)

4. In addition to shifting the production function upward, an increase in the capital stock will ordinarily make workers more productive and shift the labor demand curve rightward. Graphically illustrate the full impact of an increase in the nation's capital stock under this assumption.

5. Show what would happen to the production function if the capital stock decreased. Suppose, too, that the decrease in the capital stock—because it made workers less productive to firms—shifted the labor demand curve leftward. Graphically illustrate the full impact of a decrease in the nation's capital stock under this assumption. What government policies could cause a decrease in the capital stock?

6. State whether each of the following statements is true or false, and explain your reasoning briefly.
   a. "A permanent increase in employment from a lower to a higher level will cause an increase in real GDP, but not continued growth in real GDP."
   b. "A permanent increase in the nation's capital stock to a new, higher level will cause an increase in real GDP, but not continued growth in real GDP."
   c. "With constant population, work hours, and technology, as long as planned investment spending continues to be greater than depreciation, real GDP will continue to grow year after year."
   d. "All else equal, a permanent increase in an economy's rate of planned investment spending will cause real GDP to grow faster each year than it would at the old, lower level of investment spending."

7. On a diagram, draw an economy's production function. On the same diagram, add curves to illustrate where the production function would be in five years under each of the following assumptions. (Label your additional curves a, b, and c, and assume nothing else affecting economic growth changes.)
   a. Planned investment remains constant at its current level, which exceeds depreciation.
   b. Planned investment remains constant at its current level, which is less than depreciation.
   c. Planned investment rises above its current level, which exceeds depreciation.

8. Complete the table on page 661, then find the growth rate of output from Year 1 to Year 2, from Year 2 to Year 3, and from Year 3 to Year 4, in terms of the percentage change in each of its components.

9. Redraw Figure 9 from the chapter, adding the new PPF the country would face in Year 2 if it produces at point *H* in Year 1. Explain your drawing. (Hint: Does a shifting PPF always mean a change in living standards?)

10. For each of the following scenarios, calculate (1) the percentage change in real GDP; (2) the percentage change in real GDP per capita.
   a. Average hours are constant; EPR, productivity, and population each increase by 2%.

|                          | Year 1          | Year 2             | Year 3          | Year 4          |
| ------------------------ | --------------- | ------------------ | --------------- | --------------- |
| Total hours worked       | 192 million     | 200 million        | 285 million     | 368 million     |
| Employment               | 1,200,000       | 1,400,000          | 1,900,000       | 2,100,000       |
| Population               | 2,000,000       | 2,500,000          | 2,900,000       | 3,200,000       |
| Productivity             | $50 per hour    | $52.50 per hour    | $58 per hour    | $60 per hour    |
| Average hours per worker |                 |                    |                 |                 |
| EPR                      |                 |                    |                 |                 |
| Total output             |                 |                    |                 |                 |

*Table for Problem 8*

b. Average hours and EPR are constant; productivity and population each increase by 2%.

c. Average hours, productivity, and population each increase by 2%; EPR is constant.

d. Average hours and EPR each decrease by 2%; productivity and population each increase by 2%.

11. Evaluate the following statement: "Continual population growth, with no other change affecting economic growth, leads to continual growth in real GDP, but a continual drop in living standards." Briefly explain why you believe the statement is true or false.

## More Challenging

12. Assume that average work hours and the employment–population ratio remain constant in a less developed country. The country initially has $100 billion in capital. For each of the following scenarios, describe what will happen over time to the LDC's (1) production possibilities frontier for capital and consumption goods; (2) capital per worker; and (3) average living standard.

a. Population grows by 2% per year, depreciation of capital stock is 2% per year, and investment (new capital production) each year is equal to 4% of capital stock at the beginning of the year.

b. Population grows by 1% per year, depreciation of capital stock is 2% per year, and investment (new capital production) each year is equal to 4% of capital stock at the beginning of the year.

c. Population is constant, depreciation of capital stock is 2% per year, and investment (new capital production) each year is equal to 1% of capital stock at the beginning of the year.

13. Economist Amartya Sen has argued that famines in underdeveloped countries are not simply the result of crop failures or natural disasters. Instead, he suggests that wars, especially civil wars, are linked to most famine episodes in recent history. Using a framework similar to Figure 10, discuss the probable effect of war on a country's PPF. Explain what would happen if the country were initially operating at or near a point like *S*, the minimum acceptable level of consumption.

# CHAPTER 9

# Economic Fluctuations

If you are like most college students, you will be looking for a job when you graduate, or you will already have one and want to keep it for a while. In either case, your fate is not entirely in your own hands. Your job prospects will depend, at least in part, on the overall level of economic activity in the country.

If the classical model of the previous two chapters described the economy at every point in time, you'd have nothing to worry about. Full employment would be achieved automatically, so you could be confident of getting a job at the going wage for someone with your skills and characteristics. Unfortunately, this is not always how the world works: Neither output nor employment grows as smoothly and steadily as the classical model predicts. Instead, as far back as we have data, the United States and similar countries have experienced *economic fluctuations*.

Look at panel (a) of Figure 1. The orange line shows estimated full-employment or potential output since 1960—the level of real GDP predicted by the classical model. As a result of economic growth, full-employment output rises steadily.

But now look at the green line, which shows *actual* output each quarter (at an annual rate). You can see that actual GDP fluctuates above and below the classical model's predictions. During *recessions*, which are shaded in the figure, output declines, occasionally sharply. During *expansions* (the unshaded periods) output rises quickly, usually faster than potential output is rising. Indeed, in the later stages of an expansion, output often *exceeds* potential output—a situation that economists call a **boom**.

**Boom** A period of time during which real GDP is above potential GDP.

Panel (b) shows another characteristic of expansions and recessions: fluctuations in employment. During expansions, such as the period from 1983 to 1990, employment grows rapidly. During recessions (shaded), such as 1990–91, employment declines.

Figure 1 shows us that employment and output move very closely together. But the figure doesn't tell us anything about the *causal* relationship between them. However, as you'll see in this chapter, we have good reason to conclude that over the business cycle, it is changes in output that cause firms to change their employment levels. For example, in a recession, many business firms lay off workers. If asked why, they would answer that they are reducing employment *because* they are producing less output.

Finally, look at Figure 2, which presents the unemployment rate over the same period as in Figure 1. Figure 2 shows a critical aspect of fluctuations—the bulge of unemployment that occurs during each recession. When GDP falls, the unemployment rate increases. In recent decades, the worst bulge in unemployment occurred in 1982, when more than 10 percent of the labor force was looking for work. In expansions, on the other hand, the unemployment rate falls. During the long expansion of the 1990s, for example, the unemployment rate fell from 7.8 percent to 4.2 percent.

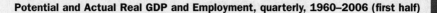

**Potential and Actual Real GDP and Employment, quarterly, 1960–2006 (first half)**    F I G U R E   1

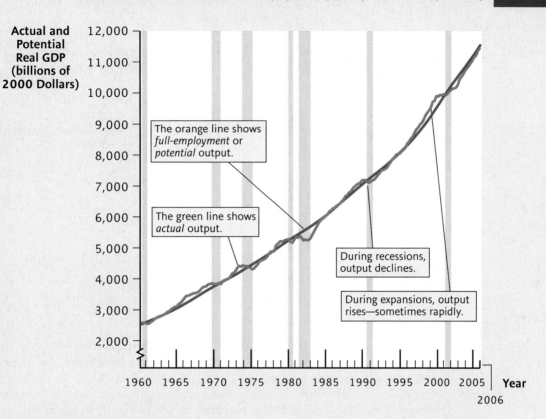

**Actual and Potential Real GDP (billions of 2000 Dollars)**

The orange line shows *full-employment* or *potential* output.

The green line shows *actual* output.

During recessions, output declines.

During expansions, output rises—sometimes rapidly.

Year
2006

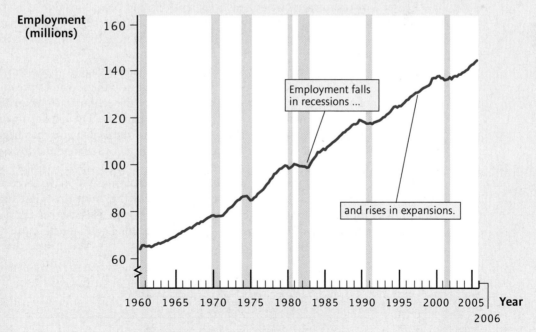

**Employment (millions)**

Employment falls in recessions ...

and rises in expansions.

Year
2006

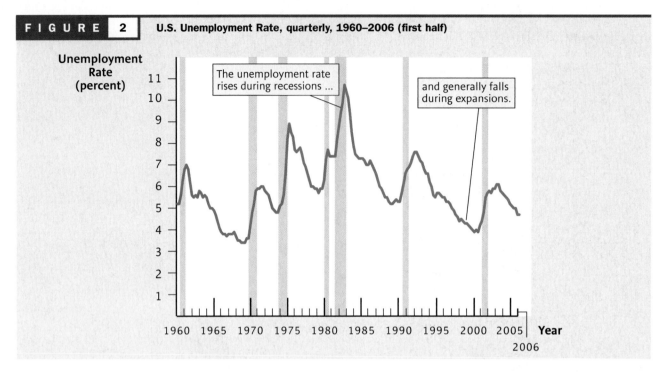

**FIGURE 2**    U.S. Unemployment Rate, quarterly, 1960–2006 (first half)

In our most recent expansion (2002–?), the unemployment rate fell from around 6 percent down to 4.6 percent (in June 2006). In some expansions, the unemployment rate can drop even lower than the full-employment level. In the sustained expansion of the late 1960s, for example, it reached a low of just over 3 percent. At the same time, output exceeded its potential, as you can verify in Figure 1.

Figure 1 also shows something else: Expansions and recessions don't last forever. Indeed, sometimes they are rather brief. The recession of 1990–91, for example, ended within a year. And the recession that began in March 2001 officially ended in November of that year.

But if you look carefully at the figure, you'll see that the back-to-back recessions of the early 1980s extended over 3 full years. And during the Great Depression of the 1930s (not shown), it took more than a decade for the economy to return to full employment. Expansions too can last for extended periods. The expansion of the 1980s lasted about 7 years, from 1983 to 1990. And the expansion that began in March 1991 turned out to be the longest expansion in U.S. economic history—a duration of 10 years.

The next several chapters deal with economic fluctuations. We have three things to explain: (1) *why* they occur in the first place, (2) why they sometimes last so long, and (3) why they do not last forever. But our first step is to ask whether the macroeconomic model you've already studied—the classical, long-run model—can explain why economic fluctuations occur.

## CAN THE CLASSICAL MODEL EXPLAIN ECONOMIC FLUCTUATIONS?

The classical model does a good job of explaining why the economy tends to operate near its potential output level, on average, over long periods of time. But can it help us understand the facts of economic fluctuations, as shown in Figures 1 and 2? More specifically, can the classical model explain why GDP and employment typically fall *below* potential during a recession and often rise above it in an expansion? Let's see.

## SHIFTS IN LABOR DEMAND

One idea, studied by a number of economists, is that a recession might be caused by a leftward shift of the labor demand curve. This possibility is illustrated in Figure 3, in which a leftward shift in the labor demand curve would move us down and to the left along the labor supply curve. In the diagram, the labor market equilibrium would move from point *E* to point *F*, employment would fall, and so would the real wage rate. Is this a reasonable explanation for recessions? Most economists feel that the answer is no, and for a very good reason.

The labor demand curve tells us the number of workers the nation's firms want to employ at each real wage rate. A leftward shift of this curve would mean that firms want to hire *fewer* workers at any given wage than they wanted to hire before. What could make them come to such a decision? One possibility is that firms are suddenly unable to sell all the output they produce. Therefore, the story would go, they must cut back production and hire fewer workers at any wage.

But as you've learned, in the classical model, total spending is *never* deficient. On the contrary, from the classical viewpoint, total spending is automatically equal to whatever level of output firms decide to produce. As you learned two chapters ago when we analyzed fiscal policy, a decrease in spending by one sector of the economy (such as the government) would cause an equal *increase* in spending by other sectors, with no change in total spending. While it is true that a decrease in output would cause total spending to decrease along with it (because Say's law tells us total spending is always equal to total output), the causation cannot go the other way in the classical model. In that model, changes in total spending cannot arise on their own. Therefore, if we want to explain a leftward shift in the labor demand curve using the classical model, we must look for some explanation other than a sudden change in spending.

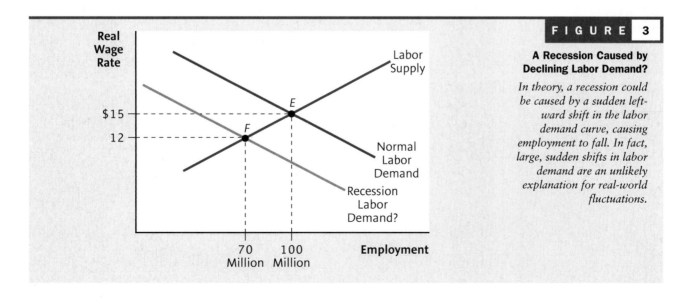

**FIGURE 3**

**A Recession Caused by Declining Labor Demand?**

*In theory, a recession could be caused by a sudden leftward shift in the labor demand curve, causing employment to fall. In fact, large, sudden shifts in labor demand are an unlikely explanation for real-world fluctuations.*

Another possibility is that the labor demand curve shifts leftward because workers have become less *productive* and therefore less valuable to firms. This might happen if there were a sudden decrease in the capital stock, so that each worker had less equipment to work with. Or it might happen if workers suddenly forgot how to do things—how to operate a computer or use a screwdriver or fix an oil rig. Short of a major war that destroys plant and equipment, or an epidemic of amnesia, it is highly unlikely that workers would become less productive so suddenly. Thus, a leftward shift of the labor demand curve is an unlikely explanation for recessions.

What about booms? Could a *rightward* shift of the labor demand curve (not shown in Figure 3) explain them? Once again, a change in total spending cannot be the answer. In the classical model, as discussed a few paragraphs ago, changes in spending are caused by changes in employment and output, not the other way around. Nor can we explain a boom by arguing that workers have suddenly become more productive. Even though it is true that the capital stock grows over time and workers continually gain new skills—and that both of these movements shift the labor demand curve to the right—such shifts take place at a glacial pace. Compared to the amount of machinery already in place, and to the knowledge and skills that the labor force already has, annual increments in physical capital or knowledge are simply too small to have much of an impact on labor demand. Thus, a sudden rightward shift of the labor demand curve is an unlikely explanation for an expansion that pushes us beyond potential output.

> *Because shifts in the labor demand curve are not very large from year to year, the classical model cannot explain real-world economic fluctuations through shifts in labor demand.*

## SHIFTS IN LABOR SUPPLY

A second way the classical model might explain a recession is through a shift in the labor supply curve. Figure 4 shows how this would work. If the labor supply curve

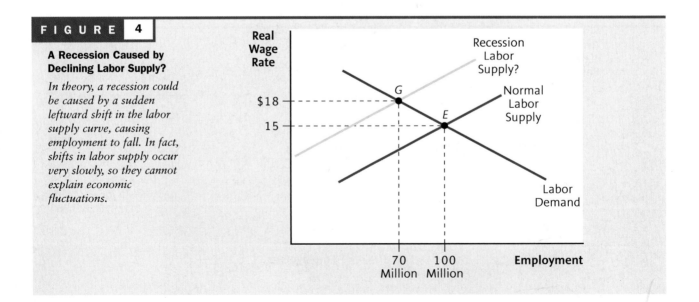

**FIGURE 4**

**A Recession Caused by Declining Labor Supply?**

*In theory, a recession could be caused by a sudden leftward shift in the labor supply curve, causing employment to fall. In fact, shifts in labor supply occur very slowly, so they cannot explain economic fluctuations.*

shifted to the left, the equilibrium would move up and to the left along the labor demand curve, from point *E* to point *G*. The level of employment would fall, and output would fall with it.

This explanation of recessions has almost no support among economists. First, remember that the labor supply schedule tells us, at each real wage rate, the number of people who *would like to* work. This number reflects millions of families' preferences about working in the market rather than pursuing other activities, such as taking care of children, going to school, or enjoying leisure time. A leftward shift in labor supply would mean that fewer people want to work at any given wage—that preferences have changed toward these other, nonwork activities. But in reality, preferences tend to change very slowly, and certainly not rapidly enough to explain recessions.

Second, even if such a shift in preferences did occur, it could not explain the facts of real-world downturns. Recessions are times when unusually large numbers of people are looking for work (see Figure 2). It would be hard to square that fact with a shift in preferences away from working.

The same arguments could be made about expansions: To explain them with labor supply shifts, we would have to believe that preferences suddenly change *toward* market work and away from other activities—an unlikely occurrence. And, in any case, expansions are periods when the unemployment rate typically falls to unusually low levels; *fewer*—not more—people are seeking work.

> *Because sudden shifts of the labor supply curve are unlikely to occur, and because they could not accurately describe the facts of the economic cycle, the classical model cannot explain fluctuations through shifts in the supply of labor.*

## VERDICT: THE CLASSICAL MODEL CANNOT EXPLAIN ECONOMIC FLUCTUATIONS

In earlier chapters, we stressed that the classical model works well in explaining the movements of the economy in the longer run. Now we see that it does a rather poor job of explaining the economy in the short run. Why is this? Largely because the classical model involves assumptions about the economy that make sense in the longer run, but not in the short run. Chief among these is the assumption that the labor market clears—that is, that the labor market operates at the point of intersection of the labor supply and labor demand curves. As long as this assumption holds, a boom or recession would have to arise from a sudden, significant *movement* in that intersection point, caused by a sudden and significant *shift* in either the labor demand curve or the labor supply curve.

But now, we've seen that such sudden shifts are very unlikely. Moreover, even if they did occur, they could not explain the changes in job-seeking activity that we observe in real-world recessions. And this, in a nutshell, is why we must reject the classical model when we turn our attention to the short run.

> *We cannot explain the facts of short-run economic fluctuations with a model in which the labor market always clears. This is why the classical model, which assumes that the market always clears, does a poor job of explaining the economy in the short run.*

## WHAT TRIGGERS ECONOMIC FLUCTUATIONS?

Recessions that bring output below potential and expansions that drive output above potential are periods during which the economy is going a bit haywire. In a recession, millions of qualified people *want* to work at the going wage rate, but firms won't hire them. Managers would *like* to hire them, but they aren't selling enough output—in part because so many people are unemployed. The macroeconomy seems to be preventing opportunities for mutual gain.

In a boom, the economy is going haywire in a different way. The unemployment rate is so low the normal job-search activity—which accounts for frictional unemployment—is short-circuited. Firms, desperate to hire workers because production is so high, are less careful about whom they hire. The result is a poorer-than-normal match between workers and their jobs. Moreover, the overheating of the economy that occurs in a boom can lead to inflation. We'll discuss how this happens a few chapters from now. But the basic outline is this: Because qualified workers are so scarce, firms must compete fiercely with each other to hire them. This drives up wage rates in the economy, raises production costs for firms, and ultimately causes firms to raise their prices.

Booms and recessions are periods during which the economy deviates from the normal, full-employment equilibrium of the classical model. The question is: Why do such deviations occur? Let's start to answer this question by looking at a world that is much simpler than our own.

### A Very Simple Economy

Imagine an economy with just two people: Yasmin and Pepe. Yasmin is especially good at making popcorn, but she eats only yogurt. Pepe, by contrast, is very good at making yogurt, but he eats only popcorn. If things are going well, Yasmin and Pepe will make suitable amounts of popcorn and yogurt and trade with each other. Because of the gains from specialization, their trade will make them both better off than if they tried to function without trading. And under ordinary circumstances, Yasmin and Pepe will take advantage of all mutually beneficial opportunities for trading. Our two-person economy will thus operate at full employment, since both individuals will be fully engaged in making products for the other. You can think of their trading equilibrium as being like the labor market equilibrium in the classical model.

Now, suppose there is a breakdown in communication. For example, Yasmin may get the impression that Pepe is not going to want as much popcorn as before. She would then decide to *make* less popcorn for Pepe. At their next trading session, Pepe will be offered less popcorn, so he will decide to produce less yogurt. The result: Total production in the economy declines, and our two traders will lose some of the benefits of trading. This corresponds to a recession.

Alternatively, suppose Yasmin thinks that Pepe will want *more* popcorn than before. This might lead her to *increase* her production, working more than she normally prefers to work so she can get more yogurt from Pepe before his demand for popcorn returns to normal. Yasmin's production of popcorn—and therefore, total output in the economy—rises even if Yasmin's expectations turn out to be wrong and Pepe does *not* want more popcorn. Temporarily, we are in a boom.

In reading the previous paragraph, you might be thinking, "Wait a minute. If either Yasmin or Pepe got the impression that the other might want less or more of the other's product, wouldn't a simple conversation between them straighten things out?" If these are your thoughts, you are absolutely right. A breakdown in communication and a sudden change in production would be extremely unlikely . . . *in a simple economy with just two people*. And therein lies the problem: The real-world economy is much more complex than the world of Yasmin and Pepe.

## THE REAL-WORLD ECONOMY

Think about the U.S. economy, with its millions of businesses producing goods and services for hundreds of millions of people. In many cases, production must be planned long before goods are actually sold. For example, from inception to final production, it takes nearly a year to build a house and two years to develop a new automobile model or produce a Hollywood film. If one firm—say, General Motors—believes that consumers will buy fewer of its cars next year, it cannot simply call a meeting of all potential customers and find out whether its fears are justified. Nor can it convince people, as Yasmin can convince Pepe, that their own jobs depend on their buying a GM car. Most potential car buyers do *not* work for General Motors and don't perceive any connection between buying a car and keeping their own jobs. Under the circumstances, it may be entirely logical for General Motors to plan for a lower production level and lay off some of its workers.

Of course, this would not be the end of the story. By decreasing its workforce, GM would create further problems for the economy. The workers it has laid off, who will earn less income or none at all, will cut back on *their* spending for a variety of consumer goods—restaurant meals, movies, vacation travel—and they will certainly postpone any large purchases they'd been planning, such as a new large-screen television or that family trip to Disney World. This will cause other firms—the firms producing these consumer goods and services—to cut back on *their* production, laying off *their* workers, and so on. In other words, what began as a perceived decrease in spending in one sector of the economy can work its way through other sectors, causing a full-blown recession.

This example illustrates a theme that we will revisit in the next chapter: the interdependence between production and income. When people spend their incomes, they give firms the revenue they need to hire workers and pay them income! If any link in this chain is broken, output and income may both decline. In our example, the link was broken because of incorrect expectations by firms in one sector of the economy. But there are other causes of recessions as well, also centering on the interdependence between production and income, and a failure to coordinate the decisions of millions of firms and households.

The classical model, however, waves these potential problems aside. It assumes that workers and firms, with the aid of markets, can work things out—like Yasmin and Pepe—and enjoy the benefits of producing and trading. And the classical model is right: People *will* work things out . . . eventually. But in the short run, we need to look carefully at the problems of coordinating production, trade, and consumption in an economy with millions of people and businesses.

A boom can arise in much the same way as a recession. It might start because of an increase in production in one sector of the economy, say, the housing sector. With more production and more workers earning higher incomes, spending increases in other sectors as well, until output rises above the classical, full-employment level.

## EXAMPLES OF RECESSIONS AND EXPANSIONS

In the preceding discussion, General Motors decided to cut back on its production of cars because its managers believed, rightly or wrongly, that the demand for GM cars had decreased. Often, many firms will face a real or predicted drop in spending at the same time. The resulting changes in production ultimately work their way through the entire economy, and often cause full-fledged macroeconomic fluctuations.

Table 1 lists some of the recessions and notable expansions of the last 50 years, along with the events and spending changes that are thought to have caused them or at least contributed heavily. You can see that each of these events first affected spending and output in one or more sectors of the economy. For example, several recessions have been set off by increases in oil prices. The initial impact of higher oil prices is often felt most strongly on energy-using goods and services, such as new

| TABLE 1 | | | | |
|---|---|---|---|---|
| **Recent Expansions and Recessions** | **Period** | | **Event** | **Major Spending Changes** |
| | Early 1950s | Expansion | Korean War | Defense spending ↑ |
| | 1953 | Recession | End of Korean War | Defense spending ↓ |
| | Late 1960s | Expansion | Vietnam War | Defense spending ↑ |
| | 1970 | Recession | Change in Federal Reserve policy | Spending on new homes ↓ |
| | 1974 | Recession | Dramatic increase in oil prices | Spending on cars and other energy-using products ↓ |
| | 1980 | Recession | Dramatic increase in oil prices | Spending on cars and other energy-using products ↓ |
| | 1981–82 | Recession | Change in Federal Reserve policy | Spending on new homes, cars, and business investment ↓ |
| | Early 1980s | Expansion | Military buildup | Defense spending ↑ |
| | Late 1980s | Expansion | Dramatic decline in oil prices | Spending on energy-using products ↑ |
| | 1990 | Recession | Large increase in oil prices; collapse of Soviet Union | Spending on cars and other energy-using products ↓; Defense spending ↓ |
| | 1991–2000 | Expansion | Technological advances in computers; development of the Internet; high wealth creation | Spending on capital equipment ↑; Consumption spending ↑ |
| | 2001 | Recession | Investment in new technology slows; technology-fueled bubble of optimism bursts; wealth destruction | Spending on capital equipment ↓ |
| | 2002–? | Expansion | Changes in fiscal and Federal Reserve policies; rapid rise in housing wealth | Consumption spending ↑ |

cars and trucks, or vacation travel. Also, because consumers spend more on expensive gasoline and other products made from oil, they have less income left over to spend on a variety of other goods and services. Other recessions were precipitated by military cutbacks. Still others came about when the Federal Reserve caused sudden increases in interest rates that led to decreased spending on new homes and other goods. (You'll learn about the Federal Reserve and its policies a few chapters from now.)

Strong expansions, on the other hand, have been caused by military buildups, by falling oil prices that stimulated consumption spending, and by bursts of planned investment spending. The long expansion of the mid- and late 1990s, for example, began when the development of the Internet, and improvements in computers more generally, led to an increase in investment spending. Once the economy began expanding, it was further spurred by other factors, such as a rise in stock prices and consumer optimism, both of which led to an increase in consumption spending.

When a decrease in spending causes production cutbacks in one or more sectors of the economy, firms will lay off workers. The laid-off workers, suffering decreases in their incomes, cut back their own spending on other products, causing further layoffs in other sectors. The economy can continue sliding downward, and remain below potential output, for a year or longer. The same process works in reverse during an expansion: Higher spending leads to greater production, higher employment, and still greater spending, possibly leading to a boom in which the economy remains overheated for some time.

Booms and recessions do not last forever, however. The economy eventually adjusts back to full-employment output. Often, a change in government macroeconomic policy helps the adjustment process along, speeding the return to full employment. Other times, a policy mistake thwarts the adjustment process, prolonging or deepening a costly recession, or exacerbating a boom and overheating the economy even more.

How does this adjustment process work? This is a question we'll be coming back to a few chapters from now, after you've learned some new tools for analyzing the economy's behavior over the short run.

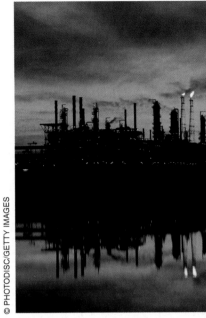

*Half of our recessions since the early 1950s have been caused, at least in part, by rapid rises in oil prices.*

## WHERE DO WE GO FROM HERE?

The classical model that you've learned in previous chapters is certainly useful: It helps us understand economic growth over time, and how economic events and economic policies affect the economy over the long run. But in trying to understand expansions and recessions—where they come from, and why they can last for one or more years—we've had to depart from the strict framework of the classical model.

One theme of our discussion has been the central role of spending in understanding economic fluctuations. In the classical model, spending could be safely ignored. First, Say's law assured us that total spending would always be sufficient to buy the output produced at full employment. Second, a change in spending—for example, a decrease in military spending by the government—would cause other categories of spending to rise by just the right amount to make up for the lower spending of the government. In the long run, we can have faith in the classical perspective on spending.

But in the short run, we've seen that changes in spending affect production, often in one or more specific sectors. When employment changes in those sectors, the spending of workers *there* will change as well, affecting demand in still other sectors. Clearly, if we want to understand fluctuations, we need to take a close look at spending. This is what we will do in the next chapter, when we study the *short-run macro model*.

## Summary

The classical model does not always do a good job of describing the economy over short time periods. Over periods of a few years, national economies experience economic fluctuations in which output rises above or falls below its long-term growth path. Significant periods of falling output are called recessions, while periods of rapidly rising output are expansions. If an expansion causes output to rise above potential (or full-employment) output, it is called a boom. When real GDP fluctuates, it causes the level of employment and the unemployment rate to fluctuate as well.

The classical model cannot explain economic fluctuations because it assumes that the labor market always clears; that is, it always operates at the point where the labor supply and demand curves intersect. Evidence suggests that this market-clearing assumption is not always valid over short time periods. And when we try to explain economic fluctuations using the classical model, we come up short. Neither shifts in the labor demand curve, nor shifts in the labor supply curve, offer a realistic explanation for what happens during a recession or a boom.

In a simple, two-person economy, decisions about spending and production could be easily coordinated, so economic fluctuations would be easy to avoid. But in a market economy with millions of people and firms, decisions about spending and production cannot be coordinated, making the economy vulnerable to changes in production that are harmful to everyone involved.

Deviations from the full-employment level of output are often caused by changes in spending that initially affect one or more sectors and then work their way through the entire economy. Decreases in spending can cause recessions, while increases in spending can cause expansions that lead to booms. Eventually, output will return to its long-run equilibrium level, but it does not do so immediately. The origins of economic fluctuations can be understood more fully with the short-run macro model, which we will study in the next chapter.

## Problem Set    *Answers to even-numbered Questions and Problems can be found on the text Web site at www.thomsonedu.com/economics/hall.*

1. Using the upper panel of Figure 1, identify two time spans during which the U.S. economy was enjoying an expansion but *not* a boom. (Hint: Reread the first page of this chapter.)

2. This chapter explains how a decrease in spending—such as investment spending—could cause a recession. But in the classical model, a decrease in investment spending could *not* cause a recession. Why not? (Hint: Use the loanable funds market diagram.)

3. "Every U.S. recession over the last 6 decades has been caused by an increase in oil prices." True or false? Explain briefly.

4. "Immediately after a recession ends, the unemployment rate begins dropping." Evaluate this statement, based on the historical record in Figure 2.

# The Short-Run Macro Model

Every December, newspapers and television news broadcasts focus their attention on spending. You might see a reporter standing in front of a Circuit City outlet, warning that unless holiday shoppers loosen their wallets and spend big on computers, DVD players, vacation trips, toys, and new cars, the economy is in for trouble.

Of course, spending matters during the rest of the year, too. But holiday spending attracts our attention because the normal forces at work during the rest of the year become more concentrated in late November and December. Factories churn out merchandise, and stores stock up at higher than normal rates. If consumers are in Scrooge-like moods, unsold goods will pile up in stores. In the months that follow, these stores will cut back on their orders for new goods. Factories will decrease production and lay off workers.

And the story will not end there. The laid-off workers—even those who collect some unemployment benefits—will see their incomes decline. As a consequence, they will spend less on a variety of consumer goods. This will cause other firms—the ones that produce those consumer goods—to cut back on *their* production.

This hypothetical example reinforces a conclusion we reached in the last chapter: Spending is very important in the short run. And it points out an interesting circularity: The more income households earn, the more they will spend. That is, *spending depends on income*. But the more households spend, the more output firms will produce—and the more income they will pay out to households that supply labor and other resources. Thus, *income depends on spending*.

> *In the short run, spending depends on income, and income depends on spending.*

In this chapter, we will explore this circular connection between spending and income. We will do so with a very simple macroeconomic model, which we'll call the **short-run macro model**. Many of the ideas behind the model were originally developed by the economist John Maynard Keynes in the 1930s. The model's perspective on the economy is in many ways opposite to that of the classical model. When we take the short-run view, total spending determines the level of production, and changes in spending play the central role in explaining economic fluctuations.

**Short-run macro model** A macroeconomic model that explains how changes in spending can affect real GDP in the short run.

To keep the model as simple as possible, we will—for the time being—ignore all influences on production *besides* spending. As a result, the short-run model may appear strange to you at first, like a drive along an unfamiliar highway. You may wonder: Where is all the scenery you are used to seeing along the classical road? Where are the labor market, the production function, the loanable funds market, and the market-clearing assumption? Rest assured that many of these concepts are still with us, lurking in the background and waiting to be exposed, and we will come back to them in later chapters. But in this chapter, we assume that spending—and *only* spending—determines how much output the economy will produce.

As we proceed, remember that we are more interested in explaining real variables (adjusted for changes in the price level) than nominal variables (measured in current dollars). Therefore, whenever we discuss any dollar-denominated variable (such as consumption spending, income, or GDP) we will always mean the *real* variable—even when the word "real" is not included.

## CONSUMPTION SPENDING

A natural place for us to begin our look at spending is with its largest component: *consumption spending*. In all, household spending on consumer goods—groceries, rent, car repairs, movies, telephone calls, and furniture—is more than two-thirds of total spending in the economy. What determines the total amount of consumption spending?

One way to answer is to start by thinking about yourself or your family. What determines your spending in any given month, quarter, or year?

*Disposable Income.* The first thing that comes to mind is your income: The more you earn, the more you spend. But in macroeconomics, small differences in language can be crucial. It's not exactly your *income* per period—what you are paid by your employer—that determines your spending, but rather what you get to *keep* from that income after deducting any taxes you have to pay. Moreover, some people receive a flow of transfer payments from the government—such as unemployment insurance benefits or Social Security payments—which they can spend in addition to any income received from an employer. If we start with the income households earn, deduct all tax payments, and then add in any transfer received, we get *disposable income*—a term introduced with the classical model. This is the income households are free to spend or save as they wish.

Disposable income = Income − Tax payments + Transfers received.

This can be rewritten as:

Disposable income = Income − (Taxes − Transfers).

Finally, remember that the term in parentheses, Taxes − Transfers, is defined as *net taxes*. So the easiest way to think of disposable income is:

Disposable income = Income − Net taxes.

All else equal, you'd certainly spend more on consumer goods with a disposable income of $50,000 per year than with $20,000 per year. And in the economy as a whole, *a rise in disposable income—with no other change—causes a rise in consumption spending*.

*Wealth.* Consumption spending is also influenced by *wealth*—the total value of household assets (home, stocks, bonds, bank accounts, and the like) minus outstanding liabilities (student loans, mortgage loans, credit card debt, and so on). Even if your disposable income stayed the same, an increase in your wealth—say, because you own stocks or bonds that have risen in value—would probably induce you to spend more. In general, *a rise in wealth, with no other change, causes a rise in consumption spending.*

*The Interest Rate.* The interest rate is the reward people get for saving, or what they have to pay when they borrow. You would probably save more each year if the interest rate was 10 percent than if it was 2 percent. But when you save more of your disposable income, you spend less. Even households with a negative net worth—who are not "savers" in the common sense of the term—are influenced by the interest rate. For example, people with credit card or other debts must decide each month how much of their debt balance to pay down. The higher the interest rate, the greater the incentive to pay back debt, and the less will be spent on consumption goods. *All else equal, a rise in the interest rate causes a decrease in consumption spending.*

*Expectations.* Expectations about the future can affect spending as well. If you become more optimistic about your job security or expect a big raise, you might spend more of your income *now.* Similarly, if you become more pessimistic—worried about losing your job or taking a pay cut—you'd probably spend less now. *All else equal, optimism about future income causes an increase in consumption spending.*

Other variables, too, can influence your consumption spending, including inheritances you expect to receive over your lifetime, and even how long you expect to live. But disposable income, wealth, the interest rate, and expectations are the key variables we'll be coming back to again and again in the short-run macroeconomic model. And just as these variables influence the consumption spending of each individual household, they also influence the consumption spending of the household sector as a whole.

Unless we're focusing on an individual household to make a point (as in the preceding paragraphs), in macroeconomics, we use phrases like "disposable income," "wealth," or "consumption spending" to mean the *total* disposable income, *total* wealth, and *total* consumption spending of all households in the economy combined. So we can state our conclusions this way:

> *All else equal, consumption spending increases when:*
>
> - *Disposable income rises*
> - *Wealth rises*
> - *The interest rate falls*
> - *Households become more optimistic about the future*

## CONSUMPTION AND DISPOSABLE INCOME

Of all the factors that influence consumption spending, the most important and stable determinant is disposable income. Figure 1 shows the relationship between (real) consumption spending and (real) disposable income in the United States from 1985 to 2005. Each point in the diagram represents a different year. For example, the point labeled "2005" represents a disposable income in that year of $8,112 billion and consumption spending of $7,857 billion. Notice that as disposable income rises, consumption spending rises as well. Indeed, almost all of the variation in consumption spending from year to year can be explained by variations in disposable income.

**FIGURE 1**   U.S. Consumption and Disposable Income, 1985–2005

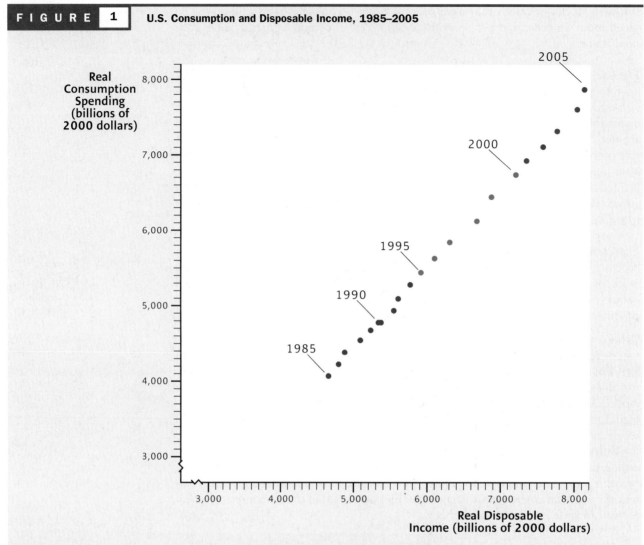

*When real consumption expenditure is plotted against real disposable income, the resulting relationship is almost perfectly linear: As real disposable income rises, so does real consumption spending.*

*Source:* Bureau of Economic Analysis, National Income and Product Accounts Tables, Tables 2.1 and 1.1.6.

Although the other factors we've discussed do affect consumption spending, their impact appears to be relatively minor.

There is something even more interesting about Figure 1: The relationship between consumption and disposable income is almost perfectly *linear;* the points lie remarkably close to a straight line. This almost-linear relationship between consumption and disposable income has been observed in a wide variety of historical periods and a wide variety of nations. This is why, when we represent the relationship between disposable income and consumption with a diagram or an equation, we use a straight line.

| Real Disposable Income (billions of dollars per year) | Real Consumption Spending (billions of dollars per year) |
|:---:|:---:|
| 0 | 2,000 |
| 1,000 | 2,600 |
| 2,000 | 3,200 |
| 3,000 | 3,800 |
| 4,000 | 4,400 |
| 5,000 | 5,000 |
| 6,000 | 5,600 |
| 7,000 | 6,200 |
| 8,000 | 6,800 |

**TABLE 1**

Hypothetical Data on Disposable Income and Consumption

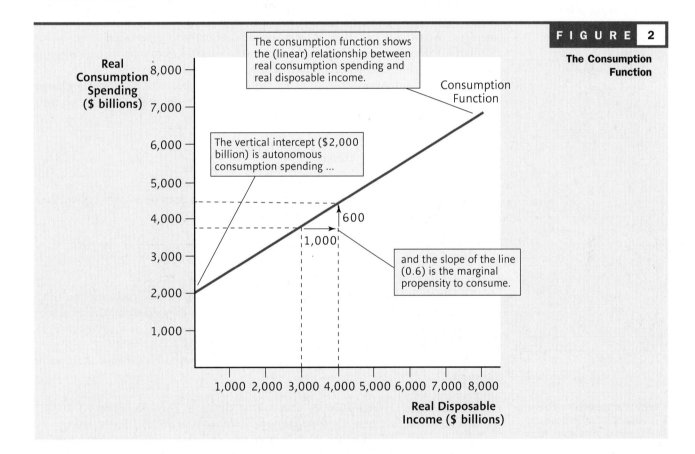

**FIGURE 2**

The Consumption Function

Our discussion will be clearer if we move from the actual data in Figure 1 to the hypothetical example in Table 1. Each row in the table represents a combination of (real) disposable income and (real) consumption we might observe in an economy. For example, the table shows us that if disposable income were equal to $7,000 billion in some year, consumption spending would equal $6,200 billion in that year. When we plot these data on a graph, we obtain the straight line in Figure 2. This line is

**Consumption function** A positively sloped relationship between real consumption spending and real disposable income.

called the **consumption function** because it illustrates the functional relationship between consumption and disposable income.

Like every straight line, the consumption function in Figure 2 has two main features: a vertical intercept and a slope. Mathematically, the intercept—in this case, $2,000 billion—tells us how much consumption spending there would be in the economy if disposable income were zero. However, the real purpose of the vertical intercept is not to identify what would actually happen at zero disposable income, but rather to help us identify the particular line that represents consumption spending in the diagram. After all, we could draw many lines that have the same slope as the one in the figure. But only one of them has a vertical intercept of $2,000.

The vertical intercept in the figure also has a name: **autonomous consumption spending**. It represents the influence on consumption spending of everything *other than* disposable income. For example, if household wealth were to increase, consumption would be greater at any level of disposable income. In that case, the entire consumption function in the figure would shift upward, so its vertical intercept would increase. We would call this *an increase in autonomous consumption spending*. Similarly, a decrease in wealth would cause a *decrease in autonomous consumption spending*, and shift the consumption function downward.

**Autonomous consumption spending** The part of consumption spending that is independent of income; also the vertical intercept of the consumption function.

The second important feature of Figure 2 is the slope, which shows the change along the vertical axis divided by the change along the horizontal axis as we go from one point to another on the line:

$$\text{Slope} = \frac{\Delta \text{Consumption}}{\Delta \text{Disposable income}}$$

As you can see in the table, each time disposable income rises by $1,000 billion, consumption spending rises by $600 billion, so that the slope is

$$\frac{\$600 \text{ billion}}{\$1,000 \text{ billion}} = 0.6$$

The slope in Figure 2 is an important feature not just of the consumption function itself, but also of the macroeconomic analysis we will build from it. This is why economists have given this slope a special name, the *marginal propensity to consume*, abbreviated *MPC*. In our example, the *MPC* is 0.6.

We can think of the *MPC* in three different ways, but each of them has the same meaning:

**Marginal propensity to consume** The amount by which consumption spending rises when disposable income rises by one dollar.

> The **marginal propensity to consume** (MPC) is (1) the slope of the consumption function; (2) the change in consumption divided by the change in disposable income; or (3) the amount by which consumption spending rises when disposable income rises by one dollar.

Logic suggests that the *MPC* should be larger than zero (when income rises, consumption spending will *rise*), but less than one (the rise in consumption will be *smaller* than the rise in disposable income). This is certainly true in our example where *MPC* is 0.6 and each one-dollar rise in disposable income causes spending to rise by 60 cents. An *MPC* between zero and one is also observed in economies throughout the world. Accordingly, we will always assume that $0 < MPC < 1$.

### Representing Consumption with an Equation

Sometimes, we'll want to use an equation to represent the straight-line consumption function. The most general form of the equation is

$$C = a + b \times \text{(Disposable income)}$$

where $C$ is consumption spending. The term $a$ is the vertical intercept of the consumption function. It represents the theoretical level of consumption spending at disposable income = 0, which you've learned is called *autonomous consumption spending*. In the equation, you can see clearly that autonomous consumption ($a$) is the part of consumption that does *not* depend on disposable income. In our example in Figure 2, $a$ is equal to $2,000 billion.

The other term, $b$, is the slope of the consumption function. This is our familiar marginal propensity to consume (*MPC*), telling us how much consumption *increases* each time disposable income rises by a dollar. In our example in Figure 2, $b$ is equal to 0.6.

## CONSUMPTION AND INCOME

The consumption function is an important building block of our analysis. Consumption is the largest component of spending, and disposable income is the most important determinant of consumption. But there is one limitation of the line as we've drawn it in Figure 2: It shows us the value of consumption at each level of *disposable* income, whereas we will need to know the value of consumption spending at each level of *income*. Disposable income, you remember, is the income that the household sector has left after deducting net taxes. How can we convert the line in Figure 2 into a relationship between consumption and income?

Table 2 illustrates the consumption–income relationship when the household sector pays net taxes. In the table, we treat net taxes as a fixed amount—in this case, $2,000 billion. Some taxes are, indeed, fixed in this way, such as the taxes assessed on real estate by local governments. Other taxes, like the personal income tax and the sales tax, rise and fall with income in the economy. Still, treating net taxes as if they are independent of income, as in Table 2, will simplify our discussion without changing our results in any important way.

Notice that the last two columns of the table are identical to the columns in Table 1: In both tables, we assume that the relationship between consumption spending and *disposable* income is the same. For example, both tables show us that, when disposable income is $7,000 billion, consumption spending is $6,200 billion. But in Table 2, we see that disposable income of $7,000 billion is associated with *income* of $9,000 billion. Thus, when income is $9,000 billion, consumption spending is $6,200 billion. By comparing the first and last columns of Table 2, we can trace out the relationship between consumption and income. This relationship—which we call the **consumption–income line**—is graphed in Figure 3.

**Consumption–income line** A line showing aggregate consumption spending at each level of income or GDP.

If you compare the consumption–income line in Figure 3 with the line in Figure 2, you will notice that both have the same slope of 0.6, but the consumption–income line is lower by $1,200 billion. Net taxes have lowered the consumption–income line. Why? Because at any level of income, taxes reduce disposable income and therefore reduce consumption spending.

But why is the consumption–income line lower by precisely $1,200 billion? We can reason it out as follows: Any increase in net taxes ($T$) will cause consumption

| TABLE 2 | Income or GDP (billions of dollars per year) | Tax Collections (billions of dollars per year) | Disposable Income (billions of dollars per year) | Consumption Spending (billions of dollars per year) |
|---|---|---|---|---|
| The Relationship Between Consumption and Income | 2,000 | 2,000 | 0 | 2,000 |
| | 3,000 | 2,000 | 1,000 | 2,600 |
| | 4,000 | 2,000 | 2,000 | 3,200 |
| | 5,000 | 2,000 | 3,000 | 3,800 |
| | 6,000 | 2,000 | 4,000 | 4,400 |
| | 7,000 | 2,000 | 5,000 | 5,000 |
| | 8,000 | 2,000 | 6,000 | 5,600 |
| | 9,000 | 2,000 | 7,000 | 6,200 |
| | 10,000 | 2,000 | 8,000 | 6,800 |

**FIGURE 3    The Consumption–Income Line**

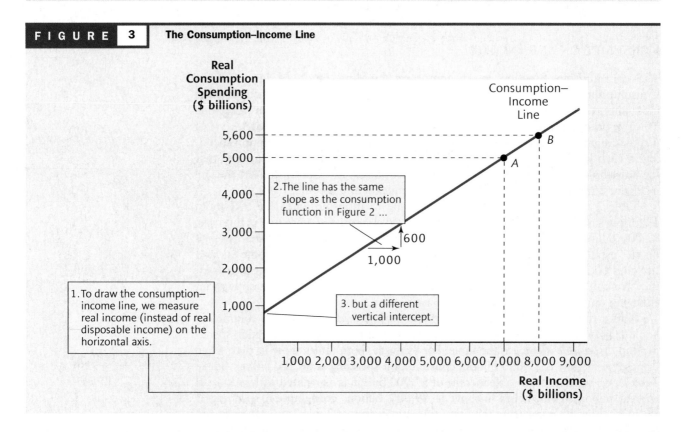

spending to fall by $MPC \times \Delta T$. In our example, when we impose taxes of $2,000 billion on the population, disposable income will drop by $2,000 billion at any level of income. With an $MPC$ of 0.6, consumption at any level of income falls by $0.6 \times \$2,000$ billion = $1,200 billion.

Finally, we noted earlier that the *slope* of the consumption–income line is unaffected by net taxes. This is because with net taxes held at a fixed amount, disposable income rises dollar-for-dollar with income. With an $MPC$ of 0.6, consumption spending will rise by 60 cents each time income rises by a dollar, just as it rises by 60 cents each time *disposable* income rises by a dollar. You can see this in Table 2: Each time income rises by $1,000 billion, consumption spending rises by $600 billion, giving the consumption–income line a slope of $600 billion/$1,000 billion = 0.6, just as in the case with no taxes. More generally,

> *when the government collects a fixed amount of taxes from households, the line representing the relationship between consumption and income is shifted downward by the amount of the tax times the marginal propensity to consume (MPC). The slope of this line is unaffected by taxes and is equal to the MPC.*

### Shifts in the Consumption–Income Line

As you've learned, consumption spending depends positively on income: If income increases and net taxes remain unchanged, disposable income will rise, and consumption spending will rise along with it. The chain of causation can be represented this way:

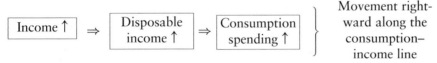

In Figure 3, this change in consumption spending would be represented by a *movement along* the consumption–income line. For example, a rise in income from $7,000 billion to $8,000 billion would cause consumption spending to increase from $5,000 billion to $5,600 billion, moving us from point *A* to point *B* along the consumption–income line.

But consumption spending can also change for reasons other than a change in income, causing the consumption–income line itself to shift. For example, a decrease in net taxes will increase *disposable* income at each level of income. Consumption spending will then increase at any income level, shifting the entire line upward. The mechanism works like this:

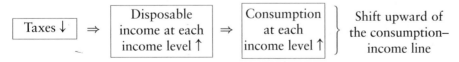

In Figure 4, a decrease in taxes from $2,000 billion to $500 billion increases spending income at each income level by $1,500 billion, and causes consumption at each income level to increase by 0.6 × $1,500 billion = $900 billion. This means that the consumption line shifts upward, to the upper line in the figure.

In addition to net taxes, all the other influences on consumption spending, other than income, shift the consumption–income line as well. But these other shift-variables work by changing the value of *autonomous consumption*, the vertical intercept of the consumption function in Figure 2. For example, an increase in household wealth would increase autonomous consumption, and shift the consumption–income line upward, as in Figure 4. Increases in autonomous consumption could also occur

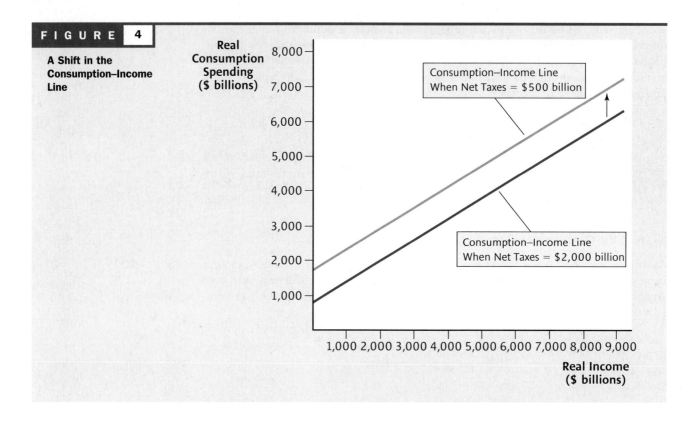

FIGURE 4

**A Shift in the Consumption–Income Line**

if the interest rate decreased, or if households became more optimistic about the future. In general, increases in autonomous consumption work this way:

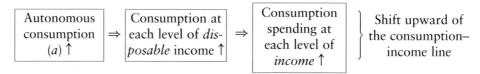

We can summarize our discussion of changes in consumption spending as follows:

> *When a change in income causes consumption spending to change, we move along the consumption–income line. When a change in anything else besides income causes consumption spending to change, the line will shift.*

Table 3 provides a more specific summary of the various changes that cause the consumption–income line to shift.

## GETTING TO TOTAL SPENDING

In addition to household consumption spending, there are three other types of spending on goods and services produced by American firms: investment, government

| Consumption–Income Line Shifts Upward When: | | Consumption–Income Line Shifts Downward When: | | TABLE 3 |
|---|---|---|---|---|
| Net taxes ↓ { Transfers ↑, Taxes ↓ | | Net Taxes ↑ { Transfers ↓, Taxes ↑ | | Shifts in the Consumption–Income Line |
| Autonomous consumption (a) ↑ { Household wealth ↑, Interest rate ↓, Greater optimism | | Autonomous Consumption (a) ↓ { Household wealth ↓, Interest rate ↑, Greater pessimism | | |

purchases, and purchases by foreigners. Let's consider each of these types of spending in turn.

## INVESTMENT SPENDING

Remember that in the definition of GDP, the word *investment* by itself (represented by the letter *I* by itself) consists of three components: (1) business spending on plant and equipment; (2) purchases of new homes; and (3) accumulation of unsold inventories. In this chapter, as we did when we studied the classical model, we focus not on investment, but on *planned investment* or *investment spending* (we'll use these two terms interchangeably).

Planned investment ($I^p$) is business purchases of plant and equipment and construction of new homes.

Why do we focus on planned investment and leave out inventory accumulation? When we look at how spending influences the economy, we are interested in the purchases households, firms, and the government *want* to make. But some inventory changes, as you learned a few chapters ago, are *unplanned* and *undesired* occurrences that firms try to avoid. While firms want to have *some* inventories on hand, sudden *changes* in inventories are typically not desirable. To keep the model simple, we treat *all* inventory changes as temporary, unplanned occurrences for the firm, and we exclude them when we measure spending in the economy.

*In the short-run macro model, (planned) investment spending ($I^p$) is plant and equipment purchases by business firms and new home construction. Inventory investment is treated as unintentional and undesired, and is therefore excluded from our definition of investment spending.*

What determines the level of investment spending in a given year? In this chapter, we will regard investment spending as a *fixed value*, determined by forces outside of our analysis. We will explore what happens when that fixed value happens to change. But we'll postpone for a couple of chapters any formal treatment of the determinants of investment spending.

*For now, we regard investment spending ($I^p$) as a given value, determined by forces outside of our model.*

## GOVERNMENT PURCHASES

Government purchases include all of the goods and services that government agencies—federal, state, and local—buy during the year. We treat government purchases in the same way as investment spending: as a given value, determined by forces outside of our analysis. Why?

The relationship between government purchases and other macroeconomic variables is rather weak. In recent decades, the biggest changes in government purchases have involved military spending. These changes have been based on world politics rather than macroeconomic conditions. So assuming that government spending is a given value, independent of the other variables in our model, is realistic.

> In the short-run macro model, government purchases are treated as a given value, determined by forces outside of the model.

As with investment spending, we'll be exploring what happens when the "given value" of government purchases changes. But we will not try to explain what causes it to change.

## NET EXPORTS

If we want to measure total spending on U.S. output, we must also consider the international sector. About 11 percent of U.S.-produced goods are sold to *foreign* consumers, *foreign* businesses, and *foreign* governments. These U.S. *exports* are as much a part of total spending on U.S. output as the other types of spending we've discussed so far. Thus, exports must be included in our measure of total spending.

International trade in goods and services also requires us to make an adjustment to the other components of spending. A portion (about 16 percent) of the output bought by *American* consumers, firms, and government agencies was produced abroad. From the U.S. point of view, these are *imports*: spending on foreign, rather than U.S., output. These imports are included in our measures of consumption, investment, and government spending, giving us an exaggerated measure of spending on *American* output. But we can easily correct for this overcount by simply deducting imported consumption goods from our measure of consumption, deducting imported investment goods from our measure of investment spending, and deducting imported government purchases from our measure of government purchases. Or, combining all these deductions together, we simply deduct *total* imports to correct our exaggerated measure of *total* spending.

In sum, to incorporate the international sector into our measure of total spending, we must add U.S. exports and subtract U.S. imports. These two adjustments can be made together by simply including *net exports* (NX) as the foreign sector's contribution to total spending.

$$\text{Net exports} = \text{Total exports} - \text{Total imports}.$$

Net exports can change for a variety of reasons: changes in tastes toward or away from a particular country's goods, changes in the price of foreign currency on world foreign exchange markets, and more. In the last chapter of this book, we'll discuss in more detail how and why net exports change. But in this chapter, to keep things simple, we assume that net exports—like investment spending and government purchases—are some given amount. We'll explore what happens when that amount changes, but we will not, in this chapter, try to explain what causes net exports to change.

> *For now, we regard net exports as a given value, determined by forces outside of our model.*

It is important to remember that net exports can be *negative;* and in the United States, they have been negative since 1982. Negative net exports means that our imports are greater than our exports. Or, equivalently, Americans are buying more foreign goods and services than foreigners are buying of ours. In that case, net exports contribute *negatively* to total spending on U.S. output.

## Summing Up: Aggregate Expenditure

Now that we've discussed all of the components of spending in the economy, we can be more precise about measuring total spending. First, we'll use the phrase *aggregate expenditure* to mean total spending on U.S. output over some period of time. More formally,

> *aggregate expenditure is the sum of spending by households, businesses, the government, and the foreign sector on final goods and services produced in the United States.*

**Aggregate expenditure (AE)** The sum of spending by households, business firms, the government, and foreigners on final goods and services produced in the United States.

Remembering that $C$ stands for household consumption spending, $I^p$ for investment spending, $G$ for government purchases, and $NX$ for net exports, we have

$$\text{Aggregate expenditure} = C + I^p + G + NX.$$

Aggregate expenditure plays a key role in explaining economic fluctuations, as you'll soon see.

## Income and Aggregate Expenditure

As we discussed earlier, the relationship between income and spending is circular: Spending depends on income, and income depends on spending. In Table 4, we take up the first part of that circle: how total spending depends on income. In the table, column 1 lists some possible income levels, and column 2 shows the level of consumption spending we can expect at each income level. These two columns are just the consumption–income relationship we introduced earlier, in Table 2.

Column 3 shows that business firms in this economy are assumed to buy $800 billion per year in plant and equipment, regardless of the level of income. Government purchases are also fixed in value, as shown by column 4: At every

**GDP versus Aggregate Expenditure** The definition of aggregate expenditure looks very similar to the definition of GDP presented in the chapter entitled "Production, Income, and Employment." Does this mean that aggregate expenditure and total output are always the same number? Not at all. There is a slight—but important—difference in the definitions. GDP is defined as $C + I + G + NX$. Aggregate expenditure, by contrast, is defined as $C + I^p + G + NX$. The difference is that GDP adds actual investment ($I$), which includes business firms' inventory investment. Aggregate expenditure adds just planned investment ($I^p$), which *excludes* inventory investment. The two numbers will not be equal unless inventory investment is zero. (We'll use this fact to help us find the equilibrium GDP in the next section.)

**DANGEROUS CURVES**

| T A B L E | 4 | The Relationship Between Income and Aggregate Expenditure |

| (1) Income or GDP (billions of dollars per year) | (2) Consumption Spending (billions of dollars per year) | (3) Investment Spending (billions of dollars per year) | (4) Government Purchases (billions of dollars per year) | (5) Net Exports (billions of dollars per year) | (6) Aggregate Expenditure (*AE*) (billions of dollars per year) | (7) Change in Inventories (billions of dollars per year) |
|---|---|---|---|---|---|---|
| 4,000 | 3,200 | 800 | 1,000 | 600 | 5,600 | −1,600 |
| 5,000 | 3,800 | 800 | 1,000 | 600 | 6,200 | −1,200 |
| 6,000 | 4,400 | 800 | 1,000 | 600 | 6,800 | −800 |
| 7,000 | 5,000 | 800 | 1,000 | 600 | 7,400 | −400 |
| **8,000** | **5,600** | **800** | **1,000** | **600** | **8,000** | **0** |
| 9,000 | 6,200 | 800 | 1,000 | 600 | 8,600 | 400 |
| 10,000 | 6,800 | 800 | 1,000 | 600 | 9,200 | 800 |
| 11,000 | 7,400 | 800 | 1,000 | 600 | 9,800 | 1,200 |
| 12,000 | 8,000 | 800 | 1,000 | 600 | 10,400 | 1,600 |

level of income, the government buys $1,000 billion in goods and services. And net exports, in column 5, are assumed to be $600 billion at each level of income. Finally, if we add together the entries in columns 2, 3, 4, and 5, we get $C + I^p + G + NX$, or aggregate expenditure, shown in column 6. (For now, ignore column 7.)

Notice that aggregate expenditure increases as income rises. But notice also that the rise in aggregate expenditure is *smaller* than the rise in income. For example, you can see that when income rises from $4,000 billion to $5,000 billion (column 1), aggregate expenditure rises from $5,600 billion to $6,200 billion (column 6). Thus, a $1,000 billion increase in income is associated with a $600 billion increase in aggregate expenditure. This is because, in our analysis, consumption is the only component of spending that depends on income, and consumption spending always increases according to the marginal propensity to consume, here equal to 0.6.

> *When income increases, aggregate expenditure (AE) will rise by the* MPC *times the change in income:* $\Delta AE = MPC \times \Delta GDP$.

Notice that we've used $\Delta GDP$ to indicate the change in total income, because GDP and total income are always the same number.

## FINDING EQUILIBRIUM GDP

Table 4 shows how aggregate expenditure depends on income. In this section, you will see how income depends on aggregate expenditure—that is, how spending determines the economy's *equilibrium income* or *equilibrium GDP*. That is, we are about to use Step 2 of our three-step process: *Find the equilibrium*. As always, the equilibrium will be a point of rest of the economy: a value for GDP that remains the same until something we've been assuming constant begins to change. That part of Step 2 will be familiar to you.

However, be forewarned: Our method of *finding* equilibrium in the short run is very different from anything you've seen before in this text.

Our starting point in finding the economy's short-run equilibrium is to ask ourselves what would happen, hypothetically, if the economy were operating at different levels of output. Let's start with a GDP of $12,000 billion. Could this be the equilibrium GDP we seek? That is, if firms were producing this level of output, would they keep doing so? Let's see.

Table 4 tells us that when GDP, and therefore income, is equal to $12,000 billion, aggregate expenditure is equal to $10,400 billion. Business firms are *producing* $1,600 billion more than they are *selling*. Since firms will certainly not be willing to continue producing output they cannot sell, we can infer that, in future periods, they will slow their production. Thus, if the economy finds itself at a GDP of $12,000 billion, it will not stay there. In other words, $12,000 billion is *not* where the economy will settle in the short run, so it is *not* our equilibrium GDP. More generally,

> *when aggregate expenditure is less than GDP, output will decline in the future. Thus, any level of output at which aggregate expenditure is less than GDP cannot be the equilibrium GDP.*

Now let's consider the opposite case: a level of GDP of $4,000 billion. At this level of output, Table 4 shows aggregate expenditure of $5,600 billion; spending is actually *greater* than output by $1,600 billion. What will business firms do in response? Since they are selling more output than they are currently producing, we can expect them to *increase* their production in future months. Thus, if GDP is $4,000 billion, it will tend to rise in the future. So $4,000 billion is *not* our equilibrium GDP.

> *When aggregate expenditure is greater than GDP, output will rise in the future. Thus, any level of output at which aggregate expenditure exceeds GDP cannot be the equilibrium GDP.*

Now consider a GDP of $8,000 billion. At this level of output, our table shows that aggregate expenditure is precisely equal to $8,000 billion: Output and aggregate expenditure are equal. Since firms, on the whole, are selling just what they produce—no more and no less—they should be content to produce that same amount in the future. We have found our equilibrium GDP:

> *In the short run, **equilibrium GDP** is the level of output at which output and aggregate expenditure are equal.*

**Equilibrium GDP** In the short run, the level of output at which output and aggregate expenditure are equal.

## INVENTORIES AND EQUILIBRIUM GDP

When firms *produce* more goods than they sell, what happens to the unsold output? It is added to their inventory stocks. When firms *sell* more goods than they produce, where do the additional goods come from? They come from firms' inventory stocks. You can see that the gap between output and spending determines what will happen to inventories during the year.

More specifically,

> *the change in inventories during any period will always equal output minus aggregate expenditure.*

For example, Table 4 tells us that if GDP is equal to $12,000 billion, aggregate expenditure is equal to $10,400 billion. In this case, we can find that the change in inventories is

$$\Delta \text{Inventories} = GDP - AE$$
$$= \$12{,}000 \text{ billion} - \$10{,}400 \text{ billion}$$
$$= \$1{,}600 \text{ billion}.$$

When GDP is equal to $4,000 billion, aggregate expenditure is equal to $5,600 billion, so that the change in inventories is

$$\Delta \text{Inventories} = GDP - AE$$
$$= \$4{,}000 \text{ billion} - \$5{,}600 \text{ billion}$$
$$= -\$1{,}600 \text{ billion}.$$

Notice the negative sign in front of the $1,600 billion; if output is $4,000 billion, then inventory stocks will *shrink* by $1,600 billion over the year.

Only when output and aggregate expenditure are equal—that is, when GDP is at its equilibrium value—will the change in inventories be zero. In our example, when GDP is at its equilibrium value of $8,000 billion, so that aggregate expenditure is also $8,000 billion, the change in inventories is equal to zero. At this output level, we have

$$\Delta \text{Inventories} = GDP - AE$$
$$= \$8{,}000 \text{ billion} - \$8{,}000 \text{ billion}$$
$$= \$0.$$

What you have just learned about inventories suggests another way to find the equilibrium GDP in the economy: Find the output level at which the change in inventories is equal to zero. Firms cannot allow their inventories of unsold goods to keep growing for very long (they would go out of business), nor can they continue to sell goods out of inventory for very long (they would run out of goods). Instead, they will desire to keep their production in line with their sales, so that their inventories do not change.

To recap,

$$AE < GDP \Rightarrow \Delta \text{Inventories} > 0 \Rightarrow GDP\downarrow \text{ in future periods.}$$
$$AE > GDP \Rightarrow \Delta \text{Inventories} < 0 \Rightarrow GDP\uparrow \text{ in future periods.}$$
$$AE = GDP \Rightarrow \Delta \text{Inventories} = 0 \Rightarrow \text{No change in } GDP$$

Now look at the last column in Table 4, which lists the change in inventories at different levels of output. This column is obtained by subtracting column 6 from column 1. The equilibrium output level is the one at which the change in inventories equals zero, which, as we've already found, is $8,000 billion.

## FINDING EQUILIBRIUM GDP WITH A GRAPH

To get an even clearer picture of how equilibrium GDP is determined, we'll illustrate it with a graph, although it will take us a few steps to get there. Figure 5 begins the process by showing how we can construct a graph of aggregate expenditure. The lowest line in the figure, labeled *C,* is our familiar consumption–income line, obtained from the data in the first two columns of Table 4.

The next line, labeled $C + I^p$, shows the *sum* of consumption and investment spending at each income level. Notice that this line is parallel to the *C* line, which means that the vertical distance between them—$800 billion—is the same at any income level. This vertical difference is investment spending, which remains the same at all income levels.

The next line adds government purchases to consumption and investment spending, giving us $C + I^p + G$. The $C + I^p + G$ line is parallel to the $C + I^p$ line. The vertical distance between them—$1,000 billion—is government purchases. Like investment spending, government purchases are the same at all income levels.

Finally, the top line adds net exports, giving us $C + I^p + G + NX$, or aggregate expenditure. The distance between the $C + I^p + G + NX$ line and the $C + I^p + G$ line—$600 billion—represents net exports, which are assumed to be the same at any level of income.

Now look just at the aggregate expenditure line—the top line—in Figure 5. Notice that it slopes upward, telling us that as income increases, so does aggregate expenditure. And the slope of the aggregate expenditure line is less than 1: When income increases, the rise in aggregate expenditure is *smaller* than the rise in income. In fact, the slope of the aggregate expenditure line is equal to the *MPC,* or 0.6 in

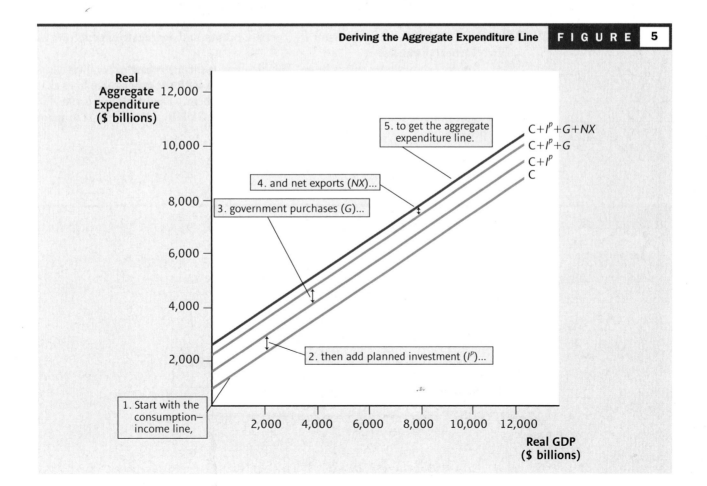

**Deriving the Aggregate Expenditure Line**   **FIGURE   5**

this example. This tells us that a one-dollar rise in income causes a 60-cent increase in aggregate expenditure. (Question: In the graph, which of the four components of aggregate expenditure rises when income rises? Which remain the same?)

Now we're almost ready to use a graph like the one in Figure 5 to locate equilibrium GDP, but first we must develop a little geometric trick.

Figure 6 shows a graph in which the horizontal and vertical axes are both measured in the same units, such as dollars. It also shows a line drawn at a 45° angle that begins at the origin. This 45° line has a useful property: Any point along it represents the same value along the vertical axis as it does along the horizontal axis. For example, look at point $A$ on the line. Point $A$ corresponds to the horizontal distance $0B$, and it also corresponds to the vertical distance $BA$. But because the line is a 45° line, we know that these two distances are equal: $0B = BA$. Now we have two choices for measuring the distance $0B$: We can measure it horizontally, or we can measure it as the vertical distance $BA$. In fact, *any* horizontal distance can also be read vertically, merely by going from the horizontal value (point $B$ in our example) up to the 45° line.

> *A 45° line is a translator line: It allows us to measure any horizontal distance as a vertical distance instead.*

Let's apply this geometric trick to help us find the equilibrium GDP. In our aggregate expenditure diagram, we want to compare output with aggregate expenditure. But output is measured horizontally, while aggregate expenditure is measured vertically. Our 45° line, however, enables us to translate output into a vertical distance, and thus permits us to compare output and aggregate expenditure as two vertical distances.

Figure 7 shows how this is done. The blue line is the aggregate expenditure line $(C + I^p + G + NX)$ from Figure 5. (We've dispensed with the other three lines that were drawn in Figure 5 because we no longer need them.) The black line is our 45° translator line. Now, let's search for the equilibrium GDP by considering a number of possibilities.

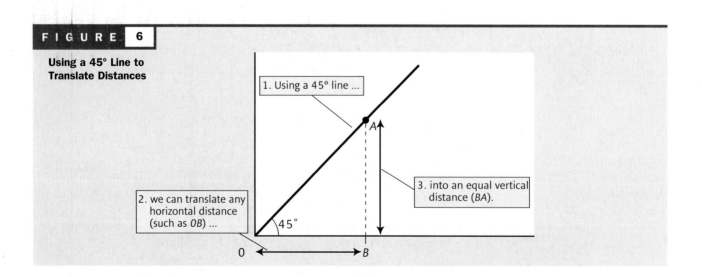

**FIGURE 6**

**Using a 45° Line to Translate Distances**

1. Using a 45° line …

2. we can translate any horizontal distance (such as *0B*) …

3. into an equal vertical distance (*BA*).

$A$

45°

0    $B$

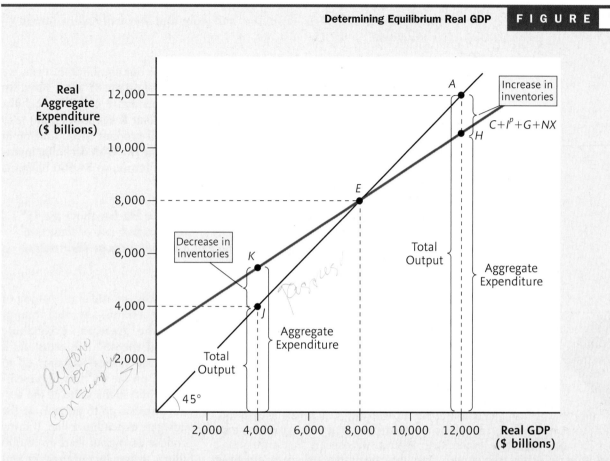

**Determining Equilibrium Real GDP** | FIGURE | 7

*At point E, where the aggregate expenditure line crosses the 45° line, the economy is in short-run equilibrium. With real GDP equal to $8,000 billion, aggregate expenditure equals real GDP. At higher levels of real GDP—such as $12,000 billion—total production exceeds aggregate expenditures, and firms will be unable to sell all they produce. Unplanned inventory increases equal to HA will lead them to reduce production. At lower levels of real GDP—such as $4,000 billion—aggregate expenditure exceeds total production. Firms find their inventories falling, and they will respond by increasing production.*

For example, could the output level $12,000 billion be our sought-after equilibrium? Let's see. We can measure the output level $12,000 billion as the vertical distance from the horizontal axis up to point *A* on the 45° line. But when output is $12,000 billion, aggregate expenditure is the vertical distance from the horizontal axis to point *H* on the aggregate expenditure line. Notice that, since point *H* lies below point *A*, aggregate expenditure is less than output. If firms *did* produce $12,000 billion worth of output, they would accumulate inventories equal to the vertical distance *HA* (the excess of output over spending). We conclude graphically (as we did earlier, using our table) that if output is $12,000 billion, firms will accumulate inventories of unsold goods and reduce output in the future. Thus, $12,000 billion is not our equilibrium. In general,

*at any output level at which the aggregate expenditure line lies* below *the 45° line, aggregate expenditure is less than GDP. If firms produce any of these output levels, their inventories will grow, and they will reduce output in the future.*

Now let's see if an output of $4,000 billion could be our equilibrium. First, we read this output level as the vertical distance up to point *J* on the 45° line. Next, we note that when output is $4,000 billion, aggregate expenditure is the vertical distance up to point *K* on the aggregate expenditure line. Point *K* lies *above* point *J*, so aggregate expenditure is greater than output. If firms *did* produce $4,000 billion in output, inventories would *decrease* by the vertical distance *JK*. With declining inventories, firms would want to increase their output in the future, so $4,000 billion is not our equilibrium. More generally,

*at any output level at which the aggregate expenditure line lies* above *the 45° line, aggregate expenditure exceeds GDP. If firms produce any of these output levels, their inventories will decline, and they will increase their output in the future.*

**What About Prices?** You may be wondering why, in the short-run macro model, a firm that produces more output than it sells wouldn't just lower the price of its goods. That way, it could sell more of them and not have to lower its output as much. Similarly, a firm whose sales exceeded its production could take advantage of the opportunity to raise its prices rather than increase production.

To some extent, firms *do* change prices—even in the short run. But they change their output levels, too. To keep things as simple as possible, this first version of the short-run macro model assumes that firms adjust *only* their output to match aggregate expenditure. That is, we assume that *prices don't change at all*. In a later chapter, we'll make the model more realistic by assuming that firms adjust both prices and output.

Finally, consider an output of $8,000 billion. At this output level, the aggregate expenditure line and the 45° line cross. As a result, the vertical distance up to point *E* on the 45° line (representing output) is the same as the vertical distance up to point *E* on the aggregate expenditure line. If firms produce an output level of $8,000 billion, aggregate expenditure and output will be precisely equal, inventories will remain unchanged, and firms will have no incentive to increase or decrease output in the future. We have thus found our equilibrium on the graph: $8,000 billion.

*Equilibrium GDP is the output level at which the aggregate expenditure line intersects the 45° line. If firms produce this output level, their inventories will not change, and they will be content to continue producing the same level of output in the future.*

## EQUILIBRIUM GDP AND EMPLOYMENT

Now that you've learned how to find the economy's equilibrium GDP in the short run, a question may have occurred to you: When the economy operates at equilibrium, will it also be operating at full employment? The answer is: *not necessarily.* Let's see why.

If you look back over the two methods we've employed to find equilibrium GDP—using columns of numbers or using a graph—you will see that in both cases we've asked only one question: How much will households, businesses, the government, and foreigners *spend* on goods produced in the United States? We did not ask any

*During the Great Depression of the 1930s, the economy's short-run equilibrium output fell far below potential, and at least a quarter of the labor force became unemployed.*

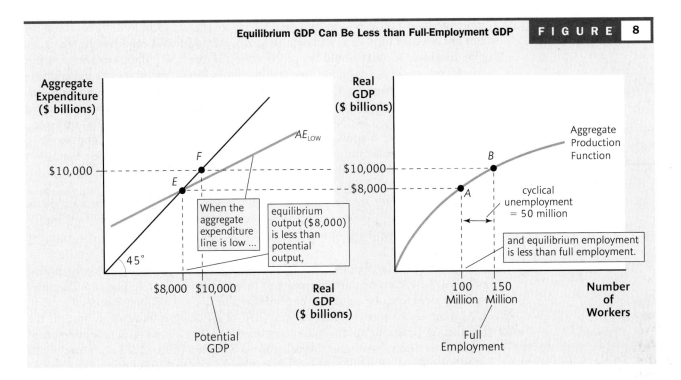

**Equilibrium GDP Can Be Less than Full-Employment GDP**    FIGURE 8

questions about the number of people who want to work. Therefore, it would be quite a coincidence if our equilibrium GDP happened to be the output level at which the entire labor force were employed.

Figure 8 illustrates the connection between employment and equilibrium GDP. We'll be going back and forth between the panels, so it's good to make sure you understand each step before going on to the next. Let's start with the right-hand panel, which shows the economy's *aggregate production function*, introduced earlier as part of the classical model. This curve tells us the relationship between any given number of workers and the level of output, with the current state of technology and given quantities of other resources. In this economy, full employment is assumed to be 150 million workers, measured along the horizontal axis. Potential output— $10,000 billion on the vertical axis—is the amount of output a fully employed labor force of 150 million workers could produce. This is also the long-run equilibrium output level that the classical model would predict for the economy.

But will $10,000 billion be the economy's equilibrium in the *short run*? Not necessarily. One possible outcome is shown in the left panel. The short-run equilibrium occurs at point *E*, where the aggregate expenditure line crosses the 45° line. At this point, output (on the horizontal axis) is $8,000 billion.

How many people will have jobs? We can answer by using the 45° line to convert the $8,000 billion from a horizontal distance to a vertical distance, then (following the dashed line) carrying that vertical distance across to the right panel. The right panel's production function tells us that to produce $8,000 billion in output, only 100 million workers are needed. In short-run equilibrium, then, only 100 million workers will have jobs. The difference between *full* employment and *actual* employment is 150 million − 100 million = 50 million, which is the amount of cyclical unemployment in the economy.

But why? What prevents firms from hiring the extra people who want jobs? After all, with more people working, producing more output, wouldn't there be more income in the economy and therefore more spending? Indeed, there would be. But not *enough* additional spending to justify the additional employment. To prove this, just look at what would happen if firms *did* hire 150 million workers. Output would rise to $10,000 billion, but at this output level, the aggregate expenditure line would lie below the 45° line so *firms would be unable to sell all their output.* Unsold goods would pile up in inventories, and firms would cut back on production until output reached $8,000 billion again, with employment back at 100 million.

In sum: Figure 8 shows that we can be in short-run equilibrium and yet have abnormally high unemployment. The reason: The aggregate expenditure line is *too low* to create an intersection at full-employment output.

> *In the short-run macro model, cyclical unemployment is caused by insufficient spending. As long as spending remains low, production will remain low, and unemployment will remain high.*

What about the opposite possibility? In the short run, is it possible for spending to be *too high,* causing unemployment to be *too low*? Absolutely. Figure 9 illustrates such a case. Here, the aggregate expenditure line and the 45° line intersect at point E′, giving us a short-run equilibrium GDP at $12,000 billion. According to the production function, producing an output of $12,000 billion requires employment of 200 million workers. Since this is greater than the economy's full employment of 150 million, we will have abnormally high employment and abnormally low *un*employment.

> *In the short-run macro model, the economy can overheat because spending is too high. As long as spending remains high, production will exceed potential output, and unemployment will be unusually low.*

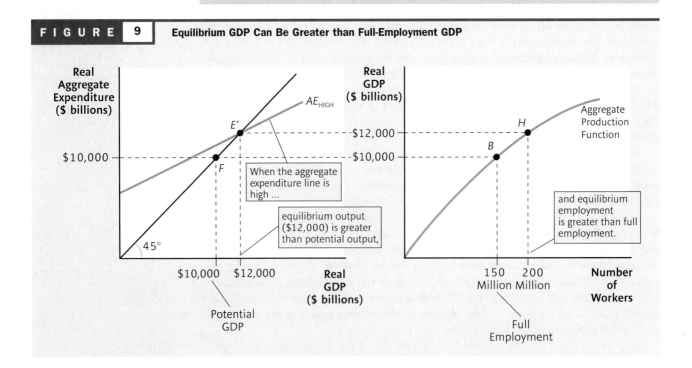

**FIGURE  9    Equilibrium GDP Can Be Greater than Full-Employment GDP**

In the previous chapter, we concluded that the classical model could not explain economic fluctuations. The short-run macro model, on the other hand, does provide an explanation: The aggregate expenditure line may be low, so that in the short run, equilibrium GDP is below full employment. Or aggregate expenditure may be high, so that in the short run, equilibrium GDP is above the full-employment level. (Of course, this is just a first step in explaining economic fluctuations. In later chapters, we'll add more realism to the model.)

## WHAT HAPPENS WHEN THINGS CHANGE?

So far, you've seen how the economy's equilibrium level of output is determined in the short run, and the important role played by spending in determining that equilibrium. But now it's time to use Step 3 and explore how a *change* in spending affects equilibrium output.

### A CHANGE IN INVESTMENT SPENDING

Suppose the equilibrium GDP in an economy is $8,000 billion and then business firms increase their investment spending on plant and equipment. This might happen because business managers feel more optimistic about the economy's future, or because there is a new "must-have" technology (such as the Internet in the late 1990s). Whatever the cause, firms decide to increase yearly planned investment purchases by $1,000 billion above the original level. What will happen?

First, sales revenue at firms that manufacture investment goods—firms like Dell Computer, Caterpillar, and Westinghouse—will increase by $1,000 billion. But remember, each time a dollar in output is produced, a dollar of income (factor payments) is created. Thus, the $1,000 billion in additional sales revenue will become $1,000 billion in additional income. This income will be paid out as wages, rent, interest, and profit to the households who own the resources these firms have purchased.[1]

What will households do with their $1,000 billion in additional income? Remember that with net taxes fixed at some value, a $1,000 billion rise in income is also a $1,000 billion rise in *disposable* income. Households are free to spend or save this additional income as they desire. What they will do depends crucially on the *marginal propensity to consume (MPC) in the economy*. If the MPC is 0.6, then consumption spending will rise by 0.6 × $1,000 billion = $600 billion. Households will save the remaining $400 billion.

But that is not the end of the story. When households spend an additional $600 billion, firms that produce consumption goods and services—firms such as McDonald's, American Airlines, and Disney—will receive an additional $600 billion in sales revenue, which, in turn, will become income for the households that supply resources to these firms. And when *these* households see *their* annual incomes rise by $600 billion, they will spend part of it as well. With an MPC of 0.6, consumption spending will rise by 0.6 × $600 billion = $360 billion, creating still more sales revenue for firms, and so on and so on. . . .

As you can see, an increase in investment spending will set off a chain reaction, leading to successive rounds of increased spending and income.

---

[1] Some of the sales revenue will also go to pay for intermediate goods, such as raw materials, electricity, and supplies. But the intermediate-goods suppliers will also pay wages, rent, interest, and profit for the resources *they* use, so that household income will still rise by the full $1,000 billion.

| TABLE 5 | Round | Additional Spending in Each Round (billions of dollars per year) | Total Additional Spending (billions of dollars per year) |
|---|---|---|---|
| **Cumulative Increases in Spending When Investment Spending Increases by $1,000 Billion** | Initial increase in investment spending | 1,000 | 1,000 |
| | Round 2 | 600 | 1,600 |
| | Round 3 | 360 | 1,960 |
| | Round 4 | 216 | 2,176 |
| | Round 5 | 130 | 2,306 |
| | Round 6 | 78 | 2,384 |
| | Round 7 | 47 | 2,431 |
| | Round 8 | 28 | 2,459 |
| | Round 9 | 17 | 2,476 |
| | Round 10 | 10 | 2,486 |
| | . . . | . . . | . . . |
| | Round 20 | 0.06 | Very close to 2,500 |

The process is illustrated in Table 5. The second column gives us the additional spending in each round of this chain reaction. The first entry shows the additional spending of $1,000 billion per year from the initial increase in investment. The next entry shows the $600 billion increase in consumption spending, then another $360 billion increase in consumption, and so on. Each successive round of additional spending is 60 percent of the round before. The third column adds up the additional spending created by all preceding rounds, to give the *total* additional spending as this chain reaction continues. For example, total additional spending after the first round is just $1,000 billion. In the second round, we add the $600 billion in additional consumption spending, to get $1,600 billion in additional spending per year. In the third round, additional spending rises to $1,960 billion per year.

Remember that each time spending rises, output rises to match it. Figure 10 illustrates what happens to GDP (at an annual rate) after each round of this chain reaction. When we analyze events like this in the U.S. economy, we find that the successive increases in spending and output occur quickly; the process is largely completed within a year. And at the end of the process, when the economy has reached its new equilibrium, total spending and total output are considerably higher.

But how much higher?

If you look at the second column of Table 5, you can see that each successive round adds less to total spending than the round before. And in Figure 10, you see that GDP rises by less and less with each round. Eventually, GDP rises by such a small amount, and the GDP will be so close to its new equilibrium value, that we can ignore any difference. In our example, when the chain reaction is virtually completed, equilibrium GDP will be $2,500 billion more than it was initially.

## THE EXPENDITURE MULTIPLIER

Let's go back and summarize what happened in our example: Business firms increased their investment spending by $1,000 billion, and as a result, spending and output rose by $2,500 billion. Equilibrium GDP increased by *more than* the initial increase in investment spending. In our example, the increase in equilibrium GDP

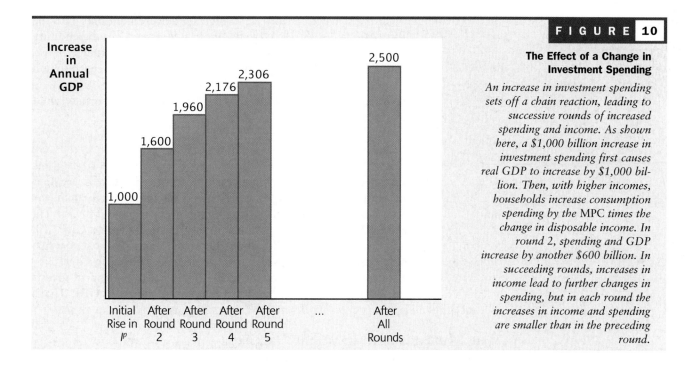

**The Effect of a Change in Investment Spending**

*An increase in investment spending sets off a chain reaction, leading to successive rounds of increased spending and income. As shown here, a $1,000 billion increase in investment spending first causes real GDP to increase by $1,000 billion. Then, with higher incomes, households increase consumption spending by the MPC times the change in disposable income. In round 2, spending and GDP increase by another $600 billion. In succeeding rounds, increases in income lead to further changes in spending, but in each round the increases in income and spending are smaller than in the preceding round.*

($2,500 billion) was two-and-a-half times the initial increase in investment spending ($1,000 billion). As you can verify, if investment spending had increased by half as much ($500 billion), GDP would have increased by 2.5 times *that* amount ($1,250 billion). In fact, *whatever* the rise in investment spending, equilibrium GDP would increase by a factor of 2.5, so we can write

$$\Delta GDP = 2.5 \times \Delta I^p.$$

In our example, the change in investment spending was *multiplied by* the number 2.5 in order to get the change in GDP that it causes. For this reason, 2.5 is called the *expenditure multiplier* in this example.

> *The **expenditure multiplier** is the number by which the change in investment spending must be multiplied to get the change in equilibrium GDP.*

**Expenditure multiplier** The amount by which equilibrium real GDP changes as a result of a one-dollar change in autonomous consumption, investment spending, government purchases, or net exports.

The value of the expenditure multiplier depends on the value of the *MPC* in the economy. If you look back at Table 5, you will see that each round of additional spending would have been larger if the *MPC* had been larger. For example, with an *MPC* of 0.9 instead of 0.6, spending in round 2 would have risen by $900 billion, in round 3 by $810 billion, and so on. The result would have been a larger ultimate change in GDP, and a larger multiplier.

There is a very simple formula we can use to determine the multiplier for *any* value of the *MPC*.

> *For any value of the* MPC, *the formula for the expenditure multiplier is*
> $$\frac{1}{(1-MPC)}.$$

In our example, the *MPC* was equal to 0.6, so the expenditure multiplier had the value 1/(1 − 0.6) = 1/0.4 = 2.5. If the *MPC* had been 0.9 instead, the expenditure multiplier would have been equal to 1/(1 − 0.9) = 1/0.1 = 10. The formula 1/(1 − *MPC*) can be used to find the multiplier for any value of the *MPC* between zero and one. If you want to see how this formula is derived, see this footnote.[2]

Using the general formula for the expenditure multiplier, we can restate what happens when investment spending increases:

$$\Delta GDP = \left[\frac{1}{(1-MPC)}\right] \times \Delta I^p.$$

The multiplier effect is a rather surprising phenomenon. It tells us that an increase in investment spending ultimately affects GDP by *more* than the initial increase in investment. Further, it tells us that as long as annual investment spending remains $1,000 billion greater than it was previously, yearly GDP will remain higher than previously—$2,500 billion higher in our example. That is, a sustained increase in investment spending will cause a sustained increase in GDP.

By contrast, a one-time increase in investment—followed by a drop in investment back to its original level—will cause only a temporary change in GDP. That's because the multiplier process works in *both* directions, as you're about to see.

## THE MULTIPLIER IN REVERSE

Suppose that, in Table 5, investment spending had *decreased* instead of increased. Then the initial change in spending would be −$1,000 billion. This would cause a $1,000 billion decrease in revenue for firms that produce investment goods, and they, in turn, would pay out $1,000 billion less in factor payments. In the next round, households, with $1,000 billion less in income, would spend $600 billion less on consumption goods, and so on. The final result would be a $2,500 billion *decrease* in equilibrium GDP.

> *Just as increases in investment spending cause equilibrium GDP to rise by a multiple of the change in spending, decreases in investment spending cause equilibrium GDP to fall by a multiple of the change in spending.*

The multiplier formula we've already established will work whether the initial change in spending is positive or negative.

---

[2] To derive the multiplier formula, let's start with our example, in which the change in GDP was:

$$\Delta GDP = (\$1,000 \text{ billion} + \$600 \text{ billion} + \$360 \text{ billion} + \$216 \text{ billion} + \dots).$$

Factoring out the $1,000 billion gives us:

$$\Delta GDP = \$1,000 \text{ billion} \times (1 + 0.6 + 0.36 + 0.216 + \dots)$$
$$= \$1,000 \text{ billion} \times (1 + 0.6 + 0.6^2 + 0.6^3 + \dots).$$

Now, in our example, $1,000 billion was the increase in investment spending and 0.6 was the *MPC*. Generalizing this for *any* change in investment or *any* MPC, we would have

$$\Delta GDP = \Delta I^p \times [1 + (MPC) + (MPC)^2 + (MPC)^3 + \dots].$$

Next, we borrow a rule from the mathematics of infinite sums (such as the sum in brackets): For any value of H between 0 and 1, the infinite sum $1 + H + H^2 + H^3 + \dots$ has the value 1/(1 − H). Replacing H with the *MPC* (which is between 0 and 1), we conclude:

$$\Delta GDP = \Delta I^p \times \left[\frac{1}{(1-MPC)}\right].$$

## OTHER SPENDING CHANGES

A change in *any* sector's spending will set off a chain of events similar to that in our investment example.

Suppose the government increased its purchases above previous levels. For example, the Department of Defense might raise its spending on new bombers, or state highway departments might hire more road-repair crews, or cities and towns might hire more teachers. If total government purchases rise by $1,000 billion, then, once again, household income will rise by $1,000 billion. As before, households will spend 60 percent of this increase, causing consumption, in the next round, to rise by $600 billion, and so on and so on. The chain of events is exactly like that of Table 5, with one exception: The first line in column 1 would read, "Initial increase in government purchases" instead of "initial increase in investment spending." Once again, output would increase by $2,500 billion.

Besides planned investment and government purchases, there are two other components of spending that can set off the same process. One is an increase in net exports (*NX*). Since *NX* = Exports − Imports, either an increase in the economy's exports or a *decrease* in imports will cause *net* exports to rise.

Finally, a change in *autonomous consumption* (*a*) can set off the process. For example, after a $1,000 billion increase in autonomous consumption spending, we would see further increases in consumption spending of $600 billion, then $360 billion, and so on. This time, the first line in column 1 of Table 5 would read, "Initial increase in autonomous consumption," but every entry in the table would be the same.

> *Changes in planned investment, government purchases, net exports, or autonomous consumption lead to a multiplier effect on GDP. The expenditure multiplier, 1/(1 − MPC), is what we multiply the initial change in spending by in order to get the change in equilibrium GDP.*

The following four equations summarize how we use the expenditure multiplier to determine the effects of different spending changes in the short-run macro model. Keep in mind that these formulas work whether the initial change in spending is positive or negative.

$$\Delta GDP = \left[ \frac{1}{(1 - MPC)} \right] \times \Delta I^p$$

$$\Delta GDP = \left[ \frac{1}{(1 - MPC)} \right] \times \Delta G$$

$$\Delta GDP = \left[ \frac{1}{(1 - MPC)} \right] \times \Delta NX$$

$$\Delta GDP = \left[ \frac{1}{(1 - MPC)} \right] \times \Delta a$$

Changes in net taxes, too, have multiplier effects, although they work more indirectly on GDP than the spending changes we've been discussing. A tax cut—by allowing households to keep more of their income—raises disposable income. As a result, consumption spending rises, creating a multiplier effect that increases equilibrium GDP. Similarly, a tax increase lowers disposable income and consumption, creating a multiplier effect that decreases equilibrium GDP. But there is a slightly different multiplier formula that applies to tax changes. We'll discuss the tax multiplier in Appendix 2 of this chapter.

## A GRAPHICAL VIEW OF THE MULTIPLIER

Figure 11 illustrates the multiplier using our aggregate expenditure diagram. The darker line is the aggregate expenditure line from Figure 7. The aggregate expenditure line intersects the 45° line at point $E$, giving us an equilibrium GDP of $8,000 billion.

Now, suppose that either autonomous consumption, investment spending, net exports, or government purchases rises by $1,000 billion. Regardless of which of these types of spending increases, the effect on our aggregate expenditure line is the same: It will *shift upward* by $1,000 billion, to the higher line in the figure. The new

---

**FIGURE  11**   **A Graphical View of the Multiplier**

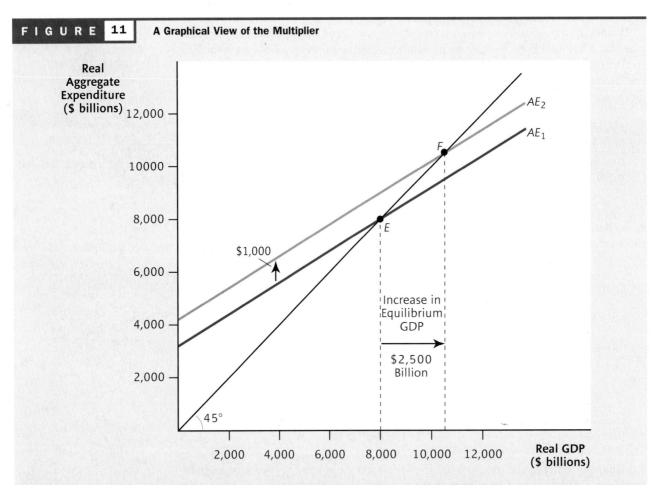

*The economy starts off at point* E *with equilibrium real GDP of $8,000 billion. A $1,000 billion increase in spending shifts the aggregate expenditure line upward by $1,000 billion, triggering the multiplier process. Eventually, the economy will reach a new equilibrium at point* F, *where the new, higher aggregate expenditure line crosses the 45° line. At* F, *real GDP is $10,500 billion, an increase of $2,500 billion.*

aggregate expenditure line intersects the 45° line at point *F*, showing that our new equilibrium GDP is equal to $10,500 billion.

What has happened? An initial spending increase of $1,000 billion has caused equilibrium GDP to increase from $8,000 billion to $10,500 billion, an increase of $2,500 billion. This is just what our multiplier of 2.5 tells us. In general,

$$\Delta GDP = \left[ \frac{1}{(1 - MPC)} \right] \times \Delta \text{Spending}$$

and in this case,

$$\$2,500 \text{ billion} = 2.5 \times \$1,000 \text{ billion}.$$

> *An increase in autonomous consumption spending, investment spending, government purchases, or net exports will shift the aggregate expenditure line upward by the initial increase in spending. Equilibrium GDP will rise by the initial increase in spending times the expenditure multiplier.*

## AUTOMATIC STABILIZERS AND THE MULTIPLIER

In this chapter, we've presented a model to help us focus on the central relationship between spending and output. To keep the model as simple as possible, we've ignored many real-world factors that interfere with, and reduce the size of, the multiplier effect. These forces are called **automatic stabilizers** because, with a smaller multiplier, spending changes will cause a much smaller change in GDP. As a result, economic fluctuations will be milder.

**Automatic stabilizers** Forces that reduce the size of the expenditure multiplier and diminish the impact of spending changes.

> *Automatic stabilizers reduce the size of the multiplier and therefore reduce the impact of spending changes on the economy. With milder fluctuations, the economy is more stable.*

How do automatic stabilizers work? They shrink the additional spending that occurs in each round of the multiplier, and thereby reduce the final multiplier effect on equilibrium GDP. In Table 5, automatic stabilizers would reduce each of the numerical entries after the first $1,000 billion, and lead to a final change in GDP smaller than $2,500 billion.

Here are some of the real-world automatic stabilizers we've ignored in the simple, short-run macro model of this chapter:

**Taxes.** We've been assuming that taxes remain constant, so that a rise in income causes an equal rise in disposable income. But some taxes (like the personal income tax) rise with income. As a result, in each round of the multiplier, the increase in disposable income will be smaller than the increase in income. With a smaller rise in disposable income, there will be a smaller rise in consumption spending as well.

**Transfer Payments.** Some government transfer payments fall as income rises. For example, many laid-off workers receive unemployment benefits, which help support them for several months while they are unemployed. When output and employment rise, newly hired workers give up their unemployment benefits. As

**The Two Kinds of Consumption Changes.** Does a change in consumption spending cause a multiplier effect? Or does the multiplier effect create a change in consumption spending? Actually, the causation runs in both directions. The key is to recognize that there are two kinds of changes in consumption spending.

One kind is a change in autonomous consumption spending (the term "*a*" in the consumption function). This change will *shift* the aggregate expenditure line up or down, telling us that total spending will be greater or smaller at *any* level of income. It is the kind of change that *causes* a multiplier effect.

But consumption also changes when something other than autonomous consumption sets off a multiplier effect. This is because consumption depends on income, and income always increases during the successive rounds of the multiplier effect. Such a change in consumption is represented by a movement *along* the aggregate expenditure line, rather than a shift.

Whenever you discuss a change in consumption spending, make sure you know whether it is a change in autonomous consumption (which shifts the *AE* line) or a change in consumption caused by a change in income (a movement along the *AE* line).

a result, a rise in income will cause a smaller rise in *disposable* income in each round, and a smaller rise in consumption.

**Interest Rates.** In a later chapter, you'll learn that an increase in output often leads to rising interest rates as well. This will crowd out some consumption and investment spending, making the increase in aggregate expenditure smaller than our simple story suggests.

**Imports.** Some additional spending is on goods and services imported from abroad. That is, instead of remaining constant as in our example, imports often rise as income rises, and net exports therefore fall as income rises. This helps to counteract any increase in spending caused by a rise in income.

**Forward-looking Behavior.** Consumers may be *forward-looking*. If they realize that the fluctuations in the economy are temporary, their consumption spending may be less sensitive to changes in their current income. Therefore, any change in income will cause a smaller change in consumption spending, and lead to a smaller multiplier effect.

Remember that each of these automatic stabilizers reduces the size of the multiplier, making it smaller than the simple formulas given in this chapter. For example, the simple formula for the expenditure multiplier is $1/(1 - MPC)$. With an $MPC$ of about 0.9—which is in the ballpark for the United States and many other countries—we would expect the multiplier to be about 10 . . . *if the simple formula were accurate*. In that case, a $1,000 billion increase in government spending would cause output to rise by $10,000 billion—quite a large multiplier effect.

But after we take account of all of the automatic stabilizers, the multiplier is considerably smaller. How much smaller? Most of the forecasting models used by economists in business and government predict that the multiplier effect takes about 9 months to a year to work its way through the economy. At the end of the process, the multiplier has a value of about 1.5. This means that a $1,000 billion increase in, say, government spending should cause GDP to increase by only about $1,500 billion in a year. This is much less than the $10,000 billion increase predicted by the simple formula $1/(1 - MPC)$ when the $MPC$ is equal to 0.9.

> *In the real world, due to automatic stabilizers, spending changes have much weaker impacts on the economy than our simple multiplier formula would suggest.*

Finally, there is one more automatic stabilizer you should know about, perhaps the most important of all: the *passage of time*. The impact of spending changes on output is *temporary*. As time passes, the classical model—lurking in the background—stands ready to take over. And if we wait long enough—a few years or so—we will return to our potential output level. So if a change in spending pulls us away from full-employment GDP, the economy will eventually return to full-employment GDP, right where it started. We thus conclude that

> *in the long run, our multipliers have a value of zero: No matter what the change in spending or taxes, output will eventually return to full employment, so the change in equilibrium GDP will be zero.*

Of course, the year or two we must wait can seem like an eternity to those who are jobless when the economy is operating below its potential. The short run is not to be overlooked. This is why, in the next several chapters, we will continue with our exploration of the short run, building on the macro model you've learned in this chapter. We'll be making the analysis more complete and more realistic by bringing in some of the real-world features that were not fully considered here.

## COUNTERCYCLICAL FISCAL POLICY

In the classical model, you saw that fiscal policy has no demand-side effects. For example, an increase in government purchases—because it crowds out an equal amount of household and business spending—does not change total spending at all. That is . . . in the long run.

But in the short run, the economy does not operate according to the mechanisms of the classical model. Instead, as you've seen, an increase in government purchases causes an increase in *total* spending and, through the multiplier, raises equilibrium GDP. That is,

> *in the short run, fiscal policy has demand-side effects on output and employment.*

This important observation suggests that fiscal policy could, in principle, improve the path of the economy. The government, by continually adjusting its own purchases or net taxes, could keep the economy closer to potential output and—in theory—smooth out the business cycle. When the government acts in this way, it is engaging in **countercyclical fiscal policy**—a change in government purchases or net taxes designed to reverse or prevent a recession or a boom.

**Countercyclical fiscal policy** A change in government purchases or net taxes designed to reverse or prevent a recession or a boom.

### HOW COUNTERCYCLICAL FISCAL POLICY WORKS

Figure 12 illustrates the idea behind countercyclical fiscal policy. It shows the aggregate expenditure line for an economy that is initially operating at point *A*, producing its potential output of $10,000 billion. Then we suppose that investment or autonomous consumption spending decreases, so the aggregate expenditure line shifts downward, and we end up with an output below potential at $9,000 billion. We are in a recession.

We could wait for a few years, knowing that recessions don't last forever. Eventually, the economy would operate according to the classical model, and we'd be back at our potential output. But why wait for the classical model to "kick in"

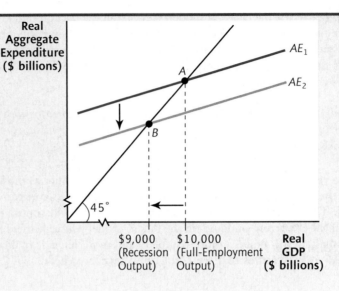

**Counterycyclical Fiscal Policy**

*Initially, the economy's equilibrium is at full-employment output of $10,000 billion (Point A). Then a decrease in investment spending shifts the aggregate expenditure line down to AE$_2$, and the economy starts heading toward point B—a recession. The government could shift the AE line back to its original position by increasing its own purchases, or by decreasing net taxes with a change in tax or transfer policies. If the change were enacted quickly enough, the government could prevent the recession.*

when we have such a powerful tool—fiscal policy—at our disposal? Why not make things better right away by, say, increasing government purchases?

Let's calculate how much government purchases (G) would have to rise in Figure 12 to bring us back to full employment. We'll start with the equation relating changes in G to changes in GDP:

$$\Delta GDP = \text{Multiplier} \times \Delta G.$$

Let's assume the multiplier in this economy is 2.5. Also, because equilibrium GDP is now at $9,000 billion, and we want it to be $10,000 billion, the required $\Delta$GDP is $1,000. Substituting these values into our equation, we have

$$\$1,000 \text{ billion} = 2.5 \times \Delta G.$$

Finally, we solve for $\Delta$G:

$$\Delta G = \frac{\$1,000 \text{ billion}}{2.5} = \$400 \text{ billion.}$$

This tells us that if the government increases its purchases by $400 billion, it will shift up the aggregate expenditure line by just enough to bring the economy back to full employment. Fiscal policy can cure the recession.

But why not go further and use countercyclical fiscal policy to *prevent* recessions from occurring in the first place? At the first sign of a contraction, the government could quickly increase its own purchases (say, hire more people to work with children in after-school programs) or cut taxes (say, offer everyone an immediate tax rebate). If successful, a government-induced increase in spending would counteract any decline in spending elsewhere in the economy. The recession would never occur.

Indeed, in the 1960s and early 1970s, this was the thinking of many economists. At the time, the popular view was that fiscal policy could effectively smooth out economic fluctuations, perhaps even eliminate them entirely. But very few economists believe this today. Why?

# PROBLEMS WITH COUNTERCYCLICAL FISCAL POLICY

While countercyclical fiscal policy is a wonderful idea in theory, it is plagued with practical problems that seriously limit its effectiveness. Here are some of them.

### Timing Problems

In most countries, it usually takes many months—or even longer—for fiscal changes to be enacted. Consider, for example, a decision to decrease taxes in the United States. A tax bill originates in the House of Representatives and then goes to the Senate, where it is usually modified. Then a conference committee irons out the differences between the House and Senate versions, and the tax bill goes back to each chamber for a vote. Once the legislation has passed, the president must sign it. Even if all goes smoothly, this process can take many months.

But in most cases, it will *not* go smoothly. First, there is the thorny question of *distributing* the benefits of any total tax cut among different groups within the country—an issue about which Democrats and Republicans rarely agree. And some senators and representatives will see the bill as an opportunity to change the tax system in more fundamental ways, causing further political debate. Because of these problems, the tax cut may not take effect until long after it is needed—stimulating the economy after it has recovered from recession, perhaps even when it is booming.

The same timing problem occurs in the opposite situation—when a tax hike is needed to counteract a boom. And these problems plague fiscal policy whether it is implemented through changes in taxes or changes in government purchases or transfers. Because of the long delays, regular use of countercyclical policy could very well be a *destabilizing* force in the economy—stepping on the gas when we should be hitting the brakes, or vice versa.

### Irreversibility

To be effective, countercyclical fiscal policy must be reversible. In our example in Figure 12, suppose the recession was caused by a sudden decrease in investment spending. Then, once investment spending returned to more normal levels, the fiscal stimulation should be reversed as well, so as not to overheat the economy.

But reversing changes in government purchases or taxes is difficult. Spending programs that create new departments or expand existing ones tend to become permanent, or at least difficult to terminate. Many "temporary" tax changes become permanent as well; the public is never happy to see a tax cut reversed, and the government is often reluctant to reverse a tax hike that could provide revenues for new government programs.

### The Reaction of the Federal Reserve

In the next chapter, you'll learn about the *Federal Reserve*—a quasi-governmental body responsible for another method of guiding the economy (monetary policy). In recent decades, the Federal Reserve has taken over the main role in reacting to and smoothing out economic fluctuations. And—for reasons you'll soon learn—the Federal Reserve can generally act more rapidly and flexibly than can Congress. In most circumstances, by the time any fiscal change would take place, the Federal Reserve would have *already* taken the steps it thought necessary to adjust aggregate expenditure. Any further changes in spending caused by fiscal policy would then be counteracted and effectively neutralized by the Federal Reserve.

## USING THE THEORY

### The Recession of 2001

Our most recent recession lasted from March 2001 to November 2001. Figure 13 tells the story. In the upper panel, you can see that investment spending—which had been drifting downward—fell sharply during the second quarter of 2001, and continued to fall throughout the year. The decrease in investment spending shifted the aggregate expenditure line downward (not shown). The middle panel shows the behavior of real GDP, which in normal times would have increased (along with potential output) at an annual rate of $80 billion each quarter. Instead, GDP fluctuated during the year, with almost no growth, and actually fell during the third quarter of 2001. As production faltered, employment fell—as seen in the bottom panel.

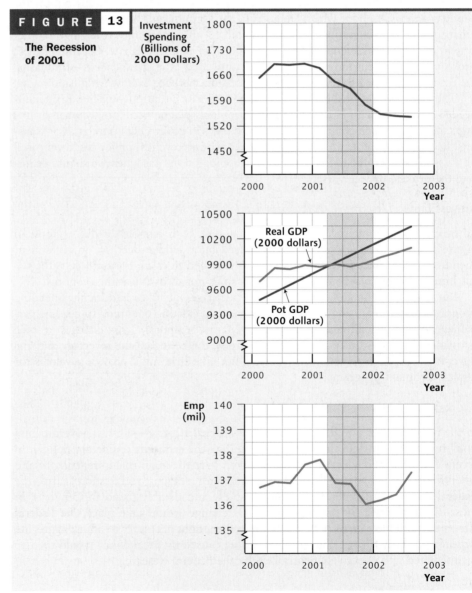

**FIGURE 13**

**The Recession of 2001**

What caused the recession of 2001? The simple answer is that the decline in investment spending, through the multiplier process, pushed down real GDP and employment. But what caused investment spending to fall in the first place?

In retrospect, we can see there were at least three causes.

First, during much of the late 1990s, there had been a boom in capital equipment spending as existing businesses rushed to incorporate the Internet into factories, offices, and their business practices in general. Firms like Avis, Wal-Mart, and Viacom needed servers and high-speed Internet connections, and the firms that supplied the new technology needed their own new offices, factories, and equipment. But as 2000 ended and 2001 began, firms had begun to catch up to the new technology. The rush ended, and investment began to fall.

Another reason for the drop in investment spending also had roots in the 1990s. During this period, the Internet and other new technologies made the public very optimistic about the future profits of American businesses, and hungry to own shares of stock in almost any company that had anything to do with the Internet. Share prices rose sky high. The optimism and high share prices encouraged entirely new businesses to start up—businesses that used the Internet to sell pet supplies, prescription drugs, and toys or to deliver videos, groceries, or even fresh hot pizzas. Of course, these new businesses needed their own capital equipment, warehouses, and office buildings, driving investment spending even further skyward in the late 1990s.

Unfortunately, in late 2000 and early 2001, reality set in. Competition was preventing many new firms from earning any profit, and many went bankrupt. Optimism shifted to pessimism. Share prices fell, and new business ventures—especially those having to do with the Internet—came to a halt. And so did the investment spending they had been undertaking.

The final reason for the change in planned investment—more accurately, an exacerbation of the change already occurring—was the infamous terrorist attacks on the World Trade Center and the Pentagon on September 11, 2001. The nation was traumatized by these events. What little optimism was left about the future of the U.S. economy turned to uncertainty and fear. Millions of potential airline passengers no longer wanted to fly, forcing airlines to cancel flights as well as orders for new aircraft. Hotel vacancy rates skyrocketed, and investment in new hotels and expansion of existing hotels came to a halt. Similar decisions were made in other industries, and investment spending fell sharply.

One abnormal feature of the recession of 2001 was the behavior of consumption spending. Ordinarily, as income falls in a recession, consumption declines along with it. This is a movement leftward and downward along the consumption–income line (such as the line in Figure 3 of this chapter). Moreover, decreases in wealth from falling stock prices, and a sharp drop in consumer confidence after September 11, would ordinarily have caused a decrease in *autonomous* consumption spending (see Table 3), *shifting* the consumption–income line downward. Yet consumption spending (not shown) actually *rose* during every quarter of 2001. Since income fell during this time, the only way that consumption spending could rise was through an upward shift of the consumption–income line.

**What Makes It a Recession?** Newspapers and television commentators often state that a recession occurs when real GDP declines for two consecutive quarters. But this is not correct.

Actually, when a U.S. recession begins and ends is determined by a committee within the National Bureau of Economic Research, an entirely private, nonprofit research organization headquartered in Boston. (For the past few decades, the NBER's Business Cycle Dating Committee has been chaired by Robert E. Hall, a coauthor of this textbook.) The committee makes its decisions by looking at a variety of factors, including employment, industrial production, sales, and personal income, all of which are reported monthly. Even though it is true that each of these measures tends to move closely with real GDP, the latter is measured only quarterly, and plays only a supporting role in dating recessions.

**DANGEROUS CURVES**

Part of the reason for the upward shift was a 10-year tax cut that went into effect in June of 2001. While this may seem like a successful example of countercyclical fiscal policy, the timing of the 2001 tax cut was actually a stroke of luck. It had been formulated by presidential candidate Bush in 2000, as a long-run growth measure, well before there was even a hint of a recession on the horizon. Policy moves by the Federal Reserve (which we'll discuss in a later chapter) played a role in boosting consumption as well.

The increase in consumption spending made the recession of 2001 more mild than it would otherwise have been. But it was not enough to prevent the recession from occurring. The decline in investment spending, and the multiplier process it initiated, were too powerful.

## Summary

In the short run, spending depends on income, and income depends on spending. The short-run macro model was developed to explore this circular connection between spending and income.

Total spending or aggregate expenditure is the sum of four other aggregates: consumption spending by households, investment spending by firms, government purchases of goods and services, and net exports. Consumption spending (C) depends primarily on *disposable income*—what households have left over after paying taxes. The *consumption function* is a linear relationship between disposable income and consumption spending. The slope of the consumption function is the *marginal propensity to consume*, a number between zero and one. It indicates the fraction of each additional dollar of disposable income that is consumed. The *consumption–income line* is the linear relationship between consumption and income. It has the same slope as the consumption function, but a different vertical intercept. For a given level of income, consumption spending can change as a result of changes in taxes, the interest rate, wealth, or expectations about the future. Each of these changes will shift the consumption–income line.

In this chapter, investment spending ($I^p$), government purchases (G), and net exports (NX) are taken as given values, determined by forces outside our analysis. Aggregate expenditure (AE) is the sum $C + I^p + G + NX$; it varies with income because consumption spending varies with income.

*Equilibrium GDP* is the level of output at which aggregate expenditure is just equal to GDP (Y). If AE exceeds Y, then firms will experience unplanned decreases in inventories. They will respond by increasing production. If AE is less than Y, firms will find their inventories increasing and will respond by reducing production. Only when AE = Y will there be no unplanned inventory changes and no reason for firms to change production. Graphically, this occurs at the point where the aggregate expenditure line intersects the 45° line.

Changes in spending will change the economy's short-run equilibrium. An increase in investment spending, for example, shifts the aggregate expenditure line upward and triggers the multiplier process. The initial increase in investment spending causes income to increase. That, in turn, leads to an increase in consumption spending, a further increase in income, more consumption spending, and so on. The economy eventually reaches a new equilibrium with a change in GDP that is a multiple of the original increase in spending. Other spending changes have similar multiplied effects on GDP. The size of the *expenditure multiplier* is determined by the marginal propensity to consume.

There are several important differences between the short-run macro model and the long-run classical model. In the long run, the economy operates at potential output; in the short run, GDP can be above or below potential. In the short run (unlike the long run), fiscal policy can have demand-side effects. A change in G or T can change total spending and change equilibrium GDP. At one time, economists believed that *countercyclical fiscal policy* could effectively prevent or smooth out business cycles. But numerous problems—including timing difficulties, irreversibility, and neutralization by the Federal Reserve—have made economists skeptical about countercyclical fiscal policy.

## Problem Set   *Answers to even-numbered Questions and Problems can be found on the text Web site at www.thomsonedu.com/economics/hall.*

1.

| Y GDP | C | $I^p$ | G | NX |
|-------|-------|-----|-----|-----|
| 3,000 | 2,500 | 300 | 500 | 200 |
| 4,000 | 3,250 | 300 | 500 | 200 |
| 5,000 | 4,000 | 300 | 500 | 200 |
| 6,000 | 4,750 | 300 | 500 | 200 |
| 7,000 | 5,500 | 300 | 500 | 200 |
| 8,000 | 6,250 | 300 | 500 | 200 |

a. What is the marginal propensity to consume implicit in these data?

b. Plot a 45° line, and then use the data to draw an aggregate expenditure line.

c. What is the equilibrium level of real GDP? Illustrate it on your diagram.

d. Suppose that investment spending increased by 250 at each level of income. What would happen to equilibrium GDP?

Terrie Cox

2. a. Complete the following table when autonomous consumption is $30 billion, the marginal propensity to consume is 0.85, and net taxes are $0.

| Real GDP ($ billions) | Autonomous Consumption | $MPC \times$ Disposable Income | Consumption = Autonomous Consumption + ($MPC \times$ Disposable Income) |
|---|---|---|---|
| $ 0 | | | |
| $100 | | | |
| $200 | | | |
| $300 | | | |
| $400 | | | |
| $500 | | | |
| $600 | | | |

b. Use your answers in part (a) and assume planned investment is $40 billion, government spending is $20 billion, exports are $20 billion, and imports are $35 billion. Complete the table at the bottom of the page.

c. Plot a 45° line, and then use your data to draw an aggregate expenditure line.

d. What is the equilibrium level of real GDP? Illustrate it on your diagram.

e. What will happen if the actual level of real GDP in this economy is $200 billion?

f. What will happen if the planned investment in this economy falls to $25 billion?

3. 

| Y | C | $I^p$ | G | NX |
|---|---|---|---|---|
| 7,000 | 6,100 | 400 | 1,000 | 500 |
| 8,000 | 6,900 | 400 | 1,000 | 500 |
| 9,000 | 7,700 | 400 | 1,000 | 500 |
| 10,000 | 8,500 | 400 | 1,000 | 500 |
| 11,000 | 9,300 | 400 | 1,000 | 500 |
| 12,000 | 10,100 | 400 | 1,000 | 500 |
| 13,000 | 10,900 | 400 | 1,000 | 500 |

a. What is the marginal propensity to consume implicit in these data?

b. What is the numerical value of the expenditure multiplier for this economy?

c. What is the equilibrium level of real GDP?

d. Suppose that government purchases (G) decreased from 1,000 to 400 at each level of income. What would happen to equilibrium real GDP?

4. Draw a graph showing a 45° line and an aggregate expenditure line.

a. Choose a point where real GDP is less than aggregate expenditure and label it $GDP^A$. Explain what will happen to inventories if the economy is operating at this point. What signal does this send to firms? Is $GDP^A$ sustainable?

b. Choose a point where real GDP is greater than aggregate expenditure and label it $GDP^B$. Explain what will happen to inventories if the economy is operating at this point. What signal does this send to firms? Is $GDP^B$ sustainable?

5. Use an aggregate expenditure diagram to show the effect of each of the following changes:

a. An increase in autonomous consumption spending due, say, to optimism on the part of consumers

b. An increase in U.S. exports

c. A decrease in taxes

d. An increase in U.S. imports

In each case, be sure to label the initial equilibrium and the new equilibrium.

6. What would be the effect on real GDP and total employment of each of the following changes?

a. As a result of restrictions on imports into the United States, net exports (NX) increase.

b. The federal government launches a new program to improve highways, bridges, and airports.

c. Banks are offering such high interest rates that consumers decide to save a larger proportion of their incomes.

7. Assuming the MPC is 0.8, construct a table similar to Table 5 in this chapter.

a. Show what would happen in the first five rounds following an increase in investment spending from $400 billion to $800 billion.

b. If investment spending stays at $800 billion, what would be the ultimate effect on real GDP?

c. How much would consumption spending rise as a result of the rise in investment spending?

8. Suppose that households become thriftier; that is, they now wish to save a larger proportion of their disposable income and spend a smaller proportion.

a. In the table in problem 1, which column of data would be affected?

Table for 2(b)

| Real GDP ($ billions) | Consumption Spending | Planned Investment | Government Spending | Net Exports | Aggregate Expenditure |
|---|---|---|---|---|---|
| $ 0 | | | | | |
| $100 | | | | | |
| $200 | | | | | |
| $300 | | | | | |
| $400 | | | | | |
| $500 | | | | | |
| $600 | | | | | |

b. Draw an aggregate expenditure diagram and show how an increase in saving can be measured in that diagram.

c. Use your aggregate expenditure diagram to show how an economy that is initially in short-run equilibrium will respond to an increase in thriftiness.

9. Calculate the change in real GDP that would result in each of the following cases:
a. Planned investment spending rises by $100 billion, and the MPC is 0.9.
b. Autonomous consumption spending decreases by $50 billion, and the MPC is 0.7.
c. Government purchases rise by $40 billion, while at the same time investment spending falls by $10 billion. The MPC is 0.6.

10. Calculate the changes in real GDP that would result in each of the following cases:
a. Government purchases rise by $7,500, and the MPC is 0.95.
b. Planned investment spending falls by $300,000 and the MPC is 0.65.
c. Export spending rises by $60 billion at the same time that import spending rises by $65 billion, and the MPC is 0.75.

11. [Requires Appendix 2] Calculate the change in real GDP that would result in each of the following cases:
a. Taxes fall by $30 billion, and the MPC is 0.8.
b. Government spending and taxes *both* rise by $100 billion and the MPC is 0.9.

12. [Requires Appendix 2] Calculate the change in real GDP that would result in each of the following cases:
a. Taxes rise by $400,000, and the MPC is 0.75.
b. Taxes and government spending both fall by $500,000, and the MPC is 0.60.

13. Reread the last few paragraphs of the Using the Theory section. Note that the consumption–income line shifted

upward during the recession of 2001. But what happened to the aggregate expenditure line? How do we reconcile the shift in *AE* with the shift in the consumption–income line?

14. "Saving is good for the economy; it increases GDP." Is this statement true, false, or sometimes true and sometimes false? Explain your reasoning. (Hint: You've now worked with two macroeconomic models: the classical/long-run model and the short-run model of this chapter.)

## More Challenging

15. [Requires Appendix 1] Suppose that $a = 600$, $b = 0.75$, $T = 400$, $I^p = 600$, $G = 700$, and $NX = 200$. Calculate the equilibrium level of real GDP. Then check that the equilibrium value equals the sum $C + I^p + G + NX$.

16. [Requires Appendix 1] Suppose that $a = 1,000$, $b = 0.65$, $T = 700$, $I^p = 800$, $G = 600$, and $NX = -200$. Calculate the equilibrium level of real GDP. Then check that the equilibrium value equals aggregate expenditures.

17. The short-run equilibrium condition that $Y = C + I^p + G + NX$ can be reinterpreted as follows. First, subtract $C$ from both sides to get $Y - C = I^p + G + NX$. Then note that all income not spent on consumption goods is either taxed or saved, so that $Y - C = S + T$. Now combine the two equations to obtain $S + T = I^p + G + NX$.

Construct a diagram with real GDP measured on the horizontal axis. Draw two lines, one for $S + T$ and the other for $I^p + G + NX$. How would you interpret the point where the two lines cross? What would happen if investment spending increased?

18. Refer to your answer to problem 12. Will your answer to part (b) change if the MPC is 0.80, rather than 0.60? Use your finding to write a general statement about changes in government spending and taxes, and the resulting change in real GDP.

## Finding Equilibrium GDP Algebraically

The chapter showed how we can find equilibrium GDP using tables and graphs. This appendix demonstrates an algebraic way of finding the equilibrium GDP.

Our starting point is the relationship between consumption and disposable income given in the chapter. Letting $Y_D$ represent disposable income:

$$C = a + bY_D$$

where $a$ represents autonomous consumption spending and $b$ represents the marginal propensity to consume. Remember that disposable income ($Y_D$) is the income that the household sector has left after net taxes. Letting $T$ represent net taxes and $Y$ represent total income or GDP, we have

$$Y_D = Y - T.$$

If we now substitute $Y_D = Y - T$ into $C = a + bY_D$, we get an equation showing consumption at each level of income:

$$C = a + b(Y - T).$$

We can rearrange this equation algebraically to read

$$C = (a - bT) + bY.$$

This is the general equation for the consumption–income line. When graphed, the term in parentheses $(a - bT)$ is the vertical intercept, and $b$ is the slope. (Figure 3 shows a specific example of this line in which $a = \$2,000$, $b = 0.6$, and $T = \$2,000$.)

As you've learned, total spending or aggregate expenditure ($AE$) is the sum of consumption spending ($C$), investment spending ($I^p$), government spending ($G$), and net exports ($NX$):

$$AE = C + I^p + G + NX.$$

If we substitute for $C$ the expression $C = (a - bT) + bY$, we get

$$AE = a - bT + bY + I^p + G + NX.$$

Now we can use this expression to find the equilibrium GDP. Equilibrium occurs when output ($Y$) and aggregate expenditure ($AE$) are the same. That is,

$$Y = AE$$

or, substituting the equation for $AE$,

$$Y = a - bT + bY + I^p + G + NX.$$

This last equation will hold true only when $Y$ is at its equilibrium value. We can solve for equilibrium $Y$ by first bringing all terms involving $Y$ to the left-hand side:

$$Y - bY = a - bT + I^p + G + NX.$$

Next, factoring out $Y$, we get

$$Y(1 - b) = a - bT + I^p + G + NX.$$

Finally, dividing both sides of this equation by $(1 - b)$ yields

$$Y = \frac{a - bT + I^p + G + NX}{1 - b}$$

This last equation shows how equilibrium GDP depends on $a$ (autonomous consumption), $b$ (the $MPC$), $T$ (net taxes), $I^p$ (investment spending), $G$ (government purchases), and $NX$ (net exports). These variables are all determined "outside our model." That is, they are given values that we use to determine equilibrium output, but they are not themselves affected by the level of output. If we use actual numbers for these given variables in the equation, we will find the same equilibrium GDP we would find using a table or a graph.

In the example we used throughout the chapter, the given values (found in Tables 1, 2, and 4) are, in billions of dollars, $a = 2,000$; $b = 0.6$; $T = 2,000$; $I^p = 800$; $G = 1,000$; and $NX = 600$. Plugging these values into the equation for equilibrium GDP, we get

$$Y = \frac{2,000 - (0.6 \times 2,000) + 800 + 1,000 + 600}{1 - 0.6}$$

$$= \frac{3,200}{0.4}$$

$$= 8,000$$

This is the same value we found in Table 4 and Figure 7.

You learned in this chapter how changes in autonomous consumption, planned investment, and government purchases affect aggregate expenditure and equilibrium GDP. But there is another type of change that can influence equilibrium GDP: a change in taxes. For this type of change, the formula for the multiplier is slightly different from the one presented in the chapter.

Let's suppose that net taxes (*T*) *decrease* by $1,000 billion. Since disposable income is equal to total income less net taxes, the immediate impact of the tax cut is to *increase* disposable income by $1,000 billion. As a result, consumption spending will increase by MPC × $1,000 billion. Using the example in the chapter, with an MPC of 0.6, consumption spending would increase by 0.6 × $1,000 billion = $600 billion. *This is the initial rise in spending caused by the tax cut.* Once consumption spending rises, the multiplier works as with any other change in spending: Consumption rises by another 0.6 × $600 billion = $360 billion in the next round, and by another 0.6 × $360 billion = $216 billion after that, and so on.

Now let's compare the full multiplier effect from a $1,000 billion cut in net taxes with the effect from a $1,000 billion increase in spending, such as planned investment spending. Look back at Table 5. There you can see that a $1,000 billion rise in investment spending causes a total increase in GDP of $1,000 billion + $600 billion + $360 billion + $216 billion + · · · = $2,500 billion. But when taxes are cut by $1,000 billion, the total increase in GDP is $600 billion + $360 billion + $216 billion + . . . . These two series of numbers are the same except that for the tax cut, the first $1,000 billion is missing. Therefore, the final rise in GDP from the tax cut must be $1,000 billion less than the final rise in GDP from the increase in investment spending. Since the $1,000 billion rise in investment spending raises GDP by $2,500 billion, a $1,000 billion cut in taxes must raise GDP by $2,500 billion − $1,000 billion = $1,500 billion.

Another way to say this is: For each dollar that taxes are cut, equilibrium GDP will increase by $1.50 rather than $2.50; the increase is one dollar less in the case of the tax cut. This observation tells us that the tax multiplier must have a numerical value *1.0 less than* the spending multiplier of the chapter.

Finally, there is one more difference between the spending multiplier of the chapter and the tax multiplier: While the spending multiplier is a positive number (because an increase in spending causes an increase in equilibrium GDP), the tax multiplier is a negative number, since a tax cut (a negative change in taxes) must be multiplied by a *negative* number to give us a *positive* change in GDP. Putting all this together, we conclude that

> the tax multiplier is 1.0 less than the spending multiplier, and negative in sign.

Thus, if the MPC is 0.6 (as in the chapter), so that the spending multiplier is 2.5, then the tax multiplier will have a value of −(2.5 − 1) = −1.5.

More generally, since the tax multiplier is 1.0 less than the spending multiplier and is also negative, we can write

Tax multiplier = − (Spending multiplier − 1).

Because the expenditure multiplier is 1/(1 − MPC), we can substitute to get

$$\text{Tax multiplier} = -\left[\frac{1}{1-MPC} - 1\right]$$
$$= -\left[\frac{1}{1-MPC} - \frac{1-MPC}{1-MPC}\right]$$
$$= \frac{-MPC}{1-MPC}.$$

Hence,

> *the general formula for the tax multiplier is*
> $$\frac{-\text{MPC}}{(1 - \text{MPC})}.$$

For any change in net taxes, we can use the formula to find the change in net equilibrium GDP as follows:

$$\Delta GDP = \frac{-MPC}{1 - MPC} \times \Delta T.$$

In our example, in which taxes were cut by \$1,000 billion, we have $\Delta T = -\$1{,}000$ billion and $MPC = 0.6$. Plugging these values into the formula, we obtain

$$\Delta GDP = \left[\frac{-0.6}{1 - 0.6}\right] \times -\$1{,}000 \text{ billion}$$

$$= \$1{,}500 \text{ billion.}$$

# The Banking System and the Money Supply

Everyone knows that money doesn't grow on trees. But where does it actually come from? You might think that the answer is simple: The government just prints it. Right?

Sort of. It is true that much of our money supply is, indeed, paper currency, provided by our national monetary authority. But most of our money is *not* paper currency at all. Moreover, the monetary authority in the United States—the Federal Reserve System—is technically not a part of the executive, legislative, or judicial branch of government. Rather, it is a quasi-independent agency that operates *alongside* the government.

In future chapters, we'll make our short-run macro model more realistic by bringing in money and its effects on the economy. This will deepen your understanding of economic fluctuations, and help you understand our policy choices in dealing with them. But in this chapter, we focus on money itself, and the institutions that help create it. We will begin, in the next section, by taking a look at the purpose and functions of a nation's monetary system.

## THE MONETARY SYSTEM

A monetary system establishes two different types of standardization in the economy. First, it establishes a **unit of value**—a common unit for measuring how much something is worth. A standard unit of value permits us to compare the costs of different goods and services and to communicate these costs when we trade.

**Unit of value** A common unit for measuring how much something is worth.

The dollar is the unit of value in the United States. If a pair of running shoes costs $120, while a round-trip airline ticket from Phoenix to Minneapolis costs $360, we know immediately that the ticket has the same value in the marketplace as three pairs of running shoes.

The second type of standardization concerns the **means of payment**, the things we can use as payment when we buy goods and services. In the United States, the means of payment include dollar bills, personal checks, money orders, and credit cards like Visa and American Express.

**Means of payment** Anything acceptable as payment for goods and services.

These two functions of a monetary system—establishing a unit of value and a standard means of payment—are closely related, but they are not the same thing. The unit-of-value function refers to the way we *think* about and record transactions; the means-of-payment function refers to how payment is actually made. The unit of value works in the same way as units of weight, volume, distance, and time.

283

In fact, the same sentence in Article I of the U.S. Constitution gives Congress the power to create a unit of value along with units of weights and measures. All of these units help us determine clearly and precisely what is being traded for what. Think about buying gas in the United States; you exchange dollars for gallons. The transaction will go smoothly and quickly only if there is clarity about both the unit of fluid volume (gallons) *and* the unit of purchasing power (dollars).

The means of payment can be different from the unit of value. For example, in some countries where local currency prices change very rapidly, it is common to use the U.S. dollar as the unit of value—to specify prices in dollars—while the local currency remains the means of payment. Even in the United States, when you use a check to buy something, the unit of value is the dollar but the means of payment is a piece of paper with your signature on it.

In the United States, the dollar is the centerpiece of our monetary system. It is the unit of value in every economic transaction, and dollar bills are very often the means of payment as well. How did the dollar come to play such an important role in the economy?

## A BRIEF HISTORY OF THE DOLLAR

Prior to 1790, each colony had its own currency. It was named the "pound" in every colony, but it had a different purchasing power in each of them. In 1790, soon after the Constitution went into effect, Congress created a new unit of value called the dollar. Historical documents show that merchants and businesses switched immediately to the new dollar, thereby ending the chaos of the colonial monetary systems. Prices began to be quoted in dollars, and accounts were kept in dollars. The dollar rapidly became the standard unit of value.

But the primary means of payment in the United States until the Civil War was paper currency issued by private banks. Just as the government defined the length of the yard but did not sell yardsticks, the government defined the unit of value but let private organizations provide the means of payment.

**Federal Reserve System** The monetary authority of the United States, charged with creating and regulating the nation's supply of money.

During the Civil War, however, the government issued the first federal currency, the greenback. It functioned as both the unit of value and the major means of payment until 1879. Then the government got out of the business of money creation for a few decades. During that time, currency was once again issued by private banks. But in 1913, a new institution called the **Federal Reserve System** was created to be the national monetary authority in the United States. The Federal Reserve was charged with creating and regulating the nation's supply of money, and it continues to do so today.

### Why Paper Currency Is Accepted as a Means of Payment

You may wonder why people are willing to accept paper dollars—or the promise of paper dollars—as a means of payment. Why should a farmer give up a chicken, or a manufacturer give up a new car, just to receive a bunch of green rectangles with words and numbers printed on them?

In fact, paper currency is a relatively recent development in the history of the means of payment. The earliest means of payment were precious metals and other valuable commodities such as furs or jewels. These were called *commodity money* because they had important uses other than as a means of payment. The nonmoney use is what gave commodity money its ultimate value. For example, people would accept furs as payment because furs could be used to keep warm.

Similarly, gold and silver had a variety of uses in industry, as religious artifacts, and for ornamentation.

Precious metals were an especially popular form of commodity money. Eventually, to make it easier to identify the value of precious metals, they were minted into coins whose weight was declared on their faces. Because gold and silver coins could be melted down into pure metal and used in other ways, they were still commodity money.

Commodity money eventually gave way to paper currency. Initially, paper currency was just a certificate representing a certain amount of gold or silver held by a bank. At any time, the holder of a certificate could go to the bank that issued it and trade the certificate for the stated amount of gold or silver. People were willing to accept paper money as a means of payment for two reasons. First, the currency could be exchanged for a valuable commodity like gold or silver. Second, the issuer—either a government or a bank—could print new money only when it acquired additional gold or silver. This put strict limits on money printing, so people had faith that their paper money would retain its value in the marketplace.

But today, paper currency is no longer backed by gold or any other physical commodity. If you have a dollar handy, put this book down and take a close look at the bill. You will not find on it any promise that you can trade your dollar for gold, silver, furs, or anything else. Yet we all accept it as a means of payment. Why?

A clue is provided by the statement in the upper left-hand corner of every bill: *This note is legal tender for all debts, public and private.* The statement affirms that the piece of paper in your hands will be accepted as a means of payment (you can "tender" it to settle any "debt, public or private") by any American because the government says so. This type of currency is called **fiat money**. *Fiat*, in Latin, means "let there be," and fiat money serves as a means of payment by government declaration.

**Fiat money** Something that serves as a means of payment by government declaration.

The government need not worry about enforcing this declaration. The real force behind the dollar—and the reason that we are all willing to accept these green pieces of paper as payment—is its long-standing acceptability by *others*. As long as you have confidence that you can use your dollars to buy goods and services, you won't mind giving up goods and services for dollars. And because everyone else feels the same way, the circle of acceptability is completed. But while the government can declare that paper currency is to be accepted as a means of payment, it cannot declare the terms. Whether a gallon of gas will cost you 1 dollar, 4 dollars, or 10 dollars is up to the marketplace.

## WHAT COUNTS AS MONEY

Consider what *is* and what is *not* thought to be money in countries around the world. For example, paper currency, travelers checks, and funds held in checking accounts are all considered to be money in nations with well-established banking systems. That makes sense, because all of these can be used as means of payment. Yet credit cards are *not* considered money, even though you can use them to buy things. Why is this?

A more formal definition of money helps to answer questions like this.

> **Money** *is an asset that is widely accepted as a means of payment in the economy.*

**Money** An asset widely accepted as a means of payment.

Let's consider this definition more closely. First, only *assets*—things of value that people own—can be considered as money. Paper currency, travelers checks, and funds held in checking accounts are all examples of assets that people own, and these are all considered money in the United States. But *the right to borrow* is not an asset, so is not considered money. This is why the credit limit on your credit card, or your ability to go into a bank and borrow funds, is not considered *money* in the economy.

Second, only things that are *widely acceptable* as a means of payment are regarded as money. Coins and paper currency (usually called *cash*), travelers checks, and personal checks can all be used to buy things or pay bills. Other assets—such as stocks and bonds or even gold bars—can*not* generally be used to pay for goods and services, and so they fail the acceptability test.

## MEASURING THE MONEY SUPPLY

**Money supply** The total amount of money held by the public.

As you will learn in the next chapter, the amount of money in circulation can affect the macroeconomy. This is why governments around the world like to know how much money is available to their citizens—the total **money supply.**

In practice, measuring the money supply is not as straightforward as it might seem, and brings up some conceptual problems. For example, consider funds you might have in a savings account. While you can't use those funds to buy things directly, you can easily *move* the funds *into* your checking account, converting them to money. You might therefore regard your savings account as part of the means of payment that are easily available to you. Should they be included as part of the money supply?

Governments recognize this and other similar sticky questions, and have decided that the best way to deal with them is to have *different* measures of the money supply—in effect, alternative ways of defining what is and what is not money. Each measure includes a selection of *assets* that are *widely acceptable as a means of payment* and, as an additional criterion, *relatively liquid.*

**Liquidity** The property of being easily converted into cash.

> An asset is considered **liquid** if it can be converted to cash quickly and at little cost. An illiquid asset, by contrast, can be converted to cash only after a delay, or at considerable cost.

Checking account balances are highly liquid because you can convert them to cash at the ATM or by cashing a check. Travelers checks are also highly liquid. But stocks and bonds are *not* as liquid as checking accounts or travelers checks. Stock- and bondholders must go to some trouble and pay brokers' fees to convert these assets into cash.

But notice the phrase "*relatively* liquid." This does not sound like a hard-and-fast rule for measuring the money supply, and indeed it is not. This is why there are different measures of the money supply: Each interprets the phrase "relatively liquid" in a different way. To understand this better, let's look at the different kinds of liquid assets that people can hold.

### ASSETS AND THEIR LIQUIDITY

Figure 1 lists a spectrum of assets, ranked according to their liquidity, along with the amounts of each asset in the U.S. public's hands on June 26, 2006. The most

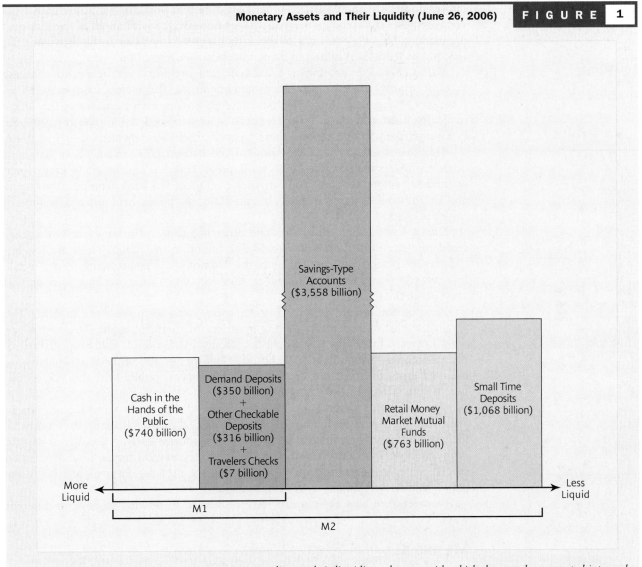

**Monetary Assets and Their Liquidity (June 26, 2006)** FIGURE 1

Savings-Type
Accounts
($3,558 billion)

Cash in the
Hands of the
Public
($740 billion)

Demand Deposits
($350 billion)
+
Other Checkable
Deposits
($316 billion)
+
Travelers Checks
($7 billion)

Retail Money
Market Mutual
Funds
($763 billion)

Small Time
Deposits
($1,068 billion)

More
Liquid

Less
Liquid

M1

M2

*Assets vary according to their liquidity—the ease with which they can be converted into cash.
Assets toward the left side of this figure are more liquid than those toward the right side.*

Source: http://www.federalreserve.gov, *Money Stock Measures.* H.6, Tables 5 and 6.

liquid asset of all is **cash in the hands of the public.** It takes no time and zero expense to convert this asset into cash, since it's *already* cash. In June 2006, the public—including residents of other countries—held about $740 billion in U.S. cash.

Next in line are three asset categories of about equal liquidity. **Demand deposits** are the checking accounts held by households and business firms at commercial banks, including huge ones like the Bank of America or Citibank, and smaller ones like Simmons National Bank in Arkansas. These checking accounts are called "demand" deposits because when you write a check to someone, that person can go into a bank and, on demand, be paid in cash. This is one reason that demand deposits are considered very liquid: The person who has your check can convert it

**Cash in the hands of the public** Currency and coins held outside of banks.

**Demand deposits** Checking accounts that do not pay interest.

into cash quickly and easily. Another reason is that you can withdraw cash from your own checking account very easily—24 hours a day with an ATM card, or during banking hours if you want to speak to a teller. As you can see in the figure, the U.S. public held $350 billion in demand deposits in mid-2006.

*Other checkable deposits* is a catchall category for several types of checking accounts that work very much like demand deposits. This includes *automatic transfers from savings accounts*, which are interest-paying savings accounts that automatically transfer funds into checking accounts when needed. On June 26, 2006, the U.S. public held $316 billion of these types of checkable deposits.

*Travelers checks* are specially printed checks that you can buy from banks or other private companies, like American Express. Travelers checks can be easily spent at almost any hotel or store. You can often cash them at a bank. You need only show an I.D. and countersign the check. In mid-2006, the public held about $7 billion in travelers checks.

*Savings-type accounts* at banks and other financial institutions (such as *savings and loan* institutions) amounted to $3,558 billion in mid-2006. These are less liquid than checking-type accounts, since they do not allow you to write checks. While it is easy to transfer funds from your savings account to your checking account, you must make the transfer yourself.

Next on the list are deposits in *retail money market mutual funds (MMMFs)*, which use customer deposits to buy a variety of financial assets. Depositors can withdraw their money by writing checks. Money market funds held in special retirement accounts—which cannot be accessed before age $59\frac{1}{2}$ without a penalty—are excluded from this measure. In mid-2006, the general public held about $763 billion in such MMMFs.

*Time deposits* (sometimes called *certificates of deposit*, or *CDs*) require you to keep your money in the bank for a specified period of time (usually six months or longer), and impose an interest penalty if you withdraw early. A *small time deposit* is any amount less than $100,000. As with money market funds, time deposits in special retirement accounts are excluded from the measure. In mid-June 2006, the public held $1,068 billion in these accounts.

Now let's see how these assets have been used to define "money" in different ways.

## M1 and M2

**M1** A standard measure of the money supply, including cash in the hands of the public, checking account deposits, and travelers checks.

The standard measure of the money stock is called **M1**. It is the sum of the first four assets in our list: cash in the hands of the public, demand deposits, other checkable deposits, and travelers checks. These are also the four most liquid assets in our list.

$$M1 = \text{Cash in the hands of the public} + \text{Demand deposits} + \\ \text{Other checkable deposits} + \text{Travelers checks}.$$

On June 26, 2006, this amounted to

$$M1 = \$740 \text{ billion} + \$350 \text{ billion} + \$316 \text{ billion} \\ + \$7 \text{ billion} = \$1{,}413 \text{ billion}.$$

When economists or government officials speak about "the money supply," they usually mean M1.

But what about the assets left out of M1? While savings accounts are not as liquid as any of the components of M1, for most of us there is hardly a difference.

All it takes is an ATM card and, presto, funds in your savings account become cash. Money market funds held by households and businesses are fairly liquid, even though there are sometimes restrictions or special risks involved in converting them into cash. And even time deposits—if they are not too large—can be cashed in early with only a small interest penalty. When you think of how much "means of payment" you have, you are very likely to include the amounts you have in these types of accounts. This is why another common measure of the money supply, **M2**, adds these assets to M1:

**M2** M1 plus savings account balances, retail money market mutual fund balances, and small time deposits.

$$M2 = M1 + \text{Savings-type accounts} + \text{Retail MMMF balances} +$$
$$\text{Small-denomination time deposits.}$$

Using the numbers for June 26, 2006, in the United States:

$$M2 = \$1,413 \text{ billion} + \$3,558 \text{ billion} + \$763 \text{ billion} + \$1,068 \text{ billion}$$
$$= \$6,802 \text{ billion.}$$

There have been other official measures of the money supply besides M1 and M2 that include assets that are less liquid than those in M2. But M1 and M2 have been the most popular, and most commonly watched, definitions.

It is important to understand that the M1 and M2 money stock measures exclude many things that people use regularly as a means of payment. Although M1 and M2 give us important information about the activities of the Fed and of banks, they do not measure all the different ways that people hold their wealth or pay for things. Credit cards, for example, are not included in any of the official measures of the money supply (they are not assets). But for most of us, unused credit *is* a means of payment, which we lump together with our cash and our checking accounts. As credit cards were issued to more and more Americans over the last several decades, the available means of payment increased considerably, much more than the money supply (as measured by M1 and M2) increased.

**Cash in Private Banks or the Fed** In our definitions of money—whether M1, M2, or some other measure—we include cash (coin and paper currency) only if it is *in the hands of the public*. The italicized words are important. Some of the nation's cash is stored in bank vaults and is released only when the public withdraws cash from their accounts. Other cash is stored in the Federal Reserve or U.S. Treasury for future release. But until this cash is released from bank vaults, the Fed, or the Treasury, it is not part of the money supply. Only the cash possessed by households, businesses, or government agencies (other than the Fed or Treasury) is considered part of the money supply.

DANGEROUS CURVES

Fortunately, the details and complexities of measuring money are not important for a basic understanding of the monetary system and monetary policy. For the rest of our discussion, we will make a simplifying assumption:

*We will assume the money supply consists of just two components: cash in the hands of the public and checkable deposits, which we'll call demand deposits.*

*Money supply = Cash in the hands of the public + Demand deposits.*

As you will see later, our definition of the money supply corresponds closely to the liquid assets that our national monetary authority—the Federal Reserve—can control. While there is not much that the Federal Reserve can do directly about the amount of funds in savings accounts, MMMFs, or time deposits, or about the ability to borrow on credit cards, it can tightly control the sum of cash in the hands of the public and demand deposits.

We will spend the rest of this chapter analyzing how money is created and what makes the money supply change. Our first step is to introduce a key player in the creation of money: the banking system.


## THE BANKING SYSTEM

Think about the last time you used the services of a bank. Perhaps you deposited a paycheck in the bank's ATM, or withdrew cash to take care of your shopping needs for the week. We make these kinds of transactions dozens of times every year without ever thinking about what a bank really is, or how our own actions at the bank—and the actions of millions of other bank customers—might contribute to a change in the money supply.

### FINANCIAL INTERMEDIARIES IN GENERAL

**Financial intermediary** A business firm that specializes in brokering between savers and borrowers.

Let's begin at the beginning: What are banks? They are important examples of **financial intermediaries**: business firms that specialize in assembling loanable funds from households and firms whose revenues exceed their expenditures, and channeling those funds to households and firms (and sometimes the government) whose expenditures exceed revenues. Financial intermediaries make the economy work much more efficiently than would be possible without them.

To understand this more clearly, imagine that Boeing, the U.S. aircraft maker, wants to borrow a billion dollars for 3 years. If there were no financial intermediaries, Boeing would have to make individual arrangements to borrow small amounts of money from thousands—perhaps millions—of households, each of which wants to lend money for, say, 3 months at a time. Every 3 months, Boeing would have to renegotiate the loans, and it would find borrowing money in this way to be quite cumbersome. Lenders, too, would find this arrangement troublesome. All of their funds would be lent to one firm. If that firm encountered difficulties, the funds might not be returned at the end of 3 months.

An intermediary helps to solve these problems by combining a large number of small savers' funds into custom-designed packages and then lending them to larger borrowers. The intermediary can do this because it can predict—from experience—the pattern of inflows of funds. While some deposited funds may be withdrawn, the overall total available for lending tends to be quite stable. The intermediary can also reduce the risk to depositors by spreading its loans among a number of different borrowers. If one borrower fails to repay its loan, that will have only a small effect on the intermediary and its depositors.

Of course, intermediaries must earn a profit for providing brokering services. They do so by charging a higher interest rate on the funds they lend than the rate they pay to depositors. But they are so efficient at brokering that both lenders and borrowers benefit. Lenders earn higher interest rates, with lower risk and greater liquidity, than if they had to deal directly with the ultimate users of funds. And borrowers end up paying lower interest rates on loans that are specially designed for their specific purposes.

The United States boasts a wide variety of financial intermediaries, including commercial banks, savings and loan associations, mutual savings banks, credit unions, insurance companies, and some government agencies. Some of these inter-mediaries—called *depository institutions*—accept deposits from the general public and lend the deposits to borrowers. *Commercial banks* are the largest group of depository institutions. They obtain funds mainly by accepting checkable deposits, savings deposits, and time deposits and use the funds to make business, mortgage, and consumer loans. Since commercial banks will play a central role in the rest of this chapter, let's take a closer look at how they operate.

## COMMERCIAL BANKS

A commercial bank (or just "bank" for short) is a private corporation, owned by its stockholders, that provides services to the public. For our purposes, the most impor-tant service is to provide checking accounts, which enable the bank's customers to pay bills and make purchases without holding large amounts of cash that could be lost or stolen. Checks are one of the most important means of payment in the economy. Every year, U.S. households and businesses write trillions of dollars' worth of checks to pay their bills, and many wage and salary earners have their pay deposited direct-ly into their checking accounts. And as you saw in Figure 1, the public holds about as much money in the form of demand deposits and other checking-type accounts as it holds in cash.

Banks provide checking account services in order to earn a profit. Where does a bank's profit come from? Mostly from lending out the funds that people deposit and charging interest on the loans, but also by charging for some services directly, such as check-printing fees or that annoying dollar or so sometimes charged for using an ATM.

## A BANK'S BALANCE SHEET

We can understand more clearly how a bank works by looking at its *balance sheet*, a tool used by accountants. A **balance sheet** is a two-column list that provides infor-mation about the financial condition of a bank at a particular point in time. In one column, the bank's *assets* are listed—everything of value that it *owns*. On the other side, the bank's *liabilities* are listed—the amounts that the bank *owes*.

**Balance sheet** A financial state-ment showing assets, liabilities, and net worth at a point in time.

Table 1 shows a simplified version of a commercial bank's balance sheet.

| Assets | | Liabilities and Net Worth | |
|---|---|---|---|
| Property and buildings | $ 5 million | Demand deposit liabilities | $100 million |
| Government and corporate bonds | $ 25 million | Net worth | $ 5 million |
| Loans | $ 65 million | | |
| Cash in vault | $ 2 million | | |
| In accounts with the Federal Reserve | $ 8 million | | |
| **Total Assets** | $105 million | **Total Liabilities plus Net Worth** | $105 million |

**TABLE 1**

**A Typical Commercial Bank's Balance Sheet**

**Bond** A promise to pay back borrowed funds, issued by a corporation or government agency.

**Loan** An agreement to pay back borrowed funds, signed by a household or noncorporate business.

Why does the bank have these assets and liabilities? Let's start with the assets side. The first item, $5 million, is the value of the bank's real estate—the buildings and the land underneath them. This is the easiest to explain, because a bank must have one or more branch offices in order to do business with the public.

Next comes $25 million in *bonds*, and $65 million in *loans*. A **bond** is a promise to pay funds to the holder of the bond, issued by a corporation or a government agency when it borrows money.[1] A bond promises to pay back the loan either gradually (e.g., each month), or all at once at some future date. **Loans** are promises, signed by households or noncorporate businesses, to pay back funds. Examples are auto loans, student loans, small-business loans, and home mortgages (where the funds lent out are used to buy a home). Both bonds and loans generate interest income for the bank.

Next come two categories that might seem curious: $2 million in "vault cash," and $8 million in "accounts with the Federal Reserve." Vault cash, just like it sounds, is the coin and currency that the bank has stored in its vault. In addition, banks maintain their own accounts with the Federal Reserve, and they add to and subtract from these accounts when they make transactions with other banks. Neither vault cash nor accounts with the Federal Reserve pay interest. Why, then, does the bank hold them? After all, a profit-seeking bank should want to hold as much of its assets as possible in interest-earning forms: bonds and loans.

There are two explanations for vault cash and accounts with the Federal Reserve. First, on any given day, some of the bank's customers might want to withdraw more cash than other customers are depositing. The bank must always be prepared to honor its obligations for withdrawals, so it must have some cash on hand to meet these requirements. This explains why it holds vault cash.

**Reserves** Vault cash plus balances held at the Fed.

**Required reserves** The minimum amount of reserves a bank must hold, depending on the amount of its deposit liabilities.

**Required reserve ratio** The minimum fraction of checking account balances that banks must hold as reserves.

Second, banks are required by law to hold **reserves,** which are defined as *the sum of cash in the vault and accounts with the Federal Reserve*. The amount of reserves a bank must hold is called **required reserves.** The more funds its customers hold in their checking accounts, the greater the amount of required reserves. The **required reserve ratio,** set by the Federal Reserve, tells banks the fraction of their checking accounts that they must hold as required reserves.

For example, the bank in Table 1 has $100 million in demand deposits. If the required reserve ratio is 0.1, this bank's required reserves are $0.1 \times \$100$ million = $10 million in reserves. The bank must hold *at least* this amount of its assets as reserves. Since our bank has $2 million in vault cash and $8 million in its reserve account with the Federal Reserve, it has a total of $10 million in reserves, the minimum required amount.

Now skip to the right side of the balance sheet. This bank's only liability is its demand deposits. Why are demand deposits a *liability*? Because the bank's customers have the right to withdraw funds from their checking accounts. Until they do, the bank *owes* them these funds.

Finally, the last entry. When we total up both sides of the bank's balance sheet, we find that it has $105 million in assets and only $100 million in liabilities. If the bank were to go out of business—selling all of its assets and using the proceeds to pay off all of its liabilities (its demand deposits)—it would have $5 million left over.

---

[1] We are using the term "bond" loosely to refer to *all* such promises issued by corporations and government agencies. Technically, a bond must be a long-term obligation to pay back money, 10 years or more from the time the money is first borrowed. Shorter-term obligations are called *notes* (between 1 and 10 years) or *bills* (1 year or less).

Who would get this $5 million? The bank's owners: its stockholders. The $5 million is called the bank's **net worth.** More generally,

$$\text{Net worth} = \text{Total assets} - \text{Total liabilities.}$$

We include net worth on the liabilities side of the balance sheet because it is, in a sense, what the bank would owe to its owners if it went out of business. Notice that, because of the way net worth is defined, both sides of a balance sheet must always have the same total: *A balance sheet always balances.*

Private banks are just one of the players that help determine the money supply. Now we turn our attention to the other key player—the Federal Reserve System.

**Net worth** The difference between assets and liabilities.

## THE FEDERAL RESERVE SYSTEM

Every large nation controls its money supply with a **central bank**—the nation's principal monetary authority and the institution responsible for controlling its money supply. Most of the developed countries established their central banks long ago. For example, England's central bank—the Bank of England—was created in 1694. France was one of the latest in Europe, waiting until 1800 to establish the Banque de France. But the United States was even later. Although we experimented with central banks at various times in our history, we did not get serious about a central bank until 1913, when Congress established the *Federal Reserve System.*

Why did it take the United States so long to create a central bank? Part of the reason is the suspicion of central authority that has always been part of U.S. politics and

**Central bank** A nation's principal monetary authority responsible for controlling the money supply.

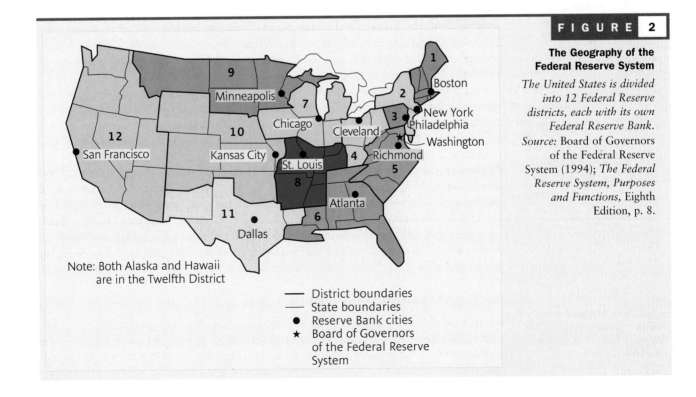

**FIGURE 2**

**The Geography of the Federal Reserve System**

*The United States is divided into 12 Federal Reserve districts, each with its own Federal Reserve Bank.*

*Source:* Board of Governors of the Federal Reserve System (1994); *The Federal Reserve System, Purposes and Functions,* Eighth Edition, p. 8.

Note: Both Alaska and Hawaii are in the Twelfth District

— District boundaries
— State boundaries
● Reserve Bank cities
★ Board of Governors of the Federal Reserve System

*The Federal Open Market Committee meets in this room, inside the Fed's headquarters in Washington, D.C. The meetings are highly secretive. No one from the media, and no one representing Congress or the president, is permitted in the room during the meetings.*

culture. Another reason is the large size and extreme diversity of our country, and the fear that a powerful central bank might be dominated by the interests of one region to the detriment of others. These special American characteristics help explain why our own central bank is different in form from its European counterparts.

One major difference is indicated in the very name of the institution: the Federal Reserve System. It does not have the word *central* or *bank* anywhere in its title, making it less suggestive of centralized power.

Another difference is the way the system is organized. Instead of a single central bank, the United States is divided into 12 Federal Reserve districts, each one served by its own Federal Reserve Bank. The 12 districts and the Federal Reserve Banks that serve them are shown in Figure 2. For example, the Federal Reserve Bank of Dallas serves a district consisting of Texas and parts of New Mexico and Louisiana, while the Federal Reserve Bank of Chicago serves a district including Iowa and parts of Illinois, Indiana, Wisconsin, and Michigan.

Another interesting feature of the Federal Reserve System is its peculiar status within the government. Strictly speaking, it is not even a *part* of any branch of government. But the *Fed* (as the system is commonly called) was created by Congress, and could be eliminated by Congress if it so desired. Second, both the president and Congress exert some influence on the Fed through their appointments of key officials in the system.

## THE STRUCTURE OF THE FED

Figure 3 shows the organizational structure of the Federal Reserve System. Near the top is the Board of Governors, consisting of seven members who are appointed by the president and confirmed by the Senate for a 14-year term. The most powerful person at the Fed is the *chairman* of the Board of Governors—one of the seven governors who is appointed by the president, with Senate approval, to a 4-year term as chair. In order to keep any president or Congress from having too much influence over the Fed, the 4-year term of the chair is *not* coterminous with the 4-year term of the president. As a result, every newly elected president inherits the Fed chair appointed by the previous president, and may have to wait several years before making an appointment of his own.

Each of the 12 Federal Reserve Banks is supervised by nine directors, three of whom are appointed by the Board of Governors. The other six are elected by private commercial banks, the official stockholders of the system. The directors of each Federal Reserve Bank choose a president of that bank, who manages its day-to-day operations.

Notice that Figure 3 refers to "member banks." Only about a third of the approximately 7,500 commercial banks in the United States are members of the Federal Reserve System. But they include all *national banks* (those chartered by the federal government) and about a thousand *state banks* (chartered by their state governments). All of the largest banks in the United States (e.g., Citibank, Bank of America, and Wells Fargo) are nationally chartered banks and therefore member banks as well.

### The Federal Open Market Committee

**Federal Open Market Committee (FOMC)** A committee of Federal Reserve officials that establishes U.S. monetary policy.

Finally, we come to what most economists regard as the most important part of the Fed, the **Federal Open Market Committee (FOMC)**. As you can see in Figure 3, the FOMC consists of all seven governors of the Fed, along with 5 of the 12 district

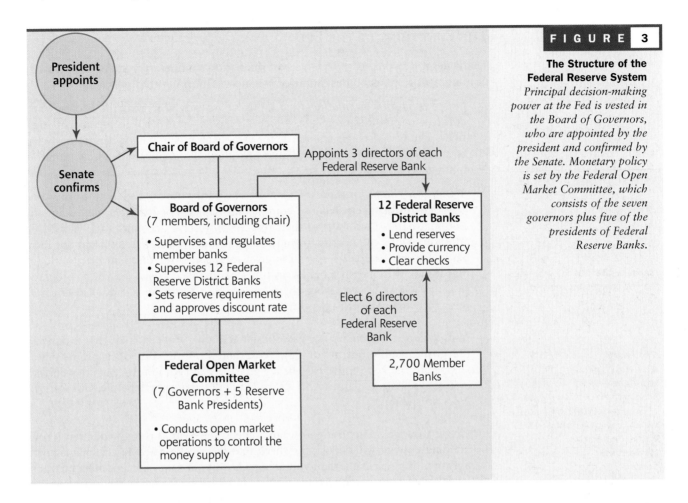

**FIGURE 3**

**The Structure of the Federal Reserve System**
*Principal decision-making power at the Fed is vested in the Board of Governors, who are appointed by the president and confirmed by the Senate. Monetary policy is set by the Federal Open Market Committee, which consists of the seven governors plus five of the presidents of Federal Reserve Banks.*

bank presidents.[2] The committee meets about eight times a year to discuss current trends in inflation, unemployment, output, interest rates, and international exchange rates. After determining the current state of the economy, the FOMC sets the general course for the nation's money supply.

The word "open" in the FOMC's name is ironic, since the committee's deliberations are private. Summaries of its meetings are published only after a delay of a month or more. In some cases, the committee will release a brief public statement about its decisions on the day they are made. But not even the president of the United States knows the details behind the decisions, or what the FOMC actually discussed at its meeting, until the summary of the meeting is finally released. The reason for the word "open" is that the committee exerts control over the nation's money supply by buying and selling bonds in the public ("open") bond market. Later, we will discuss how and why the FOMC does this.

---

[2] Although all Reserve Bank presidents attend FOMC meetings, only 5 of the 12 presidents can vote on FOMC decisions. The president of the Federal Reserve Bank of New York has a permanent vote because New York is such an important financial center. But the remaining four votes rotate among the other district presidents.

## THE FUNCTIONS OF THE FED

The Federal Reserve, as the overseer of the nation's monetary system, has a variety of important responsibilities. Some of the most important are listed here.

*Supervising and Regulating Banks.* We've already seen that the Fed sets and enforces reserve requirements, which all banks—not just Fed members—must obey. The Fed also sets standards for establishing new banks, determines what sorts of loans and investments banks are allowed to make, and closely monitors many banks' financial activities.

*Acting as a "Bank for Banks."* Commercial banks use the Fed in much the same way that ordinary citizens use commercial banks. For example, we've already seen that banks hold most of their reserves in reserve accounts with the Fed. In addition, banks can borrow from the Fed, just as we can borrow from our local bank. The Fed charges a special interest rate, called the discount rate, on loans that it makes to member banks. In times of financial crisis, the Fed is prepared to act as lender of last resort, to make sure that banks have enough reserves to meet their obligations to depositors.

**Discount rate** The interest rate the Fed charges on loans to banks.

*Issuing Paper Currency.* The Fed doesn't actually *print* currency; that is done by the government's Bureau of Engraving and Printing. But once printed, it is shipped to the Fed (under *very* heavy guard). The Fed, in turn, puts this currency into circulation. This is why every U.S. bill carries the label *Federal Reserve Note* on the top.

*Check Clearing.* Suppose you write a check for $1,000 to pay your rent. Your building's owner will deposit the check into *his* checking account, which is probably at a different bank than yours. Somehow, your rent payment must be transferred from your bank account to your landlord's account at the other bank, a process called *check clearing.* In some cases, the services are provided by private clearinghouses. But in many other cases—especially for clearing out-of-town checks—the Federal Reserve System performs the service by transferring funds from one bank's reserve account to another's.

*Controlling the Money Supply* The Fed, as the nation's monetary authority, is responsible for controlling the money supply. Since this function is so important in macroeconomics, we explore it in detail in the next section.

## THE FED AND THE MONEY SUPPLY

Suppose the Fed wants to change the nation's money supply. (*Why* would the Fed want to do this? The answer will have to wait until the next chapter.) There are many ways this could be done. To increase the money supply, the Fed could print up currency and give it to Fed officials, letting them spend it as they wish. Or it could hold a lottery and give all of the newly printed money to the winner. To decrease the money supply, the Fed could require that all citizens turn over a portion of their cash to Fed officials who would then feed it into paper shredders.

These and other methods would certainly work, but they hardly seem fair or orderly. In practice, the Fed uses a more organized, less haphazard method to change the money supply: *open market operations.*

> *When the Fed wishes to increase or decrease the money supply, it buys or sells* government bonds *to bond dealers, banks, or other financial institutions. These actions are called* **open market operations.**

**Open market operations**
Purchases or sales of bonds by the Federal Reserve System.

We'll make two special assumptions to keep our analysis of open market operations simple for now:

1. Households and businesses are satisfied holding the amount of cash they are currently holding. Any additional funds they might acquire are deposited in their checking accounts. Any decrease in their funds comes from their checking accounts.
2. Banks never hold reserves in excess of those legally required by law.

Later, we'll discuss what happens when these simplifying assumptions do not hold. We'll also assume that the required reserve ratio is 0.1, so that each time deposits rise by $1,000 at a bank, its required reserves rise by $100.

## HOW THE FED INCREASES THE MONEY SUPPLY

To increase the money supply, the Fed will *buy* government bonds. This is called an *open market purchase.* Suppose the Fed buys a government bond worth $1,000 from Lehman Brothers, a bond dealer that has a checking account at First National Bank.[3] The Fed will pay Lehman Brothers with a $1,000 check, which the firm will deposit into its account at First National. First National, in turn, will send the check to the Fed, which will credit First National's reserve account by $1,000.

These actions will change First National's balance sheet as follows:

**CHANGES IN FIRST NATIONAL BANK'S BALANCE SHEET**

| Action | Changes in Assets | Changes in Liabilities |
|---|---|---|
| Fed buys $1,000 bond from Lehman Brothers, which deposits $1,000 check from Fed into its checking account. | +$1,000 in reserves | +$1,000 in demand deposits |

Notice that here we show only *changes* in First National's balance sheet. Other balance sheet items—such as property and buildings, loans, government bonds, or net worth—are not immediately affected by the open market purchase, so they are not listed here. As you can see, First National gains an asset—reserves—so we enter "+$1,000 in reserves" on the left side of the table. But there are also additional liabilities: the $1,000 that is now in Lehman Brothers' checking account and which First National owes to that firm. The additional liabilities are represented by the entry "+$1,000 in demand deposits" on the right side. Since First National's balance sheet was in balance before Lehman Brothers' deposit, and since assets and liabilities both grew by the same amount ($1,000), we know that the balance sheet is still in balance. Total assets are again equal to total liabilities plus net worth.

Before we go on, let's take note of two important things that have happened. First, the Fed, by conducting an open market purchase, has injected *reserves* into the banking system. So far, these reserves are being held by First National in its reserve account with the Fed.

---

[3] We'll limit our analysis to commercial banks, which hold demand deposits, although our story would be similar if other types of depository institutions were involved.

The second thing to notice is something that is easy to miss: *The money supply has increased.* How do we know? Because demand deposits are part of the money supply, and they have increased by $1,000. As you are about to see, even more demand deposits will be created before our story ends.

To see what will happen next, let's take the point of view of First National Bank's manager. He might reason as follows: "My demand deposits have just increased by $1,000. Since the required reserve ratio is 0.1, I must now hold $0.1 \times \$1,000 = \$100$ in additional reserves. But my *actual* reserves have gone up by more than $100; in fact, they have gone up by $1,000. Therefore, I have **excess reserves**—reserves above those I'm legally required to hold—equal to $1,000 − $100, or $900. Since these excess reserves are earning no interest, I should lend them out." Thus, we can expect First National, in its search for profit, to lend out $900 at the going rate of interest.

**Excess reserves** Reserves in excess of required reserves.

How will First National actually make the loan? It could lend out $900 in *cash* from its vault. It would be more typical, however, for the bank to issue a $900 *check* to the borrower. When the borrower deposits the $900 check into his own bank account (at some other bank), the Federal Reserve—which keeps track of these transactions for the banking system—will deduct $900 from First National's reserve account and transfer it to the other bank's reserve account. This will cause a further change in First National's balance sheet, as follows:

**CHANGES IN FIRST NATIONAL BANK'S BALANCE SHEET**

| Action | Changes in Assets | Changes in Liabilities |
|---|---|---|
| Fed buys $1,000 bond from Lehman Brothers, which deposits $1,000 check from Fed into its checking account. | +$1,000 in reserves | +$1,000 in demand deposits |
| First National lends out $900 in excess reserves. | −$900 in reserves +$900 in loans | |
| Total effect on First National from beginning to end. | +$100 in reserves +$900 in loans | +$1,000 in demand deposits |

Look at the highlighted entries in the table. By making the loan, First National has given up an asset: $900 in reserves. This causes assets to change by −$900. But First National also gains an asset of equal value—the $900 loan. (Remember: While loans are liabilities to the borrower, they are assets to banks.) This causes assets to change by +$900. Both of these changes are seen on the assets side of the balance sheet.

Now look at the bottom row of the table. This tells us what has happened to First National from beginning to end. We see that, after making its loan, First National has $100 more in reserves than it started with, and $900 more in loans, for a total of $1,000 more in assets. But it also has $1,000 more in liabilities than it had before: the additional demand deposits that it owes to Lehman Brothers. Both assets and liabilities have gone up by the same amount. Notice, too, that First National is once again holding exactly the reserves it must legally hold. It now has $1,000 more in demand deposits than it had before, and it is holding $0.1 \times \$1,000 = \$100$ more in reserves than before. First National is finished ("loaned up") and cannot lend out any more reserves.

But there is still more to our story. Let's suppose that First National lends the $900 to the owner of a local business, Paula's Pizza, and Paula deposits her loan check into *her* bank account at Second United Bank. The Fed will transfer $900 in reserves from First National's reserve account to that of Second United. Second United's balance sheet will change as follows:

### CHANGES IN SECOND UNITED'S BALANCE SHEET

| Action | Changes in Assets | Changes in Liabilities |
|---|---|---|
| Paula deposits $900 loan check into her checking account. | + $900 in reserves | + $900 in demand deposits |

Second United now has $900 more in assets—the increase in its reserve account with the Federal Reserve—and $900 in additional liabilities—the amount added to Paula's checking account.

Now consider Second United's situation from its manager's viewpoint. He reasons as follows: "My demand deposits have risen by $900, which means my required reserves have risen by $0.1 \times \$900 = \$90$. But my reserves have *actually* increased by $900. Thus, I have *excess reserves* of $\$900 - \$90 = \$810$, which I will lend out." After making the $810 loan, Second United's balance sheet will change once again (look at the highlighted entries):

### CHANGES IN SECOND UNITED'S BALANCE SHEET

| Action | Changes in Assets | Changes in Liabilities |
|---|---|---|
| Paula deposits $900 loan check into her checking account. | +$900 in reserves | +$900 in demand deposits |
| Second United lends out $810 in excess reserves. | − $810 in reserves<br>+ $810 in loans | |
| Total effect on Second United from beginning to end. | + $ 90 in reserves<br>+ $810 in loans | + $900 in demand deposits |

In the end, as you can see in the bottom row of the table, Second United has $90 more in reserves than it started with, and $810 more in loans. Its demand deposit liabilities have increased by $900. The money supply has increased once again—this time, by $900.

Are you starting to see a pattern? Let's carry it through one more step. Whoever borrowed $810 from Second United will put it into his or her checking account at, say, Third State Bank. This will give Third State excess reserves that it will lend out. Its balance sheet will change as follows:

### CHANGES IN THIRD STATE'S BALANCE SHEET

| Action | Changes in Assets | Changes in Liabilities |
|---|---|---|
| Borrower from Second United deposits $810 loan check into checking account. | + $810 in reserves | +$810 in demand deposits |
| Third State lends out $729 in excess reserves. | − $729 in reserves<br>+ $729 in loans | |
| Total effect on Third State from beginning to end. | + $ 81 in reserves<br>+ $729 in loans | +$810 in demand deposits |

As you can see, demand deposits increase each time a bank lends out excess reserves. In the end, they will increase by a *multiple* of the original $1,000 in reserves injected into the banking system by the open market purchase. Does this process sound familiar? It should. It is very similar to the explanation of the *expenditure multiplier* in the previous chapter, where in each round, an increase in spending led to an increase in income, which caused spending to increase again in the next round. Here, instead of spending, it is the *money supply*—or more specifically, *demand deposits*—that increase in each round.

## THE DEMAND DEPOSIT MULTIPLIER

By how much will demand deposits increase in total? If you look back at the balance sheet changes we've analyzed, you'll see that each bank creates less in demand deposits than the bank before. When Lehman Brothers deposited its $1,000 check from the Fed at First National, $1,000 in demand deposits was created. This led to an additional $900 in demand deposits created by Second United, another $810 created by Third State, and so on. In each round, a bank lent 90 percent of the deposit it received. Eventually the additional demand deposits will become so small that we can safely ignore them. When the process is complete, how much in additional demand deposits has been created?

Table 2 provides the answer. Each row of the table shows the additional demand deposits created at each bank, as well as the running total. The last row shows that, in the end, $10,000 in new demand deposits has been created.

Let's go back and summarize what happened in our example. The Fed, through its open market purchase, injected $1,000 of reserves into the banking system. As a result, demand deposits rose by $10,000—10 times the injection in reserves. As you can verify, if the Fed had injected twice this amount of reserves ($2,000), demand deposits would have increased by 10 times *that* amount ($20,000). In fact, *whatever* the injection of reserves, demand deposits will increase by a factor of 10, so we can write

$$\Delta DD = 10 \times \text{Reserve injection}$$

| TABLE 2 | Round | Additional Demand Deposits Created by Each Bank | Additional Demand Deposits Created by *All* Banks |
|---|---|---|---|
| **Cumulative Increases in Demand Deposits After a $1,000 Open Market Purchase** | First National Bank | $1,000 | $1,000 |
| | Second United | $ 900 | $1,900 |
| | Third State | $ 810 | $2,710 |
| | Bank 4 | $ 729 | $3,439 |
| | Bank 5 | $ 656 | $4,095 |
| | Bank 6 | $ 590 | $4,685 |
| | . . . | | |
| | Bank 10 | $ 387 | $6,511 |
| | . . . | | |
| | Bank 20 | $ 135 | $8,784 |
| | . . . | | |
| | Bank 50 | very close to zero | very close to $10,000 |

where *DD* stands for demand deposits. The injection of reserves must be *multiplied by* the number 10 in order to get the change in demand deposits that it causes. For this reason, 10 is called the **demand deposit multiplier** in this example.

The size of the demand deposit multiplier depends on the value of the required reserve ratio set by the Fed. If you look back at Table 2, you will see that each round of additional deposit creation would have been smaller if the required reserve ratio had been larger. For example, with a required reserve ratio of 0.2 instead of 0.1, Second United would have created only $800 in deposits, Third State would have created only $640, and so on. The result would have been a smaller cumulative change in deposits, and a smaller multiplier.

There is a very simple formula we can use to determine the value of the demand deposit multiplier for *any* value of the required reserve ratio:

> *For any value of the required reserve ratio (RRR), the formula for the demand deposit multiplier is 1/RRR.*

In our example, the *RRR* was equal to 0.1, so the demand deposit multiplier had the value 1/0.1 = 10. If the *RRR* had been 0.2 instead, the demand deposit multiplier would have been equal to 1/0.2 = 5. To see how this formula is derived, read this footnote.[4]

Using our general formula for the demand deposit multiplier, we can restate what happens when the Fed injects reserves into the banking system as follows:

$$\Delta DD = \left(\frac{1}{RRR}\right) \times \Delta\text{Reserves}.$$

This formula tells us the change in demand deposits. But because we've been assuming that the amount of cash in the hands of the public (the other component of the money supply) does not change, we can also write

$$\Delta DD = \Delta\text{Money supply} = \left(\frac{1}{RRR}\right) \times \Delta\text{Reserves}.$$

**Demand deposit multiplier** The number by which a change in reserves is multiplied to determine the resulting change in demand deposits.

[4] To derive the formula for the demand-deposit multiplier, let's start with our numerical example, in which the change in demand deposits ($\Delta DD$) is

$$\Delta DD = (\$1,000 + \$900 + \$810 + \$729 + \cdots).$$

Factoring out $1,000 gives us

$$\Delta DD = \$1,000 \times (1 + 0.9 + 0.81 + 0.729 + \cdots)$$
$$= \$1,000 \times (1 + 0.9 + 0.9^2 + 0.9^3 + \cdots).$$

In this example, $1,000 is the initial injection of reserves, and 0.9 is the fraction of its new reserves that each bank lends out, which is 1 *minus* the required reserve ratio. Generalizing this for *any* change in reserves ($\Delta$Reserves) or *any* required reserve ratio (*RRR*), we have

$$\Delta DD = \Delta\text{Reserves} \times [1 + (1-RRR) + (1-RRR)^2 + (1-RRR)^3 + \cdots].$$

Now we use a rule from the mathematics of infinite sums (such as the sum in brackets): For any value of $H$ between 0 and 1, the infinite sum $1 + H + H^2 + H^3 + \cdots$ has the value $1/(1-H)$.

Replacing $H$ with the value $1 - RRR$ (which is between 0 and 1), we get

$$\Delta DD = \Delta\text{Reserves} \times \{1/[1-(1-RRR)]\}$$

or

$$\Delta DD = \Delta\text{Reserves} \times (1/RRR).$$

## THE FED'S INFLUENCE ON THE BANKING SYSTEM AS A WHOLE

We can also look at what happened to total demand deposits and the money supply from another perspective. When the Fed bought the $1,000 bond from Lehman Brothers, it injected $1,000 of reserves into the banking system. That was the only increase in reserves that occurred in our story. Where did the additional $1,000 in reserves end up? If you go back through the changes in balance sheets, you'll see that First National ended up with $100 in additional reserves, Second United ended up with $90, Third Savings with $81, and so on. Each of these banks is required to hold more reserves than initially, because its demand deposits have increased. In the end, *the additional $1,000 in reserves will be distributed among different banks in the system as required reserves.*

> *After an injection of reserves, the demand deposit multiplier stops working—and the money supply stops increasing—only when all the reserves injected are being held by banks as* required *reserves.*

This observation helps us understand the demand deposit multiplier in another way. In our example, the deposit-creation process will continue until the entire injection of $1,000 in reserves becomes *required* reserves. But with an *RRR* of 0.1, each dollar of reserves entitles a bank to have $10 in demand deposits. Therefore, by injecting $1,000 of reserves into the system, the Fed has enabled banks, in total, to hold $10,000 in additional demand deposits. Only when $10,000 in deposits has been created will the process come to an end.

**"Creating Money" Doesn't Mean "Creating Wealth"** Demand deposits are a means of payment, and banks create them. This is why we say that banks "create deposits" and "create money." But don't fall into the trap of thinking that banks create wealth. No one gains any additional wealth as a direct result of money creation.

To see why, think about what happened in our story when Lehman Brothers deposited the $1,000 check from the Fed into its account at First National. *Lehman Brothers* was no wealthier: It gave up a $1,000 check from the Fed and ended up with $1,000 more in its checking account, for a net gain of zero. Similarly, the *bank* gained no additional wealth: It had $1,000 more in cash, but it also *owed* Lehman Brothers $1,000—once again, a net gain of zero.

The same conclusion holds for any other step in the money-creation process. When Paula borrows $900 and deposits it into her checking account at Second United, she is no wealthier: She has $900 more in her account, but owes $900 to First National. And once again, the bank is no wealthier: It has $900 more in demand deposits, but owes this money to Paula.

Always remember that when banks "create money," they do not create wealth.

Just as we've looked at balance sheet changes for each bank, we can also look at the change in the balance sheet of the *entire banking system*. The Fed's open market purchase of $1,000 has caused the following changes:

### CHANGES IN THE BALANCE SHEET OF THE ENTIRE BANKING SYSTEM

| Changes in Assets | Changes in Liabilities |
|---|---|
| + $1,000 in reserves<br>+ $9,000 in loans | + $10,000 in demand deposits |

In the end, total reserves in the system have increased by $1,000—the amount of the open market purchase. Each dollar in reserves supports $10 in demand deposits, so we know that total deposits have increased by $10,000. Finally, we know that a balance sheet always balances. Because liabilities increased by $10,000, loans must have increased by $9,000 to increase total assets (loans and reserves) by $10,000.

## HOW THE FED DECREASES THE MONEY SUPPLY

Just as the Fed can increase the money supply by purchasing government bonds, it can also *decrease* the money supply by *selling* government bonds—an *open market sale*.

Where does the Fed get the government bonds to sell? It has trillions of dollars' worth of government bonds from open market *purchases* it has conducted in the past. Since, on average, the Fed tends to increase the money supply each year, it conducts more open market purchases than open market sales, and its bond holdings keep growing. So we needn't worry that the Fed will run out of bonds to sell.

Suppose the Fed sells a $1,000 government bond to a bond dealer, Merrill Lynch, which—like Lehman Brothers in our earlier example—has a checking account at First National Bank. Merrill Lynch pays the Fed for the bond with a $1,000 check drawn on its account at First National. When the Fed gets Merrill Lynch's check, it will present the check to First National and deduct $1,000 from First National's reserve account. In turn, First National will deduct $1,000 from Merrill Lynch's checking account.

After all of this has taken place, First National's balance sheet will show the following changes:

### CHANGES IN FIRST NATIONAL BANK'S BALANCE SHEET

| Action | Changes in Assets | Changes in Liabilities |
|---|---|---|
| Fed sells $1,000 bond to Merrill Lynch, which pays with a $1,000 check drawn on First National. | −$1,000 in reserves | −$1,000 in demand deposits |

Now First National has a problem. Since its demand deposits have decreased by $1,000, it can legally decrease its reserves by 10 percent of that, or $100. But its reserves have *actually* decreased by $1,000, which is $900 more than they are allowed to decrease. First National has *deficient reserves*—reserves smaller than those it is legally required to hold. How can it get the additional reserves it needs?

First National will have to *call in a loan* (ask for repayment) in the amount of $900.[5] A loan is usually repaid with a check drawn on some other bank. When First National gets this check, the Federal Reserve will add $900 to its reserve account, and deduct $900 from the reserve account at the other bank. This is how First National brings its reserves up to the legal requirement. After it calls in the $900 loan, First National's balance sheet will change as follows:

---

[5] In reality, bank loans are for specified time periods, and a bank cannot actually demand that a loan be repaid early. But most banks have a large volume of loans outstanding, with some being repaid each day. Typically, the funds will be lent out again the very same day they are repaid. A bank that needs additional reserves will simply reduce its rate of new lending on that day, thereby reducing its total amount of loans outstanding. This has the same effect as "calling in a loan."

**CHANGES IN FIRST NATIONAL BANK'S BALANCE SHEET**

| Action | Changes in Assets | Changes in Liabilities |
|---|---|---|
| Fed sells $1,000 bond to Merrill Lynch, which pays with a $1,000 check drawn on First National. | − $1,000 in reserves | − $1,000 in demand deposits |
| First National calls in loans worth $900. | + $ 900 in reserves<br>− $ 900 in loans | |
| Total effect on First National from beginning to end. | − $ 100 in reserves<br>− $ 900 in loans | − $1,000 in demand deposits |

Look at the highlighted terms. After First National calls in the loan, the composition of its assets will change: $900 more in reserves and $900 less in loans. The last row of the table shows the changes to First National's balance sheet from beginning to end. Compared to its initial situation, First National has $100 less in reserves (it lost $1,000 and then gained $900), $900 less in loans, and $1,000 less in demand deposits.

As you might guess, this is not the end of the story. Remember that whoever paid back the loan to First National did so by a check drawn on another bank. That other bank, which we'll assume is Second United Bank, will lose $900 in reserves and experience the following changes in its balance sheet:

**CHANGES IN SECOND UNITED BANK'S BALANCE SHEET**

| Action | Changes in Assets | Changes in Liabilities |
|---|---|---|
| Someone with an account at Second United Bank writes a $900 check to First National. | −$900 in reserves | −$900 in demand deposits |

Now Second United Bank is in the same fix that First National was in. Its demand deposits have decreased by $900, so its reserves can legally fall by $90. However, its actual reserves have decreased by $900, which is $810 too much. Now it is Second United's turn to call in a loan. (On your own, fill in the rest of the changes in Second United Bank's balance sheet as it successfully brings its reserves up to the legal requirement.)

As you can see, the process of calling in loans will involve many banks. Each time a bank calls in a loan, demand deposits are destroyed—the same amount as were created in our earlier story, in which each bank *made* a new loan. The total decline in demand deposits will be a multiple of the initial withdrawal of reserves. Keeping in mind that a withdrawal of reserves is a *negative change in reserves*, we can still use our demand deposit multiplier—$1/RRR$—and our general formula:

$$\Delta DD = \left(\frac{1}{RRR}\right) \times \Delta \text{Reserves}.$$

Applying it to our example, we have

$$\Delta DD = \left(\frac{1}{0.1}\right) \times (-\$1,000) = -\$10,000.$$

In words, the Fed's $1,000 open market sale causes a $10,000 decrease in demand deposits. Since we assume that the public's cash holdings do not change, the money supply decreases by $10,000 as well.

To the banking system as a whole, the Fed's bond sale has done the following:

**CHANGES IN BALANCE SHEET FOR THE ENTIRE BANKING SYSTEM**

| Changes in Assets | Changes in Liabilities |
|---|---|
| −$1,000 in reserves<br>−$9,000 in loans | −$10,000 in demand deposits |

## SOME IMPORTANT PROVISOS ABOUT THE DEMAND DEPOSIT MULTIPLIER

Although the process of money creation and destruction as we've described it illustrates the basic ideas, our formula for the demand deposit multiplier—$1/RRR$—is oversimplified. In reality, the multiplier is likely to be smaller than our formula suggests, for two reasons.

First, we've assumed that as the money supply changes, the public does *not* change its holdings of cash. But in reality, as the money supply increases, the public typically will want to hold part of the increase as demand deposits and part of the increase as cash. As a result, in each round of the deposit-creation process, some reserves will be *withdrawn* in the form of cash. This will lead to a smaller increase in demand deposits than in our story.

Second, we've assumed that banks will always lend out all of their excess reserves. In reality, banks often *want* to hold excess reserves, for a variety of reasons. For example, they may want some flexibility to increase their loans in case interest rates—their reward for lending—rise in the near future. Or they may prefer not to lend the maximum legal amount during a recession, because borrowers are more likely to declare bankruptcy and not repay their loans. If banks increase their holdings of excess reserves as the money supply expands, they will make smaller loans than in our story, and in each round, demand deposit creation will be smaller.

**Selling Bonds: Fed versus Treasury** In this section, you learned how the Fed sells government bonds to decrease the money supply. It's easy to confuse this with another type of government bond sale, which is done by the U.S. Treasury.

The U.S. Treasury is the branch of government that collects tax revenue, disburses money for government purchases and transfer payments, and borrows money to finance any government budget deficit. The Treasury borrows funds by issuing *new* government bonds and *selling* them to the public—to banks, other financial institutions, and bond dealers. What the public pays for these bonds is what they are lending the government.

When the Fed conducts open market operations, however, it does not buy or sell *newly* issued bonds, but "secondhand bonds"—those already issued by the Treasury to finance past deficits. Thus, open market sales are *not* government borrowing; they are strictly an operation designed to change the money supply, and they have no direct effect on the government budget.

DANGEROUS CURVES

## OTHER TOOLS FOR CONTROLLING THE MONEY SUPPLY

Open market operations are the Fed's primary means of controlling the money supply. But there are two other tools that the Fed can use to increase or decrease the money supply.

- *Changes in the required reserve ratio.* In principle, the Fed can set off the process of deposit creation, similar to that described earlier, by lowering the required reserve ratio. Look back at Table 1, which showed the balance sheet of a bank facing a required reserve ratio of 0.1 and holding exactly the amount of reserves required by law—$10 million. Now suppose the Fed lowered the required reserve ratio to 0.05. Suddenly, the bank would find that its required reserves were only $5 million; the other $5 million in reserves it holds would become excess reserves. To earn the highest profit possible, the bank would increase its lending by $5 million. At the same time, all other banks in the country would find that some of their formerly required reserves were now excess reserves, and they would increase their lending. The money supply would increase.

On the other hand, if the Fed *raised* the required reserve ratio, the process would work in reverse: All banks would suddenly have reserve deficiencies and be forced to call in loans. The money supply would decrease.

- *Changes in the discount rate.* The discount rate, mentioned earlier, is the rate the Fed charges banks when it lends them reserves. In principle, a lower discount rate, by enabling banks to borrow reserves from the Fed more cheaply, might encourage banks to borrow more. An increase in borrowed reserves works just like any other injection of reserves into the banking system: It increases the money supply.

On the other side, a *rise* in the discount rate would make it more expensive for banks to borrow from the Fed, and decrease the amount of borrowed reserves in the system. This withdrawal of reserves from the banking system would lead to a decrease in the money supply.

Changes in either the required reserve ratio or the discount rate *could* set off the process of deposit creation or deposit destruction in much the same way as is outlined in this chapter. In reality, neither of these policy tools is used very often. The most recent change in the required reserve ratio was in April 1992, when the Fed lowered the required reserve ratio for most demand deposits from 12 percent to 10 percent. Changes in the discount rate are more frequent, but it is not unusual for the Fed to leave the discount rate unchanged for a year or more.

Why are these other tools used so seldom?

First, frequent changes in the required reserve ratio could create problems for the banking industry. Remember that banks earn their revenue by lending out deposits for interest, and that deposits held as reserves pay no interest at all. A rise in the required reserve ratio would immediately require banks to convert interest-earning funds to non-interest earning funds, decreasing their revenue and profits. A drop in the required reserve ratio would have the opposite effect. Thus, if the Fed relied on frequent changes in the required reserve ratio, bank profits would be more unstable.

Changes in the discount rate are problematic for a different reason. Traditionally, bank managers have preferred *not* to borrow reserves from the Fed, since it would put them under closer Fed scrutiny. And in the past, the Fed discouraged banks from borrowing reserves from it, unless the bank was in difficulty. Thus, a small change in the discount rate was unlikely to have much of an impact on bank borrowing of reserves, and therefore on the money supply.

In January 2003, however, the Fed changed its discount policy, and began to *encourage* banks to borrow. It established two different discount rates—one for banks in excellent financial condition and another, higher rate for banks considered more at risk. Banks in sound condition could borrow freely at the lower rate without Fed scrutiny. As a result, the discount rate may become a more effective, and more frequently used, policy tool in the future.

Still, open market operations will almost certainly remain the Fed's *principal* tool for controlling the money supply. The main reason is that they are so efficient in accomplishing the Fed's goals. Open market operations, unlike the other tools, can be adjusted frequently—even minute-by-minute. They enable the Fed to use trial and error—buying or selling bonds and then observing the effects—to fine-tune the money supply to any desired level.

# USING THE THEORY

## Bank Failures and Banking Panics

A bank becomes *insolvent* when its total assets are less than its total liabilities (or, equivalently, when its net worth becomes negative). When an insolvent bank goes out of business—usually after a regulatory agency steps in—we say that the bank has *failed*. What causes a bank to become insolvent? The most frequent reason is the bankruptcies of businesses and households that have borrowed money from the bank.

Table 3 shows how such bankruptcies would affect a bank's balance sheet. The original (black-type) entries in the table are taken from the balance sheet in Table 1. Initially, the bank has $65 million in loans that appear on the assets side. These loans—as long as the bank expects them to be repaid—are something of value that the bank owns. Notice that the bank begins with a positive net worth of $5 million. If the bank's owners decided to cease operations and sell off all of the bank's assets and pay off all of its liabilities, the $5 million in net worth would be left, and would go to the bank's owners.

Now suppose that the bank gets some bad news: $15 million of its loans will never be paid back because the businesses and households that owed the money have declared bankruptcy. As a result, $15 million in loans must be "written off" of the balance sheet; they are now worthless to the bank. The new (red-type) entries show how the balance sheet will change. On the left side, outstanding loans are reduced from $65 million to $50 million, so total assets decrease from

| Assets | | Liabilities and Net Worth | | TABLE 3 |
|---|---|---|---|---|
| | | | | **How Borrower Bankruptcies Affect a Bank's Balance Sheet** |
| Property and buildings | $5 million | Demand deposit liabilities | $100 million | |
| Government and corporate bonds | $25 million | Net worth | ~~$5 million~~ −$10 million | |
| Loans | ~~$65 million~~ $50 million | | | |
| Reserves | $10 million | | | |
| **Total Assets** | ~~$105 million~~ $90 million | **Total Liabilities plus Net Worth** | ~~$105 million~~ $90 million | |

© BETTMANN/CORBIS

$105 million to $90 million. On the right side, the bank continues to owe the same $100 million to its depositors. The only change is the bank's net worth. Subtracting the bank's liabilities ($100 million) from its assets (now $90 million), net worth has become negative, equal to −$10 million. At this point, even if the bank were to sell all of its assets to other banks, it would not have enough funds to honor all of its liabilities. The bank is *insolvent*.

What will happen?

In the old days, before the banking system was regulated and strict financial reporting was enforced, an insolvent bank could continue to operate for some time. That's because on any given day only a small fraction of its checking account balances would be withdrawn. So as long as the bank had enough cash on hand to meet normal requests for withdrawals, its day of reckoning could be postponed.

Until, that is, word of the bank's insolvency leaked out. At that point, all of the depositors would want to be first in line to withdraw their funds. They would know that banks meet requests for withdrawals on a first-come, first-served basis, and those who wait might not get any cash at all. We call this situation—in which all depositors try to withdraw their funds at once—a **run on the bank.**

Ironically, even a bank in good financial health, with more than enough assets to cover its liabilities, could find itself in trouble from a run on the bank. As you've seen in this chapter, even a solvent bank does not keep enough reserves on hand to cover all of its demand deposit liabilities. Unless it could sell all of its assets quickly and get the cash needed to honor withdrawals, it would have to close its doors and refuse (at least for a while) some of its customers' requests. Thus, a mere *rumor* of insolvency could force a bank to close. And the bank's closure would likely add fuel to the rumors that the bank was in trouble.

A **banking panic** occurs when a run on many banks occurs simultaneously. In the past, a typical panic would begin with some unexpected event, such as the failure of a large bank. During recessions, for example, many businesses go bankrupt, so fewer bank loans are repaid. A bank that had an unusual number of "bad loans" would be in trouble, and if the public found out about this, there might be a run on that bank. The bank would fail, and many depositors would find that they had lost their deposits.

But that would not be the end of the story. Hearing that their neighbors' banks were short of cash might lead others to question the health of their own banks. Just to be sure, they might withdraw their own funds, preferring to ride out the storm and keep their cash at home. As we've seen, even healthy banks cannot withstand the pressure of a bank run. They, too, would have to close their doors, stoking the rumor mill even more, and so on.

Banking panics can cause serious problems for the nation. First, there is the hardship suffered by people who lose their accounts when their bank fails. Second, the withdrawal of cash decreases the banking system's reserves. As we've seen, the withdrawal of reserves leads—through the demand deposit multiplier—to a larger decrease in the money supply. In the next chapter, you will learn that a decrease in the money supply can cause a recession. In a banking panic, the money supply can decrease suddenly and severely, causing a serious recession.

There were five major banking panics in the United States from 1863 to 1907. Indeed, it was the banking panic of 1907 that convinced Congress to establish the Federal Reserve System. From the beginning, one of the Fed's primary functions was to act as a lender of last resort, providing banks with enough cash to meet their obligations to depositors.

**Run on the bank** An attempt by many of a bank's depositors to withdraw their funds.

**Banking panic** A situation in which depositors attempt to withdraw funds from many banks simultaneously.

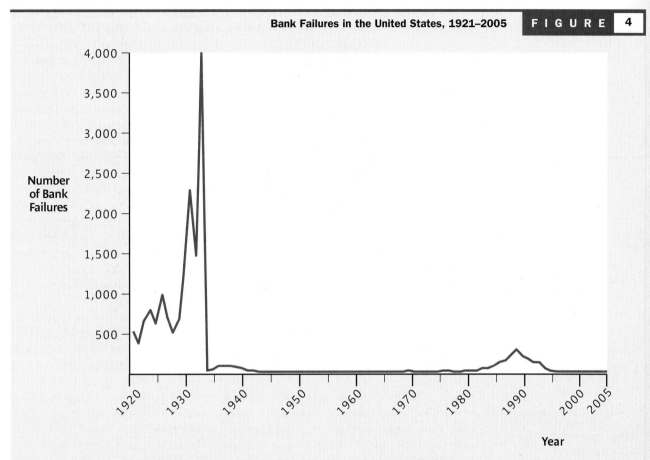

**Bank Failures in the United States, 1921–2005**   F I G U R E   4

*Bank failures continued after the Fed was created in 1913. During the Great Depression, a large number of banks failed. The creation of the Federal Deposit Insurance Corporation in 1933 strengthened faith in the stability of the banking system. Few banks have failed since that time.*

But the creation of the Fed did not, in itself, solve the problem. Figure 4 shows the number of bank failures each year since 1921. As you can see, banking panics continued to plague the financial system even after the Fed was created. The Fed did not always act forcefully enough or quickly enough to prevent the panic from spreading.

The Great Depression is a good example of this problem. In late 1929 and 1930, many banks began to fail because of bad loans. Then, from October 1930 until March 1933, more than one-third of all banks shut down as frantic depositors stormed bank after bank, demanding to withdraw their funds—even from banks that were in reasonable financial health. Many economists believe that the banking panic of 1930–1933 turned what would have been just a serious recession into the Great Depression. Officials of the Federal Reserve System, not quite grasping the seriousness of the problem, stood by and let it happen.[6]

[6] Milton Friedman and Anna Jacobson Schwartz, *A Monetary History of the United States, 1867–1960* (Princeton, NJ: Princeton University Press, 1963), especially p. 358.

As you can see in Figure 4, banking panics were largely eliminated after 1933. There was a moderate increase in failures during the late 1980s and early 1990s (more on this a bit later). But otherwise, the system has been almost failure free. In fact, for the six-year period ending in June 2006, a total of 24 banks failed—an average of just 4 per year. Why the dramatic improvement?

Largely for two reasons. First, the Federal Reserve learned an important lesson from the Great Depression, and it now stands ready to inject reserves into the system more quickly in a crisis. Moreover, in 1933 Congress created the Federal Deposit Insurance Corporation (FDIC) to reimburse those who lose their deposits. If your bank is insured by the FDIC (today, accounts are covered in 99 percent of all banks) and cannot honor its obligations for any reason—bad loans, poor management, or even theft—the FDIC will reimburse you up to the first $100,000 you lose in each of your bank accounts.[7]

The FDIC has had a major impact on the psychology of the banking public. Imagine that you hear your bank is about to go under. As long as you have less than $100,000 in your account, you will not care. Why? Because even if the rumor turns out to be true, you will be reimbursed in full. The resulting calmness on your part, and on the part of other depositors, will prevent a run on the bank. This makes it very unlikely that bank failures will spread throughout the system.

FDIC protection for bank accounts has not been costless. Banks must pay insurance premiums to the FDIC, and they pass this cost on to their depositors and borrowers by charging higher interest rates on loans and higher fees for their services. And there is a more serious cost. If you are thoroughly protected in the event of a bank failure, your bank's managers have little incentive to develop a reputation for prudence in lending funds, since you will be happy to deposit your money there anyway. Without government regulations, banks could act irresponsibly, taking great risks with your money, and you would remain indifferent. Many more banks would fail, the FDIC would have to pay off more depositors, and banks—and their customers—would bear the burden of higher FDIC premiums.

This is the logic behind the Fed's continuing regulation of bank lending. Someone must watch over the banks to keep the failure rate low. If the public has no incentive to pay attention, the Fed must do so. Most economists believe that if we want the freedom from banking panics provided by the FDIC, we must also accept the strict regulation and close monitoring of banks provided by the Fed and other agencies.

Look again at Figure 4 and notice the temporary rise in bank failures of the late 1980s and the early 1990s. Most of these failures occurred in state-chartered banks. These banks are less closely regulated by the Fed, and are often insured by state agencies instead of the FDIC. When a few banks went bankrupt because highly speculative loans turned sour, insurance funds in several states were drained. Citizens in those states began to fear that insufficient funds were left to insure their own deposits, and the psychology of banking panics took over. To many observers, the experience of the late 1980s and early 1990s was a reminder of the need for a sound insurance system and close monitoring of the banking system.

---

[7] If you are fortunate enough to be worried about this limit, keep in mind that it applies to each *account*, not to each household or individual. Anyone can protect more than $100,000 by creating multiple accounts. And in mid-2006, Congress was considering raising the limit to $200,000. The current limits and other relevant facts can be found at *www.fdic.gov/deposit/deposits/insuringdeposits/index.html*.

# Summary

A nation's monetary system provides two important functions. First, it creates a *unit of value* that helps us compare the costs of different goods and services. Second, it provides for a generally acceptable *means of payment*. In the United States, the unit of value is the dollar, and the means of payment includes paper currency, checking accounts, travelers checks, and credit cards.

Money is an asset that is also widely accepted as a means of payment. In the United States, the standard measure of money—M1—includes currency, checking account balances, and travelers checks. Each of these assets is liquid and widely acceptable as a means of payment. Other, broader measures go beyond M1 to include funds in savings accounts and other deposits.

The amount of money circulating in the economy is controlled by the Federal Reserve, operating through the banking system. Banks and other financial intermediaries are profit-seeking firms that collect loanable funds from households and businesses; then they repackage them to make loans to other households, businesses, and governmental agencies.

The Federal Reserve injects money into the economy by altering banks' balance sheets. In a balance sheet, assets always equal liabilities plus net worth. One important kind of asset is *reserves*—funds that banks are required to hold in proportion to their demand deposit liabilities. When the Fed wants to increase the money supply, it buys bonds in the open market and pays for them with a check. This is called an *open market purchase*. When the Fed's check is deposited in a bank, the bank's balance sheet changes. On the asset side, reserves increase; on the liabilities side, demand deposits (a form of money) also increase. The bank can lend some of the reserves, and the funds lent out will end up in some other banks where they support creation of still more demand deposits. Eventually, demand deposits, and the M1 money supply, increase by some multiple of the original injection of reserves by the Fed. The *demand deposit multiplier*, the inverse of the required reserve ratio, gives us that multiple.

The Fed can decrease the money supply by selling government bonds—an *open market sale*—causing demand deposits to shrink by a multiple of the initial reduction in reserves. The Fed can also change the money supply by changing either the required reserve ratio or the discount rate it charges when it lends reserves to banks. These tools are used much less frequently than open market operations.

# Problem Set     *Answers to even-numbered Questions and Problems can be found on the text Web site at www.thomsonedu.com/economics/hall.*

1. Suppose the required reserve ratio is 0.2. If an extra $20 billion in reserves is injected into the banking system through an open market purchase of bonds, by how much can demand deposits increase? Would your answer be different if the required reserve ratio were 0.1?

2. If the Fed buys $50 million of government securities, by how much can the money supply increase if the required reserve ratio is 0.15? How will your answer be different if the required reserve ratio is 0.18?

3. Which of the following is considered part of the U.S. money supply? (Use the M1 measures.)
   a. A $10 bill you carry in your wallet
   b. A $100 travelers check you bought but did not use
   c. A $100 bill in a bank's vault
   d. The $325.43 balance in your checking account
   e. A share of General Motors stock worth $40

4. Given the following data (in billions of dollars), calculate the value of the M1 money supply and the value of the M2 money supply.

   | | |
   |---|---:|
   | Bank reserves | 50 |
   | Cash in the hands of the public | 400 |
   | Demand deposits | 400 |
   | Retail MMMF balances | 880 |
   | Other checkable deposits | 250 |
   | Savings-type account balances | 1,300 |
   | Small time deposits | 950 |
   | Travelers checks | 10 |

5. Suppose bank reserves are $100 billion, the required reserve ratio is 0.2, and excess reserves are zero. Calculate how many dollars, worth of demand deposits are being supported. Now suppose that the required reserve ratio is lowered to 0.1 and that banks once again become fully "loaned up" with no excess reserves. What is the new level of demand deposits?

6. Suppose bank reserves are $200 billion, the required reserve ratio is 0.2, and excess reserves are zero. Calculate how many dollars, worth of demand deposits are being supported. If the Fed wants to decrease demand deposits by $50 billion by changing the required reserve ratio, what new required reserve ratio should it set?

7. Suppose that the money supply is $1 trillion. Decision makers at the Federal Reserve decide that they wish to use open market operations to reduce the money supply by $100 billion, or by 10 percent. If the required reserve ratio is 0.05, what does the Fed need to do to carry out the planned reduction?

8. Suppose that the money supply is $3.2 trillion. Decision makers at the Federal Reserve decide that they wish to use open market operation to increase the money supply by $500 billion. If the required reserve ratio is 0.10, what does the Fed need to do to carry out the planned increase? What if the required reserve ratio is 0.15?

9. For each of the following situations, determine whether the money supply will increase, decrease, or stay the same.

a. Depositors become concerned about the safety of depository institutions.

b. The Fed lowers the required reserve ratio.

c. The economy enters a recession and banks have a hard time finding creditworthy borrowers.

d. The Fed sells $100 million of bonds to First National Bank of Ames, Iowa.

10. Suppose that the Fed decides to increase the money supply. It purchases a government bond worth $1,000 from a private citizen. He deposits the check in his account at First National Bank, as in the chapter example. But now, suppose that the required reserve ratio is 0.2, rather than 0.1 as in the chapter.

a. Trace the effect of this change through three banks—First National, Second United, and Third State. Show the changes to each bank's balance sheet as a result of the Fed's action.

b. By how much does the money supply change in each of these first three rounds?

c. What will be the ultimate change in demand deposits in the entire banking system?

11. Suppose accountants at the bank whose balance sheet is depicted in Table 1 discover that they've made an error: Cash in vault is only $1 million, not $2 million.

a. Which other entries in the bank's balance sheet will change as a consequence of correcting this error?

b. If the required reserve ratio is 0.10, does this bank now have excess reserves or deficient reserves? Of what value?

12. Assume that the Fed wants to keep the size of the money supply constant by adjusting the required reserve ratio only. How will it have to adjust the required reserve ratio to achieve this goal if

a. People decide to hold more of their money as cash rather than as demand deposits?

b. Bankers decide to decrease their holdings of excess reserves?

13. Suppose a bank has the following entries on its balance sheet: $20 million in property and buildings; $200 million in government bonds; $300 million in loans; $5 million cash in vault; $95 million in accounts with the Federal Reserve; $550 million in demand deposit liabilities. There are no other entries on the balance sheet except for net worth.

a. What is this bank's net worth?

b. What is the maximum value of the bank's loans that could be "written off" due to bankruptcies before the bank would become insolvent?

## More Challenging

14. Sometimes banks wish to hold reserves in excess of the legal minimum. Suppose the Fed makes an open market purchase of $100,000 in government bonds. The required reserve ratio is 0.1, but each bank decides to hold additional reserves equal to 5 percent of its new deposits.

a. Trace the effect of the open market purchase of bonds through the first three banks in the money expansion process. Show the changes to each bank's balance sheet.

b. Derive the demand deposit multiplier in this case. Is it larger or smaller than when banks hold no excess reserves?

c. What is the ultimate change in demand deposits in the entire banking system?

15. Suppose the Fed buys $100,000 in government bonds from Jonathan, and that the required reserve ratio is 0.1. Assume that Jonathan and each additional depositor always hold half of their money as cash.

a. Trace the effect of this open market purchase through the first three banks in the money expansion process. Show the changes to each bank's balance sheet.

b. Derive the demand deposit multiplier in this case. How does it compare with the demand deposit multiplier when depositors hold no cash?

c. What is the ultimate change in demand deposits in the entire banking system?

# The Money Market and Monetary Policy

Which of the following two newspaper headlines might you see in your daily paper?

1. "Motorists Fear Department of Energy Will Raise Gasoline Prices"
2. "Wall Street Expects Fed to Raise Interest Rates"

You probably know the answer: The first headline is entirely unrealistic. The Department of Energy, the government agency that makes energy policy, has no authority to set prices in any market. The Federal Reserve, by contrast, has full authority to influence the interest rate—the price of borrowing money. And it exercises this authority every day. This is why headlines such as the second one appear in newspapers so often.

In this chapter, you will learn how the Fed, through its control of the money supply, also controls the interest rate and uses it to influence real GDP.

## THE DEMAND FOR MONEY

Reread the title of this section. Does it appear strange to you? Don't people always want as much money as possible?

Indeed, they do. But when we speak about the *demand* for something, we don't mean the amount that people would desire if they could have all they wanted, without having to sacrifice anything for it. Instead, economic decision makers always face constraints: They must sacrifice one thing in order to have more of another. Thus, the *demand for money* does not mean how much money people would *like* to have in the best of all possible worlds. Rather, it means *how much money people would like to hold, given the constraints that they face*. Let's first consider the demand for money by an individual, and then turn our attention to the demand for money in the entire economy.

### AN INDIVIDUAL'S DEMAND FOR MONEY

Money is one of the forms in which people hold their wealth. Unfortunately, at any given moment, the total amount of wealth we have is given; we can't just snap our fingers and have more of it. Therefore, if we want to hold more wealth in the form of money, we must hold less wealth in other forms: savings accounts, money market funds, time deposits, stocks, bonds, and so on. Indeed, people exchange one kind of wealth for another millions of times a day—in banks, stock markets, and bond markets. If you sell shares in the stock market, for example, you give up wealth in the form of corporate stock and acquire money. The buyer of your stock gives up money and acquires the stock.

These two facts—that wealth is given, and that you must give up one kind of wealth in order to acquire more of another—determine an individual's **wealth constraint.** Whenever we speak about the demand for money, the wealth constraint is always in the background, as in the following statement:

**Wealth constraint** At any point in time, total wealth is fixed.

> *An individual's* quantity of money demanded *is the amount of wealth that the individual chooses to hold as money, rather than as other assets.*

Why do people want to hold some of their wealth in the form of money? The most important reason is that money is a *means of payment;* you can buy things with it. Other forms of wealth, by contrast, are *not* used for purchases. (For example, we don't ordinarily pay for our groceries with shares of stock.) However, the other forms of wealth provide a financial return to their owners. For example, bonds, savings deposits, and time deposits pay interest, while stocks pay dividends and may also rise in value (which is called a *capital gain*). Money, by contrast, pays very little interest (some types of checking accounts) or none at all (cash and most checking accounts). Thus,

> *when you hold money, you bear an opportunity cost—the interest you could have earned by holding other assets instead.*

Each of us must continually decide how to divide our total wealth between money and other assets. The upside to money is that it can be used as a means of payment. The more of our wealth we hold as money, the easier it is to buy things at a moment's notice, and the less often we will have to pay the costs (in time, trouble, and commissions to brokers) to change our other assets into money. The downside to money is that it pays little or no interest.

To keep our analysis as simple as possible, *we'll use bonds as our representative nonmoney asset.* We'll also assume that all assets considered to be money pay no interest at all. In our discussion, therefore, people will choose between two assets that are mirror images of each other. Specifically,

> *individuals choose how to divide wealth between two assets: (1) money, which can be used as a means of payment but earns no interest; and (2) bonds, which earn interest, but cannot be used as a means of payment.*

This choice involves a clear tradeoff: The more wealth we hold as money, the less often we will have to go through the inconvenience of changing our bonds into money . . . but the less interest we will earn on our wealth.

What determines how much money an individual will decide to hold? While tastes vary from person to person, three key variables have rather predictable impacts on most of us.

- *The price level.* The greater the number of dollars you spend in a typical week or month, the more money you will want to have on hand to make your purchases. A rise in the price level, which raises the dollar cost of your purchases, should therefore increase the amount of money you want to hold.
- *Real income.* Suppose the price level remains unchanged, but your income increases. Your purchasing power or *real* income will increase, and so will the

number of dollars you spend in a typical week or month. Once again, since you are spending more dollars, you will choose to hold more of your wealth in the form of money.

- *The interest rate.* Interest payments are what you give up when you hold money—the *opportunity cost* of money. The greater the interest rate, the greater the opportunity cost of holding money. Thus, a rise in the interest rate *decreases* your quantity of money demanded.

The effect of the interest rate on the quantity of money demanded will play a key role in our analysis. But before we go any further, you may be wondering whether it is realistic to think that changes in the interest rate—which are usually rather small—would have any effect at all. Here, as in many aspects of economic life, you may not consciously think about the interest rate in deciding how to adjust your money-holding habits. Similarly, you may not rethink all your habits about using lights and computers every time the price of electricity changes. But in both cases, you may respond more casually. And when we add up everybody's behavior, we find a noticeable and stable tendency for people to hold less money when it is more expensive to hold it—that is, when the interest rate is higher.

### The Demand for Money by Businesses

Our discussion of money demand has focused on the typical individual. But some money (not a lot in comparison to what individuals hold) is held by businesses. Stores keep some currency in their cash registers, and firms generally keep funds in business checking accounts. Businesses face the same types of constraints as individuals: They have only so much wealth, and they must decide how much of it to hold as money rather than other assets. The quantity of money demanded by businesses follows the same principles we have developed for individuals: They want to hold more money when real income or the price level is higher, and less money when the opportunity cost (the interest rate) is higher.

## THE ECONOMY-WIDE DEMAND FOR MONEY

When we use the term *quantity of money demanded* without the word *individual*, we mean the total demand for money by all wealth holders in the economy—businesses and individuals. And just as each person and each firm in the economy has only so much wealth, so, too, there is a given amount of wealth in the economy as a whole at any given time. In our analysis, this total wealth must be held in one of two forms: money or bonds.

> *The (economy-wide) quantity of money demanded is the amount of total wealth in the economy that all households and businesses, together, choose to hold as money rather than as bonds.*

The demand for money in the economy depends on the same three variables that we discussed for individuals. In particular, (1) a rise in the price level will increase the demand for money; (2) a rise in real income (real GDP) will increase the demand for money; and (3) a rise in the interest rate will *decrease* the quantity of money demanded.

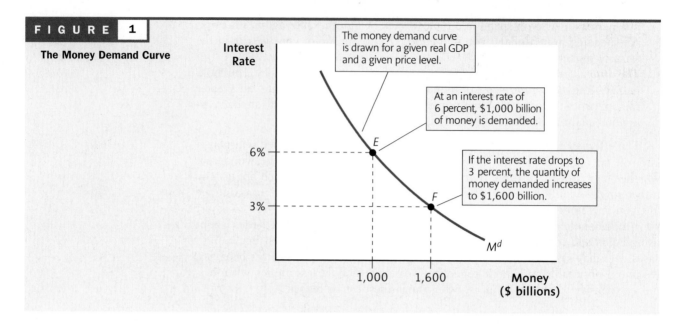

**FIGURE 1**

**The Money Demand Curve**

## THE MONEY DEMAND CURVE

**Money demand curve** A curve indicating how much money will be demanded at each interest rate.

Figure 1 shows a **money demand curve**, which tells us *the total quantity of money demanded in the economy at each interest rate*. Notice that the curve is downward sloping. As long as the other influences on money demand don't change, a drop in the interest rate—which lowers the opportunity cost of holding money—will increase the quantity of money demanded.

Point *E*, for example, shows that when the interest rate is 6 percent, the quantity of money demanded is $1,000 billion. If the interest rate falls to 3 percent, we move to point *F*, where the quantity demanded is $1,600 billion. As we move along the money demand curve, the interest rate changes, but other determinants of money demand (such as the price level and real income) are assumed to remain unchanged.

### Shifts in the Money Demand Curve

What happens when something *other* than the interest rate changes the quantity of money demanded? Then the curve shifts. For example, suppose that real income increases. Then, at each interest rate, individuals and businesses will want to hold *more* of their wealth in the form of money. The entire money demand curve will shift rightward. This is illustrated in Figure 2, where the money demand curve shifts rightward from $M_1^d$ to $M_2^d$. At an interest rate of 6 percent, the quantity of money demanded rises from $1,000 billion to $1,400 billion; if the interest rate were 3 percent, the amount of money demanded would rise from $1,600 billion to $2,000 billion.

In general,

> *a change in the interest rate moves us along the money demand curve. A change in money demand caused by something other than the interest rate (such as real income or the price level) will cause the curve to shift.*

Figure 3 summarizes how the key variables we've discussed so far affect the demand for money.

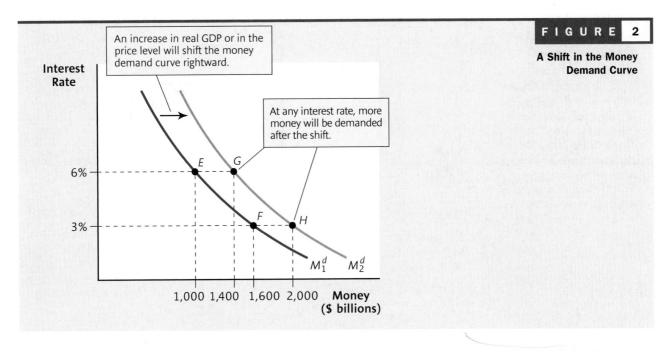

**FIGURE 2**

**A Shift in the Money Demand Curve**

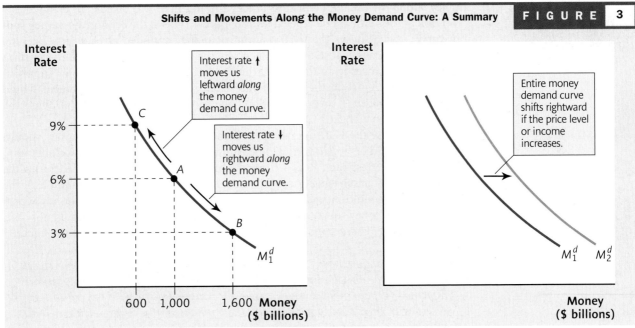

**FIGURE 3**

Shifts and Movements Along the Money Demand Curve: A Summary

## THE SUPPLY OF MONEY

Just as we did for money demand, we would like to draw a curve showing the quantity of money *supplied* at each interest rate. In the previous chapter, you learned how the Fed controls the money supply: It uses open market operations to inject or withdraw reserves from the banking system and then relies on the demand deposit multiplier to do the rest. Since the Fed decides what the money supply will

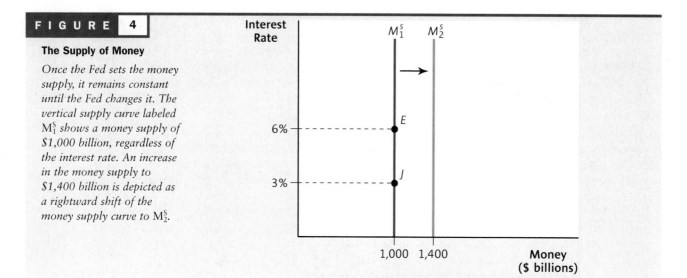

**Money supply curve** A line showing the total quantity of money in the economy at each interest rate.

be, we treat it as a fixed amount. That is, the interest rate can rise or fall, but the money supply will remain constant unless and until the Fed decides to change it.

Look at the vertical line labeled $M_1^S$ in Figure 4. This is the economy's **money supply curve**, which shows the total amount of money supplied at each interest rate. The line is vertical because once the Fed sets the money supply, it remains constant until the Fed changes it. In the figure, the Fed has chosen to set the money supply at $1,000 billion. A rise in the interest rate from, say, 3 percent to 6 percent would move us from point *J* to point *E* along the money supply curve $M_1^S$, leaving the money supply unchanged.

Now suppose the Fed, for whatever reason, were to *change* the money supply. Then there would be a *new* vertical line, showing a different quantity of money supplied at each interest rate. Recall from the previous chapter that the Fed raises the money supply by purchasing bonds in an open market operation. For example, if the demand deposit multiplier is 10, and the Fed purchases government bonds worth $40 billion, the money supply increases by 10 × $40 billion = $400 billion. In this case, the money supply curve shifts rightward, to the vertical line labeled $M_2^S$ in the figure.

> *Open market purchases of bonds inject reserves into the banking system, and shift the money supply curve rightward by a multiple of the reserve injection. Open market sales have the opposite effect: They withdraw reserves from the system and shift the money supply curve leftward by a multiple of the reserve withdrawal.*

## EQUILIBRIUM IN THE MONEY MARKET

Now let's combine money demand and money supply to find the equilibrium interest rate in the economy (Step two in the three-step process). But before we do, a question may have occurred to you. Haven't we already discussed how the interest rate is determined? Indeed, we have. The classical model tells us that the interest rate

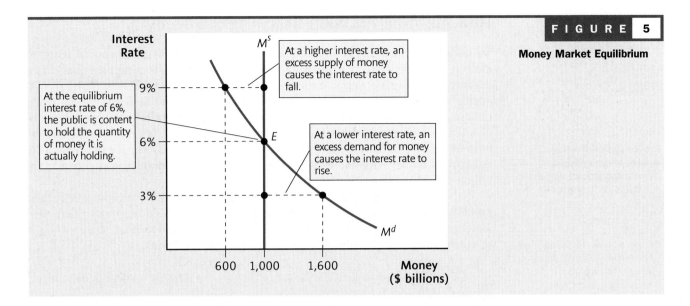

Interest Rate

At a higher interest rate, an excess supply of money causes the interest rate to fall.

$M^s$

9%

At the equilibrium interest rate of 6%, the public is content to hold the quantity of money it is actually holding.

6%        E

At a lower interest rate, an excess demand for money causes the interest rate to rise.

3%

$M^d$

600   1,000   1,600        Money ($ billions)

is determined by equilibrium in the *loanable funds market,* where a flow of loanable funds is offered by lenders to borrowers. But remember: The classical model tells us how the economy operates in the *long run.* We can rely on its mechanisms to work only over long periods of time. Here, we are interested in how the interest rate is determined in the *short run,* so we must change our perspective. Toward the end of the chapter, we'll come back to the classical model and explain why its theory of the interest rate does not apply in the short run.

In the short run—our focus here—we look for the equilibrium interest rate in the *money market:* the interest rate at which the quantity of money demanded and the quantity of money supplied are equal. Figure 5 combines the money supply and demand curves. Equilibrium occurs at point *E,* where the two curves intersect. At this point, the quantity of money demanded and the quantity supplied are both equal to $1,000 billion, and the equilibrium interest rate is 6 percent.

It is important to understand what equilibrium in the money market actually means. First, remember that the money supply curve tells us the quantity of money, determined by the Fed, that *actually exists* in the economy. Every dollar of this money—either in cash or in checking account balances—is held by *someone.* Thus, the money supply curve, in addition to telling us the quantity of money supplied by the Fed, also tells us the quantity of money that people *are actually holding* at any given moment. The money demand curve, on the other hand, tells us how much money people *want* to hold at each interest rate. Thus, when the quantity of money supplied and the quantity demanded are equal, all of the money in the economy is being *willingly held.* That is, people are satisfied holding the money that they are *actually* holding.

*Equilibrium in the money market occurs when the quantity of money people are* actually *holding (quantity supplied) is equal to the quantity of money they* want *to hold (quantity demanded).*

Can we have faith that the interest rate will reach its equilibrium value in the money market, such as 6 percent in our figure? Indeed we can. In the next section, we explore the forces that drive the money market toward its equilibrium.

## How the Money Market Reaches Equilibrium

To understand how the money market reaches its equilibrium, suppose that the interest rate, for some reason, were *not* at its equilibrium value of 6 percent in Figure 5. For example, suppose the interest rate were 9 percent. As the figure shows, at this interest rate the quantity of money demanded would be $600 billion, while the quantity supplied would be $1,000 billion. Or, put another way, people would *actually* be holding $1,000 billion of their wealth as money, but they would *want* to hold only $600 billion as money. There would be an **excess supply of money** (the quantity of money supplied would exceed the quantity demanded) equal to $1,000 billion − $600 billion = $400 billion.

Now comes an important point. Remember that in our analysis, money and bonds are the only two assets available. If people want to hold *less* money than they are currently holding, then, by definition, they must want to hold *more* in bonds than they are currently holding—an **excess demand for bonds.**

> *When there is an excess supply of money in the economy, there is also an excess demand for bonds.*

To understand this more clearly, imagine that instead of the money market, which can seem rather abstract, we were discussing something more concrete: the arrangement of books in a bookcase. Suppose that you have a certain number of books, and you have only two shelves on which to place all of them: top and bottom. One day, you look at the shelves and decide that, the way you've arranged things, the top shelf has *too many* books. Then, by definition, you must also feel that the bottom shelf has *too few* books. That is, an excess supply of books on the top shelf (it has more books than you want there) is the same as an excess demand for books on the bottom shelf (it has fewer books than you want there).

A similar conclusion applies to the money market. People allocate a given amount of wealth between two different assets: money and bonds. Too much in one asset implies too little in the other.

So far, we've established that if the interest rate were 9 percent, which is higher than its equilibrium value, there would be an excess supply of money, and an excess demand for bonds. What would happen? The public would demand more bonds. Just as there is a market for money, there is also a market for bonds. And as the public begins to demand more bonds, making them scarcer, *the price of bonds will rise.* We can illustrate the steps in our analysis so far as follows:

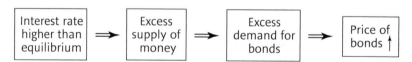

We conclude that, when the interest rate is higher than its equilibrium value, the price of bonds will rise. Why is this important? In order to take our story further, we must first take a detour for a few paragraphs.

### An Important Detour: Bond Prices and Interest Rates

A bond, in the simplest terms, is a promise to pay back borrowed funds at a certain date or dates in the future. There are many types of bonds. Some promise to make

**Excess supply of money** The amount of money supplied exceeds the amount demanded at a particular interest rate.

**Excess demand for bonds** The amount of bonds demanded exceeds the amount supplied at a particular interest rate.

payments each month or each year for a certain period and then pay back a large sum at the end. Others promise to make just one payment—perhaps 1, 5, 10, or more years from the date the bond is issued. When a large corporation or the government wants to borrow money, it issues a new bond and sells it in the marketplace; the amount borrowed is equal to the price of the bond.

Let's consider a very simple example: a bond that promises to pay to its holder $1,000 exactly 1 year from today. Suppose that you purchase this bond from the issuer—a firm or government agency—for $800. Then you are lending $800 to the issuer, and you will be paid back $1,000 one year later. What interest rate are you earning on your loan? Let's see: You will be getting back $200 more than you lent, so that is your *interest payment*. The annual interest *rate* is the interest payment over the year divided by the amount of the loan, or $200/$800 = 0.25 or 25 percent.

Now, what if instead of $800, you paid a price of $900 for this very same bond? The bond still promises to pay $1,000 one year from now, so your annual interest payment would now be $100, and your interest rate would be $100/$900 = 0.11 or 11 percent—a considerably lower interest rate. As you can see, the interest rate that you will earn on your bond depends entirely on the *price* of the bond. *The higher the price, the lower the interest rate.*

This general principle applies to virtually all types of bonds, not just the simple one-time-payment bond we've considered here. Bonds promise to pay various sums to their holders at different dates in the future. Therefore, the more you pay for any bond, the lower your overall rate of return, or interest rate, will be. Thus,

> *when the price of bonds rises, the interest rate falls; when the price of bonds falls, the interest rate rises.*[1]

The relationship between bond prices and interest rates helps explain why the government, the press, and the public are so concerned about the *bond market*, where bonds issued in previous periods are bought and sold. This market is sometimes called the *secondary* market for bonds, to distinguish it from the *primary* market where newly issued bonds are bought and sold. When you hear that "the bond market rallied" on a particular day of trading, it means that prices rose in the secondary bond market. This is good news for bondholders. But it is also good news for any person or business that wants to borrow money. When prices rise in the secondary market, they immediately rise in the primary market as well, because newly issued bonds and previously issued bonds are almost perfect substitutes for each other. Therefore, a bond market rally not only means lower interest rates in the secondary market, it also means lower interest rates in the primary market, where firms borrow money by issuing new bonds. Sooner or later, it will also lead to a drop in the interest rate on mortgages, car loans, credit card balances, and even many student loans. This is good news for borrowers. But it is bad news for anyone wishing to lend money, for now they will earn less interest.

Now that you understand the relationship between bond prices and interest rates, let's return to our analysis of the money market.

---

[1] In our macroeconomic model of the economy, we refer to *the* interest rate. In the real world, there are many types of interest rates: a different one for each type of bond, and still other rates on savings accounts, time deposits, car loans, mortgages, and more. However, all of these interest rates usually move up and down together, even though some may lag behind a few days, weeks, or months. Thus, when bond prices rise, interest rates *generally* will fall, and vice versa.

**Back to the Money Market**

Look back at Figure 5, and let's recap what you've learned so far. If the interest rate were 9 percent, there would be an excess supply of money, and therefore an excess demand for bonds. The price of bonds would rise. Now we can complete the story. As you've just learned, a rise in the price of bonds means a *decrease* in the interest rate. The complete sequence of events is

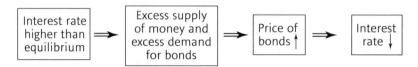

Thus, if the interest is 9 percent in our figure, it will begin to fall. Therefore, 9 percent is *not* the equilibrium interest rate.

How far will the interest rate fall? As long as there continues to be an excess supply of money, and an excess demand for bonds, the public will still be trying to acquire bonds, and the interest rate will continue to fall. But notice what happens in the figure as the interest rate falls: The quantity of money demanded *rises*. Finally, when the interest rate reaches 6 percent, the excess supply of money, and therefore the excess demand for bonds, is eliminated. At this point, there is no reason for the interest rate to fall further, so 6 percent is, indeed, our equilibrium interest rate.

We can also do the same analysis from the other direction. Suppose the interest rate were *lower* than 6 percent in the figure—say, 3 percent. Then, as you can see in Figure 5, there would be an *excess demand for money*, and an *excess supply of bonds*. In this case, the following would happen:

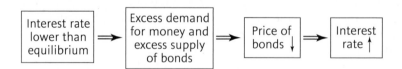

The interest rate would continue to rise until it reached its equilibrium value: 6 percent.

## WHAT HAPPENS WHEN THINGS CHANGE?

Now that we have seen how the interest rate is determined in the money market, we turn our attention to *changes* in the interest rate. We'll focus on two questions: (1) What *causes* the equilibrium interest rate to change? and (2) What are the *consequences* of a change in the interest rate? As you are about to see, the Fed can change the interest rate as a matter of policy, or the interest rate can change on its own, as a by-product of other events in the economy. We'll begin with the Fed.

### HOW THE FED CHANGES THE INTEREST RATE

Suppose the Fed wants to *lower* the interest rate. Fed officials cannot just declare that the interest rate should be lower. To change the interest rate, the Fed must change the *equilibrium* interest rate in the money market, and it does this by changing the money supply.

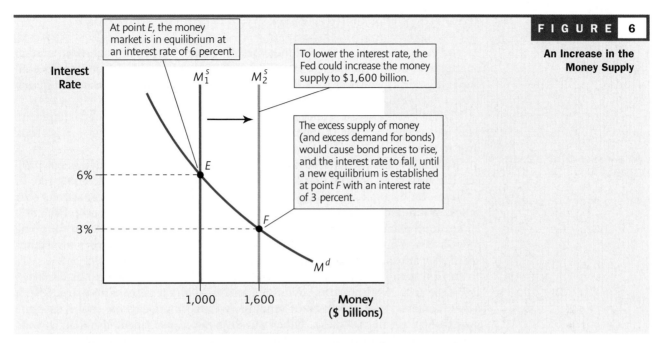

**FIGURE 6**

**An Increase in the Money Supply**

Look at Figure 6. Initially, with a money supply of $1,000 billion, the money market is in equilibrium at point *E*, with an interest rate of 6 percent. To lower the interest rate, the Fed *increases* the money supply through open market purchases of bonds. In the figure, the Fed raises the money supply to $1,600 billion, shifting the money supply curve rightward. (This is a much greater shift than the Fed would ever actually engineer in practice, but it makes the graph easier to read.) At the old interest rate of 6 percent, there would be an excess supply of money and an excess demand for bonds. This will drive the interest rate down until it reaches its new equilibrium value of 3 percent, at point *F*. The process works like this:

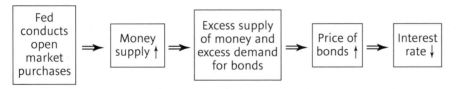

The Fed can *raise* the interest rate as well, through open market *sales* of bonds. In this case, the money supply curve in Figure 6 would shift leftward (not shown), setting off the following sequence of events:

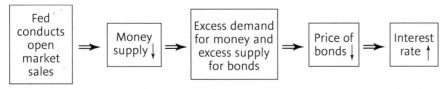

*If the Fed increases the money supply by buying government bonds, the interest rate falls. If the Fed decreases the money supply by selling government bonds, the interest rate rises. By controlling the money supply through purchases and sales of bonds, the Fed can also control the interest rate.*

## HOW DO INTEREST RATE CHANGES AFFECT THE ECONOMY?

As you've just learned, if the Fed increases the money supply through open market purchases of bonds, the interest rate will fall. But what then? How is the macroeconomy affected? The answer is: *A drop in the interest rate will boost several different types of spending in the economy.*

First, a lower interest rate stimulates business spending on plant and equipment. This idea came up a few chapters ago in the classical model, but we will go back over it here.

Remember that the interest rate is one of the key costs of any investment project. If a firm must borrow funds, it will have to pay for them at the going rate of interest—for example, by selling a bond at the going price. If the firm uses its *own* funds, so it doesn't have to borrow, the interest rate *still* represents a cost: Each dollar spent on plant and equipment *could* have been lent to someone else at the going interest rate. Thus, the interest rate is the *opportunity cost* of the firm's own funds when they are spent on plant and equipment.

A firm deciding whether to spend on plant and equipment compares the benefits of the project—the increase in future income—with the costs of the project. With a lower interest rate, the costs of funding investment projects are lower, so more projects will get the go-ahead. Other variables affect investment spending as well. But all else equal, a drop in the interest rate will cause an increase in spending on plant and equipment.

Interest rate changes also affect another kind of investment spending: spending on new houses and apartments that are built by developers or individuals. Most people borrow to buy houses or condominiums, and most developers borrow to build apartment buildings. The loan agreement for housing is called a *mortgage,* and mortgage interest rates tend to rise and fall with other interest rates. Thus, when the Fed lowers the interest rate, families find it more affordable to buy homes, and developers find it more profitable to build new apartments. Total investment in new housing increases.

Finally, in addition to investment spending, the interest rate affects consumption spending on big-ticket items such as new cars, furniture, and dishwashers. Economists call these *consumer durables* because they usually last several years. People often borrow to buy consumer durables, and the interest rate they are charged tends to rise and fall with other interest rates in the economy. Spending on new cars, the most expensive durable that most of us buy, is especially sensitive to interest rate changes. Since a lower interest rate causes higher consumption spending at *any* level of disposable income, it causes a *shift* of the consumption function, not a movement along it. Therefore, we consider this impact on consumption to be a rise in autonomous consumption spending, called *a* in our discussion of the consumption function.

We can summarize the impact of money supply changes as follows:

> *When the Fed increases the money supply, the interest rate falls, and spending on three categories of goods increases: plant and equipment, new housing, and consumer durables (especially automobiles). When the Fed decreases the money supply, the interest rate rises, and these categories of spending fall.*

# MONETARY POLICY

Two chapters ago, you learned that changes in aggregate expenditure cause changes in real GDP through the multiplier process. In this chapter, you've learned that the Federal Reserve, through its control of the money supply, can change the interest rate, and therefore influence aggregate expenditure. Thus, the Fed—through its control of the money supply—has the power to influence real GDP.

When the Fed controls or manipulates the money supply in order to achieve any macroeconomic goal—such as a change in the level of real GDP—it is engaging in **monetary policy.** Let's put all the pieces of our analysis together and see how monetary policy works.

**Monetary policy** Control or manipulation of the money supply by the Federal Reserve designed to achieve a macroeconomic goal.

## HOW MONETARY POLICY WORKS

In Figure 7, we revisit the short-run macro model, but we now include the money market in our analysis. In panel (a), the Fed has initially set the money supply at $1,000 billion. Equilibrium is at point $A$, with an interest rate ($r$) of 6 percent. Panel (b) shows the familiar short-run aggregate expenditure diagram, with equilibrium at point $E$, and equilibrium GDP equal to $8,000 billion.

But notice the new labels in the figure. The aggregate expenditure line has the subscript "$r = 6\%$," Why this additional label?

As you are about to see, a change in the interest rate will cause the aggregate expenditure line to shift. Therefore, our aggregate expenditure line is drawn for a particular interest rate, the one determined in the money market, or 6 percent.

Now we suppose that the Fed increases the money supply to $1,600 billion. (Again, this is an unrealistically large change in the money supply, but it makes it easier to see the change in the figure.) In the upper panel, the money market equilibrium moves from point $A$ toward point $B$, and the interest rate drops to 3 percent. The drop in the interest rate causes planned investment spending on plant and equipment and on new housing to rise. It also causes an increase in consumption spending—especially on consumer durables like automobiles—to rise at any level of income. This is an increase in autonomous consumption spending ($a$). In the lower panel, the rise in spending causes the aggregate expenditure line to shift upward, setting off the multiplier effect and increasing equilibrium GDP. The new equilibrium in the lower panel is point $F$, with real GDP at $10,000 billion. In the end, we see that the Fed, by increasing the money supply and lowering the interest rate, has increased the level of output.

**Shift versus Movement Along the AE Line** When thinking about the effects of monetary policy, try not to confuse movements *along* the aggregate expenditure line with *shifts* of the line itself. We move *along* the line only when a change in *income* causes spending to change. The line shifts when something *other* than a change in income causes spending to change.

When the Fed changes the interest rate, both types of changes occur, but it's important to keep the order straight. *First,* the drop in the interest rate (something other than income) causes interest-sensitive spending to change, *shifting* the aggregate expenditure line. *Then,* increases in income in each round of the multiplier cause further increases in spending, moving us *along* the new aggregate expenditure line.

DANGEROUS CURVES

We've covered a lot of ground to reach our conclusion, so let's review the highlights of how monetary policy works. This is what happens when the Fed conducts open market purchases of bonds:

**Monetary Policy and the Economy**

*Initially, the Fed has set the money supply at $1,000 billion, so the interest rate is 6 percent (point A). Given that interest rate, aggregate expenditure is AE$_{r=6\%}$ in panel (b), and real GDP is $8,000 billion (point E).*

*If the Fed increases the money supply to $1,600 billion, money market equilibrium moves to point B in panel (a). The interest rate falls to 3% (point B), stimulating interest-sensitive spending and driving aggregate expenditures upward in panel (b). Through the multiplier process, real GDP increases to $10,000 billion (point F).*

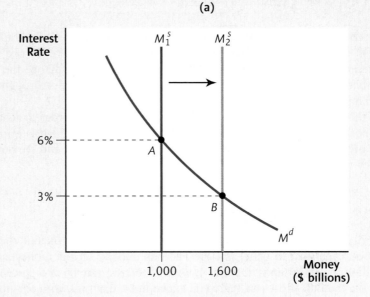

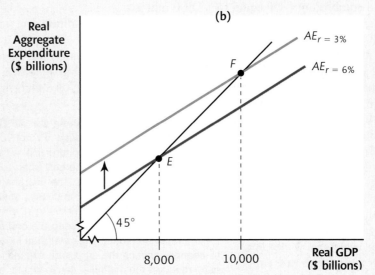

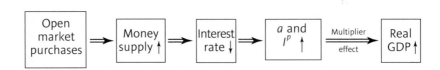

Open market *sales* by the Fed have exactly the opposite effects. In this case, the money supply curve in Figure 7 would shift leftward (not shown), driving the interest rate up. The rise in the interest rate would cause a decrease in interest-sensitive spending (*a* and *I$^p$*), shifting the aggregate expenditure line downward. Equilibrium GDP would fall by a multiple of the initial decrease in spending.

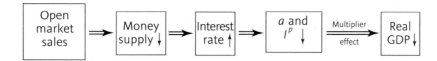

## Feedback Effects?

If you've been paying close attention, you may have a question about Figure 7. We've shown how changes in the upper panel (an increase in the money supply) cause changes in the lower panel (equilibrium GDP rises). But what about effects that go in the other direction? Shouldn't the rise in income in the lower panel increase the demand for money in the upper panel?

In Figure 7, we have ignored this "feedback effect" from changes in income to changes in money demand. Including this effect would make our analysis of monetary policy a bit more complicated, and alter the *size* of the changes in real GDP and the interest rate. But it would not alter the direction of the changes, or any of the conclusions we've reached about monetary policy.

The appendix to this chapter provides a more detailed analysis of monetary policy, incorporating the effect of income on money demand. It also takes another look at fiscal policy, which becomes a bit more complicated when the money market is included.

## MONETARY POLICY IN PRACTICE

You've just seen how changes in the interest rate can shift the *AE* line and change equilibrium GDP. It is not surprising that the Fed regards the interest rate as its main policy instrument in influencing the economy.

In practice, the interest rate that the Fed watches most closely is the rate in the *federal funds market*. In this market, banks with excess reserves lend them out to other banks for very short periods, usually a day. The interest rate in the federal funds market is called the **federal funds rate**. Although it is just an interest rate for lending among banks, many other interest rates in the economy vary with it closely. When the Fed changes the federal funds rate, other interest rates—such as those on automobile loans, business loans, mortgages, and home equity loans—change as well. They may change less or more than the federal funds rate has changed, but they virtually always move in the same direction.

During most periods, the Fed tries to prevent unnecessary fluctuations in the federal funds rate in order to avoid unnecessary shifts in the *AE* line. The Fed does this by targeting a specific value for the federal funds rate, and adjusting the money supply as needed to keep the funds rate at the target level.

At other times, the Fed *wants* the federal funds rate (and other interest rates) to change, in order to *cause* a shift in the *AE* line—say, to bring it closer to full employment than it would be otherwise. At such times, the Fed will *change* its target rate.

Note that the money supply itself plays a subservient role in the Fed's thinking about monetary policy. The money supply is simply increased or decreased as needed to keep the federal funds rate at its target. Since 1994, the Federal Open Market Committee has formalized this practice, by publicly announcing its target for the federal funds rate when it meets every six weeks or so. The FOMC then instructs its open market operations desk, operating out of the New York Federal Reserve Bank, to adjust the money supply as needed (with open market operations) to reach and maintain the announced target.

**Federal funds rate** The interest rate charged for loans of reserves among banks.

To see how this works, let's consider two different situations: one in which the Fed wants to *maintain* the interest rate at its target level, and one in which the Fed wants to *change* the target level.

### Maintaining an Interest Rate Target

Figure 8 shows an economy that is initially operating at full employment output. In the upper panel, the money market is in equilibrium at point *A*, with the interest rate (federal funds rate) at its target of 5 percent. The money supply is $1,000 billion, which is just the amount needed to maintain the target. In the lower panel, the

---

**FIGURE 8**

**Maintaining an Interest Rate Target**

*Initially, the money market in panel (a) is at point A, with the interest rate at its target of 5 percent. In panel (b), this interest rate positions the AE line to create equilibrium output of $10,000 billion, which results in full employment.*

*An increase in money demand from $M_1^d$ to $M_2^d$ in panel (a), with no action by the Fed, would drive the interest rate up to 8 percent, and shift the AE line in panel (b) downward. To prevent this, the Fed increases the money supply from $1,000 billion ($M_1^S$) to $1,400 billion ($M_2^S$), moving the money market equilibrium to point C. This maintains the interest rate at its target of 5 percent, and prevents any change in equilibrium output in panel (b).*

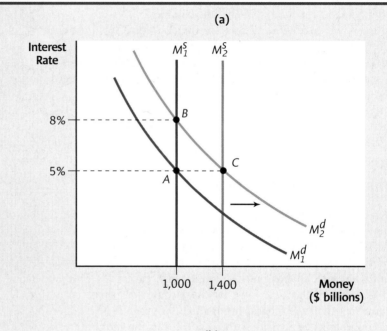

(a)

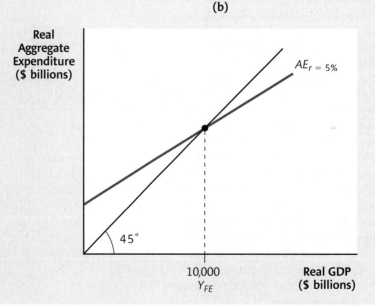

(b)

aggregate expenditure line for an interest rate of 5 percent ($AE_{r\,=\,5\%}$) intersects the 45° line to create equilibrium output of $10,000 billion. We assume that this happens to be the economy's full-employment output ($Y_{FE}$) as well.

Now suppose that public preferences change: People suddenly want to hold more of their wealth in money, which means less in bonds. (Perhaps it's the holiday shopping season, and people need to hold more wealth as money because they are making more purchases.) Because people want to hold more money at every interest rate, the money demand curve shifts rightward. If the Fed did nothing and left the money supply unchanged, the money market equilibrium would move to point B, with an interest rate of 8 percent. But this rise in the interest rate would cause the AE line in the lower panel to shift downward (not shown), and cause equilibrium GDP to fall below $Y_{FE}$—a recession.

To prevent any drop in GDP, the Fed has a simple task: to maintain its target interest rate. It does so by increasing the money supply (from $1,000 billion to $1,400 billion in the figure), shifting the money supply curve rightward from $M_1^s$ to $M_2^s$. After the shift, the new equilibrium in the money market occurs at point C, with the interest rate back to its target rate of 5 percent.

In general,

*to prevent fluctuations in money demand from affecting the economy, the Fed simply adjusts the money supply to maintain its interest rate target.*

## Changing the Interest Rate Target

Figure 9 illustrates a case where the Fed would want to *change* its interest rate target. Initially, things are fine. In the upper panel, the Fed is maintaining a target interest rate of 5 percent, at point A. In the lower panel, the aggregate expenditure line for that interest rate ($AE_1$) creates full-employment output of $10,000 billion.

Then something happens: Some sector of the economy reduces its spending. Perhaps pessimism about the future has caused a decrease in investment spending or autonomous consumption spending. Or perhaps the government has increased net taxes. Regardless of the cause, the aggregate expenditure line in the lower panel shifts downward, to $AE_2$. Equilibrium output falls to $9,000 billion at point F— below potential output. We are in a recession.

The Fed knows that a lower interest rate would stimulate additional investment and consumption spending, and could shift the AE line back up to its original position. So now the Fed will *lower* its interest rate target. For example, suppose the Fed believes an interest rate of 3 percent will move the aggregate expenditure line back to its original position. To achieve this new target, the Fed increases the money supply as necessary (to $1,300 billion in the figure).

In practice, the Fed would use a trial-and-error procedure to find the appropriate target. Every six weeks or so, it would lower the federal funds rate by a small amount, observe how the change is affecting other interest rates in the economy, and try to gauge the ultimate impact on the aggregate expenditure line and equilibrium GDP. This trial-and-error approach is not perfect, and the Fed has made mistakes— overshooting full employment in some periods and not quite hitting it in others. We'll explore some of the Fed's problems in conducting monetary policy in a later chapter.

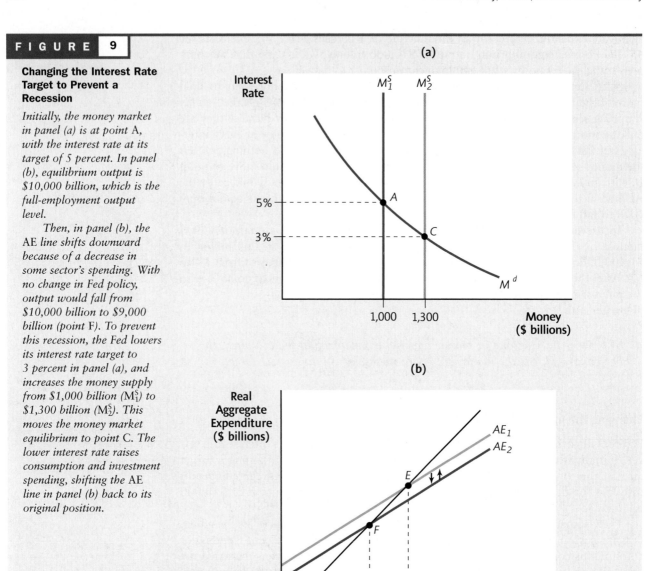

FIGURE  9

**Changing the Interest Rate Target to Prevent a Recession**

*Initially, the money market in panel (a) is at point A, with the interest rate at its target of 5 percent. In panel (b), equilibrium output is $10,000 billion, which is the full-employment output level.*

*Then, in panel (b), the AE line shifts downward because of a decrease in some sector's spending. With no change in Fed policy, output would fall from $10,000 billion to $9,000 billion (point F). To prevent this recession, the Fed lowers its interest rate target to 3 percent in panel (a), and increases the money supply from $1,000 billion ($M_1^S$) to $1,300 billion ($M_2^S$). This moves the money market equilibrium to point C. The lower interest rate raises consumption and investment spending, shifting the AE line in panel (b) back to its original position.*

## ARE THERE TWO THEORIES OF THE INTEREST RATE?

At the beginning of this chapter, you were reminded that you had already learned a different theory of how the interest rate is determined in the economy. In the classical model, the interest rate is determined in the *market for loanable funds*. In this chapter, you learned that the interest rate is determined in the *money market*, where people make decisions about holding their wealth as money and bonds. Which theory is correct?

The answer is: Both are correct. The classical model, you remember, tells us what happens in the economy in the *long run*. Therefore, when we ask what changes the interest rate over long periods of time—many years or even a decade—we should think about the market for loanable funds. But over shorter time periods—days, weeks, or months—we should use the money market model presented in this chapter.

Why don't we use the classical loanable funds model to determine the interest rate in the short run? Because, as you've seen, the economy behaves differently in the short run than it does in the long run. For example, in the classical model, output is automatically at full employment. But in the short run, output changes as the economy goes through booms and recessions. These changes in output affect the loanable funds market in ways that the classical model does not consider. For example, flip back to the chapter on the classical model and look at Figure 8 there. Recessions, which decrease household income, would also decrease household saving at any given interest rate: With less income, households will spend less *and* save less. The supply of loanable funds curve would shift leftward in the diagram, and the interest rate would rise. The classical model—because it ignores recessions—ignores these short-run changes in the supply of loanable funds.

The classical model also ignores an important idea discussed in this chapter: that the public continuously chooses how to divide its wealth between money and bonds. In the short run, the public's preferences over money and bonds can change, and this, in turn, can change the interest rate. This idea does not appear in the classical model.

Of course, in the long run, the classical model gives us an accurate picture of how the economy and the interest rate behave. Recessions and booms don't last forever, so the economy returns to full employment. Thus, in the long run we needn't worry about recessions causing shifts in the supply of loanable funds curve. Also, changes in preferences for holding money and bonds are rather short-lived. We can ignore these changes when we take a long-run view.

> *In the long run, we view the interest rate as determined in the market for loanable funds, where household saving is lent to businesses and the government. In the short run, we view the interest rate as determined in the money market, where wealth holders adjust their wealth between money and bonds, and the Fed participates by controlling the money supply.*

## USING THE THEORY

### The Fed and the Recession of 2001

Two chapters ago, we began an analysis of our most recent recession, which officially lasted from March to November of 2001. We saw that a drop in investment spending caused a decrease in aggregate expenditure, which in turn caused equilibrium GDP and employment to drop. But we left two questions unanswered: (1) What did policy makers do to try to prevent the recession, and to deal with it once it started? and (2) Why did consumption spending behave abnormally, rising as income fell and preventing the recession from becoming a more serious downturn? Now that you've learned about monetary policy, we can begin to answer these questions.

Starting in January 2001—three months before the official start of the recession—the Fed began to worry. Although the economy was operating at or even above its potential output (the unemployment rate the previous month was 3.9 percent), there was danger on the horizon: Investment spending had declined from the previous quarter. This had started a negative multiplier effect, which was working its way through the economy and could ultimately cause a recession. Other factors made the Fed worry that investment spending could decrease further. And a sharp decrease in stock prices over the previous year—which had destroyed billions of dollars in household wealth—suggested that consumption spending might begin to fall as well.

The lower right panel (d) of Figure 10, which shows the aggregate expenditure diagram, illustrates the situation. Initially, the economy was at point E, with real GDP in January of 2001 (for this example, measured in 1996 dollars) equal to $9,242 billion.[2] The Fed feared that if it did nothing, the investment slowdown would shift the aggregate expenditure line downward, moving the equilibrium to a point like F, with GDP falling (in our diagram) to $9,000 billion.

The Fed decided to take action, indicated in panels (a), (b), and (c) of Figure 10. Panel (a) shows how the publicly announced federal funds rate target changed through the period. As you can see, the Fed repeatedly lowered the target, from 6.5 percent (prior to January 2001) down to 1.75 percent by the end of the year.

The lower left panel (b) tracks the money supply measure M1 (monthly). It shows that the Fed, beginning in January 2001, continually increased M1 in order to hit its (falling) interest rate target.

Now look at the upper right panel (c), which shows a before-and-after view of the money market. In January 2001, the money market was in equilibrium at point A, with the M1 measure of the money supply at $1,093 billion and a federal funds rate of 6.5 percent. By the end of 2001, the money supply had increased to $1,170 billion—just enough to maintain the Fed's federal funds rate target of 1.75 percent (point B).

Finally, look again at panel (d) in the lower right corner. It shows the impact of this monetary policy on equilibrium GDP. Instead of falling to point F, the economy ended up at point H, with real GDP hitting bottom at about $9,125 billion in September 2001. Although the Fed's policy moves did not completely prevent the recession, it no doubt saved the economy from a more severe and longer-lasting one. The lower interest rate was especially helpful in maintaining new-home construction, a category of investment spending that is especially sensitive to the interest rate.

The Fed's policy also helps us understand the other question we raised about the 2001 recession: the continued rise in consumption spending throughout the period. Lower interest rates, as you've now learned, stimulate consumption spending on consumer durables, especially automobiles. Indeed, helped by lower interest rates, auto sales rose in every quarter of 2001.

Moreover, when interest rates drop dramatically and rapidly—as they did in 2001—a frenzy of *home mortgage refinancing* can occur: Households rush to exchange their existing, higher-interest-rate mortgages for new mortgages at a lower interest rate. After a refinance, monthly mortgage payments are reduced, freeing up disposable income to be spent on goods and services. But many households go further, taking advantage of the refinancing to borrow even more than they owed on

[2] This example makes use of monthly real GDP estimates in 1996 dollars provided by Macroeconomic Advisors, a private consulting firm, to the National Bureau of Economic Research (NBER) (available at *http://www.nber.org/cycles/hall.pdf*).

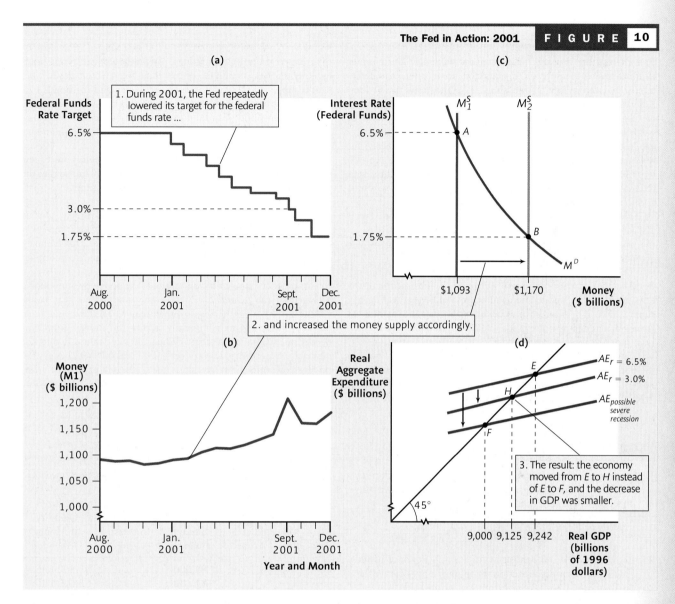

**The Fed in Action: 2001**    FIGURE 10

(a)

Federal Funds Rate Target

1. During 2001, the Fed repeatedly lowered its target for the federal funds rate …

6.5%

3.0%

1.75%

Aug. 2000    Jan. 2001    Sept. 2001    Dec. 2001

(c)

Interest Rate (Federal Funds)

$M_1^S$    $M_2^S$

6.5%    A

1.75%    B

$M^D$

$1,093    $1,170    Money ($ billions)

2. and increased the money supply accordingly.

(b)

Money (M1) ($ billions)

1,200

1,150

1,100

1,050

1,000

Aug. 2000    Jan. 2001    Sept. 2001    Dec. 2001

Year and Month

(d)

Real Aggregate Expenditure ($ billions)

E    $AE_r = 6.5\%$

$AE_r = 3.0\%$

H

F    $AE_{possible\ severe\ recession}$

45°

3. The result: the economy moved from E to H instead of E to F, and the decrease in GDP was smaller.

9,000 9,125 9,242    Real GDP (billions of 1996 dollars)

their original mortgage. This provides them with a one-time burst of cash to spend. Home refinancing and additional borrowing on homes seemed to play a major role in boosting consumption spending during the recession of 2001.

As you've read these pages, some questions may have formed in your mind. Why wasn't the Fed able to prevent the recession entirely? Couldn't the Fed have reduced the interest rate even more rapidly than it did?

There are, in general, good reasons for the Fed to be somewhat cautious in reducing interest rates. Over the next two chapters, you'll learn some of the reasons for the Fed's caution, and why most economists—despite the recession of 2001— give the Fed high marks for its actions during *that year*.

But you'll also learn that Fed policies during the year or so *before* 2001 may have actually contributed to the recession.

# Summary

The interest rate is a key macroeconomic variable. This chapter explores how the supply and demand for money interact to determine the interest rate in the short run, and how the Federal Reserve can adjust the money supply to change the interest rate.

An individual's *demand for money* indicates the amount of wealth that person wishes to hold in the form of money, at different interest rates. Money is useful as a means of payment, but holding money means sacrificing the interest that could be earned by holding bonds instead. The higher the interest rate, the larger the fraction of their wealth people will hold in the form of bonds, and the smaller the fraction they will hold as money.

The demand for money is sensitive to the interest rate, but it also depends on the price level, and real income. An increase in the price level, or higher real income, can each shift the money demand curve to the right.

The money supply is under the control of the Fed. Equilibrium in the money market occurs at the intersection of the downward-sloping money demand curve and the vertical money supply curve. The interest rate will adjust so that the quantity of money demanded by households and firms just equals the quantity of money supplied by the Fed and the banking system.

Conditions in the money market mirror conditions in the bond market. If the interest rate is above equilibrium in the money market, there will be an *excess supply of money* there. People are holding more of their wealth in the form of money

than they *want* to hold as money. This means that they are holding less of their wealth in bonds than they would desire. (An excess supply of money means an excess demand for bonds.) As people move to acquire bonds, the price of bonds will rise and the interest rate will fall. Thus, an excess supply of money will cause the interest rate to fall. Similarly, an excess demand for money will cause the interest rate to rise.

The Fed can increase the money supply, creating an excess supply of money. Very quickly, the interest rate will fall so that the public is willing to hold the now-higher money supply.

Changes in the interest rate affect interest-sensitive forms of spending—firms' spending on plant and equipment, new housing construction, and households' purchases of "big-ticket" consumer durables. By lowering the interest rate, the Fed can stimulate aggregate expenditures and increase GDP through the multiplier process.

In practice, the Fed conducts monetary policy by announcing a target for the *federal funds rate*—the interest rate that banks charge for lending reserves to other banks. The Fed uses open market operations to continually adjust the money supply as needed to maintain the target. When the Fed wants to shift the aggregate expenditure line and influence real GDP, it changes the target. Lowering the target shifts the aggregate expenditure line upward and raises real GDP; raising the target has the opposite effects.

# Problem Set   *Answers to even-numbered Questions and Problems can be found on the text Web site at www.thomsonedu.com/economics/hall.*

1. Assume the demand deposit multiplier is 10. For each of the following, state the impact on the money supply curve (the direction it will shift, and the amount of the shift).
   a. The Fed purchases bonds worth $10 billion.
   b. The Fed sells bonds worth $5 billion.

2. Assume the demand deposit multiplier is 7. For each of the following, state the impact on the money supply curve (the direction it will shift, and the amount of the shift).
   a. The Fed purchases bonds worth $28 million.
   b. The Fed sells bonds worth $17 million.

3. A bond promises to pay its owner $500 one year from now. For the following prices, find the corresponding interest payments and interest rates that the bond offers.

   | Price | Amount Paid in 1 Year | Interest Payment | Interest Rate |
   |-------|-----------------------|------------------|---------------|
   | $375  | $500                  | _____          | _____       |
   | $425  | $500                  | _____          | _____       |
   | $450  | $500                  | _____          | _____       |
   | $500  | $500                  | _____          | _____       |

   As the price of the bond rises, what happens to the bond's interest rate?

4. A bond promises to pay its owner $20,000 one year from now.
   a. Complete the following chart.

   | Price | Amount Paid in 1 Year | Interest Payment | Interest Rate | Quantity of Money Demanded |
   |-------|------------------------|------------------|---------------|----------------------------|
   |       | $2,000                 |                  |               | $2,300 billion             |
   |       | $1,500                 |                  |               | $2,600 billion             |
   |       | $1,000                 |                  |               | $2,900 billion             |
   |       | $ 500                  |                  |               | $3,200 billion             |
   |       | $ 0                    |                  |               | $3,500 billion             |

   b. Draw a graph of the money market, assuming that it is currently in equilibrium at an interest rate of 5.26 percent. What is the price of this bond? How large is the money supply?
   c. Find the new interest rate and the new bond price if the money supply increases by $300 billion. Show this on your graph.

5. A fellow student in your economics class stops you in the hallway and says: "An increase in the demand for money causes the interest rate to rise. But a rise in the interest rate causes people to demand *less* money. Therefore, increases in money demand largely cancel themselves out, and have very

little effect on the interest rate." Is this correct? Why or why not? (Hint: Draw a graph.)

6. For each of the following events, state (1) the impact on the money demand curve, and (2) whether the Fed should increase or decrease the money supply if it wants to keep the interest rate unchanged. (Hint: It will help to draw a diagram of the money market for each case.)

    a. People start making more of their purchases over the Internet, using credit cards.

    b. Greater fear of credit card fraud makes people stop buying goods over the Internet with credit cards, and discourages the use of credit cards in other types of purchases as well.

    c. A new type of electronic account is created in which your funds are held in bonds up to the second you make a purchase. Then—when you buy something— just the right amount of bonds are transferred to the ownership of the seller. (Hint: Would you want to increase or decrease the amount of your wealth in the form of money after this new type of account were available?)

7. Suppose that you own a bond that matures in one year, and promises to pay you $1,000 at that time. The current one-year interest rate in the economy is 6 percent.

    a. What is the price that someone would pay for your bond?

    b. Suppose that in the next few days, you *expect* the Fed to raise its interest rate target, causing the 1-year interest rate to rise to 8 percent. What is the price that you *expect* someone would pay for your bond after the Fed acts?

    c. If you have confidence in your expectation, which of the following will you want to do *now* (before the Fed acts): (1) acquire more bonds like the one you have; (2) sell your bond now; (3) neither? Explain briefly.

    d. If most other people develop the same expectations about the Fed that you have, what will likely happen to the money demand curve *now* (before the Fed acts)? Illustrate on a diagram of the money market.

    e. If the Fed wants to maintain the interest rate at its current target level, what must the Fed do? Illustrate by adding to your diagram of the money market.

8. Suppose that, in an attempt to prevent the economy from overheating, the Fed raises the interest rate. Illustrate graphically, using a diagram similar to Figure 7 in this chapter, the effect on the money supply, interest rate, and GDP.

9. In a later chapter, you will learn that a drop in the interest rate has *another* channel of influence on real GDP: It causes a depreciation of the dollar (that is, it makes the dollar cheaper to foreigners), which, in turn, increases U.S. net exports.

    a. When we take account of the effect on net exports, does a given change in the money supply have *more* or *less* impact on real GDP?

    b. Suppose that the Fed wants to stimulate the economy as during 2001. Should the Fed lower the interest rate by more or by less when it takes the impact on net exports into account (compared to the case of no impact on net exports)? Explain.

## More Challenging

10. [Requires appendix] As in problem 8, suppose that the Fed raises the interest rate to prevent the economy from over-heating. Using a diagram that includes feedback effects (similar to Figure A.1 in the appendix), illustrate the impact on the money supply, interest rate, and real GDP.

11. [Requires appendix] Determine whether *fiscal policy* is *more* or *less* effective in changing GDP when autonomous consumption and investment spending are *very sensitive* to changes in the interest rate, and explain your reasoning.

12. Figure 10(b) shows a spike in money growth during September 2001. Using what you know about bonds versus money and the money demand curve, explain why this spike might have occurred.

# APPENDIX

## *Feedback Effects from GDP to the Money Market*

In the body of this chapter, you learned how changes in the money market affect equilibrium GDP. But we ignored how changes in equilibrium GDP affect the money market and cause further changes in the interest rate. In this appendix, we'll incorporate these feedback effects from GDP to the money market into our analysis. This will give us a more complete picture of how monetary policy works. We'll also take another look at fiscal policy, this time incorporating the money market into the analysis.

### A MORE COMPLETE VIEW OF MONETARY POLICY

Figure A.1 revisits the economy shown in Figure 7. The upper panel shows the initial situation in the money market. The Fed has initially set the money supply at $1,000 billion, so the money supply curve is $M_1^s$. The money supply curve and money demand curve initially intersect at point A, resulting in an interest rate of 6 percent. But notice the label on the initial money demand curve "Y = $8,000 billion." In this appendix, the money demand curve will shift if there is a change in real income. Therefore, our money demand curve is drawn for a particular level of real income—the level of income determined in panel (b) at point E. Notice that the aggregate expenditure line in panel (b) has the subscript "r = 6%" because that is the interest rate found in panel (a). As you can see, the two panels are *interdependent*: The equilibrium in each one depends on the equilibrium in the other. When we draw the diagrams, we have to make sure that the money demand curve is consistent with the level of income found in the aggregate expenditure diagram, and that the aggregate expenditure line is consistent with the interest rate found in the money market diagram.

Now, let's see how monetary policy works when the two panels are interdependent in this way. Suppose the Fed increases the money supply to $1,600 billion. In the upper panel, the money supply curve shifts rightward, to $M_2^s$. The equilibrium starts to move toward

point B, with the interest rate heading down toward 3 percent.

But it will not actually get there. As the interest rate begins to drop, the aggregate expenditure line in the lower panel begins to rise. This causes equilibrium GDP to rise. As equilibrium GDP (which is the same as income) rises, people will want to hold more of their wealth in the form of money. So, in the upper panel, *the rise in equilibrium GDP shifts the money demand curve to the right.*

Where will we end up? To locate the exact final equilibrium, we would need quite a bit of detailed information about the economy. For example, we would need to know how sensitive aggregate expenditure is to changes in the interest rate, and how sensitive money demand is to changes in income. But even without these details, we know what must be true in the final equilibrium: Income will be higher than initially, because the aggregate expenditure line will have shifted upward. And the interest rate will be lower than initially, because the money supply will have increased.[3] Figure A.1 illustrates just one possibility, in which the new equilibrium is point C in the money market (upper panel), and point H in the aggregate expenditure diagram (lower panel). At this new equilibrium, the interest rate ends up at 4.5 percent, so our new aggregate expenditure line has the label "r = 4.5%." Equilibrium GDP has risen to $9,000 billion, so the new, higher money demand curve has the label "Y = $9,000 billion."

If you compare the final equilibrium in Figure A.1 to that in Figure 7, you'll see that the same increase in the money supply (from $1,000 billion to $1,600 bil-

---

[3] You might think that the interest rate could end up *higher* than initially, if the rightward shift in money demand is great enough—in particular, if the money demand curve shifts by more than the money supply curve. But this cannot happen. The money demand curve can shift rightward *only if* income rises. And income rises *only if* the AE line shifts upward. And the AE line shifts upward *only if* the interest rate falls. And the interest rate falls *only if* the shift in money demand is smaller than the shift in money supply. So to argue that the shift in money demand is so great that the interest rate actually rises is a logical contradiction. It would eliminate the reason for the money demand curve to shift rightward in the first place.

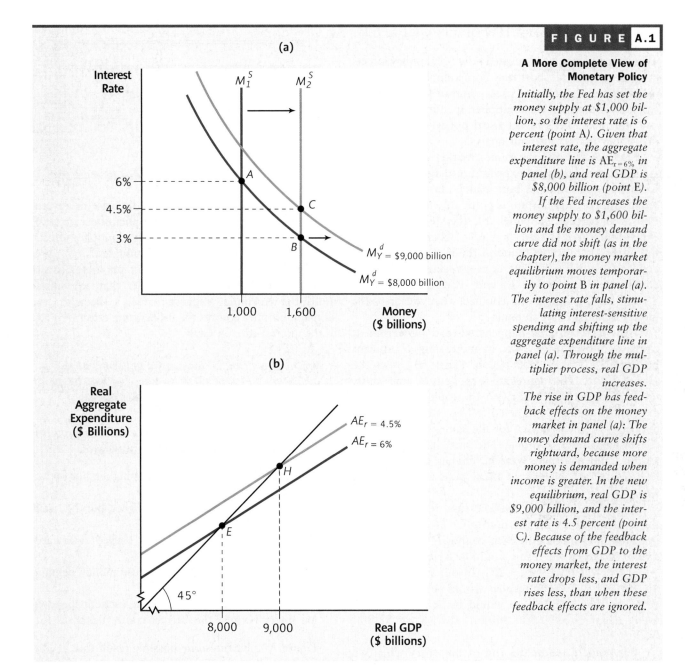

**FIGURE A.1**

**A More Complete View of Monetary Policy**

*Initially, the Fed has set the money supply at $1,000 billion, so the interest rate is 6 percent (point A). Given that interest rate, the aggregate expenditure line is $AE_{r=6\%}$ in panel (b), and real GDP is $8,000 billion (point E).*

*If the Fed increases the money supply to $1,600 billion and the money demand curve did not shift (as in the chapter), the money market equilibrium moves temporarily to point B in panel (a). The interest rate falls, stimulating interest-sensitive spending and shifting up the aggregate expenditure line in panel (a). Through the multiplier process, real GDP increases.*

*The rise in GDP has feedback effects on the money market in panel (a): The money demand curve shifts rightward, because more money is demanded when income is greater. In the new equilibrium, real GDP is $9,000 billion, and the interest rate is 4.5 percent (point C). Because of the feedback effects from GDP to the money market, the interest rate drops less, and GDP rises less, than when these feedback effects are ignored.*

lion) has somewhat different effects. In Figure 7, the interest rate dropped all the way to 3 percent, and real GDP increased all the way to $10,000 billion. In Figure A.1, the interest rate still drops, but by less: to just 4.5 percent. And income still rises, but by less: to just $9,000 billion. Thus, including feedback effects makes monetary policy a little less potent, but it does not really change the way it works. If the Fed wants to hit any given interest rate target (say, 3 percent), the feedback effects will require it to

raise the money supply by more than it otherwise would. But it can still hit any desired target.

*When the feedback effects from income to the money market are included, a given change in the money supply will cause a smaller change in the interest rate. Or, equivalently, to achieve any given change in the interest rate requires a larger change in the money supply.*

## A MORE COMPLETE VIEW OF FISCAL POLICY

Two chapters ago, we discussed how fiscal policy affects the economy in the short run. For example, an increase in government purchases causes output to rise, and in successive rounds of the multiplier, spending and output rise still more. Let's revisit fiscal policy, incorporating the money market into our analysis.

Figure A.2 shows the money market and the familiar short-run aggregate expenditure diagram. Initially, we have equilibrium in both panels. In panel (a), the money market equilibrium is point $A$, with the interest rate at 6 percent. In panel (b), the initial aggregate expenditure line, labeled "$r = 6\%$," is consistent with the interest rate we've found in the money market. As you can see, with this aggregate expenditure line, the equilibrium is at point $E$, with real GDP equal to $8,000 billion, just as we assumed when we drew the money demand curve in panel (a).

Now let's see what happens when the government changes its fiscal policy, say, by increasing government purchases ($G$) by $1,000 billion. Panel (b) shows the initial effect: The aggregate expenditure line shifts upward, by $1,000 billion, to the topmost aggregate expenditure line (unlabeled). This new aggregate expenditure line is drawn for the same interest rate as the original line: $r = 6\%$. The shift illustrates what *would* happen if there were no change in the interest rate, as in our analysis of fiscal policy two chapters ago.

As you've learned, the increase in government purchases will set off the multiplier process, increasing GDP and income in each round. *If this were the end of the story*, the result would be a rise in real GDP equal to $[1/(1 - MPC)] \times \Delta G$. In our example, with an $MPC$ of 0.6, the multiplier would be $1/(1 - 0.6) = 2.5$. The new equilibrium would be at point $F$, with GDP equal to $10,500 billion—a rise of $2,500 billion.

But point $F$ is *not* the end of our story when we include effects in the money market. As income increases, the money demand curve in panel (a) will shift rightward, raising the interest rate. As a result, autonomous consumption ($a$) and investment spending ($I$) will decrease and shift the aggregate expenditure line downward. That is, *an increase in government purchases, which by itself shifts the aggregate expenditure line upward, also sets in motion forces that shift it downward*. We can outline these forces as follows:

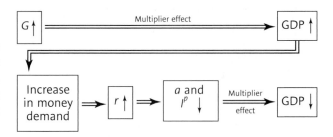

Net Effect: GDP↑, but by less due to effect of $r$↑

Thus, at the same time that the increase in government purchases has a *positive* multiplier effect on GDP, the decrease in $a$ and $I^p$ have *negative* multiplier effects. But the positive multiplier effect dominates.[4]

Thus, an increase in government purchases causes GDP to rise. But the rise is smaller than the simple multiplier formula suggests. That's because the simple multiplier ignores the moderating effect of a rise in the interest rate on GDP.

> *In the short run, an increase in government purchases causes real GDP to rise, but not by as much as if the interest rate had not increased.*

Let's sum up the characteristics of the new equilibrium after an increase in government purchases:

- The aggregate expenditure line is higher, but by less than $\Delta G$.
- Real GDP and real income are higher, but the rise is less than $[1/(1 - MPC)] \times \Delta G$.
- The money demand curve has shifted rightward, because real income is higher.
- The interest rate is higher, because money demand has increased.
- Autonomous consumption and investment spending are lower, because the interest rate is higher.

Figure A.2 indicates one possible result that is consistent with all of these requirements. In the figure, the new equilibrium occurs at point $B$ in the upper panel

[4] To prove this to yourself, remember that the negative multiplier effect is created *only if* the interest rate rises. And the interest rate rises *only if* the money demand curve shifts rightward. And the money demand curve shifts rightward *only if* income rises—that is, only if the positive multiplier effect is greater than the negative multiplier effect. So to argue that the negative multiplier effect dominates and income falls is a logical contradiction. It would eliminate the reason for the negative multiplier effect to occur in the first place.

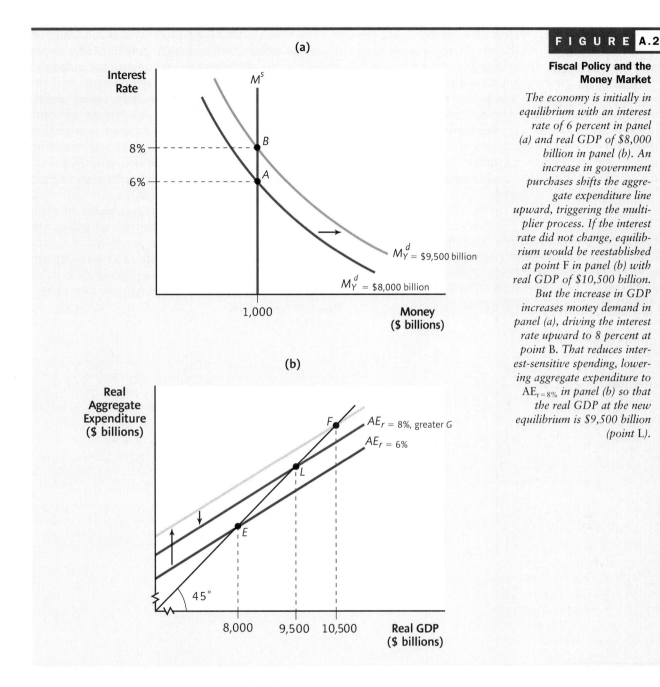

**FIGURE A.2**

**Fiscal Policy and the Money Market**

The economy is initially in equilibrium with an interest rate of 6 percent in panel (a) and real GDP of $8,000 billion in panel (b). An increase in government purchases shifts the aggregate expenditure line upward, triggering the multiplier process. If the interest rate did not change, equilibrium would be reestablished at point F in panel (b) with real GDP of $10,500 billion. But the increase in GDP increases money demand in panel (a), driving the interest rate upward to 8 percent at point B. That reduces interest-sensitive spending, lowering aggregate expenditure to $AE_{r = 8\%}$ in panel (b) so that the real GDP at the new equilibrium is $9,500 billion (point L).

and L in the lower panel. The new equilibrium GDP is $9,500 billion, and the new equilibrium interest rate is 8 percent. Notice that real GDP has risen, but by only $1,500 billion—not the $2,500 billion suggested by the simple multiplier formula. Moreover, the two panels of the diagram are consistent with each other. The aggregate expenditure line (labeled "$r = 8\%$") corresponds to the equilibrium interest rate in the money market.

The money demand curve (labeled "$Y = \$9,500$ billion") corresponds to the equilibrium GDP in the aggregate expenditure diagram.

### Crowding Out Once Again

Our analysis illustrates an interesting by-product of fiscal policy. Comparing our initial equilibrium to the final equilibrium, we see that government purchases increase. But because of the rise in the interest rate, *investment spending has decreased.*

What about consumption spending? It is influenced by two opposing forces. The rise in the interest rate causes *some* types of consumption spending (e.g., on automobiles) to decrease, but the rise in *income* makes other types of consumption spending *increase*. Thus, an increase in government purchases may increase or decrease consumption spending, depending on which effect is stronger.

Summing up:

> *When effects in the money market are included in the short-run macro model, an increase in government purchases raises the interest rate and* crowds out *some private investment spending. It may also crowd out consumption spending.*

This should sound familiar. In the classical, long-run model, an increase in government purchases also causes crowding out. But there is one important difference between crowding out in the classical model and the effects we are outlining here. In the classical model, there is *complete crowding out:* Investment spending and consumption spending fall by the same amount that government purchases rise. As a result, total spending does not change at all, and neither does real GDP. This is why, in the *long run,* we expect fiscal policy to have no demand-side effects on real GDP.

In the short run, however, our conclusion is somewhat different. While we expect *some* crowding out from an increase in government purchases, *it is not complete*. Investment spending falls, and consumption spending *may* fall, but together, they do not drop by as much as the rise in government purchases. In the short run, real GDP rises.

# Aggregate Demand and Aggregate Supply

Economic fluctuations are facts of life. If you need a reminder, look back at Figure 1 in the chapter titled "Economic Fluctuations." There you can see that while potential GDP tends to move upward year after year due to economic growth, *actual* GDP tends to rise above and fall below potential over shorter periods.

But the figure also reveals another important fact about the economy: Deviations from potential output don't last forever. When output dips below or rises above potential, the economy returns to potential output after a few quarters or years. True, in some of these episodes, government policy—either fiscal or monetary—helped the economy return to full employment more quickly. But even without corrective policies—such as during long parts of the Great Depression of the 1930s—the economy shows a remarkable tendency to begin moving back toward potential output. Why? And what, exactly, is the mechanism that brings us back to our potential when we have strayed from it? These are the questions we will address in this chapter. And we'll address them by studying the behavior of a variable that we've put aside for several chapters: the price level.

The chapter begins by exploring the relationship between the price level and output. This is a two-way relationship, as you can see in Figure 1 in *this* chapter. On the one hand, changes in the price level cause changes in real GDP. This causal relationship is illustrated by the *aggregate demand curve*, which we will discuss shortly. On the other hand, changes in real GDP cause changes in the price level. This relationship is summarized by the *aggregate supply curve*, to which we will turn later.

Once we've developed the aggregate demand and supply curves, we'll be able to use them to understand how changes in the price level—sometimes gently, other times more harshly—steer the economy back toward potential output.

## THE AGGREGATE DEMAND CURVE

Our first step in understanding how the price level affects the economy is an important fact: When the price level rises, the money demand curve shifts rightward. Why? Remember that the money demand curve tells us how much of their wealth people want to hold as money (as opposed to bonds) at each interest rate. People hold bonds because of the interest they pay; people hold money because of its convenience. Each day, as we make purchases, we need cash or funds in our checking account to pay for them. If the price level rises, so that our purchases become more expensive, we'll need to hold more of our wealth as money just to achieve the same

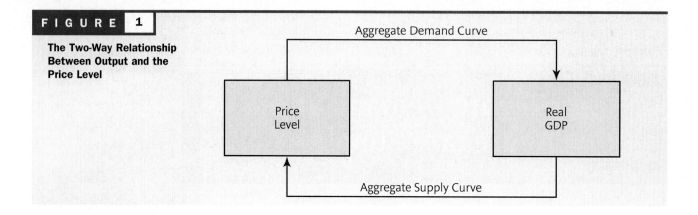

**FIGURE 1**

**The Two-Way Relationship Between Output and the Price Level**

level of convenience. Thus, at any given interest rate, the demand for money increases, and the money demand curve shifts rightward.

The shift in money demand, and its impact on the economy, is illustrated in Figure 2. Panel (a) has our familiar money market diagram. We'll assume that, initially, the price level in the economy is equal to 100. With this price level, the money market is in equilibrium at point *A*, with an interest rate of 6 percent.

In panel (b), equilibrium GDP is at point *E*, with output equal to $10 trillion. The aggregate expenditure line is marked "*r* = 6%," which is the equilibrium interest rate we just found in the money market.

Now let's imagine a rather substantial rise in the price level, from 100 to 140. What will happen in the economy? The initial impact is in the money market. The money demand curve will start to shift rightward. For now, we'll assume the Fed does *not* change the money supply, so the interest rate will rise. Next, in panel (b), the higher interest rate decreases interest-sensitive spending—business investment, new housing, and consumer durables. The aggregate expenditure line shifts downward, and equilibrium real GDP decreases. All of these changes continue until we reach a new, consistent equilibrium in both panels. Compared with our initial position, this new equilibrium has the following characteristics:

- The money demand curve has shifted rightward.
- The interest rate is higher.
- The aggregate expenditure line has shifted downward.
- Equilibrium GDP is lower.

Remember that all of these changes are caused by a rise in the price level.

Panels (a) and (b) show one possible new equilibrium that meets these requirements. In panel (a), the money demand curve has shifted to $M_2^d$. The interest rate has risen to 9 percent. The aggregate expenditure line has shifted downward, to the one marked "*r* = 9%." Finally, equilibrium output has fallen to $6 trillion.

Now recall the initial event that caused real GDP to fall: a rise in the price level. We've thus established an important principle:

*A rise in the price level causes a decrease in equilibrium GDP.*

## Deriving the Aggregate Demand Curve

In panel (c), we introduce a new curve that directly shows the negative relationship between the price level and equilibrium GDP. In this panel, the price level is measured

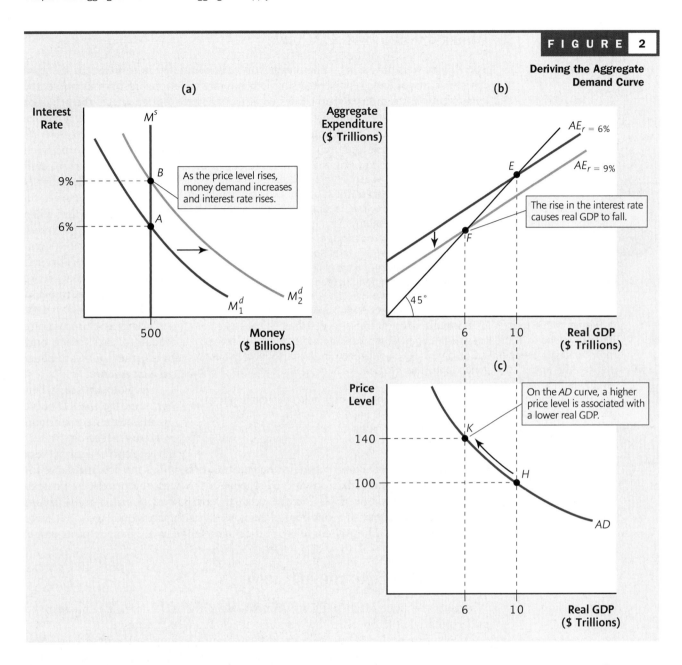

FIGURE 2

Deriving the Aggregate Demand Curve

**(a)**

Interest Rate

$M^s$

$B$

9%

As the price level rises, money demand increases and interest rate rises.

$A$

6%

$M_1^d$

$M_2^d$

500

Money ($ Billions)

**(b)**

Aggregate Expenditure ($ Trillions)

$AE_{r\,=\,6\%}$

$E$

$AE_{r\,=\,9\%}$

The rise in the interest rate causes real GDP to fall.

$F$

45°

6    10

Real GDP ($ Trillions)

**(c)**

Price Level

On the *AD* curve, a higher price level is associated with a lower real GDP.

$K$

140

$H$

100

$AD$

6    10

Real GDP ($ Trillions)

along the vertical axis, while real GDP is on the horizontal. Point *H* represents our initial equilibrium, with *P* = 100 and equilibrium GDP = $10 trillion. Point *K* represents the new equilibrium, with *P* = 140 and equilibrium GDP = $6 trillion. If we continued to change the price level to other values—raising it further to 150, lowering it to 85, and so on—we would find that each different price level results in a different equilibrium GDP. This is illustrated by the downward-sloping curve in the figure, which we call the *aggregate demand curve.*

*The **aggregate demand** (**AD**) **curve** tells us the equilibrium real GDP at any price level.*

**Aggregate demand (*AD*) curve** A curve indicating equilibrium GDP at each price level.

## UNDERSTANDING THE *AD* CURVE

The *AD* curve is unlike any other curve you've encountered in this text. In all other cases, our curves have represented simple behavioral relationships. For example, the demand curve for maple syrup shows us how a change in price affects the behavior of buyers in a market. Similarly, the aggregate expenditure line shows how a change in income affects total spending in the economy.

But the *AD* curve represents more than just a behavioral relationship between two variables. Each point on the curve represents a short-run *equilibrium* in the economy. For example, point *H* on the *AD* curve in Figure 2 tells us that when the price level is 100, *equilibrium* GDP is $10 trillion. Thus, point *H* doesn't just tell us that total spending is $10 trillion; rather, it tells us that when *P* = 100, spending and output are equal to each other only when they *both* are equal to $10 trillion.

**Two Misconceptions About the *AD* Curve** Watch out for two common mistakes. The first is thinking that the *AD* curve is simply a "total demand" or "total spending" curve for the economy. This is an oversimplification. Rather, the *AD* curve tells us the *equilibrium* real GDP at each price level. This is the level of output at which total spending *equals* total output. Thus, total spending is only part of the story behind the *AD* curve: The other part is the requirement that total spending and total output be equal.

A second, related mistake is thinking that the *AD* curve slopes downward for the same reason that a microeconomic demand curve slopes downward. This, too, is wrong. In the market for maple syrup, for example, a rise in price causes quantity demanded to decrease, mostly because people switch to *other* goods that are now relatively cheaper. But along the *AD* curve, a rise in the price level generally causes the prices of *all* goods to increase *together*. There are no relatively cheaper goods to switch to!

The *AD* curve works in an entirely different way from microeconomic demand curves. Along the *AD* curve, an increase in the price level raises the interest rate in the money market, which decreases spending on interest-sensitive goods, causing a drop in equilibrium GDP.

As you can see, a better name for the *AD* curve would be the "equilibrium-output-at-each-price-level" curve—not a very catchy name. The *AD* curve gets its name because it *resembles* the demand curve for an individual product. It's a downward-sloping curve, with the price level (instead of the price of a single good) on the vertical axis and *equilibrium total output* (instead of the quantity of a single good demanded) on the horizontal axis. But there the similarity ends. The *AD* curve is not a demand curve at all, in spite of its name.

## MOVEMENTS ALONG THE *AD* CURVE

Whenever the price level changes, we move *along* the *AD* curve. It's important to understand what happens in the economy as we make such a move.

Look again at the *AD* curve in panel (c) of Figure 2. Suppose the price level rises, and we move from point *H* to point *K* along this curve. Then the following sequence of events occurs: The rise in the price level increases the demand for money, raises the interest rate, decreases autonomous consumption (*a*) and investment spending ($I^p$), and works through the multiplier to decrease equilibrium GDP. The process can be summarized as follows:

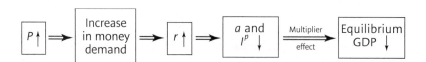

The opposite sequence of events will occur if the price level falls, moving us rightward along the *AD* curve:

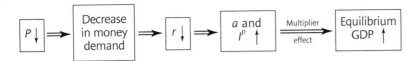

## SHIFTS OF THE *AD* CURVE

When we move along the *AD* curve in Figure 2, we assume that the price level changes but that other influences on equilibrium GDP are constant. When any of these other influences on GDP changes, the *AD* curve will shift. The distinction between movements along the *AD* curve and shifts of the curve itself is very important. Always keep the following rule in mind:

> *When a change in the price level causes equilibrium GDP to change, we move along the* AD *curve. Whenever anything other than the price level causes equilibrium GDP to change, the* AD *curve itself shifts.*

What are these other influences on GDP? They are the very same changes you learned about in previous chapters. Specifically, equilibrium GDP will change whenever there is a change in any of the following:

- Government purchases
- Taxes
- Autonomous consumption spending
- Investment spending
- Net exports
- The money supply

Let's consider some examples and see how each causes the *AD* curve to shift.

### An Increase in Government Purchases

In Figure 3, we assume that the economy begins at a price level of 100. In the money market (not shown), the equilibrium interest rate is 6 percent and equilibrium output—given by point *E* in panel (a)—is $10 trillion. Panel (b) shows the same equilibrium as represented by point *H* on $AD_1$.

Now let's repeat an experiment from an earlier chapter: We'll increase government purchases by $1 trillion and ask what happens to equilibrium GDP. As we do this, we'll assume that *the price level remains at 100*. If the MPC is 0.6, and our simple multiplier formula applies, the value of the multiplier will be $1/(1 - 0.6) = 2.5$. Therefore, GDP will rise by $1 trillion $\times$ 2.5 = $2.5 trillion. Our new value for equilibrium GDP is $12.5 trillion. This new equilibrium is also shown in panel (a) of Figure 3. The aggregate expenditure line shifts upward to $AE_2$, and the equilibrium moves to point *F*. With the price level remaining at 100, equilibrium GDP increases.

Now look at panel (b) in Figure 3. There, the new equilibrium is represented by point *J* (*P* = 100, real GDP = $12.5 trillion). This point lies to the right of our original curve $AD_1$. Point *J*, therefore, must lie on a *new AD* curve—a curve that tells

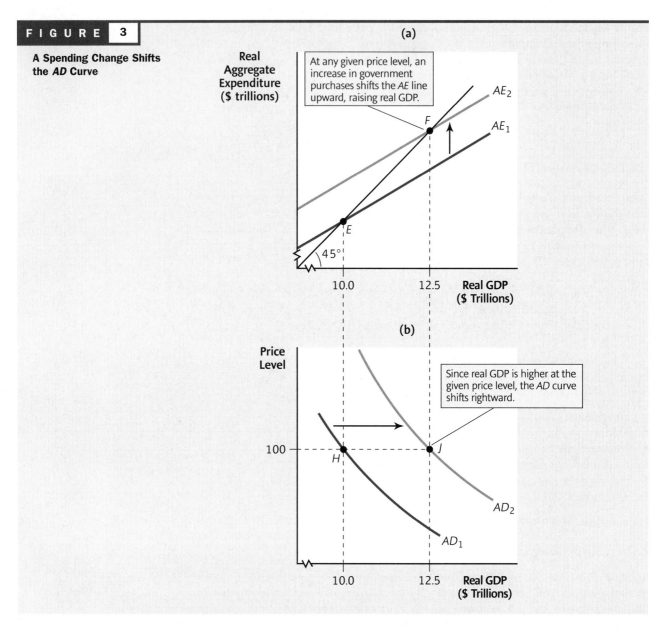

**FIGURE 3**

**A Spending Change Shifts the *AD* Curve**

**(a)**

At any given price level, an increase in government purchases shifts the *AE* line upward, raising real GDP.

**(b)**

Since real GDP is higher at the given price level, the *AD* curve shifts rightward.

us equilibrium GDP at any price level *after the increase in government spending.* The new *AD* curve is the one labeled $AD_2$, which goes through point *J.* What about the other points on $AD_2$? They tell us that, if we had started at any *other* price level, an increase in government spending would have increased equilibrium GDP at that price level, too. We conclude that *an increase in government purchases shifts the entire* AD *curve rightward.*

Any other factor that initially shifts the aggregate expenditure line upward will shift the AD curve rightward, just as in Figure 3. More specifically,

*the* AD *curve shifts rightward when government purchases, investment spending, autonomous consumption spending, or net exports increase, or when net taxes decrease.*

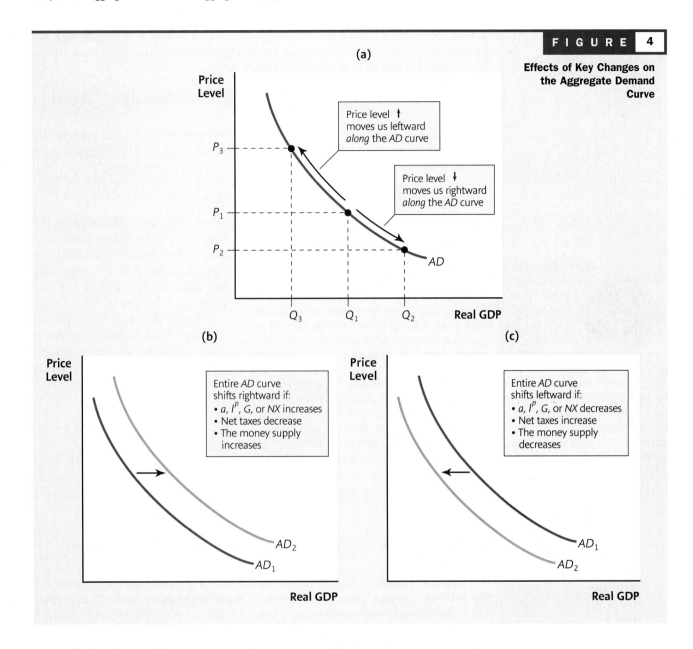

**FIGURE 4**

**Effects of Key Changes on the Aggregate Demand Curve**

(a)

Price level ↑ moves us leftward *along* the AD curve

Price level ↓ moves us rightward *along* the AD curve

(b)

Entire AD curve shifts rightward if:
• a, $I^p$, G, or NX increases
• Net taxes decrease
• The money supply increases

(c)

Entire AD curve shifts leftward if:
• a, $I^p$, G, or NX decreases
• Net taxes increase
• The money supply decreases

Our analysis also applies in the other direction. For example, at any given price level, a *decrease* in government spending shifts the aggregate expenditure line *downward,* decreasing equilibrium GDP. This in turn shifts the AD curve leftward.

## Changes in the Money Supply

Changes in the money supply will also shift the aggregate demand curve. To see why, let's imagine that the Fed conducts open market operations to *increase* the money supply. As you learned in the previous chapter, this will cause the interest rate to decrease, increasing investment spending and autonomous consumption spending. Together, these spending changes will shift the aggregate expenditure line upward, just as in panel (a) of Figure 3, and increase equilibrium GDP. Since this change in equilibrium output is caused by something *other* than a change in the price level, the *AD* curve shifts. In this case, because the money supply *increased*, the *AD* curve shifts *rightward*, just as in panel (b) of Figure 3.

> *An increase in the money supply shifts the* AD *curve rightward.*

A decrease in the money supply would have the opposite effect: The interest rate would rise, the aggregate expenditure line would shift downward, and *equilibrium GDP at any price level would fall.*

### Shifts versus Movements Along the *AD* Curve: A Summary

Figure 4 summarizes how some events in the economy cause a movement along the *AD* curve, and other events shift the *AD* curve. You can use the figure as an exercise, drawing diagrams similar to Figures 2 and 3 to illustrate why we move along or shift the *AD* curve in each case.

Notice that panels (b) and (c) of Figure 4 tell us how a variety of events affect the *AD* curve, but *not* how they affect *real GDP*. The reason is that, even if we know which *AD* curve we are on, we could be at *any point* along that curve, depending on where the price level ends up.

But where will the price level end up? To answer that question, we must understand the other side of the relationship between GDP and the price level.

**Confusion over Spending Changes.** In this chapter, you've learned that changes in autonomous consumption (*a*) and planned investment spending ($I^p$), like other spending changes, can shift the *AD* curve. And they can. But these two variables also change whenever we move *along* the *AD* curve. (Remember: As we move along the *AD* curve, a rise in the price level increases money demand, raises the interest rate, and decreases autonomous consumption and $I^p$).

Therefore, a change in *a* or $I^p$ shifts the *AD* curve only if it is *not* initiated by a change in the price level. For example, if businesses and households become more optimistic and thus increase their spending, the *AD* curve will shift, because increased optimism is something other than a change in the price level. When a change in the price level initiates a change in *a* and $I^p$, there is no shift of the *AD* curve, but rather a movement along it.

DANGEROUS CURVES

## THE AGGREGATE SUPPLY CURVE

Look back at Figure 1, which illustrates the *two-way* relationship between the price level and output. On the one hand, changes in the price level affect output. This is the relationship, summarized by the *AD* curve, which we've just explored in the previous section. On the other hand, changes in output affect the price level. This relationship—summarized by the *aggregate supply curve*—is the focus of this section.

The effect of changes in output on the price level is complex, involving a variety of forces. Current research is helping economists get a clearer picture of this relationship. Here, we will present a simple model of the aggregate supply curve that focuses on the link between prices and costs. Toward the end of the chapter, we'll discuss some additional ideas about the aggregate supply curve.

### COSTS AND PRICES

The price *level* in the economy results from the pricing behavior of millions of individual business firms. In any given year, some of these firms will raise their prices, and some will lower them. For example, during the early 2000s, laptop computers and long-distance telephone calls came down in price, while college tuition and the prices of movies rose. These types of price changes are subjects for *microeconomic* analysis, because they involve individual markets.

But often, all firms in the economy are affected by the same *macroeconomic* event, causing prices to rise or fall throughout the economy. This change in the price *level* is what interests us in macroeconomics.

To understand how macroeconomic events affect the price level, we begin with a very simple assumption:

> *A firm sets the price of its products as a markup over cost per unit.*

For example, if it costs Burger King $2.50, on average, to produce a Whopper (cost per unit is $2.50), and Burger King's percentage markup is 10 percent, then it will charge $2.50 + (0.10 × $2.50) = $2.75 per Whopper.[1]

The percentage markup in any particular industry will depend on the degree of competition there. If there are many firms competing for customers in a market, all producing very similar products, then we can expect the markup to be relatively small. Thus, we expect a relatively low markup on fast-food burgers or personal computers. In industries where there is less competition—such as daily newspapers or jet aircraft—we would expect higher percentage markups.

In macroeconomics, we are not concerned with how the markup varies among different industries, but rather with the *average percentage markup* in the economy:

> *The average percentage markup in the economy is determined by competitive conditions in the economy. The competitive structure of the economy changes very slowly, so the average percentage markup should be somewhat stable from year to year.*

But a stable markup does not necessarily mean a stable price level, because unit costs can change. For example, if Burger King's markup remains at 10 percent, but the unit cost of a Whopper rises from $2.50 to $3.00, then the price of a Whopper will rise to $3.00 + (0.10 × $3.00) = $3.30. Extending this example to all firms in the economy, we can say:

> *In the short run, the price level rises when there is an economy-wide increase in unit costs, and the price level falls when there is an economy-wide decrease in unit costs.*

## GDP AND THE PRICE LEVEL

Our primary concern in this chapter is the impact of *total output or real GDP* on unit costs and, therefore, on the price level. Why should a change in output affect unit costs and the price level? We'll focus on three key reasons.

© SUSAN VAN ETTEN

*Fast-food restaurants, like other firms in the economy, charge a markup over cost per unit. The average markup in the economy is determined by competitive conditions and tends to change slowly over time.*

---

[1] In microeconomics, you learn more sophisticated theories of how firms' prices are determined. But our simple markup model captures a central conclusion of those theories: that an increase in costs will result in higher prices.

As total output increases:

*Greater amounts of inputs may be needed to produce a unit of output.* As output increases, firms hire new, untrained workers who may be less productive than existing workers. Firms also begin using capital and land that are less well suited to their industry. As a result, greater amounts of labor, capital, land, and raw materials are needed to produce each unit of output. Even if the prices of these inputs remain the same, unit costs will rise.

For example, imagine that Intel increases its output of computer chips. Then it will have to be less picky about the workers it employs, hiring some who are less well suited to chip production than those already working there. Thus, more labor hours will be needed to produce each chip. Intel may also have to begin using older, less-efficient production facilities, which require more silicon and other raw materials per chip. Even if the prices of all of these inputs remain unchanged, unit costs will rise.

*The prices of nonlabor inputs rise.* In addition to needing greater quantities of inputs, firms will have to pay a higher price for them. This is especially true of inputs like land and natural resources, which may be available only in limited quantities in the short run. An increase in the output of final goods raises the demand for these inputs, causing their prices to rise. Firms that produce final goods experience an increase in unit costs, and raise their own prices accordingly.

*The nominal wage rate rises.* Greater output means higher employment, leaving fewer unemployed workers looking for jobs. As firms compete to hire increasingly scarce workers, they must offer higher nominal wage rates to attract them. Higher nominal wages increase unit costs, and therefore result in a higher price level. Notice that we use the nominal wage, rather than the real wage we've emphasized elsewhere in this book. That's because we are interested in explaining how firms' prices are determined. Since price is a nominal variable, it is marked up over *nominal* costs.

A decrease in output affects unit costs through the same three forces, but with the opposite result. As output falls, firms can be more selective in hiring the best, most efficient workers and in choosing other inputs, decreasing their input requirements per unit of output. Decreases in demand for land and natural resources will cause their prices to drop. And as unemployment rises, wages will fall as workers compete for jobs. Each of these forces contributes to a drop in unit costs, and a decrease in the price level.

## Short Run versus Long Run

All three of our reasons are important in explaining why a change in output affects the price level. However, they operate within different time frames. When total output increases, new, less-productive workers will be hired rather quickly. Similarly, the prices of certain key inputs—such as lumber, land, oil, and wheat—may rise within a few weeks or months.

But our third explanation—changes in the nominal wage rate—is a different story. While wages in some lines of work might respond very rapidly, we can expect wages in many industries to change very little or not at all for a year or more after a change in output.

> *For a year or so after a change in output, changes in the average nominal wage are less important than other forces that change unit costs.*

Here are some of the more important reasons why wages in many industries respond so slowly to changes in output:

- Many firms have union contracts that specify wages for up to three years. Although wage increases are often built into these contracts, a rise in output will not affect the amount of the wage increase. When output rises or falls, these firms continue to abide by the contract.
- Wages in many large corporations are set by slow-moving bureaucracies.
- Wage changes in either direction can be costly to firms. Higher wages to attract new workers must be widely publicized in order to raise the number of job applicants at the firm. Lower wages can reduce the morale of workers—and their productivity. Thus, many firms are reluctant to change wages until they are reasonably sure that any change in their output will be long lasting.
- Firms may benefit from developing reputations for paying stable wages. A firm that raises wages when output is high and labor is scarce may have to lower wages when output is low and labor is plentiful. Such a firm would develop a reputation for paying unstable wages, and have difficulty attracting new workers.

For now, we focus exclusively on the short run—a time horizon of a year or so after a change in output. Since the average nominal wage rate changes very little over the short run, we'll make the following simplifying assumption: *The nominal wage rate is fixed in the short run.* More specifically,

> *we assume that changes in output have no effect on the nominal wage rate in the short run.*

Keep in mind, though, that our assumption of a constant wage holds only in the *short run.* As you will see later, wage changes play a very important role in the economy's adjustment over the long run.

Since we assume a constant nominal wage in the short run, a change in output will affect unit costs through the other two factors we mentioned earlier. Specifically, in the short run, a rise in real GDP raises firms' unit costs because (1) input requirements per unit of output rise, and (2) the prices of nonlabor inputs rise. With a constant percentage markup, the rise in unit costs translates into a rise in the price level. Thus,

> *in the short run, a rise in real GDP, by causing unit costs to increase, will also cause a rise in the price level.*

In the other direction, a *drop* in real GDP lowers unit costs because (1) input requirements per unit of output fall, and (2) the prices of nonlabor inputs fall. With a constant percentage markup, the drop in unit costs translates into a drop in the price level.

> *In the short run, a fall in real GDP, by causing unit costs to decrease, will also cause a decrease in the price level.*

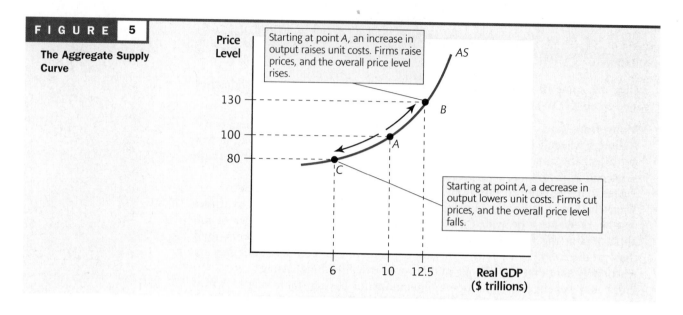

**FIGURE 5**

The Aggregate Supply
Curve

## DERIVING THE AGGREGATE SUPPLY CURVE

Figure 5 summarizes our discussion about the effect of output on the price level in the short run. Suppose the economy begins at point *A*, with output at $10 trillion and the price level at 100. Now suppose that output rises to $12.5 trillion. What will happen in the short run? Even though wages are assumed to remain constant, the price level will rise because of the other forces we've discussed. In the figure, the price level rises to 130, indicated by point *B*. If, instead, output *fell* to $6 trillion, the price level would fall—to 80 in the figure, indicated by point *C*.

As you can see, each time we change the level of output, there will be a new price level in the short run, giving us another point on the figure. If we connect all of these points, we obtain the economy's *aggregate supply curve*:

**Aggregate supply (*AS*) curve** A curve indicating the price level consistent with firms' unit costs and markups for any level of output over the short run.

> *The **aggregate supply curve** (or **AS curve**) tells us the price level consistent with firms' unit costs and their percentage markups at any level of output over the short run.*

A more accurate name for the *AS* curve would be the "short-run-price-level-at-each-output-level" curve, but that is more than a mouthful. The *AS* curve gets its name because it *resembles* a microeconomic market supply curve. Like the supply curve for maple syrup we discussed in Chapter 3, the *AS* curve is upward sloping, and it has a price variable (the price level) on the vertical axis and a quantity variable (total output) on the horizontal axis. But there, the similarity ends.

## MOVEMENTS ALONG THE *AS* CURVE

When a change in output causes the price level to change, we *move along* the economy's *AS* curve. But what happens in the economy as we make such a move?

Look again at the *AS* curve in Figure 5. Suppose we move from point *A* to point *B* along this curve in the short run. The increase in output raises the prices of raw materials and other (nonlabor) inputs and also raises input requirements per unit of output at many firms. Both of these changes increase costs per unit. As long as the markup remains somewhat stable, the rise in unit costs will lead firms to raise their prices, and the price level will increase. Thus, as we move upward along the *AS* curve, we can represent what happens as follows:

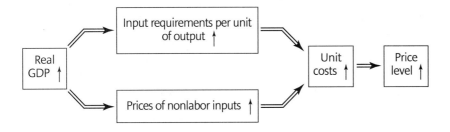

The opposite sequence of events occurs when real GDP falls, moving us downward along the *AS* curve:

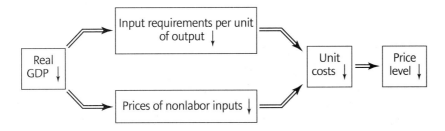

## SHIFTS OF THE *AS* CURVE

When we drew the *AS* curve in Figure 5, we assumed that a number of important variables remained unchanged. In particular, we assumed that the only changes in unit costs were those caused by a change in output. But in the real world, unit costs sometimes change for reasons *other* than a change in output. When this occurs, unit costs—*and* the price level—will change at *any* level of output, so the *AS* curve will shift.

In general, we distinguish between a movement along the *AS* curve, and a shift of the curve itself, as follows:

> *When a change in real GDP causes the price level to change, we move along the* AS *curve. When anything other than a change in real GDP causes the price level to change, the* AS *curve itself shifts.*

Figure 6 illustrates the logic of a shift in the *AS* curve. Suppose the economy's initial *AS* curve is $AS_1$. Now suppose that some economic event *other* than a change in output—for the moment, we'll leave the event unnamed—causes firms to raise their prices. Then the price level will be higher at *any* level of output we might imagine, so the *AS* curve must shift *upward*—for example, to $AS_2$ in the figure. At an output level of $10 trillion, the price level would rise from 100 to 140. At any other output level, the price level would also rise.

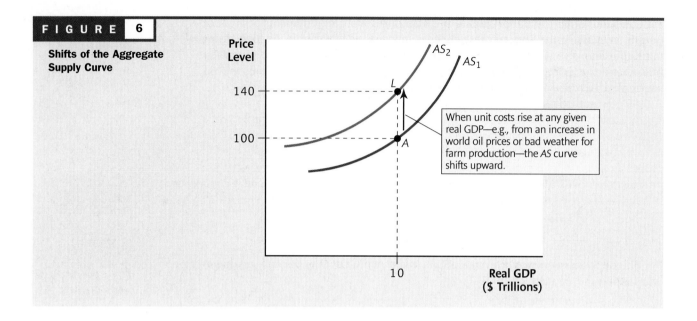

**FIGURE 6**

**Shifts of the Aggregate Supply Curve**

When unit costs rise at any given real GDP—e.g., from an increase in world oil prices or bad weather for farm production—the *AS* curve shifts upward.

What can cause unit costs to change at any given level of output? The following are some important examples:

- *Changes in world oil prices.* Oil is traded on a world market, where prices can fluctuate even while output in the United States does not. And changes in world oil prices have often caused shifts in the *AS* curve. For example, from January 2005 to July 2006, the price of oil rose from about $43 per barrel to more than $70. (The reasons included geopolitical instability in the Middle East, and the rapidly rising demand for oil in fast-growing economies such as China and India.) Some firms—especially those that use relatively large quantities of oil, gasoline, or jet fuel (including FedEx, UPS, and American Airlines)—

**A Misconception About the *AS* Curve** A common mistake about the *AS* curve is thinking that it describes the same kind of relationship between price and quantity as a microeconomic supply curve. There are two reasons why this is wrong.

First, the direction of causation between price and output is reversed for the *AS* curve. For example, when we draw the supply curve for maple syrup, we view changes in the price of maple syrup as causing a change in output supplied. But along the *AS* curve, it's the other way around: A change in *output* causes a change in the *price level*.

Second, the basic assumption behind the *AS* curve is very different from that behind a single market supply curve. When we draw the supply curve for an individual product, we assume that the prices of inputs used in producing the good remain fixed. This is a sensible thing to do because an increase in production for a single good is unlikely to have much effect on input prices in the economy as a whole.

But when we draw the *AS* curve, we imagine an increase in *real GDP*, in which *all* firms are increasing their output. This will significantly raise the demand for inputs, so it is unrealistic to assume that input prices will remain fixed. Indeed, the rise in input prices is one of the important reasons for the *AS* curve's upward slope.

raised prices right away, as did gasoline retailers. If oil prices had remained elevated, many other firms throughout the economy would have raised their prices as well, shifting the *AS* curve noticeably upward, as in Figure 6. (Fortunately, by October 2006, oil prices began coming down again, moderating this upward shift.)

Conversely, oil prices fell sharply during 1997 and 1998. This caused unit costs to decrease at many firms, shifting the *AS* curve downward.

- *Changes in the weather.* Good crop-growing weather increases farmers' yields for any given amounts of land, labor, capital, and other inputs used. This decreases farms' unit costs, and the price of agricultural goods falls. Since many of these goods are final goods (such as fresh fruit and vegetables), the price drop will contribute directly to a drop in the price level and a downward shift of the *AS* curve. Additionally, agricultural products are important inputs in the production of many other goods. (For example, corn is an input in beef production.) Good weather thus leads to a drop in input prices for many other firms in the economy, causing their unit costs, and their prices, to decrease. For these reasons, we can expect good weather to shift the *AS* curve downward. Bad weather, which decreases crop yields, increases unit costs at any level of output and shifts the *AS* curve upward.

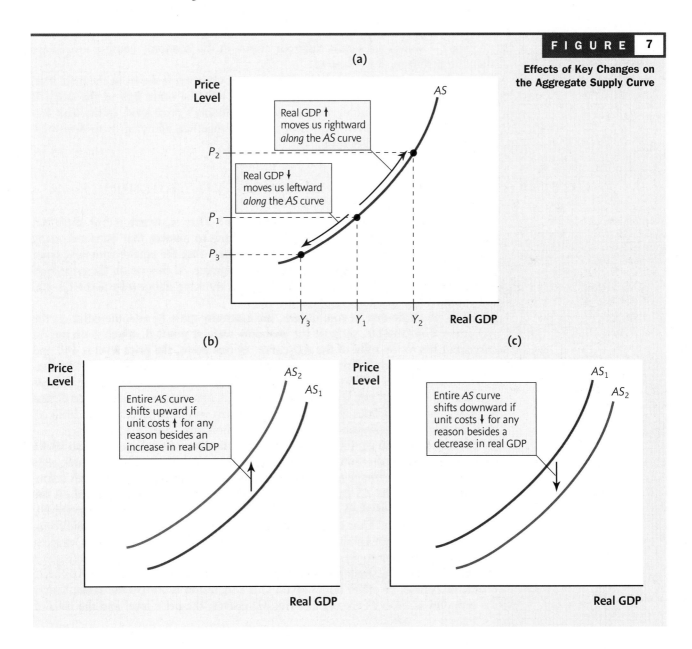

FIGURE 7

**Effects of Key Changes on the Aggregate Supply Curve**

- *Technological change.* New technologies can enable firms to produce any given level of output at lower unit costs. In recent years, for example, we've seen revolutions in telecommunications, information processing, and medicine. The result has been steady downward shifts of the *AS* curve.

- *The nominal wage.* Remember that in our short-run analysis we're assuming the nominal wage rate does *not* change. As we move along the *AS* curve, we hold the nominal wage rate constant. But later in the chapter—when we extend our time horizon beyond a year or so—you'll see that changes in the nominal wage are an important part of the economy's long-run adjustment process. Here we just point out that, *if* the nominal wage were to increase for any reason, it would raise unit costs for firms at any level of output and therefore *shift* the *AS* curve *upward*. Similarly, *if* the nominal wage rate were to fall for any reason, it would *decrease* unit costs at any level of output and shift the *AS* curve downward. We'll come back to this important fact later.

Figure 7 summarizes how different events in the economy cause a movement along, or a shift in, the *AS* curve.

But the *AS* curve tells only half of the economy's story: It shows us the price level *if* we know the level of output. The *AD* curve tells the other half of the story: It shows us the level of output *if* we know the economy's price level. In the next section, we finally put the two halves of the story together, allowing us to determine both the price level and output.

## AD AND AS TOGETHER: SHORT-RUN EQUILIBRIUM

**Short-run macroeconomic equilibrium** A combination of price level and GDP consistent with both the *AD* and *AS* curves.

Where will the economy settle in the short run? That is, where is our **short-run macroeconomic equilibrium**? Figure 8 shows how to answer that question, using both the *AS* curve and the *AD* curve. If you suspect that the equilibrium is at point *E*, the intersection of these two curves, you are correct. At that point, the price level is 100 and output is $10 trillion. But it's worth thinking about *why* point *E*—and only point *E*—is our short-run equilibrium.

First, we know that in equilibrium, the economy must be at some point on the *AD* curve. For example, suppose the economy were at point *B*, which is on the *AS* curve, but lies to the right of the *AD* curve. At this point, the price level is 140 and output is $14 trillion. But the *AD* curve tells us that with a price level of 140, *equilibrium* output is $6 trillion. Thus, at point *B*, real GDP would be greater than its equilibrium value. As you learned several chapters ago, this situation cannot persist for long, since inventories would pile up and firms would be forced to cut back on their production. Thus, point *B* cannot be our short-run equilibrium.

Second, short-run equilibrium requires that the economy be operating on its *AS* curve. Otherwise, firms would not be charging the prices dictated by their unit costs and the average percentage markup in the economy. For example, point *F* lies *below* the *AS* curve. But the *AS* curve tells us that if output is $14 trillion, based on the average percentage markup and unit costs, the price level should be 140 (point *B*), not something lower. That is, the price level at point *F* is *too low* for equilibrium. This situation will not last long either, since firms will want to raise prices, causing the overall price level to rise.

We could make a similar argument for any other point that is off the *AS* curve, off the *AD* curve, or off of both curves. Our conclusion is always the same: Unless the economy is on *both* the *AS* and the *AD* curves, the price level and the level of

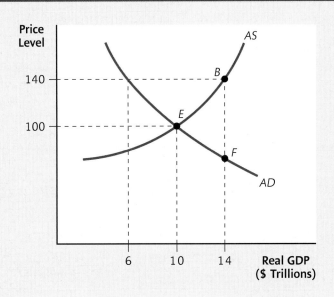

F I G U R E   8

**Short-Run Macroeconomic Equilibrium**

*Short-run equilibrium occurs where the AD and AS curves intersect. At point E, the price level of 100 is consistent with an output of $10 trillion along the AD curve. The output level of $10 trillion is consistent with a price level of 100 along the AS curve. At any other combination of price level and output, such as point F or point B, at least one condition for equilibrium will not be satisfied.*

output will change. Only when the economy is at point *E*—on *both* curves—can we have a sustainable level of real GDP and the price level.

## WHAT HAPPENS WHEN THINGS CHANGE?

Now that we know how the short-run equilibrium is determined, and armed with our knowledge of the *AD* and *AS* curves, we are ready to put the model through its paces. In this section, we'll explore how different types of events cause the short-run equilibrium to change.

Our short-run equilibrium will change when either the *AD* curve, the *AS* curve, or both, *shift*. Since the consequences for the economy are very different for shifts in the *AD* curve as opposed to shifts in the *AS* curve, economists have developed a shorthand language to distinguish between them:

> *An event that causes the* AD *curve to shift is called a* **demand shock.** *An event that causes the* AS *curve to shift is called a* **supply shock.**

**Demand shock** Any event that causes the *AD* curve to shift.

**Supply shock** Any event that causes the *AS* curve to shift.

In this section, we'll first explore the effects of demand shocks, both in the short run and during the adjustment process to the long run. Then, we'll take up the issue of supply shocks.

### DEMAND SHOCKS IN THE SHORT RUN

Figure 4, which lists the causes of a shift in the *AD* curve, also serves as a list of demand shocks to the economy. Let's consider some examples.

#### An Increase in Government Purchases

You've learned that an increase in government purchases shifts the *AD* curve rightward. Now we can see how it affects the economy in the short run. Figure 9 shows

FIGURE 9

**The Effect of a Demand Shock**

*Starting at point E, an increase in government purchases would shift the AD curve rightward to AD₂. Point J illustrates where the economy would move if the price level remained constant. But as output increases, the price level rises. Thus, the economy moves along the AS curve from point E to point N.*

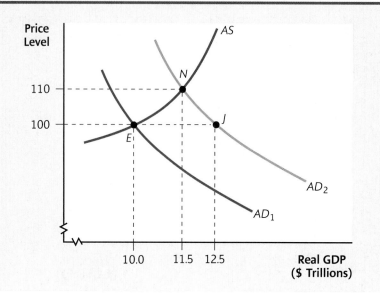

the initial equilibrium at point *E*, with the price level equal to 100 and output at $10 trillion. Now, suppose that government purchases rise by $1 trillion. Figure 4(b) tells us that the *AD* curve will shift rightward. What will happen to equilibrium GDP?

Back in Figure 3, this $1 trillion rise in government purchases increased output to $12.5 trillion. But that analysis did not consider any change in the price level. Thus, the rise in output to $12.5 trillion makes sense *only if the price level does not change*. Here, in Figure 9, this *would* be a movement rightward, from point *E* to point *J*. However, *point J does not describe the economy's short-run equilibrium*. Why not? Because it ignores two facts that you've learned about in this chapter: The rise in output will change the price level, and the change in the price level will, in turn, affect equilibrium GDP.

To see this more clearly, let's first suppose that the price level did *not* rise when output increased, so that the economy actually *did* arrive at point *J* after the *AD* shift. Would we stay there? Absolutely not. Point *J* lies below the *AS* curve, telling us that when GDP is $12.5 trillion, the price level consistent with firms' unit costs and average markup is *greater* than 100. Firms would soon raise prices, and this would cause a movement leftward along *AD₂*. The price level would keep rising and output would keep falling, until we reached point *N*. At that point, with output at $11.5 trillion, we would be on both the *AS* and *AD* curves, so there would be no reason for a further rise in the price level and no reason for a further fall in output.

However, the process we've just described is not entirely realistic. It assumes that when government purchases rise, *first* output increases (the move to point *J*) and *then* the price level rises (the move to point *N*). In reality, output and the price level tend to rise *together*. Thus, the economy would likely *slide along* the *AS* curve from point *E* to point *N*. As we move along the *AS* curve, output rises, increasing unit costs and the price level. At the same time, the rise in the price level *reduces equilibrium GDP* (the level of output toward which the economy is heading on the *AD* curve) from point *J* to point *N*.

We can summarize the impact of a rise in government purchases this way:

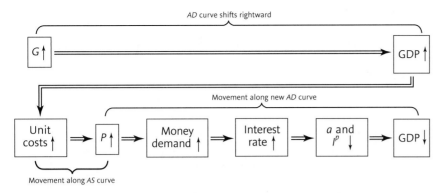

Net Effect: GDP ↑, but by less due to effect of P ↑

Let's step back a minute and get some perspective about this example of fiscal policy. When you first learned about fiscal policy, we used the simple multiplier formula to determine the impact of an increase in $G$ on real GDP. Now you've learned that a rise in government purchases will increase the price level. This, in turn, raises the interest rate in the money market and crowds out some interest-sensitive spending, thus making the rise in GDP smaller than it would be otherwise. We know that the crowding out is not complete, because GDP still rises. This tells us that the drop in consumption and investment spending must be smaller than the rise in government purchases. But this partial crowding out reduces the impact of fiscal policy on GDP. When the partial crowding out of $C$ and $I^p$ is included, the expenditure multiplier is smaller than our simple multiplier formula $[1/(1 - MPC)]$ suggests.[2]

We can summarize the impact of price-level changes this way:

> *When government purchases increase, the horizontal shift of the* AD *curve measures how much real GDP* would *increase if the price level remained constant.* But because the price level rises, real GDP rises by *less than the horizontal shift in the* AD *curve.*

Now let's switch gears into reverse: How would we illustrate the effects of a *decrease* in government purchases? In this case, the *AD* curve would shift *leftward*, causing the following to happen:

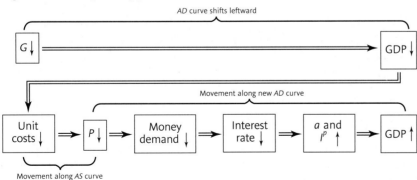

Net Effect: GDP ↓, but by less due to effect of P ↓

[2] If you've read the appendix to the chapter on "The Money Market and Monetary Policy," you learned that—even with no change in the price level—there is a feedback effect from the money market to GDP. This effect, too, reduces the size of the multiplier. The partial crowding out described here—caused by a rise in the price level—is *in addition* to the crowding out described in that appendix. It reduces the size of the multiplier further.

As you can see, the same sequence of events occurs in the same order, but each variable moves in the opposite direction. A decrease in government purchases decreases equilibrium GDP, but the multiplier effect is smaller because the price level falls.

### An Increase in the Money Supply

Although monetary policy stimulates the economy through a different channel than fiscal policy, once we arrive at the *AD* and *AS* diagram, the two look very much alike. For example, an increase in the money supply, which reduces the interest rate, will stimulate interest-sensitive consumption and investment spending. Real GDP then increases, and the *AD* curve shifts rightward, just as in Figure 9. Once output begins to rise, we have the same sequence of events as in fiscal policy: The price level rises, so the increase in GDP will be smaller. We can represent the situation as follows:

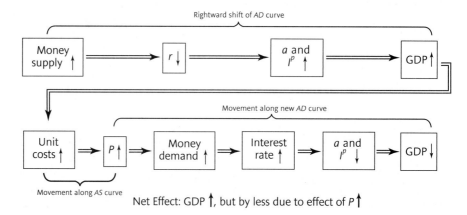

### Other Demand Shocks

On your own, try going through examples of different demand shocks (see the list in Figures 4(b) and (c)) and explain the sequence of events in each case that causes output and the price level to change. This will help you verify the following general conclusion about demand shocks:

> *A positive demand shock—one that shifts the* AD *curve rightward—increases both real GDP and the price level in the short run. A negative demand shock—one that shifts the* AD *curve leftward—decreases both real GDP and the price level in the short run.*

### An Example: The Great Depression

As mentioned at the beginning of the chapter, the U.S. economy collapsed far more seriously during the period 1929 through 1933—the onset of the Great Depression—than it did at any other time in the country's history. Because the price level fell during this time, we know that the contraction was caused by an adverse demand shock. (An adverse supply shock would have caused the price level to *rise* as GDP fell, as you will see in a few pages.)

What do we know about the demand shocks that caused the depression? This question has been debated by economists almost continuously over the past 70 years. The candidates are numerous, and it appears that a combination of events was responsible. The 1920s were a period of optimism, with high levels of investment by businesses and spending by families on houses and cars. The stock market soared. In the fall of 1929, the bubble of optimism burst. The stock market crashed, and investment and consumption spending plummeted. Similar events occurred in other countries, and the demand for products exported by the United States fell. The Fed—then only 16 years old—reacted by cutting the money supply sharply, which added an adverse monetary shock to all of the cutbacks in spending. Each of these events contributed to a leftward shift of the *AD* curve, causing both output and the price level to fall.

## DEMAND SHOCKS: ADJUSTING TO THE LONG RUN

In Figure 9, point N shows the new equilibrium after a positive demand shock *in the short run*—a year or so after the shock. But point N is not necessarily where the economy will end up in the long run. For example, suppose full-employment output is $10 trillion, and point N—representing an output of $11.5 trillion—is *above full-employment output*. Then, with employment unusually high and unemployment unusually low, business firms will have to compete to hire scarce workers, driving up the wage rate. It might take a year or more for the wage rate to rise significantly (recall our earlier list of reasons that wages adjust only slowly). But extending our horizon to several years or more, if output is above its potential, the wage rate will rise. Since the *AS* curve is drawn for a given wage, a rise in the wage rate will *shift* the curve upward, changing our equilibrium.

Alternatively, we could imagine a situation in which short-run equilibrium GDP was *below* its potential. In this case, with abnormally high unemployment, workers would compete to get scarce jobs, and eventually the wage rate would fall. Then the *AS* curve would shift downward, once again changing our equilibrium GDP.

> *In the short run, we treat the wage rate as given. But in the long run, the wage rate can change. When output is above full employment, the wage rate will rise, shifting the AS curve upward. When output is below full employment, the wage rate will fall, shifting the AS curve downward.*

Now we are ready to explore what happens over the long run in the aftermath of a demand shock. Figure 10 shows an economy in equilibrium at point *E*. We assume that the initial equilibrium is at full-employment output ($Y_{FE}$) because—as you are about to see—this is where the economy always ends up after the long-run adjustment process is complete. To make our results as general as possible, we'll use symbols, rather than numbers, to represent output and price levels.

Now suppose the *AD* curve shifts rightward due to, say, an increase in government purchases. In the short run, the equilibrium moves to point N, with a higher price level ($P_2$) and a higher level of output ($Y_2$). Point N tells us where the economy will be about a year after the increase in government purchases, before the wage rate has a chance to adjust. (Remember, along any given *AS* curve, the wage rate is assumed to be constant.)

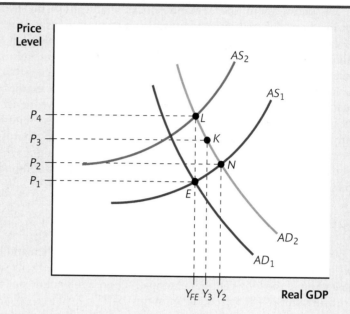

**FIGURE 10**

**Long-Run Adjustment After a Positive Demand Shock**

*Beginning at point E, a positive demand shock would shift the aggregate demand curve to $AD_2$, raising both output and the price level. At point N, output is above the full-employment level, $Y_{FE}$. Firms will compete to hire scarce workers, thereby driving up the wage rate. The higher wage rate will shift the AS curve to $AS_2$. Only when the economy returns to full-employment output at point L will there be no further shifts in AS.*

But now let's extend our analysis beyond a year. Notice that $Y_2$ is greater than $Y_{FE}$. Eventually, the wage will begin to rise, raising unit costs at any given output level and causing firms to raise prices. In the figure, the *AS* curve would begin shifting upward. Point *K* shows where the shifting aggregate supply curve might be 2 years after the shock, after the long-run adjustment process has begun. (You might want to pencil this intermediate *AS* curve into the figure, so that it intersects $AD_2$ at point *K*.) At this point, output would be at $Y_3$, and the rise in the price level has moved us along the new aggregate demand curve, $AD_2$.

But point *K* cannot be our final, long-run equilibrium. At $Y_3$, output is *still* greater than $Y_{FE}$, so the wage rate will continue to rise and the *AS* curve will continue to shift upward. At point *K*, the long-run adjustment process is not yet complete. When will the process end? Only when the wage rate stops rising, that is, only when output has returned to $Y_{FE}$. This occurs when the *AS* curve has shifted all the way to $AS_2$, moving the economy to point *L*—our new, long-run equilibrium.

As you can see, the increase in government purchases has no effect on equilibrium GDP in the long run: The economy returns to full employment, which is just where it started. This is why the long-run adjustment process is often called the economy's **self-correcting mechanism.** And this mechanism applies to any demand shock, not just an increase in government purchases:

**Self-correcting mechanism**
The adjustment process through which price and wage changes return the economy to full-employment output in the long run.

> *If a demand shock pulls the economy away from full employment, changes in the wage rate and the price level will eventually cause the economy to correct itself and return to full-employment output.*

For a positive demand shock that shifts the *AD* curve rightward, the self-correcting mechanism works like this:

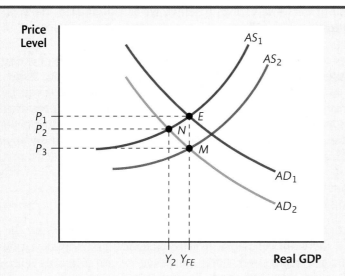

**Long-Run Adjustment After
a Negative Demand Shock**

*Starting from point* E, *a
negative demand shock shifts
the* AD *curve to* AD$_2$, *lowering GDP and the price level.
At point* N, *output is below
the full-employment level.
With unemployed labor
available, wages and unit
costs will fall, causing firms
to lower their prices. The* AS
*curve shifts downward until
full employment is regained
at point* M, *with a lower
price level.*

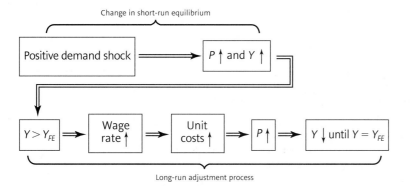

Figure 11 illustrates the case of a negative demand shock, in which the *AD* curve shifts leftward. Starting at point *E*, the short-run equilibrium moves to point *N*, with real GDP *below* $Y_{FE}$. Over the long run, high unemployment drives the wage rate down, shifting the *AS* curve down as well. The price level decreases, causing equilibrium GDP to rise along the $AD_2$ curve. The process comes to a halt only when output returns to $Y_{FE}$. Thus, in the long run, the economy moves from point *E* to point *M*, and the negative demand shock causes no change in equilibrium GDP.

The complete sequence of events after a negative demand shock looks like this:

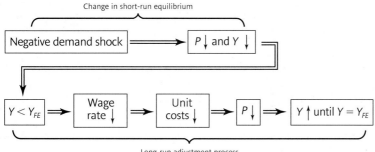

Pulling all of our observations together, we can summarize the economy's self-correcting mechanism as follows:

> *Whenever a demand shock pulls the economy away from full employment, the self-correcting mechanism will eventually bring it back. When output exceeds its full-employment level, wages will eventually rise, causing a rise in the price level and a drop in GDP until full employment is restored. When output is less than its full-employment level, wages will eventually fall, causing a drop in the price level and a rise in GDP until full employment is restored.*

### The Long-Run Aggregate Supply Curve

The self-correcting mechanism provides an important link between the economy's long-run and short-run behaviors. It helps us understand why deviations from full employment don't last forever. Often, however, we are primarily interested in the long-run effects of a demand shock. In these cases, we may want to skip over the self-correcting mechanism and go straight to its end result. A new version of the *AS* curve helps us do this.

Now look at Figure 12, which illustrates the impact of a positive demand shock like the one in Figure 10. The economy begins at full employment at point *E*, then moves to point *N* in the short run (before the wage rate rises), and then goes to point

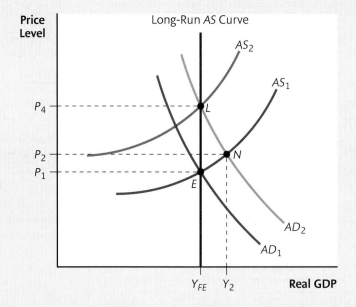

**FIGURE 12**

**The Long-Run *AS* Curve**

*This figure, like Figure 10, illustrates a positive demand shock, but focuses on the long-run effects. The initial equilibrium is at point E, with output at full employment ($Y_{FE}$) and price level $P_1$. After the positive demand shock and all the long-run adjustments to it, the economy ends up at point L with a higher price level ($P_4$), but the same full-employment output level ($Y_{FE}$). The long-run AS curve—a vertical line—shows all possible combinations of price level and output for the economy, skipping over the short-run changes. The vertical, long-run AS curve shows that in the long run, demand shocks can affect the price level but not output.*

*L* in the long run (after the rise in wages). If we skip over the short-run equilibrium, we find that the positive demand shock has moved the economy from *E* to *L*, which is vertically above *E*. That is, in the long run, the price level rises but output remains unchanged.

Now look at the vertical line in Figure 12, which shows another way of illustrating this long-run result. In the figure, the vertical line is the economy's **long-run aggregate supply curve**. It summarizes all possible output and price-level combinations at which the economy could end up in the long run. It is vertical because, in the long run, GDP will be the same—full-employment output—*regardless* of the position of the *AD* curve. The price level, however, will depend on the position of the *AD* curve. In the long run, a positive demand shock shifts the *AD* curve rightward, moving the economy from *E* to *L*: a higher price level, but the same level of output. Similarly, in Figure 11, a negative demand shock—which shifts the *AD* curve leftward—moves the economy from *E* to *M* in the long run: a lower price level with the same level of output. (You may want to pencil in a vertical long-run aggregate supply curve in Figure 11 to help you see that it is the same curve as the one drawn in Figure 12.)

The long-run aggregate supply curve tells us something very important about the economy: In the long run, after the self-correcting mechanism has done its job, *the economy behaves as the classical model predicts*. In particular, the classical model tells us that demand shocks cannot change equilibrium GDP in the long run. Figure 12 brings us to the same conclusion: While demand shocks shift the *AD* curve, this only moves the economy up or down along a vertical long-run *AS* curve, leaving output unchanged.[3]

The long-run aggregate supply curve also illustrates another classical conclusion. In the classical model, an increase in government purchases causes *complete crowding out*; the rise in government purchases is precisely matched by a drop in consumption and investment spending, leaving total output and total spending unchanged. In Figure 12, the same result holds in the long run. How do we know? The figures tell us that, in the long run, the rise in government purchases causes no change in GDP. But if GDP is the same, and government purchases are higher, then other components of GDP—consumption and investment—must decrease by the amount that government purchases increased.[4]

> *The self-correcting mechanism shows us that, in the long run, the economy will eventually behave as the classical model predicts.*

But notice the word *eventually* in the previous statement. It can take several years before the economy returns to full employment after a demand shock. This is why governments around the world are reluctant to rely on the self-correcting mechanism alone to keep the economy on track. Instead, they often use fiscal and monetary policies in an attempt to return the economy to full employment more quickly. We'll explore fiscal and monetary policies in more detail in the next two chapters.

**Long-run aggregate supply curve**
A vertical line indicating all possible output and price-level combinations at which the economy could end up in the long run.

---

[3] Of course, full-employment output can increase from year to year, as you learned in the chapter on economic growth. When the economy is growing, the long-run *AS* curve will shift rightward. In that case, the level of output at which the economy will eventually settle increases from year to year.

[4] Net exports can be crowded out as well. In a later chapter, you'll learn that a higher interest rate causes a currency's value to increase relative to foreign currencies. This causes exports to fall and imports to rise.

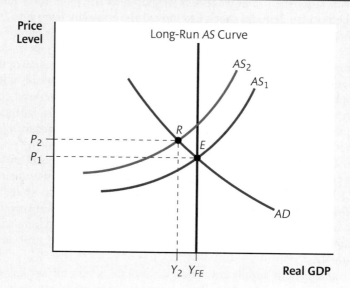

| FIGURE 13 |
| --- |

**The Effect of a Negative Supply Shock**

*A negative supply shock would shift the AS curve upward from $AS_1$ to $AS_2$. In the short-run equilibrium at point R, the price level is higher and output is below $Y_{FE}$. Eventually, wages will fall, causing unit costs to fall, and the AS curve will shift back to its original position. A positive supply shock would have just the opposite effect.*

## SUPPLY SHOCKS

In recent decades, supply shocks have been important sources of economic fluctuations. The most dramatic supply shocks have resulted from sudden changes in world oil prices. As you are about to see, supply shocks affect the economy differently than demand shocks.

### Short-Run Effects of Supply Shocks

Figure 13 shows an example of a supply shock: an increase in world oil prices that shifts the aggregate supply curve upward, from $AS_1$ to $AS_2$. As rising oil prices increase unit costs, firms will begin raising prices, and the price level will increase. The rise in the price level decreases equilibrium GDP along the $AD$ curve. In the short run, the price level will continue to rise, and the economy will continue to slide upward along its $AD$ curve, until we reach the $AS_2$ curve at point R. At this point, the price level is consistent with firms' unit costs and average markup (we are on the $AS$ curve), and total output is equal to total spending (we are on the $AD$ curve). As you can see, the short-run impact of higher oil prices is a rise in the price level and a fall in output. We call this a *negative* supply shock, because of the negative effect on output.

> In the short run, a negative supply shock shifts the AS curve upward, decreasing output and increasing the price level.

Notice the sharp contrast between the effects of negative supply shocks and negative demand shocks in the short run. After a negative demand shock (see, for example, Figure 11), both output and the price level fall. After a negative supply shock, output falls but the price level rises. Economists and journalists have coined the term **stagflation** to describe a *stagnating* economy experiencing in*flation*.

**Stagflation** The combination of falling output and rising prices.

> A negative supply shock causes stagflation *in the short run.*

Stagflation caused by increases in oil prices is not just a theoretical possibility. Three of our recessions in the last quarter century—in 1973–74, 1980, and 1990–91—followed increases in world oil prices. And each of these three recessions also saw jumps in the price level.

A *positive supply shock* would increase output by shifting the *AS* curve *downward*. (We call it positive, because of its effect on output.) As you can see if you draw such a shift on your own,

> *a positive supply shock shifts the* AS *curve downward, increasing output and decreasing the price level.*

Examples of positive supply shocks include unusually good weather, a drop in oil prices, and a technological change that lowers unit costs. In addition, a positive supply shock can sometimes be caused by government policy. A few chapters ago, we discussed how the government could use tax incentives and other policies to increase the rate of economic growth. These policies work by shifting the *AS* curve downward, thus increasing output while tending to decrease the price level.

## Long-Run Effects of Supply Shocks

What about the effects of supply shocks in the long run? In some cases, we need not concern ourselves with this question, because some supply shocks are temporary. For example, periods of rising oil prices are often followed by periods of falling oil prices. Similarly, supply shocks caused by unusually good or bad weather, or by natural disasters, are always short-lived. A temporary supply shock causes only a temporary shift in the *AS* curve; over the long run, the curve simply returns to its initial position, and the economy returns to full employment. In Figure 13, the *AS* curve would shift back from $AS_2$ to $AS_1$, the price level would fall, and the economy would move from point *R* back to point *E*.

In other cases, however, a supply shock can last for an extended period. One example was the rise in oil prices during the 1970s, which persisted for several years. In cases like this, is there a self-correcting mechanism that brings the economy back to full employment after a long-lasting supply shock? Indeed, there is, and it is the same mechanism that brings the economy back to full employment after a demand shock.

Look again at Figure 13. At point *R*, output is below full-employment output. In the long run, as workers compete for scarce jobs, the wage rate will decline. This will cause the *AS* curve to shift *downward*. The wage will continue to fall until the economy returns to full employment, that is, until we are back at point *E*.

> *In the long run, the economy self-corrects after a long-lasting supply shock, just as it does after a demand shock. When output differs from its full-employment level, the wage rate changes, and the* AS *curve shifts until full employment is restored.*

# USING THE THEORY

### The Story of Two Recessions

The aggregate demand and aggregate supply curves are more than just abstract graphs; they're tools to help us understand important economic events. For example, they can help us understand why the economy suffered its two most recent recessions, and also how and why these recessions differed from one another.

## THE RECESSION OF 1990–91

The story of the 1990–91 recession begins in mid-1990, when Iraq invaded Kuwait, a major oil producer. During this conflict, Kuwait's oil was taken off the world market, and so was Iraq's. The reduction in oil supplies resulted in a rapid and substantial increase in the price of oil, a key input to many industries. From the second to the fourth quarter of 1990, the price of oil doubled.

The left-hand panel of Figure 14 shows our *AS–AD* analysis of the shock. Initially, the economy was on both $AD_{1990}$ and $AS_{1990}$. Equilibrium was at point *E*, and output was at the full-employment level. Then, the oil price shock shifted the *AS* curve upward, to $AS_{1991}$, while leaving the *AD* curve more or less unchanged. As the short-run equilibrium moved to point *R*, real GDP fell and the price level *rose*. Now look at the left side of the next figure (Figure 15). The upper panel shows the behavior of GDP during the period leading up to, and during, the recession. As you can see, consistent with our *AS–AD* analysis, real GDP fell—from a high of $7.13 trillion in the third quarter of 1990 to a low of $7.04 trillion in the first quarter of 1991 (a decrease of 1.3 percent). The lower panel shows the behavior of the Consumer Price Index (CPI). While the CPI was rising modestly before the recession began, it rose more rapidly during the second half of 1990, as the recession took hold. Once again, this is consistent with what our *AS–AD* analysis predicts for a negative supply shock, such as the rise in oil prices in 1990.

What about the recovery that followed this recession? Once you know what the Fed did, you have all the tools to answer this question yourself. Problem 7 at the end of this chapter takes you through the process.

## THE RECESSION OF 2001

The story of the 2001 recession was quite different. This time, there was no spike in oil prices and no other significant supply shock to plague the economy. Rather, there was a demand shock, and a Federal Reserve policy during the year before the recession that might have made it a bit worse.

In earlier chapters, you learned that the major cause of the recession was a decrease in investment spending. To review: In the years leading up to 2001, businesses rushed to acquire and develop new equipment needed to exploit new technologies, such as the Internet and wireless communication. By 2001, many firms had sufficiently "caught up" and the flow of investment spending—while still positive and high—began to decrease relative to previous years. This decrease in investment spending was a demand shock to the economy: In 2001, the *AD* curve shifted leftward.

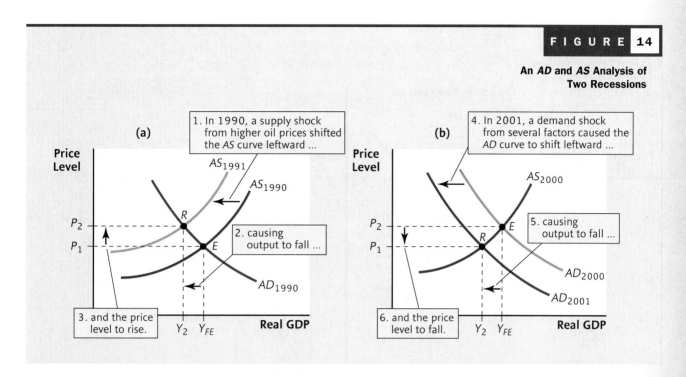

FIGURE 14

An *AD* and *AS* Analysis of
Two Recessions

**(a)**

**Price Level**

1. In 1990, a supply shock from higher oil prices shifted the *AS* curve leftward ...

$AS_{1991}$

$AS_{1990}$

$R$

$P_2$

$P_1$

$E$

2. causing output to fall ...

$AD_{1990}$

3. and the price level to rise.

$Y_2$   $Y_{FE}$

**Real GDP**

**(b)**

**Price Level**

4. In 2001, a demand shock from several factors caused the *AD* curve to shift leftward ...

$AS_{2000}$

$P_2$

$E$

$P_1$

$R$

5. causing output to fall ...

$AD_{2000}$

$AD_{2001}$

6. and the price level to fall.

$Y_2$   $Y_{FE}$

**Real GDP**

Now we can introduce another force that may have contributed to the recession of 2001: the policy of the Fed. During the late 1990s, the Fed had become concerned that the investment boom and consumer optimism were shifting the *AD* curve rightward too rapidly, creating a danger that we would overshoot potential GDP and set off higher inflation. The Fed responded by tightening up on the money supply and raising the interest rate. From mid-1999 to mid-2000, the Fed raised its federal funds rate target six times—a total of almost two full percentage points in less than a year. The Fed then held the rate at a relatively high 6.50 percent for another 6 months until early 2001. In retrospect, the Fed may have continued raising and holding the rate high a bit too long, even after the *AD* curve stopped moving rightward. And the effects of this policy may have continued into early 2001, exacerbating the decrease in investment that was occurring for other reasons. In this way, the rate hikes themselves may have contributed to a further leftward shift of the *AD* curve.

The right-hand panel of Figure 14 shows our *AS–AD* analysis of this period. Initially, the economy was on both $AD_{2000}$ and $AS_{2000}$, with equilibrium at point *E* and output roughly at the full-employment level. Then, the decrease in investment spending—helped along by the Fed—shifted the *AD* curve leftward, to $AD_{2001}$, while leaving the *AS* curve more or less unchanged. As the short-run equilibrium moved to point *R*, real GDP fell. This is mirrored in Figure 15, where the upper right-hand panel shows the behavior of GDP during the period leading up to, and during, the 2001 recession. As you can see, consistent with our *AS–AD* analysis, real GDP did fall in the first quarter of 2001, although it sputtered upward in the second quarter before falling again in the third.

But what about the price level? Here, we need to recognize that there is a slight difference between what our *AS–AD* analysis predicts and what actually happened.

FIGURE 15

FIGURE 15

**GDP and the Price Level in Two Recessions**

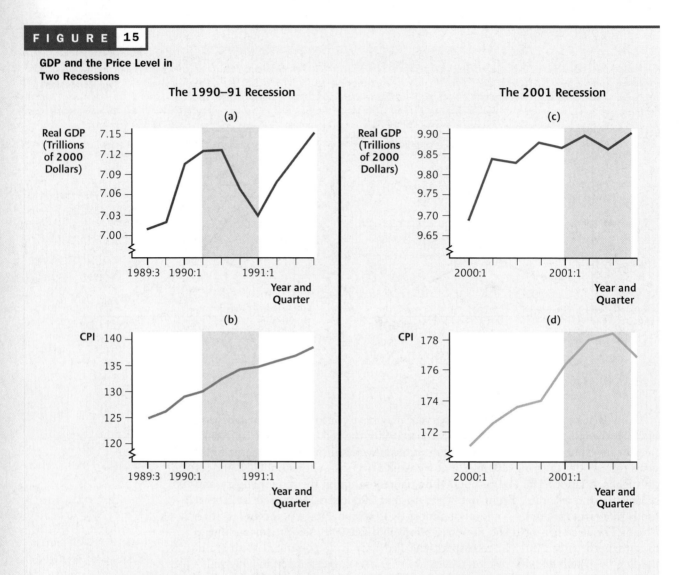

In the right panel of Figure 14, the price level falls. And indeed, in the lower right panel of Figure 15, you can see that the price level eventually fell—in the fourth quarter of 2001. But for much of the recession, instead of the price level falling we can see that it was rising, but more slowly as 2001 continued. In the next chapter, you will learn that inflation often has some momentum: When it's been rising at a certain rate for some time, then—left alone—it will continue to rise at that rate. The leftward shift in the *AD* curve meant that inflation was *not* left alone in early 2001, so while prices continued to rise, they rose more slowly due to the *AD* shift. And, as you can see, the downward pressure on prices from the shifting *AD* curve eventually overcame the inflationary momentum, causing a drop in the price level toward the end of 2001. This is just what we'd expect from our *AS–AD* analysis.

## Summary

The model of aggregate supply and demand explains how the price level and output are determined in the short run—a period of a year or so following a change in the economy—and how the economy adjusts over longer time periods as well.

The *aggregate demand* (AD) *curve* shows how changes in the price level affect equilibrium real GDP. A change in the price level shifts the money demand curve and alters the interest rate in the money market. The change in the interest rate, in turn, affects interest-sensitive forms of spending, shifts the aggregate expenditure curve, triggers the multiplier process, and leads to a new level of equilibrium real GDP. A lower price level means a higher equilibrium real GDP, and a higher price level means lower GDP. A change in government purchases, net taxes, autonomous consumption, planned investment, net exports, or the money supply will cause the AD curve to shift.

The *aggregate supply* (AS) *curve* summarizes the way changes in output affect the price level. To draw the AS curve, we assume that firms set the price of individual products as a markup over their costs per unit, and that the economy's average markup is determined by competitive conditions. We also assume that the nominal wage rate is fixed in the short run. As we move upward along the AS curve, a rise in real GDP, by raising unit costs, causes the price level to increase. When anything other than a change in real GDP causes the price level to change, the entire AS curve shifts.

AD and AS together determine real GDP and the price level. The economy must be on the AD curve, or real GDP would not be at its equilibrium level. It must be on the AS curve or firms would not be charging prices dictated by their unit costs and markups. Both conditions are satisfied at the intersection of the two curves.

The AD–AS equilibrium can be disturbed by a *demand shock*. An increase in government purchases, for example, shifts the AD curve rightward. As a result, the price level rises, and so does real GDP. In the long run, if GDP is above potential, wages will rise. This causes unit costs to rise and shifts the AS curve upward. Eventually, GDP will return to potential and the only long-run result of the demand shock is a higher price level. This implies that the economy's long-run aggregate supply curve is vertical at potential output.

The short-run AD–AS equilibrium can also be disturbed by a *supply shock*, such as an increase in world oil prices. With unit costs higher at each level of output, the AS curve shifts upward, decreasing real GDP and increasing the price level. Eventually, the shock will be self-correcting: With output below potential, the wage rate will fall, unit costs will decrease, and the AS curve will shift back downward until full employment is restored.

## Problem Set
*Answers to even-numbered Questions and Problems can be found on the text Web site at www.thomsonedu.com/economics/hall.*

1. Redraw Figure 2, showing how a decrease in the price level will lead to an increase in equilibrium real GDP.

2. With a three-panel diagram—one panel showing the money market, one showing the aggregate expenditure diagram, and one showing the AD curve—show how a *decrease* in the money supply shifts the AD curve leftward.

3. Suppose firms become pessimistic about the future and consequently investment spending falls. With an AD and AS graph, describe the short-run effects on real GDP and the price level. If the price level were constant, how would your answer change?

4. With an AD and AS diagram, explain the short-run effect of a decrease in the money supply on real GDP and the price level. What is the effect in the long run? Assume the economy begins at full employment.

5. Use an AD and AS graph to explain the short-run and long-run effects on real GDP and the price level of an increase in autonomous consumption spending. Assume the economy begins at full employment.

6. A new government policy successfully lowers firms' unit costs. What are the short-run and the long-run effects of such a policy? (Assume that full-employment output does not change.)

7. Make two copies of Figure 14(a) on a sheet of paper. Add curves to illustrate your answer to (a) on one copy and (b) on the other:
   a. What *would* have happened in the years after 1991 if the Fed had done nothing and the economy had relied solely on the self-correcting mechanism to return to full employment?
   b. What *did* happen as a result of the Fed bringing down the interest rate to end the recession?
   c. Is there a difference in the behavior of the price level during the recovery in these two cases? Explain.

8. Make two copies of Figure 14(b) on a sheet of paper. Add curves to illustrate the impacts of Fed policy for (a) on one copy and (b) on the other:
   a. What *would* have happened in the years following 2001 if the Fed had done nothing and the economy had relied solely on the self-correcting mechanism to return to full employment?
   b. What *did* happen as a result of the Fed's actual policy in 2001 (successive cuts in the interest rate throughout the year)?
   c. Is there a difference in the behavior of the price level during the recovery in these two cases? Explain.

9.  Increased international trade has forced many U.S. firms to compete with foreign producers. The increased competition has likely affected the average markup in the U.S. economy. Use *AS* and *AD* curves to illustrate the short-run impact on the economy if, at the same time,
    a.  The Fed does nothing.
    b.  The Fed pursues a policy that successfully achieves the highest possible level of GDP with no rise in the price level.
10. a.  Graphically show the effects of a temporary decrease in nonlabor input prices.
    b.  How will your results change if this decrease lasts for an extended period?
    c.  How would your results differ if the Fed intervened to keep the economy at full employment?

### More Challenging

11. Suppose that wages are slow to adjust downward but rapidly adjust upward. What would the *AS* curve look like? How would this affect the economy's adjustment to demand shocks (compared to the analysis given in the chapter)?
12. During the 1990s, because of technological change, the *AS* curve was shifting downward, but—except for a few months—the price level did not fall. Why not? (Hint: What was the Fed doing?)

# Inflation and Monetary Policy

In the late 1970s, the annual inflation rate in the United States reached 13 percent. At the time, polls showed that the public considered inflation the most serious economic problem facing the country. From 1991 to 2005, however, the annual inflation rate never exceeded 3.5 percent in any year, and the problem receded as a matter of public concern. Bringing the inflation rate down, and keeping it low, was one of the solid victories of national economic policy.

But in 2006, inflation began to creep up again, reaching 4.9 percent (at an annual rate) during the first half of the year.

Why was the inflation rate so high in the 1970s? How did the Fed bring the rate down? Why did it begin to plague the economy again in early 2006? And finally, how should the Fed respond to future economic disturbances?

In this chapter, we'll be addressing these and other questions as we take a closer look at the Fed's conduct of monetary policy. Our earlier discussions of monetary policy were somewhat limited, because we lacked the tools—aggregate demand and aggregate supply—to explain changes in the price level. In this chapter, we'll explore monetary policy more fully, making extensive use of the *AD* and *AS* curves.

## THE OBJECTIVES OF MONETARY POLICY

The Fed's objectives have changed over the years. When the Fed was first established in 1913, its chief responsibility was to ensure the stability of the banking system. By acting as a *lender of last resort*—injecting reserves into the banking system in times of crisis—the Fed was supposed to alleviate financial panics.

By the 1950s, the stability of the banking system was no longer a major concern, largely because the United States had not had a banking panic in decades. (Deposit insurance programs had effectively eliminated panics.) Accordingly, the Fed's objective in the 1950s and 1960s changed to keeping the interest rate low and stable. In the 1970s, the Fed's objectives shifted once again. As stated in the Federal Reserve Banking Act of 1978, which is still in force, the Fed is now responsible for achieving a low, stable rate of inflation, as well as full employment of the labor force. Let's consider each of these goals in turn.

### LOW, STABLE INFLATION

Why is a low rate of inflation important? Several chapters ago, we reviewed the social costs of inflation. When the inflation rate is high, society uses up resources coping with it—resources that could have been used to produce goods and services. Among these resources are the labor needed to update prices at stores and factories, as well as the additional time spent by households and businesses to manage their wealth and protect it from a loss of purchasing power.

In addition to keeping the inflation rate low, the Fed tries to keep it *stable* from year to year. For example, the Fed would prefer a steady yearly inflation rate of 3 percent to an inflation rate of 5 percent half the time, and 1 percent the other half, even though the average inflation rate would be 3 percent in both cases. The reason is that unstable inflation is difficult to predict accurately; it will often turn out higher or lower than people expected. As you learned several chapters ago, an inflation rate higher than expected redistributes real income from lenders to borrowers, while an inflation rate lower than expected has the opposite effect. Thus, unstable inflation adds to the risk of lending and borrowing, and interferes with long-run financial planning.

The Fed, as a public agency, chooses its policies with the costs of inflation in mind. And the Fed has another concern: Inflation is very unpopular with the public. Surveys show that most people associate high rates of inflation with a general breakdown of government and the economy.[1] A Fed chairman who delivers low rates of inflation is seen as popular and competent, while one who tolerates high inflation goes down in history as a failure.

## FULL EMPLOYMENT

"Full employment" means that unemployment is at normal levels. But what, exactly, is a *normal* amount of employment?

Recall that there are different types of unemployment. Some of the unemployed in any given month will find jobs after only a short time of searching. This *frictional* unemployment is part of the normal workings of the labor market and is not a serious social problem. Other job seekers will spend many months or years out of work because they lack the skills that employers require, or because they lack information about available jobs. While this *structural* unemployment is a serious social problem, it is best solved with *micro*economic policies, such as job-training programs or improved information flows.

*Cyclical* unemployment, by contrast, is a *macro*economic problem. It occurs during a recession, in which millions of workers lose their jobs and remain unemployed as they seek new ones. This is why macroeconomists use the term "full employment" to mean *the absence of cyclical unemployment*. When the economy achieves full employment according to this definition, macroeconomic policy has done all that it can do.

The Fed is concerned about cyclical unemployment for two reasons. First is its *opportunity cost*: the output that the unemployed could have produced if they were working. Part of this opportunity cost is paid by the unemployed themselves, in the form of lost earnings, and part is paid by people who remain employed but pay higher taxes to provide unemployment benefits to job losers. By maintaining full employment, the Fed can help society avoid this cost.

Second, cyclical unemployment represents a social failure. In a recession, people who have the right skills and who could be working actually *lose* their jobs. Excess

[1] Robert J. Shiller, "Public Resistance to Inflation: A Puzzle," *Brookings Papers on Economic Activity,* 1997.

unemployment lingers for several years after a recession strikes. Thus, cyclical unemployment caused by a recession is a partial breakdown of the system. The economy is not doing what it should do: provide a job for anyone who wants to work and who has the needed skills.

But why should the Fed try to eliminate only *cyclical* unemployment? Why not go further and push output above its full-employment level? After all, at higher levels of output, business firms would be more willing to hire *any* available workers. The frictionally unemployed would find jobs more easily, and some of the structurally unemployed would be hired as well. If unemployment is a bad thing, shouldn't the Fed aim for the lowest possible unemployment rate?

The answer is no. If the unemployment rate falls too low, GDP rises beyond its potential, full-employment level. As you learned in the last chapter, this causes the economy's self-correcting mechanism to kick in: The *AS* curve shifts upward, increasing the price level. Thus, unemployment that is too low compromises the Fed's other chief goal by creating inflation. And, as you will see later in the chapter, the Fed cannot keep the economy operating above full employment for more than a short time anyway. In the long run, its attempts to push the economy too hard would only create more inflation and would not succeed in lowering unemployment.

The unemployment rate at which GDP is at its full-employment level—that is, with no cyclical unemployment—is sometimes called the **natural rate of unemployment**.

> *When the unemployment rate is below the natural rate, GDP is greater than potential output. The economy's self-correcting mechanism will then create inflation. When the unemployment rate is above the natural rate, GDP is below potential output. The self-correcting mechanism will then put downward pressure on the price level.*

**Natural rate of unemployment** The unemployment rate when there is no cyclical unemployment.

The word *natural* must be interpreted with care. The natural unemployment rate is not etched in stone, nor is it the outcome of purely natural forces that can't be influenced by public policy. But it is determined by rather slow-moving forces in the economy: how frequently workers move from job to job, how efficiently the unemployed can search for jobs and firms can search for new workers, and how well the skills of the unemployed match the skills needed by employers.

Still, the natural rate can change when any of these underlying conditions change. And it can also be influenced by government policies that provide incentives or disincentives for workers to find jobs quickly, or for employers to hire them. Indeed, economists generally believe that over the past decade, the natural rate has decreased in the United States—from 6 or 6.5 percent in the mid-1980s to perhaps as low as 4.5 percent today. Meanwhile, in some European economies, the natural rate of unemployment increased during the 1990s and remains stuck at high levels—close to 10 percent in France and Spain. The causes of these changes in the natural rate, as well as the *extent* of the changes, are hotly debated by economists. But there is general agreement that the rate has come down in the United States and remained high in continental Europe.

Why use the term *natural* for such a changeable feature of the economy? The term makes sense only from the perspective of *macroeconomic* policy. Simply put, there isn't much that macroeconomic policy can do about the natural rate. Stimulating the economy with fiscal or monetary policy may bring the *actual* unemployment rate down for a time, but it will not change the natural rate itself. And pushing unemployment below the natural rate would cause inflation. Thus, the natural rate of unemployment can be seen as a kind of goalpost for the Fed. The location of the goalpost may change over the years, but during any given year, it tells us where the Fed is aiming.

## THE FED'S PERFORMANCE

How well has the Fed achieved its goals? Panel (a) of Figure 1 shows the annual inflation rate since 1950, as measured by the Consumer Price Index. You can see that monetary policy permitted extended periods of high inflation in the 1970s and

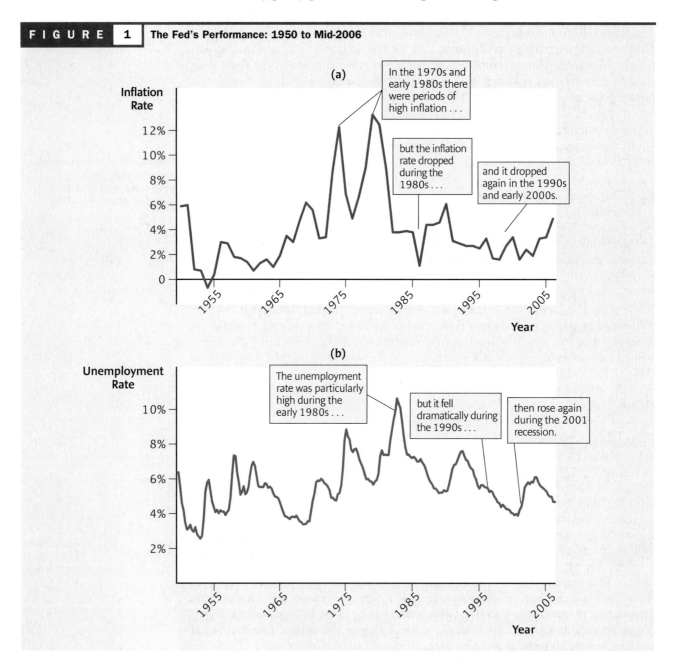

**FIGURE 1**  The Fed's Performance: 1950 to Mid-2006

early 1980s. You can also see, as noted at the beginning of the chapter, that the Fed has achieved great success in controlling inflation since then. Indeed, in the 20 years leading up to 2006, the annual inflation rate exceeded 4.6 percent only once—in 1990, during the supply shock caused by higher oil prices. And in recent years, inflation near or under 3.0 percent has become the norm.

Panel (b) shows the quarterly rate of unemployment since 1950. Over the last 20 years of that period, the Fed has succeeded in keeping inflation in check. But its performance on unemployment has been somewhat mixed. From mid-1986 to mid-2006, the unemployment rate was 6.5 percent or greater—significantly above its natural rate—more than one-fifth of the time. But notice the remarkable improvement from mid-1992 and after, as the Fed slowly inched the unemployment rate down to 4 percent *without* heating up inflation. The Fed even managed to keep the unemployment rate hovering near 4 percent for more than 2 years until it began to rise during the recession of 2001.

As you can see, the Fed has mostly had a good—and improving—record in recent years. The inflation rate has been kept low and relatively stable, and—except for our most recent recession—unemployment has been near and even below most estimates of the natural rate. How has the Fed done it? Are there any general conclusions we can reach about how a central bank should operate to achieve the twin goals of full employment and a stable, low inflation rate? Indeed there are, as you'll see in the next section.

## FEDERAL RESERVE POLICY: THEORY AND PRACTICE

The Fed's job is not an easy one. It must constantly respond to macroeconomic events with its twin goals in mind: low inflation and full employment. In some cases, the correct response—at least in theory—is clear, because the same action that maintains full employment also helps maintain low inflation. But in other cases, the Fed must trade off one goal for another: Responses that maintain full employment will worsen inflation, and responses that alleviate inflation will create more unemployment.

We'll make a temporary simplifying assumption in this section: that the Fed's goal for the inflation rate is *zero*. In reality, the Fed's goal is *low*, but not zero, inflation. Later, we'll discuss why the Fed prefers a low inflation rate to a zero rate, and how this modifies our analysis.

### RESPONDING TO DEMAND SHOCKS

In the last chapter, you learned that a demand shock is a change in spending that shifts the economy's aggregate demand (*AD*) curve. Suppose an economy is operating at its potential output, and then it is hit with a *positive* demand shock. The shock might come from fiscal policy (an increase in government purchases or a tax cut) or from the private sector (an increase in autonomous consumption, investment, or net exports). In theory, how should the Fed respond?

Let's consider three possible responses: Maintaining the money supply, maintaining the interest rate, and neutralizing the shock. As you'll see, the first two responses would be poor choices for the Fed. The last one does the best job in achieving the Fed's goals.

### Hypothetical Response: Constant Money Supply

Figure 2 illustrates an economy that is initially operating at full employment. Panel (a) shows the money market, with an equilibrium interest rate of 5 percent (point A). Panel (b) shows the aggregate demand and aggregate supply diagram. The equilibrium (point E) is a price level of 100 and an output of $10 trillion—the assumed full-employment level. Points A and E represent a *long-run* equilibrium for this economy—with output at its potential and, therefore, unemployment at its natural rate, the economy is at rest.

Then a positive demand shock (an increase in spending) hits the economy, setting off the multiplier process. The AD curve shifts rightward, from $AD_1$ to $AD_2$. At every price level, equilibrium GDP is greater than before. If, for example, the price level stayed at 100, the figure tells us that equilibrium GDP would rise to $12.5 trillion (point F). But that is not necessarily where the economy will end up; it depends on the actions of the Fed.

In the last chapter, we assumed that the Fed's response to a demand shock was to hold the money supply constant and allow the interest rate to rise automatically to its new equilibrium level. That is not a realistic description of Fed policy, but it served as a benchmark case. In Figure 2, we once again explore this benchmark case.

In panel (b), the rise in GDP causes a movement along the economy's AS curve, and the price level rises. In the money market in panel (a), the rise in the price level shifts the money demand curve rightward, driving the interest rate up to 7 percent (point B). This crowds out some consumption and investment spending, so that GDP does not rise by as much as it otherwise would. But it still rises. In panel (b),

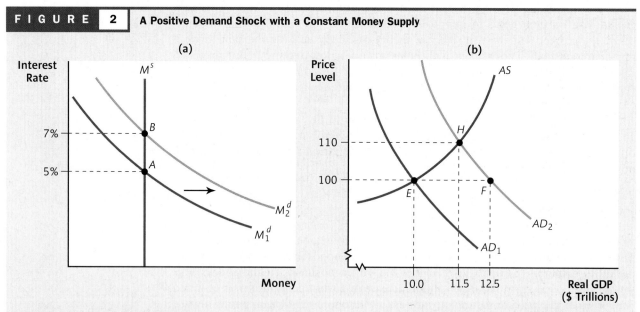

| FIGURE | 2 | A Positive Demand Shock with a Constant Money Supply |

*A positive demand shock would shift the AD curve rightward to $AD_2$ in panel (b), causing both the price level and output to rise. If the Fed maintains a constant money supply, the rise in the price level causes the money demand curve to shift to $M_2^d$ in panel (a), driving the interest rate up from 5 percent to 7 percent. A higher interest rate causes some crowding out of consumption and investment spending, but not complete crowding out. In panel (b), output ends up higher than initially, and the price level rises as well (point H).*

we end up at point $H$, with the price level rising to 110, and real GDP rising to $11.5 trillion.

As you can see, the Fed would not want to respond to a positive demand shock by holding the money supply constant as in the figure. Output would rise above potential, bringing the unemployment rate below its natural rate. The price level would rise as well—to 110 in the figure. And in the long run, the price level would rise further, as the self-correcting mechanism returned the economy to full employment (by shifting the $AS$ curve upward—not shown).

> *If a fully employed economy experiences a positive demand shock, and the Fed responds by holding the money supply constant, output will overshoot its potential. The price level will rise in the short run, and rise further in the long run.*

Since we are assuming, for now, that one of the Fed's goals is zero inflation, holding the money supply constant would not be an advisable response.

### Hypothetical Response: Constant Interest Rate

Two chapters ago, you learned that, in practice, the Fed conducts monetary policy by setting an interest rate target. It then adjusts the money supply as necessary to hit the desired target. What would happen if the Fed, in response to a positive demand shock, chose to maintain a constant interest rate target?

Figure 3 provides the answer. In panel (a), the interest rate is initially at its target rate of 5 percent. In panel (b), the economy is at full employment with output of $10.0 trillion. When the positive demand shock hits, the $AD$ curve begins to shift rightward in panel (b). We've included $AD_2$ in the figure, to show where the $AD$ curve would be if the Fed did not change the money supply (as in the last example). But this time, as the money demand curve shifts rightward in panel (a), and the interest rate rises, the Fed increases the money supply (shifting the money supply curve to $M_2^s$). This will maintain the interest rate at its target of 5 percent (point $C$).[2]

An increase in the money supply, as you've learned, is one of the factors that shifts the $AD$ curve rightward. So now, in panel (b), the $AD$ curve will shift out further than it did before—all the way to $AD_3$. (The spending change first shifts it to $AD_2$; the increase in the money supply shifts it further, to $AD_3$.) In effect, by maintaining the interest rate target at 5 percent, the Fed prevents *any* crowding out of consumption or investment that would otherwise result from a higher interest rate. Instead, it allows the economy to experience the full effect of the multiplier, so output rises all the way to $12.5 trillion (point $J$).

But notice the consequence: In Figure 3, the price level rises even more (in comparison with the constant-money-supply policy of Figure 2). By maintaining its interest rate target, the Fed pushes output even further beyond its potential, causing an even greater rise in the price level both in the short run (to 130 in the figure) and in the long run (as the economy self-corrects—not shown).

---

[2] You might have noticed that in panel (a) of Figure 3, the money demand curve shifts out further than in Figure 2. This is because in Figure 3, the price level ends up higher, so the increase in money demand is greater.

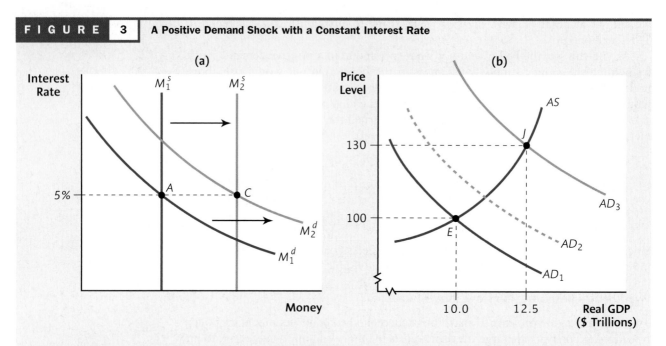

**FIGURE 3** **A Positive Demand Shock with a Constant Interest Rate**

*A positive demand shock initially shifts the AD curve rightward to AD₂ in panel (b), causing both the price level and output to rise. The rise in the price level shifts the money demand curve rightward to M²ᵈ in panel (a), which would ordinarily cause the interest rate to rise. But if the Fed maintains a constant interest rate target, it will increase the money supply to prevent any rise in the interest rate. There will be no crowding out of consumption or investment spending, so the AD curve in panel (b) shifts further rightward (to AD₃). As a result, the economy ends up at point J, with output and the price level rising by more than under a constant-money-supply policy.*

> *If a fully employed economy experiences a positive demand shock, a constant interest rate creates an even greater overshooting of potential output than a constant money supply. The result is an even greater rise in the price level.*

You can see that maintaining a constant interest rate would be an even poorer choice for the Fed than maintaining a constant money supply.

### Best Response: Neutralization

A third possible response to a demand shock—and the best one—is for the Fed to prevent any shift in the *AD* curve at all. That is, the Fed should completely neutralize the demand shock.

This is illustrated in Figure 4. Once again, in panel (b), an increase in spending begins to shift the *AD* curve rightward (as indicated by the rightward arrow). But this time, instead of keeping the money supply constant (so the interest rate rises enough for *partial* crowding out) or keeping the interest rate constant (preventing *any* crowding out at all), the Fed now creates *complete crowding out.* That is, it raises its interest rate target by just enough to make spending fall as much as it initially rose from the demand shock. In this way, total spending remains unchanged, and the *AD* curve does not shift at all. In the figure, this is indicated by arrows showing the *AD* curve first shifts rightward, and then leftward back to its original position.

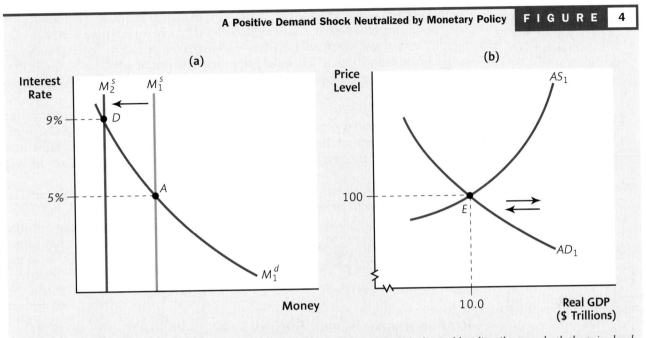

**A Positive Demand Shock Neutralized by Monetary Policy**   FIGURE   4

*A positive demand shock begins to shift the AD curve rightward in panel (b), which would ordinarily cause both the price level and output to rise. But the Fed can neutralize the shock by increasing its interest rate target enough to cause complete crowding out of consumption and investment spending. To reach the new, higher interest rate target, the Fed must decrease the money supply in panel (a), moving the money market equilibrium to a point like D. This reverses (or prevents) the shift in the AD curve, so the economy ends up at point E in panel (b), at its initial output and price level.*

Panel (a) shows what happens in the money market as the Fed raises its interest rate target. In order to neutralize the demand shock completely, the Fed must raise the interest rate *higher* than it rose in Figure 2 (which caused only partial crowding out). In Figure 4, we assume that an interest rate of 9 percent will do the trick. The Fed shifts the money supply curve leftward, from $M_1^s$ to $M_2^s$, moving the money market equilibrium to point $D$. Note that the money demand curve does not shift in this case. This is because, in the end, we are back at our original price level.

If the Fed acts quickly enough, it could prevent the demand shock from shifting the $AD$ curve at all, keeping the economy at point $E$ in panel (b). The Fed could thus prevent *any* rise in the price level. At the same time, it could keep the economy at full employment.

If a *negative* demand shock hits the economy, shifting the $AD$ curve leftward, the Fed should respond with the opposite policy: lowering its interest rate target by *increasing* the money supply. The lower interest rate will stimulate additional consumption and investment spending, and can prevent the $AD$ curve from shifting leftward.

> *To maintain full employment and price stability after a demand shock, the Fed must change its interest rate target. A positive demand shock requires an increase in the target; a negative demand shock requires a decrease in the target.*

In recent years, the Fed has changed its interest rate target as frequently as needed to keep the economy on track. If the Fed observes that the economy is overheating—and that the unemployment rate has fallen below its natural rate—it will raise its target. The Fed, believing that the *AD* curve was shifting rightward too rapidly, reacted this way from June 2004 to June 2006, raising its federal funds rate target 17 times in 2 years. When the Fed raises its target, it responds to forces that shift the *AD* curve rightward by creating an opposing force—a higher interest rate—to prevent the shift.

When the Fed observes that the economy is sluggish—and the unemployment rate has risen above its natural rate—the Fed will lower its target. The Fed did this aggressively throughout 2001, dropping its federal funds rate target 12 times that year. In this way, the Fed created a force opposing the leftward shift of the *AD* curve.

As you can see, demand shocks present the Fed with a no-lose situation: The same policy that helps to keep unemployment at its natural rate also helps to maintain a stable price level. However, these shocks present a challenge to the Fed that it doesn't face during other, less-eventful periods. To change the interest rate target by just the right amount, the Fed needs accurate information about how the economy operates. We'll return to this and other problems in conducting monetary policy a bit later.

## RESPONDING TO SUPPLY SHOCKS

So far in this chapter, you've seen that demand shocks, in general, present the Fed with easy policy choices. By changing its interest rate target from time to time, it can deal with demand shocks, such as those caused by changes in aggregate expenditure. For demand shocks, the very same policy that maintains a stable price level also helps to maintain full employment.

But adverse or negative *supply* shocks present the Fed with a true dilemma: If the Fed tries to preserve price stability, it will worsen unemployment; if it tries to maintain high employment, it will worsen inflation. And even though supply shocks are usually temporary, the shocks themselves—and the Fed's response—can affect the economy for several quarters or even years.

Figure 5 illustrates the Fed's dilemma when confronting an adverse supply shock. Initially, the economy is at point *E* (full employment). Then, a supply shock—say, a rise in world oil prices—shifts the *AS* curve up to $AS_2$. One possible response for the Fed is to keep the *AD* curve at $AD_1$. It would do this by holding the *money supply* constant as the price level rose, allowing the interest rate to rise (not shown) and allowing the economy to move along $AD_1$. The short-run equilibrium would then move from point *E* to point *R*, and the economy would experience *stagflation*—both inflation and a recession—with output falling to $Y_2$ and the price level rising to $P_2$.

But the Fed can instead respond by *shifting* the *AD* curve, changing the money supply in order to alter the short-run equilibrium. Which policy should it choose? The answer will depend on whether it is mostly concerned about rising prices or rising unemployment. Let's start by imagining two extreme positions.

First, the Fed could prevent inflation entirely by decreasing the money supply, shifting the *AD* curve leftward to the curve labeled $AD_{\text{no inflation}}$. This would move the short-run equilibrium to point *T*. Notice, though, that while the price level remains at $P_1$, output decreases to $Y_3$, exacerbating the recession.

At the other extreme, the Fed could prevent any fall in output. To accomplish this, the Fed would *increase* the money supply and shift the *AD* curve rightward, to $AD_{\text{no recession}}$. The equilibrium would then move to point *V*, keeping output at its full-

FIGURE 5

**Responding to Supply Shocks**

*Starting at point E, a negative supply shock shifts the AS curve upward to $AS_2$. With a constant money supply, a new short-run equilibrium would be established at point R, with a higher price level ($P_2$) and a lower level of output ($Y_2$). The Fed could prevent inflation by decreasing the money supply and shifting AD to $AD_{no\ inflation}$, but output would fall to $Y_3$. At the other extreme, it could increase the money supply and shift the AD curve to $AD_{no\ recession}$. This would keep output at the full-employment level, but at the cost of a higher price level, $P_3$.*

FIGURE 5

**Responding to Supply Shocks**

*Starting at point E, a negative supply shock shifts the AS curve upward to $AS_2$. With a constant money supply, a new short-run equilibrium would be established at point R, with a higher price level ($P_2$) and a lower level of output ($Y_2$). The Fed could prevent inflation by decreasing the money supply and shifting AD to $AD_{no\ inflation}$, but output would fall to $Y_3$. At the other extreme, it could increase the money supply and shift the AD curve to $AD_{no\ recession}$. This would keep output at the full-employment level, but at the cost of a higher price level, $P_3$.*

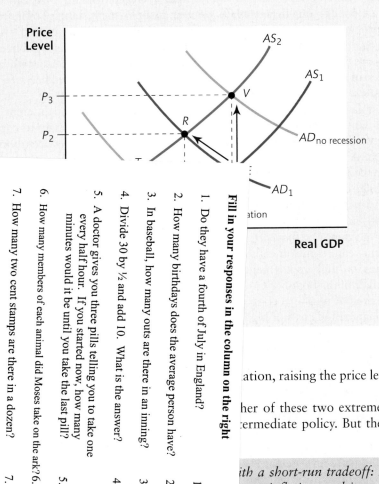

emp... ...ation, raising the price level all the way...

wit... ...her of these two extremes to deal ...termediate policy. But the extreme pos...

*...ith a short-run tradeoff: It can ...nore inflation; and it can limit ...ession.*

... one. After supply shocks, there are often debates within the Fed—and in the p... arena—about how best to respond. Inflation *hawks* lean in the direction of price stability and are willing to tolerate more unemployment in order to achieve it. In the face of an adverse supply shock, hawks would prefer a response that shifts the *AD* curve closer to $AD_{no\ inflation}$, even though it means higher unemployment. Inflation *doves* lean in the direction of a milder recession, and are more willing to tolerate the cost of higher inflation. They would prefer a response that brings the *AD* curve closer to $AD_{no\ recession}$.

## Choosing Between Hawk and Dove Policies

When a supply shock hits, should the Fed use a hawk policy, should it employ a dove policy, or should it keep the *AD* curve unchanged? That depends. Over time, as the economy is hit by supply shocks, the hawk policy maintains more stability in the

*Significant supply shocks—which have often been caused by higher oil prices—force the Fed to choose between lower output or a higher inflation rate.*

price level but less stability in output and employment. The dove policy gives the opposite result: more stability in output and less stability in the price level. The Fed should choose a hawkish policy if it cares more about price stability, and a dovish policy if it cares more about the stability of output and employment. Or it can pick an intermediate policy—one that balances price and employment stability more evenly.

The proper choice depends on how the Fed weights the harm caused by unemployment against the harm caused by inflation. And since the Fed is a public institution, its views should reflect the assessment of society as a whole. This is why supply shocks present such a challenge to the Fed: The public itself is divided between hawks and doves.

Both inflation and unemployment cause harm, but of very different kinds. Inflation imposes a more general cost on society: the resources used up to cope with it. If the inflation is unexpected, it will also redistribute income between borrowers and lenders. And, as you'll see in the next section, if inflation continues, people will expect it to continue into the future. At that point, prices and wages will begin to rise automatically, even if we are back at the natural rate of unemployment. The costs of unemployment are borne largely by the unemployed themselves—who suffer the harm of job loss—but partly by taxpayers, who provide funds for unemployment insurance. Balancing the gains and losses from hawk and dove policies is no easy task.

In recent years, some officials at the Fed have argued that having two objectives—stable prices *and* full employment—is unrealistic when there are supply shocks. The previous chair of the Board of Governors, Alan Greenspan, asked Congress to change the Fed's mandate to one of controlling inflation, period. But it would be difficult for the Fed to ignore the costs of higher unemployment, even if it were legally permitted to do so. Others have proposed that the Fed follow a predetermined rule, spelling out just how hawkish or dovish its response to supply shocks will be. We'll come back to this controversial idea later in the chapter.

## EXPECTATIONS AND ONGOING INFLATION

So far in this chapter, we've assumed that the Fed strives to maintain *zero* inflation, and that the price level remains constant when the economy reaches its long-run, full-employment equilibrium. But as we discussed earlier, this is not entirely realistic. Look again at panel (a) of Figure 1. There you can see that the U.S. economy has been characterized by *ongoing inflation*. Even in the 1990s and into early 2001—with unemployment at (or very close to) its natural rate—the annual inflation rate hovered around 2 to 3 percent. This means that, even though the economy was at full employment (so the economy's self-correcting mechanism was not operating), prices were *continually rising*.

Even when the unemployment rate is *above* its natural rate—as in 2002 and 2003—prices keep rising. Why? And how does ongoing inflation change our analysis of the effects of monetary policy or the guidelines that the Fed should follow? We'll consider these questions next.

### How Ongoing Inflation Arises

The best way to begin our analysis of ongoing inflation is to explore how it arises in an economy. We can do this by revisiting the 1960s, when the inflation rate rose steadily, and ongoing inflation first became a public concern.

What was special about the economy in the 1960s? First, it was a period of exuberance and optimism, for both businesses and households. Business spending on plant and equipment rose, and household spending on new homes and automobiles rose as well. At the same time, government spending rose—both military spending for the war in Vietnam and social spending on programs to help alleviate poverty. These increases in spending all contributed to rightward shifts of the $AD$ curve; they were positive demand shocks. The unemployment rate fell below the natural rate—hovering around 3 percent in the late 1960s. And, as expected, the economy's self-correcting mechanism kicked in: Higher wages shifted the $AS$ curve upward, causing the price level to rise.

As you've learned in this chapter, the Fed could have neutralized the positive demand shocks by raising its interest rate target (as in Figure 4), shifting the $AD$ curve back to its original position. Alternatively, the Fed could have allowed the self-correcting mechanism to bring the economy back to full employment with a higher—but stable—price level. But in the late 1960s, the Fed made a different choice: It maintained its low interest rate target. This required the Fed to increase the money supply, thus adding its *own* positive demand shock to the spending shocks already hitting the economy. In Figure 3, this was the equivalent of moving the $AD$ curve all the way out to $AD_3$, preventing any rise in interest rates but overheating the economy even more.

Why did the Fed act in this way? No one knows for sure, but one likely reason is that, in the 1960s, the Fed saw its job differently than it does today. The Fed tried to keep the interest rate stable and low, both to maintain high investment spending and to avoid instability in the financial markets. This is what it had been doing for years, with good effect: Americans had prospered in the previous decade, the 1950s, and financial markets were, indeed, stable.

But even though this policy worked well in the 1950s, it did not serve the economy well during and after the demand shocks of the 1960s. That's because the Fed's policy—year after year—prevented the self-correcting mechanism from bringing the economy back to full employment. Instead, each time the price level began rising, and the economy began to self-correct, the Fed would increase the money supply *again*, causing output to remain *continually* above its potential output. And that, in turn, meant that the price level would continue to rise, year after year.

Now comes a crucial part of the story: As the price level continued to rise in the 1960s, the public began to *expect* it to rise at a similar rate in the future. This illustrates a more general principle:

> *When inflation continues for some time, the public develops expectations that the inflation rate in the future will be similar to the inflation rates of the recent past.*

Why are expectations of inflation so important? Because when managers and workers expect inflation, it gets built into their decision-making process. Union contracts that set wages for the next 3 years will include automatic increases to compensate for the anticipated loss of purchasing power caused by future inflation. Nonunion wages will tend to rise each year as well, to match the wages in the unionized sector. And contracts for future delivery of inputs—like lumber, cement, and unfinished goods—will incorporate the higher prices everyone expects by the date of delivery. For reasons like these, *a continuing, stable rate of inflation gets built into the economy. The built-in rate is usually the rate that has existed for the past few years.*

## BUILT-IN INFLATION

Once there is built-in inflation, the economy continues to generate inflation even *after* the self-correcting mechanism has finally been allowed to do its job and bring us back to potential output. To see why, look at Figure 6. It shows what might happen over the year in an economy with built-in inflation. In the figure, output is at its full-employment level. But over the year, the *AS* curve shifts upward and the *AD* curve shifts rightward, so the equilibrium moves from A to B and the price level rises from $P_1$ to $P_2$. Why does all this happen when there is built-in inflation?

Let's start with the reason for the upward shift of the *AS* curve. Unemployment is at its natural rate, so the self-correction mechanism is no longer contributing to any rise in wages or unit costs. But something else is causing unit costs to increase: inflationary expectations. Based on recent experience, the public expects the price level to rise as it has been rising in the past, so wages (and other input prices) will continue to increase, *even though real GDP is equal to potential output.* Thus,

*in an economy with built-in inflation, the* AS *curve will shift upward each year, even when output is at potential and unemployment is at its natural rate. The upward shift of the* AS *curve will equal the built-in rate of inflation.*

For example, if the public expects inflation of 6 percent during the year, then contracts will call for wages and input prices to rise by 6 percent that year. This means that unit costs will increase by 6 percent. Firms—marking up prices over unit costs—will raise their prices by 6 percent as well, and the *AS* curve will shift upward by 6 percent.

Explaining why the *AS* curve shifts upward is only half the story in Figure 6. We must also explain why the *AD* curve shifts rightward. The simple answer is: The *AD*

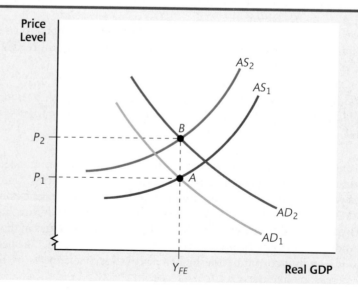

**FIGURE 6**

**Long-Run Equilibrium with Built-In Inflation**

*During the year, the aggregate supply curve shifts upward by the built-in rate of inflation. To keep the economy at full employment, the Fed shifts the AD curve rightward by increasing the money supply.*

curve shifts rightward because the Fed increases the money supply. But *why* does the Fed shift the *AD* curve rightward, when it knows that doing so only prolongs inflation? One reason is that reducing inflation would be *costly* to the economy.

Imagine what would happen if the Fed decided *not* to shift the *AD* curve rightward during the year. The *AS* curve will shift upward anyway, by a percentage shift equal to the built-in rate of inflation. This will happen *no matter what the Fed does* because the shift is based on expected inflation, which, in turn, is based on past experiences of inflation. There is nothing the Fed can do today to affect what has happened in the past, so it must accept the upward shift of the *AS* curve as a given. So if, during the year, the Fed maintains the *AD* curve at $AD_1$, the new equilibrium (not labeled in the figure) will be at the intersection of $AD_1$ and $AS_2$. The Fed would achieve its goal of reducing inflation that year—the price level would rise from $P_1$ to something less than $P_2$ instead of all the way to $P_2$. But the drop in inflation would come with a cost: The economy's output will decline below $Y_{FE}$—a recession.

> *In the short run, the Fed can reduce the rate of inflation below the built-in rate, but only at the cost of creating a recession.*

Would the Fed ever purposely create a recession to reduce inflation? Indeed it would, and it has—more than once. By far the most important episode occurred during the early 1980s. As Figure 1 shows, annual inflation reached the extraordinary level of 13.3 percent in 1979. Soon after, with some support from the newly elected President Reagan, the Fed embarked on an aggressive campaign to bring inflation down. The Fed stopped increasing the money supply and stopped shifting the *AD* curve rightward, and a recession began in July of 1981. Unemployment peaked, as shown earlier in Figure 1, at 10.7 percent at the end of 1982. With tremendous slack in the economy, the inflation rate fell rapidly, to below 4 percent in 1982. The Fed deliberately created a serious recession, but it brought down the rate of inflation.

Creating a recession is not a decision that the Fed takes lightly. Recessions are costly to the economy and painful to those who lose their jobs. The desire to avoid a recession is one reason that the Fed tolerated ongoing inflation for years and continued to play its role by shifting the *AD* curve rightward. We'll discuss other reasons for the Fed's tolerance of ongoing inflation a bit later.

## ONGOING INFLATION AND THE PHILLIPS CURVE

Ongoing inflation changes our analysis of monetary policy. For one thing, it forces us to recognize a subtle, but important, change in the Fed's objectives: While the Fed still desires full employment, its other goal—price stability—is not zero inflation, but rather a *low and stable inflation rate*.

Another difference is in the graphs we use to illustrate the Fed's policy choices. Instead of continuing to analyze the economy with *AS* and *AD* graphs, when there is ongoing inflation, we usually use another powerful tool.

This tool is the *Phillips curve*—named after the late economist A. W. Phillips, who did early research on the relationship between inflation and unemployment. The **Phillips curve** illustrates the Fed's choices between inflation and unemployment in the short run, for a given built-in inflation rate.

Figure 7 shows a Phillips curve for the U.S. economy. The inflation rate is measured on the vertical axis; the unemployment rate on the horizontal. Point *E* shows

**Phillips curve** A curve indicating the Fed's choices between inflation and unemployment in the short run.

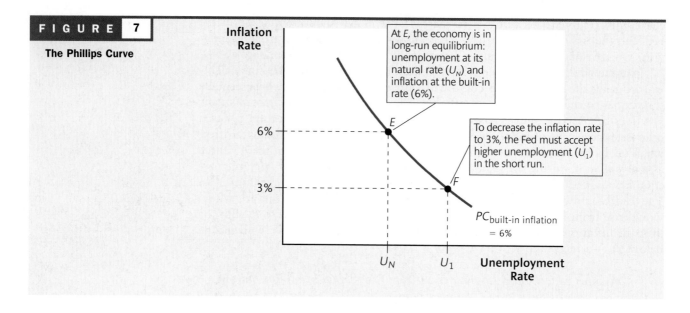

**F I G U R E  7**

**The Phillips Curve**

At *E*, the economy is in long-run equilibrium: unemployment at its natural rate ($U_N$) and inflation at the built-in rate (6%).

To decrease the inflation rate to 3%, the Fed must accept higher unemployment ($U_1$) in the short run.

$PC_{\text{built-in inflation}}$
$= 6\%$

the long-run equilibrium in the economy when the built-in inflation rate is 6 percent. At point *E*, unemployment is at its natural rate—$U_N$—and inflation remains constant from year to year at the built-in rate of 6 percent.

Notice that the Phillips curve is downward sloping. Why? Because it tells the same story we told earlier—with *AD* and *AS* curves—about the Fed's options in the short run. If the Fed wants to decrease the rate of inflation from 6 percent to 3 percent, it must slow the rightward shifts of the *AD* curve. This would cause a movement *along* the Phillips curve from point *E* to point *F*. As you can see, in moving to point *F*, the economy experiences a recession: Since output falls, unemployment rises above the natural rate.

> *In the short run, the Fed can move along the Phillips curve by adjusting the rate at which the* AD *curve shifts rightward. When the Fed moves the economy downward and rightward along the Phillips curve, the unemployment rate increases, and the inflation rate decreases.*

### A Downward Shift in the Phillips Curve

Suppose the Fed moves the economy downward along the Phillips curve, from point *E* to point *F*, and then keeps it at point *F*. In the long run, the public—observing a 3 percent inflation rate—will come to expect 3 percent inflation into the future. Thus, in the long run, 3 percent will become the economy's built-in rate of inflation. Figure 8 shows the effect on the Phillips curve. When the economy's built-in inflation rate drops from 6 percent to 3 percent, the Phillips curve shifts downward, to the lower curve. At any unemployment rate, the inflation rate will be lower, now that the public expects inflation of only 3 percent rather than 6 percent.

> *In the long run, a decrease in the inflation rate leads to a lower built-in inflation rate, and the Phillips curve shifts downward.*

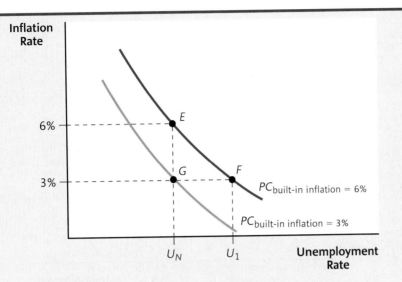

FIGURE 8

**The Phillips Curve Shifts Downward**

*Initially, the economy is at point E, with inflation equal to the built-in rate of 6%. If the Fed moves the economy to point F and keeps it there for some time, the public will eventually come to expect 3% inflation in the future. The built-in inflation rate will fall and the Phillips curve will shift downward to PC$_{built-in\ inflation\ =\ 3\%}$. The economy will move to point G in the long run, with unemployment at the natural rate and an actual inflation rate equal to the built-in rate of 3%.*

Once the Fed has reduced the built-in inflation rate, it can locate anywhere on the new Phillips curve by adjusting how rapidly it lets the money supply grow (and, therefore, how rapidly the *AD* curve shifts rightward each year). Therefore, the Fed can choose to bring the economy back to full employment (point *G*), with a new, lower inflation rate of 3 percent rather than the previous 6 percent.

### An Upward Shift in the Phillips Curve

The process we've described—moving down the Phillips curve and thereby causing it to shift downward—also works in reverse: Moving *up* the Phillips curve will, in the long run, shift the curve *upward*. Figure 9 illustrates this case. Once again, assume the economy begins at point *E*, with a built-in inflation rate of 6 percent and unemployment at its natural rate. Now suppose the Fed begins to increase the money supply *more rapidly* than in the past, and begins shifting the *AD* curve further rightward than in Figure 6. In the short run, the economy would move *along* the Phillips curve from point *E* to point *H* in Figure 9. The inflation rate would rise to 9 percent, and the unemployment rate would fall below its natural rate—in the short run.

But suppose the Fed keeps the economy at point *H* for some time, continuing to shift the *AD* curve rightward at a faster rate than before. Then, in the long run, the public will begin to expect 9 percent inflation, and that will become the new built-in rate of inflation. The Phillips curve will then shift upward. At this point, if the Fed returns the economy to full employment, we end up at point *J*. The economy will be back in long-run equilibrium—but with a higher built-in inflation rate.

*In the long run, an increase in the inflation rate leads to a higher built-in inflation rate, and the Phillips curve shifts upward.*

**The Phillips Curve Shifts Upward**

*Initially, the economy is at point E, with inflation equal to the built-in rate of 6%. If the Fed moves the economy to point H and keeps it there for some time, the public will eventually come to expect 9% inflation in the future. The built-in inflation rate will rise and the Phillips curve will shift upward to* $PC_{built\text{-}in\ inflation\ =\ 9\%}$. *The economy will move to point J in the long run, with unemployment at the natural rate and an actual inflation rate equal to the built-in rate of 9%.*

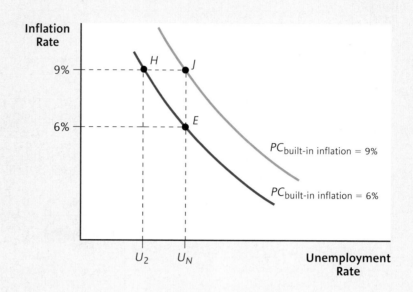

## THE LONG-RUN PHILLIPS CURVE

Figure 10 combines the previous two figures, showing the policy choices for the Fed and their consequences. We assume, as before, that we are initially at point *E* on the middle Phillips curve. The built-in inflation rate is 6 percent, and the economy is operating at full employment. In the short run, the built-in inflation rate will remain at 6 percent, so the Fed can freely move along the middle Phillips curve, say, to point *H* or point *F*. In doing so, the Fed exploits the short-run tradeoff between unemployment and inflation. But in the long run—once the public's expectations of inflation adjust to the new reality—the built-in inflation rate will change, and the Phillips curve will shift. Indeed, the Phillips curve will *keep* shifting whenever the unemployment rate is kept above or below the natural rate. (To see why, ask yourself what would happen in the future if the Fed tried to keep the unemployment rate *permanently* at a level like $U_2$—below the natural rate.) Thus, the economy cannot be in long-run equilibrium until the unemployment rate returns to its natural rate, and output is back to its potential level. In the long run, when we are at the natural rate of unemployment, the Fed can only choose *which* Phillips curve the economy will be on.

> *In the short run, there is a tradeoff between inflation and unemployment: The Fed can choose lower unemployment at the cost of higher inflation, or lower inflation at the cost of higher unemployment. But in the long run, since unemployment always returns to its natural rate, there is no such tradeoff.*

Now look at the vertical line. It tells us how monetary policy affects the economy in the long run, without the distractions of the short-run story. The vertical line is the

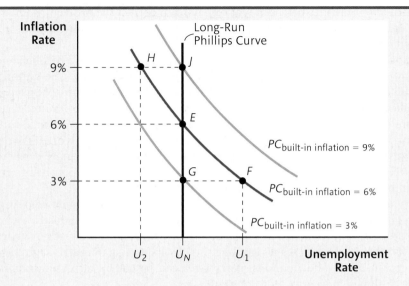

FIGURE 10

**The Long-Run Phillips Curve**

*The vertical line is the economy's long-run Phillips curve, showing all combinations of unemployment and inflation the Fed can choose in the long run. The curve is vertical because in the long run, the unemployment rate must equal the natural rate. Starting at point E with 6% inflation, the Fed can choose unemployment at the natural rate with either a higher rate of inflation (point J) or a lower rate of inflation (point G). But points off of the vertical line are not sustainable in the long run.*

economy's *long-run Phillips curve*, which tells us the combinations of unemployment and inflation that the Fed can choose in the long run.

To see why, suppose the Fed moves the economy from point $E$ to point $H$ in the short run. Then in the long run, we will end up at point $J$ on the vertical line: The economy will be back at the natural rate of unemployment, but with a higher inflation rate (9 percent). Suppose, on the other hand, the Fed moves us from point $E$ to point $F$ in the short run. Then in the long run, we will once again be on the vertical line, but this time at point $G$. Unemployment is at its natural rate, but with a lower inflation rate (3 percent). No matter what the Fed does, unemployment will always return to the natural rate, $U_N$, in the long run. However, the Fed can use monetary policy to select any rate of inflation it wants.

> *The **long-run Phillips curve** is a vertical line at the natural rate of unemployment. It shows us that, in the long run, the Fed can change the rate of inflation, but not the rate of unemployment.*

**Long-run Phillips curve** A vertical line indicating that in the long run, unemployment must equal its natural rate, regardless of the rate of inflation.

## WHY THE FED ALLOWS ONGOING INFLATION

Since the Fed can choose any rate of inflation it wants, and since inflation is costly to society, we might think that the Fed would aim for an inflation rate of zero. But a look back at panel (a) of Figure 1 shows that this is not what the Fed has chosen to do. In recent years, with unemployment very close to its natural rate, the Fed has maintained annual inflation at around 2 or 3 percent. Why doesn't the Fed eliminate inflation from the economy entirely?

One reason is a widespread belief that the Consumer Price Index (CPI) and other measures of inflation actually *overstate* the true rate of inflation in the economy. As you've learned, many economists believe that the CPI has overstated the true annual inflation rate by 1 to 2 percent—or more—in recent decades. Although the

Bureau of Labor Statistics has been working hard to correct the problem, some significant upward bias remains. Thus, the Fed is effectively eliminating *actual* inflation when it keeps the *measured* rate low.

But some economists have offered another explanation for the Fed's behavior: Low, stable inflation makes the labor market work more smoothly. The argument goes as follows: While no one wants a cut in his or her real wage rate, people seem to react differently, depending on *how* the real wage is decreased. For example, suppose there is an excess supply of workers in some industry, and a real wage cut of 3 percent would bring that labor market back to equilibrium. Workers would strongly resist a 3 percent cut in the nominal wage. But they would more easily tolerate a freeze in the nominal wage while the price level rises by 3 percent, even though in both scenarios, the real wage falls by 3 percent.

If this argument is correct, then a low or modest inflation rate would help wages adjust in different markets, helping to ensure that workers move to industries where they would be most productive as the structure of the economy changes over time. In some labor markets, real wages can be raised by increasing nominal wages faster than prices. In other labor markets, real wages can be cut by increasing nominal wages more slowly than prices, or not at all.

> *The Fed has tolerated measured inflation at 2 to 3 percent per year because it knows that the true rate of inflation is lower, and because low rates of inflation may help labor markets adjust more easily.*

## CHALLENGES FOR MONETARY POLICY

So far in this chapter, we've described some clear-cut guidelines the Fed *can* and *does* follow in conducting monetary policy. We've seen that the proper response to demand shocks is a change in the interest rate target. Dealing with a supply shock is more problematic because it requires the Fed to balance its goal of low, stable inflation with its goal of full employment. But even here, once the Fed decides on the proper balance, its policy choice is straightforward: Shift the *AD* curve to achieve the desired combination of inflation and unemployment in the short run, and then guide the economy back to full employment in the long run.

One might almost conclude that monetary policy is akin to operating a giant machine—adjusting this or that knob, and making the occasional repair by consulting the manual. And policy making might appear rather uncontroversial, other than the occasional debate between those who favor hawkish and dovish policies toward inflation after a supply shock.

But the truth is very much the opposite. First, the Fed faces frequent criticism from members of Congress, the business community, the media, and some academic economists—over not just its policy choices but also the *way* it arrives at them. Second, the Fed, rather than operating a well-understood machine, must conduct monetary policy with highly imperfect information about the economy's course and precisely how its policies will alter that course. Let's consider some of the challenges facing the Fed.

### INFORMATION PROBLEMS

The Federal Reserve has hundreds of economists carrying out research and gathering data to improve its understanding of how the economy works, and how monetary policy affects the economy. Research at the Fed is widely respected and has made great progress. But because the economy is complex and constantly changing, serious gaps remain. Two of the most important gaps concern the time lag before monetary policy affects the economy, and knowledge of the natural rate of unemployment (or—equivalently—the economy's potential output).

## Uncertain and Changing Time Lags

Suppose that we are in the midst of an expansion, and Fed officials begin to worry that the economy is about to overheat. They respond by raising their interest rate target. Eventually, the higher interest rate will dampen planned investment and consumption spending and cool the economy off. But when?

Monetary policy works with a time lag. Even after a rise in the interest rate, business firms will likely continue to build the new plants and new homes they've already started constructing. The most powerful effects on investment spending will be the cancellation of *new* projects currently being planned—projects that *would* have entered the pipeline of new spending many months later. The same applies in the other direction: When the Fed lowers the interest rate to stimulate additional spending, the full effects will be felt many months later, after new investment projects are planned and firms begin making the associated purchases.

The time lag in the effectiveness of monetary policy can have serious consequences. For example, by the time a higher interest rate target has its maximum effect, the economy may already be returning to full employment on its own, or it may be hit by a negative demand shock. In this case, the Fed—by raising its interest rate target—will be reining in the economy at just the wrong time, causing a recession.

Economists often use an analogy to describe this problem. Imagine that you are trying to drive a car with a special problem: When you step on the gas, the car will go forward . . . but not until 5 minutes later. Similarly, when you step on the brake, the car will slow, but also with a 5-minute lag. It would be very difficult to maintain an even speed with this car: You'd step on the gas, and when nothing happened, you'd be tempted to step on it harder. By the time the car begins to move, you will have given too much gas and find yourself speeding down the road. So you try to slow down, but once again, hitting the brakes makes nothing happen. So you brake harder, and when the car finally responds, you come to a dead halt.

The Fed can make—and, in the past, has made—similar mistakes. When it tries to cool off an overheated economy, it may find that nothing is happening. Is it just a long time lag, or has the Fed not hit the brakes hard enough? If it hits the brakes harder, it runs the risk of braking the economy too much; if it doesn't, it runs the risk of continuing to allow the economy to overheat. Even worse, the time lag before monetary policy affects prices and output can change over the years: Just when the Fed may think it has mastered the rules of the game, the rules change.

## The Natural Rate of Unemployment

In our Phillips curve analysis, we've assumed that the economy's natural rate of unemployment is known and remains constant, signified by the vertical long-run Phillips curve at some value $U_N$. In this case, once the economy achieved a long-run equilibrium, the Fed's job would be relatively straightforward: to shift the $AD$ curve rightward by just the right amount each period to maintain the natural rate of unemployment with an acceptable rate of inflation.

But even though there is wide agreement that the natural rate rose in the 1970s and has fallen since the late 1980s, economists remain uncertain about its value during any given period. Many economists believe that today the natural rate is between 4.5 and 5 percent, but no one is really sure.

Why is this a problem? It's very much like the two mountain climbers who become lost. One of them pulls out a map. "Do you see that big mountain over there?" he says, pointing off into the distance. "Yes," says the other. "Well," says the first, "according to the map, we're standing on top of it." In order to achieve its twin goals of full employment and a stable, low rate of inflation, the Fed tries to maintain the unemployment rate as close to the natural rate as possible. If its estimate of the natural rate is wrong, it may believe it has succeeded when, in fact, it has not.

For example, suppose the Fed believes the natural rate of unemployment is 5 percent, but the rate is really 4.5 percent. Then—at least for a time—the Fed will be steering the economy toward an unemployment rate that is unnecessarily high and an output level that is unnecessarily low. We've already discussed the costs of cyclical unemployment. An overestimate of the natural rate makes society bear these costs needlessly. On the other hand, if the Fed believes the natural rate is 4.5 percent when it is really 5 percent, it will overheat the economy. This will raise the inflation rate—and a costly recession may be needed later in order to reduce it.

Trial and error can help the Fed determine the true natural rate. If the Fed raises unemployment above the true natural rate, the inflation rate will drop. If unemployment falls below the true natural rate, the inflation rate will rise. But (as we discussed earlier) trial and error works best when there is continual and rapid feedback. It can take some time for the inflation rate to change—6 months, a year, or even longer. In the meantime, the Fed might believe it has been successful, even while causing avoidable unemployment, or planting the seeds for a future rise in the inflation rate.

Estimating the natural rate of unemployment is made even more difficult because the economy is constantly buffeted by shocks of one kind or another. If the Fed observes that the inflation rate is rising, does that mean that unemployment is below the natural rate? Or is the higher inflation being caused by a negative supply shock? Or by the Fed's response to an earlier, negative demand shock? This information is difficult to sort out, although the Fed has become increasingly sophisticated in its efforts to do so.

## RULES VERSUS DISCRETION

Over the last several decades, the Federal Reserve has formulated monetary policy using *discretion*: responding to demand and supply shocks in the way that Fed officials thought best at the time. In some cases, this seems to have helped the economy's performance, as when the Fed aggressively cut interest rates during 2001 and helped to make the recession of that year shorter and milder than it would otherwise have been. In other cases, discretion has worked less well. During the late 1970s, frequent changes in monetary policy contributed to wide fluctuations in output and a rapidly rising inflation rate that reached 13.3 percent in 1979. A more recent example is the Fed's policy in 2000. It raised interest rates and, in retrospect, waited too long before bringing them down again, missing an opportunity to begin an early fight against the recession of 2001.

Should the Federal Reserve have complete discretion to change its interest rate target in response to demand and supply shocks as it sees fit? Or should it stick to rules or guidelines in making monetary policy—rules that it announces in advance, with a justification required for any departure? Some economists have suggested that the Fed's performance on average would be better with less discretion and more deference to predetermined rules.

## The Taylor Rule

The most often discussed rule for monetary policy is the **Taylor rule**, originally proposed by economist John Taylor. Under this rule, the Fed would be required to announce a target for the inflation rate (say, 2 percent per year) and another target for real GDP (equal to the Fed's estimate of potential GDP in that period). Then the Fed would be required to change its interest rate target by some predetermined amount whenever either output or inflation (or both) deviated from their respective targets.

**Taylor rule** A proposed rule that would require the Fed to change the interest rate by a specified amount whenever real GDP or inflation deviates from its pre-announced target.

For example, suppose the economy began to overheat from a positive demand shock. Then at some point either real GDP would rise above potential, or the inflation rate would rise above its target rate, or both would occur. The Fed would then be obligated to raise its interest rate target by an amount that everyone knew in advance, depending on the changes observed in output and inflation. On the other side, if a negative demand shock started to threaten a recession, changes in inflation and/or output would commit the Fed to *lower* its interest rate target, and stimulate the economy back toward full employment.

What about a negative supply shock—such as a rise in oil prices—that causes the inflation rate to rise and output to fall? In this case, inflation would rise *higher* than its target, and output would fall *below* it. But the rule would identify in advance just how the Fed would respond. It would raise or lower the interest rate target depending on which variable—output or inflation—deviated the most, and depending on the response to each variable that the rule calls for. Thus, the hawk–dove debate that follows every supply shock would be settled—publically—in advance.

What would be the advantage of such a rule? First, if the Federal Reserve were committed to respond to the first signs of a boom, the public would know that the Fed would *not* allow the economy to continue overheating. This would discourage the formation of inflationary expectations. In effect, the Fed would be saying to the public, "Even though the inflation rate just rose, you know the rules. We have to bring the inflation rate back down, so don't get any ideas that we're going to let this continue." Similarly, if a negative demand shock sends the economy into a recession, and the Fed begins to stimulate the economy, the public needn't wonder whether the Fed will go too far and create ongoing, higher inflation. The rule says that the Fed will stimulate the economy only until we are back at potential output.

Second, the Taylor rule would give the Fed ammunition to fight inflation with a higher interest rate even when doing so might prove unpopular at the time. The Fed would only be following the rule that everyone understood in advance. This would help discourage the sort of discretion, and political pressure, that contributed to the high inflation rates of the late 1970s.

The Taylor rule is controversial. Opponents argue that it implies more advanced knowledge about the economy—and what an appropriate future response should be—than is realistically possible. And unless the rule were written into law—which only a few economists would advocate—the Fed would not be obligated to follow it. Since the public would know this, the existence of the rule might not be a strong deterrent to inflationary expectations.

Interestingly, the Fed's behavior under Alan Greenspan (1987–2005) followed reasonably close to the specific numerical rule that Taylor originally proposed. Whether the economy performed better or worse due to Greenspan's *deviations* from the rule remains controversial.

As you can see, conducting monetary policy is not easy. The Fed has hundreds of economists carrying out research and gathering data to improve its information about the status of the economy and its understanding of how the economy works. And the effort seemed to have paid off during the decade leading up to 2001. But some economists believe that the Fed, in retrospect, could have done more to offset the forces that caused the recession that began in March 2001. They believe that the Fed raised the interest rate too high in 2000 and waited too long before starting to lower the interest rate in January 2001. This is an easy conclusion to come to with hindsight. But given the uncertainties faced by the Fed in conducting monetary policy, most economists have expressed approval of the Fed's performance under the chairmanship of Alan Greenspan. In mid-2006, economists were also giving high marks to Ben Bernanke, who took over Greenspan's job in February of that year.

# USING THE THEORY

## Expectations and the Importance of Words

*Alan Greenspan, Fed Chair from 1987 through 2005.*

Alan Greenspan—the Chair of the Federal Reserve Board from 1987 through 2005—was famous for his style of speaking. When testifying before Congress, giving a speech, or granting an interview, he spoke in sentences that gave English teachers heartache. They were long, complex, and packed with specifics. At the same time, they seemed carefully designed to allow for multiple interpretations.

A famous example occurred after Greenspan spoke to reporters on June 7, 1995. The next morning, the headline in the *New York Times* was, "Greenspan Sees Chance of Recession," while in the *Washington Post,* it was, "Recession Is Unlikely, Greenspan Concludes." Greenspan's wife, NBC reporter Andrea Mitchell, has said that he had to propose to her three times before she understood what he meant.

Most economists understood why Greenspan spoke in that style—at least about the economy. Words matter. And the words of the Fed chair matter a lot. A Fed chair who speaks *too* clearly and gives *too* much new information about a future change in monetary policy can destabilize financial markets.

To understand why, let's first review how changes in monetary policy affect the bond market. Recall that the interest rate and the price of bonds are negatively related. When the Fed raises interest rates, bond prices drop. Because the public holds trillions of dollars in government and corporate bonds, even a small rise in the interest rate—say, a quarter of a percentage point—decreases the value of the public's bond holdings by billions of dollars.

The stock market is often affected in a similar way. People hold stocks because they entitle the owner to a share of a firm's profits, and because stock prices are usually expected to rise as the economy grows and firms become more profitable. But stocks must offer a competitive rate of return to bonds, or else no one would hold them. The lower the price of a share of stock, the more attractive the stock is to a potential buyer.

When the Fed raises interest rates, and the rate of return on bonds increases, bonds become more attractive to potential buyers. As a result, stock prices must fall, so that stocks, too, will become more attractive to hold. And that is typically what happens. Unless other events are affecting the stock market, a rise in the interest rate causes people to try to sell their stocks in order to acquire the suddenly more attractive bonds. This causes stock prices to fall, until stocks are once again as attractive as bonds.

Thus, a rise in the interest rate (federal funds rate) target—which causes interest rates in general to rise—causes stock prices, as well as bond prices, to fall.

> *The stock and bond markets move in the opposite direction to the Fed's interest rate target. Ceteris paribus, when the Fed raises its target, stock and bond prices fall. When the Fed lowers its target, stock and bond prices rise.*

The potentially destabilizing effect on stock and bond markets is one reason why, in normal times, the Fed prefers not to change its interest rate target very often. Frequent changes in the target would make prices in financial markets less stable and the public more hesitant to supply funds to business firms by buying stocks and bonds.

But financial markets are also affected by *expected* changes in the interest rate target—whether or not they actually occur. If you expect the Fed to raise its target, you also expect stock and bond prices to fall. Therefore, you would want to dump these assets *now*, before their price drops. Similarly, an expectation of a drop in the interest rate target would make you want to buy stocks and bonds now, before their prices rise. Thus, changes in expectations about the Fed's future actions can be as destabilizing as the actions themselves.

Once you understand the Fed's logic in changing its interest rate target, you can understand a phenomenon that—at first glance—appears mystifying: Stock and bond prices often fall when good news about the economy is released, and rise when bad news is released. For example, if the Bureau of Labor Statistics announces a sudden, unexpected drop in the unemployment rate, or the Commerce Department announces that real GDP grew more rapidly during the previous quarter than had been thought, stock and bond prices may plummet. Why? Because owners of stocks and bonds believe that the Fed might interpret the good news as evidence that the economy is overheating. They would then expect the Fed to raise its interest rate target, so they try to sell their stocks and bonds before the Federal Open Market Committee even meets.

> *Good news about the economy sometimes leads to new expectations that the Fed, fearing inflation, will raise its interest rate target. This is why good economic news can cause stock and bond prices to fall. Similarly, bad news about the economy sometimes leads to expectations that the Fed, fearing recession, will lower its interest rate target. This is why bad economic news sometimes causes stock and bond prices to rise.*

Now let's go back to the importance of words. The members of the FOMC are well aware that the public speculates about what the committee will do at its next meeting, and that FOMC announcements and speeches by Fed officials are carefully studied. This creates both an opportunity and a challenge.

The opportunity is that words themselves are another Fed tool (in addition to its interest rate target) for influencing the direction of the economy. For example, if the FOMC hints at a *slight* increase in the likelihood of a lower interest rate target at the next meeting, there will likely be *some* increase in stock and bond buying. Because stocks and bonds are important components of household wealth, households—now wealthier—will increase their consumption spending. In this way the Fed, if it is careful, can gradually shift the aggregate expenditure line by phrasing its announcements carefully. On occasion, the Fed may want to engineer a more dramatic change in aggregate expenditure and will use stronger, more definitive phrasing.

Over the years, the Fed has experimented with different strategies for managing expectations. Greenspan was widely considered a master of this craft. His statements, while complex, often contained hints—sometimes subtle, sometimes more pronounced—of a change in policy.

The challenge for Fed officials—especially the Fed chair—is that if they are not careful, and tip their hand too suddenly or too strongly, there can be huge, undesired price swings in financial markets. Indeed, stock and bond prices often jump around in the days leading up to meetings of the FOMC, as statements made by Fed officials are parsed especially closely.

Ben Bernanke replaced Alan Greenspan as Fed chair in February 2006.[3] And he was quickly reminded about the importance of words. In Congressional testimony just 2 months after taking office, Bernanke—who had promised greater "transparency" about Fed decision making—mused about policy in a rather straightforward manner. Financial market analysts interpreted his remarks to mean that the Fed would not continue its recent interest rate hikes, as had been expected. Stock and bond prices jumped up.

A week later, at a White House correspondent's dinner, Bernanke told CNBC reporter Maria Bartiromo (in what he *may* have thought was a private conversation) that the markets had misinterpreted his testimony. He had been musing only about the *possibility* of a *temporary* pause in rate hikes. Bartiromo, in turn, broadcast her account of the conversation at 3:15 P.M. the next day. Suddenly, expectations changed: Now everyone believed that the FOMC *would* raise interest rates at its next meeting. Stock and bond prices—which had been rising until that very minute—turned on a dime and ended up lower for the day.

A few weeks later, when asked about the incident in a Senate hearing, Bernanke vowed that "in the future, my communications with the public and with the markets will be entirely through regular and formal channels."[4] Those formal channels consist mostly of the carefully worded statements released by the FOMC after each of its meetings. They are most often designed to calm and occasionally nudge—rather than startle or stir up—the financial markets. Typically, that means they must defy clear interpretation.

For example, consider the statement released by the Bernanke FOMC after its meeting on June 29, 2006. Here is the key section that is always studied most closely by journalists and market analysts, who are looking for hints of the Fed's next move. Take a deep breath.

*Although the moderation in the growth of aggregate demand should help to limit inflation pressures over time, the Committee judges that some inflation risks remain. The extent and timing of any additional firming that may be*

*Ben Bernanke became the new Fed Chair in February 2006.*

© JOSHUA ROBERTS/REUTERS/CORBIS

---

[3] Before Ben Bernanke was nominated by President Bush, Glenn Hubbard—Dean of the Columbia Business School—was also thought to be a candidate. When Hubbard wasn't chosen, Columbia students made a music video featuring a jealous Hubbard look-alike. It is well worth watching. You can find it at *www.cbsfollies.com*, then find the entry for "Every Breath You Take," and select "View."

[4] Nell Henderson, "Fed Chief Calls His Remarks a Mistake," *Washington Post*, May 24, 2006, p. D01.

*needed to address these risks will depend on the evolution of the outlook for both inflation and economic growth, as implied by incoming information. In any event, the Committee will respond to changes in economic prospects as needed to support the attainment of its objectives.*

A statement like this does not give much of a hint about the Fed's future moves. It is difficult to read, and even harder to interpret. Alan Greenspan couldn't have phrased it any better.

## Summary

As the nation's central bank, the Federal Reserve bears primary responsibility for maintaining a low, stable rate of inflation and for maintaining full employment of the labor force as the economy is buffeted by a variety of shocks.

Demand shocks can shift the *AD* curve, causing output to deviate from its full-employment level. The Fed can neutralize these shocks by adjusting its interest rate target—changing the money supply to shift the *AD* curve back to its original position.

The Fed's most difficult problem is responding to supply shocks. A negative supply shock—an upward shift of the *AS* curve—presents the Fed with a dilemma. In the short run, it must choose a point along that new *AS* curve. If it wishes to maintain price stability, it must shift the *AD* curve to the left and accept higher unemployment. If the Fed wishes to maintain full employment, it must shift the *AD* curve to the right and accept a higher rate of inflation. A "hawk" policy puts greater emphasis on price stability, while a "dove" policy emphasizes lower unemployment.

If Fed policy leads to ongoing inflation, then businesses and households come to expect the prevailing inflation rate to continue. As a result, the *AS* curve continues to shift upward at that built-in expected inflation rate. To maintain full employment, the Fed must shift the *AD* curve rightward, creating an inflation rate equal to the expected rate.

If the Fed wishes to change the built-in inflation rate, it must first change the expected inflation rate. For example, to lower the expected inflation rate, the Fed will slow down the rightward shifts of the *AD* curve. The actual inflation rate will fall, and expectations will eventually adjust downward. While they do so, however, the economy will experience a recession. The Fed's short-run choices between inflation and unemployment can be illustrated with the Phillips curve. In the short run, the Fed can move the economy along the downward-sloping *Phillips curve* by adjusting the rate at which the *AD* curve shifts. If the Fed moves the economy to a new point on the Phillips curve and holds it there, the built-in inflation rate will eventually adjust and the Phillips curve will shift. In the long run, the economy will return to the natural rate of unemployment with a different inflation rate. The *long-run Phillips curve* is a vertical line at the natural rate of unemployment.

In conducting monetary policy, the Fed faces several challenges. It has imperfect information about the time required for its policies to affect the economy, and also about the economy's potential GDP (or its natural rate of unemployment) during any given period. The Fed often faces criticism for using discretion rather than following rigid rules, especially when the economy does not perform well.

## Problem Set   *Answers to even-numbered Questions and Problems can be found on the text Web site at www.thomsonedu.com/economics/hall.*

1. Suppose that a law required the Fed to do everything possible to keep the inflation rate equal to zero. Using *AD* and *AS* curves, illustrate and explain how the Fed would deal with (a) a negative demand shock from a decrease in investment spending and (b) an adverse aggregate supply shock. What would the costs and benefits of such a law be?

2. Suppose that, in a world with *no* ongoing inflation, the government raises taxes. Using *AD* and *AS* curves, describe the effects on the economy if the Fed decides to keep the money supply constant. Alternatively, how could the Fed use active policy to neutralize the demand shock?

3. Suppose that initially the price level is $P_1$ and GDP is $Y_1$, with no built-in inflation. The Fed reacts to a negative demand shock by shifting the aggregate demand curve in the appropriate direction. The next time the Fed receives data on GDP and the price level, it finds that the price level is above $P_1$ and GDP is above $Y_1$. Give a possible explanation for this finding.

4. Suppose the economy has been experiencing a low inflation rate. A new chair of the Federal Reserve is named, and he or she is known to be sympathetic to dove policies. Explain the possible effects on the Phillips curve.

5. "The idea of the Fed having to choose between hawk and dove policies in Figure 5 is silly. All the Fed has to do is

shift the *AS* curve back to its original position, which would prevent *both* recession *and* inflation." Do you agree? Why or why not?

6. Using a graph similar to Figure 9, and some additional curves, show what would happen in the future if the Fed tried to keep the unemployment rate *permanently* at a level like $U_2$—below the natural rate.

## More Challenging

7. Suppose the economy is experiencing ongoing inflation. The Fed wants to reduce expected inflation, so it announces that in the future it will tolerate less inflation. How does the Fed's credibility affect the success of the reduction? How can the Fed build its credibility? Are there costs to building credibility? If so, what are they?

8. This chapter mentioned what would happen if the Fed over- or underestimated the natural rate of unemployment. Using the *AD–AS* model, suppose the economy is at the true natural rate of unemployment, so that GDP is at its potential level. Suppose, too, that the Fed wrongly believes that the natural rate of unemployment is higher (potential GDP is lower) and acts to bring the economy back to its supposed potential. What will the Fed do? What will happen in the short run? If the Fed continues to maintain output below potential, what will happen over the long run?

# Spending, Taxes, and the Federal Budget

Almost every year throughout the 1980s and early 1990s, a best-selling book would be published that predicted economic disaster for the United States and the world. In most of these books, the U.S. federal government played a central role. Arguments and statistics were offered to show that federal government spending—which was growing by leaps and bounds—was out of control, causing us to run budget deficits year after year. As a result, the United States was facing a growing debt burden that would soon swallow up all of our incomes, sink the United States economy, and bring about a worldwide depression.

During the late 1990s, as the federal budget picture improved, these disaster books quietly disappeared. Now, the federal government was running *surpluses*—raising more funds in tax revenues than it was spending. Moreover, the surpluses were projected to continue for at least a decade. News articles and public statements described a bright economic future in which our most pressing problem would be: What shall we do with our mounting budget surpluses?

Then, in 2002, another flip-flop: The government began running deficits again, with continued deficits projected through the end of the decade and beyond. Once again, concern over the budget and growing U.S. debt saturated the media, and the word *disaster* reappeared in the media.

What caused these flip-flops in the government's budget? And why should we care?

In this chapter, we'll take a close look at the government's role in the macro-economy. You'll learn how to interpret trends in the government's budget, and how to identify the causes and effects of those trends. You'll also learn how economists differentiate between debt burdens that are not really problematic, those that are cause for concern, and those that can truly be described as disastrous.

## THINKING ABOUT THE NUMBERS

Let's start with some simple numbers. In 1959, the federal government's total outlays for goods and services, transfer payments, and interest on its debt was $92 billion. By 2006, the total had grown to about $2,700 billion, an increase of more than 2,800 percent. Does this show that government spending is out of control?

Or consider the **national debt**—the total amount that the federal government owes to the general public from past borrowing in years in which it ran a budget deficit. In 1959, the national debt was $235 billion; by mid-2005, it had grown to $4,900 billion. Is this evidence that debt is crushing the economy?

**National debt** The total amount the federal government still owes to the general public from past borrowing.

Actually, these figures don't tell us much of anything. First, prices rose during that period, so *real* government outlays and the *real* national debt rose considerably less than these nominal figures suggest. In addition, from 1959 to 2006, the U.S. population grew, the labor force grew, and the average worker became more productive. As a result, real GDP and real income more than quadrupled during this period. Why is that important? Because *spending and debt should be viewed in relation to income.*

We automatically recognize this principle when we think about an individual family or business. Suppose you are told that a family is spending $50,000 each year on goods and services, and has a total debt—a combination of mortgage debt, car loans, student loans, and credit card balances—of $200,000. Is this family acting responsibly? Or is its spending and borrowing out of control? That depends. If the income of the household is less than its spending—say, $40,000—and is expected to remain so, then there is serious trouble. A family that continues to spend more than it earns would see its debt grow every year until it could not handle the monthly interest payments.

But what if the family's income is $800,000 per year? Then our conclusion would change dramatically: We'd wonder why this family spends so *little*. And if it owed $200,000, we would not think it irresponsible at all. After all, the family could pay the interest on its debt with a tiny fraction of its income.

What is true for an individual family is also true for the nation. Spending and debt are *relative* concepts. As a country's total income grows, it will want more of the things that government can provide—education, high environmental standards, domestic security, programs to help the needy, and more. Therefore, we expect government spending to rise as a nation becomes richer. Moreover, as its income grows, a country can *handle* higher interest payments on its debt. Government spending and the total national debt, considered in isolation, tell us nothing about how responsibly or irresponsibly the government is behaving.

> *Budget-related figures such as government outlays, tax revenues, or government debt should be considered relative to a nation's total income—as percentages of GDP.*

Viewing budget-related figures relative to GDP helps to put things in perspective. In 1959, the federal government's total outlays were 19 percent of GDP. In 2006, they were 20.6 percent—reflecting a slight upward drift, but far from out of control. And relative to GDP, the national debt in the hands of the public was lower in 2006 than in 1959, shrinking from about 48 percent to 37 percent of GDP. This doesn't suggest that everything is fine with the federal budget, and we'll discuss some causes for concern in this chapter. But our concerns should be based on, and expressed with, the proper perspective.

In the rest of this chapter, as we explore recent trends in fiscal behavior and their effects on the economy, we'll do so with these lessons in mind. Accordingly, we'll look at fiscal variables as *percentages of GDP*.[1]

---

[1] It makes no difference whether we divide *nominal* government outlays by *nominal* GDP, or *real* government outlays by *real* GDP; we get the same answer for government outlays as a percentage of GDP. When we measure a variable as a percentage of GDP, we are adjusting for inflation *and* for growth in real income at the same time.

# THE FEDERAL BUDGET AND ITS COMPONENTS

Our ultimate goal in this chapter is to understand how fiscal changes have affected, and continue to affect, the macroeconomy. But before we do this, some background will help. What has happened to the *composition* of government spending in recent decades? How does the U.S. tax system work, and what has happened to the government's tax revenues? Why has the national debt decreased in some years, risen slowly in other years, and risen very rapidly in still others? This section provides answers to these and other questions about the government's finances. Although state and local spending also play an important role in the macroeconomy, most of the significant macroeconomic changes in recent decades have involved the *federal* government. This is why we'll focus on spending, taxing, and borrowing at the federal level.

## GOVERNMENT OUTLAYS

The federal government's *outlays*—the total amount spent or disbursed by the federal government in all of its activities—can be divided into three categories:

- *Government purchases*—the total value of the goods and services that the government buys (corresponding to "*G*" in GDP = $C + I + G + NX$)
- *Transfer payments*—income supplements the government provides to people, such as Social Security benefits, unemployment compensation, and welfare payments
- *Interest on the national debt*—the interest payments the government must make to those who hold government bonds

### Government Purchases

Until the mid-1970s, government purchases of goods and services were the largest component of government spending. To understand how these purchases have changed over time, it's essential to divide them into two categories: military and nonmilitary. Figure 1 shows total federal purchases, as well as federal military and nonmilitary purchases, from 1959 to 2006.

One fact stands out from the figure: The federal government uses up only a tiny fraction of our national resources for nonmilitary purposes. These nonmilitary purchases include the salaries paid to all government workers outside the Defense Department (for example, federal judges, legislators, and the people who run federal agencies), as well as purchases of buildings, equipment, and supplies. It also includes the spending of the new Homeland Security Department (established in 2003). Added together, all the different kinds of nonmilitary government purchases account for a stable, low fraction of GDP—about 2 percent.

This strongly contradicts a commonly held notion: that government spending is growing by leaps and bounds because of bloated federal bureaucracies. While it's true that government outlays have drifted upward over the last several decades, nonmilitary purchases have not been the cause.

> *As a percentage of GDP, nonmilitary government purchases have remained very low and stable. They have not contributed to growth in total government outlays.*

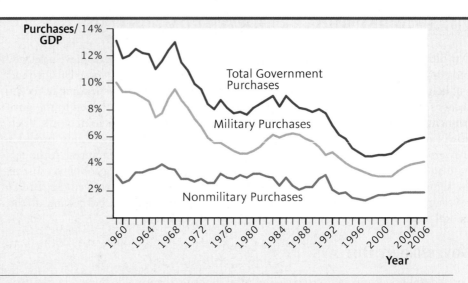

**FIGURE 1**

**Federal Government Purchases as a Percentage of GDP**

*Over the last several decades, total government purchases have trended downward largely because nonmilitary purchases remained a stable, small percentage of GDP while military purchases have steadily decreased. Exceptions were the late 1960s (Vietnam War), 1980s (Reagan defense buildup) and the early 2000s (Bush defense buildup after September 11, 2001).*

*Source* for this and most of the other figures in this chapter: Office of Management and Budget, *The Budget for Fiscal Year 2007, Historical Tables* (especially Tables 1.1, 1.3, 2.1, 2.3, 6.1, and 7.1). Data for 2006 are estimates.

© GEORGE HALL/CORBIS

What about military purchases? Here, we come to an even stronger conclusion:

> *As a percentage of GDP, military purchases trended sharply downward over the past several decades. Like nonmilitary purchases, they have not contributed to the long-term upward drift in government outlays.*

The decline in military purchases is shown by the middle line in Figure 1. They were around 10 percent of GDP in 1959, fell almost continuously to about 3 percent in the late 1990s, then rose again from 2001 to 2006. In between, there were two large military buildups—one associated with the Vietnam War in the late 1960s and the other during the Reagan administration in the 1980s. But both of these buildups were temporary. From 1959 to 2001, the decline of military spending freed up resources amounting to 6½ to 7 percent of GDP (often called the "peace dividend" from the ending of the cold war). As you can see in Figure 1, the more recent rise in military purchases has taken back only a small part of the peace dividend.

It is too early to say whether the current rise in military purchases will be temporary, or how large it will become. But given the current U.S. role in global politics, significant future cuts seem highly unlikely. The implications are tremendously important for thinking about the recent past and the future of the federal government's role in the economy:

> *The decline in military spending in relation to GDP since the early 1960s has made huge amounts of resources available for other purposes. Because military spending has little room to fall further and is likely to rise over the next decade, there will not be any similar freeing up of resources in coming years.*

The resources released from military spending eased many otherwise tough decisions about resource allocation in the economy. In particular, they made it easy

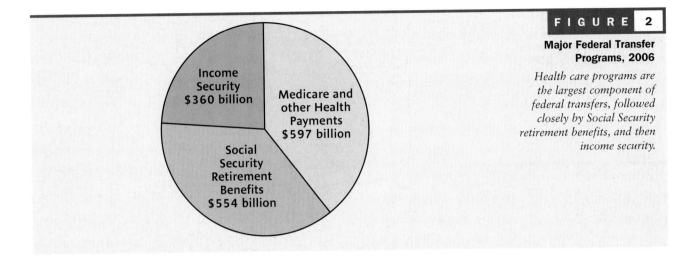

**FIGURE** 2

**Major Federal Transfer Programs, 2006**

*Health care programs are the largest component of federal transfers, followed closely by Social Security retirement benefits, and then income security.*

for the federal government to provide increases in resources to some parts of the population, through transfer payments. Now that this trend has ended, the government will be presented with difficult budget choices.

### Social Security and Other Transfers

Transfer programs provide cash and in-kind benefits to people whom the federal government designates as needing or entitled to help. Figure 2 shows the three major categories of transfers.

The largest category of transfers—and the fastest-growing—occurs in health programs. Medicare (officially part of the Social Security system) provides health-related benefits to everyone aged 62 and over. It covers care at hospitals and nursing facilities, covers outpatient physician services, and began in 2006 to cover prescription medication. Efforts have been made to control Medicare's rapidly rising costs, but they have continued to rise as a percentage of GDP. They are expected to rise even more rapidly over the next decade as the baby-boom generation begins retiring. In addition to funding Medicare, the federal government helps finance state-operated health plans for the poor, through a program called Medicaid. The costs of these programs have been rising rapidly as well.

The second largest category is retirement benefits—the payments made by the Social Security system to retired people. Although the benefits are loosely related to past contributions to the Social Security system, workers whose earnings are low receive benefits that are worth far more than their contributions. And after age 72, even someone with no history of contributions receives the minimum benefit. Social Security outlays have grown rapidly over the last few decades, and are expected to rise even more rapidly as the baby-boom generation begins retiring and collecting benefits around 2010.

**Government "Outlays" versus Government "Purchases"**
Don't confuse government outlays with government purchases, which are just one component of the government's outlays. The other components are transfer payments and interest on the debt.

The third and smallest of the three categories of transfers is *income security*—a catch-all for some federal retirement programs, as well as programs to help the poor and the unemployed, such as unemployment insurance, food stamps, and welfare.

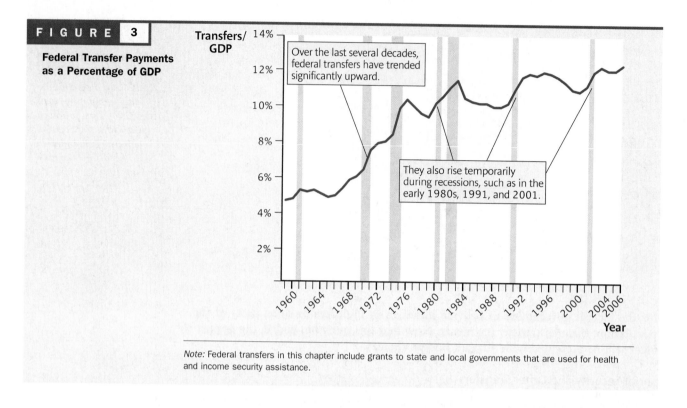

**FIGURE 3**

**Federal Transfer Payments as a Percentage of GDP**

Transfers/GDP

Over the last several decades, federal transfers have trended significantly upward.

They also rise temporarily during recessions, such as in the early 1980s, 1991, and 2001.

Year

*Note:* Federal transfers in this chapter include grants to state and local governments that are used for health and income security assistance.

Have transfer payments been growing as a fraction of GDP? Indeed, they have. All three categories of transfer programs have grown rapidly in recent decades. Figure 3 shows how *total* transfer payments as a percentage of GDP have trended upward.

*In recent decades, transfers have been the fastest growing part of federal government outlays and are currently equal to about 12.4 percent of GDP.*

Growth in transfers relative to GDP was most rapid in the 1970s during the Nixon administration. During this period, government-financed retirement benefits became much more generous, food stamps were introduced, and Medicare expanded. Since then, transfers have continued to rise modestly but are projected to soar as baby boomers retire and receive Social Security and Medicare benefits.

Notice, too, that transfers are sensitive to the ups and downs of the economy. Transfers as a fraction of GDP rise during recessions, as in 1974, 1981, 1991, and 2001. This is for two reasons. First, the number of needy recipients rises in a recession, so transfer payments—the numerator of the fraction—increase. Second, GDP—the denominator—typically falls in a recession. Similarly, transfers as a fraction of GDP tend to fall during expansions, such as the long expansion that ran from 1991 through early 2001. During expansions, the numerator of this fraction falls (why?), and the denominator rises. We will come back to these movements in transfers toward the end of the chapter.

### Interest on the National Debt

Figure 4 shows the behavior of the third and smallest category of government spending: interest on the national debt. As you can see, interest as a percentage of

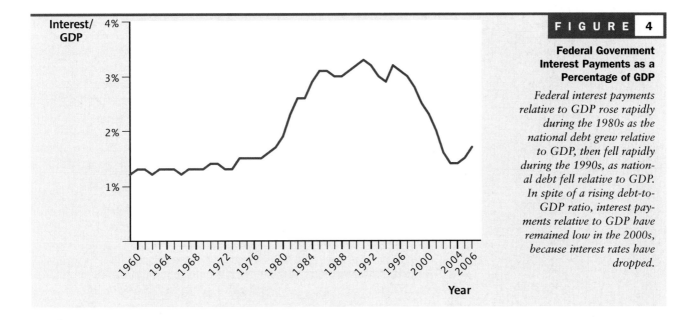

**FIGURE 4**

**Federal Government Interest Payments as a Percentage of GDP**

*Federal interest payments relative to GDP rose rapidly during the 1980s as the national debt grew relative to GDP, then fell rapidly during the 1990s, as national debt fell relative to GDP. In spite of a rising debt-to-GDP ratio, interest payments relative to GDP have remained low in the 2000s, because interest rates have dropped.*

GDP grew rapidly in the early 1980s, when the debt was growing and interest rates were rising. In the 1990s, interest as a fraction of GDP fell slowly at first, as growth in the debt slowed, and then fell dramatically as the national debt dropped from 1998 to 2001. Interest relative to GDP has remained low in the early 2000s even though the national debt has been rising, because the Federal Reserve repeatedly lowered interest rates in 2001, and they remained low through most of 2004.

### Total Government Outlays

Figure 5 shows total outlays in relation to GDP over the past several decades. There are two important things to notice in the figure. The first is the *fluctuations* in government outlays over the period. There was a sharp increase in outlays in each recession (shaded) due to the jump in transfers that we saw in Figure 3. The recession of 1981–82 is a striking example. Also visible is the increase in military spending for the Vietnam War in the late 1960s.

The second thing to notice is the trends. First, for several decades up to the early 1990s, federal outlays as a percentage of GDP drifted upward (due mainly to increases in transfers and interest payments). Then, from 1992 to 2000, federal outlays relative to GDP declined (due mainly to the "peace dividend" and falling transfers during a long economic expansion).

However, Figure 5 also shows the appearance of a likely new trend:

*From 2001 to 2006, due to the ending of the "peace dividend" and continued increases in transfers, federal government outlays as a percentage of GDP have been rising, and seem likely to continue rising through the decade.*

These trends in government outlays have important implications, but they are only half of the story. In order to understand their impact on the budget and the macroeconomy, we must look at the other side of the budget: tax revenue.

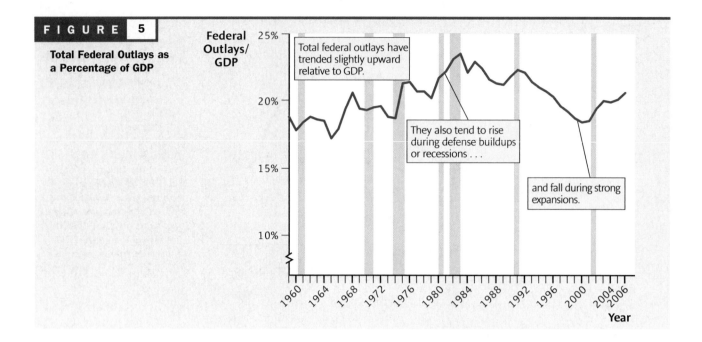

### FIGURE 5

**Total Federal Outlays as a Percentage of GDP**

Federal Outlays/GDP

Total federal outlays have trended slightly upward relative to GDP.

They also tend to rise during defense buildups or recessions . . .

and fall during strong expansions.

Year

## FEDERAL TAX REVENUE

The federal government obtains most of its revenue from two sources: the personal income tax and the Social Security tax.

### The Personal Income Tax

The personal income tax is the most important source of revenue for the federal government and also the most conspicuous and painful. Almost every adult has to file Form 1040 or one of its shorter cousins. One of the signs of success as an American is seeing your federal tax return swell to the size of a magazine. Proposals to reduce both the amount of taxes people pay and the complexity of the tax forms are immensely popular.

**Progressive tax** A tax whose rate increases as income increases.

The personal income tax is designed to be **progressive**, to tax those at the higher end of the income scale at higher rates than those at the lower end of the scale, and to excuse the poorest families from paying any tax at all. Table 1 shows how the income tax works, in theory, by computing the amount of tax a family of four should have paid on its 2005 income if it took the standard deduction.[2] The table also shows the **average tax rate**—the fraction of total income a family pays in taxes—and the **marginal tax rate**—the tax rate paid on *each additional dollar* of income.

**Average tax rate** The fraction of a given income paid in taxes.

**Marginal tax rate** The fraction of an additional dollar of income paid in taxes.

We can see from Table 1 that the income tax is designed to be quite progressive. In principle, a family in the middle of the income distribution for married couples, earning $65,000 per year, should have paid about 9 percent of its income in taxes, while a family near the top should have paid almost 30 percent of its income in

[2] The federal government allows households to deduct certain expenses (like medical care or the costs of moving to a new job) from their income before calculating the tax that they owe. Alternatively, they may deduct a standard amount (the *standard deduction*) from their income, regardless of their spending patterns.

| Income | Tax | Average Tax Rate | Marginal Tax Rate | **TABLE** **1** |
|---|---|---|---|---|
| | | | | **The 2005 Personal Income Tax for a Married Couple with Two Children** |
| $ 20,000 | $        0 | 0% | 0% | |
| $ 30,000 | $     723 | 2.4% | 10% | |
| $ 50,000 | $   3,354 | 6.7% | 15% | |
| $ 75,000 | $   7,104 | 9.5% | 15% | |
| $150,000 | $ 25,348 | 16.9% | 28% | |
| $250,000 | $ 63,092 | 25.2% | 33% | |
| $400,000 | $110,563 | 27.6% | 35% | |

*Source:* Calculated from the 2005 Form 1040 tax table with the standard deduction of $10,000. First column shows total income before standard deduction or deduction for dependents.

taxes. The table also shows that marginal tax rates on families with the highest income are in the range of 33 to 35 percent.

But the tax system shown in the table does not reflect the ways that people can avoid tax. Many people have deductions far above the standard deduction. Some people earn income that they never report to the government, thereby evading taxes entirely. And people can shelter income in their employer's retirement plan or in a plan of their own. Studies have shown that higher-income households avoid more taxes than poorer families and that the federal tax system—while still progressive— is much less progressive than suggested by Table 1.

Also, remember that we are looking at the *federal personal income* tax only. Households pay other taxes related to their income, some of which are **regressive**— taking a lower percentage in taxes as household income rises. For example, state and local sales taxes are regressive: Lower-income households *spend* a larger fraction of their incomes, so they pay a higher percentage of that income in sales taxes. Another example of a regressive tax is the federal payroll tax, earmarked to fund Social Security and Medicare, which we'll turn to now.

**Regressive tax** A tax that collects a lower percentage of income as income rises.

### The Social Security Tax

The Social Security tax applies to wage and salary income only. It was put in place in 1936, to finance the Social Security system created in that year. Whereas the personal income tax is a nightmare of complex forms and rules, the Social Security tax is remarkably simple. The current tax rate (including the Medicare part of the tax) is a flat 15.3 percent,[3] except for one complication: Most of the tax is applied only on earnings below a certain amount ($94,200 in 2006, although the cap rises each year).

Because the payroll tax applies only to earnings below a certain level, it is regressive. For example, employees earning $94,200 or below in 2006 paid the full 15.3 percent of their income in taxes, while those who earned twice that amount— $188,400—paid only 7.65 percent (since the tax applied to only half of their earnings). The Social Security tax is actually the largest tax paid by many Americans,

[3] If you look at your own paycheck, it may seem that the Social Security tax (including Medicare) is only 7.65 percent instead of the 15.3 percent we've just mentioned. The reason is that your employer pays half the tax and you pay the other half. But the amount paid on your earnings is the sum, 15.3 percent.

especially those with lower incomes. These families pay little or no income tax, but pay the Social Security tax on all of their wage earnings. For example, a family with $30,000 of earnings in Table 1 would pay $723 in federal income tax, but Social Security taxes on those earnings would be $4,590.

## Other Federal Taxes

The federal government also collects around $503 billion annually from other sources. The most important of these is the *corporate profits tax,* which raised $332 billion in 2006 by taxing the profits earned by corporations at a rate of 35 percent.

The corporate profits tax is often criticized by economists because of two important problems. First, it applies only to corporations. Thus, a business owner can avoid it completely by setting up a sole proprietorship or partnership instead of a corporation. As a result, the tax causes many businesses to forego the benefits of being corporations because of the extra tax they would have to pay.

Second, the corporation tax results in *double taxation* on the portion of corporate profits that corporations pay to their owners. This portion of profits is taxed once when the corporation is taxed and again when the profits are included as part of the owners' personal income. The corporation tax is thus a prime target for tax reform. Almost all reform proposals put forward by economists involve integrating the taxation of corporations into the tax system in a way that avoids these two distortions.

The federal government also taxes the consumption of certain products, such as gasoline, alcohol, tobacco, and air travel. These are called *excise taxes.* Excise taxes raise additional revenue for the government, but they are usually put in place for other, nonrevenue reasons as well. The excise tax on gasoline is seen, in part, as a fee on drivers for the use of federal highways. The taxes on alcohol and tobacco are intended to discourage consumption of these harmful products.

## Trends in Federal Tax Revenue

The top line in Figure 6 shows total federal government revenue, as a percentage of GDP, from all of the taxes we've discussed. Until recently, there was an upward trend. More specifically,

> *federal revenue trended upward from around 18 percent of GDP in the early 1960s to around 21 percent in the late 1990s.*

But notice the sharp drop in the early 2000s. This was partly due to the very slow recovery from the 2001 recession, and partly due to significant long-term reductions in tax rates proposed by the Bush administration, and passed by Congress, in 2001 and 2003. We'll have more to say about these tax cuts at the end of this chapter.

Notice, also, that the *composition* of total federal revenue has changed dramatically. The lower two lines in Figure 6 show the part of federal revenue that comes from Social Security taxes and all other taxes. Notice the steady upward trend in Social Security tax revenue. Also notice that all other sources of revenue have trended slightly downward over the same period even before the sharp drop of the 2000s.

Why have Social Security taxes grown in importance? First, a little background. The Social Security system operates on a pay-as-you-go principle: It taxes people who are working now in order to pay benefits to those who worked earlier and are

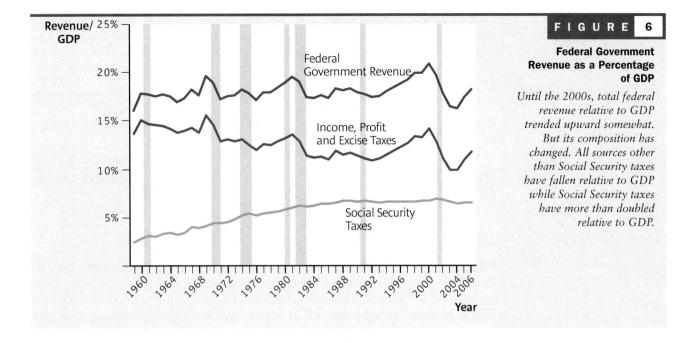

**FIGURE 6**

**Federal Government Revenue as a Percentage of GDP**

*Until the 2000s, total federal revenue relative to GDP trended upward somewhat. But its composition has changed. All sources other than Social Security taxes have fallen relative to GDP while Social Security taxes have more than doubled relative to GDP.*

now retired. For the first several decades after the system was established (in 1935), there were so few retirees that benefits could be funded with very low payroll tax rates on those currently working.

But now, demographic trends are working against the system. First, improved health is allowing people to spend a larger fraction of their lives in retirement. That is good from a human perspective, but from an accounting point of view, it means that the average retiree is drawing more benefits. At the same time, the baby boomers will begin retiring en masse around 2010, which means greater *numbers* of people drawing benefits. Finally, these increased benefits will be funded by a smaller number of working taxpayers.

Anticipating these trends, the government had been raising Social Security tax rates for years, not just to keep the system solvent, but to go further—building up reserves in a separate government account (called the Social Security Trust Fund) for retiring baby boomers. This helped to create the rising Social Security tax line in Figure 6.

But the trust fund has imposed no constraints on Congress, legal or economic. In fact, the reserves built up in the trust fund have been (and continue to be) borrowed by the Treasury and spent on other government programs. Meanwhile, Congress has been (and continues to be) free to raise or lower Social Security benefits as it wishes, regardless of the balance in the trust fund.

Thus, the rising Social Security tax line in Figure 6—while it helped to fund past government outlays—did not "solve" the real Social Security problem. That problem is: Scheduled Social Security benefits as a percentage of GDP will begin rising (due to retiring baby boomers) around 2010. At the same time, payroll tax revenues as a percentage of GDP will begin falling (fewer baby boomers working and paying taxes). Similar but even larger changes will be occurring in Medicare, the government health program for retirees.

This combination—greater total benefits relative to GDP, and lower payroll taxes relative to GDP to pay for them—forces the country to choose among four unpleasant alternatives:

- Raise the payroll tax rate (or other tax rates) on current workers
- Cut future retirement and/or health benefits as a fraction of GDP (say, by raising the retirement age, or cutting projected benefits for each retiree)
- Reduce *other* government outlays relative to GDP to pay the greater benefits
- Allow the overall annual budget deficit relative to GDP to rise

The last option occurs automatically if none of the others is chosen. By mid-2006, it was still unclear which one (or combination) of these unpleasant options the country would ultimately choose.

## THE FEDERAL BUDGET AND THE NATIONAL DEBT

Finally, we can bring together what we've learned about the government's tax revenue with what we've learned about the government's outlays. Look first at the upper panel in Figure 7. This shows total federal outlays (from Figure 5) and total federal revenue (from the top line in Figure 6). The difference between these two lines in any year is the federal budget deficit (when outlays exceed revenue) or surplus (when revenue exceeds outlays).

$$\text{Budget surplus} = \text{Tax revenue} - \text{Outlays}$$

$$\text{Budget deficit} = \text{Outlays} - \text{Tax revenue}^4$$

The bottom panel shows the history of the budget in recent decades, with surpluses as positive values and deficits as negative values.[5] The lower panel looks much choppier because the scale of the diagram is different there. But you can see that there was a dramatic change in the behavior of the budget around 1975. Until that year, the government mostly ran deficits, but rarely more than 2 percent of GDP. But from 1975 until 1993, the deficit grew significantly. During that period, it was usually greater than 3 percent of GDP, and often more than 4 percent. Notice, for example, the especially large rise in the deficit that occurred in the early 1980s. This was the combined result of a severe recession, which caused transfers to rise as shown in Figure 3, the buildup in military spending shown in Figure 1, and a large cut in income taxes during President Reagan's first term in office.

---

[4] If we consider interest payments as part of transfer payments, these are the same definitions given earlier in the text. To see this, start with our current definition of the deficit:

$$\text{Budget deficit} = \text{Outlays} - \text{Tax revenue}$$
$$= (\text{Government purchases} + \text{Transfers}) - \text{Tax revenue}$$
$$= \text{Government purchases} - (\text{Tax revenue} - \text{Transfers})$$
$$= G - T$$

The last line is the definition for the deficit given in the chapter on the classical model, where $G$ is government purchases in GDP and $T$ is net taxes.

[5] To measure the deficit or surplus, we have included all sources of federal revenue and all types of spending, whether part of the official federal budget or not. In particular, we've included Social Security taxes and Social Security payments even though they are officially considered "off budget" in U.S. government statistics.

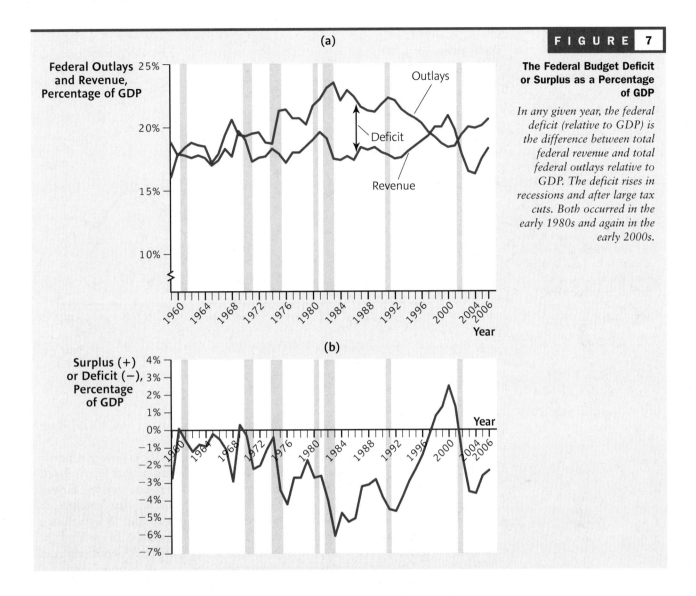

**(a)**

**Federal Outlays and Revenue, Percentage of GDP**

Outlays

Deficit

Revenue

**(b)**

**Surplus (+) or Deficit (−), Percentage of GDP**

Year

**FIGURE 7**

**The Federal Budget Deficit or Surplus as a Percentage of GDP**

*In any given year, the federal deficit (relative to GDP) is the difference between total federal revenue and total federal outlays relative to GDP. The deficit rises in recessions and after large tax cuts. Both occurred in the early 1980s and again in the early 2000s.*

In the mid-1990s, the deficit began to come down, and finally, in the late 1990s, the federal government began running budget surpluses for a few years. But from 2002 to 2006, the budget was back into deficit, and the deficits were projected to continue through the end of the decade. Even though the world has changed much since the 1980s, the reasons for the recent deficits seem like a repeat of history: a recession, increased military spending, and a sizable, multiyear tax cut.

### The National Debt

Before we consider the government's budget further, we need to address some common confusion among three related, but very different, terms: the federal *deficit*, the federal *surplus*, and the national *debt*. The federal deficit and surplus are *flow* variables: They measure the difference between government spending and tax revenue *over a given period*, usually a year. The national debt, by contrast, is a *stock* variable: It measures the total amount that the federal government owes *at a given point*

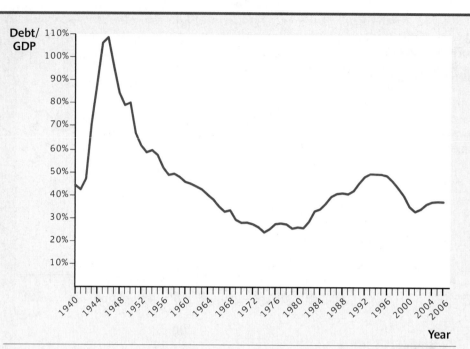

**FIGURE 8**

**Federal Debt as a Percentage of GDP**

*Federal debt (the national debt) relative to GDP soared during World War II then fell steadily for several decades. It rose during the 1980s due to a combination of tax cuts and defense buildups during the Reagan administration, then fell during the shrinking deficits and expansion of the 1990s. In the early 2000s, a combination of recession and slow recovery, tax cuts, and defense spending caused the debt–GDP ratio to begin rising.*

*Source:* Office of Management and Budget. *Historical Tables, Budget of the United States Government, Fiscal Year 2007,* Table 7.1.

*in time.* (See the chapter "Economic Growth and Rising Living Standards" if you need a refresher on stocks and flows.)

The relationship between these terms is this: Each year that the government runs a deficit, it must borrow funds to finance it, *adding to the national debt.* For example, in 1996, the federal government ran a deficit of $107 billion. During that year, it issued about $107 billion in new government bonds, adding that much to the national debt. On the other hand, if the government runs a surplus, it uses the surplus to *pay back* some of the national debt. For example, in 2000, the federal government ran a surplus of about $236 billion. That year, it purchased about that much in government bonds it had issued in the past, thus reducing the national debt.[6]

We can measure the national debt as the total value of government bonds held by the public. Thus,

> *deficits—which add to the public's holdings of federal government bonds— add to the national debt. Surpluses—which decrease the public's bond holdings —subtract from the national debt.*

Since the cumulative total of the government's deficits has been greater than its surpluses, the national debt has grown over the past several decades. In the 1980s and early 1990s, it also grew relative to GDP, as shown in Figure 8.

The rise and fall in the national debt also explains another trend we discussed earlier: the rise and fall in *interest payments* the government must make to those who hold government bonds. All else equal, the larger the national debt, the greater

---

[6] The increase or decrease in the national debt is never exactly the same as the annual deficit or surplus, because of accounting details.

will be the government's yearly interest payments on the debt. As you saw in Figure 4, total interest payments rose rapidly during the 1980s—the same period in which the national debt zoomed upward. In the 1990s, as the national debt decreased relative to GDP, so did interest payments on the debt. If you compare Figure 4 with Figure 8, however, you'll see that, as a percentage of GDP, the national debt rose in the early 2000s while yearly interest payments fell. That's because all else was *not* equal during this period: As mentioned earlier, the Federal Reserve dramatically lowered interest rates in the early 2000s, which reduced the government's interest payments on each dollar of newly issued debt.

Now that we've outlined the recent history of federal government spending, taxes, and debt, we turn our attention to the relationship between fiscal changes and the economy.

## FISCAL CHANGES IN THE SHORT RUN

In the short run, there is a two-way relationship between the government's budget and the macroeconomy. On the one hand, changes in the economy affect the government's outlays and taxes; on the other hand, changes in outlays and taxes affect the economy. Let's begin by considering how economic fluctuations affect the government's budget.

### How Economic Fluctuations Affect the Federal Budget

Economic fluctuations affect both transfer payments and tax revenues. In a recession, in which many people lose their jobs, the federal government contributes larger amounts to state-run unemployment insurance systems and pays more in transfers to the poor, since more families qualify for these types of assistance. Thus, a recession causes transfer payments to rise. Recessions also cause a drop in tax revenue, because household income and corporate profits—two important sources of tax revenue—decrease during recessions.

*In a recession, because transfers rise and tax revenue falls, the federal budget deficit increases (or the surplus decreases).*

An expansion has the opposite effect on the federal budget: With lower unemployment and higher levels of output and income, federal transfers decrease and tax revenues increase. Thus,

*in an expansion, because transfers decrease and tax revenue rises, the budget deficit decreases (or the surplus increases).*

Because the business cycle has systematic effects on the budget, economists find it useful to divide the deficit into two components. The **cyclical deficit** is the part that can be attributed to the current state of the economy. We have a cyclical deficit when output is below potential GDP, and a cyclical surplus when output is above potential. When the economy is operating just at full employment, the cyclical deficit is, by definition, zero.

The **structural deficit** is the part of the deficit that is *not* caused by economic fluctuations. As the economy recovers from a recession, for example, the cyclical deficit goes away, but any structural deficit in the budget will remain.

**Cyclical deficit** The part of the federal budget deficit that varies with the business cycle.

**Structural deficit** The part of the federal budget deficit that is independent of the business cycle.

Cyclical changes in the budget are not a cause for concern because they average out to about zero, as output fluctuates above and below potential output. Thus, the cyclical deficit should not contribute to a long-run rise in the national debt.

## How the Budget Affects Economic Fluctuations

There are two types of budget changes that can affect the macroeconomy. One is a change in total government purchases or net taxes *not* caused by the business cycle. These are *policy* changes, and they affect the *structural* budget deficit. For example, an increase in government purchases will raise the budget deficit we would have at *any* level of GDP.

As you learned in earlier chapters, fiscal policy can affect total spending and have a multiplier affect on GDP in the short run. In theory, fiscal policy could even change the course of the business cycle itself. However, as discussed in an earlier chapter ("The Short-Run Macro Model"), counter-cyclical fiscal policy is problematic, and is no longer regarded as the most effective tool to counter the business cycle.

A second type of budgetary change that affects the macroeconomy was introduced in this chapter: changes in taxes or transfers that are *caused* by the business cycle itself. These are not policy changes; rather, they occur *automatically* as income rises or falls during the business cycle. They affect the cyclical, but not the structural, deficit.

Such changes in the cyclical deficit have an important impact: They help to make economic fluctuations milder than they would otherwise be. Recall that changes in spending have a multiplier effect on output. The larger the multiplier, the greater will be the fluctuations in output caused by any given change in spending. But changes in the cyclical deficit make the multiplier *smaller*, and thus act as an *automatic stabilizer*. How?

Let's use unemployment insurance as an example. In normal times, with the unemployment rate at around, say, 4.5 percent or lower, federal transfers for unemployment insurance are modest. But when the economy goes into recession, and output and income begin to fall, the unemployment rate rises. Federal transfers for unemployment insurance rise *automatically*. Without assistance from the government, many of the newly unemployed would have to cut back their consumption spending substantially. But unemployment insurance cushions the blow for many such families—at least for six months or sometimes longer—allowing them to make smaller cutbacks in consumption during that time. As a result, the total decline in consumption is smaller and GDP declines by less. Unemployment insurance thus reduces the multiplier.

Other transfer programs have a similar stabilizing effect on output. More people receive food stamps during recessions. Consequently, their consumption falls by less than it would if they did not have this help. And the tax system contributes to economic stability in a similar way. Income tax payments, for example, fall during a recession. With the government siphoning off a smaller amount of income from the household sector, the drop in consumption is smaller than it would be if tax revenues remained constant.

The same principle applies during an expansion. Transfer payments automatically decline, as the unemployed find jobs and fewer families qualify for government assistance. And tax revenues automatically rise, since income rises. As a result, the rise in GDP is smaller than it would otherwise be.

> *Many features of the federal tax and transfer systems act as automatic stabilizers. As the economy goes into a recession, these features help to reduce the decline in consumption spending, and they also cause the cyclical deficit to rise. As the economy goes into an expansion, these features help to reduce the rise in consumption spending, and they also cause the cyclical deficit to fall.*

## FISCAL CHANGES IN THE LONG RUN

Fiscal changes have important effects on the economy over the long run. And, as you've learned, the classical model—which focuses on the determinants of potential output—provides a useful framework for analyzing these long-run effects.

Let's first list three important conclusions about fiscal policy in the classical model that you learned in earlier chapters:

- The government's tax and transfer policies can influence employment. For example, higher tax rates on labor income (or household income, generally) or more generous transfers can reduce the employment–population ratio and *decrease* the average standard of living. Lower tax rates or less generous transfers can raise the employment–population ratio and raise the standard of living.
- The government's tax policies can directly influence the rate of investment spending on new capital and R&D. Higher tax rates on the profits from investment projects will lower investment spending and lead to slower growth in the average standard of living. Lower tax rates or other investment incentives will increase investment spending and lead to faster growth in living standards.
- The government's budget deficit can influence investment spending as well. An increase in the budget deficit causes the government to demand more loanable funds. This raises the interest rate, lowers investment spending, and slows the growth in living standards. Lower budget deficits reduce the government's demand for loanable funds, resulting in a lower interest rate, greater investment spending, and faster growth in living standards.

And, from this chapter, you've learned the following:

- Budget deficits add to the national debt.

But what are the *consequences* of adding to the national debt?

### THE NATIONAL DEBT

On a billboard in midtown Manhattan, a giant clocklike digital display tracks the U.S. national debt up to the second. In mid-2006, as the clock headed toward $8.5 trillion (rising by $951,000 per minute), the last four digits on the display changed so rapidly that they appeared as a blur.

The national debt clock is one of several public relations campaigns that spread fear among the American public.[7] How can we ever hope to repay all of this debt? Surely, we must be speeding toward a debt disaster.

---

[7] You can find similar debt clocks on the Web (google "national debt clock"). But keep in mind that they all exaggerate the burden by using "total national debt," which includes amounts that one government agency owes to another. In mid-2006, when "total national debt" was approaching $8.5 trillion, the more relevant "publicly held debt" (what the government owed to everyone but itself) was approaching $4.9 trillion.

Economists do have concerns about the national debt. But they are very different from the concerns suggested by the national debt clock or other similar gimmicks.

### Mythical Concerns About the National Debt

What bothers many people about a growing national debt is the belief that one day we will have to pay it all back. But although we might *choose* to repay the national debt, we do not have to. *Ever.* Moreover, there is nothing automatically wrong with a national debt that *grows* every year. That may sound surprising. How could a government keep borrowing funds without ever paying them back? Surely, no business could behave that way.

But actually, many successful businesses *do* behave that way. For example, the debt of many major corporations—like Pfizer and Verizon—continues to grow, year after year. While they continue to pay interest on their debt, they may have no plans to pay back the amount originally borrowed. As these companies' bonds become due, they simply *roll them over;* they issue new bonds to pay back the old ones.

Why don't these firms pay back their debt? Because they believe they have a better use for their funds: investing in new capital equipment and research and development to expand their businesses. This will lead to higher future profits.

Of course, this does not mean that *any* size debt would be prudent. Recall the important principle we discussed earlier in the chapter: *Debt and interest payments have meaning only in relation to income.* If a firm's income is growing by 5 percent each year, but its interest payments are growing by 10 percent per year, it would eventually find itself in trouble. Each year, its interest payments would take a larger and larger fraction of its income, and at some point interest payments would exceed total income. But even *before* this occurred, the firm would find itself in trouble. Lenders, anticipating the firm's eventual inability to pay interest, would cut the firm off. At that point, the firm would reach its *credit limit*—the maximum amount it can borrow based on lenders' willingness to lend. Since it could no longer roll over its existing debt with further borrowing, it would have to pay back any bonds coming due until its debt was comfortably below its credit limit.

All of these observations apply to the federal government as well. As long as the nation's total income is rising, the government can safely take on more debt. More specifically, if the nation's income is growing at least as fast as total interest payments, the debt can continue to grow indefinitely, without putting the government in danger.

The federal government *could* pay back the national debt—by running budget surpluses for many years. But the government could also choose to behave like most corporations and *not* pay back its debt. In fact, the government would better serve the public by not paying down the debt if it has better uses for its revenue than debt repayment.

But how rapidly could the government continue to accumulate debt? Or, equivalently, how large could annual deficits be without making the national debt a looming danger?

Let's see. As long as total national income grows at least as fast as interest payments on the debt, the ratio of interest payments to income will not grow. In that case, we could continue to pay interest without increasing the average tax rate on U.S. citizens.

Let's use some round numbers to make this clearer. Suppose that the nominal GDP is $10 trillion and the national debt is $5 trillion. And suppose that annual interest payments average out to 7 percent of the national debt, or $350 billion.

Then the ratio of interest payments to nominal GDP would be \$350 billion/\$10 trillion = 0.035 or 3.5 percent of GDP. So the government must collect tax revenue equal to 3.5 percent of GDP to cover the interest payments for the year. Now suppose that, over some period of time, both nominal GDP and the national debt double, to \$20 trillion and \$10 trillion, respectively. Then interest payments would double as well, to \$700 billion. But the ratio of interest payments to nominal GDP would remain constant, at \$700 billion/\$20 trillion = 0.035. The same tax rate of 3.5 percent still covers the interest payments.

More generally,

> *as long as the debt grows by the same percentage as nominal GDP, the ratios of debt to GDP and interest payments to GDP will remain constant. In this case, the government can continue to pay interest on its rising debt without increasing the average tax rate in the economy.*

## GENUINE CONCERNS ABOUT THE NATIONAL DEBT

When *should* we be concerned about a growing national debt? Our previous discussion has hinted at three scenarios that should cause concern.

### A National Debt That Is Growing Too Rapidly

An important *minimal guideline* for responsible government is that the debt should grow no faster than nominal GDP. Whenever that guideline is violated, interest payments as a fraction of GDP rise, and the average tax burden on the public—taxes relative to GDP—grows. The violation cannot go on forever because the tax burden has a mathematical upper limit of 100 percent of GDP. And even before that limit was reached, tax rates would become oppressive, harming growth and—if pushed too high—actually reducing living standards. However, if the violation of the guideline is temporary, and the debt begins growing at the same rate as nominal GDP again, tax payments as a fraction of GDP could stop rising.

This has two important implications. First, to prevent a long-term disaster after too-rapid growth in the debt, we do not have to run budget surpluses. A surplus is only necessary if the goal is to reduce the *total* debt. But all that is required to put the economy on a *responsible path* is a reduction of the growth rate of the debt back to the growth rate of nominal GDP. After that, we can keep running deficits and the debt can keep rising indefinitely, as long as it rises no faster than nominal GDP.

But there is a second implication as well: Even a temporary violation of the guideline is costly. During the time that debt grows faster than nominal GDP, tax rates must rise to cover the rising interest burden as a fraction of total income. After the debt starts growing at the same rate as nominal GDP again, then the tax rate can stop rising—but *the tax rate will remain at its new, higher level.* Thus, while a temporary violation of the guideline does not mean a disaster, it *does* leave us with a permanently elevated tax burden . . . at least, until we do something about it.

How can the tax burden be brought back down after a temporary violation of the guideline? There are only two basic ways: (1) raise the growth rate of nominal GDP *above* the growth rate of the debt for some time; or (2) lower the growth rate of the debt below the growth rate of nominal GDP for some time. Either of these solutions could return the debt-to-GDP ratio back to its original level, so that interest payments relative to GDP and the tax rate needed to cover them could return to their original levels as well.

But these solutions are costly to society. Let's first consider raising the growth rate of nominal GDP. Since policy has only limited ability to influence the growth rate of *real* GDP over long periods, the only practical method to ensure a higher growth rate of *nominal* GDP is faster growth in the price level. This means allowing the inflation rate to rise for some time. But we've already seen that allowing the inflation rate to rise can be costly for society in numerous ways—including the buildup of inflationary expectations that would be difficult to reverse.

Now consider the second option: slowing down the growth rate of the debt below the growth rate of nominal GDP. The only way to do this is to run *smaller deficits* as a fraction of GDP than we would otherwise be able to run. And the only way to reduce the deficit for some length of time is to raise tax rates or reduce government outlays during that period.

Thus,

> *a debt that rises too fast—faster than nominal GDP—for some period of time will impose an opportunity cost in the future. The cost will be either a permanently higher tax burden, a period of inflation, or a temporary period of reduced government outlays or higher taxes relative to GDP.*

This is not just theoretical, as the U.S. experience during the 1970s and 1980s demonstrates. During this time, nominal GDP was growing at about 9 percent per year—mostly due to increases in the price level. But the debt grew by an average of 11 percent per year, beyond the minimal guidelines for responsible government. The debt-to-GDP ratio therefore rose (see Figure 8) and so did interest payments relative to GDP (see Figure 4). This could not go on indefinitely, or interest payments on the debt would rise to an ever-larger share of GDP, and ever-higher tax rates would be needed to cover them. How did we solve the problem? As we entered the 1990s, we gradually shrunk the budget deficit with higher tax rates and strict limits on the growth of government spending. Fortunately, the 1990s was a period of prolonged expansion and reduced military purchases, so lowering the deficit was not as painful as it might otherwise have been.

### A Debt Approaching a National Credit Limit

If debt were to rise *too* rapidly relative to GDP, for *too* long, there is a theoretical danger of reaching the nation's credit limit—the amount of debt that would make lenders worry about the government's ability to continue paying interest. If this credit limit were approached, a nation would be truly flirting with disaster: a tiny increase in the ratio of debt to GDP would lead to a cutoff of further lending and require that the budget be balanced immediately. It could also cause a financial panic, with everyone trying to sell their government bonds at the same time, causing bond prices to fall and household wealth to plummet.

While this is *theoretically* possible, it's doubtful the United States will be anywhere near that type of limit in the next decade. Look at Figure 8. At the end of World War II, the debt reached 109 percent of GDP—almost triple its current percentage. Even then, no one doubted the U.S. government would continue to honor its obligations.

However, since the late 1990s, economists have had another concern: More than half of the national debt held by the public is in foreign hands. While foreigners still have faith that the United States will honor its obligations, they may nevertheless have an upper limit on the proportion of total wealth they want to hold in dollar-denominated assets (say, to limit their risk in case the dollar falls in value against their own currency). If U.S. debt grows too rapidly, and foreigners find themselves with too much dollar-denominated wealth, they could suddenly, simultaneously, begin selling their U.S. bonds.

*It is highly unlikely U.S. debt levels will approach an absolute credit limit based on loss of faith in the U.S. government. A more realistic concern is that rapidly rising debt causes foreign wealth portfolios to become too "dollar-heavy," leading to a destabilizing sell-off of U.S. bonds.*

We'll come back to this foreign-held debt in the next chapter.

## Failing to Account for Future Obligations

Many students reading this book are getting financial help from their parents to pay the costs of college. If so, your parents probably began planning for this obligation very early—perhaps even before you knew what college was. This makes sense: If a family wants to avoid a drastic decrease in its standard of living in the future, it should start accounting for future obligations early.

The federal government is in an analogous situation. It has effectively promised to provide Medicare and Social Security payments to millions of people at some time in the future. If we assume no changes in scheduled benefit policies, and if current cost trends continue, Social Security, Medicare, and Medicaid benefits are projected to rise significantly—from 8.5 percent of GDP in 2005 to around 19 percent of GDP in 2050.[8] (By comparison, remember that *total* federal outlays are currently about 20 percent of GDP.) If the federal government is to act like a responsible household, it should take these future obligations into account in its planning process. Otherwise, we may have to dramatically decrease *other* government outlays, dramatically increase taxes, or have an ever-rising debt-to-GDP ratio, leading to the dangers discussed earlier.

Of course, trying to project total federal revenues and outlays over the next 50 years is guesswork at best. Even official forecasts of *10-year* projections are typically widely off the mark. In 1989, for example, when the government made its fiscal projections for 1990–1999, no one could have predicted the development of the Internet and other technologies, and the rapid economic growth that would accompany them. And in 1999, when projections for 2000–2009 were completed, who could have predicted the events of September 11, 2001, and how they would change our spending on national defense and homeland security?

This uncertainty over future projections has led to divergent views about policy. Some argue that a responsible government should be exceedingly cautious, running

[8] *The Long-Term Budget Outlook: A CBO Study*, Congressional Budget Office, December 2005. The 19 percent of GDP figure is actually somewhat conservative. It assumes that medical costs per enrollee will grow 1 percentage point faster than GDP per capita through 2050. From 1970 to 2005, spending per enrollee actually rose 2.9 percentage points faster than GDP per capita.

budget surpluses now, paying down the national debt, and leaving us better prepared for any dramatic future rise in government outlays. Others argue that preparing for the worst would require huge sacrifices in the present—sacrifices that might be unnecessary in hindsight.

These divergent views formed part of the background for the controversy over the Bush tax cuts.

© WWW.OMB.GOV

# USING THE THEORY

## The Bush Tax Cuts of 2001 and 2003

In 2001, the Bush administration cut taxes over 10 years by $1.35 trillion, and in 2003, by another $350 billion. Marginal tax rates were reduced on all income brackets, as were tax rates on capital gains and dividends. There were additional reductions for taxpayers with children, and a reduction of the "marriage penalty" that taxed married couples at higher rates than if they were single. Also, the tax cuts in 2003 accelerated some of the 2001 reductions that had originally been postponed until 2006 and beyond.

Much of the debate over the tax reductions had to do with distribution: whether the cuts were apportioned fairly among different income groups. But they also raised two important macroeconomic issues that we've discussed in this and other chapters.

### THE SHORT RUN: COUNTERCYCLICAL FISCAL POLICY?

The tax cuts of 2001 and 2003 seem, at first glance, like perfect examples of well-timed countercyclical fiscal policy. After all, the first cuts were put in place in June 2001—in the middle of a recession that began just three months earlier. And the cuts in May 2003 took effect as the economy was still struggling with a weak expansion. Does this show that countercyclical fiscal policy works?

Not really, because a closer look suggests that neither tax cut was really designed for that purpose. The tax cut of June 2001 had actually been proposed more than 18 months earlier by presidential candidate Bush as a long-run policy measure, to promote growth in potential output. At the time, the economy was in a boom, and the Federal Reserve was actively trying to slow it down. The fact that the tax cut was enacted during a recession was a stroke of luck, not an example of well-timed short-run fiscal policy.

Moreover, remember that countercyclical fiscal policy requires that changes in taxes be reversible when economic conditions change. But both of the Bush tax cuts were *long-term* policy changes: Some of their provisions applied through the end of the decade, and the others were expected to be extended at least that long, and probably beyond.

As so often happens in macroeconomic debates, however, politics took over. As the economy entered the recession of 2001, the debate over the 2001 tax cut quickly shifted to its short-run stimulus potential. And the 2003 cut—weighted heavily toward long-run reforms in the tax code—was both touted and opposed almost entirely on the basis of its ability to create jobs in the short run, during a slow recovery.

In between these two cuts, however, the Bush administration proposed a purely countercyclical, $60 billion tax cut. This was formulated and designed as an emergency measure, shortly after September 11, 2001, to prevent the economy from sliding further into recession. Timing was crucial, and the administration urged quick passage by Congress. If there was ever an opportunity to showcase the effectiveness of countercyclical fiscal policy, this was it. But the tax bill was debated for a full 6 months in the House and Senate, and was not signed by the president until March 2002. During these 6 months of debate, the Fed reduced its interest rate target four times, illustrating the greater flexibility of monetary policy as a countercyclical tool.

## THE LONG RUN: THE TAX CUTS AND THE NATIONAL DEBT

Now let's consider the long-run macroeconomic controversies raised by the tax cuts. Table 2 shows two different projections of budget deficits and the national debt, both issued less than 2 months after the 2003 tax cuts were signed into law. It also shows what actually happened during the first 4 years after those tax cuts.

Let's start with the left-most columns in the table, which show numbers released by the Bush administration's Office of Management and Budget (OMB) as part of its midyear budget update in July 2003. The second column shows the projected deficit in each fiscal year, ending in September of the year indicated. For example, back in 2003, the OMB projected a deficit of $304 billion in 2005.

The third column shows the projected national debt as a percentage of GDP at the end of each fiscal year. For the end of 2005, the OMB was predicting the national debt at 40.3 percent of GDP.

Judging by the OMB's numbers, it appeared that the administration's fiscal policy was an example of a temporary violation of the guideline for responsible

| | OMB Projections Made in 2003 | | Democratic Caucus Projections Made in 2003 | | What Actually Happened | |
|---|---|---|---|---|---|---|
| Fiscal Year | Federal Budget Deficit ($ Billions) | Debt as a Percentage of GDP | Federal Budget Deficit ($ Billions) | Debt as a Percentage of GDP | Federal Budget Deficit ($ Billions) | Debt as a Percentage of GDP |
| 2002 | $158 | 33.9% | $158 | 33.9% | $158 | 33.9% |
| 2003 | $455 | 37.5% | $416 | 36.8% | $378 | 36.2% |
| 2004 | $475 | 39.6% | $489 | 39.4% | $413 | 37.2% |
| 2005 | $304 | 40.3% | $364 | 40.5% | $318 | 37.4% |
| 2006 | $238 | 40.4% | $345 | 41.3% | $296 | 37.3% |
| 2007 | $213 | 40.2% | $329 | 41.8% | — | — |
| 2008 | $226 | 40.1% | $343 | 42.4% | — | — |
| . . . . | | | | | | |
| 2013 | — | — | $476 | 44.3% | — | — |

**TABLE  2**

**Fiscal Projections After the Tax Cuts of 2001 and 2003**

*Sources:* Office of Management and Budget, *Fiscal Year 2004 Mid-Session Review* (Summary Table 7) and *Fiscal Year 2007 Mid-Session Review* (Historical Tables 1.1 and 7.1), and House Budget Committee, Democratic Caucus, "Deficits Hit Record Levels," Press Release, July 16, 2003. 2002 figures are actual data, known at time of projections.

government: Debt was projected to rise faster than GDP through 2006, and then stabilize and descend through 2008. (Starting in 2003, the administration began issuing only 5-year projections, instead of the usual 10 years, citing uncertainties over the military occupation of Iraq and the war on terrorism.)

What did these numbers imply? Certainly not a debt disaster. But a fiscal policy with future costs. By raising the national debt as a percentage of GDP, interest payments relative to GDP and the tax burden would rise. Afterward, the debt-to-GDP ratio would come down a bit, but not enough to bring the tax burden back to where it was originally.

Where would this rise in the debt come from? Some of the early rise would come from *cyclical* deficits. Because of the economy's slow recovery after the recession in 2001, it was expected to remain below potential even into 2004, with lower tax revenues and higher transfers than would occur at full employment. But the continued deficits in 2006 and beyond—when the economy was assumed to have recovered— would be mostly *structural* deficits. According to the OMB's estimates, the two Bush tax cuts would account for about 25 percent of the total rise in the national debt over the projection period.

Now look at the next two columns. They show the numbers put out by the Democratic Caucus of the House Budget Committee in a press release, within days of the OMB document's release. It shows a more sharply rising deficit, and what looks like a *long-run* violation of the guideline for responsible government. The debt-to-GDP ratio was projected to rise continually, with no end in sight. Note that the Democratic Caucus projected 10 years forward instead of 5. But that accounted for only part of the dramatic difference in the fiscal story each side told. What accounted for the rest?

The answer is: the assumptions behind the numbers. The OMB deficit numbers left out estimates of government outlays for military operations in Iraq or Afghanistan beyond 2003. It also assumed that any provisions of the two tax cuts that were legally set to expire between 2004 and 2008 would, in fact, expire, thereby boosting tax revenues.

The Democrats made different assumptions. On the outlays side, they included the estimated cost of Iraq and Afghanistan from 2004 through 2006, and projected greater increases in other national defense spending. They also added the expenses of the proposed prescription drug benefit plan for Medicare, starting in 2006. (The plan did, in fact, go into effect in 2006.) On the revenue side, the Democrats not only assumed that expiring provisions of the tax cuts would be renewed, but that further changes in the tax code favored by the administration would also be enacted.

Using the Democratic numbers, virtually *all* of the rise in the debt during their 11-year projection period could be attributed to tax cuts of some form—either the original cuts in 2001 and 2003, or expected extensions and further expected reductions.

Note that, based on *either* set of numbers, we would be entering a period of rising debt that would entail the kinds of future costs we've discussed in the chapter. Under the Democrats' assumptions, the path would be unsustainable in the long run: Debt and interest payments would rise faster than GDP for 10 years and perhaps beyond. Under the Bush administration's assumptions, the path would be costly, but sustainable, with debt and interest payments topping out in 2006.

How did the first 4 years of these projections actually play out? Look at the last two columns, which show the actual numbers through fiscal year 2006. As you can see, in each of those years, the budget deficit was actually lower than the Democrats projected, and in some years, even lower than the administration itself projected. Throughout this period, government outlays exceeded what both sides expected, largely because of spending for the war in Iraq and, in 2006, funds spent in the wake of Hurricanes Katrina and Rita. But federal tax revenues also grew faster than expected—so fast, in fact, that the sum of the annual deficits during all 4 years fell below even the administration's own projections.

Now look at the last column, which shows the actual behavior of the national debt as a percentage of GDP. These numbers were also lower than either side expected— significantly so. For 2006, the debt stood at 38.5 percent of GDP, whereas the administration and the Democratic Caucus had forecast 40.4 percent and 41.3 percent, respectively.

What accounts for this disparity? Part of the answer is the smaller deficits just discussed. But even more significant was the behavior of GDP itself. Remember that debt relative to GDP will grow more slowly when GDP rises more rapidly. And during this period, the nation's total output grew much faster than either side had predicted. (Indeed, this was the main reason that tax revenues grew faster than projected.)

But now look just at the last column, and ignore all of the projections. You can see that total debt has been growing faster than GDP in recent years. As a result, the debt as a percentage of GDP rose from 33.9 percent in 2002 to 37.3 percent in 2006. Even if the percentage stays at this level, this past increase in debt has imposed a cost on our society. As you've learned, the cost will be paid in a permanently higher tax burden, a period of inflation, or a temporary period of reduced government outlays or higher taxes to bring the debt-to-GDP ratio back down.

What about the future? In mid-2006, the administration and its critics were once again at odds. The administration, projecting out five years, saw rapidly falling deficits and a rapidly declining debt-to-GDP ratio through 2011.[9] The House Democratic Caucus, projecting out to 2017, saw much larger deficits and only a slow drop in the debt-to-GDP ratio.[10] And neither side's projections included the serious fiscal problem facing the nation beyond 2017, when its ongoing obligations to aging baby boomers will continue to rise.

Clearly, the tax cuts of 2001 and 2003 have created a cost for society. But ultimately, our assessment about any economic policy must compare costs with benefits. And views about the benefits of the administration's tax and spending policies diverge even more widely than views about its costs.

Was the tax cut distributed in the right way? Should the United States have gone to war in Iraq? In the future, how much should younger workers be asked to sacrifice to care for retiring baby boomers? How one answers questions like these ultimately determines whether the costs of higher debt—whatever they turn out to be—are justified. But this is where a purely economic analysis makes its exit, and political and ideological differences take center stage.

---

[9] Office of Management and Budget, *Fiscal Year 2007 Mid-Session Review,* July 2006, Table S-13.
[10] House Budget Committee, Democratic Caucus, "Administration's Mid-Session Review of the Budget," Press Release, July 11, 2006.

# Summary

The U.S. federal government finances its spending through a combination of taxes and borrowing. When government outlays exceed tax revenue, the government runs a budget deficit. It finances that deficit by selling bonds, thereby adding to the national debt. When government outlays are less than tax revenue, the government runs a budget surplus. It uses that surplus to buy back bonds it has issued in the past, thus shrinking the national debt.

Federal government outlays consist of three broad categories: government purchases of goods and services, transfer payments, and interest on the national debt. Nonmilitary government purchases have traditionally accounted for a stable, low 2 percent of real GDP. Military purchases vary according to global politics; in recent years, they have begun rising relative to GDP. Transfer programs—such as Social Security and Medicare—have been the fastest-growing part of government outlays. They currently equal about 12.5 percent of GDP.

On the revenue side, the government relies primarily on personal and corporate income taxes and Social Security taxes. Federal revenue was trending mildly upward until the early 2000s; then it jumped downward, due to a recession and a significant cut in income tax rates.

From 1970 through the mid-1990s, federal outlays exceeded federal revenues every year, so the government ran budget deficits.

Particularly large deficits occurred in the early 1980s. But in the 1990s, the deficit declined, and in 1998 the government began running yearly budget surpluses. In 2002, the budget picture flip-flopped again, as deficits were projected for several years.

In the short run, there is a two-way relationship between government outlays and taxes on the one hand and the level of output on the other. In recessions, for example, government tax revenues fall and transfer payments rise. In this way, the tax and transfer system acts as an automatic stabilizer, helping to smooth out fluctuations in output.

Fiscal changes have important long-run effects on the economy. All else equal, we can expect larger budget deficits to slow growth in living standards, and smaller budget deficits or surpluses to speed the growth of living standards.

Over the 1970s and, especially, the 1980s, the average federal budget deficit was so large, and the national debt growing so rapidly, that interest payments were rising relative to GDP. While we were not on the brink of disaster, the deficits and the growing national debt did require a future sacrifice, which we paid in the 1990s by reducing the deficit through tight fiscal policy. The same scenario of high deficits and rising debt-to-GDP ratio occurred in the early 2000s. Even if temporary, it will require future sacrifices.

# Problem Set    *Answers to even-numbered Questions and Problems can be found on the text Web site at www.thomsonedu.com/economics/hall.*

1. "The U.S. spends more on national defense than it does helping people who are poor, retired, and unemployed." Was this statement *ever* true during the past five decades? Is it true today? (Hint: Use Figures 1 and 3.)

2. Look at Figures 3, 5, and 6, and project forward for the next several decades. For each figure, what will be the *direct* effects (if any) as the baby-boom generation begins to retire around 2010? (Assume there is no change in policy related to Social Security or Medicare and no change in tax rates.)

3. Use the following statistics, in billions of units, to calculate the real national debt and the debt relative to GDP in 1990 and 2000 for this hypothetical country. Which figures would you use to compare the national debt in the 2 years?

   | | |
   |---|---|
   | National debt in 1990: | 1.2 |
   | National debt in 2000: | 13.8 |
   | Nominal GDP in 1990: | 101.7 |
   | Nominal GDP in 2000: | 552.2 |
   | Price index in 1990: | 35.2 |
   | Price index in 2000: | 113.3 |

4. You are running for president of the small nation of Utopia. You promise to cut tax rates, increase transfers and government purchases, reduce the government's budget deficit, and reduce the government's debt as a fraction of GDP. If elected, is it possible for you to keep all of your campaign promises in the short run? What about in the long run?

5. You are running for reelection as president of the nation of Utopia. Your opponents have criticized you for allowing the national debt to grow by almost 50 percent over the last 4 years. Use the following statistics, measured in millions of dollars, to defend yourself to Utopia's voters:

   | | |
   |---|---|
   | National debt in year 1 of your presidency: | $152 |
   | National debt in year 4 of your presidency: | $200 |
   | Nominal GDP in year 1 of your presidency: | $3,042 |
   | Nominal GDP in year 4 of your presidency: | $4,098 |
   | Price index in year 1 of your presidency: | 45 |
   | Price index in year 4 of your presidency: | 72 |

6. Suppose there is a country with 30 households divided into three categories (A, B, and C), with 10 households of each type. If a household earns 20,000 zips (the country's currency) or more in a year, it must pay 15 percent of its income in taxes. If the household earns less than 20,000 zips, it doesn't pay any tax. When the economy is operating at full employment, household income is 250,000 zips per year for each type A household, 50,000 zips for type B households, and 20,000 zips for type C households.

   a. If the economy is operating at full employment, how much revenue does the government collect in taxes for the year?

   b. Suppose a recession hits and household income falls for each type of household. Type A households now earn 150,000 zips, type B households earn 30,000 zips, and type C households earn 10,000 zips for the year. How much does the government collect in tax revenue for the year? Assume the government spends all of the revenue it would have collected if the economy had been operating at full employment. Under this assumption, what is the effect of the recession on the government budget deficit (i.e., the effect on the cyclical deficit)?

c. Suppose instead that the economy expanded and household incomes rose to 400,000 zips, 75,000 zips, and 30,000 zips, respectively, for the year. How much tax would the government collect for the year? What is the effect on the cyclical deficit (assume again that the government spends exactly the amount of revenue it collects when household income is at the values in part (a))?

d. What does this problem tell you about the relationship between shocks to the economy and the budget deficit? The structural deficit?

7. Are either of the following countries violating the minimal guidelines for responsible government as outlined in this text?

**Country A**
**(Figures in Billions of $)**

|      | Debt | GDP |
|------|------|-----|
| 1999 | 1    | 100 |
| 2000 | 2    | 110 |
| 2001 | 3    | 150 |

**Country B**
**(Figures in Billions of $)**

|      | Debt  | GDP   |
|------|-------|-------|
| 1999 | 1,236 | 1,400 |
| 2000 | 1,346 | 1,550 |
| 2001 | 1,406 | 1,707 |

8. Assume that the unemployment rate in the small country of Economica is currently 6 percent, and that in this country government purchases = $10 million, tax revenue = $17 million, transfers and interest payments = $5 million. Also assume that at full employment, the unemployment rate would be *less* than 6 percent.
   a. Find the size of Economica's budget deficit.
   b. What can you tell about Economica's cyclical deficit and its structural deficit?

9. Suppose a nation's government purchases are equal to $2 trillion, regardless of the state of the economy. However, its taxes and transfers depend on economic conditions. When the economy is at potential output, net taxes (taxes minus transfers) equal $2.2 trillion. However, for each 1 percent GDP falls below potential output, net taxes fall by 5 percent.
   a. Suppose the economy was operating at potential output. What would be the structural deficit? The cyclical deficit?
   b. Suppose that real GDP was 5 percent below potential output. What would be the cyclical deficit? The structural deficit?

10. Complete the table below for the small country of Microland. Assume that Microland started Year 1 with no federal debt. What is the relationship between the deficit and the debt? How can the real national debt fall even in years when the budget is balanced or in deficit? Explain briefly.

[Table for Problem 10]

|                                | Year |      |      |      |      |      |        |
|--------------------------------|------|------|------|------|------|------|--------|
|                                | 1    | 2    | 3    | 4    | 5    | 6    | 7      |
| Price index                    | 100  | 103  | 105  | 110  | 118  | 133  | 140    |
| Nominal GDP                    | $400 | $500 | $600 | $700 | $800 | $900 | $1,000 |
| Outlays                        | $105 | $126 | $130 | $135 | $133 | $130 | $ 130  |
| Tax revenue                    | $100 | $120 | $125 | $132 | $134 | $138 | $ 130  |
| Deficit/Surplus                |      |      |      |      |      |      |        |
| National debt (end of year)    |      |      |      |      |      |      |        |
| Real national debt (end of year) |    |      |      |      |      |      |        |
| Debt to GDP                    |      |      |      |      |      |      |        |

## More Challenging

11. Suppose the United States were running a budget surplus and decided to eliminate it by increasing government purchases.
    a. Compared to a policy of just accruing surpluses and paying down the national debt, what will this policy do to U.S. real GDP and interest rates in the *short run*? Illustrate your answer graphically. (Hint: Which macro model, and which graphs, should you use to illustrate effects on output and interest rates in the short run? Assume the Fed maintains a constant interest rate.)
    b. Compared to a policy of just accruing surpluses and paying down the national debt, what will this policy do to U.S. real GDP and interest rates in the *long run*? Illustrate your answer graphically.
    c. Going back to the short run, suppose the Fed responds by neutralizing the impact of the fiscal change in part (a). What will happen to real GDP and interest rates in the short run?

# Exchange Rates and Macroeconomic Policy

If you've ever traveled to a foreign country, you were a direct participant in the **foreign exchange market**—a market in which one country's currency is traded for that of another. For example, if you traveled to Mexico, you might have stopped near the border to exchange some dollars for Mexican pesos.

But even if you have never traveled abroad, you've been involved, at least indirectly, in all kinds of foreign exchange dealings. For example, suppose you buy some Mexican-grown tomatoes at a store in the United States, where you pay with dollars. A Mexican farmer grew the tomatoes; Mexican truckers transported them to the distribution center in the nearest large city; and Mexican workers, machinery, and raw materials were used to package them. All of these people need to be paid in Mexican pesos, regardless of who buys the final product. After all, they live in Mexico, so they need pesos to buy things there. But you, as an American, want to pay for your tomatoes with dollars.

Let's think about this for a moment. You want to pay for the tomatoes in dollars, but the Mexicans who produced them want to be paid in pesos. How can this happen?

The answer: *Someone,* here or abroad, must use the foreign exchange market to exchange dollars for pesos. For example, it might work like this: You pay dollars to your supermarket, which pays dollars to a U.S. importer, who pays dollars to the distributor in Mexico, who—finally—turns the dollars over to a Mexican bank in exchange for pesos. Finally, the Mexican distributor uses these pesos to pay the Mexican farmer.

In this chapter, we'll look at the markets in which dollars are exchanged for foreign currency. We'll also expand our macroeconomic analysis to consider the effects of changes in exchange rates. As you'll see, what happens in the foreign exchange market affects the economy, and changes in the economy affect the foreign exchange market. This has implications for the Fed as it tries to use monetary policy to steer the economy and keep it growing smoothly. Finally, we'll turn our attention to an analysis of the large and growing U.S. trade deficit.

**Foreign exchange market** The market in which one country's currency is traded for another country's.

## FOREIGN EXCHANGE MARKETS AND EXCHANGE RATES

Every day, all over the world, more than a hundred different national currencies are exchanged for one another in banks, hotels, stores, and kiosks in airports and train stations. Traders exchange dollars for Mexican pesos, Japanese yen, European euros, Indian rupees, Chinese yuan, and so on. In addition, traders exchange each of these foreign currencies for one another: pesos for euros, yen for yuan, euros for yen. . . . There are literally thousands of combinations. How can we hope to make sense of these markets—how they operate and how they affect us?

Our basic approach is to treat each pair of currencies as a separate market. That is, there is one market in which dollars are exchanged for euros, another in which Angolan kwanzas trade for yen, and so on. The physical locations where the trading takes place do not matter: Whether you exchange your dollars for yen in France, Germany, the United States, or even in Ecuador, you are a trader in the same dollar–yen market.

**Exchange rate** The amount of one country's currency that is traded for one unit of another country's currency.

In any foreign exchange market, the rate at which one currency is traded for another is called the **exchange rate** between those two currencies. For example, if you happened to trade dollars for British pounds on July 28, 2006, each British pound would have cost you about $1.86. On that day, the exchange rate was 1.8629 dollars per pound.

## DOLLARS PER POUND OR POUNDS PER DOLLAR?

Table 1 lists exchange rates between the dollar and various foreign currencies on a particular day in 2006. But notice that we can think of any exchange rate in two ways: as so many units of foreign currency per dollar, or so many dollars per unit of foreign currency. For example, the table shows the exchange rate between the British pound and the dollar as 0.5368 pounds per dollar, or 1.8629 dollars per pound. We can always obtain one form of the exchange rate from the other by taking its reciprocal: $1/0.5368 = 1.8629$, and $1/1.8629 = 0.5368$.

In this chapter, we'll always define the exchange rate as "dollars per unit of foreign currency," as in the last column of the table. That way, from the American point of view, the exchange rate is just another *price*. The same way you pay a certain number of dollars for a gallon of gasoline (the price of gas), so, too, you pay a certain number of dollars for a British pound (the price of pounds).

> *The exchange rate is the price of foreign currency in dollars.*

Table 1 raises some important questions: Why, in mid-2006, did a pound cost $1.86? Why not $1? Or $5? Why did one Japanese yen cost less than a penny? And a Russian ruble about four cents?

| TABLE 1 Foreign Exchange Rates, July 28, 2006 | Country | Name of Currency | Symbol | Units of Foreign Currency per Dollar | Dollars per Unit of Foreign Currency |
|---|---|---|---|---|---|
| | Brazil | real | R | 2.1739 | $0.4600 |
| | China | yuan | Y | 7.971 | $0.1255 |
| | European Monetary Union Countries | euro | € | 0.7843 | $1.2751 |
| | Great Britain | pound | £ | 0.5368 | $1.8629 |
| | India | rupee | R | 46.53 | $0.02149 |
| | Japan | yen | ¥ | 114.77 | $0.008713 |
| | Mexico | peso | P | 10.858 | $0.09210 |
| | Russia | ruble | R | 26.81 | $0.03730 |

The answers to these questions certainly affect Americans who travel abroad. Suppose you are staying in a hotel in London that costs 100 pounds per night. If the price of the pound is $1, the hotel room will cost you $100, but if the price is $5, the room will cost you $500. And exchange rates affect Americans who stay at home, too. They influence the prices of many goods we buy in the United States, and they help determine which of our industries will expand and which will contract.

How are all these exchange rates determined? In most cases, they are determined by the familiar forces of supply and demand. As in other markets, each foreign exchange market reaches an equilibrium at which the quantity of foreign exchange demanded is equal to the quantity supplied.

In the next several sections, we'll build a model of supply and demand for a representative foreign exchange market: the one in which U.S. dollars are exchanged for British pounds. Taking the American point of view, we'll call this simply "the market for pounds." The other currency being traded—the dollar—will always be implicit.

## THE DEMAND FOR BRITISH POUNDS

To analyze the demand for pounds, we start with a very basic question: *Who is demanding them?* The simple answer is, anyone who has dollars and wants to exchange them for pounds. But the most important buyers of pounds in the pound–dollar market will be American households and businesses. When Americans want to buy things from Britain, they will need to acquire pounds. To acquire them, they will need to offer U.S. dollars. To keep our analysis simple, we'll focus on just these American buyers. We'll also—for now—ignore any demand for pounds by the U.S. government.

> *In our model of the market for pounds, we assume that American households and businesses are the only buyers.*

Why do Americans want to buy pounds? There are two reasons:

- *To buy goods and services from British firms.* Americans buy sweaters knit in Edinburgh, airline tickets sold by Virgin Airways, and insurance services offered by Lloyd's. American tourists also stay in British hotels, use British taxis, and eat at British restaurants. To buy goods and services from British firms, Americans need to acquire pounds in order to pay for them.
- *To buy British assets.* Americans buy British stocks, British corporate or government bonds, and British real estate. In each case, the British seller will want to be paid in pounds, so the American buyer will have to acquire them.

### The Demand for Pounds Curve

Panel (a) of Figure 1 shows an example of a **demand curve for foreign currency,** in this case, the demand curve for pounds. The curve tells us *the quantity of pounds Americans will want to buy in any given period, at each different exchange rate.* Notice that the curve slopes downward: The lower the exchange rate, the greater the quantity of pounds demanded. For example, at an exchange rate of $2.25 per pound, Americans would want to purchase £200 million (point *A*). If the exchange rate fell to $1.50 per pound, Americans would want to buy £300 million (point *E*).

**Demand curve for foreign currency** A curve indicating the quantity of a specific foreign currency that Americans will want to buy, during a given period, at each different exchange rate.

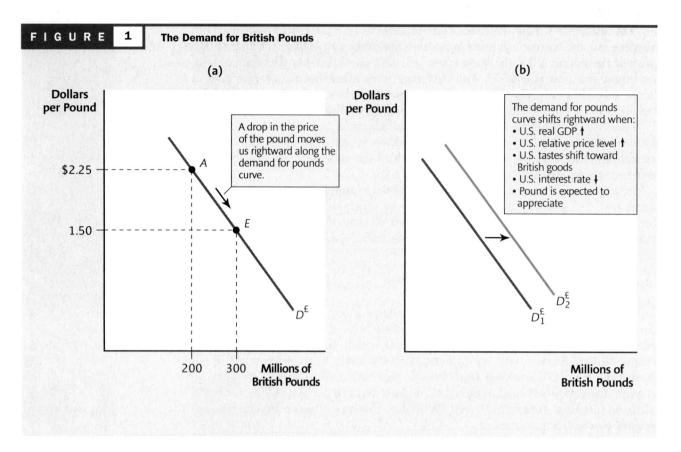

**FIGURE 1**    The Demand for British Pounds

**(a)**

**Dollars per Pound**

A drop in the price of the pound moves us rightward along the demand for pounds curve.

$2.25 ----- A

1.50 ----- E

$D^£$

200    300    **Millions of British Pounds**

**(b)**

**Dollars per Pound**

The demand for pounds curve shifts rightward when:
• U.S. real GDP ↑
• U.S. relative price level ↑
• U.S. tastes shift toward British goods
• U.S. interest rate ↓
• Pound is expected to appreciate

$D_2^£$

$D_1^£$

**Millions of British Pounds**

Why does a lower exchange rate—a lower price for the pound—make Americans want to buy more of them? Because the lower the price of the pound, the less expensive British goods are to American buyers. Remember that Americans think of prices in dollar terms. A British compact disc that sells for £8 will cost an American $18 at an exchange rate of $2.25 per pound, but only $12 if the exchange rate is $1.50 per pound.

Thus, as we move rightward *along* the demand for pounds curve, as in the move from point *A* to point *E*:

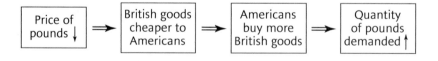

| Price of pounds ↓ | ⇒ | British goods cheaper to Americans | ⇒ | Americans buy more British goods | ⇒ | Quantity of pounds demanded ↑ |

### Shifts in the Demand for Pounds Curve

In panel (a), you saw that a change in the exchange rate moves us *along* the demand for pounds curve. But other variables besides the exchange rate influence the demand for pounds. If any of these other variables changes, the entire curve will shift. As we consider each of these variables, keep in mind that we are assuming that only one of them changes at a time; we suppose the rest to remain constant.

**U.S. Real GDP.** Suppose real GDP and real income in the United States rise—say, because of continuing economic growth or a recovery from a recession. Then, Americans will buy more of everything, including goods and services from Britain. Thus, at any given exchange rate, Americans will demand more pounds. This is illustrated, in panel (b), as a rightward shift of the demand curve from $D_1^£$ to $D_2^£$.

**Relative Price Levels.** Suppose that the U.S. price level rises by 8 percent, while that in Britain rises by 5 percent. Then U.S. prices will rise *relative* to British prices. Americans will shift from buying their own goods toward buying the relatively cheaper British goods, so their demand for pounds will rise. That is, the demand for pounds curve will shift rightward.

**Americans' Tastes for British Goods** All else being equal, would you prefer to drive a General Motors Corvette or a Jaguar? Do you prefer British-made films, like *Pride and Prejudice* or *Harry Potter and the Goblet of Fire*, or America's offerings, such as *Superman Returns* or *Million Dollar Baby*? These are matters of taste, and tastes can change. If Americans develop an increased taste for British cars, films, tea, or music, their demand for these goods will increase, and the demand for pounds curve will shift rightward.

**Relative Interest Rates.** Because financial assets must remain competitive in order to attract buyers, the rates of return on different financial assets—such as stocks and bonds—tend to rise and fall together. Thus, when one country's interest rate is high relative to that of another country, the first country's assets, *in general*, will have higher rates of return.

Now, suppose you're an American trying to decide whether to hold some of your wealth in British financial assets or in American financial assets. You will look very carefully at the rate of return you expect to earn in each country. All else being equal, a lower U.S. interest rate, relative to the British rate, will make British assets more attractive to you. Accordingly, as you and other Americans demand more British assets, you will need more pounds to buy them. The demand for pounds curve will shift rightward.

**Expected Changes in the Exchange Rate.** Once again, imagine you are an American deciding whether to buy an American or a British bond. Suppose British bonds pay 10 percent interest per year, while U.S. bonds pay 5 percent. All else equal, you would prefer the British bond, since it pays the higher rate of return. You would then exchange dollars for pounds at the going exchange rate and buy the bond.

But what if the price of the pound falls before the British bond becomes due? Then, when you cash in your British bond for pounds, and convert the pounds back into dollars, you'll be *selling your pounds at a lower price* than you bought them for. While you'd benefit from the higher interest rate on the British bond, you'd lose on the foreign currency transaction—buying pounds when their price is high and selling them when their price is low. If the foreign currency loss is great enough, you would be better off with U.S. bonds, even though they pay a lower interest rate.

As you can see, it is not just relative interest rates that matter to wealth holders; it is also *expected changes in the exchange rate*. An expectation that the price of the pound will fall will make British assets less appealing to Americans, since they will expect a foreign currency loss. In this case, the demand for pounds curve will shift leftward.

The opposite holds as well. If Americans expect the price of the pound to *rise*, they will expect a foreign currency *gain* from buying British assets. This will cause the *demand for pounds curve to shift rightward.*

## THE SUPPLY OF BRITISH POUNDS

The demand for pounds is one side of the market for pounds. Now we turn our attention to the other side: the supply of pounds. And we'll begin with our basic question: *Who* is supplying them?

In the real world, pounds are supplied from many sources. Anyone who has pounds and wants to exchange them for dollars can come to the market and supply pounds. But the most important sellers of pounds are British households and businesses, who naturally have pounds and need dollars in order to make purchases from Americans. To keep our analysis simple, we'll focus on just these British sellers, and we'll ignore—for now—any pounds supplied by the British government:

> *In our model of the market for pounds, we assume that British households and firms are the only sellers.*

The British supply pounds in the dollar–pound market for only one reason: because they want dollars. Thus, to ask why the British supply pounds is to ask why they want dollars. We can identify two separate reasons:

- *To buy goods and services from American firms.* The British buy airline tickets on United Airlines, computers made by Hewlett-Packard and Apple, and the rights to show films made in Hollywood. British tourists stay in American hotels and eat at American restaurants. The British demand dollars—and supply pounds—for all of these purchases.
- *To buy American assets.* The British buy American stocks, American corporate or government bonds, and American real estate. In each case, the American seller will want to be paid in dollars, and the British buyer will acquire dollars by offering pounds.

### The Supply of Pounds Curve

**Supply curve for foreign currency** A curve indicating the quantity of a specific foreign currency that will be supplied, during a given period, at each different exchange rate.

Panel (a) of Figure 2 shows an example of a **supply curve for foreign currency**—here, British pounds. The curve tells us *the quantity of pounds the British will want to sell in any given period, at each different exchange rate.* Notice that the curve slopes upward: The higher the exchange rate, the greater is the quantity of pounds supplied. For example, at an exchange rate of $1.50 per pound, the British would want to supply £300 million (point *E*). If the exchange rate rose to $2.25 per pound, they would supply £400 million (point *F*).

Why does a higher exchange rate—a higher price for the pound—make the British want to sell more of them? Because the higher the price for the pound, the more dollars someone gets for each pound sold. This makes U.S. goods and services less expensive to British buyers, who will want to buy more of them—and who will therefore need more dollars.[1]

To summarize, as we move rightward *along* the supply of pounds curve, such as the move from point *E* to point *F*:

## Shifts in the Supply of Pounds Curve

When the exchange rate changes, we *move along* the supply curve for pounds, as in panel (a) of Figure 2. But other variables can affect the supply of pounds besides the exchange rate. When any of these variables change, the supply of pounds curve will shift, as shown in panel (b). What are these variables?

*Real GDP in Britain.* If real GDP and real income rise in Britain, British residents will buy more goods and services, including those produced in the United States. Because

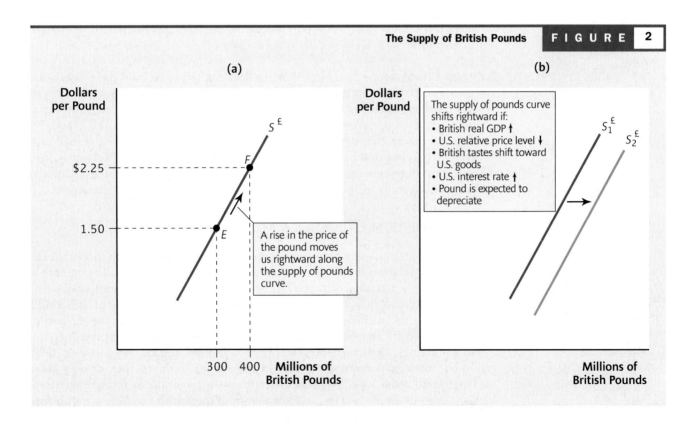

**The Supply of British Pounds**   **FIGURE 2**

[1] Actually, it is not a logical necessity for the supply of pounds curve to slope upward. Why not? When the price of the pound rises, it is true that the British will buy more U.S. goods and need more dollars to buy them. However, each dollar they buy costs *fewer pounds.* It might be that, even though the British obtain more dollars, they actually supply fewer pounds to get them at the higher exchange rate. In this **case,** the supply of pounds curve would slope downward. Economists believe, however, that a downward-sloping supply curve for foreign currency—while theoretically possible—is very rare.

they will need more dollars to buy U.S. goods, they will supply more pounds. In panel (b) this causes a rightward shift of the supply curve, from $S_1^£$ to $S_2^£$.

***Relative Price Levels.*** Earlier, you learned that a rise in the relative price level in the United States makes British goods more attractive to Americans. But it also makes *American* goods *less* attractive to the British. Since the British will want to buy fewer U.S. goods, they will want fewer dollars and will supply fewer pounds. Thus, a rise in the relative U.S. price level shifts the supply of pounds curve leftward.

***British Tastes for U.S. Goods.*** Recall our earlier discussion about the effect of American tastes on the demand for pounds. The same reasoning applies to the effect of British tastes on the *supply* of pounds. The British could begin to crave things American—or recoil from them. A shift in British tastes *toward* American goods will shift the supply of pounds curve rightward. A shift in tastes *away* from American goods will shift the curve leftward.

***Relative Interest Rates.*** You've already learned that a rise in the relative U.S. interest rate makes U.S. assets more attractive to Americans. It has exactly the same effect on the British. As the U.S. interest rate rises, and the British buy more U.S. assets, they will need more dollars and will supply more pounds. The supply of pounds curve will shift rightward.

***Expected Change in the Exchange Rate.*** In deciding where to hold their assets, the British have the same concerns as Americans. They will look, in part, at rates of return; but they will *also* think about possible gains or losses on foreign currency transactions. Suppose the British *expect the price of the pound to fall*. Then, by holding U.S. assets, they can anticipate a foreign currency gain—selling pounds at a relatively high price and buying them back again when their price is relatively low. The prospect of foreign currency gain will make U.S. assets more attractive, and the British will buy more of them. *The supply of pounds curve will shift rightward.*

## THE EQUILIBRIUM EXCHANGE RATE

**Floating exchange rate** An exchange rate that is freely determined by the forces of supply and demand.

Now we will make an important—and in most cases, realistic—assumption: that the exchange rate between the dollar and the pound *floats*. A **floating exchange rate** is one that is freely determined by the forces of supply and demand, without government intervention to change it or keep it from changing. Indeed, many of the world's leading currencies, including the Japanese yen, the British pound, the 12-nation euro, and the Mexican peso, do float freely against the dollar most of the time.

In some cases, however, governments do not allow the exchange rate to float freely, but instead manipulate its value by intervening in the market, or even *fix* it at a particular value. We'll discuss government intervention in foreign exchange markets later. In this section, we assume that both the British and U.S. governments leave the dollar–pound market alone.

When the exchange rate floats, the price will settle at the level where quantity supplied and quantity demanded are equal. Here, buyers and sellers are trading British pounds, and the price is the exchange rate—the *price of the pound*.

Look at panel (a) of Figure 3. The equilibrium in the market for pounds occurs at point *E*, where the supply and demand curves intersect. The equilibrium price is $1.50 per pound. As you can verify, if the exchange rate were *higher*, say, $2.25 per

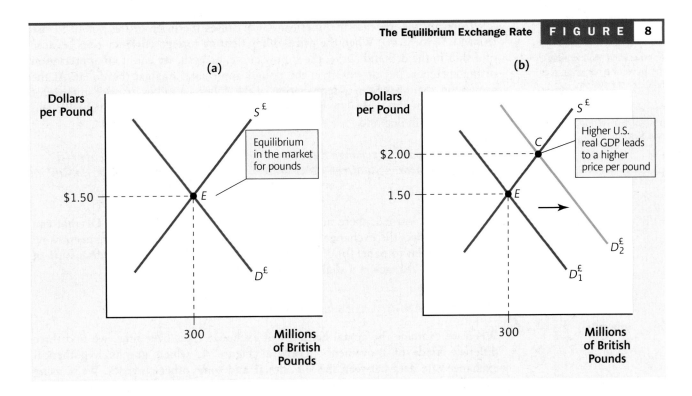

**The Equilibrium Exchange Rate** FIGURE 8

pound, there would be an *excess supply* of pounds, forcing the price of the pound back down to $1.50. If the exchange rate were *lower* than the equilibrium price of $1.50, there would be an *excess demand* for pounds, driving the price back up to $1.50.

> *When the exchange rate floats—that is, when the government does not intervene in the foreign currency market—the equilibrium exchange rate is determined at the intersection of the demand curve and the supply curve.*

## WHAT HAPPENS WHEN THINGS CHANGE?

What would cause the price of the pound to rise or fall? The simple answer to this question is, anything that shifts the demand for pounds curve, or the supply of pounds curve, or both curves together. Have another look at the right-hand panels of Figures 1 and 2. They summarize the major factors that can shift the demand and supply curves for pounds and therefore change the floating exchange rate.

Let's illustrate with a simple example. In panel (b) of Figure 3, the initial equilibrium in the market for pounds is at point *E*, with an exchange rate of $1.50 per pound. Now suppose that real GDP rises in the United States. As you've learned (see Figure 1), this rise in U.S. GDP will shift the demand for pounds curve rightward, from $D_1^£$ to $D_2^£$ in the figure. At the old exchange rate of $1.50 per pound, there would be an excess demand for pounds, which would drive the price of the pound higher. The new equilibrium—where the quantities of pounds supplied and demanded are equal—occurs at point *C*, and the new equilibrium exchange rate is $2.00 per pound.

**Appreciation** An increase in the price of a currency in a floating-rate system.

**Depreciation** A decrease in the price of a currency in a floating-rate system.

To recap, the increase in American GDP causes the price of the pound to rise from $1.50 to $2.00. When the price of any floating foreign currency rises because of a shift in the demand curve, the supply curve, or both, we call it an **appreciation** of the currency. In our example, the pound appreciates against the dollar. At the same time, there has been a **depreciation** of the dollar—a fall in its price in terms of pounds. (To see this, calculate the price of the dollar in terms of pounds before and after the shift in demand.)

> *When a floating exchange rate changes, one country's currency will appreciate (rise in price) and the other country's currency will depreciate (fall in price).*

As you've learned, there are many other variables besides U.S. GDP that can change and affect the exchange rate. We could analyze each of these changes, using diagrams similar to panel (b) of Figure 3. However, we'll organize our discussion of exchange rate changes in a slightly different way.

## HOW EXCHANGE RATES CHANGE OVER TIME

When we examine the actual behavior of exchange rates over time, we find three different kinds of movements. Look at Figure 4, which graphs hypothetical exchange rate data between the U.S. dollar and some other currency. We're using hypothetical data to make these three kinds of movements stand out more clearly than they usually do in practice.

Notice first the sharp up-and-down spikes. These fluctuations in exchange rates occur over the course of a few weeks, a few days, or even a few minutes—periods of time that we call the *very short run*.

Second, we see a gradual rise and fall of the exchange rate over the course of several months or a year or two. An example is the appreciation of the foreign currency from point A to B and its depreciation from point B to C. These are *short-run* movements in the exchange rate.

Finally, notice that while the price of the foreign currency fluctuates in the very short run and the short run, we can also discern a general *long-run* trend: This nation's currency seems to be depreciating in the figure. This long-run trend is illustrated by the dashed line connecting points A and E.

In this section, we'll explore the causes of movements in the exchange rate over all three periods: the very short run, the short run, and the long run.

## THE *VERY* SHORT RUN: "HOT MONEY"

Banks and other large financial institutions collectively have trillions of dollars worth of funds that they can move from one type of investment to another at very short notice. These funds are often called "hot money." If those who manage hot money perceive even a tiny advantage in moving funds to a different country's assets—say, because its interest rate is slightly higher—they will do so. Often, decisions to move billions of dollars are made in split seconds, by traders watching computer screens showing the latest data on exchange rates and interest rates around the world. Because these traders move such large volumes of funds, they have immediate effects on exchange rates.

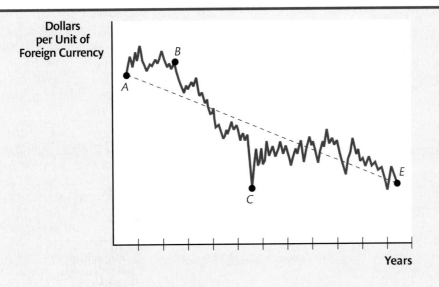

**FIGURE 4**

**Hypothetical Exchange Rate Data Over Time**

*These hypothetical data show typical patterns of exchange rate fluctuations. Over the course of a few minutes, days, or weeks, the exchange rate can experience sharp up-and-down spikes. Over several months or a year or two, the exchange rate may rise or fall, as in the appreciation of the foreign currency from points A to B and the depreciation from B to C. Over the long run, there may be a general upward or downward trend, like the depreciation of the foreign currency illustrated by the dashed line connecting points A and E.*

Let's consider an example. Suppose that the relative interest rate in the United States suddenly rises. Then, as you've learned, U.S. assets will suddenly be more attractive to residents of both the United States and England, including managers of hot-money accounts in both countries. As these managers shift their funds from British to United States assets, they will be dumping billions of pounds on the foreign exchange market in order to acquire dollars to buy U.S. assets. This will cause a significant rightward shift of the supply of pounds curve.

In addition to affecting managers of hot-money accounts, the higher relative interest rate in the United States will affect ordinary investors. British investors will want to buy more American assets, helping to shift the supply of pounds curve further rightward. And American investors will want to buy fewer British assets than before, causing some decrease in the *demand* for pounds. Thus, in addition to the very large rightward shift in the supply of pounds, there will be a more moderate leftward shift in the demand for pounds.

Both of these shifts are illustrated in Figure 5: The supply of pounds curve shifts from $S_1^{\pounds}$ to $S_2^{\pounds}$, and the demand for pounds curve shifts from $D_1^{\pounds}$ to $D_2^{\pounds}$. The result is easy to see: The equilibrium in the market for pounds moves from point $E$ to point $G$, and the price of the pound *falls* from $1.50 to $1.00. The pound depreciates and the dollar appreciates.

Expectations about future exchange rates can also trigger huge shifts of hot money, and Figure 5 also illustrates what would happen if American and British residents suddenly *expect* the pound to depreciate against the dollar. In this case, it would be the anticipation of foreign currency gains from holding U.S. assets, rather than a higher U.S. interest rate, that would cause the supply and demand curves to

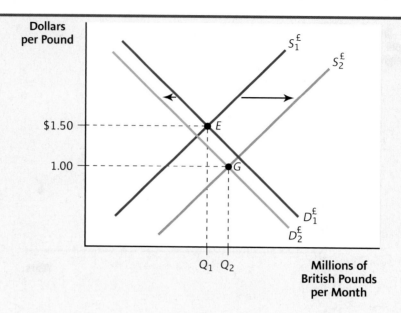

**Hot Money in the Very Short Run**

*The market for pounds is initially in equilibrium at point E, with an exchange rate of $1.50 per pound. A rise in the U.S. interest rate relative to the British rate will make U.S. assets more attractive to both Americans and Britons. Hot-money managers in both countries will shift funds from British to U.S. assets, causing a rightward shift of the supply of pounds curve. American investors will want to buy fewer British assets, causing a decrease in the demand for pounds. The net effect is a lower exchange rate—$1.00 per pound at point G.*

shift. As you can see in Figure 5, the expectation that the pound will depreciate actually *causes* the pound to depreciate—a self-fulfilling prophecy.

Sudden changes in relative interest rates, as well as sudden expectations of an appreciation or depreciation of a nation's currency, occur frequently in foreign exchange markets. They can cause massive shifts of hot money from the assets of one country to those of another in very short periods of time. For this reason,

*relative interest rates and expectations of future exchange rates are the dominant forces moving exchange rates in the very short run.*

## THE SHORT RUN: MACROECONOMIC FLUCTUATIONS

Look again at Figure 4. What explains the movements in the *short-run* rate—the changes that occur over several months or a few years? In most cases, the causes are economic fluctuations taking place in one or more countries.

Suppose, for example, that both Britain and the United States are in a recession, and the U.S. economy begins to recover while the British slump continues. As real GDP rises in the United States, so does Americans' demand for foreign goods and services, including those from Britain. The demand for pounds curve will shift rightward, and—as shown in panel (a) of Figure 6—the pound will appreciate.

A year or so later, when Britain recovers from *its* recession, its real GDP will rise. British residents will begin to buy more U.S. goods and services, and supply more pounds so they can acquire more dollars. The supply of pounds curve will shift

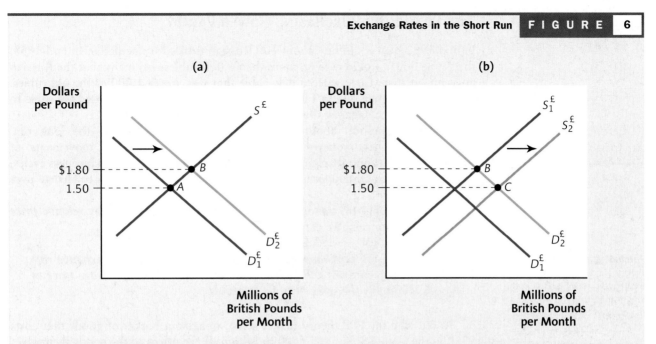

**Exchange Rates in the Short Run** | F I G U R E | 6

**(a)**

**(b)**

Panel (a) shows a situation in which the United States recovers from a recession first. U.S. demand for foreign goods and services increases, shifting the demand for pounds curve to the right. The equilibrium moves from A to B—an appreciation of the
pound. Panel (b) shows Britain's subsequent recovery from its recession. As the British begin to buy more U.S. goods and
services, the supply of pounds curve shifts rightward. The equilibrium moves from B to C, causing the pound to depreciate.

rightward, and—as shown in panel (b) of Figure 6—the pound will depreciate.
Thus,

> in the short run, movements in exchange rates are caused largely by econom-
> ic fluctuations. All else equal, a country whose GDP rises relatively rapidly
> will experience a depreciation of its currency. A country whose GDP falls
> more rapidly will experience an appreciation of its currency.

This observation contradicts a commonly held myth: that a strong (appreciating)
currency is a sign of economic health and a weak (depreciating) currency denotes a
sick economy. The truth may easily be the opposite. Over the course of several
quarters or a few years, the dollar could appreciate because the U.S. economy is
*weakening*—entering a serious recession. This would cause Americans to cut back
spending on domestic *and* foreign goods, and decrease the demand for foreign currency. Similarly, a *strengthening* U.S. economy—in which Americans are earning and
spending more—would increase the U.S. demand for foreign currency and (all else
equal) cause the dollar to depreciate.

Keep in mind, though, that other variables can change over the business cycle
besides real GDP, including interest rates and price levels in the two countries. For
example, a recession can be caused by a monetary contraction that raises the relative
interest rate in a country. Or a monetary stimulus in the midst of a recession could
result in a relatively low interest rate. These changes, too, will influence exchange
rates over the business cycle.

# THE LONG RUN: PURCHASING POWER PARITY

In mid-1992, you could buy about 100 Russian rubles for one dollar. In mid-1998, that same dollar would get you more than 6,000 rubles—so many that the Russian government that year created a new ruble that was worth 1,000 of the old rubles. (The ruble exchange rate in Table 1 is for the new ruble.) What caused the ruble to depreciate so much against the dollar during those 6 years?

This is a question about exchange rates over many years—the long run. Movements of hot money—which explain sudden, temporary movements of exchange rates—cannot explain this kind of long-run trend. Nor can business cycles, which are, by nature, temporary. What, then, causes exchange rates to change over the long run?

In general, long-run trends in exchange rates are determined by *relative price levels* in two countries. We can be even more specific:

**Purchasing power parity (PPP) theory** The idea that the exchange rate will adjust in the long run so that the average price of goods in two countries will be roughly the same.

> *According to the **purchasing power parity** (PPP) **theory**, the exchange rate between two countries will adjust in the long run until the average price of goods is roughly the same in both countries.*

To see why the PPP theory makes sense, imagine a basket of goods that costs $750 in the United States and £500 in Britain. If the prices of the goods themselves do not change, then, according to the PPP theory, the exchange rate will adjust to $750/£500 = $1.5 dollars per pound. Why? Because at this exchange rate, $750 can be exchanged for £500, so the price of the basket is the same to residents of either country—$750 for Americans and £500 for the British.

Now, suppose the exchange rate was *below* its PPP rate of $1.50 per pound—say, $1 per pound. Then a trader could take $500 to the bank, exchange it for £500, buy the basket of goods in Great Britain, and sell it in the United States for $750. She would earn a profit of $250 on each basket of goods traded. In the process, however, traders would be increasing the demand for pounds and raising the exchange rate. When the price of the pound reached $1.50, purchasing power parity would hold, and special trading opportunities would be gone. As you can see, trading activity will tend to drive the exchange rate toward the PPP rate. (On your own, explain the adjustment process when the exchange rate starts *higher* than the PPP rate.)

The PPP theory has an important implication:

> *In the long run, the currency of a country with a higher inflation rate will depreciate against the currency of a country whose inflation rate is lower.*

Why? Because in the country with the higher inflation rate, the relative price level will be rising. As that country's basket of goods becomes relatively more expensive, only a depreciation of its currency can restore purchasing power parity. And traders—taking advantage of opportunities like those just described—would cause the currency to depreciate.

## Purchasing Power Parity: Some Important Caveats

While purchasing power parity is a good general guideline for predicting long-run trends in exchange rates, it does not work perfectly. For a variety of reasons, exchange rates can deviate from their PPP values for many years.

First, some goods—by their very nature—are difficult to trade. Suppose a haircut costs £5 in London and $30 in New York, and the exchange rate is $1.50 per pound. Then British haircuts are cheaper for residents of both countries. Could traders take advantage of this? Not really. They cannot take $30 to the bank in exchange for £20, buy four haircuts in London, ship them to New York, and sell them for a total of $120 there. Haircuts and most other personal services are nontradable.

Second, high transportation costs can reduce trading possibilities even for goods that *can* be traded. Our earlier numerical example would have quite a different ending if moving the basket of goods between Great Britain and the United States involved $500 of freight and insurance costs.

Third, artificial barriers to trade, such as special taxes or quotas on imports, can hamper traders' ability to move exchange rates toward purchasing power parity.

Still, the purchasing power parity theory is useful in many circumstances. Under floating exchange rates, a country whose relative price level is rising rapidly will almost always find that the price of its currency is falling rapidly. If not, all of its tradable goods would soon be priced out of the world market.

Indeed, we often observe that countries with very high inflation rates have currencies depreciating against the dollar by roughly the amount needed to preserve purchasing power parity. For example, we've already mentioned the sharp depreciation of the Russian ruble from 1992 to 1998. During those 6 years, the number of rubles that exchanged for a dollar rose from around 100 to about 6,000. Over the same period, the annual inflation rate averaged about 200 percent in Russia, but only about 3 percent in the United States. And in Zimbabwe, which experienced hyperinflation in the early 2000s, the number of Zimbabwean dollars required to purchase one U.S. dollar went from about 1,000 in mid-2002 to more than 100,000 in mid-2006.

## GOVERNMENT INTERVENTION IN FOREIGN EXCHANGE MARKETS

As you've seen, when exchange rates float, they can rise and fall for a variety of reasons. But a government may not be content to let the forces of supply and demand change its exchange rate. If the exchange rate rises, the country's goods will become much more expensive to foreigners, causing harm to its export-oriented industries. If the exchange rate falls, goods purchased from other countries will rise in price. Since many imported goods are used as inputs by U.S. firms (such as oil from the Middle East and Mexico or computer screens from Japan), a drop in the exchange rate will cause a rise in the U.S. price level. Finally, if the exchange rate is too volatile, it can make trading riskier or require traders to acquire special insurance against foreign currency losses, which costs them money, time, and trouble. For all of these reasons, governments sometime *intervene* in foreign exchange markets involving their currency.

### MANAGED FLOAT

Many governments let their exchange rate float *most of the time,* but will intervene on occasion when the floating exchange rate moves in an undesired direction or becomes too volatile. For example, look back at Figure 5, where the price of the British pound falls to $1 as hot money is shifted out of British assets. Suppose the British government does not want the pound to depreciate. Then its central bank— the Bank of England—could begin trading in the dollar–pound market itself. It would buy British pounds with dollars, thereby shifting the demand for pounds curve rightward. If it buys just the right amount of pounds, it can prevent the pound from depreciating at all. Alternatively, the U.S. government might not be happy with the *appreciation* of the dollar in Figure 5. In that case, the Federal Reserve can enter the market and buy British pounds with dollars, once again shifting the demand for pounds curve rightward.

The central banks of many countries—including the Federal Reserve—will sometimes intervene in this way in foreign exchange markets. When a government buys or sells its own currency or that of a trading partner to influence exchange rates, it is engaging in a "managed float" or a "dirty float."

**Managed float** A policy of frequent central bank intervention to move the exchange rate.

> Under a **managed float,** a country's central bank actively manages its exchange rate, buying its own currency to prevent depreciations, and selling its own currency to prevent appreciations.

Managed floats are used most often in the very short run, to prevent large, sudden changes in exchange rates. For example, during the week after the terror attacks of September 2001, the Bank of Japan (Japan's central bank) sold 2 trillion yen (about $17 billion worth) in order to stop a rapid *appreciation* of the yen against the dollar. On the other side—and on a smaller scale—Argentina's central bank purchased 15 million Argentinian pesos (about $9 million worth at the time) on January 15, 2002, in order to slow the *depreciation* of the peso against the dollar.

That last example raises a question. When a country—such as Argentina— wants to prevent or slow a depreciation against the dollar, it has to buy its own currency with dollars. Where does it get those dollars? Unfortunately for Argentina, it cannot print dollars; only the U.S. Federal Reserve can do that. Instead, Argentina must use its *reserves* of dollars—the dollars its central bank keeps on hand specifically to intervene in the dollar–peso market.

Almost every nation holds reserves of dollars—as well as euros, yen, and other key currencies—just so it can enter the foreign exchange market and sell them for its own currency when necessary. Under a managed float, periods of selling dollars are usually short-lived, and alternate with periods of buying dollars. Thus, countries rarely use up all of their dollar reserves when they engage in managed floats.

Managed floats are controversial. Some economists believe they help to avoid wide swings in exchange rates, and thus reduce the risks for international traders and investors. But others are critical of how managed floats often work out in practice. They point out that countries often intervene when the forces behind an appreciation or depreciation are strong. In these cases, the intervention only serves to delay inevitable changes in the exchange rate—sometimes, at great cost to a country's reserves of dollars and other key currencies.

## FIXED EXCHANGE RATES

**Fixed exchange rate** A government-declared exchange rate maintained by central bank intervention in the foreign exchange market.

A more extreme form of intervention is a **fixed exchange rate,** in which a government declares a particular value for its exchange rate with another currency. The government, through its central bank, then commits itself to intervene in the foreign exchange market any time the *equilibrium* exchange rate differs from the *fixed* rate.

For example, from 1987 to 1997, the government of Thailand fixed the value of its currency—the *baht*—at $0.04 per baht. The two panels of Figure 7 show the different types of intervention that might be necessary in the baht–dollar market to maintain this fixed exchange rate. Each panel shows a different set of supply and demand curves—and a different equilibrium exchange rate that might exist for the baht. Look first at panel (a). Here, we assume that the equilibrium exchange rate is $0.06 per baht, so that the fixed rate is *lower* than the equilibrium rate. At the fixed rate of $0.04 per baht, 400 million baht would be demanded each month, but only 100 million would be supplied. There would be an *excess demand* of 300 million baht, which would ordinarily drive the exchange rate back up to its equilibrium value of $0.06. But the Thai government prevents this by entering the market and *selling* just enough baht to cover the excess demand. In panel (a), the Central Bank of Thailand would sell 300 million baht per month to maintain the fixed rate.

> When a country fixes its exchange rate below the equilibrium value, the result is an excess demand for the country's currency. To maintain the fixed rate, the country's central bank must sell enough of its own currency to eliminate the excess demand.

Panel (b) shows another possibility, where the equilibrium exchange rate is $0.02, so that the same fixed exchange rate of $0.04 per baht is now *above* the equilibrium rate. There is an excess *supply* of 300 million baht. In this case, to prevent the excess supply from driving the exchange rate down, the Central Bank of Thailand must *buy* the excess baht.

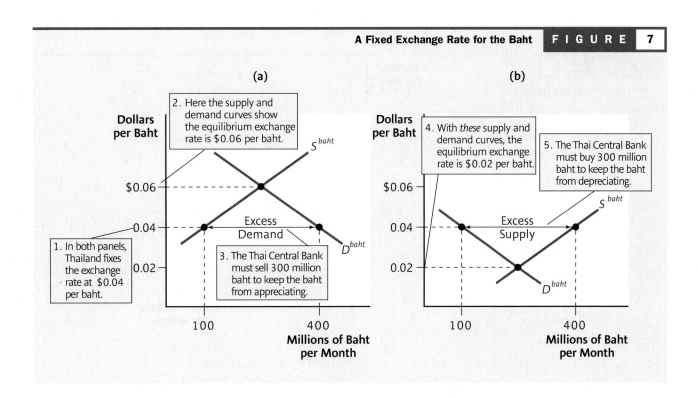

**A Fixed Exchange Rate for the Baht**    FIGURE 7

> *When a country fixes its exchange rate above the equilibrium value, the result is an excess supply of the country's currency. To maintain the fixed rate, the country's central bank must buy enough of its own currency to eliminate the excess supply.*

Fixed exchange rates present little problem for a country as long as the exchange rate is fixed at or very close to its equilibrium rate. But when the equilibrium exchange rate moves away from the fixed rate—as in the two panels of Figure 7—governments often try to maintain their fixed rate anyway, sometimes for long periods. This can create problems, especially when the exchange rate is fixed *above* the equilibrium rate.

## FOREIGN CURRENCY CRISES, THE IMF, AND MORAL HAZARD

To see how a fixed exchange rate can be problematic, look at Figure 8. Initially, the supply and demand curves for baht are given by $S_1$ and $D_1$, respectively, so that the equilibrium exchange rate, $0.04, is equal to the fixed exchange rate. At this point, the central bank is neither selling nor buying baht. Now, suppose that, for some reason (we'll be more specific in a few paragraphs), the supply and demand curves shift to $S_2$ and $D_2$, respectively. The equilibrium rate falls, so the fixed rate of $0.04 is above the equilibrium rate of $0.02. The Central Bank of Thailand must now *buy* its own currency with dollars—at the rate of 300 million baht per month. Each baht costs the central bank 4 cents, so as the months go by, its dollar reserves are being depleted at the rate of 300 million $\times$ $0.04 = $12 million per month. Once those reserves are gone, Thailand will have only two choices: to let its currency float

---

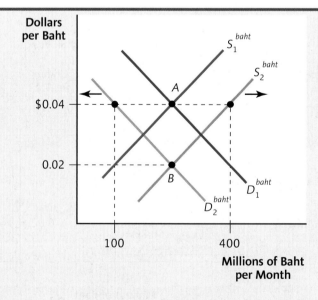

**FIGURE 8**

**A Foreign Currency Crisis**

*Initially, the baht is fixed at the equilibrium rate of $0.04. When the supply and demand curves shift to $D_2$ and $S_2$, the equilibrium exchange rate falls to $0.02. If Thailand continues to fix the rate at $0.04, it will have to buy up the excess supply of 300 million baht per month, using dollars. As its dollar reserves dwindle, traders will anticipate a drop in the value of the baht, shifting the curves out further, as indicated by the arrows.*

(which means an immediate depreciation to the lower, equilibrium rate) or to declare a new, lower fixed rate—a **devaluation** of its currency.

Of course, at a certain point, foreign exchange speculators and traders would see that Thailand doesn't have many dollars left. (Most countries' central banks regularly report their holdings of key currencies, and economists can estimate the holdings of countries that don't.) Looking ahead, these speculators and traders will begin to *anticipate* a drop in the baht. And—as you've learned in this chapter—expected changes in the exchange rate *shift* supply and demand curves for foreign currency. In this case, an expected fall in the baht causes the supply curve for baht to shift further rightward and the demand curve to shift further leftward, as indicated by the heavy arrows in the diagram. In Figure 8, these shifts will *decrease* the equilibrium value of the baht, increase the *excess supply* of baht, and make the fixed rate of $0.04 even harder to maintain. The country is now experiencing a *foreign currency crisis.*

> A *foreign currency crisis* arises when people no longer believe that a country can maintain a fixed exchange rate above the equilibrium rate. As a consequence, the supply of the currency increases, demand for it decreases, and the country must use up its reserves of dollars and other key currencies even faster in order to maintain the fixed rate.

**Devaluation** A change in the exchange rate from a higher fixed rate to a lower fixed rate.

**Foreign currency crisis** A loss of faith that a country can prevent a drop in its exchange rate, leading to a rapid depletion of its foreign currency (e.g., dollar) reserves.

Once a foreign currency crisis arises, a country typically has no choice but to devalue its currency or let it float and watch it depreciate. And ironically, because the country waited for the crisis to develop, the exchange rate may for a time drop even lower than the original equilibrium rate. For example, in Figure 8, an early devaluation to $0.02 per dollar might prevent a crisis from occurring at all. But once the crisis begins, and the supply and demand curves shift out further than $S_2$ and $D_2$, the currency will have to drop *below* $0.02 to end the rapid depletion of dollar reserves.

Our analysis of a foreign currency crisis used the example of the Thai baht for good reason. In 1997 and 1998, Thailand was at the center of a financial crisis that rocked the world.

The crisis began when a lack of confidence in Thailand's financial system led to dramatic shifts in the supply and demand curves for baht—just as in Figure 8. While the *equilibrium* exchange rate fell, Thailand continued to fix the *actual* exchange rate at $0.04 per baht, above the equilibrium rate. As a result, Thailand's central bank was depleting its reserves of dollars and other foreign currencies. This, of course, led currency traders to anticipate a devaluation, shifting the supply and demand curves even further. Finally, in July 1997, the Thai central bank simply ran out of foreign currency reserves, and was forced to let its currency float. The baht immediately depreciated from $0.04 to $0.02.

But this was only the beginning of the story. Many of Thailand's banks—counting on the fixed exchange rate—had borrowed heavily in dollars, yen, and other foreign currencies, but then lent funds to Thai businesses in baht. Once the baht depreciated, these banks were obligated to make unchanged dollar and yen payments on their debts, while continuing to receive unchanged baht payments on the funds they had lent. The problem was that, after the depreciation, the baht coming in would no longer cover the dollars going out. Thailand's banks were in trouble.

And the trouble spread. Investors began to wonder if banks in *other* nearby countries were similarly vulnerable, and began to dump the foreign exchange of

**International Monetary Fund
(IMF)** An international
organization founded in 1945 to
help stabilize the world monetary
system.

Indonesia, South Korea, Malaysia, and the Philippines. Before the crisis ended, it had even spread to several Latin American countries.

What ended the crisis? In large part, the crisis was resolved by the **International Monetary Fund (IMF)**, an international organization formed in 1945 in large part to help nations avoid such foreign currency crises and help them recover when crises occur. In 1998, the IMF—in cooperation with the U.S. government—orchestrated a rescue package of more than $100 billion to cover the Asian economies' foreign debt.

The rescue was controversial, however. Why? Helping a troubled country leads other countries to expect that they, too, will get help if they pursue untenable policies and get themselves into trouble. This is an example of a more general problem which economists call *moral hazard*.

**Moral hazard** When decision
makers—expecting assistance in
the event of an unfavorable
outcome—change their behavior
so that the unfavorable outcome
is more likely.

> *Moral hazard occurs when a decision maker (such as an individual, firm, or government) expects to be rescued in the event of an unfavorable outcome, and then changes its behavior so that the unfavorable outcome is more likely.*

Moral hazard plagues the insurance industry (are you as likely to lock your car if you're insured against theft?), efforts to care for the unemployed (will you look as hard for a new job after being laid off if you are collecting unemployment insurance?), and troubled business firms (will mega-corporations be careful not to take risks if they expect the government to rescue them in the event of a disaster?).

But here, our focus is on the international financial system. The problem of moral hazard helps explain the very different response of the IMF when, in late 2001 and early 2002, Argentina faced a somewhat similar foreign currency crisis. Like the Asian countries a few years earlier, Argentina needed billions of dollars of help to prevent it from devaluing its currency and defaulting on its foreign debt. This time, however, it was felt that Argentina's problems were unique, and so its foreign currency crisis—unlike the Asian crisis a few years earlier—was unlikely to spread to other countries. Accordingly, the Bush administration—concerned about the moral hazard problem—encouraged the IMF to take a tough stand. There was no rescue, and Argentina was forced into devaluation *and* default in January 2002.

*The IMF headquarters building in Washington, D.C.*

# EXCHANGE RATES AND THE MACROECONOMY

Exchange rates can have important effects on the macroeconomy—largely through their effect on net exports. And although we've included net exports in our short-run macro model, we haven't yet asked how exchange rates affect them. That's what we'll do now.

## EXCHANGE RATES AND DEMAND SHOCKS

Suppose that the dollar depreciates against the foreign currencies of its major trading partners. (We'll discuss *why* that might happen in a later section.) Then U.S. goods would become cheaper to foreigners, and net exports would rise at each level of output. This increase in net exports is a positive demand shock to the economy—it increases aggregate expenditure and shifts the aggregate demand curve to the right. And, as you've learned, positive demand shocks increase GDP in the short run.

> *A depreciation of the dollar causes net exports to rise—a positive demand shock that increases real GDP in the short run. An appreciation of the dollar causes net exports to drop—a negative demand shock that decreases real GDP in the short run.*

The impact of net exports on equilibrium GDP—often caused by changes in the exchange rate—helps us understand one reason why governments are often concerned about their exchange rates. An unstable exchange rate can result in repeated shocks to the economy. At worst, this can cause fluctuations in GDP; at best, it makes the central bank's job more difficult as it tries to keep the economy on an even keel.

## EXCHANGE RATES AND MONETARY POLICY

In several earlier chapters, we've explored how the Fed tries to keep the U.S. economy on an even keel with monetary policy. The central banks around the world are engaged in a similar struggle, and face many of the same challenges as the Fed. One challenge to central banks is that monetary policy causes changes in exchange rates, and thus has additional effects on real GDP that we have not yet considered.

To understand this, let's run through an example. Suppose the United States is in a recession, and the Fed decides to increase equilibrium GDP. As you've learned, the Fed—by increasing the money supply—brings down the interest rate. Interest-sensitive spending rises, and so does aggregate expenditure. When we consider the foreign exchange market, however, there is an additional effect on aggregate expenditure.

By lowering the U.S. interest rate, the Fed makes *foreign* financial assets more attractive to Americans, which raises their demand for foreign currency. In the market for pounds, for example, this will shift the demand for pounds curve rightward. At the same time, U.S. financial assets become less attractive to foreigners, which decreases the supply of foreign exchange (in the market for pounds, a leftward shift in the supply of pounds curve). If you sketch out these shifts right now, you'll see that, as long as the exchange rate floats, the result is a *depreciation of the dollar* against the pound.

Now let's see how the depreciation of the dollar affects the economy. With dollars now cheaper to foreigners, they will buy more U.S. goods, raising U.S. exports. At the same time, with foreign goods and services more expensive to Americans, U.S. imports will decrease. Both the increase in exports and the decrease in imports contribute to a rise in net exports, *NX*. This, in turn, increases aggregate expenditure.

Thus, as you can see, the expansionary monetary policy causes aggregate expenditures to rise in two ways: first, by increasing interest-sensitive spending and, second, by increasing net exports. As a result, equilibrium GDP rises by more—and monetary policy is more effective—when the effects on exchange rates are included.

The channels through which monetary policy works are summarized in the following schematic:

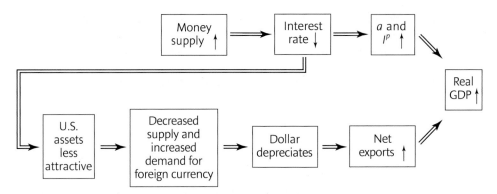

Net Effect: GDP ↑ by more when the exchange rate's effect on net exports is included

The top line shows the familiar effect on interest-sensitive spending: An increase in the money supply causes a drop in the interest rate, which increases autonomous consumption spending ($a$) and investment spending ($I^p$). The bottom line shows the *additional* effect on net exports through changes in the exchange rate—the effects we've been discussing.

The analysis of contractionary monetary policy is the same, but in reverse. A decrease in the money supply will not only decrease interest-sensitive spending, it will also cause the dollar to appreciate and net exports to drop. Thus, it will cause equilibrium GDP to fall by more than in earlier chapters, where we ignored the foreign exchange market.

The channel of monetary influence through exchange rates and the volume of trade is an important part of the full story of monetary policy in the United States. And in countries where exports are relatively large fractions of GDP—such as those of Europe—the trade channel is even more important. It is the main channel through which monetary policy affects the economy.

> *Monetary policy has a stronger effect when we include the impact on exchange rates and net exports, rather than just the impact on interest-sensitive consumption and investment spending.*

## EXCHANGE RATES AND THE TRADE DEFICIT

The U.S. trade deficit is often in the news. But what, exactly, is it?

The trade deficit is the extent to which a country's imports exceed its exports:

**Trade deficit** = Imports − Exports

**Trade deficit** The excess of a nation's imports over its exports during a given period.

On the other hand, when exports exceed imports, a nation has a trade surplus:

**Trade surplus** = Exports − Imports

**Trade surplus** The excess of a nation's exports over its imports during a given period.

As you can see, the trade surplus is nothing more than a nation's net exports ($NX$). And when net exports are negative, we have a trade deficit.

The United States has had large trade deficits with the rest of the world since the early 1980s. In 2005, the trade deficit was $716 billion. Simply put, Americans bought $716 billion more goods and services from other countries than their residents bought from the United States.

Why does the United States have a trade deficit with the rest of the world? A variety of explanations have been offered in the media, including poor U.S. marketing savvy in selling to foreigners, and a greater degree of protectionism in foreign markets.

But economists believe that there is a much more important reason.

## THE ORIGINS OF THE U.S. TRADE DEFICIT

To keep our analysis simple, we'll start by looking at the U.S. trade deficit with just one country—Japan—but our results will hold more generally to the trade deficit with many other countries as well.

Before we analyze the causes of the trade deficit, we need to do a little math. Let's begin by breaking down the total quantity of yen demanded by Americans ($D^¥$) into two components: the yen demanded to purchase Japanese goods and services (U.S. imports from Japan) and the yen demanded to buy Japanese assets:

$$D^¥ = \text{U.S. imports from Japan} + \text{U.S. purchases of Japanese assets.}$$

Similarly, we can divide the total quantity of yen supplied by the Japanese ($S^¥$) into two components: the yen exchanged for dollars to purchase American goods (U.S. exports to Japan) and the yen exchanged for dollars to purchase American assets like stocks, bonds, or real estate:

$$S^¥ = \text{U.S. exports to Japan} + \text{Japanese purchases of U.S. assets.}$$

As long as the yen floats against the dollar without government intervention—which it does during most periods—we know that the exchange rate will adjust until the quantities of yen supplied and demanded are equal, or $D^¥ = S^¥$. Substituting the foregoing breakdowns into this equation, we have

$$\left\{ \begin{array}{l} \text{U.S. imports from Japan} \\ + \text{ U.S. purchases of Japanese assets} \end{array} \right\} = \left\{ \begin{array}{l} \text{U.S. exports to Japan} \\ + \text{ Japanese purchases of U.S. assets} \end{array} \right\}.$$

Now let's rearrange this equation—subtracting U.S. exports from both sides and subtracting American purchases of Japanese assets from both sides—to get

$$\left\{ \begin{array}{l} \text{U.S. imports from Japan} \\ - \text{ U.S. exports to Japan} \end{array} \right\} = \left\{ \begin{array}{l} \text{Japanese purchases of U.S. assets} \\ - \text{ U.S. purchases of Japanese assets} \end{array} \right\}.$$

The term on the left should look familiar: It is the U.S. trade deficit with Japan. And since a similar equation must hold for every country, we can generalize it this way:

$$\left\{ \begin{array}{l} \text{U.S. imports from other countries} \\ - \text{ U.S. exports to other countries} \end{array} \right\} = \left\{ \begin{array}{l} \text{foreign purchases of U.S. assets} \\ - \text{ U.S. purchases of foreign assets} \end{array} \right\}.$$

But what is the expression on the right? It tells us the extent to which foreigners are buying more of our assets than we are buying of theirs. It is often called the **net financial inflow** into the United States, because when the residents of other countries buy U.S. assets, funds flow into the U.S. financial market, where they are made available to U.S. firms and the U.S. government. Thus, the equation we've derived—which must hold true when exchange rates float—can also be expressed as

$$\text{U.S. trade deficit} = \text{U.S. net financial inflow}$$

**Net financial inflow** An inflow of funds equal to a nation's trade deficit.

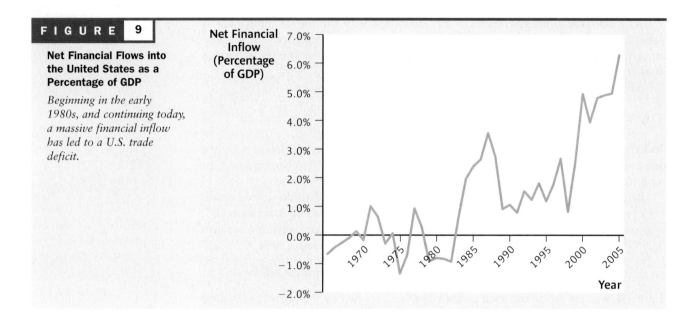

**FIGURE 9**

**Net Financial Flows into the United States as a Percentage of GDP**

*Beginning in the early 1980s, and continuing today, a massive financial inflow has led to a U.S. trade deficit.*

Why have we bothered to derive this equation? Because it tells us two very important things about the U.S. trade deficit. First, it tells us how the trade deficit is *financed*. Think about it: If the United States is running a trade deficit with, say, Japan, it means that the Japanese are providing more goods and services to Americans—more automobiles, VCRs, memory chips, and other goods—than Americans are providing to them. The Japanese are not doing this out of kindness. They must be getting *something* in return for the extra goods we are getting, and the equation tells us just what that is: U.S. assets. This is one reason why the trade deficit concerns U.S. policy makers: It results in a transfer of wealth from Americans to foreign residents.

The second important insight provided by the equation is that a trade deficit can arise *because* of forces that cause a financial inflow. That is, if forces in the global economy make the right side of the equation positive, then the left side must be positive as well, and we will have a trade deficit.

Indeed, economists believe this is just what has happened to the United States: that the U.S. trade deficit has been caused by the desire of foreigners to invest in the United States. The result was a massive financial inflow and trade deficit that arose in the early 1980s, as illustrated in Figure 9. This financial inflow was unprecedented in size and duration, and it reversed a long-standing pattern of ownership between the United States and other countries. For decades, American holdings of foreign assets far exceeded foreign holdings of U.S. assets. But the financial inflows of the 1980s changed that: By 1988, foreigners held about $500 billion more in U.S. assets than Americans held in foreign assets. By the end of 2005, the difference in asset holdings increased more than fivefold, and exceeded $2.7 trillion.

But how do the forces that create a financial inflow also *cause* a trade deficit?

## HOW A FINANCIAL INFLOW CAUSES A TRADE DEFICIT

Figure 10 illustrates this process, using the yen–dollar market. We'll assume that initially, neither the Japanese nor the Americans are buying *assets* from the other country. Only goods and services are traded. Point *A* shows the initial equilibrium under

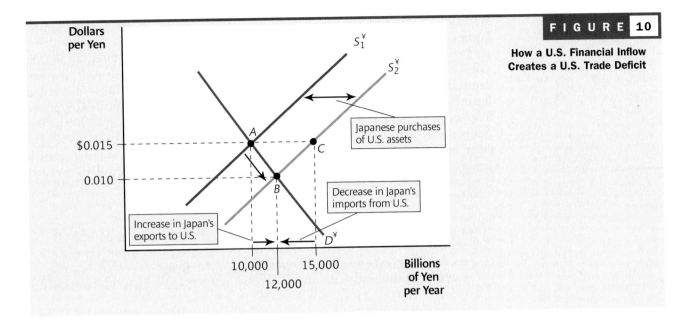

**FIGURE 10**

**How a U.S. Financial Inflow Creates a U.S. Trade Deficit**

this special assumption. Under these circumstances, the demand curve for yen would reflect U.S. *imports* of goods and services from Japan, and the supply curve would reflect U.S. *exports* of goods and services to Japan. The exchange rate would be $0.015 per yen (one-and-a-half cents per yen), and each year, 10,000 billion yen would be traded in exchange for 10,000 × 0.015 = 150 billion dollars. Since the quantities of yen demanded and supplied are equal in equilibrium, there is no trade deficit: The United States buys $150 billion in goods from Japan, and Japan buys $150 billion in goods from the United States.

Now suppose that the Japanese start to buy U.S. stocks, bonds, and real estate. Specifically, they want to purchase 5,000 billion yen worth of these assets from Americans each year. To do so, they need dollars, so they must supply additional yen to the foreign exchange market to get them. Accordingly, the supply of yen curve shifts rightward by 5,000 billion yen. The market equilibrium moves from point A to point B, and the new exchange rate is $0.01 per yen. The yen depreciates against the dollar, and the dollar appreciates against the yen.

But something interesting happens in the market as the exchange rate changes. First, there is a *movement along the demand curve* for yen, from point A to point B. Why? The yen is now cheaper, so Americans—finding Japanese goods and services cheaper—buy more of them. Thus, the movement along the demand curve represents an *increase in Japan's exports to the U.S.* (valued in yen, the units on the horizontal axis). In the figure, Japan's exports—the quantity of yen demanded—rise by 2,000 billion yen as we move from A to B.

But there is a second movement as well. After the shift in the supply curve, *and at the old exchange rate of $0.015*, the Japanese want to supply 15,000 billion yen to the market (point C). But as the exchange rate falls, there is a movement from point C to point B—the quantity of yen supplied decreases. Why does this happen? Because as the yen depreciates (the dollar appreciates), U.S. goods and services become more expensive to the Japanese. Accordingly, they purchase fewer U.S. goods. Assuming that the Japanese still want to purchase the same 5,000 billion yen in U.S. *assets*, the entire decrease in the quantity of yen supplied as we move from C to B represents a *decrease in Japan's imports from the United States* (valued in yen). In the figure, Japan's imports decrease by 3,000 billion yen.

Let's recap: Because the Japanese wanted to purchase 5,000 billion yen in U.S. assets (a net financial inflow to the United States of 5,000 billion yen), the yen depreciated. This, in turn, made Japanese goods cheaper for Americans—increasing Japan's exports (U.S. imports) by 2,000 billion yen per year. It also made U.S. goods more expensive in Japan, decreasing Japan's imports (U.S. exports) by 3,000 billion yen per year. Since U.S. imports have risen by 2,000 billion ¥ and U.S. exports have fallen by 3,000 billion ¥, the United States—which initially had no trade deficit with Japan at point *A*—now has a trade deficit equal to 5,000 billion yen. This is exactly equal to the financial inflow—Japan's purchases of U.S. assets.

More generally,

> *an increase in the desire of foreigners to invest in the United States contributes to an appreciation of the dollar. As a result, U.S. exports—which become more expensive for foreigners—decline. Imports—which become cheaper to Americans—increase. The result is a rise in the U.S. trade deficit.*

## EXPLAINING THE NET FINANCIAL INFLOW

What explains the huge financial inflow that began in the 1980s and has since grown larger? In the 1980s, an important part of the story was *a rise in U.S. interest rates relative to interest rates abroad*, which made U.S. assets more attractive to foreigners, and foreign assets less attractive to Americans. In the 1990s, however, U.S. interest rates were low relative to rates in other countries, yet the inflow continued. Why?

Even when U.S. interest rates are lower than abroad, it seems that foreign residents have a strong preference for holding American assets. In part, this is because of a favorable investment climate. The United States is a stable country with a long history of protecting individual property rights. People know that if they buy American stocks or bonds, unless they violate U.S. criminal law, the U.S. government is very unlikely to confiscate foreign-owned assets or suddenly impose punitive taxes when foreigners want to repatriate the funds to their home countries. This asymmetrical foreign preference for American assets helps explain why the U.S. net financial inflow has been *persistent*.

But why the recent *surge* in the inflow? One reason is that Americans have been saving less, and foreigners have been saving more. (In Europe and in Japan, aging populations have been saving heavily for retirement, while developing country governments have been reducing debt and building up financial reserves.) All of this new foreign wealth needs to be held in *some* country's assets, and—for reasons discussed earlier—the U.S. seems to be the favorite.[2]

At the same time, the *demand* for loanable funds in the U.S. has been growing rapidly. Part of this greater demand for funds arose from new investment opportunities, causing business firms to issue new shares of stock and new bonds in order to finance projects. This was especially true in the late 1990s, during the Internet boom. And when the boom turned to a bust in the early 2000s, a new demand for funds arose: The government needed to finance large budget deficits.

---

[2] For a complete explanation of this argument, see the speech by Federal Reserve Governor Ben S. Bernanke, "The Global Saving Glut and the U.S. Current Account Deficit," April 14, 2005 (*www. federalreserve.gov/boarddocs/speeches/2005*).

Remember that, under floating exchange rates, the financial inflow equals the trade deficit. Thus, the story of the U.S. financial inflow of the 1980s, 1990s, and early 2000s is also the story of the U.S. trade deficit:

> *We can trace the rise in the trade deficit during recent decades to two important sources: first, relatively high interest rates in the 1980s and, second, a long-held preference for American assets that grew stronger in the 1990s. Each of these contributed to a large financial inflow, a higher value for the dollar, and a trade deficit.*

In addition to a strong desire to buy U.S. assets, a trade deficit can arise from another cause: a foreign currency fixed at an artificially low value. In the minds of many economists, this has contributed to the United States' growing trade deficit with China. We will explore the U.S. trade deficit with China in our Using the Theory section. But first, let's look at why many economists are concerned about the large U.S. trade deficit.

## CONCERNS ABOUT THE TRADE DEFICIT

Should we be concerned about the U.S. trade deficit? To most economists, the answer is yes. But the reasons are different from those typically offered in public debate.

To many *non*-economists, the U.S. trade deficit is viewed as bad because it makes Americans poorer. We get VCRs, toys, and T-shirts from the rest of the world. But we don't pay for all of these things with our own goods and services. To make up the difference, we sell assets: We turn over ownership of our factories and real estate to the rest of the world, and also accumulate debt to them (when we sell them bonds). According to this view, the U.S. trade deficit means declining American wealth.

Although the first part of this analysis is correct (the United States *does* finance its trade deficit by selling assets to the rest of the world), it does not necessarily follow that the trade deficit makes American households poorer. That would follow if the total amount of wealth in the U.S. economy were fixed, so that any wealth sold to foreigners meant less wealth in American hands. But, in fact, total U.S. wealth grows every year, as new factories and new homes are built, new intellectual property is developed, and more. And even after deducting the wealth that the rest of the world acquires, what is left in American hands continues to grow every year as well.

What *does* follow from this analysis is that, *because of the trade deficit, U.S. wealth owned by the U.S. public grows more slowly than it otherwise would.* Slower growing wealth is a choice made by U.S. households (choosing to buy more toys and T-shirts instead of saving more) and the U.S. government (choosing to pay for part of its expenditure by borrowing instead of taxing). Economists continue to debate the wisdom or lack of wisdom behind these choices, but slower growing wealth is not the main reason for economists' concern.

The real problem, as economists view it, is the trade deficit's *sustainability*.

Why might the trade deficit not be sustainable? As the U.S. trade deficit continues year after year, foreign holdings of U.S. assets continue to accumulate—rapidly. And the *proportion* of the rest of the world's total wealth that is held in dollar-denominated assets grows as well. At some point, the rest of the world's wealth holders may decide that their portfolios are too "dollar heavy," and that the time

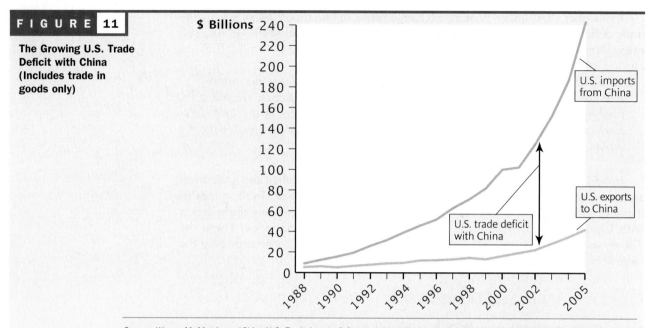

**FIGURE 11**

**The Growing U.S. Trade Deficit with China (Includes trade in goods only)**

Source: Wayne M. Morrison, "China-U.S. Trade Issues," Congressional Research Service, Library of Congress, Updated May 16, 2003; *Economic Report of the President*, 2006; and Bureau of Economic Analysis, "U.S. International Transactions by Area."

has come to diversify. This would mean a slowdown—or possibly a halt—in new purchases of U.S. assets. If this occurs, we can imagine two possibilities.

### The Soft-Landing Scenario

In the benign, soft-landing scenario, the U.S. and world economies would gradually adjust to a slowdown in foreign purchases of U.S. assets. A decline in the demand for U.S. assets, as you've learned, would cause the dollar to depreciate. Imports would become more expensive for U.S. residents, and U.S. exports would become cheaper to the rest of the world, so the trade deficit would gradually shrink.

At the same time, the U.S. interest rate would rise. (From a long-run, loanable funds perspective, the interest rate would rise because the supply of funds to the U.S. loanable funds market is shrinking. From a short-run perspective, the Fed would raise its interest rate target to prevent the rise in net exports from overheating the U.S. economy.)

The rise in the U.S. interest rate would contribute to the gradualness of the adjustment. First, a higher interest rate would mean more saving by Americans, enabling them to buy some of the assets foreigners are no longer buying. Second, higher interest rates would help make U.S. assets more attractive to foreigners.

The soft-landing scenario would not be painless. It would require structural changes in the U.S. economy as the export- and import-competing industries expanded, while interest-sensitive industries such as home building declined. But it would not be a disaster.

### The Hard-Landing Scenario

The more dangerous, hard-landing scenario works much like the soft-landing scenario, except that the changes are much larger and more sudden. Once again, we start with a decline in the demand for U.S. assets by foreigners. Only this time, as the dollar begins to depreciate, foreigners anticipate *further* depreciation in the future. They begin to dump dollar-denominated assets *en masse*, before the anticipated decline in their value. Hot money flows out of the dollar and into other currencies. The dollar doesn't just depreciate—it plummets. And the more it does, the more foreign wealth holders want to get rid of their dollars.

The interest rate would rise. (See the soft-landing scenario.) But in this case, with the dollar depreciating so rapidly, substitute the word "skyrocket" for "rise." With soaring interest rates, spending on interest-sensitive goods, such as new factories and homes, would disappear. Moreover, as you learned a few chapters ago, the rise in interest rates would cause stock and bond prices to fall—a decline in household wealth. Consumption spending would fall across the board.

In the most pessimistic form of the hard-landing scenario, the United States would experience a very serious recession—one that the Fed would be unable to prevent. If the Fed tried to lower the interest rate to prevent the recession entirely, it would have to allow the dollar to continue plummeting. This would make the price of imports rise rapidly and cause unacceptable inflation. And even if the Fed decided to take this course, the dramatic changes in the economy would make any Fed response particularly error-prone.

Which of these two scenarios is most likely to occur? In mid-2006, economists continued to debate the probabilities. Some argued that the hard-landing scenario was unrealistic. It assumes that central banks in the rest of the world would *allow* the dollar to plummet, even though this would devastate their own export industries and decrease the value of their remaining dollar-denominated assets. Surely, so the soft-landers say, these central banks would intervene in the foreign exchange market, by purchasing dollars to prop up its value. If the hard-landing scenario begins to occur, we will see if they are right.

# USING THE THEORY

## The U.S. Trade Deficit with China

The growing U.S. trade deficit with China has become one of the most controversial issues of U.S. public policy. Figure 11 shows United States imports to, and exports from, China from 1988 to 2005. (The figure excludes trade in services, but this has little effect on the numbers.) Trade in both directions expanded dramatically. But while U.S. exports to China increased tenfold, U.S. *imports* from China increased 28-fold, from $8.5 billion in 1988 to $243 billion in 2005. During this period, China went from being a relatively unimportant trading partner of the United States to the fourth-largest trading partner. In the figure, the growing trade deficit is the increasing distance between the (higher) imports line and the (lower) exports line. In 2005, the United States had a larger trade deficit with China—$202 billion—than with any other country.

The U.S. trade deficit with China has been soaring for a variety of reasons, including special trade agreements during this period that gave China new access to U.S. markets, and Chinese trade policies that have encouraged exports and discouraged imports. But another factor, as mentioned earlier, is China's undervalued exchange rate. China has fixed the value of its currency (the yuan) against the dollar—at about

© SUSAN VAN ETTEN

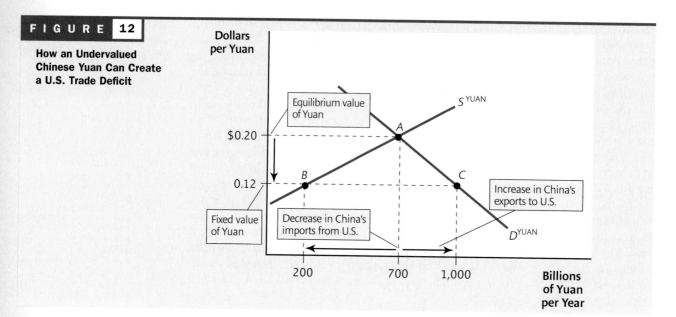

**FIGURE 12**

**How an Undervalued Chinese Yuan Can Create a U.S. Trade Deficit**

$0.12 per yuan for most of the past decade. This is widely believed to be far below the yuan's equilibrium value. In mid-2005, China revalued the yuan slightly (by 2.1 percent) and announced that it would move to a managed float, allowing its currency to rise slowly. In fact, the rise has been *so* slow (about another 2 percent from mid-2005 to mid-2006) that, effectively, we can continue to regard the yuan–dollar exchange rate as fixed.

Figure 12 illustrates how an undervalued yuan can create a trade deficit for the United States. We'll assume that if the exchange rate were floating, the market equilibrium would be at point *A*, with an exchange rate of $0.20 per yuan. In this case, 700 billion yuan would be exchanged for 700 × .02 = 140 billion dollars each year.

Now we introduce the lower, fixed exchange rate of $.12 per yuan. Compared to the equilibrium exchange rate, the fixed exchange rate causes a movement along the *demand* for yuan curve, from point *A* to point *C*. The yuan is now cheaper, which makes Chinese goods and services cheaper to Americans, who buy more of them. Measured along the horizontal axis, *China's exports to the U.S. increase* by 300 billion yuan per year.

There is also a move from point *A* to point *B* along the *supply* curve; the quantity of yuan supplied decreases. A lower-valued yuan makes U.S. goods and services more expensive to Chinese households and businesses, so they purchase fewer of them. Along the horizontal axis, *China's imports from the U.S. decrease* by 500 billion yuan.

Since the fixed exchange rate has caused *China's imports from the U.S. to decrease* by 500 billion yuan, and *China's exports to the U.S. to increase* by 300 billion yuan, the U.S. trade deficit with China—valued in yuan—rises by 500 + 300 or 800 billion yuan per year. (If you convert the U.S. trade deficit to dollars, you'll see that our example comes close to the actual U.S. trade deficit with China.)

But wait . . . doesn't the rise in the U.S. trade deficit have to equal the rise in the net financial inflow? Indeed it does. Figure 11 shows an *excess demand for yuan* of 1,000 − 200 = 800 billion at the fixed exchange rate. The Chinese government must supply these yuan, selling them for U.S. dollars. These dollars are then used to purchase U.S. assets, contributing to the U.S. net financial inflow.

> *When a U.S. trading partner fixes the dollar price of its currency below its equilibrium value, U.S. exports—which become more expensive to foreigners—decline. U.S. imports—which become cheaper to Americans—increase. The result is a rise in the U.S. trade deficit.*

China's fixed exchange rate with the dollar is the source of considerable tension between the two countries. On the one hand, it enables Americans to purchase goods from China at even lower prices than otherwise. But rapidly growing trade with China also disrupts production in the U.S. economy, as U.S. businesses that produce sandals, shoes, suits, electronic goods, toys, and textiles find they are unable to compete with cheaper goods from China. The fixed exchange exacerbates their problem. By giving China an even *greater* cost advantage than it would otherwise have, U.S. firms and workers that compete in these markets must adjust more rapidly—and painfully—to the new pattern of international trade.

## Summary

When residents of two countries trade with one another, one party ordinarily makes use of the foreign exchange market to trade one national currency for another. In this market, suppliers of a currency interact with demanders to determine an *exchange rate*—the price of one currency in terms of another.

In the market for U.S. dollars and British pounds, for example, demanders are mostly Americans who wish to obtain pounds in order to buy goods and services from British firms, or to buy British assets. A higher dollar price for the pound will lead Americans to demand fewer pounds—the demand curve slopes downward. Changes in U.S. real GDP, the U.S. price level relative to the British price level, Americans' tastes for British goods, interest rates in the United States relative to Britain, or expectations regarding the exchange rate can each cause the demand curve to shift.

Suppliers of pounds are mostly British residents who wish to buy American goods, services, or assets. A higher dollar price for the pound will lead Britons to supply more pounds—the supply curve slopes upward. The supply curve will shift in response to changes in British real GDP, prices in Britain relative to the United States, British tastes for U.S. goods, the British interest rate relative to the U.S. rate, and expectations regarding the exchange rate.

When the exchange rate floats, the equilibrium rate is determined where the supply and demand curves cross. If the equilibrium is disturbed by, say, a rightward shift of the demand curve, then the currency being demanded will *appreciate*—the exchange rate will rise. (The other country's currency will *depreciate*.) In a similar way, a rightward shift of the supply curve will cause the currency being supplied to depreciate.

Governments often intervene in foreign exchange markets. Many countries manage their float, buying and selling their own currency to alter the exchange rate. Some countries fix their exchange rate to the dollar or the currency of a major trading partner.

When a currency depreciates, its net exports rise—a positive demand shock. Monetary policy, in addition to its impact on interest-sensitive spending, also changes the exchange rate and net exports, adding to changes in output. This monetary policy is more effective in changing GDP when its effects on net exports are included.

The United States has had a persistent—and growing—*trade deficit* with the rest of the world. Much of this trade deficit can be explained by the growing U.S. *financial inflow* from the rest of the world. U.S. assets have been consistently more attractive to foreigners than foreign assets have been to Americans. The U.S. financial inflow causes the dollar to appreciate, which decreases U.S. exports and increases U.S. imports. In addition, when an exchange rate is fixed, an undervalued foreign currency can create a U.S. trade deficit. By making the U.S. dollar artificially more expensive to residents of the foreign country, it causes U.S. exports to decline and U.S. imports to rise.

# Problem Set
*Answers to even-numbered Questions and Problems can be found on the text Web site at www.thomsonedu.com/economics/hall.*

1. Do the following events cause the dollar to appreciate against the euro or to depreciate?
   a. Health experts discover that red wine, especially French and Italian red wine, lowers cholesterol.
   b. GDP in nations across Europe falls.
   c. The United States experiences a higher inflation rate than Europe does.
   d. The U.S. budget deficit rises. (Hint: What happens to the U.S. interest rate?)

2. Let the monthly demand for British pounds and the monthly supply of British pounds be described by the following equations:

   $$\text{Demand for pounds} = 10 - 2e$$

   $$\text{Supply of pounds} = 4 + 3e$$

   where the quantities are in millions of pounds, and $e$ is dollars per pound.
   a. Find the equilibrium exchange rate.
   b. Suppose the U.S. government intervenes in the foreign currency market and uses U.S. dollars to buy 2 million pounds each month. What happens to the exchange rate? Why might the U.S. government do this?

3. Let the demand and supply of Philippine pesos each month be described by the following equations:

   $$\text{Demand for pesos} = 100 - 2000e$$

   $$\text{Supply of pesos} = 20 + 3000e$$

   where the quantities are millions of pesos, and $e$ is dollars per peso.
   a. Find the equilibrium exchange rate.
   b. Suppose the Philippine central bank wants to fix the exchange rate at 50 pesos per dollar and keep it there. Should the Philippine central bank buy or sell its own currency? How much per month?

4. Suppose the United States and Mexico are each other's sole trading partners. The Fed, afraid that the economy is about to overheat, raises the U.S. interest rate.
   a. Will the dollar appreciate or depreciate against the Mexican peso? Illustrate with a diagram of the dollar–peso foreign exchange market.
   b. What will happen to equilibrium GDP in the United States?
   c. How would your analyses in (a) and (b) change if, at the same time that the Fed was increasing the U.S. interest rate, the Mexican central bank increased the Mexican interest rate by an equivalent amount?

5. Jordan fixes its national currency—the dinar—against the dollar. In June 2006, the fixed rate was 1.41 dinars per dollar.
   a. Draw a diagram illustrating the market in which Jordanian dinars are traded for U.S. dollars, assuming that the equilibrium exchange rate is 1.00 dinar per dollar. (In your diagram, put the number of dinars per month on the horizontal axis.)
   b. Under the assumption in (a), would Jordan's central bank be buying or selling Jordanian dinars in this market? Indicate the number of dinars per month that the central bank must buy or sell as a distance on your graph.
   c. Based on your diagram and your answers so far, could Jordan continue to fix its currency at 1.41 dinars per dollar forever? Why or why not?
   d. Suppose that foreign currency traders believe that Jordan will soon allow the dinar to float. How would this affect the current supply and demand curves for dinars? (Draw new curves to indicate the impact.)
   e. How would the events in (d) affect the number of dinars that Jordan's central bank must buy or sell?

6. As in problem 5, note that Jordan fixes its national currency—the dinar—against the dollar at 1.41 dinars per dollar.
   a. Draw a diagram illustrating the market in which Jordanian dinars are traded for U.S. dollars, assuming that the equilibrium exchange rate is 2.00 dinars per dollar. (Put the number of dinars per month on the horizontal axis.)
   b. Under the assumption in (a), would Jordan's central bank be buying or selling Jordanian dinars in this market? Indicate the number of dinars per month that the central bank must buy or sell as a distance on your graph.
   c. Based on your diagram and your answers so far, could Jordan continue to fix its currency at 1.41 dinars per dollar forever? Why or why not?
   d. Suppose that foreign currency traders believe that Jordan will soon allow the dinar to float. How would this affect the current supply and demand curves for dinars? (Draw new curves to indicate the impact.)
   e. How would the events in (d) affect the number of dinars that Jordan's central bank must buy or sell?

7. Some nations that fix their exchange rates make their currency more expensive for foreigners (an overvalued currency), while others make their currency artificially cheap to foreigners (an undervalued currency).
   a. Why would a country want an overvalued currency? How, specifically, would the country benefit? Would the policy cause harm to anyone in the country? Explain briefly.
   b. Why would a country want an undervalued currency? How, specifically, would the country benefit? Would the policy cause harm to anyone in the country? Explain briefly.

8. If the inflation rate in Country A is 4 percent and the inflation rate in Country B is 6 percent, explain what will happen to the relative value of each country's currency.

9.  a. Use the information in the following table to find the exchange rate if the euro and the U.S. dollar are allowed to float freely.

| Dollars per Euro | Quantity of Euros Demanded | Quantity of Euros Supplied |
|---|---|---|
| $1.20 | 500 million | 2,600 million |
| $1.10 | 1,000 million | 2,400 million |
| $1.00 | 1,500 million | 2,200 million |
| $0.90 | 2,000 million | 2,000 million |
| $0.80 | 2,500 million | 1,800 million |

b. What will happen to the exchange rate if the demand for euros rises by 700 million at each price if there is no intervention?

c. Assume that the European central bank currently owns 400 million dollars and the Fed currently owns 300 million euros. If the demand for euros rises by 700 million at each price, what would the European central bank have to do to maintain a fixed exchange rate equal to the exchange rate you found in part (a)? Is this possible?

10. Refer to Figure 10 in the chapter. Remember that there was no trade deficit at point *A*. What is the U.S. trade deficit with Japan in *dollars* at point *B*?

## More Challenging

11. It is often stated that the U.S. trade deficit with Japan results from Japanese trade barriers against U.S. goods.

a.  Suppose that Japan and the United States trade goods but not assets. Show—with a diagram of the dollar–yen market—that a U.S. trade deficit is impossible as long as the exchange rate floats. (Hint: With no trading in assets, the quantity of yen demanded at each exchange rate is equal in value to U.S. imports, and the quantity of yen supplied at each exchange rate is equal in value to U.S. exports.)

b.  In the diagram, illustrate the impact of a reduction in Japanese trade barriers. Would the dollar appreciate or depreciate against the yen? What would be the impact on U.S. net exports?

c.  Now suppose that the United States and Japan also trade assets, but that the Japanese buy more U.S. assets than we buy of theirs. Could the elimination of Japanese trade barriers wipe out the U.S. trade deficit with Japan? Why, or why not? (Hint: What is the relationship between the U.S. trade deficit and U.S. net financial inflow?)

12. Suppose that the U.S. government raises spending without increasing taxes. Will there be any effects on the foreign exchange market? (Hint: What does this policy do to U.S. interest rates?) When we add in the effects from the foreign exchange market and net exports, is fiscal policy more effective or less effective in changing equilibrium GDP in the short run?

# CHAPTER 17

# Comparative Advantage and the Gains from International Trade

Consumers love bargains. And the rest of the world offers U.S. consumers bargains galore: cars from Japan, computer memory chips from Korea, shoes and clothing from China, tomatoes from Mexico, lumber from Canada, and sugar from the Caribbean. But Americans' purchases of foreign-made goods have always been a controversial subject. Should we let these bargain goods into the country? Consumers certainly benefit when we do so. But don't cheap foreign goods threaten the jobs of American workers and the profits of American producers? How do we balance the interests of specific workers and producers on the one hand with the interests of consumers in general? These questions are important not just in the United States, but in every country of the world.

Over the post–World War II period, there has been a worldwide movement toward a policy of *free trade*—the unhindered movement of goods and services across national boundaries. An example of this movement was the creation—in 1995—of a new international body: the World Trade Organization (WTO). The WTO's goal is to help resolve trade disputes among its members and to reduce obstacles to free trade around the world.

And to some extent it has succeeded: Import taxes, import limitations, and all kinds of crafty regulations designed to keep out imports are gradually falling away. Today, almost one-third of the world's production is exported to other countries. One hundred forty-nine countries have joined the WTO, including the most recent member, Saudi Arabia. Some 26 other countries, including Russia and Vietnam, are eager to join the free trade group.

But even though many barriers have come down, others remain—and new ones have come up. As of 2006, the United States was still refusing to eliminate its long-standing quota on sugar imports as well as more recent barriers to importing shrimp from Vietnam, Brazil, Thailand, and several other countries. The European Union continued to restrict the sale of U.S. beef, high-tech equipment, and entertainment programming. China was trying to keep out American-made automobile parts.

Looking at the contradictory mix of trade policies that exist in the world, we are left to wonder: Is free international trade a good thing that makes us better off, or is it bad for us and something that should be kept in check? In this chapter, you'll learn to apply the tools of economics to issues surrounding international trade. Most important, you'll see how we can extend economic analysis to a global context, in which markets extend across international borders.

# THE LOGIC OF FREE TRADE

Many of us like the idea of being self-reliant. A very few even prefer to live by themselves in a remote region of Alaska or the backcountry of Montana. But consider the defects of self-sufficiency: If you lived all by yourself, you would be poor. You could not *export* or sell to others any part of your own production, nor could you *import* or buy from others anything they have produced. You would be limited to consuming the goods and services that you produced. Undoubtedly, the food, clothing, and housing you would manage to produce by yourself would be small in quantity and poor in quality—nothing like the items you currently enjoy. And there would be many things you could not get at all—electricity, television, cars, airplane trips, or the penicillin that could save your life.

The defects of self-sufficiency explain why most people do not choose it. Rather, people prefer to specialize and trade with each other. In Chapter 2, you learned that specialization and exchange enable us to enjoy greater production and higher living standards than would otherwise be possible.

This principle applies not just to individuals, but also to *groups* of individuals, such as those living within the boundaries that define cities, counties, states, or nations. That is, just as we all benefit when *individuals* specialize and exchange with each other, so, too, we can benefit when *groups* of individuals specialize in producing different goods and services, and exchange them with other *groups*.

Imagine what would happen if the residents of your state switched from a policy of open trading with other states to one of self-sufficiency, refusing to import anything from "foreign states" or to export anything to them. Such an arrangement would be preferable to individual self-sufficiency; at least there would be specialization and trade *within* the state. But the elimination of trading between states would surely result in many sacrifices. Lacking the necessary inputs for their production, for instance, your state might have to do without bananas, cotton, or tires. And the goods that *were* made in your state would likely be produced inefficiently. For example, while residents of Vermont *could* drill for oil, and Texans *could* produce maple syrup, they could do so only at great cost of resources.

Thus, it would make no sense to insist on the economic self-sufficiency of each of the 50 states. And the founders of the United States knew this. They placed prohibitions against tariffs, quotas, and other barriers to interstate commerce right in the U.S. Constitution. The people of Vermont and Texas are vastly better off under free trade among the states than they would be if each state were self-sufficient.

What is true for states is also true for entire nations. The members of the WTO have carried the argument to its ultimate conclusion: National specialization and exchange can expand world living standards through free *international* trade. Such trade involves the movement of goods and services across national boundaries. Goods and services produced domestically, but sold abroad, are called **exports;** those produced abroad, but consumed domestically, are called **imports.** The long-term goal of the WTO is to remove all barriers to exports and imports in order to encourage among nations the specialization and trade that have been so successful within nations.

**Exports** Goods and services produced domestically, but sold abroad.

**Imports** Goods and services produced abroad, but consumed domestically.

## THE THEORY OF COMPARATIVE ADVANTAGE

In Chapter 2, you learned about absolute and comparative advantage for trade between individuals. Now we'll apply these concepts to trade between nations.

Economists who first considered the benefits of international trade focused on a country's absolute advantage. Using the definition from Chapter 2, but applying it to nations rather than individuals, we say that

> *A country has an absolute advantage in a good when it can produce it using* fewer resources *than another country.*

As the early economists saw it, the citizens of every nation could improve their economic welfare by specializing in the production of goods in which they had an absolute advantage and exporting them to other countries. In turn, they would import goods from countries that had an absolute advantage in those goods.

In 1817, however, the British economist David Ricardo disagreed. Absolute advantage, he argued, was not a necessary ingredient for mutually beneficial international trade. The key was *comparative advantage:*

> *A nation has a comparative advantage in producing a good if it can produce it at a* lower opportunity cost *than some other country.*

Notice the difference between the definitions of absolute advantage and comparative advantage. While absolute advantage in a good is defined by the resources used to produce it, comparative advantage is based on the *opportunity cost* of producing it. The opportunity cost of producing something is the *other goods* that these resources *could* have produced instead.

Ricardo argued that a potential trading partner could be absolutely inferior in the production of every single good—requiring more resources per unit of each good than any other country—and still have a comparative advantage in some good. The comparative advantage would arise because the country was *less* inferior at producing some goods than others. Likewise, a country that had an absolute advantage in producing everything could—contrary to common opinion—still benefit from trade. It would have a comparative advantage only in some, but not all, goods.

### DETERMINING COMPARATIVE ADVANTAGE

To illustrate Ricardo's insight, let's consider a hypothetical world that has only two countries: the United States and China. Both are producing only two goods: soybeans and T-shirts. And—to keep things as simple as possible—we'll imagine that these goods are being produced with just one resource: labor.

Table 1 shows the amount of labor, in hours, required to produce one bushel of soybeans or one T-shirt in each country. We assume that hours per unit remain *constant,* no matter how much of a good is produced. For example, the entry "5 hours" tells us that it takes 5 hours of labor to produce one bushel of soybeans in China. This will be true no matter how many bushels China produces.

In the table, we've given the United States an *absolute advantage* in producing both goods. That is, it takes fewer resources (less labor time) to produce either soybeans or T-shirts in the United States than in China. But—as you are about to see—China will still have a *comparative* advantage in one of these goods.

| Labor Requirements per: | United States | China |
|---|---|---|
| Bushel of soybeans | $\frac{1}{2}$ hour | 5 hours |
| T-shirt | $\frac{1}{4}$ hour | 1 hour |

**TABLE 1**

**Labor Requirements per Unit**

To determine comparative advantage, we'll use the information in Table 1 to calculate opportunity costs. Let's first find the opportunity cost of one more bushel of soybeans in the United States. In order to produce this bushel, the United States would have to divert a half hour of labor from making T-shirts. Since each T-shirt requires a $\frac{1}{4}$ hour of labor, taking away $\frac{1}{2}$ hour would reduce production of T-shirts by 2. Thus, the opportunity cost of one more bushel of soybeans in the United States is 2 T-shirts. This opportunity cost is recorded in Table 2; check the table and make sure you can find the entry.

Now let's do the same for China. There, producing an additional bushel of soybeans requires 5 hours of labor, which would have to be diverted from the T-shirt industry. Since each T-shirt requires 1 hour of labor in China, taking away 5 hours would mean 5 fewer T-shirts. Thus, in China, the opportunity cost of one bushel of soybeans is 5 T-shirts, which can also be found in Table 2.

Summing up, we see that the opportunity cost of a bushel of soybeans is 2 T-shirts in the United States and 5 T-shirts in China. Therefore, the United States—with the lower opportunity cost—has a comparative advantage in producing soybeans.

Notice that in Table 2, we do similar calculations for the opportunity cost of T-shirts, measuring the opportunity cost in terms of bushels of soybeans *foregone*. These computations are summarized in the last row of the table. Make sure you can use these numbers to verify that China has a comparative advantage in producing T-shirts.

Now we can use our conclusions about comparative advantage to show how both countries can gain from trade. The explanation comes in two steps. First, we show that if China could be persuaded to produce more T-shirts and the United States more soybeans, the world's total production of both goods will increase. Second, we show how each country can come out ahead by trading with the other.

## HOW SPECIALIZATION INCREASES WORLD PRODUCTION

Figure 1 shows production possibilities frontiers for the United States and China. In the left panel, we assume that the United States has 100 million hours of labor per year, which it must allocate between soybeans (on the horizontal axis) and T-shirts (on the vertical axis). To obtain the PPF for the United States, we first suppose that all 100 million hours of labor were allocated to T-shirts. The United States could then produce 400 million of them per year (because each one requires $\frac{1}{4}$ hour of

| Opportunity Costs per: | United States | China |
|---|---|---|
| Bushel of soybeans | 2 T-shirts | 5 T-shirts |
| T-shirt | $\frac{1}{2}$ bushel of soybeans | $\frac{1}{5}$ bushel of soybeans |

**TABLE 2**

**Opportunity Costs**

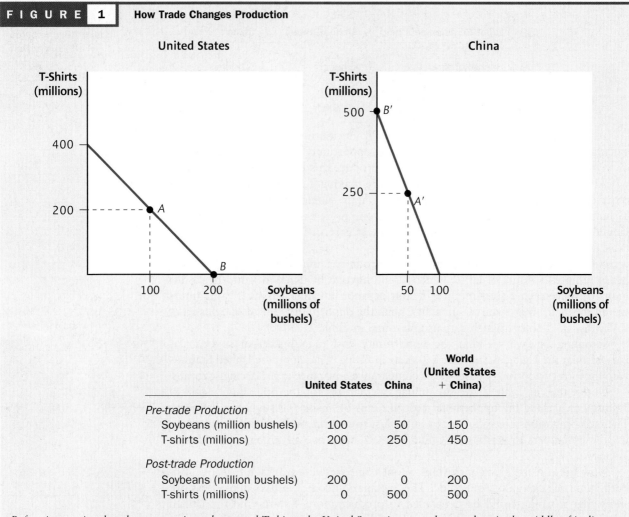

| F I G U R E   1 | How Trade Changes Production |

**United States**

T-Shirts (millions)

**China**

T-Shirts (millions)

|                                      | United States | China | World (United States + China) |
|--------------------------------------|:-------------:|:-----:|:-----------------------------:|
| *Pre-trade Production*               |               |       |                               |
|    Soybeans (million bushels) | 100 | 50 | 150 |
|    T-shirts (millions)        | 200 | 250 | 450 |
|                                      |               |       |                               |
| *Post-trade Production*              |               |       |                               |
|    Soybeans (million bushels) | 200 | 0 | 200 |
|    T-shirts (millions)        | 0 | 500 | 500 |

*Before international trade opens up in soybeans and T-shirts, the United States is assumed to produce in the middle of its linear PPF at point A, representing 100 million bushels of soybeans and 200 million T-shirts. Similarly, China is assumed to produce at point A', representing 50 million bushels of soybeans and 250 million T-shirts.*

*After trade, each country will completely specialize in its comparative advantage good. The United States will shift all resources into soybeans (200 million bushels) at point B, and China will put all resources into T-shirts (500 million) at point B'. The result is greater world production of both goods. World soybean production rises from 150 million to 200 million bushels, and world T-shirt production rises from 450 million to 500 million.*

labor). Accordingly, the upper-most point on the PPF represents 400 million T-shirts and zero bushels of soybeans.

To get the rest of the points, remember that the opportunity cost of one more bushel of soybeans is 2 T-shirts. Therefore, each time we move rightward by one unit (one more bushel), we must move downward by 2 units (2 fewer T-shirts). Accordingly, the PPF for the United States will be a straight line, with a slope of $-2$. The PPF ends where the United States would be allocating all of its 100 million hours to soybeans, producing 200 million bushels.

Notice that this PPF is a straight line, unlike the curved PPFs in Chapter 2. A linear PPF follows from our assumption that hours per unit—and therefore opportunity costs—remain constant no matter how much of either good is produced. Essentially, to keep things simple, we are assuming *constant opportunity costs*, rather than increasing opportunity cost as in the PPFs drawn in Chapter 2. (We'll discuss the implications of this in a few pages.)

The right panel shows China's PPF, under the assumption that China has 500 million hours of labor per year. On your own, be sure you can see how the two endpoints of China's PPF are determined. Also, be sure you understand why the slope of China's PPF will be −5. (Hint: What is the opportunity cost of another bushel of soybeans in China?)

Before international trade occurs, we assume (arbitrarily) that both countries are operating in the middle of their respective PPFs. The United States is at point *A*, producing 100 million bushels of soybeans and 200 million T-shirts each year. This combination of goods is also U.S. *consumption* per year: Without trade, you can only consume what you produce. In the right panel, China is at point *A'*, producing and consuming 50 million bushels of soybeans and 250 million T-shirts.

Now look at the table that accompanies the figure. The first two rows tell us the production of each good in each country before trade opens up, and also world production of each good. As you can see, with the United States producing at point *A* along its PPF and China producing at point *A'*, the world (the United States and China combined) produces 150 million bushels of soybeans and 450 million T-shirts per year.

Let's now see what happens to world *production* when trade opens up. We'll have each country devote *all* of its resources to the good in which it has a comparative advantage. The United States, with a comparative advantage in soybeans, moves to point *B* on its PPF, producing 200 million bushels of soybeans and zero T-shirts. China moves to point *B'* on its PPF, producing 500 million T-shirts and zero soybeans. The new production levels for each country are entered in the last two rows of the table in Figure 1.

Finally, look at the last column of numbers in the table. For both goods, world production has increased. Soybean output is up from 150 million to 200 million bushels, and T-shirt production is up from 450 million to 500 million. This increase in world production has been accomplished without adding any resources to either country. The world's resources are simply being used more efficiently.

Although our example has just two countries and two goods, it illustrates a broader conclusion:

> *When countries specialize according to their comparative advantage, the world's resources are used more efficiently, enabling greater production of every good.*

## HOW EACH NATION GAINS FROM INTERNATIONAL TRADE

Now let's show that both countries can gain from trade. As you've seen, when the two countries specialize in their comparative advantage good, they produce more of that good but none of the other. For example, China produces more T-shirts but no soybeans. However, by trading some of its comparative advantage good for the other good, each country can *consume* more of both goods.

Table 3 illustrates this conclusion. The first row of numbers shows how specialization has changed production in each country, based on the movement along the PPF in Figure 1. To get from changes in production to changes in consumption, we have to consider what each country is exporting and importing. The second row in the table shows one possible example. We suppose that the United States will exchange 80 million bushels of soybeans for 240 million T-shirts from China.

| **TABLE 3** | | United States | | | China | | |
|---|---|---|---|---|---|---|---|
| **The Gains from Specialization and Trade** | | Soybeans (million bushels) | T-Shirts (millions) | | Soybeans (million bushels) | T-Shirts (millions) | |
| Change in Production | | +100 | −200 | | −50 | +250 | |
| Exports (−) or Imports (+) | | −80 | +240 | | +80 | −240 | |
| Net Gain in Consumption | | +20 | +40 | | +30 | +10 | |

A country's exports are represented with a minus sign (they contribute negatively to consumption) and its imports with a plus sign (they add to consumption). The third row shows how consumption of each good changes after considering both production changes and international trade.

Let's first consider the United States. When it moved from point $A$ to point $B$ along its PPF, soybean production increased from 100 million to 200 million bushels—an increase of 100 million, hence the entry +100 in the first row. But it exported 80 million bushels (−80 in the second row), leaving the United States to consume 20 more bushels than it had before trade (+20 in the third row). Similarly, U.S. production of T-shirts decreased from 200 million to zero (−200), but the United States imports 240 million (+240), for a net gain of 40 million T-shirts (+40).

In China, soybean production has decreased by 50 million bushels (−50), but imports are 80 million. Therefore, China ends up with 30 million more bushels of soybeans. China has also increased production of T-shirts by 250 million, but exports 240 million of those, so it is left with 10 million more after trade.

These changes in consumption are illustrated Figure 2. Once again, we show the PPFs for the United States and China. But now we compare consumption in each country before trade with consumption *after* trade. The United States began with 100 million bushels of soybeans and 200 million T-shirts (point $A$). After specialization and trade, it moves to 120 million bushels of soybeans and 240 million T-shirts (point $C$). Similarly, China began by consuming 50 million bushels of soybeans and 250 million T-shirts (point $A'$). After specialization and trade, it consumes 80 million bushels of soybeans and 260 million T-shirts (point $C'$).

Notice that points $C$ and $C'$ lie *beyond* each country's PPF. While the PPF still shows possibilities for *production* of the two goods, *consumption* is no longer limited to what is produced. Instead, with trade, a country can consume more of both goods than it would be capable of producing and consuming on its own.

Let's take a step back and consider what we've discovered. First, look back at Table 1. Based on the required labor hours, the United States has an *absolute advantage* in both goods: It can produce both soybeans and T-shirts using fewer hours of labor than can China. But in Table 2, we saw that the United States has a *comparative advantage* in only *one* of these goods—soybeans—and China has a comparative advantage in the other—T-shirts. This is because the *opportunity costs* of each good differ in the two countries. Then, in Figure 1, we saw how world production of both goods increases when each country shifts its resources toward its comparative advantage good. Finally, in the last row of Table 3 and in Figure 2, we saw that *international trade* can enable *each* country to end up with more of *both* goods.

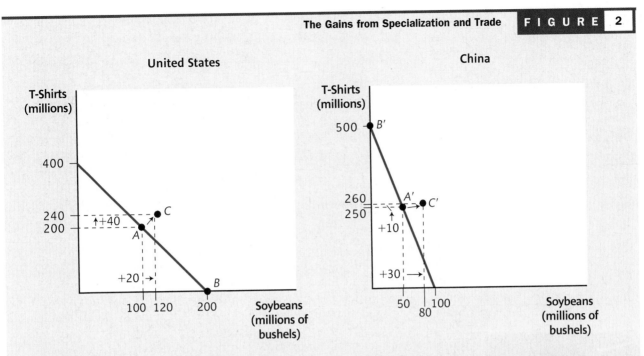

**The Gains from Specialization and Trade** FIGURE 2

With international trade, *the U.S. moves production from point A to point B, but consumes at point C—beyond its PPF. Soybean production increases from 100 million (at point A) to 200 million (at point B). After exporting 80 million bushels to China, the United States is left with 120 million (at point C), for a net gain of 20 million bushels. With terms of trade assumed to be 3 T-shirts for 1 bushel of soybeans, the United States trades its soybeans for 240 million T-shirts. United States T-shirt consumption rises from 200 million (point A) to 240 million (point C).*

*In China, production moves from point A' to point B', but consumption is at point C'. T-shirt production rises from 250 million (at point A') to 500 million (at point B'). After exporting 240 million T-shirts to the United States, China is left with 260 million (point C'), for a net gain of 10 million. China trades its T-shirts for 80 million bushels of soybeans from the United States, so China's soybean consumption rises from 50 million (at point A') to 80 million (at point C').*

*As long as opportunity costs differ, specialization and trade can be beneficial to all involved. This remains true whether the parties are different nations, different states, different counties, or different individuals. It remains true even if one party has an all-round absolute advantage or disadvantage.*

## THE TERMS OF TRADE

In our ongoing example, China exports 240 million T-shirts in exchange for 80 million bushels of soybeans. This exchange ratio (240 million to 80 million, or 3 to 1) is knows as the **terms of trade**—the quantity of one good that is exchanged for one unit of the other.

The terms of trade determine how the gains from international trade are *distributed* among countries. Our particular choice of 3 to 1 apportioned the gains as shown in the last row of Table 3. But with different terms of trade, the gains would have been apportioned differently. In the problems at the end of this chapter, you will be asked to recalculate the gains for each country with different terms of trade. You'll see that with different terms of trade, both countries still gain, but the distribution of the gains between countries changes.

**Terms of trade** The ratio at which a country can trade domestically produced products for foreign-produced products.

But notice that the terms of trade were not even *used* in our example until we arrived at Table 3. The gains from trade for the *world as a whole* were demonstrated in Figure 1, and were based entirely on the increase in world production when countries specialize according to comparative advantage.

> For the world as a whole, the gains from international trade are due to increased production as nations specialize according to comparative advantage. How *those* world gains are distributed among specific countries depends on the terms of trade.

We won't consider here precisely *how* the terms of trade are determined (it's a matter of supply and demand). But we *will* establish the limits within which the terms of trade must fall.

Look again at Table 2. China would never give up *more* than 5 T-shirts to import 1 bushel of soybeans. Why not? Because it could always get a bushel for 5 T-shirts *domestically*, simply by shifting resources into soybean production.

Similarly, the United States would never export a bushel of soybeans for *fewer* than 2 T-shirts because it could get 2 T-shirts for a bushel domestically (again, by shifting resources). Therefore, when these two nations trade, we know the terms of trade will lie *somewhere between* 5 T-shirts for 1 bushel and 2 T-shirts for 1 bushel. Outside of that range, one of the two countries would refuse to trade. Note that in our example, we assume terms of trade of 3 T-shirts for 1 bushel—well within the acceptable range.

## SOME PROVISOS ABOUT SPECIALIZATION

Our simple example seems to suggest that countries should specialize *completely*, producing *only* the goods in which they have a comparative advantage. That is, it seems that China should get out of soybean production *entirely*, and the United States should get out of T-shirt production *entirely*.

The real world, however, is more complicated than our simplified example might suggest. Despite divergent opportunity costs, sometimes it does *not* make sense for two countries to trade with each other, or it might make sense to trade, but *not* completely specialize. Following are some real-world considerations that can lead to reduced trade or incomplete specialization.

### Costs of Trading

If there are high transportation costs or high costs of making deals across national boundaries, trade may be reduced and even become prohibitively expensive. High transportation costs are especially important for perishable goods, such as ice cream, which must be shipped frozen, and most personal services, such as haircuts, eye exams, and restaurant meals. These goods are less subject to trade according to comparative advantage. (Imagine the travel cost for a U.S. resident to see an optometrist in China, where eye exams are less expensive.)

The costs of making deals are generally higher for international trade than for trade within domestic borders. For one thing, different laws must be dealt with and different business and marketing customs must be mastered. In addition, international trade involves the exchange of one country's currency for another. This can introduce additional costs and risks that don't exist for domestic trade, because exchange rates can change before a contract is settled with payment. High trans-

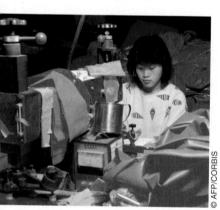

Countries can gain when they shift production toward their comparative advantage goods (such as textiles in China), and trade them for other goods from other countries.

portation costs and high costs of making deals help explain why nations continue to produce some goods in which they do not have a comparative advantage and why there is less than complete specialization in the world.

### Sizes of Countries

Our earlier example featured two large economies capable of fully satisfying each other's demands. But sometimes a very large country, such as the United States, trades with a very small one, such as the Pacific island nation of Tonga. If the smaller country specialized completely, its output would be insufficient to fully meet the demand of the larger one. While the smaller country would specialize *completely*, the larger country would not. Instead, the larger country would continue to produce both goods. This helps to explain why the United States continues to produce bananas, even though we do so at a much higher opportunity cost than many small Latin American nations.

### Increasing Opportunity Cost

In all of our tables, we have assumed that opportunity cost remains constant as production changes. For example, in Table 2, the opportunity cost of a bushel of soybeans remains at 2 T-shirts for the United States, regardless of how many bushels it produces. But more typically, the opportunity cost of a good rises as more of it is produced. (Why? You may want to review the law of increasing opportunity cost in Chapter 2.) In that case, each step on the road to specialization would change the opportunity cost. A point might be reached—before complete specialization—in which opportunity costs became *equal* in the two countries, and there would be no further mutual gains from trading. (Remember: Opportunity costs must *differ* between the two countries in order for trade to be mutually beneficial.) In the end, while trading will occur, there will not be complete specialization. Instead, each country will produce both goods, just as China and the United States each produce T-shirts *and* soybeans in the real world.

### Government Barriers to Trade

Governments can enact barriers to trading. In some cases, these barriers increase trading costs; in other cases, they make trade impossible. Since this is such an important topic, we'll consider government-imposed barriers to trade in a separate section, later in the chapter.

## THE SOURCES OF COMPARATIVE ADVANTAGE

We've just seen how nations can benefit from specialization and trade when they have comparative advantages. But what determines comparative advantage in the first place?

In many cases, the answer is the *resources* a country has at its disposal.

*A country that has relatively large amounts of a particular resource at its disposal will tend to have a comparative advantage in goods that make heavy use of that resource.*

This is most easy to see when the relevant resources are *gifts of nature*, such as a specific natural resource or a climate especially suited to a particular product.

| TABLE 4 | | |
|---|---|---|
| **Examples of National Specialties in International Trade** | **Country** | **Specialization Resulting from Natural Resources or Climate** |
| | Saudi Arabia | Oil |
| | Canada | Timber |
| | United States | Grain |
| | Spain | Olive oil |
| | Mexico | Tomatoes |
| | Jamaica | Aluminum ore |
| | Italy | Wine |
| | Israel | Citrus fruit |
| | Niger | Uranium |
| | **Country** | **Specialization *Not* Based on Natural Resources or Climate** |
| | Japan | Cars, consumer electronics |
| | United States | Software, movies, music, aircraft |
| | Switzerland | Watches |
| | Korea | Cars, steel, ships |
| | China | Textiles, toys, shoes |
| | Great Britain | Financial services |
| | Pakistan | Textiles |

The top part of Table 4 contains some examples. Saudi Arabia has a comparative advantage in the production of oil because it has oil fields with billions of barrels of oil that can be extracted at low cost. The United States' comparative advantage in crops such as wheat and soybeans is partly explained by its abundant farmland. Canada is a major exporter of timber because its climate and geography make its land more suitable for growing trees than other crops. Canada is a good example of comparative advantage without absolute advantage: It grows a lot of timber, not because it can do so using fewer resources than other countries, but because its land is even more poorly suited to growing other things.

But now look at the bottom half of Table 4. It shows examples of international specialization that arise from some cause *other* than natural resources. Japan has a strong comparative advantage in making automobiles. Yet none of the *natural* resources needed to make cars are available in Japan; the iron ore, coal, and oil needed to produce cars are all imported.

What explains the cases of comparative advantage in the bottom half of Table 4? In part, it is due to resources *other* than natural resources or climate. The United States is rich in both physical capital and human capital. As a result, the United States tends to have a comparative advantage in goods and services that make heavy use of computers, tractors, and satellite technology, as well as goods that require highly skilled labor. This, in part, explains the U.S. comparative advantage in the design and production of aircraft, a good that makes heavy use of physical capital (such as computer-based design systems) and human capital (highly trained engineers).

In less developed countries, by contrast, capital and skilled labor are relatively scarce, but less-skilled labor is plentiful. Accordingly, these countries tend to have a comparative advantage in products that make heavy use of less-skilled labor, such as textiles and light manufacturing. Note, however, that as a country develops—and acquires more physical and human capital—its pattern of comparative advantage can change. Japan, Korea, and Singapore, after a few decades of very rapid development, acquired a comparative advantage in several goods that, at one time, were specialties of the United States and Europe—including automobiles, steel, and sophisticated consumer electronics.

But another aspect of the bottom half of Table 4 is harder to explain: Why do specific countries develop a *particular* specialty? For example, if you think you know why Japan dominates the world market for VCRs and other consumer electronics—say, some unique capacity to mass-produce precision products—be sure you can explain why Japan is a distant second in computer printers. The company that dominates the market for printers—Hewlett Packard—is a U.S. firm.

Similarly, we take the worldwide dominance of American movies for granted. But if you try to explain it based on the availability of resources like physical capital or highly skilled labor, or cultural traditions that encouraged artists, writers, or actors, then why not Britain or France? At the time the film industry developed in the United States, these two countries had similar endowments of physical and human capital, and much older and stronger theatrical traditions than the United States. Yet their film industries—in spite of massive government subsidies—are a very distant second and third compared to that of the United States.

In even the most remote corner of the world, the cars, cameras, and VCRs will be Japanese, the movies and music American, the clothing from Hong Kong or China, and the bankers from Britain. These specialties are certainly *consistent* with the capital and other resources each nation has at its disposal, but explaining why each *specific* case of comparative advantage arose in the first place is not easy.

We can, however, explain why a country *retains* its comparative advantage once it gets started. Japan today enjoys a huge comparative advantage in cars and consumer electronics in large part because it has accumulated a capital stock—both physical capital and human capital—well suited to producing those goods. The physical capital stock includes the many manufacturing plants and design facilities that the Japanese have built over the years.

But Japan's human capital is no less important. Japanese managers know how to anticipate the features that tomorrow's buyers of cars and electronic products will want around the world. And Japanese workers have developed skills adapted for producing these products. The stocks of physical and human capital in Japan sustain its comparative advantage just as stocks of natural resources lead to comparative advantages in other countries. More likely than not, Japan will continue to have a comparative advantage in cars and electronics, just as the United States will continue to have a comparative advantage in making movies.

> *Countries often develop strong comparative advantages in the goods they have produced in the past, regardless of why they began producing those goods in the first place.*

## WHY SOME PEOPLE OBJECT TO FREE TRADE

Given the clear benefits that nations can derive by specializing and trading, why would anyone ever *object* to free international trade? Why do the same governments that join the WTO turn around and create roadblocks to unhindered trade? The answer is not too difficult to find: Despite the benefit to the nation as a whole, some groups within the country, in the short run, are likely to lose from free trade, even while others gain a great deal more. Unfortunately, instead of finding ways to compensate the losers—to make them better off as well—we often allow them to block free trade policies. The simple model of supply and demand helps illustrate this story.

Figure 3 shows the market for shrimp in the United States. Both the supply and demand curve in the figure represent the *domestic* market only. That is, the supply curve tells us the quantity supplied at each price by U.S. producers; the demand curve tells us quantity demanded at each price by U.S. consumers. With no international trade in shrimp, the U.S. market would achieve equilibrium at point *A*, at a price of $7 per pound. This relatively high price reflects the relatively high opportunity cost of producing shrimp in the United States. Both production and consumption would be 400 million pounds per year.

The United States does not have a comparative advantage in shrimp. Other countries that *do* have a comparative advantage (such as Vietnam, Thailand, and Brazil) would like to sell it to us. Moreover, because their opportunity cost of producing shrimp is less than in the United States, their price tends to be lower as well. Let's suppose that the *world price* of shrimp—the price at which other countries offer to sell it to Americans—is $3 per pound. To keep our example simple, we'll also assume this price remains constant, no matter how much shrimp Americans buy from the rest of the world. (In effect, we're assuming that under international trade, the United States would be a relatively small buyer in a much larger world market.)

Now let's open up free trade in shrimp. Because Americans can buy unlimited quantities of imported shrimp at $3, domestic producers will have to lower their price to $3 as well in order to sell any. So the price of *all* shrimp in the U.S. market falls to $3 per pound—the same as the world price.

As the price drops, two things happen. On the one hand, we move along the demand curve from point *A* to point *C*: U.S. consumers buy more shrimp (900 million pounds) because it is cheaper. On the other hand, we move along the supply curve from point *A* to point *B*: U.S. producers decrease their quantity supplied (to

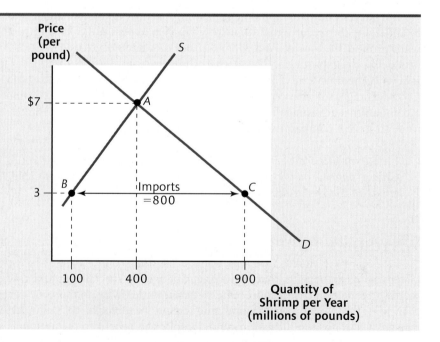

**FIGURE 3**

**The Impact of Trade**

*With no international trade, equilibrium in the U.S. market for shrimp is at point A, where domestic quantity supplied equals domestic quantity demanded. Price is $7 per pound, and 400 million pounds are consumed each year.*

*When U.S. consumers can import shrimp at the lower world price of $3.00 per pound, quantity supplied falls to 100 million pounds, while quantity demanded rises to 900 million. The difference—800 million pounds—is imports from the world market.*

*Consumers of shrimp gain from trade—they enjoy a greater quantity at a lower price. But producers lose—they sell less at a lower price.*

100 million pounds). The difference between domestic supply of 100 million and domestic demand of 900 million is the amount of shrimp the United States imports each year: 800 million pounds.

You've already learned (in the last section) that international trade according to comparative advantage makes a country better off: It increases total world production and enables consumers to enjoy greater quantities of goods and services. But not *everyone* is better off. It is easy to figure out who will be happy and who will be unhappy in the United States. American consumers are delighted: They are buying more shrimp at a lower price. American producers are miserable: They are selling less shrimp at a lower price.

> *International trade makes each country, as a whole, better off. But not everyone gains, because cheap imports from abroad—while beneficial to domestic consumers—are harmful to domestic producers.*

## THE ANTITRADE BIAS AND SOME ANTIDOTES

Imagine that a bill comes before Congress to prohibit or restrict the sale of cheap shrimp from abroad, so that its U.S. price can rise above $3.00. Domestic producers would favor the bill. Domestic consumers would oppose it. But not with equally loud voices. After all, the harm to consumers from this restriction of trade would be spread widely among *all* U.S. consumers. The loss to any individual would be very small. For example, if the total loss to U.S. consumers were $200 million per year, the total harm to any single consumer would be less than a dollar. As a result, no individual consumer of shrimp has a strong incentive to lobby Congress, or to join a dues-paying organization that would act on behalf of shrimp consumers to oppose this antitrade bill.

By contrast, the benefits from this restriction of trade would be highly concentrated on a much smaller group of people: those who work in or own firms in the domestic shrimp industry. They have a powerful incentive to lobby against free trade in shrimp. Not surprisingly, when it comes to trade policy, the voices raised *against imports* are loud and clear, while those *for imports* are often nonexistent. Since a country has the power to restrict imports from other countries, the lobbying can—and often does—lead to a restriction on free trade. The United States, for example, continues to restrict imports of shrimp from low-cost producers, largely due to powerful lobbying by the U.S. shrimp industry.

A similar process works against U.S. *exports* to other countries. In this case, the foreign producers who would have to compete with U.S. goods will complain loudest, while foreign consumers who stand to gain will be mostly silent. The U.S. exporters—who are not constituents of these foreign governments—will have little influence in the debate. Thus, just as there is a policy bias against U.S. imports in the United States, there is a policy bias against U.S. exports in other countries.

> *The distribution of gains and losses creates a policy bias against free trade. Consumers who benefit from buying a specific product have little incentive to lobby for imports of that product. But domestic producers harmed by the imports have a powerful incentive to lobby against them.*

There are, however, three antidotes to this policy bias.

## All or Nothing Trade Agreements

In a bilateral or multilateral trade agreement, two or more countries agree to trade freely in many goods—or even all goods—simultaneously. These agreements are typically negotiated by government officials and then presented to legislatures as "all-or-nothing" deals: The agreement must be approved or rejected as a whole, without any amendments that make exceptions for specific industries.

Such agreements can bring in another constituent to lobby for free trade: *exporters* in both countries. Ordinarily, exporters have no ability to influence the debate because their ability to export is decided in the *importing* country, where they have little influence. But in an all-or-nothing free trade deal, they can lobby their *own* country to allow imports as a way of enabling them to sell their exports. In this way, a balance of forces is created. Domestic producers threatened by imports will lobby against trade agreements in each country. But potential exporters will lobby just as strongly *for* the agreement.

An example was the North American Free Trade Agreement (NAFTA) between the United States, Canada, and Mexico, which went into effect in 1994, and has eliminated barriers on most products produced by the three nations. NAFTA was hotly opposed in all three countries by many producers and some labor unions who stood to lose from imports, but was just as hotly favored by producers and workers who stood to gain from exports. (The biggest gainers—consumers in the three countries—were hardly involved in the debate, for reasons we've discussed.)

More recently, a similar conflict arose over the Dominican Republic–Central American Free Trade Agreement (DR-CAFTA). In each country (including the U.S.) producers who would have to compete with imports lobbied against the bill, while exporters in each country lobbied for it. In mid-2005, the U.S. Congress narrowly approved the agreement; by mid-2006, most of the other countries involved had given their approval as well.

## The World Trade Organization

Another antidote to antitrade bias is the World Trade Organization. By setting standards for acceptable and unacceptable trade restrictions and making rulings in specific cases, the WTO has some power to influence nations' trade policies. But its influence is limited because the WTO has no enforcement power. For example, the WTO has ruled several times against European trade barriers against U.S. beef, with little effect. Still, a negative WTO ruling puts public relations pressure on a country, and allows a nation harmed by restrictions on its exports to retaliate, in good conscience, with its own trade barriers.

## Industries as Consumers

Whenever we use the word *consumer*, we naturally think of a household buying products for its own enjoyment. But the term can apply to any buyer of a product, including a firm that uses it as an input. If these firms are among the "consumers" who benefit from cheaper imports, and if the good is an important part of these firms' costs, they have an incentive to lobby for free trade in the good. For example, in late 2004, the textile industry lobbied the Bush administration to slow the rise in clothing imports from China. But U.S. clothing retailers and importers—for whom clothing is an input—lobbied strongly *against* any trade barriers. While the retailers and importers ultimately lost the battle in May 2005, their opposition delayed the restrictions for months and influenced the final policy adopted.

# HOW FREE TRADE IS RESTRICTED

So far in this chapter, you've learned that specialization and trade according to comparative advantage can dramatically improve the well-being of entire nations. This is why governments generally favor free trade. Yet international trade can, in the short run, hurt particular groups of people. These groups often lobby their government to restrict free trade.

When governments decide to accommodate the opponents of free trade, they are apt to use one of two devices to restrict trade: tariffs or quotas.

## TARIFFS

A **tariff** is a tax on imported goods. It can be a fixed dollar amount per physical unit, or it can be a percentage of the good's value. In either case, the effect in the tariff-imposing country is similar.

**Tariff** A tax on imports.

Figure 4 illustrates the effect of a U.S. tariff of $2 per pound on imported shrimp. Before the tariff is imposed, the price of shrimp under free trade is the world price: $3 per pound. The U.S. imports 800 million pounds per year (the distance *BC*). When the tariff is imposed, U.S. importers must still pay the same $3 per pound to their foreign suppliers. But now they must also pay $2 per pound to the U.S. government. Thus, the price of imported shrimp will rise from $3 to $5 per pound to cover the additional cost of the tariff.[1]

The higher price for imported shrimp allows U.S. producers to charge $5 for their domestic shrimp as well. As the price of shrimp rises, domestic quantity supplied

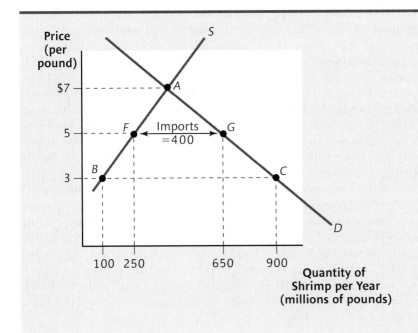

**FIGURE 4**

**The Effects of a Tariff**

*With free trade in shrimp, the price in the United States is the same as the world price: $3.00 per pound. U.S. imports are equal to the distance from B to C, 800 million pounds per year.*
*A tariff of $2.00 per pound raises the price of imported shrimp to $5.00 per pound, and the price of domestically produced shrimp rises to the same level. Domestic quantity supplied increases from 100 million to 250 million (the move from A to B), while domestic quantity demanded falls from 900 million to 650 million (the move from C to G). The result is lower imports of 400 million pounds. Domestic suppliers gain from the tariff: They sell more shrimp at a higher price. But domestic consumers lose: They pay a higher price and consume less.*

[1] If the United States is a large buyer in the world market for shrimp, the reduction in imports caused by the tariff would cause the world price to fall. This would change the quantitative results in our example. However, the price in the United States would still rise above $3.00, and all of our conclusions about the impact of tariffs would still hold.

increases (a movement along the supply curve from point *B* to point *F*). At the same time, domestic quantity demanded *decreases* (a movement along the demand curve from point *C* to point *G*). The final result is a reduction in imports, from 800 million before the tariff to 400 million after the tariff.

As you can see, American consumers are worse off: They pay more for shrimp and enjoy less of it. But U.S. producers are better off: They sell more shrimp at a higher price.

But we also know this: Since the volume of trade has decreased, the gains from trade according to comparative advantage have been reduced as well. The United States, as a whole, is worse off as a result of the tariff.

> *Tariffs reduce the volume of trade and raise the domestic prices of imported goods. In the country that imposes the tariff, producers gain, but consumers lose. The country as a whole loses, because tariffs decrease the volume of trade and therefore decrease the gains from trade.*

## QUOTAS

**Quota** A limit on the physical volume of imports.

A **quota** is a government decree that limits the imports of a good to a specified maximum physical quantity, such as 400 million pounds of shrimp per year. Because the goal is to restrict imports, a quota is set below the level of imports that would occur under free trade. Its general effects are very similar to the effects of a tariff.

Figure 4, which we used to illustrate tariffs, can also be used to analyze the impact of a quota. In the figure, we start with our free trade price of $3. Consumers are buying 900 million pounds, and domestic producers are selling 100 million pounds per year. The difference of 800 million pounds is satisfied by imports.

Now suppose the United States imposes a quota of 400 million pounds (equal to the distance *FG* in the figure). At $3 per pound, the gap between the domestic supply curve and the domestic demand curve would still be 900 million pounds, which is more than the 400 million pounds of foreign shrimp allowed into the country. There is an excess demand for shrimp, which drives up the price. The price will keep rising until the gap between the supply and demand curves shrinks to the quantity allowed under the quota. As you can see in the figure, only when the price rises to $5 would the gap shrink to 400 million pounds. Thus, a quota of 400 million gives us exactly the same result as did a tariff of $2: In both cases, the price rises to $5, and yearly imports shrink to 400 million pounds.

The previous discussion seems to suggest that tariffs and quotas are pretty much the same. But even though the price and level of imports may end up being the same, there is one important difference between these two trade-restricting policies. A tariff, after all, is a *tax* on imported goods. Therefore, when a government imposes a tariff, it collects some revenue every time a good is imported. Even though the country loses from a tariff, it loses a bit less (compared to a quota) because at least it collects some revenue from the tariff. This revenue can be used to fund government programs or reduce other taxes, to the benefit of the country as a whole. When a government imposes a quota, however, it typically gains no revenue at all.

> *Quotas have effects similar to tariffs: They reduce the quantity of imports and raise domestic prices. While both measures help domestic producers, they reduce the benefits of trade to the nation as a whole. However, a tariff has one saving grace: increased government revenue.*

Economists, who generally oppose measures such as quotas and tariffs to restrict trade, argue that, if one of these devices must be used, tariffs are the better choice. While both policies reduce the gains that countries can enjoy from specializing and trading with each other, the tariff provides some compensation in the form of additional government revenue.

# PROTECTIONISM

This chapter has outlined the *gains* that arise from international trade, but it has also outlined some of the *pain* trade can cause to different groups within a country. While the country as a whole benefits, those who own or work in firms that have to compete with cheap imports will be harmed. The groups who suffer from trade with other nations have developed a number of arguments against free trade. Together, these arguments form a position known as **protectionism**—the belief that a nation's industries should be *protected* from free trade with other nations.

**Protectionism** The belief that a nation's industries should be protected from foreign competition.

## PROTECTIONIST MYTHS

Some protectionist arguments are rather sophisticated and require careful consideration. We'll consider some of these a bit later. But antitrade groups have also promulgated a number of myths to support their protectionist beliefs. Let's consider some of these myths.

**Myth #1** "A HIGH-WAGE COUNTRY CANNOT AFFORD FREE TRADE WITH A LOW-WAGE COUNTRY. THE HIGH-WAGE COUNTRY WILL EITHER BE UNDERSOLD IN EVERYTHING AND LOSE ALL OF ITS INDUSTRIES, OR ELSE ITS WORKERS WILL HAVE TO ACCEPT EQUALLY LOW WAGES AND EQUALLY LOW LIVING STANDARDS."

It's true that some countries have much higher wages than others. Here are 2004 figures for average hourly wages of manufacturing workers, including benefits such as holiday pay and health insurance: Germany, $32.53; United States, $23.17; Japan, $21.90; Italy, $20.48; Korea, $11.52; Singapore, $7.45; Brazil, $3.03; Mexico, $2.50; and less than a dollar in China, India, and Bangladesh. This leads to the fear that the poorer countries will be able to charge lower prices for their goods, putting American workers out of jobs unless they, too, agree to work for low wages.

But this argument is incorrect, for two reasons. First, it is true that American workers are paid more than Chinese workers, but this is because the average American worker is more *productive* than his or her Chinese counterpart. After all, the American workforce is more highly educated, and American firms provide their workers with more sophisticated machinery than do Chinese firms. If an American can produce more output than a Chinese worker in an hour, then even though wage rates in the United States may be greater, cost *per unit* produced can still be lower in the United States.

But suppose the cost per unit *were* lower in China. Then there is still another, more basic argument against the fear of a general job loss or falling wages in the United States: comparative advantage. Let's take an extreme case. Suppose that labor productivity were the same in the United States and China, so that China—with lower wages—could produce *everything* more cheaply than the United States could. Both countries would still gain if China specialized in products in which its cost advantage was relatively large and the United States specialized in goods in which China's cost advantage was relatively small. That is, the United States would still have a comparative advantage in some things and there would be mutual gains from trade.

**Myth #2** "A LOW-PRODUCTIVITY COUNTRY CANNOT AFFORD FREE TRADE WITH A HIGH-PRODUCTIVITY COUNTRY. THE FORMER WILL BE CLOBBERED BY THE LATTER AND LOSE ALL OF ITS INDUSTRIES."

This argument is the flip side of the first myth. Here, it is the poorer, less-developed country that is supposedly harmed by trade with a richer country. But this myth confuses absolute advantage with comparative advantage. Suppose the high-productivity country (say, the United States) could produce *every* good with fewer resources than the low-productivity country (say, China). Once again, the low-productivity country would *still* have a comparative advantage in *some* goods. It would then gain by producing those goods and trading with the high-productivity country. This is the case in our hypothetical example that began with Table 1. In that example, the United States has an absolute advantage in both goods, yet—as we've seen—trade still benefits both countries.

To make the point even clearer, let's bring it closer to home. Suppose there is a small, poor town in the United States where workers are relatively uneducated and work with little capital equipment, so their productivity is very low. Would the residents of this town be better off sealing their borders and not trading with the rest of the United States, which has higher productivity? Before you answer, think what this would mean: The residents of the poor town would have to produce everything on their own: grow their own food, make their own cars and television sets, and even provide their own entertainment. Clearly, they would be worse off in isolation. And what is true *within* a country is also true *between* different countries: Closing off trade will make a nation, as a whole, worse off, regardless of its level of wages or productivity. Even a low-productivity country is made better off by trading with other nations.

**Myth #3** INTERNATIONAL TRADE DECREASES THE TOTAL NUMBER OF JOBS IN A COUNTRY. It is true that a sudden opening up of trade temporarily disrupts markets. There can even be a temporary drop in employment as jobs are lost in some sectors before they are created in other sectors. But neither logic nor observation supports the view that international trade causes any long-lasting drop in total employment. In the United States, for example, as international trade has expanded rapidly in recent decades, total employment has risen steadily. And the U.S. unemployment rate has trended downward, not upward.

This myth about losses in total employment comes from looking at only one side of the international trade coin: imports. It is true that international trade destroys jobs in those industries that now have to compete with cheaper imports from abroad. But trade also creates *new* jobs in the export sector. When trade is balanced—exports and imports are equal—there is no reason to expect the jobs lost in the import-competing sector to exceed the jobs gained in the export sector.

What about when trade is unbalanced, as when a country runs a *trade deficit* (the value of imports exceeds the value of exports)? Even in this case, there is no reason for total employment to decrease. The United States has run a trade deficit every year for decades: We spend more dollars buying imports from other countries than they return to us by buying our products. As a result, producers in these other countries start to pile up dollar balances. But they don't just hold onto these dollar balances, which pay no interest or other return. Instead, they invest these dollars in U.S. financial markets, purchasing stocks and bonds and making bank deposits. The funds are then lent out to U.S. firms and households who, in turn, spend them—on new capital equipment, new housing construction, or other things. In this way, while some jobs are lost when Americans spend their dollars on imports rather than U.S. goods, other jobs are created when the dollars flow back into the U.S. through the financial markets. A trade deficit can cause other problems for a country (as you will learn when you study macroeconomics), but it does not reduce total employment.

**Myth #4** "IN RECENT TIMES, THE DECLINING WAGES OF AMERICA'S UNSKILLED WORKERS ARE DUE TO EVER-EXPANDING TRADE BETWEEN THE UNITED STATES AND OTHER COUNTRIES." True enough, unskilled workers have lost ground over the past 25 years. College graduates have enjoyed growing purchasing power from their earnings, while those with only a high school education or less have lost purchasing power. Rising trade with low-wage countries has been blamed for this adverse trend.

But before we jump to conclusions, let's take a closer look. Our discussion earlier in this chapter tells us where to look for effects that come through trade. If the opening of trade has harmed low-skilled workers in the United States, it would have done so by lowering the prices of products that employ large numbers of those workers. A study taking this approach found almost no change in the relative prices of products in the United States that employ large numbers of unskilled workers. Studies that take other approaches have found only modest effects. In general, economists who have looked at the impact of trade on U.S. labor markets have concluded that foreign trade is a small contributor to the depressed earnings of low-wage workers. A much more important factor is technological change, and the greater skills needed to work with new technologies.[2]

## SOPHISTICATED ARGUMENTS FOR PROTECTION

While most of the protectionist arguments we read in the media are based on a misunderstanding of comparative advantage, some more recent arguments for protecting domestic industries are based on a more sophisticated understanding of how markets work. These arguments have become collectively known as *strategic trade policy*. According to its proponents, a nation can gain in some circumstances by assisting certain *strategic industries* that benefit society as a whole, but that may not thrive in an environment of free trade.

Strategic trade policy is most effective in situations where a market is dominated by a few large firms. With few firms, the forces of competition—which ordinarily reduce profits in an industry to very low levels—will not operate. Therefore, each firm in the industry may earn high profits. These profits benefit not only the owners of the firm but also the nation more generally, since the government will be able to capture some of the profit with the corporate profits tax. When a government helps an industry compete internationally, it increases the likelihood that high profits—and the resulting general benefits—will be shifted from a foreign country to its own country. Thus, interfering with free trade—through quotas, tariffs, or even a direct subsidy to domestic firms—might actually benefit the country.

An argument related to strategic trade policy is the **infant industry argument.** This argument begins with a simple observation: In order to enjoy the full benefits of trade, markets must allocate resources toward those goods in which a nation has a comparative advantage. This includes not only markets for resources such as labor

**Infant industry argument** The argument that a new industry in which a country has a comparative advantage might need protection from foreign competition in order to flourish.

[2] See, for example, Gary Burtless, Robert Lawrence, Robert Litan, and Robert Shapiro, *Globaphobia: Confronting Fears About Free Trade* (Washington, DC: The Brookings Institution Press, 1998). See also the recent survey by Bernard Hoekman and L. Alan Winters, "Trade and Employment: Stylized Facts and Research Findings," mimeo, World Bank Development Research Group, March 2005.

and land, but also *financial markets,* where firms obtain funds for new products. But in some countries—especially developing countries—financial markets do not work very well. Poor legal systems or incomplete information about firms and products may prevent a new industry from obtaining financing, even though the country would have a comparative advantage in that industry once it was formed. In this case, protecting the infant industry from foreign competition may be warranted until the industry can stand on its own feet.

Strategic trade policy and support for infant industries are controversial. Opponents of these ideas stress three problems:

1. Once the principle of government assistance to an industry is accepted, special-interest groups of all kinds will lobby to get the assistance, whether it benefits the general public or not.
2. When one country provides assistance to an industry by keeping out foreign goods, other nations may respond in kind. If they respond with tariffs and quotas of their own, the result is a shrinking volume of world trade and falling living standards. If subsidies are used to support a strategic industry, and another country responds with its own subsidies, then both governments lose revenue, and neither gains the sought-after profits.
3. Strategic trade policy assumes that the government has the information to determine which industries, infant or otherwise, are truly strategic and which are not.

Still, the arguments related to strategic trade policy suggest that government protection or assistance *may* be warranted in some circumstances, even if putting this support into practice proves difficult. Moreover, the arguments help to remind us of the conditions under which free trade is most beneficial to a nation:

> *Production is most likely to reflect the principle of comparative advantage when firms can obtain funds for investment projects and when they can freely enter industries that are profitable. Thus, free trade, without government intervention, works best when markets are working well.*

This may explain, in part, why the United States, where markets function relatively well, has for decades been among the strongest supporters of the free trade ideal.

## PROTECTIONISM IN THE UNITED STATES

Americans can enjoy the benefits of importing many of the products listed in Table 4: olive oil from Spain, watches from Switzerland, tomatoes from Mexico, cars and VCRs from Japan. But on the other side of the ledger, U.S. consumers have suffered and U.S. producers have gained from some persistent barriers to trade. Table 5 lists some examples of American protectionism—through tariffs, quotas, or similar policies—that have continued for years.

As you can see, protection is costly. Quotas and tariffs on apparel and textiles, the most costly U.S. trade barrier, force American consumers to pay $33.6 billion more for clothes each year. And while protection saves an estimated 168,786 workers in this industry from having to make the painful adjustment of finding other work, it does so at an annual cost of $199,241 per worker. Both workers and consumers could be made better off if textile workers were paid any amount up to $199,241 *not* to work and consumers were allowed to buy inexpensive textiles from abroad.

| | TABLE 5 |
|---|---|
| | Some Examples of U.S. Protectionism |

| Protected Industry | Annual Cost to Consumers | Number of Jobs Saved | Annual Cost per Job Saved |
|---|---|---|---|
| Apparel and Textiles | $33,629 million | 168,786 | $ 199,241 |
| Maritime Services | $ 2,522 million | 4,411 | $ 571,668 |
| Sugar | $ 1,868 million | 2,261 | $ 826,104 |
| Dairy Products | $ 1,630 million | 2,378 | $ 685,323 |
| Softwood Lumber | $ 632 million | 605 | $1,044,271 |
| Women's Nonathletic Footwear | $ 518 million | 3,702 | $ 139,800 |
| Glassware | $ 366 million | 1,477 | $ 247,889 |
| Luggage | $ 290 million | 226 | $1,285,078 |
| Peanuts | $ 74 million | 397 | $ 187,223 |

*Source: The Fruits of Free Trade, Federal Reserve Bank of Dallas, Annual Report, 2002, Exhibit 11.*

In some cases, the cost per job saved is staggering. The table shows that trade barriers preventing Americans from buying inexpensive luggage save just a couple of hundred jobs, at a yearly cost of more than $1 million each. Trade barriers on sugar are almost as bad: While 2,261 jobs are saved, the annual cost per job is $826,104.

In addition to the dozens of industries in the United States permanently protected from foreign competition, dozens more each year are granted temporary protection when the U.S. government finds a foreign producer or industry guilty of *dumping*— selling their products in the United States at "unfairly" low prices that harm a U.S. industry. Most economists believe that these low prices are most often the result of comparative advantage, and that the United States as a whole would gain from importing the good. Vietnam, for example, has a clear comparative advantage in producing shrimp. But in 2005, based on a complaint by the Southern Shrimp Alliance, the U.S. government imposed tariffs of up to 26 percent on Vietnamese shrimp.

In the Using the Theory section that follows, we take a closer look at one of the longest-running examples of protectionism in the United States.

# USING THE THEORY

## The U.S. Sugar Quota[3]

The United States has protected U.S. sugar producers from foreign competition since the 1930s. Since the 1980s, the protection has been provided in the form of a price guarantee. Essentially, the government has promised U.S. sugar beet and sugar cane producers and processors that they can sell their sugar at a predetermined price—22 cents a pound— regardless of the world price of sugar.

© RICHARD LORD/PHOTOEDIT, INC.

[3] Information in this section is based on: Mark A. Groombridge, "America's Bittersweet Sugar Policy," *Trade Briefing Paper No. 13*, Cato Institute, December 4, 2001; Lance Gay, "Soured on Sugar Prices, Candy Makers Leave the U.S.," *Scripps Howard News Service*, June 18, 2003; "Closing the 'Stuffed Molasses' Loophole," *White Paper*, United States Sugar Corporation (*http://www.ussugar.com/pressroom/white_papers/stuffed_molasses.html*); and Remy Jurenas, "Sugar Policy Issues," *CRS Issue Brief for Congress*, Congressional Research Service, February 16, 2006.

This may not sound like a high price for sugar. But in the rest of the world, people and businesses can buy sugar for a lot less. From 2000 to 2005, the world price of sugar has averaged about 9 cents a pound, while Americans have continued to pay 22 cents. Even in 1985, when the world price of sugar plunged to just 4 cents a pound—a bonanza for sugar buyers around the world—American buyers were not invited to the party: The United States price remained at 22 cents.

Because the world price of sugar is so consistently below the U.S. price, the government cannot keep its promise to support sugar prices while simultaneously allowing free trade in sugar. With free trade, the price of sugar in the United States would plummet. The government's solution is a sugar quota. More accurately, the government decides how much foreign sugar it will allow into the United States each year, free of any tariff; all sugar beyond the allowed amount is hit with a heavy tariff of about 16 cents a pound. Since the tariff is so high, no one in the United States imports sugar beyond the allowed amount. So, in effect, the United States has a sugar quota.

The *primary* effects of the sugar quota are on sugar producers and sugar consumers. As you've learned, an import quota raises the domestic price of sugar (the quota's purpose). Sugar producers benefit. But sugar consumers are hurt even more.

And the harm is substantial. Table 5 shows that American consumers pay almost $2 billion more each year for sugar and products containing sugar due to the sugar quota. But spread widely over the U.S. population, this amounts to less than $15 per person per year. This probably explains why you haven't bothered to lobby for free trade in sugar.

But the costs of the sugar quota go beyond ordinary consumers. Industrial sugar users—such as the ice cream industry—are affected by the higher price too, not all of which can be passed on to consumers. So they try to avoid the quota's harm in other ways. One way is to waste resources buying sugar abroad disguised as other products. In the late 1990s and early 2000s, U.S. firms bought about 125,000 tons of sugar each year mixed with molasses, which was not restricted by the sugar quota. The sugar was then separated from the molasses. Even with these additional (and wasteful) processing costs, it was still a better deal to buy the disguised sugar abroad than to buy it through regular channels in the United States.

And sometimes a firm decides it's just not worth it anymore. In June 2003, Lifesavers was added to the list of other candy and baked-goods manufacturers who simply gave up trying to buy sugar in the United States, and moved their production facilities to Canada. In Canada, which doesn't have a quota, sugar can be purchased at the lower, world price.

Taxpayers, too, pay a cost for the sugar quota because as part of its price support program, the U.S. government must occasionally buy excess sugar from producers. In 2005, the U.S. government was storing about 759,000 tons of sugar at a cost of more than $1 million per month. The government must also hire special agents to detect and prevent sugar from entering the country illegally.

A final cost of the sugar quota is one that we have not yet considered in our discussion of international trade. In Figure 4, when a U.S. tariff or quota caused imports to shrink, we assumed that the world price of the good remained unchanged. But when a country is a very large buyer in the world market, a reduction in its purchases can cause the world price to drop. Essentially, the quota—by keeping sugar out—causes greater quantities of sugar to be dumped onto the world market, depressing its price. This hurts the poorest countries in the world that rely on sugar as an important source of export revenue. The sugar quota's harm to these countries has been estimated at about $1.5 billion per year.

Why do we bear all of these costs? Because of lobbying by groups who enjoy highly concentrated benefits. There are about 13,000 sugar farms in the United States. When the $2 billion in additional spending by U.S. consumers is spread among this small number of farms, the additional revenue averages out to more than $150,000 per farm per year. Those benefits are sizable enough to mobilize sugar producers each time their protection is threatened.

And mobilize they do. In 2004, the United States negotiated a free trade agreement with Australia that eliminated barriers on almost every good or service . . . except sugar. In 2005, the United States approved DR-CAFTA—a free trade agreement with five Central American countries and the Dominican Republic. Once again, sugar was an exception: Additional sugar imports from all six countries combined were restricted to less than 2 percent of the U.S. market.

There is another group that receives concentrated benefits from the sugar quota: producers of high-fructose corn syrup, the closest substitute for sugar. Because of the sugar quota, high-fructose corn syrup can be sold at a substantially higher price.

Not surprisingly, the largest producer of high-fructose corn syrup in the U.S. market—the Archer Daniels Midland (ADM) company—has funded organizations that lobby Congress and try to sway public opinion in the United States. Occasionally, you may see a full-page newspaper advertisement paid for by one of these groups, arguing that sugar in the United States is cheap. And it is . . . until you find out what the country next door is paying.

## Summary

A country has a *comparative advantage* in a good when it can produce it at a lower opportunity cost than another country. When countries specialize in the production of their comparative advantage goods, world production rises. Both countries benefit as consumption rises in each country. The distribution of the benefits between countries depends on the *terms of trade*—the rate at which the imported goods are traded for the exported goods.

Despite the benefits to each nation as a whole, those who supply goods that must compete with cheaper imports are harmed. Because the gains from trade are spread widely while the harm is concentrated among a smaller number of people, the latter have an incentive to lobby against free trade. Those harmed often encourage government to block or reduce trade through the use of *tariffs* (taxes on imported goods) and *quotas* (limits on the volume of imports).

A variety of arguments have been proposed in support of protectionism. Some are clearly invalid and fail to recognize the principle that both sides gain when countries trade according to their comparative advantage. More sophisticated arguments for restricting trade may have merit in certain circumstances. These include strategic trade policy—the notion that governments should assist certain strategic industries—and the idea of protecting infant industries when financial markets are imperfect.

## Problem Set  *Answers to even-numbered Questions and Problems can be found on the text Web site at www.thomsonedu.com/economics/hall.*

1. Suppose that the costs of production of winter hats and wheat in two countries are as follows:

   |  | United States | Russia |
   | --- | --- | --- |
   | Per winter hat | $10 | 5,000 rubles |
   | Per bushel of wheat | $1 | 2,500 rubles |

   a. What is the opportunity cost of producing one more winter hat in the United States? In Russia?
   b. What is the opportunity cost of producing one more bushel of wheat in the United States? In Russia?
   c. Which country has a comparative advantage in winter hats? In wheat?

2. Suppose that the Marshall Islands does not trade with the outside world. It has a competitive domestic market for

VCRs. The market supply and demand curves are reflected in this table:

| Price ($/VCR) | Quantity Demanded | Quantity Supplied |
|---|---|---|
| 500 | 0 | 500 |
| 400 | 100 | 400 |
| 300 | 200 | 300 |
| 200 | 300 | 200 |
| 100 | 400 | 100 |
| 0 | 500 | 0 |

a. Plot the supply and demand curves and determine the domestic equilibrium price and quantity.

b. Suddenly, the islanders discover the virtues of free exchange and begin trading with the outside world. The Marshall Islands is a very small country, and so its trading has no effect on the price established in the world market. It can import as many VCRs as it wishes at the world price of $100 per VCR. In this situation, how many VCRs will be purchased in the Marshall Islands? How many will be produced there? How many will be imported?

c. After protests from domestic producers, the government decides to impose a tariff of $100 per imported VCR. Now how many VCRs will be purchased in the Marshall Islands? How many will be produced there? How many will be imported?

d. What is the government's revenue from the tariff described in part (c)?

e. Compare the effect of the tariff described in part (c) with a quota that limits imports to 100 VCRs per year.

3. The following table gives information about the supply and demand for beef in the European Union. The prices are in euros, and quantities are millions of pounds of beef per month. (You may wish to draw the supply and demand curves to help you visualize what is happening.)

| Price | Quantity Supplied | Quantity Demanded |
|---|---|---|
| 0 | 0 | 160 |
| 2 | 20 | 140 |
| 4 | 40 | 120 |
| 6 | 60 | 100 |
| 8 | 80 | 80 |
| 10 | 100 | 60 |
| 12 | 120 | 40 |

a. In the absence of international trade, what is the equilibrium price and quantity of beef?

b. If trade opens up, and the world price of beef is (and remains) 2 euros per pound of beef, how much beef will EU producers supply? How much beef will EU consumers demand? How much beef will be imported?

c. Within the EU, who gains and who loses when trade opens up?

4. Using the data on supply and demand in problem 3, suppose the EU imposed a tariff of 2 euros on each pound of beef.

a. How much beef would EU producers supply?

b. How much beef would EU consumers demand?

c. How much beef would the EU import?

d. How much total revenue would EU government authorities collect from the tariff?

5. Using the data on supply and demand in problem 3, suppose the EU imposed a quota on imports of beef equal to 40 million pounds of beef per month.

a. What would be the price of beef in the EU?

b. How much beef would EU producers supply?

c. How much beef would EU consumers demand?

6. Refer to Table 3 in the chapter. Suppose the terms of trade are *two and a half* T-shirts for each bushel of soybeans (instead of three for one as in the chapter). As in the chapter, assume the United States increases soybean production by 100 million bushels and exports 80 million of them to China, and that China decreases its own soybean production by 50 million bushels. Some of the remaining numbers in the table will have to change to be consistent with these new specifications. Then, answer each of the following questions.

a. Does China still gain from trade? Explain briefly.

b. Does the United States still gain from trade? Explain briefly.

c. Compare the effects of trade for China under the new and old terms of trade. In which case does China fare better? Explain briefly.

d. Compare the effects of trade for the United States under the new and old terms of trade. In which case does the United States fare better? Explain briefly.

7. Refer to Table 3 in the chapter. Suppose the terms of trade are *four* T-shirts for each bushel of soybeans (instead of three for one as in the chapter). Assume the United States increases soybean production by 100 million bushels and exports 60 million to China. China increases its T-shirt production by 250 million. Some of the remaining numbers in the table will have to change, to be consistent with these new specifications. Then, answer each of the following

questions.

a. Does China still gain from trade? Explain briefly.

b. Does the United States still gain from trade? Explain briefly.

c. Compare the effects of trade for China under the new and old terms of trade. In which case does China fare better? Explain briefly.

d. Compare the effects of trade for the United States under the new and old terms of trade. In which case does the United States fare better? Explain briefly.

8. Redraw the PPFs for the United States and China from Figure 2 in the chapter. Assume that the initial production and consumption points ($A$ and $A'$) and the new production points ($B$ and $B'$) are the same as in that figure. Plot the new consumption points ($C$ and $C'$) that correspond to your results from the previous problem (7).

9. The following table shows the hypothetical labor requirements per ton of wool and per hand-knotted rug, for New Zealand and for India.

**Labor Requirements per Unit**

|  | New Zealand | India |
| --- | --- | --- |
| Per ton of wool | 10 hours | 40 hours |
| Per hand-knotted rug | 60 hours | 80 hours |

a. Which country has an absolute advantage in each product?

b. Calculate the opportunity cost in each country for each of the two products. Which country has a comparative advantage in each product?

c. If India produces one more rug and exports it to New Zealand, what is the lowest price (measured in tons of wool) that it would accept? What is the highest price that New Zealand would pay? Within what range will the equilibrium terms of trade lie?

10. Using the data from problem 9, suppose that New Zealand has 300 million hours of labor per period, while India has 800 million hours.

a. Draw PPFs for both countries for the two goods (put quantity of wool on the vertical axis).

b. Suppose that, before trade, each country uses half of its labor to produce wool and half to produce rugs. Locate each country's production point on its PPF (label it $A$ for New Zealand, and $A'$ for India).

c. After trade opens up and each country specializes in its comparative advantage good, locate each country's production point on its PPF (label it $B$ for New Zealand, and $B'$ for India).

## More Challenging

11. This problem uses the data from problem 9, and the graphs you drew in problem 10. Suppose that the terms of trade end up at 4 tons of wool for 1 hand-knotted rug. Suppose, too, that New Zealand decides to export 12 million tons of wool to India.

a. How many rugs will New Zealand import from India?

b. What will be New Zealand's consumption of each good after trade?

c. What will be India's consumption of each good after trade?

d. On the PPFs you drew for problem 10, plot each country's consumption point after trade. Label it $C$ for New Zealand, and $C'$ for India.

12. In Figures 3 and 4, we assumed that the world price of a good was fixed, and not affected by the quantity of imports a country chooses. But if a country is large relative to the world market, its imports can influence the world price.

Suppose the market for good X involves only two large countries (A and B), with supply and demand schedules as shown below:

| Country A | | | Country B | | |
| --- | --- | --- | --- | --- | --- |
| Price per Unit of Good X (measured in dollars) | Quantity Demanded of Good X | Quantity Supplied of Good X | Price per Unit of Good X (measured in dollars) | Quantity Demanded of Good X | Quantity Supplied of Good X |
| $10 | 1 | 25 | $10 | 5 | 11 |
| 9 | 2 | 22 | 9 | 6 | 10 |
| 8 | 3 | 19 | 8 | 7 | 9 |
| 7 | 4 | 16 | 7 | 8 | 8 |
| 6 | 5 | 13 | 6 | 9 | 7 |
| 5 | 6 | 10 | 5 | 10 | 6 |
| 4 | 7 | 7 | 4 | 11 | 5 |
| 3 | 8 | 4 | 3 | 12 | 4 |

a. Plot the supply and demand curves for each country.

b. Before international trade, what is the equilibrium price and quantity in each country?

*For the remaining questions, assume that the two countries can trade in good X.*

c. Which country will export good X?

d.  What will be the equilibrium world price? (Hint: This will be the price at which the quantity of exports from one country equals the quantity of imports to the other.)

e.  What will happen to production and consumption in Country A?

f.  What will happen to production and consumption in Country B?

g.  What quantity will be exported (and also imported) in equilibrium?

h.  On your graph, label the new levels of production and consumption in each country, as well as distances representing exports and imports.

# Glossary

## A

**Absolute advantage** The ability to produce a good or service, using fewer resources than other producers use.

**Aggregate demand (AD) curve** A curve indicating equilibrium GDP at each price level.

**Aggregate expenditure (AE)** The sum of spending by households, business firms, the government, and foreigners on final goods and services produced in the United States.

**Aggregate production function** The relationship showing how much total output can be produced with different quantities of labor, with quantities of all other resources held constant.

**Aggregate supply (AS) curve** A curve indicating the price level consistent with firms' unit costs and markups for any level of output over the short run.

**Aggregation** The process of combining different things into a single category.

**Alternate goods** Other goods that a firm could produce, using some of the same types of inputs as the good in question.

**Alternate market** A market other than the one being analyzed in which the same good could be sold.

**Appreciation** An increase in the price of a currency in a floating-rate system.

**Automatic stabilizers** Forces that reduce the size of the expenditure multiplier and diminish the impact of spending shocks.

**Autonomous consumption spending** The part of consumption spending that is independent of income; also the vertical intercept of the consumption function.

**Average standard of living** Total output (real GDP) per person.

**Average tax rate** The fraction of a given income paid in taxes.

## B

**Balance sheet** A financial statement showing assets, liabilities, and net worth at a point in time.

**Banking panic** A situation in which depositors attempt to withdraw funds from many banks simultaneously

**Bond** A promise to pay back borrowed funds, issued by a corporation or government agency.

**Boom** A period of time during which real GDP is above potential GDP.

**Budget deficit** The excess of government purchases over net taxes.

**Budget surplus** The excess of net taxes over government purchases.

**Business cycles** Fluctuations in real GDP around its long-term growth trend.

**Business demand for funds curve** Indicates the level of investment spending firms plan at various interest rates.

## C

**Capital** Something produced that is long-lasting and used to produce other goods.

**Capital gains tax** A tax on profits earned when a financial asset is sold at more than its acquisition price.

**Capital per worker** The total capital stock divided by total employment.

**Capital stock** The total value of all goods that will provide useful services in future years.

**Capitalism** A type of economic system in which most resources are owned privately.

**Cash in the hands of the public** Currency and coins held outside of banks.

**Central bank** A nation's principal monetary authority responsible for controlling the money supply.

**Ceteris paribus** Latin for "all else remaining the same."

**Change in demand** A shift of a demand curve in response to a change in some variable other than price.

**Change in quantity demanded** A movement along a demand curve in response to a change in price.

**Change in quantity supplied** A movement along a supply curve in response to a change in price.

**Change in supply** A shift of a supply curve in response to some variable other than price.

**Circular flow** A simple model that shows how goods, resources, and dollar payments flow between households and firms.

**Classical model** A macroeconomic model that explains the long-run behavior of the economy.

**Command or centrally planned economy** An economic system in which resources are allocated according to explicit instructions from a central authority.

**Communism** A type of economic system in which most resources are owned in common.

**Comparative advantage** The ability to produce a good or service at a lower opportunity cost than other producers.

**Complement** A good that is used together with some other good.

**Complete crowding out** A dollar-for-dollar decline in one sector's spending caused by an increase in some other sector's spending.

**Consumer Price Index** An index of the cost, through time, of a fixed market basket of goods purchased by a typical household in some base period.

**Consumption (C)** The part of GDP purchased by households as final users.

**Consumption function** A positively sloped relationship between real consumption spending and real disposable income.

**Consumption tax** A tax on the part of their income that households spend.

**Consumption-income line** A line showing aggregate consumption spending at each level of income or GDP.

**Corporate profits tax** A tax on the profits earned by corporations.

**Countercyclical fiscal policy** A change in government purchases or net taxes designed to reverse or prevent a recession or a boom.

**Critical assumption** Any assumption that affects the conclusions of a model in an important way.

**Crowding out** A decline in one sector's spending caused by an increase in some other sector's spending.

**Cyclical deficit** The part of the federal budget deficit that varies with the business cycle.

**Cyclical unemployment** Joblessness arising from changes in production over the business cycle.

## D

**Deflation** A *decrease* in the price level from one period to the next.

**Demand curve** The graphical depiction of a demand schedule; a curve showing the quantity of a good or service demanded at various prices, with all other variables held constant.

**Demand curve for foreign currency** A curve indicating the quantity of a specific foreign currency that Americans will want to buy, during a given period, at each different exchange rate.

**Demand deposit multiplier** The number by which a change in reserves is multiplied to determine the resulting change in demand deposits.

**Demand deposits** Checking accounts that do not pay interest.

**Demand schedule** A list showing the quantities of a good that consumers would choose to purchase at different prices, with all other variables held constant.

**Demand shock** Any event that causes the *AD* curve to shift.

**Demand-side effects** Macroeconomic policy effects on total output that work through changes in total spending.

**Depreciation** A decrease in the price of a currency in a floating-rate system.

**Depression** An unusually severe recession.

**Devaluation** A change in the exchange rate from a higher fixed rate to a lower fixed rate.

**Discount rate** The interest rate the Fed changes on loans to banks.

**Discouraged workers** Individuals who would like a job, but have given up searching for one.

**Disposable income** Household income minus net taxes, which is either spent or saved.

## E

**Economic growth** The increase in our production of goods and services that occurs over long periods of time.

**Economic system** A system of resource allocation and resource ownership.

**Economics** The study of choice under conditions of scarcity.

**Employment–population ratio (EPR)** The percentage of the population that wants to be working.

**Entrepreneurship** The ability and willingness to combine the other resources—labor, capital, and natural resources—into a productive enterprise.

**Equilibrium GDP** In the short run, the level of output at which output and aggregate expenditure are equal.

**Equilibrium price** The market price that, once achieved, remains constant until either the demand curve or supply curve shifts.

**Equilibrium quantity** The market quantity bought and sold per period that, once achieved, remains constant until either the demand curve or supply curve shifts.

**Excess demand** At a given price, the excess of quantity demanded over quantity supplied.

**Excess demand for bonds** The amount of bonds demanded exceeds the amount supplied at a particular interest rate.

**Excess reserves** Reserves in excess of required reserves.

**Excess supply** At a given price, the excess of quantity supplied over quantity demanded.

**Excess supply of money** The amount of money supplied exceeds the amount demanded at a particular interest rate.

**Exchange** The act of trading with others to obtain what we desire.

**Exchange rate** The amount of one currency that is traded for one unit of another currency.

**Expansion** A period of increasing real GDP.

**Expenditure approach** Measuring GDP by adding the value of goods and services purchased by each type of final user.

**Expenditure multiplier** The amount by which equilibrium real GDP changes as a result of a one-dollar change in autonomous consumption, investment spending, government purchases, or net exports.

**Explicit cost** The dollars sacrificed-and actually paid out—for a choice.

**Exports** Goods and services produced domestically, but sold abroad.

**F**

**Factor payments** Payments to the owners of resources that are used in production

**Factor payments approach** Measuring GDP by summing the factor payments earned by all households in the economy.

**Federal funds rate** The interest rate charged for loans of reserves among banks.

**Federal Open Market Committee** A committee of Federal Reserve officials that established U.S. monetary policy.

**Federal Reserve System** The monetary authority of the United States, charged with creating and regulating the nation's supply of money.

**Fiat money** Something that serves as a means of payment by government declaration.

**Final good** A good sold to its final user.

**Financial intermediary** A business firm that specializes in brokering between savers and borrowers.

**Fiscal policy** A change in government purchases or net taxes designed to change total output.

**Fixed exchange rate** A government-declared exchange rate maintained by central bank intervention in the foreign exchange market.

**Floating exchange rate** An exchange rate that is freely determined by the forces of supply and demand.

**Flow variable** A variable measuring a process over some period

**Foreign currency crisis** A loss of faith that a country can prevent a drop in its exchange rate, leading to a rapid depletion of its foreign currency (e.g., dollar) reserves.

**Foreign exchange market** The market in which one country's currency is traded for another country's.

**Frictional unemployment** Joblessness experienced by people who are between jobs or who are just entering or reentering the labor market.

**Full employment** A situation in which there is no cyclical unemployment.

**G**

**GDP price index** An index of the price level for all final goods and services included in GDP.

**Government demand for funds curve** Indicates the amount of government borrowing at various interest rates.

**Government purchases (G)** Spending by federal, state, and local governments on goods and services.

**Gross domestic product (GDP)** The total value of all final goods and services produced for the marketplace during a given year, within the nation's borders.

**Growth equation** An equation showing the percentage growth rate of output as the sum of the growth rates of productivity, average hours, the employment–population ratio, and population.

**H**

**(Household) saving** The portion of after-tax income that households do not spend on consumption.

**Human capital** The skills and training of the labor force.

**I**

**Imperfectly competitive market** A market in which a single buyer or seller has the power to influence the price of the product.

**Implicit cost** The value of something sacrificed when no direct payment is made.

**Imports** Goods and services produced abroad, but consumed domestically.

**Income** The amount that a person or firm earns over a particular period.

**Index** A series of numbers used to track a variable's rise or fall over time.

**Indexation** Adjusting the value of some nominal payment in proportion to a price index, in order to keep the real payment unchanged.

**Indexed payment** A payment that is periodically adjusted in proportion with a price index.

**Infant industry argument** The argument that a new industry in which a country has a comparative advantage might need protection from foreign competition in order to flourish.

**Inferior good** A good that people demand less of as their income rises.

**Inflation rate** The percent change in the price level from one period to the next.

**Injections** Spending from sources other than households.

**Input** Anything (including a resource) used to produce a good or service.

**Intermediate goods** Goods used up in producing final goods.

**International Monetary Fund (IMF)** An international organization founded in 1945 to help stabilize the world monetary system.

**Investment tax credit** A reduction in taxes for firms that invest in capital.

**Involuntary part-time workers** Individuals who would like a full-time job, but who are working only part time.

# L

**Labor** The time human beings spend producing goods and services.

**Labor demand curve** Indicates how many workers firms will want to hire at various real wage rates.

**Labor force** Those people who have a job or who are looking for one.

**Labor productivity** The output produced by the average worker in an hour.

**Labor supply curve** Indicates how many people will want to work at various real wage rates.

**Land** The physical space on which production takes place, as well as the natural resources that come with it.

**Law of demand** As the price of a good increases, the quantity demanded decreases.

**Law of supply** As the price of a good increases, the quantity supplied increases.

**Leakages** Income earned, but not spent, by households during a given year.

**Liquidity** The property of being easily converted into cash.

**Loan** An agreement to pay back borrowed funds, signed by a household or noncorporate business.

**Loanable funds market** The market in which households make their saving available to borrowers.

**Long-run aggregate supply curve** A vertical line indicating all possible output and price-level combinations at which the economy could end up in the long run.

**Long-run Phillips curve** A vertical line indicating that in the long run, unemployment must equal its natural rate, regardless of the rate of inflation.

# M

**M1** A standard measure of the money supply, including cash in the hands of the public, checking account deposits, and travelers checks.

**M2** M1 plus savings account balances, noninstitutional money market mutual fund balances, and small time deposits.

**Macroeconomics** The study of the behavior of the overall economy.

**Managed float** A policy of frequent central bank intervention to move the exchange rate.

**Marginal propensity to consume** The amount by which consumption spending rises when disposable income rises by one dollar.

**Marginal tax rate** The fraction of an additional dollar of income paid in taxes.

**Market** A group of buyers and sellers with the potential to trade with each other.

**Market clearing** Adjustment of prices until quantities supplied and demanded are equal.

**Market economy** An economic system in which resources are allocated through individual decision making.

**Means of payment** Anything acceptable as payment for goods and services.

**Microeconomics** The study of the behavior of individual households, firms, and governments; the choices they make; and their interaction in specific markets.

**Model** An astract representation of reality.

**Monetary policy** Control or manipulation of the money supply by the Federal Reserve designed to achieve a macroeconomic goal.

**Money** An asset widely accepted as a means of payments.

**Money demand curve** A curve indicating how much money will be willingly held at each interest rate.

**Money supply** The total amount of money held by the public.

**Money supply curve** A line showing the total quantity of money in the economy at each interest rate.

**Moral hazard** When decision makers—expecting assistance in the event of an unfavorable outcome—change their behavior so that the unfavorable outcome is more likely.

# N

**National debt** The total amount the federal government still owes to the general public from past borrowing.

**Natural rate of unemployment** The unemployment rate when there is no cyclical unemployment.

**Net exports** (*NX*) Total exports minus total imports.

**Net financial inflow** An inflow of funds equal to a nation's trade deficit.

**Net investment** Investment minus depreciation.

**Net taxes** Government tax revenues minus transfer payments.

**Net worth** The difference between assets and liabilities.

**Nominal interest rate** The annual percent increase in a lender's dollars from making a loan.

**Nominal variable** A variable measured without adjustment for the dollar's changing value.

**Nonmarket production** Goods and services that are produced but not sold in a market.

**Normal good** A good that people demand more of as their income rises.

**Normative economics** The study of what *should be*; it is used to make judgments about the economy and prescribe solutions.

# O

**Open market operations** Purchases or sales of bonds by the Federal Reserve System.

**Opportunity cost** What is given up when taking an action or making a choice.

# P

**Patent protection** A government grant of exclusive rights to use or sell a new technology.

**Perfectly competitive market** A market in which no buyer or seller has the power to influence the price.

**Phillips curve** A curve indicating the Fed's choice between inflation and unemployment in the short run.

**Physical capital** The part of the capital stock consisting of physical goods, such as machinery, equipment, and factories.

**Planned investment spending** Business purchases of plant and equipment.

**Positive economics** The study of how the economy works.

**Potential output** The level of output the economy could produce if operating at full employment.

**Price** The amount of money that must be paid to a seller to obtain a good or service.

**Price level** The average level of dollar prices in the economy.

**Private investment (I)** The sum of business plant, equipment, and software purchases, new-home construction, and inventory changes; often referred to as just investment.

**Production possibilities frontier (PPF)** A curve showing all combinations of two goods that can be produced with the resources and technology currently available.

**Productively inefficient** A situation in which more of at least one good can be produced without sacrificing the production of any other good.

**Progressive tax** A tax whose rate increases as income increases.

**Protectionism** The belief that a nation's industries should be protected from foreign competition.

**Purchasing power parity (PPP) theory** The idea that the exchange rate will adjust in the long run so that the average price of goods in two countries will be roughly the same.

# Q

**Quantity demanded** The amount of a good that all buyers in a market would choose to buy during a period of time, given their constraints.

**Quantity supplied** The specific amount of a good that all sellers in the market would choose to sell over some time period, given (1) a particular price for the good; (2) all other constraints on firms.

**Quota** A limit on the physical volume of imports.

# R

**Real interest rate** The annual percent increase in a lender's purchasing power from making a loan.

**Real variable** A variable adjusted for changes in the dollar's value.

**Recession** A period of significant decline in real GDP.

**Regressive tax** A tax that collects a lower percentage of income as income rises.

**Required reserve ratio** The minimum fraction of checking account balances that banks must hold as reserves.

**Required reserves** The minimum amount of reserves a bank must hold, depending on the amount of its deposit liabilities.

**Reserves** Vault cash plus balances held at the Fed.

**Resource allocation** A method of determining which goods and services will be produced, how they will be produced, and who will get them.

**Resource markets** Markets in which households that own resources sell them to firms.

**Resources** The labor, capital, land and natural resources, and entrepreneurship that are used to produce goods and services.

**Run on the bank** An attempt by many of a bank's depositors to withdraw their funds.

# S

**Say's law** The idea that total spending will be sufficient to purchase the total output produced.

**Scarcity** A situation in which the amount of something available is insufficient to satisfy the desire for it.

**Seasonal unemployment** Joblessness related to changes in weather, tourist patterns, or other seasonal factors.

**Self-correcting mechanism** The adjustment process through which price and wage changes return the economy to full-employment output in the long run.

**Short-run macro model** A macroeconomic model that explains how changes in spending can affect real GDP in the short run.

**Short-run macroeconomic equilibrium** A combination of price level and GDP consistent with both the *AD* and *AS* curves.

**Simplifying assumption** Any assumption that makes a model simpler without affecting any of its important conclusions.

**Socialism** A type of economic system in which most resources are owned by the state.

**Specialization** A method of production in which each person concentrates on a limited number of activities.

**Stagflation** The combination of falling output and rising prices.

**Stock variable** a variable measuring a quantity at a moment in time.

**Structural deficit** The part of the federal budget deficit that is independent of the business cycle.

**Structural unemployment** Joblessness arising from mismatches between workers' skills and employers' requirements or between workers' locations and employers' locations.

**Substitute** A good that can be used in place of some other good and that fulfills more or less the same purpose.

**Supply curve** A graphical depiction of a supply schedule; a curve showing the quantity of a good or service supplied at various prices, with all other variables held constant.

**Supply curve for foreign currency** A curve indicating the quantity of a specific foreign currency that will be supplied, during a given period, at each different exchange rate.

**Supply of funds curve** Indicates the level of household saving at various interest rates.

**Supply schedule** A list showing the quantities of a good or service that firms would choose to produce and sell at different prices, with all other variables held constant.

**Supply shock** Any event that causes the *AS* curve to shift.

**Supply-side effects** Macroeconomic policy effects on total output that work by changing the quantities of resources available.

# T

**Tariff** A tax on imports.

**Taylor rule** A proposed rule that would require the Fed to change the interest-rate by a specified amount whenever real GDP or inflation deviate from their preannounced targets.

**Technological change** The invention or discovery of new inputs, new outputs, or new production methods.

**Terms of trade** The ratio at which a country can trade domestically produced products for foreign-produced products.

**Total demand for funds curve** Indicates the total amount of borrowing at various interest rates.

**Trade deficit** The excess of a nation's imports over its exports during a given period.

**Trade surplus** The excess of a nation's exports over its imports during a given period.

**Traditional economy** An economy in which resources are allocated according to long-lived practices from the past.

**Transfer payment** Any payment that is not compensation for supplying goods or services.

# U

**Unemployment rate** The fraction of the labor force that is without a job.

**Unit of value** A common unit for measuring how much something is worth.

# V

**Value added** The revenue a firm receives minus the cost of the intermediate goods it buys.

**Value-added approach** Measuring GDP by summing the value added by all firms in the economy.

# W

**Wealth** The total value of everything a person or firm owns, at a point in time, minus the total value of everything owed.

**Wealth constraint** At any point in time, wealth is fixed.

# Index